GOLF magazine's ENCYCLOPEDIA OF GOLF

GOLF magazine's

1817

ENCYCLOPEDIA

OF GOLF

UPDATED AND REVISED

Edited by John M. Ross

and the Editors of GOLF magazine

HARPER & ROW, PUBLISHERS

NEW YORK, HAGERSTOWN, SAN FRANCISCO, LONDON

GOLF MAGAZINE'S ENCYCLOPEDIA OF GOLF *(Updated and Revised).* Copyright © 1979 by Times Mirror Magazines, Inc. All rights reserved. Printed in the United States of America. No part of this book may be used or reproduced in any manner whatsoever without written permission except in the case of brief quotations embodied in critical articles and reviews. For information address Harper & Row, Publishers, Inc., 10 East 53rd Street, New York, N.Y. 10022. Published simultaneously in Canada by Fitzhenry & Whiteside Limited, Toronto.

LIBRARY OF CONGRESS CATALOG CARD NUMBER: 77-11818

ISBN: 0-06-011552-1

79 80 81 82 83 10 9 8 7 6 5 4 3 2 1

Contents

Acknowledgments, vii

Section I. The History of Golf, 1

Early Days of Golf in the British Isles—Golf Begins in the United States—Before World War I—Between the Wars—The Modern Era—The Wide World of Golf

Section II. Major Results of Tournaments and Golf Championships, 31

USGA Competitions—U.S. National Open Championship—U.S. National Amateur Championship—U.S. Women's Amateur Championship—U.S. Women's Open Championship—Amateur Public Links Championship—Junior Amateur Championship—Girls' Junior Championship—Senior Amateur Championship—Senior Women's Amateur Championship—PGA Competitions—PGA Championship—PGA Seniors' Championship—PGA Tour, 1955 to 1977—Masters Tournament—LPGA Competitions—LPGA Championship—LPGA Tour, 1970 to 1977—Other Major United States Championships—National Collegiate Athletic Association (NCAA) Championship—Women's National Intercollegiate Championship—Porter Cup Tournament—Sunnehanna Amateur Championship—Doherty Tournament—U.S. Seniors' Championship—U.S. National Senior Open—Western Amateur—Western Open—Western Junior—Western Women's Amateur—Western Junior Girls'—Men's North and South Amateur—Women's North and South Amateur—North and South Seniors' —Trans-Mississippi Amateur—Women's Trans-National Amateur—Southern Amateur—Women's Southern Amateur—Major International Golf Events—British Open —British Amateur—British Ladies Amateur—Argentine Open—Australian Open—Brazilian Open—Canadian Open—Canadian Amateur—Women's Canadian Open Amateur—Dutch Open—French Open—German Open—Hong Kong Open—India Open—Italian Open—Japanese Open—Korea Open—Malaysian Open—New Zealand Open—Philippine Open—Portuguese Open—Singapore Open—South African Open —Spanish Open—Swiss Open—Taiwan (China) Open—Thailand Open—World Senior Amateur Championship—World Series of Golf (Men)—Piccadilly World Match Play Championship—International Team Matches—The Walker Cup Match —The Curtis Cup Match—World Amateur Team Championship—Women's World Amateur Team Championship—The Ryder Cup Match—The World Cup Match

Section III. Golfdom's Who's Who, 125

Great Golfers of All Time—Current Touring Professionals (Men)—Current Touring Professionals (Women)—Recent PGA Tournament Winners—Recent LPGA Tournament Winners—Money-Winning Records—Modern-Era Leading Money Winners (Men) and Prior to 1955—All-Time Leading Money Winners (Men)—Leading Money Winners (Women)—All-Time Leading Money Winners (Women)—All-Time Records—Professional—Hall of Fame (PGA)—Hall of Fame (LPGA)—World Golf Hall of Fame—Trophy and Award Winners

Section IV. Golf Equipment, 207

The Evolution of Golf Equipment—The Golf Ball—The Golf Club—Types of Golf Clubs—The Woods—The Irons—Manufacture of Golf Equipment—The Golf Clubs —The Golf Ball—Selection of Golf Equipment—A Set of Clubs—The Putter—The Golf Ball—The Golf Bag—Golf Carts—Golf Clothing and Golfing Accessories— Care of Golf Equipment—The Golf Clubs—The Golf Balls—The Golf Bag and Accessories

Section V. Principles of Golf, 243

Fundamentals of Golf—The Grip—The Stance—The Swing—Wood Shots—The Tee Shot—The Fairway Shot—Common Wood-Shot Errors—Iron Shots—The Long Irons —The Middle Irons—The Short Irons—Chip and Pitch Shots—The Trouble Shots— Common Iron-Shot Errors—Putting—Reading the Greens—Judging Distance and Break—Putting Strokes—Golf Strategy—The Weather Conditions—Wet-Weather Play—Windy-Day Strategy—Practice Strategy—How to Take a Lesson

Section VI. Rules and Etiquette of Golf, 305

The Rules of Golf—Golf Etiquette—The Caddie and the Golfer—Golf Carts and the Golfer—Etiquette and the Spectator—Safety First on the Golf Course—Competitive Golf—Computation of Handicaps—Types of Play—Tournaments and Competitions— Special or Novelty Events—How to Win Golf Matches—Why Golfers Bet—And How —Country Club Membership

Section VII. Championship Golf Courses, 365

Outstanding Golf Courses—United States—Canada—England—Scotland--Ireland— Japan—Australia—Most Interesting Golf Holes in the World—The Most Challenging Courses in the United States—The World's Toughest Holes—Golf Resorts—United States—Canada—Bahamas, Bermuda, Caribbean Islands, and Mexico—Packaged Golf Vacations

Section VIII. Glossary of Golf Terms, 419

Index, 431

Acknowledgments

The compilation of this volume required the help of many people. Members of the staff of *Golf* magazine who were exceedingly co-operative were Vincent J. Pastena and Desmond Tolhurst. Writers and contributing editors of this publication who were also helpful include Herb Graffis, Gene Sarazen, Charles Price, Bob Cooke, Paul Gardner, Will Grimsley, Charlie Bartlett, Oscar Fraley, Joseph C. Dey, Jr., Harry Obitz, Dick Farley, Dom Lupo, Bob Gorham, Herbert Warren Wind, and the various professional instruction editors.

Although the vast majority of the material in this book appeared in one form or another in *Golf* magazine during the more than nineteen years of its publication, some material was contributed from other sources. We would like to thank, for instance, *The Golf Journal* (the official publication of the United States Golf Association) and its editor, Robert Sommers, for material that appears in Sections I, IV, VI, and VII; *The Professional Golfer* (the official publication of the PGA) for material in Sections I, II, III, and IV; Acushnet Process Company for information on golf balls that appears in Section IV; PGA–Victor Golf, Inc., for material on golf clubs that appears in Section IV; the National Golf Foundation for data in Sections I and VI; Herbert Warren Wind for permission to reprint in Section VII an excerpt by Robert Trent Jones that appeared in Wind's book, *The Complete Golfer;* and the United States Golf Association for permission to reprint the *Rules of Golf* and material on golf course rating and handicapping that appears in Section VI. In addition, we would like to thank the following associations and their personnel for assistance in compiling the data in Sections II and III: Doc Giffin; Connie Madsen and Pat McCarthy of the Professional Golfers' Association; the Ladies Professional Golfers' Association; and Janet Seagle of the United States Golf Association.

To the others who, inadvertently, may have been omitted from the above thank yous, please accept our deep apologies for such omissions.

The Editors

SECTION I

The History of Golf

The royal and ancient game of golf is one of the oldest of our modern sports. But its exact beginnings are lost in antiquity. Some historians trace golf back to the Stone Age, while others tell us that the sport had its origin with the idle antics of shepherd boys knocking small stones into crude holes in the ground with a crook, while their flocks grazed lazily in nearby fields. It is known, however, that the Romans, in their day of empire, played a game called *paganica,* which involved the use of open countryside, a bent stick, and a ball stuffed with feathers. In the first century before Christ, Romans overran Europe, crossed the English Channel, and occupied parts of England and Scotland. They did not withdraw until the fourth century after Christ. It is therefore assumed by most historians that their game of *paganica,* with its feather ball, was the forerunner not only of golf but of kindred games played in Holland, Belgium, France, and England. For instance, people in Holland and northern France played a game on a flat rectangular area, generally on ice, of 60 by 25 feet. Clubs with brass or wood heads and shaped like hockey sticks were used to strike a ball at a post at each end of the field. It was much like croquet, but it was called *kolf.* French and Belgians played a similar game in the fields called *choulla* or *choulle.*

While there is controversy over whether golf originated in the Low Countries or in Scotland, the latter is credited by all authorities with devising, in the fourteenth or fifteenth century, the game as we now know it and with fostering its development and growth. From its inception, even in its early Scottish days, golf was a game of accuracy. The purpose of the modern game, quite obviously, is to get a small, hard ball into a hole or cup of 4¼ inch diameter sunk into the ground on the green in the fewest possible strokes from the time the ball has been played from the tee. To accomplish this, you use wood- or iron-headed clubs, varying in design according to the intended purpose, to hit the ball. You keep count of *all* attempts to hit the ball and report the total to the scorekeeper after "holing out." The scorekeeper (generally one of the players themselves) records each player's score on a card provided by the course management. Special penalties and rules for playing the ball in certain situations are sometimes assessed. You progress from one hole to the next over a specified course until eighteen holes are played. The object of the game, as we all know, is to tour the course in as few strokes as possible. Par, based on the distance to be covered from the tee to green, plus an allowance of two strokes on the green, is the standard used to measure one's excellence. Obstacles such as rough, traps, and bunkers, and natural hazards such as creeks, ponds, and trees, are strategically placed to penalize inaccurate play. As many as four players can play together. Competition is usually based on individual play, although a few events are arranged for competition by teams of two.

Early Days of Golf in the British Isles

The sport as played in the fifteenth century

Charles I, one of Great Britain's many golfing monarchs through the centuries, receives the news of the outbreak of the Irish Rebellion in 1646 while he is playing on the links of Leith, near Edinburgh.

by the Scots was by no means as refined as the modern game of golf just described. Their equipment was still crude: a leather bag stuffed with feathers for a ball and a club cut from a bent tree branch. Nor did they have any set golf courses. But the Scots enjoyed their "golfe" so much that, in 1457, Scotland's Parliament of King James II declared it illegal. Anyone caught playing the game was fined and imprisoned because the King was afraid skill at golf would replace skill with the bow and arrow which was necessary to the defense of the realm. Remember that this was a time when men went to war with bows and arrows, and hitting a bull's-eye was more important than sinking a golf shot.

But you cannot keep a game like golf down. In spite of the ban, the noblemen continued to play in pastures by the sea, and the game continued to be a popular amusement in Scotland. The proscription against golf apparently remained in effect until the introduction of gunpowder near the end of the fifteenth century lessened the importance of archery and restored golf as legal sport to the people in the mid-1500's.

Golf was the sport of the people, and there appear to have been no social barriers among those who played. Royalty and commoners

often played together. As proof, we may cite the first international match of record. Back in 1682, when the then Prince of Wales, later James II, was living at Holyrood, he engaged certain English noblemen in a controversy over the game's historic background and as an outcome challenged them to a foursome. He chose as his partner a poor Edinburgh shoemaker, John Paterson by name. The battle was staged at Links of Leith, near Edinburgh. The Prince and John were the winners. There are no details of how much the Prince contributed to the victory, but he did give the stakes to Paterson, with which John built a house in Canongate, Edinburgh, which stood until 1961, when it was demolished to make way for a housing project.

The first known organized golf club was founded in 1744 with the establishment of the Honourable Company of Edinburgh Golfers. The same year this golf society held its first annual tournament and awarded to the winner a silver club. The winner was also designated as the Captain of Golf for the coming year. The Honourable Company used the famous Links of Leith (the same course the Prince and John played their match on) and survived until 1831, when it ceased operations. In 1836, the society was reactivated, this time using the

Musselburgh links as its course and head-quarters for its tournaments.

Ten years after the Honourable Company was formed, the St. Andrews Society of Golfers came into existence. This organization, now known as the Royal and Ancient Golf Club of St. Andrews, has been in continuous operation since its activation in 1754. This, combined with other circumstances, obviously contributed to the recognition of the Royal and Ancient Golf Club as the Mecca of golf.

While during the latter half of the eighteenth century the rules, standards, and fashions of golf were set by the Honourable Company of Edinburgh Golfers, this leadership was gradually taken over by the members of the Royal and Ancient Golf Club. Here are basic rules, translated from the archaic English, as originally played at St. Andrews:

1. You must tee your ball within a club length of the hole.
2. Your tee must be upon the ground.
3. You are not to change the ball which you strike off the tee.
4. You are not to remove stones, bones, or any break-club for the sake of playing your ball, except upon the fair green, and that only within a club length of your ball.
5. If your ball come among water or any watery filth, you are at liberty to take out your ball and throw it behind the hazard six yards at least; you may play it with any club, and allow your adversary a stroke for so getting out your ball.
6. If your balls be found anywhere touching one another, you are to lift the first ball until you play the last.
7. At holing you are to play your ball honestly for the hole, and not to play upon your adversary's ball, not lying in your way to the hole.
8. If you should lose your ball by its being taken up or any other way, you are to go back to the spot where you struck last and drop another ball and allow your adversary a stroke for the misfortune.
9. No man at holing his ball is to be allowed to mark his way to the hole with his club or anything else.
10. If a ball is stopped by any person, horse, dog, or anything else, the ball so stopped must be played where it lies.
11. If you draw your club in order to strike and proceed so far with your stroke as to be bringing down your club, if then your club should break in any way, it is to be accounted a stroke.
12. He whose ball lies farthest from the hole is obliged to play first.
13. Neither trench, ditch, nor dike made for the preservation of the links, nor the Scholars' Holes, nor the Soldiers' Lines, shall be accounted a hazard, but the ball is to be taken out, teed, and played with any iron club.

Many of these early regulations are still in the *Rules of Golf*.

Many other traditions of golf can be traced to St. Andrews. Until the middle of the eighteenth century, for instance, golf had been played over courses of no established length. Leith, for example, had only five holes. Blackheath, another ancient club, had seven, which was the most fashionable number; but other courses had as many as twenty-five. Possibly seven would have remained as the traditional number for a round had it not been for the example of St. Andrews.

At the time the members of the Society of St. Andrews Golfers laid down the rules previously mentioned, the course at St. Andrews —what would now be the famous Old Course —had twelve holes. The first eleven traveled straight out to the end of a small peninsula. After playing these, the golfers returned to the clubhouse by playing the first ten greens backward, plus a solitary green by the clubhouse. Thus, a "round" of golf at St. Andrews consisted of twenty-two holes. That is, the golfers played "out" until they reached the End Hole. There they turned around and played "in" to the same holes. If two groups approached a green simultaneously, preferencé was given to those playing "out." The outgoing holes were marked with a small iron pin with white flags, while the incoming holes were marked with a red flag.

In 1764, however, the Royal and Ancient resolved that the first four holes should be converted into two. Since this change automatically converted the same four holes into two on the way back, the "round" was reduced from twenty-two holes to eighteen. And since St. Andrews was soon to become the arbiter of all that was correct about golf, eighteen holes soon came to be accepted as standard

One of the earliest known photographs of golf, dated 1858. Robert Chambers is shown at St. Andrews winning a tournament that was a forerunner of the British Amateur Championship.

throughout Scotland and England and eventually throughout the world.

Golf, of course, found its way down into England. It is written that the game was played at Blackheath, near London, in 1608. Actually, the Honourable Company of Golfers at Blackheath was established in 1766 and became the first club formed outside of Scotland. During the first half of the nineteenth century, through the 1850's, approximately thirty-five golf clubs were started in the British Isles. Some of these organizations soon disbanded, while others grew to great prominence. The first golf society founded on the European continent was the Pau Golf Club of France in 1856.

The history of golf is closely integrated with the history of its equipment. Actually, the history of golf, as we know it, could be divided into three periods, based on the type of ball employed. The standard missile during the early times was, as previously stated, a leather-covered ball stuffed with feathers. "Featheries," as these balls were known, required a great deal of tedious and skillful craftsmanship, and most ball makers could only make four to six top-quality ones a day. In addition, quite frequently even the best

balls would burst on club-head impact, and the feathers would fly off in all directions. The "feather-ball period" of golf came to an end in about 1848 with the introduction of the gutta-percha ball. Gutta-percha is a resin or gum from certain types of Malaysian trees of the sapodilla family; it is generally brownish in color and resembles rubber in many ways. The "gutties," as these balls were called, popularized the game greatly. They were much lower in price, lasted longer, gave improved flight, and ran a great deal truer on the greens. The "gutta-percha ball period" lasted until the turn of the century, when we entered the "rubber-ball period," or present era of golf. More details on the evolution of the golf ball, as well as the clubs, may be found in Section IV.

During the first half of the nineteenth century, clubs came to be divided into four classes: drivers, spoons, irons, and putters. Drivers were distinguished by their long, tapering, and flexible shafts and their small, raking heads. They comprised "play clubs," which had more loft and were designed for use over safe ground only, and "grassed drivers," which had more loft and were designed to lift a ball from a heavy or downhill lie or over a hazard. Spoons were of four types: long spoons, middle spoons, short spoons, and baffing spoons, the distinctions being in the degree of loft. For a time there was also a fifth spoon, the niblick, a well-lofted club with a small head designed to drive a ball out of a rut or cup. Irons were three in number: driving irons, cleek, and bunker irons. There were two types of putters: driving putters, for approach work over unencumbered terrain, and green putters, for use on putting greens. With these sets, players negotiated their feather balls over holes measuring 80 to 400 yards.

In the era of the feather ball there were no championships as we now know them, but four of the great professional players of the period returned this card in a feather-ball match at St. Andrews in 1849:

pany of Edinburgh Golfers, while Allan Robertson and Tom Morris were the professionals at St. Andrews. Incidentally, the score below was part of a four-ball match held over three courses—Musselburgh, St. Andrews, and North Berwick—in which Robertson and Morris defeated the Dunns by a single hole and won the imposing sum of £400 (about $1,600) which was posted by the members of the two clubs involved.

Most golf clubs in the 1850's had professional golfers present. Their duties included greenkeeping, instructing, custodial, and even, in some cases, caddying. Occasionally, these early pros played in challenge matches for prizes offered by the "gentlemen golfers" of the various clubs. It was these amateurs who helped finance early golf competition.

	Out	
Willie and Jamie Dunn	6 5 4 6 6 6 4 4 5—46	
Allan Robertson and Tom Morris, Sr.	6 5 6 5 5 5 5 4 4—45	
	In	
Willie and Jamie Dunn	5 3 5 6 5 5 5 6 6—46—92	
Allan Robertson and Tom Morris, Sr.	6 4 5 6 5 5 5 6 6—48—93	

The Dunns represented the Honourable Com-

While several so-called national champion-

In this photograph, taken in the early 1860's at St. Andrews, a group of leading amateurs (gentlemen golfers) and professionals watch George Glennie putt. Sir Hugh Playfair is in the top hat behind Glennie, while Willie Dunn, one of the first pros, is the third from the left, holding the club in his right hand.

ships were held previously, the first British Open Championship was organized at the Prestwick Golf Club in Ayrshire, Scotland, on October 17, 1860. Eight professionals formed the first field, which was won by Willie Park of Musselburgh. He played three rounds, all in one day, over the twelve-hole course in 174 strokes. Below are the names, *estimated* par, and length of the holes at Prestwick:

Hole No.	Name	Length	Modern-day Par
1	Start	577	5
2	Alps	385	4
3	Tunnel Out	169	3
4	Stone Dike	447	4
5	Sea He'therick	440	4
6	Tunnel In	314	4
7	Green Hollow	145	3
8	Station	167	3
9	Burn	396	4
10	Sauch House	213	3
11	Short Hole	132	3
12	Home Hole	418	4
		3,803	44

Ironically, Willie Park received no money for his triumph. His prize was the Championship Challenge Belt, fashioned of red morocco leather and silver, donated by the Earl of Eglinton. However, Park, his brother Mungo, and his son, Willie, Jr., who accounted for seven British Open titles among them, became a legendary trio of winners of money matches for large private stakes.

The Belt remained the championship trophy until 1870, when Tom Morris, Jr., earned permanent possession of it by scoring his third consecutive triumph. The British Open, which was by now "open" to the world, including amateurs, was held in abeyance for the year 1871. Competition for a new trophy, The Championship Challenge Cup, was resumed in 1872. Young Tom Morris, Jr. (at the age of twenty-one), won that, too, the only golfer in British Open history to win four in succession. His father, "old" Tom Morris, also won it four times, but not in succession.

Soon after Young Tom's death in 1875, two

Ladies' day at Minchinhampton, England, in 1890.

other professionals came close to duplicating his feat of four successive victories in the British Open, which was now being rotated between Prestwick, St. Andrews, and Musselburgh. Jamie Anderson of St. Andrews won it from 1877 to 1879. He was succeeded by Bob Ferguson, from Musselburgh, who won it three times and lost a fourth title in a row in a play-off. Peter Thomson of Australia duplicated Anderson's and Ferguson's feat from 1954 to 1956.

Scotland had exclusive possession of the British Open for the first thirty-four years. In 1894, the championship was held at the Royal St. Georges Golf Club in Sandwich, England. The first Englishman to win the British Open, as well as the first amateur, was John Ball, Jr., in 1890. The only other amateur to win this event was an Englishman, Harold H. Hilton, who captured it in 1892 and 1897. The three dominant professionals in the British Isles at the turn of the century were John Henry Taylor, Harry Vardon, and James Braid. This famed trio, better known as the Great Triumvirate, won sixteen British Opens among them. The first international professional match was held at Prestwick in 1903, where Scotland defeated England by 9 and 8.

While each club held its own amateur championship and there were numerous interclub matches, the first British Amateur championship was conducted by the Royal Liverpool Golf Club at Hoylake, England, with an informal competition in the summer of 1885. The success of this first competition prompted the host club to suggest that St. Andrews sponsor an annual amateur championship. A. E. MacFie, the 1885 winner over a field of forty-four, was finally recognized in 1922 by the Royal and Ancient Club at St. Andrews as the first official champion.

The early years of the British Amateur were dominated by one golfer, John Ball, Jr., who grew up near the Royal Liverpool links and took part in the British Open at fifteen. Ball won the Amateur crown eight times between 1888 and 1912. He played in his last Amateur in 1921, reaching the sixth round at the age of sixty-one.

In the 1880's and 1890's golf courses, clubs, and facilities improved greatly and club membership increased rapidly in both Scot-

Alex "Sandy" Herd (right) and John H. Taylor (left) were two of the top professionals at the turn of the century in England.

land and England. The game expanded into Ireland, Canada, and some of the British colonies. It was inevitable that golf would migrate to the United States.

Golf Begins in the United States

Golf was played in the United States before 1888, but it was not until that year that the St. Andrew's Golf Club of Yonkers, the first permanent American golf club, was organized. Actually, the legendary beginnings of golf in the United States go back to the 1780's at Harleston Green in Charleston, South Carolina. In the *South Carolina and Georgia Almanac* of 1793 there is reference to formation of a golf club in Charleston in 1786. Newspaper reference to golf in Charleston appears in 1788. Biographical material mentions the playing of golf at Harleston Green in 1791. Historians, among them H. B. Martin in his exhaustive study of *Fifty Years of American*

Golf, pinpoint golf as lasting about twenty-five years at Harleston Green, ending at about the time of the War of 1812.

A golf club also came into being in Savannah, Georgia, before 1800—probably about 1795—and references to it continue until 1811. Apparently, the War of 1812 served to kill off the desire to continue play because not until after the Civil War was interest rekindled in the Americas.

The oldest continuous club in North America is the Royal Montreal Golf Club, organized in 1873. By 1880, four other Canadian golf clubs had been formed: Royal Quebec in 1874, Toronto Golf Club and Niagara-on-the-Lake Golf Club in 1876; Brantford Golf Club in 1879.

Charles Blair Macdonald, a great mover in early American golf, recalled playing golf in the Chicago area around 1875. In 1883 or 1884, Colonel J. Hamilton Gillespie, a Scotsman who went into the lumber business in Florida, hit golf balls in a field that now is the main street of Sarasota. In 1881, one Andrew Bell of Burlington, Iowa, went to Scotland to attend the University of Edinburgh and, returning home in 1883, laid out four informal

golf holes and played a few rounds with his friends.

In 1884, Russell W. Montague, a New Englander, got together with four friends from Scotland, organized a club at his summer home at Oakhurst, West Virginia—some two miles from White Sulphur Springs—designed a course, and played for two or three summers.

Soldiers stationed near the Rio Grande in 1886 played golf on a course they laid out. In 1887 a Scotsman turned cowboy, Alex Findlay, spent some of his leisure hitting a golf ball around the Nebraska prairies. Golf turned up at Rockwell's Woods, near Norwich, Connecticut, in 1888, but lasted only three years.

Records clearly establish the start of golf at the Tuxedo Club, Tuxedo, New York, in 1889; it was being played in 1890 at clubs in Newport, Rhode Island, the Lake Champlain Hotel Course at Bluff Point, New York, and Middlesboro, Kentucky, along the old Daniel Boone Trail. Middlesboro traces its beginning to 1889. Predating all of these was the St. Andrew's Golf Club of Yonkers, New York.

Although the actual formation of the golf club at Yonkers did not occur until Novem-

Taken in November, 1888, at the St. Andrew's Golf Club in Yonkers, New York, this is the earliest known photograph of golf being played in the United States. John Reid, the "father of American golf" and the giant of St. Andrew's early days, is at the right. J. B. Upham is putting, while Harry Holbrook (left) and A. P. Kinnan look on. The caddies are Warren and Frederick Holbrook. Reid and Upham played the first actual golf match at St. Andrew's earlier that year.

ber 14, 1888, golf at St. Andrew's had its beginning nearly nine months before: on Washington's Birthday, February 22, 1888, when John Reid invited some neighbors to his cow pasture across the road from his home in Yonkers-on-the-Hudson. Reid, born in Scotland, had come to the United States as a youth and had brought with him an interest in a game by then well established in his native

During the next three years, St. Andrew's made two more moves: to Grey Oaks, three miles distant, where the first United States championship, unofficial to be sure, was held in September of 1894, and in 1897 to its present site, Mount Hope at Hastings-on-Hudson, where it was expanded to eighteen holes. All this, and more, of St. Andrew's early days was carefully documented in minutes kept by Up-

Shinnecock Hills Country Club in 1892. In the background, the clubhouse, designed by Stanford White.

land. In 1887, Bob Lockhart, a friend of Reid's, made a trip to Scotland and at Reid's request brought back with him a few golf clubs and some gutta-percha balls. Three improvised holes were laid out in the pasture, and on Washington's Birthday, Reid and neighbor John B. Upham gave an exhibition of the Scottish game. Watching as spectators —their interest soon to develop to the point of participation—were four other neighbors, Henry O. Tallmadge, Harry Holbrook, Kingman Putnam, and Alexander P. W. Kinnan.

Within a few months, more balls and clubs arrived from Scotland and the original three holes proved inadequate. The men of St. Andrew's made their first move, setting up their patch of recreation on a thirty-acre meadow owned by a local butcher, John C. Shotts. By the end of the summer of 1888, it became evident to Reid and his cronies that this was a game that would stay. That led to the dinner party at Reid's home on November 14 at which St. Andrew's was formally organized. The minutes were kept by John B. Upham. Reid was elected President, with Upham as Secretary.

ham, Reid, and their successors. This fact is most important in light of recent claims by the Dorset Field Club (Dorset, Vermont) and Foxburg Country Club (Foxburg, Pennsylvania). The former claims to have had a golf course in 1886 and the latter one year later. While either may well be the oldest golf club and course in the United States, no minutes or other documentation of date at the time has been unearthed.

In any event, by 1895 golf and golf clubs were flourishing throughout the country. As of the end of that year, at least seventy-five clubs were in operation. The need for an organization to administer the game had been met with creation in 1894 of the Amateur Golf Association of the United States, later to become the United States Golf Association (USGA). The five charter member clubs were St. Andrew's, Newport, Shinnecock Hills on Long Island, the Chicago Golf Club, and The Country Club at Brookline, Massachusetts. The latter's role in early golf sometimes is misunderstood, since the Club was formed in 1882. Golf, however, was not played there until 1893.

It was really a mix-up involving championships that led to the creation of the USGA. In 1894, before there was a USGA, two different clubs in the East each held what it called the Amateur Championship of the United States. They were the Newport Golf Club in Rhode Island and the St. Andrew's Golf Club of Yonkers. W. G. Lawrence won at Newport in September, with a score of 188 for 36 holes and, in October, L. B. Stoddard won at St. Andrew's, at match play. Thus, there were two so-called National Amateur Champions.

To avoid such an embarrassing condition thereafter, Henry O. Tallmadge, Secretary of the St. Andrew's Club, conceived the idea of a national association of clubs to establish uniform golf rules and to conduct championships. He invited representatives of the five clubs to a dinner in New York on December 22, 1894. This meeting led to the first official USGA Championships, both amateur and open, at the Newport Golf Club in October of 1895.

Thirty-two players started in the Amateur Championship, entirely at match play, and the winner was Charles B. Macdonald, a Chicago Scotsman. One player, Richard Peters, carried a billiard cue and putted with it, in all seriousness. He went out in the first round before the more righteous play of a clergyman, the Rev. William Rainsford.

From a newspaper point of view, the social aspects of the Championship were perhaps more important than the golf, for the New York *Herald* published this thrilling account:

> At three o'clock society began to appear and fully 100 of the spectators were soon tramping over the hills. It was a bright scene; the ladies in their silks and the men in their red golfing coats made a scene of color seldom witnessed in outdoor sports. The game of the morning was C. B. Macdonald, the probable champion, against Laurence Curtis. The latter was not in any way in the game with Macdonald, for he has a low short drive compared to a long well directed drive of his opponent.

The first U.S. Open was played the day after the Amateur ended, also at Newport. It

Winners of the first USGA Amateur Championships in 1895: Mrs. Charles S. Brown (left) and Charles Blair Macdonald (right).

was at 36 holes, and the winner was the twenty-one-year-old assistant pro at Newport, Horace Rawlins. He scored 91–82–173 for the two rounds which were held in a day. Ten professionals and one amateur competed. Horace Rawlins's prizes were a $50 gold medal and $150 in cash.

In November of the same year—1895— the USGA held its first women's amateur championships at Meadowbrook on Long Island. The winner, Mrs. Charles Brown, had 69 before lunch and 63 after lunch, and her 18-hole score of 132 made her the Champion. Thus, with the Amateur, the Open, and the Women's Amateur Championships, the USGA was launched. The USGA also drew up the Rules of the Game under which golf was to be played in the United States. Actually, the American rules followed those of the Royal and Ancient Golf Club of St. Andrews, Scotland, except for a few minor modifications.

The game of golf grew rapidly in America. In 1895 there were some 75 clubs in the United States; five years later there were more than 1,000. The state of New York had at least 160 courses, while Massachusetts boasted of some 155.

While the USGA grew in stature on the national level, several sectional golf associations were formed and held district tournaments. Among the leading associations still in existence are: The Metropolitan Golf Association (1897), The Pacific Northwest Golf Association (1899), The Western Golf Association (1899), The Trans-Mississippi Golf Association (1901), and The Southern Golf Association (1902).

Before World War I

Because of the great popularity of golf in the United States, many professional golfers from the United Kingdom came to America to lend their technical skills to course construction and teaching. Many of them remained and formed the nucleus of the early professional competition. Harry Vardon, one of the famed "Trio" and considered by many as the world's greatest player of this era, came to the United States in 1900 for exhibitions sponsored by A. G. Spalding & Bros., the sporting-goods firm, in hopes that his heroics might sell the public on the virtues of their

Teeing off on the first tee of Midlothian Country Club in 1908. It was at this club in Illinois that Walter Hagen won his first National Open in 1914. The tee "box" is of packed sand.

new guttie golf ball, the *Vardon Flyer*. As far as Spalding Brothers were concerned the trip was not very successful because just about that time the rubber ball was introduced and the gutta-percha period of golf came to an end. However, Vardon's tour was no failure to American golf. He won the United States Open in 1900, and his exhibitions created a great deal of interest in golf in America.

The first decade of the twentieth century of American golf was ruled by foreign-born players. Willie Anderson, a native-born Scotsman, won four National Opens, three of them in a row (1903–1905), before he died at the age of thirty-two. His record of four victories has since been tied by Bobby Jones and later by Ben Hogan (and surpassed by nobody), but Anderson's feat of three consecutive Open wins has yet to be duplicated.

Alex Smith, one of five brothers, all fine professionals who migrated to America from Carnoustie, Scotland, captured the United States Open in 1906 and 1910. While Anderson, Smith, and the other winners—Aleck Ross, Fred McLeod, Lawrence Auchterlonie, and George Sargent—were now United States residents, they were born in the British Isles. Actually, Johnny McDermott, who reputedly could pitch a mashie shot onto a handkerchief,

Mrs. Dorothy Campbell Hurd, one of America's first great women golfers, won three United States and two British titles.

was the first American homebred to win the Open. He did it in 1911 and again in 1912.

Then, in 1913, came the bombshell that literally put golf on Page One in America. A twenty-year-old amateur, a former caddie, Francis Ouimet, defeated the great British professionals, Harry Vardon and Ted Ray, in a play-off for the Open Championship and thus became the first amateur to win the Open. As a matter of fact, an amateur won two of the next three Opens; Charles Evans in 1916 won both the U.S. Open and the Amateur, to become the first golfer to accomplish this feat.

Of all America's early golfers, one of the most interesting was the amateur Walter J. Travis. Born in Australia, Travis, better known as the "Old Man," came to the United States while still a boy and took up golf at the age of thirty-five. He won the United States Amateur three times and the British Amateur in his first and only attempt in 1904. Actually, he became the first "outsider" to win this

British championship. Travis was one of the most accomplished putters in the game.

In the early part of our present century, amateur golf had a greater appeal to the imagination of Americans than professional golf. The reason was that the amateurs were homebred—not imported from the British Isles. Prior to the coming of Francis Ouimet and Charles Evans, Robert Gardner, Jerome Travers, Chandler Egan, and William Fownes were some of the amateurs along with Travis who held the amateur spotlight in the United States.

Women's competitive golf started in Britain with the first championship of the Ladies Golf Union in 1894. This event was won by Lady Margaret Scott. As a matter of fact, Lady Margaret won the championship two more consecutive times and then retired from competitive play. Other heroines of British golf were Rhona Adair, of Ireland; May Hezlet, also of Ireland; Dorothy Campbell, of Scotland, who won two British and two American championships between 1909 and 1911 and thirteen years later, as an American citizen married to a man named Hurd, won a third American amateur title; and Cecil Leitch, of England, who played golf like a man. Miss Leitch used a wide stance and played the ball well away from herself, had a strong palm grip, and did not consider it unfeminine to punch an iron shot. She won the first of her three championships of the Ladies Golf Union in 1914.

Women's golf in America was dominated almost from its beginning by a teenager named Beatrix Hoyt. Starting with the second Women's Amateur in 1896, she won the title three straight times and was medalist five straight times. She still remains the youngest winner, at age sixteen, of the Championship and retired from competition at the "old" age of twenty-one. The Misses Margaret and Harriot Curtis won four Amateur titles between them prior to World War I. Miss Campbell, as previously mentioned, was the first woman to win both the American and British Championships in the same year, 1909. Miss Gladys Ravenscroft won the British title in 1912 and the American one in 1913.

Before 1916, professional golfers were an obscure, poorly paid, lowly regarded lot. They

The end of what was perhaps the most significant round of golf ever played. Amateur Francis Ouimet (kneeling) lines up the four-footer which dropped to decisively defeat Harry Vardon and Ted Ray during a play-off for the 1913 National Open.

were truly second-class citizens. Unsuccessful attempts to organize the pros were made early in this century. In 1907, a regional association was formed in Chicago. It died shortly afterward. A New England association, organized in 1914, met the same fate. Then a Philadelphia department store magnate with $2,580 to spend finally got the show on the road. The date was January 17, 1916. Rodman Wanamaker, son of merchant John Wanamaker, called a meeting of professionals at the Teplow Club in New York. "Gentlemen," Wanamaker told the small gathering, "I think you should have a national organization. If you are interested, I will donate $2,580 as prize money for a tournament. I would suggest that the tournament be patterned after News of the World Match Play Championship in Britain."

Among those at the meeting were John G. Anderson, A. H. Tillinghast, Joseph Appel, W. W. Harris, Jason Rogers, P. C. Pulver, and the eminent amateur Francis Ouimet. They were all enthusiastic. An organizing committee was selected with James Hepburn as Chairman, Herbert W. Strong as Secretary, and James Maiden, Robert White, Gilbert Nicholls, Jack Mackie, and Jack Hobens as other members. On January 24, 1916, they named Rogers, Hobens, Mackie, Strong, and G. C. Ennever to a committee to draft a constitution. The constitution was approved in New York on February 24, 1916. A total of 82 charter members, including 78 in Class A, were elected April 10, 1916. An additional 145 members—139 in Class A, 3 in Class C, and 3 in Class D—were added June 5, 1916.

The Association's first annual meeting was held June 26–28 at the Radisson Hotel in Minneapolis. Thirty-nine members were present. Robert White was elected the first President, George Fotheringham and James Maiden Vice-Presidents, and Herbert Strong Secretary and Treasurer. A twenty-four-man Executive Committee was set up, consisting of nine members from the New York Metropolitan section, six from the Middle States, three from New England, three from the Southeast, one from the Central section, one from the Northwest, and one from the Pacific Southwest. Later that fall, the new organization decided to take Wanamaker up on his proposal to donate $2,580 as prize money for a tournament. A meeting was held at Garden City, New York, on July 14, 1916. It was decided that the tournament should be called the Championship of the Professional Golfers' Association of America. A trophy and a gold medal would go to the winner, a silver medal to the runner-up, and a bronze medal to each of the semifinalists. The first tournament was staged at the Siwanoy Country Club in Bronxville, New York, October 10–16. Thirty-one PGA members competed. The winner was the late Long Jim Barnes, who beat Jock Hutchison, Sr., in the final match, 1 up. The winner's prize was $500.

To be eligible to apply for membership in the PGA, an applicant must be twenty-one years old, a citizen of the United States, a high school graduate or higher, a golf professional or employed as an assistant to a Class A member of the PGA, or an approved tournament player (one who has earned his eligibility to play the PGA Tour). He must have been employed as an assistant to a Class A professional for a period of six months and upon application become an apprentice. As an apprentice he must earn 32 credits over a period of three or more years by attending business schools, serving his apprenticeship, and receiving college credit. Prior to approval of his application he must also satisfactorily complete a playing test and oral examination.

The PGA, by its own definition, is a voluntary, incorporated, nonprofit membership

British essayist Bernard Darwin, a grandson of the famed evolutionist, was for more than sixty years the game's most eloquent spokesman. Darwin covered the initial Walker Cup match between the United States and Great Britain at The National Golf Links in 1922 as sportswriter. When a member of the British team became ill, Darwin substituted for him and won his match handily from a former National Amateur Champion, William C. Fownes, Jr.

association of golf professionals banded together in mutual interests. It lists its objectives as these:

1. To elevate the standards of the profession.
2. To promote interest in the game.
3. To protect the mutual interests of members.
4. To promote tournaments.

Between the Wars

In Britain no championships were held from 1915 to 1919, while in the United States championships were postponed during 1917 and 1918. Following the Armistice, the reign of the Great Triumvirate came to an end, and the brand of play of professionals and ama-

The seal of the PGA, a widely respected golf emblem

teurs from the British Isles was on the down-grade. On the other hand, America's golfers were on the upgrade, and by 1923 it had become obvious even to the British that the leadership of the game had passed to the United States.

The rise in the superiority of American golfers during the roaring twenties, sport's golden decade, was spectacular. One of the reasons for this increase in prestige of United States golf was Walter Hagen, undoubtedly the most colorful golfer of all time. He is considered by most experts as being the world's greatest match player. The Haig, as he was popularly known, won a record number of five PGA titles and a total of eleven major championships, plus capturing sixty-odd other tournaments and playing in more than 1,500 exhibitions. He was the first professional to win—and spend—a million dollars. The stories of his antics, both on the golf course and off, could fill many books.

One of the greatest accomplishments of Hagen is that he almost singlehandedly lifted the pro out of the caddie shack and into the clubhouse and first-class status. When The Haig went overseas for the British Open in 1922, he was informed coolly that he would have to dress in the pro shop, where it was necessary to hang his fancy knickers, silk shirts, and fleecy sweaters on a hook. Because he was a professional—and thus not a gentleman—he could not sully the sanctity of the clubhouse. Hagen met the situation by having his chauffeur drive his black limousine up to the front of the clubhouse and changing clothes in the back seat of the car. The stuffy British soon got the message. Barriers to the pros came down.

When Hagen won the British Open that year, he became the first native-born American to win this famed prize. (In 1921, Jock Hutchison, an American citizen, was the first person from the United States to win the Open.) Incidentally, The Haig won three more British Opens before he gave up the tournament procession just before World War II. The last tournament he won was the Gasparilla Open in 1935.

The twenties had other pros of great renown.

Jerome Travers drives at the peak of his career. Watching him are (from left): Max R. Marston (1923 National Amateur Champion), W. J. Thompson, Oswald Kirkby, John G. Anderson, and Robert A. Gardner (National Amateur Champion 1909 and 1915). Gardner, at 19 years, 5 months, was the youngest Amateur Champion when he won in 1909. Jack Nicklaus, at 19 years, 8 months when he won the 1959 Championship, was the second youngest.

Jess Sweetser (right) defeated Charles "Chick" Evans (left) in the finals of the 1922 National Amateur Championship at The Country Club. Sweetser also won the British Amateur title the same year.

Tommy Armour, Gene Sarazen, Macdonald Smith, Joe Kirkwood, Bobby Cruickshank, Leo Diegel, Jim Barnes, Jock Hutchison, Johnny Farrell, Al Espinosa, Horton Smith, Ted Ray, Denny Shute, and Joe Turnesa are a few of the more prominent names. The British professionals, during this period of time, could not make a dent in America. When Ted Ray won the National Open in 1920, that occasion marked the second time (Harry Vardon won it in 1900) that the trophy ever left the United States. Gary Player, of South Africa, in 1965, became the third foreign winner. On the other hand, except for 1923, the Championship Challenge Cup—symbol of the British Open—remained in American hands from 1921 to 1933.

In the amateur ranks, the greatest amateur of all times, Robert Tyre Jones, Jr., blossomed forth in the early twenties. From 1923 to 1930, he won thirteen national Championships: four United States National Opens, three British Opens, five United States National Amateurs, and one British Amateur. His skill is pointed up most sharply by the fact that in eight out of nine straight United States Opens he was first or second; he won four and was runner-up in four. The climax of his career came in 1930, when he scored his Grand Slam, the four leading major golf championships of the world—the British and the American Opens and Amateurs—all in the same year. This record, as well as his thirteen major championship wins, is un-matched. In 1930, after his Grand Slam, he retired from competitive golf at the age of twenty-eight.

In 1922, the Walker Cup Match came into being between selected British and American amateur teams. Possession of the Walker Cup was decided by four foursome matches and eight singles matches. The Americans won the trophy the first three years, and thereafter the matches were held every other year. Ten matches were held before the British finally took the cup in 1938. The only other time the trophy has left the shores of the United States was in 1971. The format of the Walker Cup competition was later used for both the Ryder Cup, among the professionals, and the Curtis Cup, among women amateurs, but both cups have taken *almost* permanent residency in America.

During the twenties the only phase of the sport where Britain had seeming superiority was in women's golf. In the early part of the decade Cecil Leitch carried on her domination of the game from the mid-1910's. Then, the incomparable Lady Heathcoat-Amory, nee Joyce Wethered, came along to become perhaps the finest female player in the history of the game. A flawless swinger, Miss Wethered at her prime was thought to be the equal of all but half a dozen men in the British Isles.

The number one woman golfer in America during this period was Glenna Collett, who later married Edwin H. Vare, Jr. In their only face-to-face meeting, Miss Wethered defeated Miss Collett 3 and 1 in the final round of the 1929 British Ladies' Amateur at St. Andrews. However, she won four United States Amateur Championships as Miss Collett and two more as Mrs. Vare. Most of Glenna's competition was furnished by such women golfers as Alexa Stirling, Edith Cummings, Marion Hollins, Maureen Orcutt, Miriam Burns, Virginia Van Wie, Mary K. Browne, and Helen Hicks.

In 1920, the membership of the USGA was 477 golf clubs. At the end of sport's golden decade, there were more than 5,700 golf courses in the United States, including approximately 4,500 private clubs, 500 municipal courses, and 700 privately owned public fee courses. There were an estimated 9,000 courses throughout the world, of which better than 2,000 were in the British Isles. The

USGA membership grew to 1,154 clubs. In 1922 the USGA started the National Amateur Public Links Championship for nonmember clubs. Also in that year, for the first time, admission fees were charged to spectators at the Open. This resulted partly from the need for controlling curiosity seekers at the Amateur the previous year.

The depression years had their effect on golf. The club members of the USGA dropped to a low of 767 in 1935. At the same time, many of the professional tournaments cut their prize purses, and some were even suspended or dropped. But, with the upturn in the country's economy in 1936, golf's popularity was on the rise, too.

The pro tours, as we know them today, really got under way. History is cloudy on exactly how and when the Tour started. Most golfers of the period traced it to informal tournaments staged in Florida before and after World War I. The prize for the first such tournaments, as recalled by Long Jim Barnes just before his untimely passing, was a layer cake. Long Jim said that he and such players as Jock Hutchison, Tommy Mc-Namara, Alex Smith, and Walter Hagen frequently got together in the days immediately following World War I—in 1919 and 1920—and played each other as if the world were at stake. "The prize," Long Jim said, "was a huge layer cake put up by one of the hotels. We washed it down with soda pop and whatever else was available."

Two of the professionals' wives—Estelle Armour, wife of Tommy Armour, and Jo Espinosa, wife of Al Espinosa—are credited with giving the Tour as much early impetus as anybody. They did it on the telephone.

Mrs. Espinosa telephoned friends in El Paso, Texas, and said that Armour, Espinosa, and Bobby Cruickshank would be happy to compete in a tournament there if sponsors could raise enough money to make the event worth while. El Paso golf enthusiasts were delighted. They got up the purse. The tournament was staged on greens of cottonseed hulls. Pros and amateurs of the area tried their skill against the three big-name competitors. The gallery was negligible. The total purse amounted to $1,000. But, the next year, the tournament was canceled. The ladies persevered. This time Mrs. Armour got on the phone. She called an influential friend in Chicago. The friend was taking health baths in Hot Springs, Arkansas. Mrs. Armour

Bobby Jones sinks his putt on the 18th green of Inwood Country Club to defeat Wee Bobby Cruickshank in a play-off for the 1923 National Open. This was the first of Jones's thirteen national titles.

Walter Hagen, capturing the British Open for the fourth time. His Majesty, The Haig, was perhaps the most colorful professional of all time.

The late Horton Smith once recalled that when he turned pro in 1926 the only other playing pros were Hagen and Joe Kirkwood, the transplanted Australian who later became famous as a trick-shot artist. Armour, Espinosa, and Cruickshank were teaching pros who made periodic forays to resort areas where their appearances were mostly exhibitions. "Leo Diegel joined us later as the private professional for millionaire Edward B. McLean," Smith said. "Then came Wild Bill Mehlhorn. We played in the LaGorce Open in 1929 and I got a check for $1,000 for winning."

The summer circuit was started in 1930. The St. Paul Junior Chamber of Commerce raised $10,000 for a tournament to follow the National Open. Much more popular than the 72-hole tournaments were exhibitions by such players as Walter Hagen. Hagen was handled by Bob Harlow, a newspaperman who served as advance agent, publicity director, and promoter.

The first actual tournament bureau organizer was Hal Sharkey, sports editor of the Newark (New Jersey) *Evening News*. Working for nothing, he lined up pro tournaments while on assignment for other events, such as the Rose Bowl game in California and the baseball training camps in Florida. It was not

called Hot Springs. With a towel wrapped around him in the steam room, the friend said, certainly, he would be glad to hold a tournament in Chicago.

That was the format of the early days of pro golf. A call to influential and wealthy golf enthusiasts in some far-off city, usually a resort area. Guarantee of a purse. Big-name pros. Such was the tournament life of the pros —fly-by-night events with small reward— until the circuit got under way. Actually, the pioneer of the winter circuit was the Texas Open, played on the public Brackenridge Course at San Antonio in 1922. A newspaperman, Jack O'Brien, got a group of wealthy Texans to put up $5,000 in prize money. Then scattered tournaments began popping up elsewhere. There was one at Sacramento, California, with $2,500 in prize money, and another in San Diego, six hundred miles to the south. The Los Angeles Open was started in 1927 with a total purse of $10,000, regarded as an earth-shaking figure.

In 1929, Johnny Goodman (left) upset Bobby Jones (right) in the first round of National Amateur. Later that same day, he was eliminated by eighteen-year-old Lawson Little, Jr. Four years later, however, Goodman won the National Open, becoming the last amateur ever to cop this event. In 1937, he added the National Amateur to his record.

Broadway turns out to welcome Bobby Jones home after his British triumphs in 1930.

ments with prize money ranging between $3,000 and $10,000. When he left ten years later, there were more than thirty tournaments with prize money totaling $750,000. Currently, the touring pros play for over $10,000,000.

One of the most important tournaments in the United States, the Masters, was inaugurated in 1934 at the Augusta National Golf Club. This course was designed by Bobby Jones and Dr. Alister MacKenzie. Today, the Augusta club has become a shrine, symbolic of beauty, dignity, good manners, and superlative golf, and yearly the players, from every age group, make their pilgrimage. The presence of Jones through the years at the Masters has sanctified the occasion. Horton Smith won the first Masters with a 284, beating Craig Wood by a stroke.

until January, 1936, that the PGA hired a full-time tournament director. He was Fred Corcoran, an Irishman out of Boston with a flair for promotional gimmicks. He took the job for $75 a week and $5 a day expenses. When he started, there were eleven tourna-

The better-known professionals of the first part of the thirties were Gene Sarazen, Tommy Armour, Leo Diegel, Denny Shute, Ed Dudley, Harry Cooper, Macdonald Smith, Olin Dutra, Horton Smith, Craig Wood, and Billy Burke. The latter part of the decade also brought to the fore the names of such

Bobby Jones (left) and O. B. Keeler, a well-known golf writer, with the Grand Slam trophies (left to right): the British Open, the National Amateur, the British Amateur, and the National Open.

In addition to his winning of thirteen major titles, Bobby Jones was runner-up to the National Open four times and the National Amateur twice. Willie Macfarlane (left) defeated him in a play-off for the 1923 National Open, and George Von Elm (right) won the finals from Jones 2 and 1 at Baltusrol Golf Club in the 1926 Amateur Championship.

pros as Jimmy Demaret, Ralph Guldahl, Jimmy Thomson, Sam Snead, Ben Hogan, Byron Nelson, John Revolta, Paul Runyan, Henry Picard, Harold McSpaden, E. J. Harrison, Vic Ghezzi, and a host of others.

In the British Isles, the American monopoly of their Open came to an end after Denny Shute's victory in 1933. The British pros, with Henry Cotton leading the way, kept the trophy in England until after World War II.

The leading amateurs after the retirement of Bobby Jones were Johnny Goodman, Lawson Little, and Bud Ward. A former caddie from Omaha, Johnny Goodman upset Bobby Jones in the first round of the 1929 National Amateur and four years later won the National Open to become the last amateur to take this event. In 1937 he added the National Amateur to his record. Lawson Little, Jr., won both the British and United States Amateurs back to back in 1934 and 1935. After this feat, he turned professional and captured the United States National Open in 1940 in a play-off with Gene Sarazen. Bud Ward won the United States Amateur title in both 1939 and 1941.

In women's golf, Virginia Van Wie, Helen Hicks, Maureen Orcutt, and Mrs. Edwin Vare still ruled the American scene in the first half of the 1930's, while Patty Berg and Betty Jameson led the way in the later half. In Great Britain, Enid Wilson, Diana Fishwick, and Pam Barton were the leaders. The latter won the British Ladies' Championship twice and was the last from foreign soil to win the United States Women's Amateur. Miss Barton lost her life in World War II.

One of the most important developments in golf during the 1930's was the replacement of hickory by steel shafts. The superiority of the steel shafts showed up in the improvement of the play of the so-called "average golfer." Pro scores also improved.

During the early years of the depression, the miniature golf course idea was started in Chattanooga, Tennessee, and spread rapidly throughout the United States. Garnet Carter is generally conceded to have thought up "Tom Thumb" golf, which required only a putter to play. But the fabulous rise of miniature golf was exceeded only by the quickness of its decline.

Four of the better-known professionals of the late 1920's and early 1930's (left to right): "Wild Bill" Mehlhorn, Tommy Armour, Gene Sarazen, and Leo Diegel.

The Modern Era

While golf in Great Britain came to a halt during the war years, competition continued in the United States, although in a limited fashion. All USGA events—the Open, Amateur, Women's Amateur, and Amateur Public Links Championship—were suspended from 1942 to 1945. However, there were plenty of tour events for those who were not in service.

The war years in golf were often called the era of Byron Nelson. His performances in 1944 and 1945, in which he swept 26 of 51 starts, should convince anyone of his greatness even though they were the war years and many of his colleagues were in the military service. Some competed now and then, however. He captured eight tournament victories in 1944 and eighteen the next year, depending on how you count the San Francisco Open, which was played in January and December of 1944. Some insist the December event was part of the 1945 tour. In any case, he took both of them. Eleven of his successes came in a row in 1945. In 1944, he also was second six times, third five times, fourth once, and sixth once. In 1945, he also was second seven times, third once, fourth twice, sixth once, and ninth once. Simple arithmetic will reveal that he placed first or second almost four of every five times he went to bat. His biggest prize in those years came in the Tam O'Shanter Open, forerunner of George S. May's so-called World Championships. It paid $13,462 in bonds in 1944 and $13,600 in bonds in 1945. Lord Byron annexed both, of course. Nobody else paid off in five figures then. He received only $1,000 for one victory, $1,333 for five others, $1,500 for another, $1,600 for one, and $2,000 for nine—all in bonds. By comparison, first money averaged $20,900 in 37 official tourneys in 1967. Harold "Jug" McSpaden was Nelson's major rival

Horton Smith putting on the 8th green during the first Masters Invitation Golf Tournament at Augusta, Georgia. Smith won the tournament with a score of 284.

Professional golf's "Field Artillery" of the 1930's (left to right): Jimmy Thomson, John Rogers, and Fred Morrison. Thomson was considered one of the greatest "long ball" hitters in golf.

The start of an international mixed foursome match in 1935 (left to right): Gene Sarazen opposed and helped in the American debut as a pro golfer of Joyce Wethered, internationally famous British golf star. Their partners were Mrs. Glenna Collett Vare and Johnny Dawson, respectively. Dawson substituted for Bobby Jones, who was to have been Miss Wethered's partner. The English star toured the United States and Canada in over thirty such exhibitions.

for money-winning honors, and the two became known as golf's "Gold Dust" twins. In other words, McSpaden won almost everything Nelson did not win during the war years.

With the concluding of the war and the return of golf to its prewar status, the sport entered the "modern era," or the present age. In Sections II and III of the *Encyclopedia of Golf* are found records of major championships and four tournaments from 1955 to the present time. Therefore, it is not necessary to dwell heavily on individuals and winners of various events. There were—and are—some professionals who dominate the modern era. These include, of course, such names as Ben Hogan, Sam Snead, Jimmy Demaret, Lloyd Mangrum, Porky Oliver, Lew Worsham, Julius Boros, Dr. Cary Middlecoff, Jay Hebert, Ted Kroll, Jack Burke, Dick Mayer, Sam Byrd (a former outfielder for the New York Yankees), Doug Ford, Tommy Bolt (with his well-known temper), Mike Souchak, Bob Toski, Art Wall, Walter Burkemo, Johnny Palmer, Gene Littler, Ken Venturi, Dow Finsterwald, Billy Casper, Arnold Palmer, Doug Sanders, Jack Nicklaus, Lee Trevino, Johnny Miller. New names can be added to this list yearly.

Foreign golf stars still invade the United States. But rather than coming from Great Britain as they did before the war, they now come from South Africa, New Zealand, and Australia. The best known of these players are Arthur "Bobby" Locke and Gary Player, both of South Africa. Locke played in the United States in 1947 and 1948, while Player is one of the present tour stars. The British Open, as well as being won by American players, has been captured by golfers from their former colonies. For instance, the best bet to catch or pass Harry Vardon's record of six British Opens was Australian Peter Thomson, who won four out of five of them between 1954 and 1958. But he never did.

In the amateur circles, the leaders of the modern era would include Skee Riegel, Willie Turnesa, Charlie Coe, Harvie Ward, Deane Beman, Dick Chapman, Billy Joe Patton, Frank Stranahan, Jack Nicklaus, Marvin Giles, to name a few. On the distaff side, the names of Babe Didrikson Zaharias (the first American to capture the British Ladies'

Sam Parks, Jr., a professional who was a member at the host club, stuns the world of golf by winning the 1935 National Open at Oakmont, near Pittsburgh. Parks was the only man in the field who was able to break 300 over Oakmont's ponderous bunkers and greens. He is shown sinking his putt on the 18th hole to win.

Amateur), Louise Suggs, Mary Lena Faulk, Barbara Romack, Patricia Lesser, Marlene Stewart, Anne Quast, Barabara McIntire, Jo-Anne Gunderson, and Mary Lou Dill are some of the important ones.

Interest in women golf professionals started after World War II. Certainly there were women professionals before that time. Helen Hicks was teaching; Babe Didrikson toured with Gene Sarazen in exhibition matches in 1935 (she applied for reinstatement as an amateur in 1943); and Joyce Wethered embarked on a tour of the United States, also in 1935, when deprived of her amateur status by the Ladies' Golf Union while working for a London sporting-goods store.

For the record, it is interesting to note that Miss Wethered and the Babe did oppose each other on two occasions that year in four-ball matches—once at Oak Park, Chicago, where the Babe shot 88 to the Britisher's 78, and again at Meadowbrook, New York, where Miss Wethered's 77 was four strokes better than the former Olympic Games gold medalist. However, it must be borne in mind that the Babe's power had not been properly harnessed at that early stage of her golfing career and that since she did not really come into her own until almost two decades after Joyce Wethered had quit tournament golf, no true comparison of these two tremendous competitors can ever be drawn. The Babe

was reinstated to her former amateur status in 1943.

A Women's Professional Golfers' Association (WPGA) was eventually formed in 1946 by a pioneer woman pro named Hope Seignious, with the help of her father. A Women's Open championship was inaugurated, and Miss Seignious also initiated a golf publication that was tantamount to a house organ for the Association. But neither the Association nor the publication was flourishing when Fred Corcoran, manager for the Babe since she turned pro again in 1948, was summoned to

Affectionately called the "three hillbillies" of the golfing world in the late 1930's, these three pros—(left to right) Johnny Bulla, Sam Snead, and Clayton Heafner—were a worth-while bet in any tournament.

The famous Turnesa golf family, who held sway from the 1930's through the 1950's. Here, Michael Turnesa shows his son "Willie" the correct way to hold a golf club as his other sons—Phil, Frank, Joe, Mike, Douglas, and Jimmy—look on.

meet with seven of the leading female pros in 1949. The women wanted leadership, proper promotion, more tournaments, and further exposure. But Miss Seignious would not relinquish the reins of the WPGA, and so there came into being a rival body, which called itself the Ladies' Professional Golf Association (LPGA) and soon became the ruling body it is to this day.

Corcoran describes how in the first tournament he set up for the women at Essex Fells, New Jersey, everyone finished in the money— even Helen Dettweiler, who received $350 without ever teeing off. Her dog was sick! But Fred gives proper credit to Alvin Handmacher, entrepreneur of Wethervane clothing, as the man who "put the LPGA in business." Handmacher, eager to promote his merchandise coast to coast, agreed to a four-stop transcontinental tournament for a total purse of $15,000, with a further bonus of $5,000 to the winner. The tournament was to start in San Francisco with stopovers in Chicago and Cleveland before finishing in New York.

Helen Lengfield, publisher of the *National Golfer* and for many years one of the most admirable benefactors of the game of golf, then stepped into the picture. She augmented a spring tour on the coast to the extent of a further $15,000, and the girls were on their way. As the tour expanded and the prize money grew over the years, more and more golfers were tempted to join the paid ranks, but in the formative years it was the Babe and personality "gal" Patty Berg who were the drawing cards at every event, with the dimin-

utive Bauer sisters adding the change of pace in glamour and approach.

The untimely passing of the Babe in 1956 robbed golf of one of its most dynamic personalities and was a distinct, if temporary, setback to the women's tour. The Babe was not merely a prodigious hitter, a player who often brought off the impossible recovery, and one who amazed everyone with her deli-

Among the top names of golf in the early 1940's was this foursome (left to right): Gene Sarazen, Jug McSpaden, Byron "Lord" Nelson, and Lawson Little.

Big names in the amateur circles of the early 1950's included (left to right): Dick Chapman, Willie Turnesa, Ted Bishop, and Robert Sweeny, Jr.

cate touch around the greens; she was also a showman through and through. She loved the limelight, and she entertained her audience to the full. Had she not been stricken at the peak of her career, there is no knowing to what further heights she might have risen as a competitor or what paths she might have opened up for her fellow LPGA members in "fringe benefits." The Babe was the most promotable commodity women's golf has ever known.

Betsy Rawls, Bev Hanson, Marlene Bauer Hagge, Louise Suggs, Kathy Whitworth, Mari-

lynn Smith, Betty Jameson, Patty Berg, and Mickey Wright are some of the outstanding female pros. Of this group, Miss Wright is really in a class by herself. Writing of her golf at Baltusrol in 1961, when she shot 69–72 on the final day to win her third Open title in four years, famed golf writer Herbert Warren said:

It is seriously to be doubted if Joyce Wethered or Babe Didrikson or any woman golfer has ever played a stretch of 36 holes with the power, accuracy, and overall command that Mickey did on that balmy July day. Her morning round was a lesson in how to score; she had no fewer than six birdies on her card. Her afternoon round was a lesson in shotmaking. . . . I wonder if any golfer has ever made the game seem easier than she did that day. With the sole exception of Hogan's historic double-round at Oakland Hills in the 1951 Open, Mickey Wright's golf at Baltusrol strikes me as perhaps the finest sustained performance I have been privileged to watch in a championship.

Incidentally, the first Women's Open held at Spokane, Washington, under the sponsorship of Women's Professional Golfers' Association, was won by Patty Berg. The WPGA conducted the championship until 1948, when the LPGA took over. In 1953, the USGA assumed the operation of the Women's Open and still conducts it. The USGA also began the Junior Amateur Championship in 1948,

George S. May, who has often been called "the father of big golf purses," talks with four of his named contestants in his World Championship, a $10,000 winner-take-all tourney at Tam O'Shanter CC in Chicago (left to right): May (kneeling), Sammy Snead, Herman Barron, Lloyd Mangrum, and Byron Nelson. Snead won the tourney with a 36-hole aggregate of 138.

The "Big Two" of the early 1950's: Ben Hogan (driving) and Sam Snead (background).

the Girls' Junior Championship in 1949, the Senior Amateur Championship in 1955, and the Senior Women's Amateur Championship in 1962. The USGA membership now stands at over 4,800 clubs. Incidentally, there are two classes of USGA membership:

1. *Regular Membership.* Open to any regularly organized golf club in the United States. A regularly organized club is a permanent club of individual dues-paying members who manage their own affairs through officers and committees whom they select. Such a club must operate permanently at one golf course, but it need not control the course where it plays. (Regular Membership is thus open to not only a private club but also a club of golfers using a public course.) Regular Membership entitles a club to all USGA privileges. Annual dues and publications cost: (1) Club at a course of eighteen holes or more, $70; (2) club at a course of less than eighteen holes, $50.

2. *Associate Membership.* Open to any golf course in the United States not controlled by a regularly organized club. (This applies mainly to public and daily fee courses and their managements, but not to regularly or-

ganized clubs operating there.)

Associate Membership entitles a course to all USGA privileges except voting rights and eligibility of the course's patrons for the USGA Amateur, Women's Amateur, Senior Amateur, and Senior Women's Amateur Championships. Annual dues and publications cost: (1) Course of eighteen holes or more, $50; (2) course of less than eighteen holes, $40.

In the modern era of golf the international - match program has more than doubled. Besides the Walker Cup, Ryder Cup, and Curtis Cup, we now have the Americas Cup, involving amateurs of Canada, Mexico, and the United States; the Eisenhower Trophy for the World Amateur Team Championship; and the Espirito Santo Trophy for the Women's World Team Championship. The USGA was instrumental in starting the two World Championships in recent years. Now there are around fifty-five countries belonging to the World Amateur Golf Council which sponsors the two Championships. The pros have the World Cup (formerly called the Canada Cup) and International Trophy Championship each year. This event attracts teams of professionals from about forty countries of the world.

The great Babe Didrikson Zaharias (right) displays her famed swing in 1952. Watching her tee off are (left to right): Peggy Kirk, Mrs. Jackie Pung, and Betty Dodd.

In the 1954 and 1955 National Opens, the underdog won. Ed Furgol (left), playing with an arm withered since childhood, proved that one good arm was good enough as he beat out ex-Amateur champion Gene Littler by one stroke with a four-over-par 284. Jack Fleck (right), who was playing his first year on the tour, was the Cinderella champ as he tied Ben Hogan on the last round, then dashed Ben's hopes of a fifth Open by winning the play-off, 69–72.

The most important increase in the sport is in the number of playing golfers. The following shows the growth since 1950 in the United States:

Year	Number of Golfers	Number of Courses
1950	3,215,160	4,931
1951	3,237,000	4,970
1952	3,265,000	5,020
1953	3,335,632	5,056
1954	3,400,000	5,076
1955	3,500,000	5,218
1956	3,680,000	5,358
1957	3,812,000	5,553
1958	3,970,000	5,745
1959	4,125,000	5,991
1960	4,400,000	6,385
1961	5,000,000	6,623
1962	5,500,000	7,070
1963	6,250,000	7,477
1964	7,000,000	7,893
1965	7,750,000	8,323
1966	8,525,000	8,672
1967	9,100,000	9,336
1968	9,300,000	9,615
1969	9,500,000	9,926
1970	9,700,000	10,188
1971	10,000,000	10,494
1972	10,400,000	10,665

During his two terms as President (1952–1960), General Dwight D. Eisenhower did a great deal to popularize golf. The World Amateur Team Championship trophy is named in his honor. Incidentally, the General was a good golfer.

Prize money in golf has advanced steadily through the years. First prize in the U.S. Open of 1895 was $150. By the middle thirties tournament winners could expect to earn about $1,500. The $10,000 of the forties was considered a major advance and in the early fifties when George S. May put his All-American and World Championships in operation a professional could take more than $100,000 out of Chicago for four days' work. May and Tam O'Shanter were the start of the big money era of modern golf. In 1958 the PGA tour passed the million mark in prizes. In 1979 the figure was expected to reach $10 million.

The average purse in an official PGA event was $12,183 in 1945, in contrast to $23,108 in 1954, $33,160 in 1961, $47,550 in 1963, $112,662 in 1967, and by 1978 it had soared to over $200,000.

Not only has tournament tour prize money increased in the past few years, but so has the attendance at these events and the size of the television viewing audience.

Year (cont.)	Number of Golfers (cont.)	Number of Courses (cont.)
1973	11,000,000	10,896
1974	11,660,000	11,134
1975	12,036,000	11,370
1976	12,328,000	11,562

Comparative Study: Private, Daily Fee, Municipal

At Private Clubs:	1974	1975	1976
Men	1,100,700	1,122,000	1,133,000
Women	494,400	534,000	571,000
Juniors	270,500	284,000	287,000
Total	1,865,600	1,940,000	1,991,000

At Daily Fee Courses:

Men	3,368,600	3,403,000	3,437,000
Women	1,107,100	1,195,000	1,279,000
Juniors	771,300	810,000	818,000
Total	5,247,000	5,408,000	5,534,000

At Municipal Courses:

Men	2,955,800	2,985,000	3,015,000
Women	1,045,900	1,130,000	1,209,000
Juniors	545,700	573,000	579,000
Total	4,547,400	4,688,000	4,803,000

At All Courses:

Men	7,425,100	7,510,000	7,585,000
Women	2,647,400	2,859,000	3,059,000
Juniors	1,587,500	1,667,000	1,684,000
Total in U.S.:	11,660,000	12,036,000	12,328,000[a]

[a] For 1976, add an additional 4,000,000 casual players.

Golf Statistics in the United States through January 1, 1977

Number of golf courses in the United States:

Regulation	10,205
Executive	526
Par-3	831
Total	11,562

Number of new facilities opened for play in 1976:

Regulation	99
Executive	15
Par-3	11
Total	125

Estimated number of acres devoted to golf facilities	1,237,500
Estimated number of golfers in the United States:	
Number playing more than 15 rounds a year each	12,328,000
Number playing less than 15 rounds a year each	4,000,000
Total	16,328,000

Estimated capital invested in golf facilities	$4,360,000,000
Estimated annual maintenance costs	$658,000,000
Estimated number of rounds of golf played in 1976	316,000,000
Estimated number of motorized golf carts in use in 1976:	
Electric	349,000
Gasoline	149,800
Total	498,800

The Wide World of Golf

Golf has gone world-wide, and it is still growing. The craze no longer is a Western addiction, confined to the British and their rebellious offspring in America. Over half a hundred nations on every continent now have citizens, many of them high in government or leaders of industry and finance, who fret over their hook or slice. Just as it was once said—not entirely in jest—that high government decisions in the United States might depend on President Eisenhower's golf score, so it is said now of a Prime Minister in Malaysia, a prince in Scandinavia, or a President in Pakistan.

A survey by *Golf* magazine discloses that golf is now thriving in about sixty countries, more than the number that signed the original United Nations charter. They range from Luxembourg, with its single Golf Club Grand-Ducal de Luxembourg, and Israel, where the first course was built at Caesarea ten years ago, to the United States, where there are more than 10,200 regulation courses, 125 new ones being built every year and still not enough to accommodate the hungry players, estimated at over 16,000,000.

The biggest boom is in the Orient, spearheaded by Japan, where the sport has become almost a religion. The largest vacuum lies behind the Iron Curtain, where the Communists once branded it with the "bourgeois" label, a game for the idle rich. There are no golf courses in the Soviet Union, although in 1975 the Russians did invite Robert Trent Jones to Moscow to select a suitable site for a golf course. Thereafter, plans moved slowly. Golf is, however, experiencing a revival in some of the satellite nations, Czechoslovakia particularly. At first, Czechoslovakian courses were confined almost entirely to personnel from foreign embassies. But then the Czechs

The "Big Two" of the 1960's. Arnold Palmer watches Jack Nicklaus blast a shot toward the green. Nicklaus continued strong throughout the 1970's, too.

themselves became more brazen and formed a small society which meets and competes regularly. And in recent years Czechoslovakia has been sending a team to compete in the World Cup tournament.

Golf magazine's survey, in which the associations were asked such intimate questions as the cost of club membership and lessons, the availability of golf cars, and the trend toward expansion, disclosed a wide variance in both interest and economics. In many of the countries, golf is a game for the well-to-do, much too expensive for the average worker or ordinary citizen. These barriers are gradually being broken down, however, with growing participation among the middle class. In places such as Finland, Belgium, Mexico, Pakistan, Peru, and Brazil, there are no public courses, but only private ones.

Golf carts are scarce outside the United States. There are few in Britain, South Africa, many parts of the Orient, Belgium, Mexico, Sweden, Norway, and Denmark. They are plentiful in Canada and scarce but available in Germany, Venezuela, and Pakistan.

Greens fees range from two rupees a day, less than 50 cents, to play the six-hole course in Ceylon to as high as $15 a round in some places. Public course fees are the most reasonable in South Africa and in Britain, where the

sport is made as available to commoners as to royalty. The Old Course at St. Andrews, the cradle of golf, is a municipally run course belonging to the township. For about $1, a citizen may test the hazards of the Principal's Nose, the famous Road Hole, and Hell's Bunker.

Britain, recognized as the birthplace of the game although it undoubtedly was played earlier on the Continent and perhaps elsewhere, must be credited with taking golf to the four corners of the world. When Britain was building its empire and sending its trade representatives to the far reaches of the globe, interest in golf went along. When Britons set up colonies in places such as India, South Africa, Hong Kong, and Australia, it was only natural that they should carry with them the love for the game that saturated their interest in their motherland. They hewed rough courses out of wildernesses, set them up on deserts, and had equipment sent to them from the shops of Scotland. Nevertheless, golf on this restricted scale in the outlands remained largely stagnant until recent years brought the advent of jet planes and television.

The jets carried the world's best players to areas where they might never have been seen or even known. Television took them into almost everybody's living room. This was true in the case of Japan, which triggered the current golfing explosion throughout the Far East. Prior to World War II and just after, the thickly populated chain of islands in the Far Pacific was a fast-moving, highly industrialized nation whose chief forms of recreation consisted of the gay geisha houses, the brightly lighted Ginza Strip, and baseball. Whereas in 1946 there were only 17 courses in all Japan, today there are fifty times that number and others in the planning stage. There are now over 3,000,000 players—second only to the United States in number. As in golf's swaddling days in the United States, the game still is confined largely to the more affluent. About 30 per cent of the courses are open to the public. Rates are high. But the Japanese were never people to do things halfway. Five hundred driving ranges have mushroomed in Tokyo alone. Because of the scarcity of space, some of them are triple-story, with enthusiasts hitting off from three different tiers.

Some observers trace the golf explosion there to Japan's spectacular victory in the World Cup matches when they were played in Tokyo in 1957. The Japanese were definite underdogs, and the unexpected triumph triggered a boom that threatened to make golf the national pastime.

It was natural that Japan's avid devotion to golf should spread to its neighbors. In Kuala Lumpur and Singapore, Malaysian politicians have taken up the game, realizing that it is their only opportunity to gain contact with the rulers. Chinese merchants are flocking in large numbers to the five courses in Hong Kong. In Burma, Thailand, and the Philippines, the game has become a necessity to businessmen and politicians. They tell the story that President Diosdado Macapagal of the Philippines had to take up golf in order to make sure that he would not miss out on important discussions by Far Eastern bigwigs. The Philippine chief of state got his first set of clubs from the prime minister of the Malaysian federation, Tunku Abdul Rahman. Tunku is credited with popularizing golf in Malaysia. He became exposed to the game upon a visit to New Zealand and returned home full of zeal. He joined the Selangor Club at Kuala Lumpur, which had lifted its restrictions against Asian membership. In deference to his age (early sixties), he was permitted to use the only electric golf car in the country.

The course at the Royal Bangkok Sports Club crosses a racing strip, and the golfers often are playing while horses are pounding around the track. There are so many canals that golfers are compelled to hire not one but two caddies: one to carry the clubs, another to retrieve the balls from the numerous canals, or klongs. In Singapore, the best courses, the Royal Singapore and the Royal Island, have a tough, matty type of grass that does not give with the ball, and crusty greens as well. It is almost impossible to get a bite on the ball, from either the rough or the fairway, and the greens are like glass. Players at the Royal Hong Kong Golf Club at Fanling may be distracted often by grazing cattle. The club pays some of its expenses by renting out the rough for pastureland. But a languid cow cannot be as distracting as a full-grown hippopotamus, which may meander across courses in East Africa. There, local rules permit the lifting from a hippo footprint and placement of the ball, without penalty, on a spot not nearer the hole.

Although equal in area to the United States, Australia has a population of only 10,000,000, about that of metropolitan New York. It has only half a million golfers, but the country boasts second place to the United States in the number of golf courses. The Australians have both excellent private club facilities and municipal courses, with the costs well below those of the United States. A player may tour one of the public courses for under $2.

Strangely, golf has not expanded in central and southern Europe as might have been expected, but there has been a definite pickup of interest. In France, until the World Cup matches were played in Paris in 1963, the Open Championship usually drew more competitors than spectators; the people considered it a game for the privileged class and lavished their attention on horse racing and tennis. So golf officials were astounded when The World Cup attracted about 15,000 fans on one day.

Economics, on the whole, has kept golf from mushrooming in South America, where a day's greens fee might pay a peon's wages for a year. Incidentally, however, a South American country, Bolivia, boasts the highest golf course in the world. It is located at Oruro, 12,149 feet above sea level. An oxygen tank would have to substitute as the fourteenth club. (The lowest course is at Kallia, on the shore of the Dead Sea. It is 1,250 feet below sea level, all sand and always hot and humid.)

SECTION II

Major Results of Tournaments and Golf Championships

USGA COMPETITIONS

As was stated in Section I, the United States Golf Association was founded December 22, 1894. The following year the Association sponsored three championships: The Open, the National Amateur, and the Women's National Amateur. It continues to govern these plus five more: The Amateur Public Links, Junior Amateur, Girls' Junior, Senior Amateur, and Senior Women's Amateur. In addition the USGA conducts several international cup events described later in this section.

U.S. National Open Championship

The first USGA Open was held on the 9-hole course of the Newport (Rhode Island) Golf Club on October 4, 1895, during the same week and on the same course as the first USGA Amateur. They had been originally scheduled for September, but were postponed because of a conflict with the America's Cup yacht races. Ten professionals and one amateur started the 36-hole, one-day competition. The winner, scoring 91–82—for a total of 173 with the gutta-percha ball, was Horace Rawlins, an English professional who had come over in January to be assistant at Newport. There were five money prizes: $150, $100, $50, $25, and $10. Rawlins also won a $50 gold medal and, for his club, the Open Championship Cup presented by the USGA.

The Open was extended to 72-hole stroke play in the fourth year, 1898, and sectional qualifying to handle the increasing entries was introduced in 1924. The format for many years, 72 holes in three days, was changed to four 18-hole daily rounds in 1965. Entries are open to professionals and to amateurs with handicaps not exceeding two strokes. One hundred fifty players are eligible for the Championship proper. The majority earn their places through two successive trials during the spring: first, in 36-hole Local Qualifying Rounds at about 55 sites in May; second, in 36-hole Sectional Qualifying Championships at approximately 15 locations in June.

In the Local Qualifying Rounds, there is a broad range of exemptions. These include all former Open, Amateur, PGA, and British Open Champions; members of the last USGA international teams and the last PGA Ryder Cup team; Open Champions of countries represented in World Amateur Golf Council; winners of PGA of America Tournament Players Division 72-hole tournaments for one year ending immediately before closing of Open entries; the 30 lowest scores in last Open; the 30 lowest scores in the last PGA Championship; the player in first place in the previous year's Continental Order of Merit, South African Order of Merit, Australian Order of Merit, and Asian Golf Circuit; the 50

Winner of the first U.S. Open, Horace Rawlins.

Approximately 20 per cent of the total entries, except those exempt from all qualifying rounds, become eligible for the second trial —a total of about 500 players. In the Sectional Qualifying Championships, exemptions are limited to the winners of the last five Opens; the fifteen lowest scorers and those tying for fifteenth place in the last Open (excluding any of the Champions in the last five years); the PGA Champion; the British Open Champion and the USGA Amateur Champion of the preceding year; and the fifteen leading money winners in the PGA official list for one year ending with the PGA tournament nearest the close of the Open Championship entries.

If a qualifier is unable to compete in the Championship, substitutes in the order of qualifying scores are invited from the Section in which he played.

All 150 starters play in the first and second 18-hole rounds. Then, the sixty lowest scorers and any tying for sixtieth place for 36 holes are eligible for the third and fourth 18-hole rounds. The champion is the player with the lowest score for 72 holes. In case of a tie, it is played off at 18 holes stroke play on Monday.

leaders on the PGA Tour under the USGA Point System for the previous calendar year; 15 leaders on the PGA Tour money list from January 1 until the close of Open entries; the British Amateur Champion of the preceding year; the PGA Club Professional Champion of the preceding year; and the head professional of the club entertaining the Championship proper.

Year	Site	Winner, Runner-Up	Score
1895	Newport GC	Horace Rawlins	173
	Newport, R.I.	Willie Dunn	175
1896	Shinnecock Hills GC	James Foulis	152[a]
	Southampton, N.Y.	Horace Rawlins	155
1897	Chicago GC	Joe Lloyd	162
	Wheaton, Ill.	Willie Anderson	163
1898	Myopia Hunt Club	Fred Herd	328
	Hamilton, Mass.	Alex Smith	335
1899	Baltimore CC	Willie Smith	315
	Baltimore, Md.	George Low	326
		Val Fitzjohn	326
		W. H. Way	326
1900	Chicago GC	Harry Vardon	313
	Wheaton, Ill.	J. H. Taylor	315
1901	Myopia Hunt Club	Willie Anderson	331–85
	Hamilton, Mass.	Alex Smith	331–86
1902	Garden City GC	Lawrence Auchterlonie	307
	Garden City, N.Y.	Stewart Gardner	313
		W. J. Travis[b]	313
1903	Baltusrol GC	Willie Anderson	307–82
	Springfield, N.J.	David Brown	307–84
1904	Glen View Club	Willie Anderson	303
	Golf, Ill.	Gil Nicholls	308
1905	Myopia Hunt Club	Willie Anderson	314
	Hamilton, Mass.	Alex Smith	316
1906	Onwentsia Club	Alex Smith	295
	Lake Forest, Ill.	William Smith	302
1907	Philadelphia Cricket Club	Aleck Ross	302
	Philadelphia, Pa.	Gil Nicholls	304

The 1913 U.S. Open was over. Francis Ouimet (center) accepts the congratulations of Harry Vardon (left) and Ted Ray (right) with both hands. Vardon won the National Open in 1900.

Charles "Chick" Evans sinking his putt on the 18th green of the Minikahda Club to win the 1916 National Open.

Lawson Little makes his putt for a 287 total to tie Gene Sarazen. The next day he won the play-off 70–73.

Sam Snead, who has won all other major tournaments, has never won the National Open.

In 1955 and 1956, Ben Hogan missed his bid to be the first man to win five Open Championships. In the 1955 Open (left), he is trying to blast the ball onto the 18th fairway from the deep rough into which he hooked his tee shot. It took him three to get out, and he finally got down in six, while his opponent, Jack Fleck, took a par four for a 69 and victory by three strokes in the 18-hole play-off. In 1956 (right), Hogan missed a short putt that cost him his chance to tie with Open winner, Cary Middlecoff.

Year	Site	Winner, Runner-Up	Score
1908	Myopia Hunt Club	Fred McLeod[e]	322–77
	Hamilton, Mass.	Willie Smith	322–83
1909	Englewood GC	George Sargent	290
	Englewood, N.J.	Tom McNamara	294
1910	Philadelphia Cricket Club	Alex Smith	298–71
	St. Martins, Pa.	John J. McDermott	298–75
		Macdonald Smith	298–77
1911	Chicago GC	John J. McDermott[d]	307–80
	Wheaton, Ill.	Michael J. Brady	307–82
		George O. Simpson	307–85
1912	CC of Buffalo	John J. McDermott	294
	Buffalo, N.Y.	Tom McNamara	296
1913	The Country Club	Francis Ouimet[e]	304–72
	Brookline, Mass.	Harry Vardon	304–77
		Edward Ray	304–78
1914	Midlothian CC	Walter Hagen	290
	Blue Island, Ill.	Charles Evans, Jr.[b]	291
1915	Baltusrol GC	Jerome D. Travers[b]	297
	Springfield, N.J.	Tom McNamara	298
1916	Minikahda Club	Charles Evans, Jr.[b]	286
	Minneapolis, Minn.	Jock Hutchison	288
1917–1918 Not played			
1919	Brae Burn CC	Walter Hagen	301–77
	West Newton, Mass.	Michael J. Brady	301–78
1920	Inverness Club	Edward Ray[e]	295
	Toledo, Ohio	Harry Vardon	296
		Jack Burke	296
		Leo Diegel	296
		Jock Hutchison	296
1921	Columbia CC	James M. Barnes	289
	Chevy Chase, Md.	Walter Hagen	298
		Fred McLeod	298
1922	Skokie CC[f]	Gene Sarazen	288
	Glencoe, Ill.	Robert T. Jones, Jr.[b]	289
		John L. Black	289
1923	Inwood CC	Robert T. Jones, Jr.[b]	296–76
	Inwood, N.Y.	Robert A. Cruickshank	296–78
1924	Oakland Hills CC	Cyril Walker	297
	Birmingham, Mich.	Robert T. Jones, Jr.[b]	300
1925	Worcester CC	William Macfarlane	291–75–72
	Worcester, Mass.	Robert T. Jones, Jr.[b]	291–75–73
1926	Scioto CC	Robert T. Jones, Jr.[b]	293
	Columbus, Ohio	Joe Turnesa	294
1927	Oakmont CC	Tommy Armour	301–76
	Oakmont, Pa.	Harry Cooper	301–79
1928	Olympia Fields CC	Johnny Farrell	294–143
	Matteson, Ill.	Robert T. Jones, Jr.[b]	294–144
1929	Winged Foot GC	Robert T. Jones, Jr.[b]	294–141
	Mamaroneck, N.Y.	Al Espinosa	294–164
1930	Interlachen CC	Robert T. Jones, Jr.[b]	287
	Minneapolis, Minn.	Macdonald Smith	289
1931	Inverness Club	Billy Burke	292–149–148
	Toledo, Ohio	George Von Elm	292–149–149
1932	Fresh Meadow	Gene Sarazen	286
	Flushing, N.Y.	Robert A. Cruickshank	289
		T. Philip Perkins	289
1933	North Shore GC	John G. Goodman[b]	287
	Glen View, Ill.	Ralph Guldahl	288

Year	Site	Winner, Runner-Up	Score
1934	Merion Cricket Club	Olin Dutra	293
	Ardmore, Pa.	Gene Sarazen	294
1935	Oakmont CC	Sam Parks, Jr.	299
	Oakmont, Pa.	Jimmy Thomson	301
1936	Baltusrol GC	Tony Manero	282
	Springfield, N.J.	Harry E. Cooper	284
1937	Oakland Hills CC	Ralph Guldahl	281
	Birmingham, Mich.	Sam Snead	283
1938	Cherry Hills Club	Ralph Guldahl	284
	Denver, Colo.	Dick Metz	290
1939	Philadelphia CC	Byron Nelson	284–68–70
	West Conshohocken, Pa.	Craig Wood	284–68–73
		Denny Shute	284–76
1940	Canterbury GC	Lawson Little	287–70
	Cleveland, Ohio	Gene Sarazen	287–73
1941	Colonial Club	Craig Wood	284
	Fort Worth, Texas	Denny Shute	287
1942–1945	Not played		
1946	Canterbury GC	Lloyd Mangrum	284–72–72
	Cleveland, Ohio	Byron Nelson	284–72–73
		Victor Ghezzi	284–72–73
1947	St. Louis CC	Lew Worsham	282–69
	Clayton, Mo.	Sam Snead	282–70
1948	Riviera CC	Ben Hogan	276
	Los Angeles, Calif.	Jimmy Demaret	278
1949	Medinah CC	Cary Middlecoff	286
	Medinah, Ill.	Sam Snead	287
		Clayton Heafner	287
1950	Merion GC	Ben Hogan	287–69
	Ardmore, Pa.	Lloyd Mangrum	287–73
		George Fazio	287–75
1951	Oakland Hills CC	Ben Hogan	287
	Birmingham, Mich.	Clayton Heafner	289
1952	Northwood Club	Julius Boros	281
	Dallas, Texas	Edward S. Oliver, Jr.	285
1953	Oakmont CC	Ben Hogan	283
	Oakmont, Pa.	Sam Snead	289
1954	Baltusrol GC	Ed Furgol	284
	Springfield, N.J.	Gene Littler	285
1955	Olympic CC	Jack Fleck	287–69
	San Francisco, Calif.	Ben Hogan	287–72
1956	Oak Hill CC	Cary Middlecoff	281
	Rochester, N.Y.	Julius Boros	282
		Ben Hogan	282
1957	Inverness Club	Dick Mayer	282–72
	Toledo, Ohio	Cary Middlecoff	282–79
1958	Southern Hills CC	Tommy Bolt	283
	Tulsa, Okla.	Gary Player	287
1959	Winged Foot CC	Billy Casper, Jr.	282
	Mamaroneck, N.Y.	Robert R. Rosburg	283
1960	Cherry Hills CC	Arnold Palmer	280
	Englewood, Colo.	Jack Nicklaus [b]	282
1961	Oakland Hills CC	Gene Littler	281
	Birmingham, Mich.	Bob Goalby	282
		Doug Sanders	282
1962	Oakmont CC	Jack Nicklaus	283–71
	Oakmont, Pa.	Arnold Palmer	283–74

Year	Site	Winner, Runner-Up	Score
1963	The Country Club	Julius Boros	293–70
	Brookline, Mass.	Jacky Cupit	293–73
		Arnold Palmer	293–76
1964	Congressional CC	Ken Venturi	278
	Washington, D.C.	Tommy Jacobs	282
1965	Bellerive CC	Gary Player	282–71
	St. Louis, Mo.	Kel Nagle	282–74
1966	Olympic CC	Billy Casper, Jr.	278–69
	San Francisco, Calif.	Arnold Palmer	278–73
1967	Baltusrol GC	Jack Nicklaus	275[a]
	Springfield, N.J.	Arnold Palmer	279
1968	Oak Hill CC	Lee B. Trevino	275[a]
	Rochester, N.Y.	Jack Nicklaus	279
1969	Champions GC	Orville Moody	281
	Houston, Texas	Deane Beman	282
		Al Geiberger	282
		Robert R. Rosburg	282
1970	Hazeltine National GC	Tony Jacklin	281
	Chaska, Minn.	Dave Hill	288
1971	Merion GC	Lee B. Trevino	280–68
	Ardmore, Pa.	Jack Nicklaus	280–71
1972	Pebble Beach Golf Links	Jack Nicklaus	290
	Monterey, Calif.	Bruce Crampton	293
1973	Oakmont CC	Johnny Miller	279
	Oakmont, Pa.	John Schlee	280
1974	Winged Foot GC	Hale Irwin	287
	Mamaroneck, N.Y.	Forrest Fezler	289
1975	Medinah CC	Lou Graham[g]	287–71
	Medinah, Ill.	John Mahaffey	287–73
1976	Atlanta AC	Jerry Pate	277
	Atlanta, Ga.	Tom Weiskopf	279
		Al Geiberger	279
1977	Southern Hills CC	Hubert Green	278
	Tulsa, Okla.	Lou Graham	279

[a] Record low score.
[b] Denotes amateur.
[c] McLeod, at 108 pounds, was the smallest Open winner.
[d] McDermott (at age of 19 years, 10 months) was the youngest Open winner.
[e] Ray (at 43 years, 4 months) was oldest Open winner.
[f] Admission charge was first levied in this Open.
[g] Won 18-hole play-off.

Note: In 1917, an Open Patriotic Tournament was conducted for the benefit of the American Red Cross at the Whitemarsh Valley CC, Philadelphia, Pa. Winner: Jock Hutchison, 292; runner-up: Tom McNamara, 299. In 1942, a Hale American National Open Golf Tournament was conducted for the benefit of the Navy Relief Society and the United Service Organizations at Ridgemoor CC, Chicago, Ill. Winner: Ben Hogan, 271; runners-up: Jimmy Demaret and Mike Turnesa, 274.

U.S. National Amateur Championship

The USGA Amateur began in 1895 at the Newport (R.I.) Golf Club and was won by Charles B. Macdonald, a founder of the Chicago Golf Club. There were 32 entries, and matches were determined by blind draw. While the field increased over the years, the Amateur remained at match play until 1965, when the format was changed to 72-hole stroke play. In 1973 it was changed back to match play.

Entries to the Amateur Championship at present are open to amateurs who have handicaps of not more than three strokes. Residents of the United States must be members of USGA Regular Member Clubs except that the first four finishers and ties in the Public Links will be invited to compete in sectional qualifying without regard to club affiliation or handicap. Two hundred players are eligible for the Championship proper.

The majority earn their places through 36-hole sectional qualifying rounds at various sites throughout the country. The winner receives a gold medal and his club receives custody of a replica of the Hovemeyer Trophy for the ensuing year.

Date	Site	Winner, Runner-Up	Score
1895	Newport GC	Charles B. Macdonald	
	Newport, R.I.	Charles E. Sands	12 & 11
	All Match Play		
1896	Shinnecock Hills GC	H. J. Whigham	
	Southampton, N.Y.	J. G. Thorp	8 & 7
	Medalist: H. J. Whigham, 163 (36)		
1897	Chicago GC	H. J. Whigham	
	Wheaton, Ill.	W. Rossiter Betts	8 & 6
	Medalist: Charles B. Macdonald, 174		
1898	Morris County GC	Findlay S. Douglas	
	Morristown, N.J.	Walter B. Smith	5 & 3
	Medalist: J. H. Choate, 175		
1899	Onwentsia Club	H. M. Harriman	
	Lake Forest, Ill.	Findlay S. Douglas	3 & 2
	Medalist: Charles B. Macdonald, 168		
1900	Garden City GC	Walter J. Travis	
	Garden City, N.Y.	Findlay S. Douglas	2 up
	Medalist: Walter J. Travis, 166		
1901	CC of Atlantic City	Walter J. Travis	
	Atlantic City, N.J.	Walter E. Egan	5 & 4
	Medalist: Walter J. Travis, 157		
1902	Glen View Club	Louis N. James	
	Golf, Ill.	Eben M. Byers	4 & 2
	Medalist: Walter J. Travis, 79 (18)		
1903	Nassau CC	Walter J. Travis	
	Glen Cove, N.Y.	Eben M. Byers	5 & 4
	All Match Play		
1904	Baltusrol GC	H. Chandler Egan	
	Springfield, N.J.	Fred Herreshoff	8 & 6
	Medalist: H. Chandler Egan, 242 (54)		
1905	Chicago GC	H. Chandler Egan	
	Wheaton, Ill.	D. E. Sawyer	6 & 5
	Medalist: Dr. D. P. Fredericks, 155 (36)		
1906	Englewood GC	Eben M. Byers	
	Englewood, N.J.	George S. Lyon	2 up
	Medalist: Walter J. Travis, 152		
1907	Euclid Club	Jerome D. Travers	
	Cleveland, Ohio	Archibald Graham	6 & 5
	Medalist: Walter J. Travis, 146		
1908	Garden City GC	Jerome D. Travers	
	Garden City, N.Y.	Max H. Behr	8 & 7
	Medalist: Walter J. Travis, 153		
1909	Chicago GC	Robert A. Gardner[a]	
	Wheaton, Ill.	H. Chandler Egan	4 & 3
	Medalist: Charles Evans, Jr., 151		
1910	The Country Club	William C. Fownes, Jr.	
	Brookline, Mass.	Warren K. Wood	4 & 3
	Medalist: Fred Herreshoff, 152		
1911	The Apawamis Club	Harold H. Hilton	
	Rye, N.Y.	Fred Herreshoff	1 up, 37 holes
	Medalist: Harold H. Hilton, 150		
1912	Chicago GC	Jerome D. Travers	
	Wheaton, Ill.	Charles Evans, Jr.	7 & 6
	Medalist: Charles Evans, Jr., 152		
1913	Garden City GC	Jerome D. Travers	
	Garden City, N.Y.	John G. Anderson	5 & 4
	Medalist: Charles Evans, Jr., 148		

Date	Site	Winner, Runner-Up	Score
1914	Ekwanok CC Manchester, Vt. Co-Medalists: R. R. Gorton W. C. Fownes, Jr., 144	Francis Ouimet[b] Jerome D. Travers	6 & 5
1915	CC of Detroit Grosse Pointe Farms, Mich. Medalist: Dudley Mudge, 152	Robert A. Gardner John G. Anderson	5 & 4
1916	Merion Cricket Club Haverford, Pa. Medalist: W. C. Fownes, Jr., 153	Charles Evans, Jr. Robert A. Gardner	4 & 3
1917–1918	Not played		
1919	Oakmont CC Oakmont, Pa. Co-Medalists: S. D. Herron J. B. Manion Paul Tewkesbury, 158	S. Davidson Herron Robert T. Jones, Jr.	5 & 4
1920	Engineers CC Roslyn, N.Y. Medalist: Robert T. Jones, Jr., 154	Charles Evans, Jr. Francis Ouimet	7 & 6
1921	St. Louis CC Clayton, Mo. Medalist: Francis Ouimet, 144	Jesse P. Guilford Robert A. Gardner	7 & 6
1922[c]	The Country Club Brookline, Mass. Medalist: Jesse P. Guilford, 144	Jess W. Sweetser Charles Evans, Jr.	3 & 2
1923	Flossmoor CC Flossmoor, Ill. Co-Medalists: Charles Evans, Jr. Robert T. Jones, Jr., 149	Max R. Marston Jess W. Sweetser	1 up, 38 holes
1924	Merion Cricket Club Haverford, Pa. Medalist: D. Clarke Corkran, 142	Robert T. Jones, Jr. George Von Elm	9 & 8
1925	Oakmont CC Oakmont, Pa. Medalist: Roland R. MacKenzie, 145	Robert T. Jones, Jr. Watts Gunn	8 & 7
1926	Baltusrol GC Springfield, N.J. Medalist: Robert T. Jones, Jr., 143	George Von Elm Robert T. Jones, Jr.	2 & 1
1927	Minikahda Club Minneapolis, Minn. Medalist: Robert T. Jones, Jr., 142	Robert T. Jones, Jr. Charles Evans, Jr.	8 & 7
1928	Brae Burn CC West Newton, Mass. Medalist: George J. Voigt, 143	Robert T. Jones, Jr. T. Philip Perkins	10 & 9
1929	Del Monte G&CC Pebble Beach Course, Calif. Co-Medalists: Robert T. Jones, Jr. Eugene V. Homans, 145	Harrison R. Johnston Dr. O. F. Willing	4 & 3
1930	Merion Cricket Club Ardmore, Pa. Medalist: Robert T. Jones, Jr., 142	Robert T. Jones, Jr. Eugene V. Homans	8 & 7
1931	Beverly CC Chicago, Ill. Co-Medalists: Arthur Yates Charles H. Seaver John E. Lehman, 148	Francis Ouimet Jack Westland	6 & 5
1932	Baltimore CC Five Farms Course, Md. Medalist: John W. Fischer, 142	C. Ross Somerville John Goodman	2 & 1
1933	Kenwood CC Cincinnati, Ohio Medalist: John W. Fischer, 141	George T. Dunlap, Jr. Max R. Marston	6 & 5

Date	Site	Winner, Runner-Up	Score
1934	The Country Club Brookline, Mass. All Match Play	W. Lawson Little, Jr. David Goldman	8 & 7
1935	The Country Club Cleveland, Ohio All Match Play	W. Lawson Little, Jr. Walter Emery	4 & 2
1936	Garden City GC Garden City, N.Y. All Match Play	John W. Fischer Jack McLean	1 up, 37 holes
1937	Alderwood CC Portland, Ore. Medalist: Roger Kelly, 142	John G. Goodman Raymond E. Billows	2 up
1938	Oakmont CC Oakmont, Pa. Medalist: Gus T. Moreland, 146	William P. Turnesa B. Patrick Abbott	8 & 7
1939	North Shore CC Glenview, Ill. Medalist: Thomas Sheehan, Jr., 139	Marvin H. Ward Raymond E. Billows	7 & 5
1940	Winged Foot GC Mamaroneck, N.Y. Medalist: Richard D. Chapman, 140	Richard D. Chapman W. B. McCullough, Jr.	11 & 9
1941	Omaha Field Club Omaha, Neb. Medalist: Stewart M. Alexander, Jr., 144	Marvin H. Ward B. Patrick Abbott	4 & 3
1942–1945	Not played		
1946	Baltusrol GC Springfield, N.J. Medalist: Robert H. (Skee) Riegel, 136[d]	Stanley E. (Ted) Bishop Smiley L. Quick	1 up, 37 holes
1947	Del Monte G&CC Pebble Beach Course, Calif. All Match Play	Robert H. (Skee) Riegel John W. Dawson	2 & 1
1948	Memphis CC Memphis, Tenn. All Match Play	William P. Turnesa Raymond E. Billows	2 & 1
1949	Oak Hill CC Rochester, N.Y. All Match Play	Charles R. Coe Rufus King	11 & 10
1950	Minneapolis GC Minneapolis, Minn. All Match Play	Sam Urzetta Frank Stranahan	1 up, 39 holes
1951	Saucon Valley CC Bethlehem, Pa. All Match Play	Billy Maxwell Joseph F. Gagliardi	4 & 3
1952	Seattle GC Seattle, Wash. All Match Play	Jack Westland[e] Al Mengert	3 & 2
1953	Oklahoma City G&CC Oklahoma City, Okla. All Match Play	Gene A. Littler Dale Morey	1 up
1954	CC of Detroit Grosse Pointe Farms, Mich. All Match Play	Arnold D. Palmer Robert Sweeny	1 up
1955	CC of Virginia Richmond, Va. All Match Play	E. Harvie Ward, Jr. Wm. Hyndman III	9 & 8
1956	Knollwood Club Lake Forest, Ill. All Match Play	E. Harvie Ward, Jr. Charles Kocsis	5 & 4
1957	The Country Club Brookline, Mass. All Match Play	Hillman Robbins, Jr. Dr. Frank M. Taylor	5 & 4

Date	Site	Winner, Runner-Up	Score
1958	Olympic CC	Charles R. Coe	
	San Francisco, Calif.	Thomas D. Aaron	5 & 4
	All Match Play		
1959	Broadmoor GC	**Jack W. Nicklaus**	
	Colorado Springs, Colo.	Charles R. Coe	1 up
	All Match Play		
1960	St. Louis CC	Deane R. Beman	
	Clayton, Mo.	Robert W. Gardner	6 & 4
	All Match Play		
1961	Pebble Beach Golf Links	Jack W. Nicklaus	
	Pebble Beach, Calif.	H. Dudley Wysong, Jr.	8 & 6
	All Match Play		
1962	Pinehurst CC	Labron E. Harris, Jr.	
	Pinehurst, N.C.	Downing Gray	1 up
	All Match Play		
1963	Wakonda Club	Deane R. Beman	
	Des Moines, Iowa	R. H. Sikes	2 & 1
	All Match Play		
1964	Canterbury GC	William C. Campbell	
	Cleveland, Ohio	Edgar M. Tutwiler	1 up
	Co-Medalists: Marvin M. Giles, III		
	Robert Greenwood, 143		
1965	Southern Hills CC	Robert J. Murphy, Jr.	291
	Tulsa, Okla.	Robert B. Dickson	292
1966	Merion GC	Gary Cowan	285–75
	Ardmore, Pa.	Deane R. Beman	285–76
1967	Broadmoor GC	Robert B. Dickson	285
	Colorado Springs, Colo.	Marvin M. Giles III	286
1968	Scioto CC	Bruce Fleisher	284*f*
	Columbus, Ohio	Marvin M. Giles III	285
1969	Oakmont CC	Steve Melnyk	286
	Oakmont, Pa.	Marvin M. Giles III	291
1970	Waverley CC	Lanny Wadkins	279
	Portland, Ore.	Thomas O. Kite, Jr.	280
1971	Wilmington CC	Gary Cowan	280
	Wilmington, Del.	Eddie Pearce	283
1972	Charlotte CC	Marvin M. Giles III	285
	Charlotte, N.C.	Ben Crenshaw	288
		Mark Hayes	288
1973	Inverness Club	Craig Stadler	
	Toledo, Ohio	David Strawn	6 & 5
1974	Ridgewood CC	Jerome K. Pate	
	Ridgewood, N.J.	John P. Grace	2 & 1
1975	CC of Virginia	Fred Ridley	
	Richmond, Va.	Keith Fergus	2 up
1976	Bel-Air CC	Bill Sander	
	Los Angeles, Calif.	C. Parker Moore, Jr.	8 & 6
1977	Aronimink GC	John Fought	
	Newton Square, Pa.	Doug Fischesser	9 & 8

a Gardner (at 19 years, 5 months) was youngest Amateur Champion.
b Ouimet was first to win both the National Amateur and Open in the same year.
c First year admission was charged.
d Record qualifying score in championship proper. Record score in sectional qualifying rounds, 131 by William C. Campbell in 1961.
e Westland (at 47) was oldest winner of Amateur Championship.
f Lowest score on record.
g Lowest score on record.

U.S. Women's Amateur Championship

The USGA Women's Amateur began at the Meadowbrook Club, Westbury, N.Y., on November 9, 1895. Thirteen women participated at 18 holes stroke play. Nine holes were played before lunch and nine holes after, and the silver pitcher was won by Mrs.

C. S. Brown of the Shinnecock Hills Golf Club. The next year it was decided to conduct the championship at match play. Twenty-nine women entered and competed for eight places in the match-play bracket. While the number of entries has increased, the format has not changed too greatly over the years.

The Women's Amateur Championship is contested at match play after 36 holes stroke play qualifying. Entries are open to women amateur golfers who have handicaps of not more than five strokes. Residents of the United States must be members of USGA Regular Member Clubs, except that the current Girls' Junior Champion and runner-up and the semi-finalists in the Women's Amateur Public Links championship will be invited to compete regardless of club affiliation or handicap. The field of 150 will be increased to accommodate them.

Year	Winner, Score	Runner-Up	Site
1895	Mrs. Charles S. Brown, 132	N. C. Sargent	Meadowbrook GC Hempstead, N.Y.
1896	Champion at 18 holes stroke play Beatrix Hoyt,[a] 2 & 1	Mrs. Arthur Turnure	Morris County GC Morristown, N.J.
1897	Medalist, Beatrix Hoyt, 95 Beatrix Hoyt, 5 & 4	N. C. Sargent	Essex CC Manchester, Mass.
1898	Medalist, Beatrix Hoyt, 108 Beatrix Hoyt, 5 & 3	Maud Wetmore	Ardsley GC Ardsley-on-the-Hudson, N.Y.
1899	Medalist, Beatrix Hoyt, 92 Ruth Underhill, 2 & 1	Mrs. Caleb Fox	Philadelphia CC Philadelphia, Pa.
1900	Medalist, Beatrix Hoyt, 97 Frances C. Griscom, 6 & 5	Margaret Curtis	Shinnecock Hills GC Southampton, N.Y.
1901	Medalist, Beatrix Hoyt, 94 Genevieve Hecker, 5 & 3	Lucy Herron	Baltusrol GC Springfield, N.J.
1902	Co-Medalists, Mary B. Adams Lucy Herron Margaret Curtis Mrs. E. A. Manio, 97 Genevieve Hecker, 4 & 3	Louisa A. Wells	The Country Club Brookline, Mass.
1903	Co-Medalists, Louisa A. Wells Margaret Curtis, 89 Bessie Anthony, 7 & 6	J. A. Carpenter	Chicago GC Wheaton, Ill.
1904	Medalist, Mrs. Caleb F. Fox, 94 Georgianna M. Bishop, 5 & 3	Mrs. E. F. Sanford	Merion Cricket Club Ardmore, Pa.
1905	Co-Medalists, Charlotte Dod Louise Vanderhoef Harriot S. Curtis, 93 Pauline Mackay, 1 up	Margaret Curtis	Morris County GC Morristown, N.J.
1906	Co-Medalists, Georgianna Bishop Margaret Curtis, 87 Harriot S. Curtis, 2 & 1	Mary B. Adams	Brae Burn CC West Newton, Mass.
1907	Medalist, Pauline Mackay, 87 Margaret Curtis, 7 & 6	Harriot S. Curtis	Midlothian CC Blue Island, Ill.
1908	Medalist, Margaret Curtis, 95 Katherine C. Harley, 6 & 5	Mrs. T. H. Polhemus	Chevy Chase Club Chevy Chase, Md.
1909	Medalist, Harriot S. Curtis, 85 Dorothy I. Campbell, 3 & 2	Mrs. R. H. Bartow	Merion Cricket Club Haverford, Pa.

Year	Winner, Score	Runner-Up	Site
	Co-Medalists, Dorothy I. Campbell Mrs. Caleb F. Fox Anita Phipps Margaret Curtis, 86		
1910	Dorothy I. Campbell, 2 & 1	Mrs. G. M. Martin	Homewood CC Flossmoor, Ill.
	Medalist, Dorothy I. Campbell, 85		
1911	Margaret Curtis, 5 & 3	Lillian B. Hyde	Baltusrol GC Springfield, N.J.
	Medalist, R. H. Barlow, 87		
1912	Margaret Curtis, 3 & 2	Mrs. R. H. Barlow	Essex CC Manchester, Mass.
	Medalist, Margaret Curtis, 88		
1913	Gladys Ravenscroft, 2 up	Marion Hollins	Wilmington CC Wilmington, Del.
	Medalist, Gladys Ravenscroft, 88		
1914	Mrs. H. Arnold Jackson,[b] 1 up	Elaine V. Rosenthal	Nassau CC Glen Cove, N.Y.
	Medalist, Georgianna Bishop, 85		
1915	Mrs. C. H. Vanderbeck, 3 & 2	Mrs. W. A. Gavin	Onwentsia Club Lake Forest, Ill.
	Medalist, Mrs. C. H. Vanderbeck, 85		
1916	Alexa Stirling, 2 & 1	Mildred Caverly	Belmont Springs CC Waverly, Mass.
1917–1918	Not played		
1919	Medalist, Mrs. J. V. Hurd,[c] 86 Alexa Stirling, 6 & 5	Mrs. W. A. Gavin	Shawnee CC Shawnee-on-Delaware, Pa.
	Co-Medalists, Alexa Stirling Mrs. W. A. Gavin, 87		
1920	Alexa Stirling, 5 & 4	Mrs. J. V. Hurd[c]	Mayfield CC Cleveland, Ohio
	Medalist, Marion Hollins, 82		
1921	Marion Hollins, 5 & 4	Alexa Stirling	Hollywood GC Deal, N.J.
	Medalist, Glenna Collett, 177 (36 holes)		
1922	Glenna Collett, 5 & 4	Mrs. W. A. Gavin	Greenbrier GC White Sulphur Springs, W. Va.
	Medalist, Glenna Collett, 81		
1923	Edith Cummings, 3 & 2	Alexa Stirling	Westchester-Biltmore CC Rye, N.Y.
	Medalist, Alexa Stirling, 84		
1924	Mrs. J. V. Hurd,[c] 7 & 6	Mary K. Browne	Rhode Island CC Nayatt, R.I.
	Medalist, Glenna Collett, 79		
1925	Glenna Collett, 9 & 8	Mrs. W. G. Fraser[d]	St. Louis CC Clayton, Mo.
	Medalist, Mrs. W. G. Fraser,[d] 77		
1926	Mrs. G. Henry Stetson, 3 & 1	Mrs. W. D. Goss, Jr.	Merion Cricket Club Haverford, Pa.
	Medalist, Glenna Collett, 81		
1927	Mrs. M. B. Horn, 5 & 4	Maureen Orcutt	Cherry Valley Club Garden City, N.Y.
	Medalist, Ada Mackenzie, 77		
1928	Glenna Collett, 13 & 12	Virginia Van Wie	Va. Hot Springs G&TC Hot Springs, Va.
	Medalist, Maureen Orcutt, 80		
1929	Glenna Collett, 4 & 3	Leona Pressler	Oakland Hills CC Birmingham, Mich.
	Co-Medalists, Helen Hicks, Virginia Van Wie, 79		

Year	Winner, Score	Runner-Up	Site
1930	Glenna Collett, 6 & 5	Virginia Van Wie	Los Angeles CC Beverly Hills, Calif.
1931	Medalist, Mrs. O. S. Hill, 79 Helen Hicks, 2 & 1	Mrs. E. H. Vare, Jr.[e]	CC of Buffalo Williamsville, N.Y.
1932	Co-Medalists, Maureen Orcutt Mrs. E. H. Vare, Jr.[e] Mrs. Harley G. Higbie Mrs. O. S. Hill, 82 Virginia Van Wie, 10 & 8	Mrs. E. H. Vare, Jr.	Salem CC Peabody, Mass.
1933	Co-Medalists, Maureen Orcutt Virginia Van Wie, 77 Virginia Van Wie, 4 & 3	Helen Hicks	Exmoor CC Highland Park, Ill.
1934	Medalist, Enid Wilson, 76 Virginia Van Wie, 2 & 1	Dorothy Traung	Whitemarsh Valley CC Chestnut Hill, Pa.
1935	Co-Medalists, Mrs. L. D. Cheney Lucille Robinson Mrs. E. H. Vare, Jr.,[e] 82 Mrs. E. H. Vare, Jr.,[e] 3 & 2	Patty Berg	Interlochen CC Hopkins, Minn.
1936	Medalist, Jean Bauer, 79 Pamela Barton, 4 & 3	Mrs. J. D. Crews	Canoe Brook CC Summit, N.J.
1937	Medalist, Mrs. J. A. Page, Jr., 78 Mrs. J. A. Page, Jr., 7 & 6	Patty Berg	Memphis CC Memphis, Tenn.
1938	Medalist, Mrs. J. A. Page, Jr., 79 Patty Berg, 6 & 5	Mrs. J. A. Page, Jr.	Westmoreland CC Wilmette, Ill.
1939	Co-Medalists, Dorothy Traung Patty Berg, 80 Betty Jameson, 3 & 2	Dorothy Kirby	Wee Burn Club Noroton, Conn.
1940	Medalist, Beatrice Barrett, 74 Betty Jameson, 6 & 5	Jane S. Cothran	Del Monte G&CC Del Monte, Calif.
1941	Medalist, Dorothy Traung, 78 Mrs. F. Newell, 5 & 3	Helen Sigel	The Country Club Brookline, Mass.
1942–1945	Co-Medalists, Grace Amory Alice O. Belanger Jean Bauer Betty Jameson, 76 Not played		
1946	Mrs. George Zaharias,[f] 11 & 9	Clara C. Sherman	Southern Hills CC Tulsa, Okla.
1947	Medalist, Dorothy Kirby, 152 (36 holes) Louise Suggs, 2 up	Dorothy Kirby	Franklin Hills CC Franklin, Mich.
1948	Medalist, Louise Suggs, 78 Mrs. G. S. Lenczyk, 4 & 3	Helen Sigel	Del Monte G&TC Del Monte, Calif.
1949	Medalist, Betty Mims White, 77 Mrs. M. A. Porter, 3 & 2 All Match Play	Dorothy Kielty	Merion GC Ardmore, Pa.
1950	Beverly Hanson, 6 & 4 All Match Play	Mae Murray	Atlanta AC (East Lake) Atlanta, Ga.

Year	Winner, Score	Runner-Up	Site
1951	Dorothy Kirby, 2 & 1	Claire Doran	Town & CC St. Paul, Minn.
	Co-Medalists, Carol Diringer Barbara Romack, 74		
1952	Jacqueline Pung, 2 & 1	Shirley McFedters	Waverley CC Portland, Ore.
	Medalist, Dorothy Kirby, 76		
1953	Mary Lena Faulk, 3 & 2	Polly Riley	Rhode Island CC West Barrington, R.I.
	All Match Play 1953 to 1963		
1954	Barbara Romack, 4 & 2	Mary K. Wright	Allegheny CC Sewickley, Pa.
1955	Patricia A. Lesser, 7 & 6	Jane Nelson	Myers Park CC Charlotte, N.C.
1956	Marlene Stewart, 2 & 1	Jo Anne Gunderson	Meridian Hills CC Indianapolis, Ind.
1957	JoAnne Gunderson, 8 & 6	Mrs. Les Johnstone	Del Paso CC Sacramento, Calif.
1958	Anne Quast, 3 & 2	Barbara Romack	Wee Burn CC Darien, Conn.
1959	Barbara McIntire, 4 & 3	JoAnne Gunderson	Congressional CC Washington, D.C.
1960	JoAnne Gunderson, 6 & 5	Jean Ashley	Tulsa CC Tulsa, Okla.
1961	Mrs. J. D. Decker,[g] 14 & 13	Phyllis Preuss	Tacoma C&GC Tacoma, Wash.
1962	JoAnne Gunderson, 9 & 8	Ann Baker	CC of Rochester Rochester, N.Y.
1963	Mrs. J. D. Welts, 2 & 1	Peggy Conley	Taconic GC Williamstown, Mass.
1964	Barbara McIntire, 3 & 2	JoAnne Gunderson	Prairie Dunes CC Hutchinson, Kans.
	Co-Medalists, JoAnne Gunderson Barbara McIntire Polly Riley, 151		
1965	Jean Ashley, 5 & 4	Mrs. J. D. Welts	Lakewood CC Denver, Colo.
	Medalist, Lida Fee Matthews, 148		
1966	Mrs. D. R. Carner,[h] 41 holes	Mrs. J. D. Streit[h]	Sewickly Heights GC Sewickly, Pa.
	Medalist, Shelley Hamlin, 143		
1967	Mary Lou Dill, 5 & 4	Jean Ashley	Annandale GC Pasadena, Calif.
	Medalist, Phyllis Preuss, 148		
1968	Mrs. D. R. Carner,[h] 5 & 4	Mrs. D. Welts	Birmingham CC Mich.
	Medalist, Catherine Lacoste, 143		
1969	Catherine Lacoste, 3 & 2	Shelley Hamlin	Las Colinas CC Irving, Texas
	Medalist, Mrs. T. Broddie, 149		
1970	Martha Wilkinson, 3 & 2	Cynthia Hill	Wee Burn CC Darien, Conn.
	Medalist, Martha Wilkinson, 150		
1971	Laura Baugh, 1 up	Beth Barry	Atlanta CC
	Co-Medalists, Connie Day Jane Bastanchury, 150		
1972	Mary Budke, 5 & 4	Cynthia Hill	St. Louis CC St. Louis, Mo.
	Medalist, Mrs. William Flennicken, Jr., 148		

1973	Medalist, Mrs. Kaye Potter, 74 Carol Semple, 1 up	Mrs. Stephen Sander[i]	Montclair GC Montclair, N.J.
1974	Medalist, Deborah Massey, 70 Cynthia Hill, 5 & 4	Carol Semple	Broadmoor GC Seattle, Wash.
1975	Medalist, Mrs. Nancy Sims, 71 Beth Daniel, 3 & 2	Donna Horton	Brae Burn CC Newton, Mass.
1976	Medalist, Beth Daniel, 70 Donna Horton, 2 & 1	Marianne Bretton	Del Paso CC Sacramento, Calif.
1977	Medalist, Mary Lawrence, 72 Beth Daniel, 3 & 1	Cathy Sherk	Cincinnati CC Cincinnati, Ohio

a Miss Hoyt, at the age of sixteen, was the youngest winner.
b Mrs. Jackson was the former Katherine Harley.
c Mrs. Hurd was the former Dorothy Campbell.
d Mrs. Fraser was the former Alexa Stirling.
e Mrs. Vare is the former Glenna Collett.
f Mrs. Zaharias was the former Mildred "Babe" Didrikson.
g Mrs. Decker was the former Anne Quast.
h Mrs. Carner is the former Jo Anne Gunderson, and Mrs. Streit is the former Marlene Stewart.
i Mrs. Stephen Sander is the former Anne Quast.

U.S. Women's Open Championship

The Women's Open championship has been sponsored by three organizations, the Women's Professional Golfers' Association from 1946 through 1948, the Ladies' PGA from 1949 through 1952, and the USGA since 1953. It is now played at 72 holes stroke play. Entries are open to professionals and to amateurs with handicaps of not more than four strokes.

Year	Winner, Score	Runner-Up, Score	Site
1946	Patty Berg, 5 & 4	Betty Jameson	Spokane CC Spokane, Wash.
1947	Medalist, Patty Berg, 145 Betty Jameson, 295	Sally Sessions, Polly Riley, 301	Starmount CC Greensboro, N.C.
1948	Mrs. George Zaharias,[a] 300	Betty Hicks, 308	Atlantic City CC Northfield, N.J.
1949	Louise Suggs, 291	Mrs. George Zaharias,[a] 305	Prince Georges G&CC Landover, Md.
1950	Mrs. George Zaharias,[a] 291	Betsy Rawls,[b] 300	Rolling Hills CC Wichita, Kans.
1951	Betsy Rawls, 293	Louise Suggs, 298	Druid Hills GC Atlanta, Ga.
1952	Louise Suggs,[c] 284	Marlene Bauer, Betty Jameson, 291	Bala GC Philadelphia, Pa.
1953	Betsy Rawls,[d] 302	Mrs. Jacqueline Pung, 302	CC of Rochester Rochester, N.Y.
1954	Mrs. George Zaharias, 291	Betty Hicks, 303	Salem CC Peabody, Mass.
1955	Fay Crocker, 299	Louise Suggs, Mary L. Faulk, 303	Wichita CC Wichita, Kans.
1956	Kathy Cornelius,[e] 302	Barbara McIntire, 302	Northland CC Duluth, Minn.
1957	Betsy Rawls, 299	Patty Berg, 305	Winged Foot GC Mamaroneck, N.Y.

Year	Winner, Score	Runner-Up, Score	Site
1958	Mary K. (Mickey) Wright, 290	Louise Suggs, 295	Forest Lake CC Bloomfield Hills, Mich.
1959	Mary K. (Mickey) Wright, 287	Louise Suggs, 289	Churchill Valley CC Pittsburgh, Pa.
1960	Betsy Rawls, 292	Joyce Ziske, 293	Worcester CC Worcester, Mass.
1961	Mary K. (Mickey) Wright, 293	Betsy Rawls, 299	Baltusrol GC Springfield, N.J.
1962	Mrs. Murie MacKenzie Lindstrom, 301	Ruth Jessen, Jo Anne Prentice, 303	Dunes G&BC Myrtle Beach, S.C.
1963	Mary Mills, 289	Sandra Haynie, Louise Suggs, 292	Kenwood CC Cincinnati, Ohio
1964	Mary K. (Mickey) Wright,[f] 290	Ruth Jessen, 290	San Diego CC Chula Vista, Calif.
1965	Carol Mann, 290	Kathy Cornelius, 292	Atlantic City CC Northfield, N.J.
1966	Sandra Spuzich, 297	Carol Mann, 298	Hazeltine Nat. GC Minneapolis, Minn.
1967	Catherine Lacoste,[g] 294	Susie Maxwell, Beth Stone, 296	Virginia Hot Springs G&TC Hot Springs, Va.
1968	Mrs. Susie Berning,[h] 289	Mary K. (Mickey) Wright, 292	Moselem Springs GC Fleetwood, Pa.
1969	Donna Caponi, 294	Peggy Wilson, 295	Scenic Hills CC Pensacola, Fla.
1970	Donna Caponi, 287	Sandra Haynie, Sandra Spuzich, 288	Muskogee CC Muskogee, Okla.
1971	Mrs. D. R. Carner,[i] 288	Kathy Whitworth, 295	Kahkwa CC Erie, Pa.
1972	Mrs. Susie Berning,[h] 299	Pam Barnett, Kathy Ahern, Judy Rankin, 300	Winged Foot GC Mamaroneck, N.Y.
1973	Mrs. Susie Berning,[h] 290	Gloria Ehret, Shelley Hamlin, 295	CC of Rochester Rochester, N.Y.
1974	Sandra Haynie, 295	Beth Stone, Carol Mann, 296	La Grange CC La Grange, Ill.
1975	Sandra Palmer, 295	Mrs. D. R. Carner,[i] Sandra Post, Nancy Lopez,[b] 299	Atlantic City CC Atlantic City, N.J.
1976	Mrs. D. R. Carner,[i] 292	Sandra Palmer, 292	Rolling Green CC Springfield, Pa.
1977	Hollis Stacy, 292	Nancy Lopez, 294	Hazeltine Nat. GC Chaska, Minn.

[a] Mrs. Zaharias was the former Mildred "Babe" Didrikson.
[b] Denotes amateur.
[c] Record low score.
[d] Betsy Rawls defeated Jacqueline Pung in the play-off, 71–77.
[e] Kathy Cornelius defeated Barbara McIntire in the play-off, 75–82.
[f] Mickey Wright defeated Ruth Jessen in the play-off, 70–72.
[g] Miss Lacoste, at twenty-two years, was youngest champion, while Miss Fay Crocker at forty years, 11 months, was the oldest. Incidentally, Miss Lacoste of France and Miss Crocker of Uruguay are the only foreign winners.
[h] Mrs. Berning is the former Susie Maxwell.
[i] Mrs. Carner is the former JoAnne Gunderson.
[j] Won 18-hole play-off.

The field is limited to 150 players; should more than 150 file entry, a draw will be conducted to determine the starting field. Players in certain categories will be exempt from the draw. These categories include former Women's Open Champions, former Women's Amateur Champions, and former LPGA Champions for the last 10 years, the 30 lowest scorers in the last three Women's Open Championships, 50 leading money winners on LPGA tour for preceding calendar year, 30 leading money winners from January 1 through closing date for Open entries, members and alternates for last previous USGA International Teams, qualifiers for match-play phase of previous Curtis Cup and Women's

Amateur Championships, quarter-finalists in the last three Women's Amateur Championships, and the current U.S. Girl's Junior Champion.

All entrants play in the first and second rounds. Only the 50 lowest scorers and any tying for the fiftieth place for 36 holes are eligible for the final 36 holes.

Amateur Public Links Championship

In 1922 the USGA started the Public Links Championship, a bona fide championship for all golfers who do not use the privileges of a private golf club during the current year. From a small beginning, the tourney has grown to more than 3,000 entries in which 150 players are eligible for the finals. The defending champion is exempt from sectional qualifying, and the remaining earn their places through 36-hole sectional qualifying rounds at various sites. In 1967, the Championship abandoned match play for stroke, but returned to match play in 1975.

Amateur Public Links Individual Champions

Year	Winner, Runner-Up	Score	Medalist
1922	Edmund R. Held, Richard J. Walsh	6 & 5	George F. Aulback, 139
1923	Richard J. Walsh, J. Steward Whitham	6 & 5	R. J. McAuliffe, 153
1924	Joseph Coble, Henry Decker	2 & 1	Earl McAleer, 150
1925	Raymond J. McAuliffe, William F. Serrick	6 & 5	Nelson Davis, 147
1926	Lester Bolstad, C. F. Kauffmann	3 & 2	R. J. Walsh, 146
1927	Carl F. Kauffmann, William F. Serrick	1 up, 37 holes	Clarke Morse, 149
1928	Carl F. Kauffmann, Phil Ogden	8 & 7	Samuel Graham, 152
1929	Carl F. Kauffmann, Milton Soncrant	4 & 3	C. F. Kauffmann, 151
1930	Robert E. Wingate, Joseph E. Greene	1 up	Al Quigley, 145
1931	Charles Ferrera, Joe Nichols	5 & 4	David Mitchell, 148
1932	R. L. Miller, Peter Miller	4 & 2	Joe Nichols, 145
1933	Cnarles Ferrera, R. L. Miller	3 & 2	Tab Boyer, 145
1934	David Mitchell, Arthur Armstrong	5 & 3	A. E. Campbell, 144
1935	Frank Strafaci, Joe Coria	1 up, 37 holes	Lloyd Nordstrom, 145
1936	B. Patrick Abbott, Claude B. Rippy	4 & 3	James J. Molinari, Claude B. Rippy, 145
1937	Bruce N. McCormick, Don Erickson	1 up	Don Erickson, 139
1938	Al Leach, Louis C. Cyr	1 up	Walter Burkemo, 141
1939	Andrew Szwedko, Philip Gordon	1 up	Luke Barnes, Jack Taulman, Arthur Armstrong, Gerry Bert, Jr., 144
1940	Robert C. Clark, Michael Dietz	8 & 6	Edward Furgol, Worth Stimits, Jr., 138
1941	William M. Welch, Jr., Jack Kerns	6 & 5	James C. Clark, Jr., 135
1942–1945	Not played		
1946	Smiley E. Quick, Louis Stafford	3 & 2	James C. Clark, Jr., 134
1947	Wilfred Crossley, Avery Beck	6 & 5	Wilfred Crossley, 139
1948	Michael R. Ferentz, Ben C. Hughes	2 & 1	All Match Play,
1949	Kenneth J. Towns, William E. Betger	5 & 4	1948–1955
1950	Stanley Bielot, John Dobro	7 & 5	
1951	Dave Stanley, Ralph Vranesic	1 up	
1952	Omer L. Boyan, Robert J. Sherer	4 & 3	
1953	Ted Richards, Jr., Irving A. Cooper	1 up	
1954	Gene Andrews, Jack E. Zimmerman	1 up	
1955	Sam D. Kocsis, Lewis T. Beam	2 up	
1956	James H. Burbaum, W. C. Scarbrough, Jr.	3 & 2	D. M. McBeath, 141
1957	Don Essig III, Gene Towry	6 & 5	Bud Kivett, 141
1958	Daniel D. Sikes, Jr., Bob Ludlow	3 & 2	Don Essig III, 144
1959	William A. Wright, Frank W. Campbell	3 & 2	D. D. Sikes, Jr., 137
1960	Verne Callison, Tyler Caplin	7 & 6	O. T. Douglass, Jr., H. Stevenson, R. Hogwood, 146
1961	Richard H. Sikes, John Molenda	4 & 3	Richard H. Sikes, 135
1962	Richard H. Sikes, Hung Soo Ahn	2 & 1	George Archer, 145
1963	Robert Lunn, Steve Oppermann	1 up	John Joseph, 141
1964	William McDonald, Dean Wilson, Jr.	5 & 3	Steve Oppermann, 135
1965	Arne Dokka, Leo Zampedro	10 & 9	S. Poploski, 144
1966	Lamott Kaser, Dave Ojala	6 & 5	Arne Dokka, 137

All Stroke Play—Winner Only,
1967–1972

1967	Verne Callison	287	
1968	Gene Towry	294	
1969	John Jackson, Jr.	292	
1970	Robert Risch	293	
1971	Fred Haney	290	All Match Play,
1972	Bob Allard	285	1975–1977
1973	Stan Stopa	294	
1974	Charles Barenaba, Jr.	290	
1975	Randy Barenaba, Allen Yamamoto	37 holes	
1976	Eddie Mudd, Archie Dadian	37 holes	
1977	Jerry Vidovic, Jeff Kern	4 & 2	

Junior Amateur Championship

The Junior Amateur Championship is now contested at match play after 36 holes of stroke play qualifying. The sixty-four players with the lowest 36-hole totals qualify for match play. All match play contests are at 18 holes, unless tied.

Entries are open to boys who will not reach their eighteenth birthday by the day of the final match and who have handicaps of not more than nine strokes. There is no club membership requirement. A total of 150 players are now eligible. All except the defending champion and the semi-finalists in the last Junior Amateur Championship, who are exempt if otherwise eligible, earn their places through 36-hole sectional qualifying rounds at various sites throughout the country. The defending champion and the semi-finalists are not exempt from qualifying at the site of the Championship.

Year	Winner, Runner-Up	Score
1948	Dean Lind, Kenneth Venturi	4 & 2
1949	Gay Brewer, Mason Rudolph	6 & 4
1950	Mason Rudolph, Charles Beville	2 & 1
1951	K. Thomas Jacobs, Jr., Floyd Addington	4 & 2
1952	Donald M. Bisplinghoff,	
	Eddie M. Meyerson	2 up
1953	Rex Baxter, Jr., George Warren III	2 & 1
1954	Foster Bradley, Jr., Allen L. Geiberger	3 & 1
1955	Billy J. Dunn, William J. Seanor	3 & 2
1956	Harland Stevenson, Jack D. Rule, Jr.	3 & 1
1957	Larry Beck, David C. Leon	6 & 5
1958	Gordon Baker, R. Douglas Lindsay	2 & 1
1959	Larry J. Lee, Michael V. McMahon	2 up
1960	William L. Tindall, Robert L. Hammer	2 & 1
1961	Charles S. McDowell, Jay Sigel	2 up
1962	James L. Wiechers, James Sullivan	4 & 3
1963	Gregg McHatton, Richard Bland	4 & 3
1964	John Miller, Enrique Sterling, Jr.	2 & 1
1965	James Masserio, Lloyd Liebler	3 & 2

1966	Gary Sanders, Ray Leach	2 up
1967	John T. Crooks, Andy North	2 & 1
1968	Eddie Pearce, William Harman, Jr.	6 & 5
1969	Aly Tompas, Eddie Pearce	3 & 1
1970	Gary Koch, Mike Nelms	8 & 6
1971	Mike Brannan, Robert Steele	4 & 3
1972	Bob Byman, Scott Simpson	2 & 1
1973	Jack Renner, Mike Brannan	1 up
		20 holes
1974	David Nevatt, Mark Tinder	4 & 3
1975	Brett Mullen, Scott Templeton	2 & 1
1976	Madden Hatchett III, Doug Clarke	3 & 2
1977	Willie Wood, David Games	4 & 3

Girls' Junior Championship

The Girls' Junior Championship is contested at match play after 36 holes of stroke play qualifying. The thirty-two players with the lowest 36-hole totals qualify for match play. Should a tie for the last qualifying place develop, it is settled immediately by a hole-by-hole play-off. All match play rounds are at 18 holes.

Entries are open to girl amateur golfers who will not reach their eighteenth birthday by the day of the final match. Entrants must have USGA handicaps of not more than 16 strokes. There is no requirement as to club affiliation. The starting field is limited to 120 players. Entries are accepted from the applicants with the lowest handicaps. Later vacancies in the field are offered to alternates, in order of handicaps. Any tie in the highest acceptable handicap class or for an alternate's position is decided by lot.

Catherine Lacoste of France, who does a knee bend and twists her putter as her putt lips the cup during the 1967 Women's Open Championship, was the first amateur to win the event.

Year	Winner, Runner-Up	Score
1949	Marlene Bauer, Barbara Bruning	2 up
1950	Patricia A. Lesser, Mary K. Wright	4 & 2
1951	Arlene Brooks, Barbara McIntire	1 up
1952	Mary K. Wright, Barbara McIntire	1 up
1953	Millie Meyerson, Holly Jean Roth	4 & 2
1954	Margaret Smith, Sue Driscoll	5 & 3
1955	Carole Jo Kabler, JoAnne Gunderson	4 & 3
1956	JoAnne Gunderson, Clifford Ann Creed	4 & 3
1957	Judy Eller, Beth Stone	1 up
		20 holes
1958	Judy Eller, Sherry Wheeler	1 up
1959	Judy Rand, Marcia Hamilton	5 & 3
1960	Carol Sorenson, Sharon Fladoos	2 & 1
1961	Mary Lowell, Margaret Martin	1 up
1962	Mary Lou Daniel, Mary Sawyer	2 up
1963	Janis Ferraris, Peggy Conley	2 up
1964	Peggy Conley, Laura MacIvor	6 & 5
1965	Gail Sykes, Mary Louise Pritchett	5 & 4
1966	Claudie Mayhew, Kathleen Ahern	3 & 2
1967	Elizabeth Story, Liana Zambresky	5 & 4
1968	Peggy Harmon, Kaye Beard	3 & 2
1969	Hollis Stacy, Mary Jane Fassinger	1 up
1970	Hollis Stacy, Janet Aulisi	1 up
1971	Hollis Stacy, Amy Alcott	1 up
		19 holes
1972	Nancy Lopez, Catherine Morse	1 up
1973	Amy Alcott, Mary Lawrence	6 & 5
1974	Nancy Lopez, Lauren Howe	7 & 5
1975	Dayna Benson, Kyle O'Brien	1 up
1976	Pilar Dorado, Kellii Doherty	3 & 2
1977	Althea Tome, Melissa McGeorge	3 & 2

Senior Amateur Championship

The Senior Amateur Championship is contested at match play after 36 holes of stroke play qualifying. The thirty-two players with the lowest 36-hole totals qualify for match play. If a tie for last qualifying place develops, it is decided immediately by a hole-by-hole play-off. All match play rounds are at 18 holes; 144 players are eligible. All except the defending champion, who is exempt, earn their places in 18-hole sectional qualifying rounds at various sites throughout the country. The defending champion is not exempt from qualifying at the site of the Championship.

Entrants must have reached their fifty-fifth birthday by the date set for sectional qualifying and must have USGA handicaps not exceeding eleven strokes. United States residents must be members of USGA Regular Member Clubs.

Year	Winner, Runner-Up	Score
1955	J. Wood Platt, George Studinger	5 & 4
1956	Frederick J. Wright, J. Clark Espie	4 & 3
1957	J. Clark Espie, Frederick J. Wright	2 & 1
1958	Thomas C. Robbins, John W. Dawson	2 & 1
1959	J. Clark Espie, J. Wolcott Brown	3 & 1
1960	Michael Cestone, David Rose	1 up
		20 holes
1961	Dexter H. Daniels, Col. William K. Lanman, Jr.	2 & 1
1962	Merrill L. Carlsmith, Willis H. Blakely	4 & 2
1963	Merrill L. Carlsmith, William Higgins	3 & 2
1964	William D. Higgins, Edward Murphy	2 & 1
1965	Robert B. Kiersky, George Beechler	1 up
		19 holes
1966	Dexter H. Daniels, George Beechler	1 up
1967	Ray Palmer, Walter D. Bronson	3 & 2
1968	Curtis Person, Ben Goodes	2 & 1
1969	Curtis Person, David Goldman	1 up
1970	Gene Andrews, James Ferrle	1 up
1971	Tom Draper, Ernest Pieper, Jr.	3 & 1
1972	Lew W. Oehmig, Ernest Pieper, Jr.	1 up
		20 holes
1973	William Hyndman III, Harry Welch	3 & 2
1974	Dale Morey, L. W. Oehmig	4 & 2
1975	William F. Colm, Stephen Stimac	4 & 3
1976	Lew W. Oehmig, John Richardon	4 & 3
1977	Dale Morey, Lew W. Oehmig	4 & 3

Senior Women's Amateur Championship

The Senior Women's Amateur Championship consists of 54 holes of stroke play. Any tie for the Championship is played off at 18 holes of stroke play; if such a play-off results in a tie, play immediately continues hole by hole until the winner is determined.

Entries are open to women amateur golfers who will have reached their fiftieth birthday by the date of the first round and have handicaps of not more than sixteen strokes under the USGA Handicap System. The field is limited to 120 players: entries are accepted from the applicants with the lowest handicaps. United States residents must be members of the USGA Regular Member Clubs.

Year	Winner, Runner-Up	Score
1962	Maureen Orcutt	240
	Mrs. Edwin H. Vare, Jr.	247
1963	Mrs. Allison Choate	239–81–17[a]
	Maureen Orcutt	239–81–19[a]
1964	Mrs. Hulet P. Smith	247
	Mrs. William Kirkland	248
1965	Mrs. Hulet P. Smith	242
	Mrs. John S. Haskell	245
1966	Maureen Orcutt	242
	Mrs. Frank Goldthwaite	248
1967	Mrs. Marge Mason	236
	Mrs. Hulet P. Smith	240
1968	Mrs. Philip Cudone	236
	Mrs. Hulet P. Smith	240
1969	Mrs. Philip Cudone	236–76
	Mrs. L. D. Brown	236–84
1970	Mrs. Phillip J. Cudone	231
	Mrs. Paulette Lee	239
1971	Mrs. Philip Cudone	236
	Mrs. Ann Gregory	237
1972	Mrs. Philip Cudone	231
	Mrs. Wayne Rutter	237
1973	Mrs. David Hibbs	229
	Mrs. Wayne Rutter	235
1974	Mrs. Justine Cushing	231
	Mrs. Philip Cudone	233
1975	Mrs. Albert B. Bower	234
	Mrs. Philip Cudone	240
1976	Mrs. Cecile Maclaurin	230
	Mrs. Lyle O. Bowman	237
1977	Mrs. Mark Porter	230
	Mrs. Paul Dye, Jr.	231

[a] Sudden Death play-off, 4 holes.

PGA COMPETITIONS

As previously stated in Section I, the Professional Golfers' Association of America was formed January 17, 1916, and one of its first projects was to arrange for an annual national PGA tournament. In addition to the PGA Championship, the Association also conducts the PGA Seniors' championships for their members over fifty. The PGA also co-sponsors the tournaments on the so-called "professional tour circuit."

PGA Championship

The Championship was started in 1916, and the trophy was provided by Rodman Wanamaker. James M. Barnes was victorious at the Siwanoy Country Club to become the first champion. The tournament was canceled in 1917 and 1918 due to World War I, but in 1919, at the Engineers Country Club in New York, Barnes successfully defended his title. The championship was again canceled in 1943 because of World War II. The Championship remained match play until 1957; then the format was changed to 72 holes of stroke play.

The field of the PGA Championship, as presently composed, is made of the following: all former PGA Championship Tournament winners, the United States Ryder Cup members of the last holding of this international event, winners of all PGA official tour events since the previous Championship, the five past winners of the U.S. Open, all current PGA Sectional Champions prior to the event, the host club's professional, the low 25 scorers and ties in the PGA Club Professionals' Championship, the current PGA Senior Champion, and generally five players of special merit who may be invited by the PGA Executive Committee. The remaining field, which is usually composed of about 144 players, earn their berth by placing among the top 70 money-winner list of tour events since the previous Championship. As a rule, the low 70 scorers and ties continue the play after the first 36 holes, but this does

Byron Nelson (left) is awarded the trophy for winning the 1940 PGA Championship by Thomas Walsh (center), President of the PGA. Sam Snead (right), who lost 1 up to Nelson in the finals, helps in the presentation.

not include all players within ten strokes of the leader—as is the custom in regular PGA tour events. Previous **PGA Championship** winners are as follows:

Year	Winner	Score	Runner-Up	Site
1916	James M. Barnes	1 up	Jock Hutchison	Siwanoy CC Bronxville, N.Y.
1917–1918	Not played			
1919	James M. Barnes	6 & 5	Fred McLeod	Engineers CC Roslyn, N.Y.
1920	Jock Hutchison	1 up	J. Douglas Edgar	Flossmoor CC Flossmoor, Ill.
1921	Walter Hagen	3 & 2	James M. Barnes	Inwood CC Inwood, N.Y.
1922	Gene Sarazen	4 & 3	Emmet French	Oakmont CC Oakmont, Pa.
1923	Gene Sarazen	1 up (38)	Walter Hagen	Pelham CC Pelham, N.Y.
1924	Walter Hagen	2 up	James M. Barnes	French Lick CC French Lick, Ind.
1925	Walter Hagen	6 & 5	Wm. Mehlhorn	Olympia Fields CC Olympia, Ill.
1926	Walter Hagen	5 & 3	Leo Diegel	Salisbury GC Westbury, L.I., N.Y.
1927	Walter Hagen	1 up	Joe Turnesa	Cedar Crest CC Dallas, Texas
1928	Leo Diegel	6 & 5	Al Espinosa	Baltimore CC Five Farms Baltimore, Md.
1929	Leo Diegel	6 & 4	Johnny Farrell	Hillcrest CC Los Angeles, Calif.
1930	Tommy Armour	1 up	Gene Sarazen	Fresh Meadow Flushing, N.Y.
1931	Tom Creavy	2 & 1	Denny Shute	Wannamoisett CC Rumford, R.I.
1932	Olin Dutra	4 & 3	Frank Walsh	Keller GC St. Paul, Minn.
1933	Gene Sarazen	5 & 4	Willie Goggin	Blue Mound CC Milwaukee, Wis.
1934	Paul Runyan	1 up (38)	Craig Wood	Park CC Williamsville, N.Y.
1935	John Revolta	5 & 4	Tommy Armour	Twin Hills CC Okla. City, Okla.
1936	Denny Shute	3 & 2	Jimmy Thomson	Pinehurst CC Pinehurst, N.C.
1937	Denny Shute	1 up (37)	Harold McSpaden	Pittsburgh CC Aspinwall, Pa.
1938	Paul Runyan	8 & 7	Sam Snead	Shawnee CC Shawnee-on-Dela., Pa.
1939	Henry Picard	1 up (37)	Byron Nelson	Pomonok CC Flushing, N.Y.
1940	Byron Nelson	1 up	Sam Snead	Hershey CC Hershey, Pa.
1941	Vic Ghezzi	1 up (38)	Byron Nelson	Cherry Hills CC Denver, Colo.
1942	Sam Snead	2 & 1	Jim Turnesa	Seaview CC Atlantic City, N.J.
1943	Not played			
1944	Bob Hamilton	1 up	Byron Nelson	Manito G&CC Spokane, Wash.
1945	Byron Nelson	4 & 3	Sam Byrd	Morraine CC Dayton, Ohio
1946	Ben Hogan	6 & 4	Ed Oliver	Portland GC Portland, Ore.

Year	Winner	Score	Runner-Up	Site
1947	Jim Ferrier	2 & 1	Chick Harbert	Plum Hollow CC Detroit, Mich.
1948	Ben Hogan	7 & 6	Mike Turnesa	Norwood Hills CC St. Louis, Mo.
1949	Sam Snead	3 & 2	Johnny Palmer	Hermitage CC Richmond, Va.
1950	Chandler Harper	4 & 3	H. Williams, Jr.	Scioto CC Columbus, Ohio
1951	Sam Snead	7 & 6	Walter Burkemo	Oakmont CC Oakmont, Pa.
1952	Jim Turnesa	1 up	Chick Harbert	Big Spring CC Louisville, Ky.
1953	Walter Burkemo	2 & 1	Felice Torza	Birmingham CC Birmingham, Mich.
1954	Chick Harbert	4 & 3	Walter Burkemo	Keller GC St. Paul, Minn.
1955	Doug Ford	4 & 3	Cary Middlecoff	Meadowbrook CC Detroit, Mich.
1956	Jack Burke, Jr.	3 & 2	Ted Kroll	Blue Hill CC Boston, Mass.
1957	Lionel Hebert	2 & 1	Dow Finsterwald	Miami Valley GC Dayton, Ohio
1958	Dow Finsterwald	276	Billy Casper, Jr.	Llanerch CC Havertown, Pa.
1959	Bob Rosburg	277	Jerry Barber Doug Sanders	Minneapolis GC St. Louis, Minn.
1960	Jay Hebert	281	Jim Ferrier	Firestone CC Akron, Ohio
1961	Jerry Barber[a]	277	Don January	Olympia Fields CC Olympia, Ill.
1962	Gary Player	278	Bob Goalby	Aronimink GC Newtown Sq., Pa.
1963	Jack Nicklaus	279	Dave Ragan, Jr.	Dallas Athletic Club GC Dallas, Texas
1964	Bob Nichols	271	Jack Nicklaus Arnold Palmer	Columbus CC Columbus, Ohio
1965	Dave Marr	280	Jack Nicklaus Billy Casper, Jr.	Laurel Valley GC Ligonier, Pa.
1966	Al Geiberger	280	Dudley Wysong	Firestone CC Akron, Ohio
1967	Don January[b]	281	Don Massengale	Columbine CC Denver, Colo.
1968	Julius Boros	281	Robert J. Charles	Pecan Valley CC San Antonio, Texas
1969	Ray Floyd	276	Gary Player	National Cash Register CC Dayton, Ohio
1970	Dave Stockton	279	Bob Murphy Arnold Palmer	Southern Hills CC Tulsa, Okla.
1971	Jack Nicklaus	281	Billy Casper	PGA National GC Palm Beach Gardens, Fla.
1972	Gary Player	281	Jim Jamieson	Oakland Hills CC Birmingham, Mich.
1973	Jack Nicklaus	277	Bruce Crampton	Canterbury GC Cleveland, Ohio
1974	Lee Trevino	276	Jack Nicklaus	Tanglewood GC Winston-Salem, N.C.
1975	Jack Nicklaus	276	Bruce Crampton	Firestone CC Akron, Ohio
1976	Dave Stockton	281	Ray Floyd Don January	Congressional CC Bethesda, Md.
1977	Lanny Wadkins[c]	282	Gene Littler	Pebble Beach GC Pebble Beach, Calif.

[a] Play-off winner: Barber, 67; January, 68.
[b] Play-off winner: January, 69; Massengale, 71.
[c] Play-off winner: Wadkins won on 3rd hole.

PGA Seniors' Championship

Year	Winner, Runner-Up	Score[a]
1945	Eddie Williams	148
	Jock Hutchison	150
1946	Eddie Williams[b]	146
	Jock Hutchison	146
1947	Jock Hutchison	145
	Ben Richter	148
1948	Charles McKenna	141
	Ben Richter	142
1949	Marshall Crichton	145
	Louis Chiapetta	146
	George Smith	146
	Jock Hutchison	146
1950	Al Watrous	142
	Bill Jelliffe	145
1951	Al Watrous[b]	142
	Jock Hutchison	142
1952	Ernest Newham	146
	Al Watrous	147
1953	Harry Schwab	142
	Gene Sarazen	145
	Charley McKenna	145
1954	Gene Sarazen	214
	Al Watrous	216
	Perry Del Vecchio	216
1955	Mortie Dutra	213
	Mike Murra	217
	Gene Sarazen	217
	Denny Shute	217
1956	Pete Burke	215
	Ock Willowett	216
1957	Al Watrous[b]	210–72
	Bob Stupple	210–75
1958	Gene Sarazen	288
	Charles Sheppard	291
1959	Willie Goggin	284
	Denny Shute	285
	Paul Runyan	285
	Duke Gibson	285
1960	Dick Metz	284
	Tony Longo	289
	Paul Runyan	289
1961	Paul Runyan	278
	Jimmy Demaret	281
1962	Paul Runyan	278
	Ernie Ball	281
	Joe Brown	281
	Dutch Harrison	281
1963	Herman Barron	272
	John Barnum	274
1964	Sam Snead	279
	John Barnum	282
1965[c]	Sam Snead	278
	Joe Lopez	282
1966	Fred Haas	286
	John Barnum	288
	Dutch Harrison	288
1967	Sam Snead	279
	Bob Hamilton	288

Year	Winner, Runner-Up	Score[a]
1968	Chandler Harper	279
	Sam Snead	283
1969	Tommy Bolt	278
	Pete Fleming	279
1970	Sam Snead	290
	Fred Haas	292
1971	Julius Boros	285
	Tommy Bolt	288
1972	Sam Snead	286
	Tommy Bolt	287
	Julius Boros	287
1973	Sam Snead	268
1974	Roberto DeVicenzo	273
1975	Charlie Sifford	280
1976	Pete Cooper	283
1977	Julius Boros	283
	Fred Haas	284

[a] In 1937 and 1954 to 1957, championship based on 54 holes; 1938 to 1953, play based on 36 holes; 1958 to date, championship based on 72 holes.
[b] Winner in play-off.
[c] Not PGA co-sponsored.

PGA Tour

Total prize money on the official PGA tour circuit in 1977, including related pro-amateur events, was over $9,000,000. The tour is the principal showpiece in the world of golf.

The *exemption point system* now in use is based on the money winnings for each player in most 72-hole tournaments. Purses won in pro-amateur events and in tour tournaments of less than 72 holes are not included for computation in the exemption point system.

The exemption point system is used in determining automatic eligibility and other privileges for leading golfers in tournaments sponsored by the PGA Tour. For instance, the total points scored will determine the 60 players who are to be immediately eligible (exempt from qualifying) for tournaments in the following year and who will receive preferred pairing and starting times. Players who are not exempt must play in a qualifying event generally on the Monday preceding the tournament. Most players are required to play in 15 events a year.

Winners of the PGA and the United States Open Championships are now eligible for ten years of exemption from qualifying in open invitational events co-sponsored by the PGA Tour. This decision did not affect the unlimited exemption of PGA and Open Champions prior to 1970.

As of 1978, the PGA Tour schedule ends with the playing of the World Series of Golf in early October. The new season starts immediately thereafter.

Today, you cannot just join the tour, as you could in years past. Since 1965, the would-be big-money winner must first attend the PGA Approved Tournament Players training program, or school, as it is commonly known. Under the current structure, applicants for the school are required to play in 72-hole regional tryouts at stroke play. The calibre of the field determines how many of the lowest scorers qualify for the school. At the qualifying school, the survivors play another tournament, attend classroom lectures, and undergo a written examination. Again, quality of play determines the number of players who receive playing credentials for the tour. Graduates of the school are on probation for one year.

Except for the USGA Open, the oldest stop on the tour circuit is the Western Open (1899). Other long-time *continuous* stops (except for war years) are the Canadian Open (1938), and Bing Crosby National Pro-Am. Here are the official PGA tour winners in the most recent years.

Date	Event	Winner	Score	1st Place Money	Total Purse
		1955 Tour			
Jan. 6–9	Los Angeles Open	Gene Littler	276	$ 5,000.00	$ 32,500.00
Jan. 14–16	Bing Crosby Pro-Am	Cary Middlecoff	209	$ 2,500.00	$ 15,000.00
Jan. 20–23	Convair–San Diego Open	Tommy Bolt	274	$ 2,400.00	$ 15,000.00
Jan. 27–30	Thunderbird Invitational	Shelley Mayfield	270	$ 2,000.00	$ 15,000.00
Jan. 27–30	Imperial Valley Open	Mike Fetchick	266	$ 1,000.00	$ 5,000.00
Feb. 3–6	Phoenix Open	Gene Littler	275	$ 2,400.00	$ 15,000.00
Feb. 10–13	Tucson Open	Tommy Bolt	266	$ 2,000.00	$ 10,000.00
Feb. 17–20	Texas Open	Mike Souchak	257	$ 2,000.00	$ 12,500.00
Feb. 24–27	Houston Open	Mike Souchak	273	$ 6,000.00	$ 30,000.00
Mar. 3–6	Baton Rouge Open	Bo Wininger	278	$ 2,200.00	$ 12,500.00
Mar. 17–20	St. Petersburg Open	Cary Middlecoff	274	$ 2,200.00	$ 12,500.00
Mar. 21–22	Seminole Pro-Am	Mike Souchak	139	$ 1,800.00	$ 10,000.00
Mar. 24–27	Miami Beach Open	Eric Monti	270	$ 2,200.00	$ 12,500.00
Mar. 31—Apr. 3	Azalea Open	Billy Maxwell	270	$ 2,200.00	$ 12,500.00

Many of the leading PGA touring pros of the early 1940's. Left to right: (front) Jimmy Demaret, Lawson Little, Gene Sarazen, Paul Runyan, Tony Penna, and Ben Hogan; (standing) Vic Ghezzi, Dick Metz, Jimmy Hines, Ed Oliver, Tournament sponsor, Clayton Heafner, Jimmy Thomson, Harold McSpaden, Horton Smith, and Ky Laffoon.

Date	Event	Winner	Score	1st Place Money	Total Purse
Apr. 7–10	Masters	Cary Middlecoff	279	$ 5,000.00	$ 10,000.00
Apr. 14–17	Greater Greensboro Open	Sam Snead	273	$ 2,200.00	$ 12,500.00
Apr. 21–24	Virginia Beach Open	Chandler Harper	260	$ 2,400.00	$ 15,000.00
Apr. 28—May 1	Tournament of Champions	Gene Littler	280	$10,000.00	$ 35,000.00
May 5–8	Colonial Invitational	Chandler Harper	276	$ 5,000.00	$ 25,000.00
May 12–15	Arlington Hotel Open	Bo Wininger	270	$ 2,400.00	$ 15,000.00
May 19–22	Kansas City Open	Dick Mayer	271	$ 4,000.00	$ 20,000.00
May 26–29	Fort Wayne Invitational	Dow Finsterwald	269	$ 2,400.00	$ 15,000.00
June 1–5	Palm Beach Invitational	Sam Snead	Plus 46	$ 3,000.00	$ 15,000.00
June 16–18	U.S. Open	Jack Fleck	287	$ 6,000.00	$ 20,000.00
June 23–26	Western Open	Cary Middlecoff	272	$ 2,400.00	$ 15,000.00
June 29—July 2	British Columbia Open	Dow Finsterwald	270	$ 2,400.00	$ 15,000.00
July 7–10	St. Paul Open	Tommy Bolt	269	$ 2,400.00	$ 15,000.00
July 14–17	Miller Open	Cary Middlecoff	265	$ 6,000.00	$ 35,000.00
July 28–31	Rubber City Open	Henry Ransom	272	$ 2,400.00	$ 15,000.00
Aug. 4–7	All American Championship	Doug Ford	277	$ 3,420.00	$ 25,000.00
Aug. 11–14	World Championship of Golf	Julius Boros	281	$50,000.00	$100,000.00
Aug. 17–20	Canadian Open	Arnold Palmer	265	$ 2,400.00	$ 15,000.00
Aug. 25–28	Labatt Open	Gene Littler	272	$ 5,000.00	$ 25,000.00
Sept. 8–11	Cavalcade of Golf	Cary Middlecoff	276	$10,000.00	$ 50,000.00
Sept. 15–18	Philadelphia Daily News Open	Ted Kroll	273	$ 4,000.00	$ 20,000.00
Sept. 22–25	Carling Golf Classic	Doug Ford	276	$ 7,000.00	$ 50,000.00
Sept. 25	Insurance City Open	Sam Snead	269	$ 4,000.00	$ 20,000.00
Sept. 29—Oct. 2	Long Island Rotary Open	Max Evans	273	$ 2,400.00	$ 15,000.00
Oct. 6–9	Eastern Open	Frank Stranahan	280	$ 3,000.00	$ 17,500.00
Dec. 1–4	Havana Invitational	Mike Souchak	273	$ 2,000.00	$ 15,000.00
Dec. 8–11	Miami Beach Open	Sam Snead	201	$ 2,200.00	$ 12,500.00
Dec. 15–18	Mayfair Inn Open	Al Balding	269	$ 2,400.00	$ 15,000.00
	1956 Tour				
Jan. 6–9	Los Angeles Open	Lloyd Mangrum	272	$ 6,000.00	$ 30,000.00
Jan. 13–15	Bing Crosby Pro-Am	Cary Middlecoff	202	$ 2,500.00	$ 15,000.00
Jan. 19–22	Caliente Open	Mike Souchak	281	$ 2,200.00	$ 12,500.00
Jan. 26–29	Thunderbird Invitational	Jimmy Demaret	269	$ 2,000.00	$ 15,200.00
Jan. 26–29	Imperial Valley Open	Paul O'Leary	271	$ 1,000.00	$ 5,000.00
Feb. 2–5	Phoenix Open	Cary Middlecoff	276	$ 2,400.00	$ 15,000.00
Feb. 9–12	Tucson Open	Ted Kroll	264	$ 2,000.00	$ 15,000.00
Feb. 16–19	Texas Open	Gene Littler	276	$ 3,750.00	$ 18,750.00
Feb. 23–26	Houston Open	Ted Kroll	277	$ 6,000.00	$ 30,000.00
Mar. 1–4	Baton Rouge Open	Shelley Mayfield	277	$ 2,200.00	$ 12,500.00
Mar. 8–11	Pensacola Open	Don Fairfield	275	$ 2,200.00	$ 12,500.00
Mar. 15–18	St. Petersburg Open	Mike Fetchick	275	$ 2,200.00	$ 12,500.00
Mar. 22–25	Miami Beach Open	Gardner Dickinson, Jr.	272	$ 2,400.00	$ 15,000.00
Mar. 29—Apr. 1	Azalea Open	Mike Souchak	273	$ 2,200.00	$ 12,500.00
Apr. 5–8	Masters	Jack Burke, Jr.	289	$ 6,000.00	$ 42,000.00
Apr. 12–15	Greater Greensboro Open	Sam Snead	279	$ 2,200.00	$ 12,500.00
Apr. 19–22	Arlington Hotel Open	Billy Maxwell	272	$ 2,400.00	$ 15,000.00
Apr. 26–29	Tournament of Champions	Gene Littler	281	$10,000.00	$ 38,500.00
May 3–6	Colonial Invitational	Mike Souchak	280	$ 5,000.00	$ 25,000.00
May 10–13	Carling Open	Dow Finsterwald	274	$ 5,000.00	$ 25,000.00
May 17–20	Kansas City Open	Bo Wininger	273	$ 4,300.00	$ 22,000.00
May 24–27	Dallas Open	Don January	268	$ 6,000.00	$ 30,000.00
June 1–4	Texas Open	Peter Thomson	267	$13,478.00	$ 67,500.00

Date	Event	Winner	Score	1st Place Money	Total Purse
June 14–16	U.S. Open	Cary Middlecoff	281	$ 6,000.00	$ 24,900.00
June 21–24	Philadelphia *Daily News* Open	Dick Mayer	269	$ 4,000.00	$ 20,000.00
June 28— July 1	Insurance City Open	Arnold Palmer	274	$ 4,000.00	$ 20,000.00
July 5–8	Canadian Open	Doug Sanders	273	Amateur	$ 15,000.00
July 12–15	Labatt Open	Billy Casper, Jr.	274	$ 5,000.00	$ 25,000.00
July 26–29	Eastern Open	Arnold Palmer	277	$ 3,800.00	$ 19,000.00
Aug. 2–5	All-American Championship	E. J. Harrison	278	$ 3,420.00	$ 25,000.00
Aug. 9–12	World Championship of Golf	Ted Kroll	273	$50,000.00	$101,200.00
Aug. 16–19	Miller Open	Ed Furgol	265	$ 6,000.00	$ 35,000.00
Aug. 23–26	St. Paul Open	Mike Souchak	271	$ 4,000.00	$ 20,000.00
Aug. 30— Sept. 2	Motor City Open	Bob Rosburg	284	$ 4,000.00	$ 20,000.00
Sept. 6–9	Rubber City Open	Ed Furgol	271	$ 3,000.00	$ 19,000.00
Sept. 13–16	Fort Wayne Open	Art Wall, Jr.	269	$ 2,400.00	$ 15,000.00
Sept. 20–23	Oklahoma City Open	Fred Hawkins	279	$ 2,400.00	$ 15,000.00
Oct. 4–7	San Diego Open	Bob Rosburg	270	$ 2,400.00	$ 15,000.00
Oct. 11–14	Western Open	Mike Fetchick	284	$ 5,000.00	$ 22,720.50
Dec. 6–9	Havana Invitational	Al Besselink	276	$ 2,500.00	$ 17,400.00
Dec. 13–16	Mayfair Inn Open	Mike Fetchick	263	$ 2,400.00	$ 15,000.00
	1957 Tour				
Jan. 4–7	Los Angeles Open	Doug Ford	280	$ 7,000.00	$ 35,000.00
Jan. 11–13	Bing Crosby Pro-Am	Jay Hebert	213	$ 2,500.00	$ 15,000.00
Jan. 17–20	Caliente Open	Ed Furgol	280	$ 2,000.00	$ 15,000.00
Jan. 24–27	Thunderbird Invitational	Jimmy Demaret	273	$ 2,000.00	$ 15,300.00
Jan. 24–27	Imperial Valley Open	Tony Lema	276	$ 1,000.00	$ 5,000.00
Jan. 31— Feb. 3	Phoenix Open	Billy Casper, Jr.	271	$ 2,000.00	$ 15,000.00
Feb. 7–10	Tucson Open	Dow Finsterwald	269	$ 2,000.00	$ 15,000.00
Feb. 14–17	Texas Open	Jay Hebert	271	$ 2,800.00	$ 20,000.00
Feb. 21–25	Houston Open	Arnold Palmer	279	$ 7,500.00	$ 37,100.00
Feb. 28— Mar. 3	Baton Rouge Open	Jimmy Demaret	278	$ 2,000.00	$ 15,000.00
Mar. 7–16	Pensacola Open	Art Wall, Jr.	273	$ 2,000.00	$ 15,000.00
Mar. 14–17	St. Petersburg Open	Pete Cooper	269	$ 1,700.00	$ 12,500.00
Mar. 23–24	Miami Beach Open	Al Balding	137	$ 1,200.00	$ 7,500.00
Mar. 28–31	Azalea Open	Arnold Palmer	282	$ 1,700.00	$ 12,500.00
Apr. 4–7	Masters	Doug Ford	283	$ 8,750.00	$ 53,300.00
Apr. 11–14	Greater Greensboro Open	Stan Leonard	276	$ 2,000.00	$ 15,000.00
Apr. 18–21	Tournament of Champions	Gene Littler	285	$10,000.00	$ 40,000.00
Apr. 24–28	Kentucky Derby Open	Billy Casper, Jr.	277	$ 4,300.00	$ 30,000.00
May 2–5	Colonial Invitational	Roberto DeVicenzo	284	$ 5,000.00	$ 25,000.00
May 9–12	Arlington Hotel Open	Jimmy Demaret	276	$ 2,800.00	$ 20,000.00
May 16–19	Greenbrier Invitational	E. J. Harrison	266	$ 2,300.00	$ 10,000.00
May 23–26	Kansas Open	Al Besselink	279	$ 2,800.00	$ 22,000.00
May 30— June 2	Palm Beach Invitational	Sam Snead	Plus 41	$ 3,000.00	$ 10,050.00
June 6–9	Rubber City Open	Arnold Palmer	272	$ 2,800.00	$ 22,000.00
June 13–15	U.S. Open	Dick Mayer	282	$ 7,200.00	$ 28,560.00
June 20–23	Carling Open	Paul Harney	275	$ 5,700.00	$ 30,000.00
June 27–30	Western Open	Doug Ford	279	$ 5,000.00	$ 25,200.00
July 4–7	Labatt Open	Paul Harney	278	$ 3,500.00	$ 29,000.00
July 10–13	Canadian Open	George Bayer	271	$ 3,500.00	$ 25,000.00
July 21	Erie Open	Paul O'Leary	137	$ 1,000.00	$ 5,000.00
July 25–28	Eastern Open	Tommy Bolt	276	$ 2,800.00	$ 20,000.00
Aug. 1–5	All-American Open	Roberto DeVicenzo	273	$ 3,500.00	$ 25,000.00

Date	Event	Winner	Score	1st Place Money	Total Purse
Aug. 8–11	World Championship of Golf	Dick Mayer	279	$50,000.00	$101,200.00
Aug. 15–18	St. Paul Open	Ken Venturi	266	$ 2,800.00	$ 20,000.00
Aug. 22–25	Miller Open	Ken Venturi	267	$ 6,000.00	$ 35,000.00
Aug. 29—Sept. 2	Insurance City Open	Gardner Dickinson, Jr.	272	$ 2,800.00	$ 20,000.00
Sept. 13–16	Dallas Open	Sam Snead	264	$ 8,000.00	$ 40,000.00
Oct. 24–27	Hesperia Open	Billy Maxwell	275	$ 2,000.00	$ 15,000.00
Oct. 30—Nov. 3	San Diego Open	Arnold Palmer	271	$ 2,800.00	$ 20,000.00
Nov. 8–10	Long Beach Open	Charles Sifford	203	$ 1,200.00	$ 10,000.00
Nov. 22–24	West Palm Beach Open	Al Balding	209	$ 1,200.00	$ 10,000.00
Nov. 28—Dec. 1	Caracas Open	Al Besselink	279	$ 4,000.00	$ 20,000.00
Dec. 5–8	Havana Invitational	Al Balding	281	$ 2,400.00	$ 14,700.00
Dec. 12–15	Mayfair Inn Open	Walter Burkemo	269	$ 2,000.00	$ 15,000.00

1958 Tour

Date	Event	Winner	Score	1st Place Money	Total Purse
Jan. 3–6	Los Angeles Open	Frank Stranahan	275	$ 7,000.00	$ 35,000.00
Jan. 9–12	Bing Crosby Pro-Am	Billy Casper, Jr.	277	$ 4,000.00	$ 50,000.00
Jan. 17–20	Tijuana Open	E. J. Harrison	280	$ 2,000.00	$ 15,000.00
Jan. 23–26	Thunderbird Invitational	Ken Venturi	269	$ 1,500.00	$ 15,000.00
Jan. 30—Feb. 2	Phoenix Open	Ken Venturi	274	$ 2,000.00	$ 15,000.00
Feb. 6–9	Tucson Open	Lionel Hebert	265	$ 2,000.00	$ 15,000.00
Feb. 13–16	Texas Open	Bill Johnston	274	$ 2,000.00	$ 15,000.00
Feb. 20–24	Houston Invitational	Ed Oliver	281	$ 4,300.00	$ 30,000.00
Feb. 27—Mar. 2	Baton Rouge Open	Ken Venturi	276	$ 2,000.00	$ 15,000.00
Mar. 1–2	Jackson Open	Fred Hawkins	140	$· 750.00	$ 5,000.00
Mar. 9–11	New Orleans Open	Billy Casper, Jr.	278	$ 2,800.00	$ 20,000.00
Mar. 13–16	Pensacola Open	Doug Ford	278	$ 2,000.00	$ 15,000.00
Mar. 20–23	St. Petersburg Open	Arnold Palmer	276	$ 2,000.00	$ 15,000.00
Mar. 28–30	Azalea Open	Howie Johnson	282	$ 2,000.00	$ 15,000.00
Apr. 3–6	Masters	Arnold Palmer	284	$11,250.00	$ 60,050.00
Apr. 11–13	Greater Greensboro Open	Bob Goalby	275	$ 2,000.00	$ 15,000.00
Apr. 17–20	Kentucky Derby Open	Gary Player	274	$ 2,800.00	$ 20,000.00
Apr. 24–27	Lafayette Open	Jay Hebert	273	$ 2,000.00	$ 15,000.00
May 1–4	Colonial Invitational	Tommy Bolt	282	$ 5,000.00	$ 25,000.00
May 8–11	Arlington Hotel Open	Julius Boros	273	$ 2,800.00	$ 20,000.00
May 15–18	Memphis Invitational	Billy Maxwell	267	$ 2,800.00	$ 20,000.00
May 15–18	Greenbrier Invitational	Sam Snead	264	$ 2,300.00	$ 10,000.00
May 22–25	Kansas City Open	Ernie Vossler	269	$ 2,800.00	$ 20,000.00
May 29—June 1	Western Open	Doug Sanders	275	$ 5,000.00	$ 25,000.00
June 5–8	Dallas Open	Sam Snead	272	$ 3,500.00	$ 25,000.00
June 13–15	U.S. Open	Tommy Bolt	283	$ 8,000.00	$ 35,000.00
June 19–23	Buick Open	Billy Casper, Jr.	285	$ 9,000.00	$ 50,000.00
June 26–29	Pepsi Open	Arnold Palmer	273	$ 9,000.00	$ 50,000.00
July 3–6	Rubber City Open	Art Wall, Jr.	269	$ 2,800.00	$ 20,000.00
July 10–13	Insurance City Open	Jack Burke, Jr.	268	$ 3,500.00	$ 25,000.00
July 17–20	PGA Championship	Dow Finsterwald	276	$ 5,500.00	$ 39,400.00
July 24–27	Eastern Open	Art Wall, Jr.	276	$ 2,800.00	$ 20,000.00
Aug. 1–4	Gleneagles-Chicago Open	Ken Venturi	272	$ 9,000.00	$ 50,000.00
Aug. 7–11	Miller Open	Cary Middlecoff	264	$ 5,300.00	$ 35,000.00
Aug. 14–17	St. Paul Open	Mike Souchak	263	$ 3,500.00	$ 25,000.00
Aug. 20–23	Canadian Open	Wes Ellis, Jr.	269	$ 3,500.00	$ 25,000.00
Aug. 28—Sept. 1	Vancouver Open	Jim Ferree	270	$ 6,400.00	$ 40,000.00
Sept. 5–8	Utah Open	Dow Finsterwald	267	$ 2,000.00	$ 15,000.00
Sept. 11–14	Denver Open	Tommy Jacobs	266	$ 2,800.00	$ 20,000.00

Two of the more consistent money winners of the late 1940's and early 1950's—Lou Worsham (left) and Johnny Palmer (right)—compare notes during the 1947 Miami Open.

Col. Robert T. Jones (left), father of Bobby Jones, presents the first prize check of $1,500 to Horton Smith (right) after the latter had won the first Master's Invitational Golf Tourney.

In the 1960's golf became a great spectator sport. Here members of Arnie's Army (Arnold Palmer's private fan club) watch him line up a putt in the 1966 National Open. Billy Casper, who is marking his ball so that Palmer can putt, won the event.

One of the best NCAA team champions was the 1958 University of Houston team (left to right): Jacky Cupit, Phil Rodgers, Jim "Babe" Hiskey, Dave Williams (Coach), Frank Wharton, and Bob Pratt.

Date	Event	Winner	Score	1st Place Money	Total Purse
Sept. 18–21	Hesperia Open	John McMullin	271	$ 2,000.00	$ 15,000.00
Nov. 5–9	Carling Open	Julius Boros	284	$ 3,500.00	$ 25,000.00
Nov. 13–16	Havana Invitational	George Bayer	286	$ 6,500.00	$ 40,000.00
Nov. 20–23	West Palm Beach Open	Pete Cooper	269	$ 2,000.00	$ 15,000.00
Dec. 4–7	Mayfair Inn Open	George Bayer	272	$ 2,000.00	$ 15,000.00
	1959 Tour				
Jan. 2–5	Los Angeles Open	Ken Venturi	278	$ 5,300.00	$ 35,000.00
Jan. 9–12	Tijuana Open	Ernie Vossler	273	$ 2,800.00	$ 20,000.00
Jan. 15–18	Bing Crosby Pro-Am	Art Wall, Jr.	279	$ 4,000.00	$ 34,999.76
Jan. 22–25	Thunderbird Invitational	Arnold Palmer	266	$ 1,500.00	$ 12,000.00
Jan. 29— Feb. 1	San Diego Open	Marty Furgol	274	$ 2,800.00	$ 20,000.00
Feb. 5–8	Phoenix Open	Gene Littler	268	$ 2,400.00	$ 17,500.00
Feb. 12–15	Tucson Open	Gene Littler	266	$ 2,000.00	$ 15,000.00
Feb. 19–22	Texas Open	Wes Ellis, Jr.	276	$ 2,800.00	$ 20,000.00
Feb. 27— Mar. 1	Baton Rouge Open	Howie Johnson	283	$ 2,000.00	$ 15,000.00
Mar. 6–9	New Orleans Open	Bill Collins	280	$ 2,800.00	$ 20,000.00
Mar. 12–15	Pensacola Open	Paul Harney	269	$ 2,000.00	$ 15,000.00
Mar. 20–23	St. Petersburg Open	Cary Middlecoff	275	$ 2,000.00	$ 15,000.00
Mar. 27–30	Azalea Open	Art Wall, Jr.	282	$ 2,000.00	$ 15,000.00
Apr. 2–5	Masters	Art Wall, Jr.	284	$15,000.00	$ 76,100.00
Apr. 9–12	Greater Greensboro Open	Dow Finsterwald	278	$ 2,000.00	$ 15,000.00
Apr. 16–19	Houston Classic	Jack Burke, Jr.	277	$ 4,300.00	$ 30,000.00
Apr. 23–26	Tournament of Champions	Mike Souchak	281	$10,000.00	$ 46,620.00
Apr. 30— May 1	Colonial National	Ben Hogan	285	$ 5,000.00	$ 27,300.00
May 7–11	Oklahoma City Open	Arnold Palmer	273	$ 3,500.00	$ 25,000.00
May 14–17	Arlington Hotel Open	Gene Littler	270	$ 2,800.00	$ 20,000.00
May 21–25	Memphis Open	Don Whitt	272	$ 3,500.00	$ 25,000.00
May 28–31	Kentucky Derby Open	Don Whitt	274	$ 2,800.00	$ 20,000.00
June 4–7	Eastern Open	Dave Ragan, Jr.	273	$ 2,800.00	$ 20,000.00
June 11–14	U.S. Open	Billy Casper, Jr.	282	$12,000.00	$ 49,200.00
June 18–21	Canadian Open	Doug Ford	276	$ 3,500.00	$ 25,000.00
June 25–28	Gleneagles-Chicago Open	Ken Venturi	273	$ 9,000.00	$ 50,000.00
July 2–5	Buick Open	Art Wall, Jr.	282	$ 9,000.00	$ 50,060.00
July 9–12	Western Open	Mike Souchak	272	$ 5,000.00	$ 25,000.00
July 16–19	Insurance City Open	Gene Littler	272	$ 3,500.00	$ 25,000.00
July 30— Aug. 2	PGA Championship	Bob Rosburg	277	$ 8,250.00	$ 51,175.00
Aug. 6–9	Carling Open	Dow Finsterwald	276	$ 3,500.00	$ 25,000.00
Aug. 13–16	Motor City Open	Mike Souchak	268	$ 3,500.00	$ 25,000.00
Aug. 20–23	Rubber City Open	Tom Nieporte	267	$ 2,800.00	$ 20,000.00
Aug. 27–30	Miller Open	Gene Littler	265	$ 5,300.00	$ 35,000.00
Sept. 4–7	Kansas City Open	Dow Finsterwald	275	$ 2,800.00	$ 20,000.00
Sept. 11–14	Dallas Open	Julius Boros	274	$ 3,500.00	$ 25,000.00
Sept. 17–20	El Paso Open	Marty Furgol	273	$ 2,800.00	$ 20,000.00
Sept. 24–27	Golden Gate Championship	Mason Rudolph, Jr.	275	$ 6,400.00	$ 40,000.00
Oct. 1–4	Portland Open	Billy Casper, Jr.	269	$ 2,800.00	$ 20,000.00
Oct. 8–11	Hesperia Open	Eric Monti	271	$ 2,000.00	$ 15,000.00
Oct. 15–18	Orange County Open	Jay Hebert	273	$ 2,000.00	$ 15,000.00
Nov. 12–15	Lafayette Open	Billy Casper, Jr.	273	$ 2,000.00	$ 15,000.00
Nov. 19–22	Mobile Open	Billy Casper, Jr.	280	$ 2,000.00	$ 15,000.00
Nov. 26–29	West Palm Beach Open	Arnold Palmer	281	$ 2,000.00	$ 15,000.00
Dec. 3–6	Coral Gables Open	Doug Sanders	273	$ 2,800.00	$ 20,000.00
	1960 Tour				
Jan. 8–9	Los Angeles Open	Dow Finsterwald	280	$ 5,500.00	$ 37,500.00
Jan. 15–18	Yorba Linda Open	Jerry Barber	278	$ 2,800.00	$ 20,000.00

Date	Event	Winner	Score	1st Place Money	Total Purse
Jan. 21–24	Bing Crosby Pro-Am	Ken Venturi	286	$ 4,000.00	$ 35,002.00
Jan. 28–31	San Diego Open	Mike Souchak	269	$ 2,800.00	$ 20,000.00
Feb. 3–7	Palm Springs Classic	Arnold Palmer	338	$12,000.00	$ 70,000.00
Feb. 11–14	Panama Open	Ernie Vossler	269	$ 1,500.00	$ 10,000.00
Feb. 11–15	Phoenix Open	Jack Fleck	273	$ 3,150.00	$ 22,500.00
Feb. 18–21	Tucson Open	Don January	271	$ 2,800.00	$ 20,000.00
Feb. 25–28	Texas Open	Arnold Palmer	276	$ 2,800.00	$ 20,000.00
Mar. 3–6	Baton Rouge Open	Arnold Palmer	279	$ 2,000.00	$ 15,000.00
Mar. 10–13	Pensacola Open	Arnold Palmer	273	$ 2,000.00	$ 15,000.00
Mar. 19–21	St. Petersburg Open	George Bayer	282	$ 2,000.00	$ 15,000.00
Mar. 24–27	DeSoto Open	Sam Snead	276	$ 5,300.00	$ 35,000.00
Mar. 31— Apr. 3	Azalea Open	Tom Nieporte	277	$ 2,000.00	$ 15,000.00
Apr. 7–10	Masters	Arnold Palmer	282	$17,500.00	$ 87,050.00
Apr. 14–17	Greater Greensboro Open	Sam Snead	270	$ 2,800.00	$ 20,000.00
Apr. 21–24	New Orleans Open	Dow Finsterwald	270	$ 3,500.00	$ 25,000.00
Apr. 28— May 2	Houston Classic	Bill Collins	280	$ 5,300.00	$ 36,440.00
May 5–8	Tournament of Champions	Jerry Barber	268	$16,000.00	$ 42,400.00
May 12–15	Colonial National	Julius Boros	280	$ 5,000.00	$ 30,000.00
May 19–22	Hot Springs Open	Bill Collins	275	$ 2,800.00	$ 20,000.00
May 26–29	"500" Open	Doug Ford	270	$ 9,000.00	$ 50,000.00
June 2–5	Memphis Open	Tommy Bolt	273	$ 4,300.00	$ 30,000.00
June 9–12	Oklahoma City Open	Gene Littler	273	$ 4,300.00	$ 30,000.00
June 16–18	U.S. Open	Arnold Palmer	280	$14,400.00	$ 60,720.00
July 1–4	Buick Open	Mike Souchak	282	$ 9,000.00	$ 50,000.00
July 6–9	Canadian Open	Art Wall, Jr.	269	$ 3,500.00	$ 25,000.00
July 14–17	Western Open	Stan Leonard	278	$ 5,000.00	$ 25,000.00
July 21–24	PGA Championship	Jay Hebert	281	$11,000.00	$ 63,130.00
July 28–31	Eastern Open	Gene Littler	273	$ 3,500.00	$ 25,000.00
Aug. 4–7	Insurance City Open	Arnold Palmer	270	$ 3,500.00	$ 25,000.00
Aug. 18–21	St. Paul Open	Don Fairchild	266	$ 4,300.00	$ 30,000.00
Aug. 25–28	Milwaukee Open	Ken Venturi	271	$ 4,300.00	$ 30,000.00
Sept. 2–5	Dallas Open	Johnny Pott	275	$ 3,500.00	$ 25,000.00
Sept. 9–12	Utah Open	Bill Johnson	262	$ 2,800.00	$ 20,000.00
Sept. 15–18	Carling Open	Ernie Vossler	272	$ 3,500.00	$ 25,000.00
Sept. 22–25	Portland Open	Billy Casper, Jr.	266	$ 2,800.00	$ 20,000.00
Sept. 30— Oct. 3	Hesperia Open	Billy Casper, Jr.	275	$ 2,000.00	$ 15,000.00
Oct. 13–16	Orange County Open	Billy Casper, Jr.	276	$ 2,000.00	$ 15,000.00
Nov. 17–20	Cajun Classic Open	Lionel Hebert	272	$ 2,000.00	$ 15,000.00
Nov. 24–27	Mobile Open	Arnold Palmer	274	$ 2,000.00	$ 15,000.00
Dec. 1–4	West Palm Beach Open	Johnny Pott	278	$ 2,000.00	$ 15,000.00
Dec. 8–11	Coral Gables Open	Bob Goalby	272	$ 2,800.00	$ 20,000.00
	1961 Tour				
Jan. 6–9	Los Angeles Open	Bob Goalby	275	$ 7,500.00	$ 45,000.00
Jan. 12–15	San Diego Open	Arnold Palmer	271	$ 2,800.00	$ 20,000.00
Jan. 19–22	Bing Crosby Pro-Am	Bob Rosburg	282	$ 5,300.00	$ 35,000.00
Jan. 26–29	Lucky International	Gary Player	272	$ 9,000.00	$ 50,000.00
Feb. 1–5	Palm Springs Classic	Billy Maxwell	345	$ 5,300.00	$ 35,000.00
Feb. 9–12	Phoenix Open	Arnold Palmer	270	$ 4,300.00	$ 30,000.00
Feb. 16–19	Tucson Open	Dave Hill	269	$ 2,800.00	$ 20,000.00
Feb. 24–26	Baton Rouge Open	Arnold Palmer	266	$ 2,800.00	$ 20,000.00
Mar. 2–5	New Orleans Open	Doug Sanders	272	$ 4,300.00	$ 30,000.00
Mar. 9–12	Pensacola Open	Tommy Bolt	275	$ 2,800.00	$ 20,000.00
Mar. 16–19	St. Petersburg Open	Bob Goalby	261	$ 2,800.00	$ 20,000.00
Mar. 23–26	Sunshine Open	Gary Player	273	$ 3,500.00	$ 25,000.00
Apr. 1–2	Azalea Open	Jerry Barber	213	$ 1,206.00	$ 12,000.00
Apr. 6–8, 10	Masters	Gary Player	280	$20,000.00	$ 99,500.00

Date	Event	Winner	Score	1st Place Money	Total Purse
Apr. 13–16	Greater Greensboro Open	Mike Souchak	276	$ 3,200.00	$ 22,500.00
Apr. 20–23	Houston Classic	Jay Hebert	276	$ 7,000.00	$ 43,570.00
Apr. 27–30	Texas Open	Arnold Palmer	270	$ 4,300.00	$ 30,000.00
May 4–7	Tournament of Champions	Sam Snead	273	$10,000.00	$ 52,000.00
May 11–14	Colonial National	Doug Sanders	281	$ 7,000.00	$ 40,000.00
May 18–21	Hot Springs Open	Doug Sanders	273	$ 2,800.00	$ 20,000.00
May 25–28	"500" Open	Doug Ford	273	$ 9,000.00	$ 50,000.00
June 1–4	Memphis Open	Cary Middlecoff	266	$14,300.00	$ 30,000.00
June 15–17	U.S. Open	Gene Littler	281	$14,000.00	$ 60,500.00
June 22–25	Western Open	Arnold Palmer	271	$ 5,000.00	$ 30,560.00
June 29— July 2	Buick Open	Jack Burke, Jr.	284	$ 9,000.00	$ 50,000.00
July 6–9	St. Paul Open	Don January	269	$ 4,300.00	$ 30,000.00
July 12–15	Canadian Open	Jacky Cupit	270	$ 4,300.00	$ 30,000.00
July 20–23	Milwaukee Open	Bruce Crampton	272	$ 4,300.00	$ 30,000.00
July 27–30	PGA Championship	Jerry Barber	277	$11,000.00	$ 64,800.00
Aug. 3–6	Eastern Open	Doug Sanders	275	$ 5,300.00	$ 35,000.00
Aug. 10–31	Insurance City Open	Billy Maxwell	271	$ 4,300.00	$ 30,000.00
Aug. 17–20	Carling Open	Gay Brewer, Jr.	277	$ 5,300.00	$ 35,000.00
Aug. 24–27	American Classic	Jay Hebert	278	$ 9,000.00	$ 50,900.00
Sept. 1–4	Dallas Open	Earl Stewart, Jr.	278	$ 4,300.00	$ 30,000.00
Sept. 7–10	Denver Open	Dave Hill	263	$ 3,500.00	$ 25,000.00
Sept. 14–17	Seattle Open	Dave Marr	265	$ 3,500.00	$ 25,000.00
Sept. 21–24	Portland Open	Billy Casper, Jr.	273	$ 3,500.00	$ 25,000.00
Sept. 28— Oct. 1	Bakersfield Open	Jack Fleck	276	$ 3,500.00	$ 25,000.00
Oct. 8	Hesperia Open	Tony Lema	138	$ 1,200.00	$ 10,000.00
Oct. 12–15	Ontario Open	Eric Monti	277	$ 2,800.00	$ 20,000.00
Oct. 19–22	Orange County Open	Bob McCallister	278	$ 2,400.00	$ 17,500.00
Nov. 2–5	Almaden Open	Jim Ferrier	279	$ 1,200.00	$ 10,000.00
Nov. 9–12	Beaumont Open	Joe Campbell	277	$ 2,800.00	$ 20,000.00
Nov. 16–19	Cajun Classic	Doug Sanders	270	$ 2,000.00	$ 15,000.00
Nov. 23–26	Mobile Open	Gay Brewer, Jr.	275	$ 2,000.00	$ 15,000.00
Nov. 30— Dec. 3	West Palm Beach Open	Gay Brewer, Jr.	274	$ 2,800.00	$ 20,000.00
Dec. 7–10	Coral Gables Open	George Knudson	273	$ 2,800.00	$ 20,000.00
	1962 Tour				
Jan. 5–8	Los Angeles Open	Phil Rodgers	268	$ 7,500.00	$ 45,000.00
Jan. 11–14	San Diego Open	Tommy Jacobs	277	$ 3,500.00	$ 25,000.00
Jan. 18–20	Bing Crosby Pro-Am	Doug Ford	286	$ 5,300.00	$ 35,000.00
Jan. 25–28	Lucky International Open	Gene Littler	274	$ 9,000.00	$ 50,000.00
Jan. 31— Feb. 4	Palm Springs Classic	Arnold Palmer	342	$ 5,300.00	$ 35,000.00
Feb. 8–11	Phoenix Open	Arnold Palmer	269	$ 5,300.00	$ 35,000.00
Feb. 15–18	Tucson Open	Phil Rodgers	263	$ 2,800.00	$ 20,000.00
Feb. 22–25	New Orleans Open	Bo Wininger	281	$ 4,300.00	$ 30,000.00
Mar. 2–4	Baton Rouge Open	Joe Campbell	274	$ 2,800.00	$ 20,000.00
Mar. 8–11	Pensacola Open	Doug Sanders	270	$ 2,800.00	$ 20,000.00
Mar. 15–18	St. Petersburg Open	Bob Nichols	272	$ 2,800.00	$ 20,000.00
Mar. 22–25	Doral Open	Billy Casper, Jr.	283	$ 9,000.00	$ 50,000.00
Mar. 29— Apr. 1	Azalea Open	Dave Marr	281	$ 2,800.00	$ 20,000.00
Apr. 5–8	Masters	Arnold Palmer	280	$20,000.00	$109,000.00
Apr. 12–15	Greater Greensboro Open	Billy Casper, Jr.	275	$ 5,300.00	$ 35,000.00
Apr. 19–22	Houston Classic	Bob Nichols	278	$ 9,000.00	$ 53,420.00
Apr. 26–29	Texas Open	Arnold Palmer	273	$ 4,300.00	$ 30,000.00
May 3–6	Tournament of Champions	Arnold Palmer	276	$11,000.00	$ 58,000.00
May 10–13	Colonial National	Arnold Palmer	281	$ 7,000.00	$ 40,000.00

Date	Event	Winner	Score	1st Place Money	Total Purse
May 17–20	Hot Springs Open	Al Johnson	273	$ 2,800.00	$ 20,000.00
May 24–27	"500" Open	Billy Casper, Jr.	264	$ 9,000.00	$ 50,000.00
May 31— June 3	Memphis Open	Lionel Hebert	267	$ 6,400.00	$ 40,000.00
June 7–10	Thunderbird Classic	Gene Littler	275	$25,000.00	$100,000.00
June 14–16	U.S. Open	Jack Nicklaus	283	$15,000.00	$ 68,800.00
June 21–24	Eastern Open	Doug Ford	279	$ 5,300.00	$ 35,000.00
June 28— July 1	Western Open	Jacky Cupit	281	$11,000.00	$ 55,000.00
July 5–8	Buick Open	Bill Collins	284	$ 9,000.00	$ 50,000.00
July 12–15	Motor City Open	Bruce Crampton	267	$ 5,300.00	$ 35,000.00
July 19–22	PGA Championship	Gary Player	278	$13,000.00	$ 72,500.00
July 26–29	Canadian Open	Ted Kroll	278	$ 4,300.00	$ 30,000.00
Aug. 2–5	Insurance City Open	Bob Goalby	271	$ 5,300.00	$ 35,000.00
Aug. 9–12	American Classic	Arnold Palmer	276	$ 9,000.00	$ 51,000.00
Aug. 16–19	St. Paul Open	Doug Sanders	269	$ 4,300.00	$ 30,000.00
Aug. 23–26	Oklahoma City Open	Doug Sanders	280	$ 5,300.00	$ 35,000.00
Aug. 31— Sep. 3	Dallas Open	Billy Maxwell	277	$ 5,300.00	$ 35,000.00
Sept. 6–9	Denver Open	Bob Goalby	277	$ 4,300.00	$ 30,000.00
Sept. 13–16	Seattle Open	Jack Nicklaus	265	$ 4,300.00	$ 30,000.00
Sept. 20–23	Portland Open	Jack Nicklaus	269	$ 3,500.00	$ 25,000.00
Sept. 28–30	Sahara Invitational	Tony Lema	270	$ 2,800.00	$ 20,000.00
Oct. 11–14	Bakersfield Open	Billy Casper, Jr.	272	$ 6,400.00	$ 40,000.00
Oct. 18–21	Ontario Open	Al Geiberger	276	$ 3,500.00	$ 25,000.00
Oct. 25–28	Orange County Open	Tony Lema	267	$ 2,800.00	$ 20,000.00
Nov. 1–4	Beaumont Open	Dave Ragan, Jr.	283	$ 2,800.00	$ 20,000.00
Nov. 8–11	Cajun Classic	John Barnum	270	$ 2,400.00	$ 17,500.00
Nov. 15–18	Mobile Open	Tony Lema	273	$ 2,000.00	$ 15,000.00
Nov. 22–25	Carling Open	Bo Wininger	274	$ 5,300.00	$ 35,000.00
Nov. 29— Dec. 2	West Palm Beach Open	Dave Ragan, Jr.	277	$ 2,800.00	$ 20,000.00
Dec. 6–9	Coral Gables Open	Gardner Dickinson, Jr.	274	$ 2,800.00	$ 20,000.00
	1963 Tour				
Jan. 4–7	Los Angeles Open	Arnold Palmer	274	$ 9,000.00	$ 50,000.00
Jan. 10–13	San Diego Open	Gary Player	270	$ 3,500.00	$ 25,000.00
Jan. 17–20	Bing Crosby Pro-Am	Billy Casper, Jr.	285	$ 5,300.00	$ 35,000.00
Jan. 24–27	Lucky International Open	Jack Burke, Jr.	276	$ 9,000.00	$ 50,000.00
Jan. 30— Feb. 3	Palm Springs Classic	Jack Nicklaus	345	$ 9,000.00	$ 50,000.00
Feb. 7–12	Phoenix Open	Arnold Palmer	273	$ 5,300.00	$ 35,000.00
Feb. 14–17	Tucson Open	Don January	266	$ 3,500.00	$ 25,000.00
Feb. 21–24	Caracas Open	Art Wall, Jr.	274	$ 1,300.00	$ 11,000.00
Mar. 1–4	New Orleans Open	Bo Wininger	279	$ 6,400.00	$ 40,000.00
Mar. 7–10	Pensacola Open	Arnold Palmer	273	$ 3,500.00	$ 25,000.00
Mar. 14–17	St. Petersburg Open	Ray Floyd	274	$ 3,500.00	$ 25,000.00
Mar. 21–24	Doral Open	Dan Sikes, Jr.	283	$ 9,000.00	$ 50,000.00
Mar. 28–31	Azalea Open	Jerry Barber	274	$ 2,800.00	$ 20,000.00
Apr. 4–7	Masters	Jack Nicklaus	286	$20,000.00	$ 94,000.00
Apr. 11–14	Greater Greensboro Open	Doug Sanders	270	$ 5,500.00	$ 37,500.00
Apr. 18–21	Houston Classic	Bob Charles	268	$ 9,000.00	$ 50,000.00
Apr. 25–28	Texas Open	Phil Rodgers	268	$ 4,300.00	$ 30,000.00
May 2–5	Tournament of Champions	Jack Nicklaus	273	$13,000.00	$ 59,000.00
May 9–12	Colonial National	Julius Boros	279	$12,000.00	$ 60,000.00
May 16–19	Oklahoma City Open	Don Fairfield	280	$ 5,300.00	$ 35,000.00
May 23–27	Memphis Open	Tony Lema	270	$ 9,000.00	$ 50,000.00
May 31— June 3	"500" Open	Dow Finsterwald	268	$10,000.00	$ 10,000.00

Date	Event	Winner	Score	1st Place Money	Total Purse
June 6–9	Buick Open	Julius Boros	274	$ 9,000.00	$ 50,000.00
June 13–16	Thunderbird Classic	Arnold Palmer	277	$25,000.00	$100,000.00
June 20–23	U.S. Open	Julius Boros	293	$16,000.00	$ 71,300.00
June 27—July 1	Cleveland Open	Arnold Palmer	273	$22,000.00	$110,000.00
July 3–6	Canadian Open	Doug Ford	280	$ 9,000.00	$ 50,000.00
July 11–14	Hot Springs Open	Dave Hill	277	$ 3,500.00	$ 25,000.00
July 18–21	PGA Championship	Jack Nicklaus	279	$13,000.00	$ 80,900.00
July 25–29	Western Open	Arnold Palmer	280	$11,000.00	$ 57,200.00
Aug. 1–4	St. Paul Open	Jack Burke, Jr.	266	$ 5,300.00	$ 35,000.00
Aug. 15–18	Insurance City Open	Billy Casper, Jr.	271	$ 6,400.00	$ 40,000.00
Aug. 22–25	American Classic	Johnny Pott	276	$ 9,000.00	$ 50,000.00
Aug. 29—Sep. 1	Denver Open	Juan Rodriguez	276	$ 5,300.00	$ 35,000.00
Sept. 5–8	Utah Open	Tommy Jacobs	272	$ 6,400.00	$ 40,000.00
Sept. 12–15	Seattle Open	Bob Nichols	272	$ 5,300.00	$ 35,000.00
Sept. 19–22	Portland Open	George Knudson	271	$ 4,300.00	$ 30,000.00
Oct. 3–6	Whitemarsh Open	Arnold Palmer	281	$26,000.00	$125,000.00
Oct. 17–20	Sahara Invitational	Jack Nicklaus	276	$13,000.00	$ 70,000.00
Oct. 24–27	Fig Garden Open	Mason Rudolph, Jr.	275	$ 3,500.00	$ 25,000.00
Oct. 31—Nov. 3	Almaden Open	Al Geiberger	277	$ 3,500.00	$ 25,000.00
Nov. 7–10	Frank Sinatra Open	Frank Beard	278	$ 9,000.00	$ 50,000.00
Nov. 21–24	Cajun Classic	Rex Baxter, Jr.	275	$ 2,800.00	$ 20,000.00

1964 Tour

Date	Event	Winner	Score	1st Place Money	Total Purse
Jan. 3–6	Los Angeles Open	Paul Harvey	280	$ 7,500.00	$ 50,000.00
Jan. 9–12	San Diego	Art Wall, Jr.	274	$ 4,000.00	$ 30,000.00
Jan. 16–19	Bing Crosby Pro-Am	Tony Lema	284	$ 5,800.00	$ 40,000.00
Jan. 23–26	Lucky International Open	Juan Rodriguez	272	$ 7,500.00	$ 50,000.00
Jan. 29—Feb. 2	Palm Springs Classic	Tommy Jacobs	353	$ 7,500.00	$ 50,000.00
Feb. 6–9	Phoenix Open	Jack Nicklaus	271	$ 7,500.00	$ 50,000.00
Feb. 13–16	Tucson Open	Jacky Cupit	274	$ 4,000.00	$ 30,000.00
Feb. 20–23	Caracas Open	George Knudson	277	$ 1,400.00	$ 11,000.00
Feb. 27—Mar. 2	New Orleans Open	Mason Rudolph, Jr.	283	$ 7,500.00	$ 50,000.00
Mar. 5–8	Pensacola Open	Gary Player	274	$ 4,000.00	$ 30,000.00
Mar. 12–15	St. Petersburg Open	Bruce Devlin	272	$ 3,300.00	$ 25,000.00
Mar. 19–22	Doral Open	Billy Casper, Jr.	277	$ 7,500.00	$ 50,000.00
Mar. 26–30	Azalea Open	Al Besselink	282	$ 2,700.00	$ 20,000.00
Apr. 2–5	Greater Greensboro Open	Julius Boros	277	$ 6,600.00	$ 45,000.00
Apr. 9–12	Masters	Arnold Palmer	276	$20,000.00	$129,800.00
Apr. 16–19	Houston Classic	Mike Souchak	278	$ 7,619.05	$ 57,500.00
Apr. 23–26	Texas Open	Bruce Crampton	273	$ 5,800.00	$ 40,000.00
Apr. 30—May 3	Tournament of Champions	Jack Nicklaus	279	$12,000.00	$ 65,000.00
May 7–10	Colonial National	Billy Casper, Jr.	279	$14,000.00	$ 75,000.00
May 14–18	Oklahoma City Open	Arnold Palmer	277	$ 5,800.00	$ 40,000.00
May 21–24	Memphis Open	Mike Souchak	270	$ 7,500.00	$ 50,000.00
May 27–31	"500" Festival	Gary Player	273	$12,000.00	$ 70,000.00
June 4–7	Thunderbird Classic	Tony Lema	276	$20,000.00	$100,000.00
June 11–14	Buick Open	Tony Lema	277	$ 8,177.42	$ 66,000.00
June 18–20	U.S. Open	Ken Venturi	278	$17,000.00	$ 87,450.00
June 25–28	Cleveland Open	Tony Lema	270	$20,000.00	$100,000.00
July 2–5	Whitemarsh Open	Jack Nicklaus	276	$24,042.12	$122,653.00
July 16–19	PGA Championship	Bob Nichols	271	$18,000.00	$100,000.00
July 23–26	Insurance City Open	Ken Venturi	273	$ 7,500.00	$ 50,000.00
July 30—Aug. 2	Canadian Open	Kel Nagle	277	$ 7,500.00	$ 50,000.00
Aug. 6–9	Western Open	Juan Rodriguez	268	$11,000.00	$ 65,010.00

Roberto DeVincenzo (left) and Bob Goalby (right), the man who won the 1968 Masters Tournament "through the back door" of error, sit together at the presentation ceremonies after the tournament. They would have faced each other in a play-off except for the fact that de Vicenzo signed an incorrect scorecard. The penalty gave the victory to Goalby.

The Bauer girls were a big attraction on the women's tour in 1950 when Alice (left) was 22 and Marlene (right) was 15. Today, they are still playing regularly, but now under the names of Mrs. (Alice) Gwinner and Mrs. (Marlene) Hagge.

Five Women's Amateur champions who eventually made it "big" on the professional tour (left to right, top to bottom): Betty Jameson (1939 and 1940), Mary Lena Faulk (1953), Barbara Romack (1954), and Grace Lenczyk (1948), who is watching Beverly Hanson (1950) drive off.

Date	Event	Winner	Score	1st Place Money	Total Purse
Aug. 13–16	St. Paul Open	Chuck Courtney	272	$11,500.00	$ 65,000.00
Aug. 20–23	American Classic	Ken Venturi	275	$ 7,500.00	$ 50,000.00
Aug. 27–30	Carling Open	Bob Nichols	278	$35,000.00	$201,600.00
Sept. 4–7	Dallas Open	Charles Coody	271	$ 5,800.00	$ 40,000.00
Sept. 17–20	Portland Open	Jack Nicklaus	275	$ 5,800.00	$ 40,000.00
Sept. 23–27	Seattle Open	Billy Casper, Jr.	265	$ 5,800.00	$ 40,000.00
Oct. 1–4	Fresno Open	George Knudson	280	$ 5,000.00	$ 35,000.00
Oct. 8–11	Sunset-Camellia Open	Bob McCallister	281	$ 3,300.00	$ 25,000.00
Oct. 15–18	Sahara Invitational	R. H. Sikes	275	$12,000.00	$ 70,000.00
Oct. 22–25	Mountain View Open	Jack McGowan	273	$ 5,800.00	$ 40,000.00
Oct. 29— Nov. 1	Almaden Open	Billy Casper, Jr.	279	$ 3,300.00	$ 25,000.00
Nov. 19–22	Cajun Classic	Miller Barber	277	$ 3,300.00	$ 25,000.00

1965 Tour

Jan. 8–11	Los Angeles Open	Paul Harney	276	$12,500.00	$ 70,000.00
Jan. 14–17	San Diego Open	Wes Ellis, Jr.	267	$ 4,850.00	$ 34,500.00
Jan. 21–24	Bing Crosby Pro-Am	Bruce Crampton	284	$ 7,500.00	$ 50,000.00
Jan. 28–31	Lucky International	George Archer	278	$ 8,500.00	$ 57,500.00
Feb. 3–7	Bob Hope Classic	Billy Casper, Jr.	348	$15,000.00	$ 80,000.00
Feb. 11–14	Phoenix Open	Rod Funseth	274	$10,500.00	$ 67,500.00
Feb. 18–21	Tucson Open	Bob Charles	271	$ 6,800.00	$ 46,000.00
Feb. 25–28	Caracas Open	Al Besselink	273	$ 2,000.00	$ 13,500.00
Mar. 4–7	Pensacola Open	Doug Sanders	277	$10,000.00	$ 65,000.00
Mar. 11–14	Doral Open	Doug Sanders	274	$11,000.00	$ 70,000.00
Mar. 18–21	Jacksonville Open	Bert Weaver	285	$ 8,500.00	$ 57,500.00
Mar. 25–28	Azalea Open	Dick Hart	276	$ 3,850.00	$ 28,750.00
Apr. 1–4	Greater Greensboro Open	Sam Snead	273	$11,000.00	$ 70,000.00
Apr. 8–11	Masters	Jack Nicklaus	271	$20,000.00	$137,675.00
Apr. 15–18	Houston Classic	Bob Nichols	273	$12,000.00	$ 75,000.00
Apr. 22–25	Texas Open	Frank Beard	270	$ 7,500.00	$ 50,000.00
May 6–11	Colonial National	Bruce Crampton	276	$20,000.00	$100,000.00
May 13–16	New Orleans Open	Dick Mayer	273	$20,000.00	$100,000.00
May 20–23	Memphis Open	Jack Nicklaus	271	$ 9,000.00	$ 60,000.00
May 27–30	"500" Festival	Bruce Crampton	279	$15,200.00	$ 87,000.00
June 3–6	Buick Open	Tony Lema	280	$20,000.00	$100,000.00
June 10–13	Cleveland Open	Dan Sikes, Jr.	272	$25,000.00	$125,000.00
June 17–20	U.S. Open	Gary Player	282	$25,000.00	$121,890.00
June 24–27	St. Paul Open	Ray Floyd	270	$20,000.00	$100,000.00
July 1–4	Western Open	Billy Casper, Jr.	270	$11,000.00	$ 70,000.00
July 14–17	Canadian Open	Gene Littler	273	$20,000.00	$100,000.00
July 22–25	Insurance City Open	Billy Casper, Jr.	274	$11,000.00	$ 70,000.00
July 29— Aug. 1	Thunderbird Classic	Jack Nicklaus	270	$20,000.00	$100,000.00
Aug. 5–8	Philadelphia Classic	Jack Nicklaus	277	$24,300.00	$121,500.00
Aug. 12–15	PGA Championship	Dave Marr	280	$25,000.00	$149,700.00
Aug. 19–23	Carling Open	Tony Lema	279	$35,000.00	$200,800.00
Aug. 26–29	American Classic	Al Geiberger	280	$20,000.00	$100,000.00
Sept. 2–5	Oklahoma City Open	Jack Rule, Jr.	283	$10,000.00	$ 65,000.00
Sept. 16–19	Portland Open	Jack Nicklaus	273	$ 6,600.00	$ 45,000.00
Sept. 23–26	Seattle Open	Gay Brewer, Jr.	279	$ 6,600.00	$ 45,000.00
Oct. 20–23	Sahara Invitational	Billy Casper, Jr.	269	$20,000.00	$100,000.00
Oct. 28–31	Almaden Open	Bob Verwey	273	$ 6,000.00	$ 46,000.00
Nov. 4–7	Hawaiian Open	Gay Brewer, Jr.	281	$ 9,000.00	$ 60,300.00
Nov. 11–14	Mexican Open	Homero Blancas	284	$ 3,000.00	$ 15,000.00
Nov. 18–21	Caracas Open	Al Besselink	275	$ 2,500.00	$ 15,000.00
Nov. 25–28	Cajun Classic	Babe Hiskey	275	$ 4,250.00	$ 32,000.00
Dec. 8–11	PGA Four-Ball	Brewer-Baird	259	$10,000.00 each	$125,000.00

1966 Tour

Jan. 6–9	Los Angeles Open	Arnold Palmer	273	$11,000.00	$ 70,000.00

Date	Event	Winner	Score	1st Place Money	Total Purse
Jan. 13–16	San Diego Open	Billy Casper, Jr.	268	$ 5,800.00	$ 40,000.00
Jan. 20–23	Bing Crosby Pro-Am	Don Massengale	283	$11,000.00	$ 70,000.00
Jan. 27–31	Lucky International	Ken Venturi	273	$ 8,500.00	$ 57,000.00
Feb. 2–6	Bob Hope Classic	Doug Sanders	349	$15,000.00	$ 80,000.00
Feb. 10–14	Phoenix Open	Dudley Wysong, Jr.	278	$ 9,000.00	$ 60,000.00
Feb. 17–20	Tucson Open	Joe Campbell	278	$ 9,000.00	$ 60,000.00
Mar. 3–7	Pensacola Open	Gay Brewer, Jr.	272	$10,000.00	$ 65,000.00
Mar. 10–13	Doral Open	Phil Rodgers	278	$20,000.00	$100,000.00
Mar. 17–20	Citrus Open	Lionel Hebert	279	$21,000.00	$110,000.00
Mar. 24–27	Jacksonville Open	Doug Sanders	273	$13,500.00	$ 82,000.00
Mar. 31—Apr. 3	Greater Greensboro Open	Doug Sanders	276	$20,000.00	$100,000.00
Apr. 7–11	Masters	Jack Nicklaus	288	$20,000.00	$152,880.00
Apr. 14–17	Azalea Open	Bert Yancey	278	$ 3,200.00	$ 22,800.00
Apr. 14–18	Tournament of Champions	Arnold Palmer	283	$20,000.00	$100,000.00
Apr. 21–26	Dallas Open	Roberto DeVicenzo	276	$15,000.00	$ 85,000.00
Apr. 28—May 1	Texas Open	Harold Henning	272	$13,000.00	$ 80,000.00
May 12–16	New Orleans Open	Frank Beard	276	$20,000.00	$100,000.00
May 19–22	Colonial National	Bruce Devlin	280	$22,000.00	$110,000.00
May 26–29	Oklahoma City Open	Tony Lema	271	$ 8,500.00	$ 57,000.00
June 2–5	Memphis Open	Bert Yancey	265	$20,000.00	$100,000.00
June 9–12	Buick Open	Phil Rodgers	284	$20,000.00	$100,000.00
June 16–20	U.S. Open	Billy Casper, Jr.	278	$25,000.00	$144,490.00
June 23–26	Western Open	Billy Casper, Jr.	283	$20,000.00	$101,800.00
July 14–17	Minnesota Classic	Bobby Nichols	270	$20,000.00	$100,000.00
July 21–24	PGA Championship	Al Geiberger	280	$25,000.00	$149,700.00
July 28–31	"500" Festival	Billy Casper, Jr.	277	$16,400.00	$ 92,000.00
Aug. 4–7	Cleveland Open	R. H. Sikes, Jr.	268	$20,000.00	$100,000.00
Aug. 11–14	Thunderbird Classic	Mason Rudolph, Jr.	278	$20,000.00	$100,000.00
Aug. 18–21	Insurance City Open	Art Wall, Jr.	266	$20,000.00	$100,000.00
Aug. 25–28	Philadelphia Classic	Don January	278	$21,000.00	$110,000.00
Aug. 31—Sept. 3	Carling Open	Bruce Devlin	286	$35,000.00	$204,800.48
Sept. 15–18	Portland Open	Bert Yancey	271	$ 6,800.00	$ 45,600.00
Sept. 22–25	Seattle-Everett Open	Homero Blancas	266	$ 6,600.00	$ 45,000.00
Sept. 29—Oct. 2	Canadian Open	Don Massengale	280	$18,300.00	$ 91,500.00
Oct. 12–15	Sahara Invitational	Jack Nicklaus	282	$20,000.00	$100,000.00
Oct. 27–30	Hawaiian Open	Ted Makalena	271	$ 8,500.00	$ 57,000.00
Nov. 3–6	Mexico Open	Bob McCallister	278	$ 3,000.00	$ 15,000.00
Nov. 10–13	Caracas Open	Art Wall, Jr.	276	$ 3,000.00	$ 15,000.00
Nov. 17–20	Houston International	Arnold Palmer	275	$21,000.00	$110,000.00
Nov. 24–27	Cajun Classic	Jacky Cupit	271	$ 4,850.00	$ 34,500.00
Dec. 7–10	PGA National Team Championship	Palmer & Nicklaus	256	$25,000.00 each	$280,000.00
1967 Tour					
Jan. 12–15	San Diego Open	Bob Goalby	269	$13,200.00	$ 66,000.00
Jan. 19–22	Bing Crosby Pro-Am	Jack Nicklaus	284	$16,000.00	$ 80,000.00
Jan. 26–29	Los Angeles Open	Arnold Palmer	269	$20,000.00	$100,000.00
Feb. 1–5	Bob Hope Classic	Tom Nieporte	349	$17,600.00	$ 88,000.00
Feb. 9–12	Phoenix Open	Julius Boros	272	$14,000.00	$ 70,000.00
Feb. 16–19	Tucson Open	Arnold Palmer	273	$12,000.00	$ 60,000.00
Mar. 2–5	Doral Open	Doug Sanders	275	$20,000.00	$100,000.00
Mar. 9–12	Florida Citrus Open	Julius Boros	274	$23,000.00	$115,000.00
Mar. 16–19	Jacksonville Open	Dan Sikes, Jr.	279	$20,000.00	$100,000.00
Mar. 23–26	Pensacola Open	Gay Brewer, Jr.	262	$15,000.00	$ 75,000.00
Mar. 30—Apr. 2	Greater Greensboro Open	George Archer	267	$25,000.00	$125,000.00

Date	Event	Winner	Score	1st Place Money	Total Purse
Apr. 6–9	Masters	Gay Brewer, Jr.	280	$20,000.00	$154,850.00
Apr. 13–16	Azalea Open	Randy Glover	278	$ 5,000.00	$ 35,000.00
Apr. 13–16	Tournament of Champions	Frank Beard	278	$20,000.00	$100,000.00
Apr. 20–23	Dallas Open	Bert Yancey	274	$20,000.00	$100,000.00
Apr. 27–30	Texas Open	Juan Rodriguez	277	$20,000.00	$100,000.00
May 4–7	Houston Championships International	Frank Beard	274	$23,000.00	$115,000.00
May 11–14	Greater New Orleans Open	George Knudson	277	$20,000.00	$100,000.00
May 18–21	Colonial National Invitational	Dave Stockton	278	$23,000.00	$115,000.00
May 25–28	Oklahoma City Open	Miller Barber	278	$13,200.00	$ 66,000.00
June 1–4	Memphis Open	Dave Hill	272	$20,000.00	$100,000.00
June 8–11	Buick Open	Julius Boros	283	$20,000.00	$100,000.00
June 15–18	U.S. Open	Jack Nicklaus	275	$30,000.00	$169,400.00
June 22–25	Cleveland Open	Gardner Dickinson, Jr.	271	$20,700.00	$103,500.00
June 29—July 2	Canadian Open	Billy Casper, Jr.	279	$27,840.00	$185,600.00
July 6–9	"500" Festival Open	Frank Beard	279	$20,000.00	$100,000.00
July 20–23	PGA Championship	Don January	281	$25,000.00	$149,100.00
July 27–30	Minnesota Golf Classic	Lou Graham	286	$20,000.00	$100,000.00
Aug. 3–6	Western Open	Jack Nicklaus	274	$20,000.00	$102,400.00
Aug. 10–13	American Golf Classic	Arnold Palmer	276	$20,000.00	$100,000.00
Aug. 17–20	Insurance City Open	Charley Sifford	272	$20,000.00	$100,000.00
Aug. 24–27	Westchester Classic	Jack Nicklaus	272	$50,000.00	$250,000.00
Aug. 30—Sept. 2	Carling World Open	Billy Casper, Jr.	281	$35,000.00	$198,600.00
Sept. 14–17	Philadelphia Classic	Dan Sikes, Jr.	276	$22,000.00	$110,000.00
Sept. 21–24	Thunderbird Classic	Arnold Palmer	283	$30,000.00	$150,000.00
Sept. 28—Oct. 1	Atlanta Classic	Robert J. Charles	282	$22,000.00	$115,000.00
Oct. 26–29	Sahara Open	Jack Nicklaus	270	$20,000.00	$100,000.00
Nov. 2–4	Hawaiian Open	Dudley Wysong, Jr.	284	$20,000.00	$100,000.00
Nov. 30—Dec. 3	Cajun Classic	Marty Fleckman	275	$ 5,000.00	$ 35,000.00
	1968 Tour				
Jan. 11–14	Bing Crosby Pro-Am	Johnny Pott	285	$16,000.00	$ 80,000.00
Jan. 18–21	Kaiser International Open	Kermit Zarley	273	$25,000.00	$120,000.00
Jan. 25–28	Los Angeles Open	Billy Casper, Jr.	274	$20,000.00	$100,000.00
Jan. 31—Feb. 4	Bob Hope Classic	Arnold Palmer	348	$20,000.00	$100,000.00
Feb. 8–11	Andy Williams–San Diego Open	Tom Weiskopf	273	$30,000.00	$100,000.00
Feb. 15–18	Phoenix Open	George Knudson	272	$20,000.00	$100,000.00
Feb. 22–25	Tucson Open	George Knudson	273	$20,000.00	$100,000.00
Mar. 7–10	Doral Open	Gardner Dickinson, Jr.	275	$20,000.00	$100,000.00
Mar. 14–17	Florida Citrus Open	Dan Sikes, Jr.	274	$23,000.00	$115,000.00
Mar. 21–25	Pensacola Open	George Archer	268	$14,000.00	$ 80,000.00
Mar. 28–31	Jacksonville Open	Tony Jacklin	273	$20,000.00	$100,000.00
Apr. 4–7	Greater Greensboro Open	Billy Casper, Jr.	267	$27,500.00	$137,500.00
Apr. 11–14	Masters	Bob Goalby	277	$20,000.00	$172,475.00
Apr. 11–14	Rebel Yell Open	Larry Mowry	279	$ 2,800.00	$ 20,000.00
Apr. 18–21	Tournament of Champions	Don January	276	$30,000.00	$100,000.00
Apr. 18–21	Azalea Open	Steve Reid	271	$ 5,000.00	$ 35,000.00
Apr. 25–28	Byron Nelson Classic	Miller Barber	270	$20,000.00	$100,000.00
May 2–5	Houston International Championships	Roberto DeVicenzo	274	$20,000.00	$100,000.00
May 9–12	Greater New Orleans Open	George Archer	271	$20,000.00	$100,000.00
May 16–19	Colonial National	Billy Casper, Jr.	275	$25,000.00	$125,000.00

Date	Event	Winner	Score	1st Place Money	Total Purse
May 16–19	Magnolia State Classic	B. R. McLendon	269	$ 2,800.00	$ 20,000.00
May 23–25	Memphis Open	Bob Lunn	268	$20,000.00	$100,000.00
May 30— June 2	Atlanta Classic	Bob Lunn	280	$23,000.00	$115,000.00
June 6–9	"500" Festival	Billy Casper, Jr.	280	$20,000.00	$100,000.00
June 13–16	U.S. Open	Lee Trevino	275	$30,000.00	$190,000.00
June 20–23	Canadian Open	Bob Charles	274	$25,000.00	$125,000.00
June 27–30	Cleveland Open	Dave Stockton	276	$22,000.00	$110,000.00
July 4–7	Buick Open	Tom Weiskopf	280	$25,000.00	$125,000.00
July 11–14	Greater Milwaukee Open	Dave Stockton	275	$40,000.00	$200,000.00
July 18–21	PGA Championship	Julius Boros	281	$25,000.00	$200,000.00
July 25–28	Minnesota Classic	Don Sikes, Jr.	272	$20,000.00	$100,000.00
Aug. 1–4	Western Open	Jack Nicklaus	273	$26,000.00	$130,000.00
Aug. 8–11	American Classic	Jack Nicklaus	280	$25,000.00	$125,000.00
Aug. 15–18	Westchester Classic	Julius Boros	272	$50,000.00	$250,000.00
Aug. 22–25	Philadelphia Classic	Bob Murphy	276	$20,000.00	$100,000.00
Aug. 30— Sept. 2	Thunderbird Classic	Bob Murphy	277	$30,000.00	$150,000.00
Sept. 5–8	Greater Hartford Open	Billy Casper, Jr.	266	$20,000.00	$100,000.00
Sept. 12–15	Kemper Open	Arnold Palmer	276	$20,000.00	$150,000.00
Sept. 19–22	PGA Nat. Team Champ.	Archer & Nichols	265	$20,000.00 each	$200,000.00
Sept. 26–29	Robinson Open	Dean Refram	279	$ 5,000.00	$ 25,000.00
Oct. 17–20	Sahara Invitational	Juan Rodriguez	274	$20,000.00	$100,000.00
Oct. 24–27	Haig Open	Bob Dickson	271	$22,000.00	$110,000.00
Oct. 31— Nov. 4	Lucky International Open	Billy Casper, Jr.	269	$20,000.00	$100,000.00
Nov. 7–10	Hawaiian Open	Lee Trevino	272	$25,000.00	$125,000.00
Nov. 21–24	Cajun Classic	Ron Cerrudo	270	$ 5,000.00	$ 35,000.00
	1969 Tour				
Jan. 9–12	Alameda Open	Dick Lotz	290	$10,000.00	$ 50,000.00
Jan. 9–12	Los Angeles Open	Charley Sifford	276	$20,000.00	$100,000.00
Jan. 16–17	Kaiser International Open	Miller Barber	135	$13,500.00 *	$135,000.00
Jan. 22–17	Bing Crosby Pro-Am	George Archer	283	$25,000.00	$125,000.00
Jan. 30— Feb. 2	Andy Williams– San Diego Open	Jack Nicklaus	284	$30,000.00	$150,000.00
Feb. 5–9	Bob Hope Desert Classic	Billy Casper, Jr.	345	$20,000.00	$100,000.00
Feb. 13–16	Phoenix Open	Gene Littler	263	$20,000.00	$100,000.00
Feb. 20–23	Tucson Open	Lee Trevino	271	$20,000.00	$100,000.00
Feb. 27— Mar. 2	Doral Open	Tom Shaw	276	$30,000.00	$150,000.00
Mar. 6–9	Florida Citrus Open	Ken Still	278	$23,000.00	$115,000.00
Mar. 13–18	Monsanto Open	Jim Colbert, Jr.	267	$20,000.00	$100,000.00
Mar. 20–23	Greater Jacksonville Open	Ray Floyd	278	$20,000.00	$100,000.00
Mar. 27–30	National Airlines Open	Bunky Henry	278	$40,000.00	$200,000.00
Apr. 3–6	Greater Greensboro Open	Gene Littler	274	$32,000.00	$160,000.00
Apr. 10–14	Magnolia Classic	Larry Mowry	272	$ 5,000.00	$ 35,000.00
Apr. 11–13	Masters	George Archer	281	$20,000.00	$149,975.00
Apr. 17–20	Tallahassee Open	Chuck Courtney	282	$ 5,000.00	$ 35,000.00
Apr. 17–20	Azalea Open	Dale Douglass	275	$ 5,000.00	$ 35,000.00
Apr. 17–20	Tournament of Champions	Gary Player	284	$30,000.00	$150,000.00
Apr. 24–27	Byron Nelson Classic	Bruce Devlin	277	$20,000.00	$100,000.00
May 1–4	Greater New Orleans Open	Larry Hinson	275	$20,000.00	$100,000.00
May 9–12	Texas Open	Deane Beman	274	$20,000.00	$100,000.00
May 15–18	Colonial National Invitational	Gardner Dickinson, Jr.	278	$25,000.00	$125,000.00
May 22–25	Atlanta Classic	Bert Yancey	277	$23,000.00	$115,000.00

Date	Event	Winner	Score	1st Place Money	Total Purse
May 29— June 1	Memphis Open	Dave Hill	265	$30,000.00	$150,000.00
June 5–8	Western Open	Billy Casper, Jr.	276	$26,000.00	$130,000.00
June 12–15	U.S. Open	Orville Moody	281	$30,000.00	$161,400.00
June 19–22	Kemper Open	Dale Douglass	274	$30,000.00	$150,000.00
June 26–29	Cleveland Open	Charles Coody	271	$22,000.00	$110,000.00
July 3–6	Buick Open	Dave Hill	277	$25,000.00	$125,000.00
July 10–13	Minnesota Classic	Frank Beard	269	$20,000.00	$100,000.00
July 17–20	Philadelphia Classic	Dave Hill	279	$30,000.00	$150,000.00
July 24–27	American Classic	Ray Floyd	268	$25,000.00	$125,000.00
July 24–27	Canadian Open	Tommy Aaron	275	$25,000.00	$125,000.00
July 31— Aug. 3	Westchester Classic	Frank Beard	275	$50,000.00	$250,000.00
Aug. 7–10	Greater Milwaukee Open	Ken Still	277	$20,000.00	$100,000.00
Aug. 14–17	PGA Championship	Ray Floyd	276	$35,000.00	$175,000.00
Aug. 14–17	Indian Ridge Hospital Open	Monty Kaser	274	$ 7,400.00	$ 35,000.00
Aug. 21–24	AVCO Classic	Tom Shaw	280	$30,000.00	$150,000.00
Aug. 29– Sept. 1	Greater Hartford Open	Bob Lunn	268	$20,000.00	$100,000.00
Sept. 4–7	Michigan Classic	Larry Ziegler	272	$20,000.00	$100,000.00
Sept. 25–28	Robinson Open	Bob Goalby	273	$15,000.00	$ 75,000.00
Oct. 16–19	Sahara Invitational	Jack Nicklaus	272	$20,000.00	$100,000.00
Oct. 23–26	Lucky International Open	Steve Spray	269	$20,000.00	$100,000.00
Oct. 30– Nov. 2	Kaiser International Open	Jack Nicklaus	273	$28,000.00	$135,000.00
Nov. 6–9	Hawaiian Open	Bruce Crampton	274	$25,000.00	$125,000.00
Nov. 27–30	Heritage Golf Classic	Arnold Palmer	283	$20,000.00	$100,000.00
Dec. 4–7	Danny Thomas– Diplomat Classic	Arnold Palmer	270	$25,000.00	$125,000.00
Dec. 4–7	West End Classic	Jim Weichers	274	$ 5,000.00	$ 25,000.00
	1970 Tour				
Jan. 8–11	Los Angeles Open	Billy Casper, Jr.	278	$20,000.00	$100,000.00
Jan. 15–18	Phoenix Open	Dale Douglass	271	$20,000.00	$100,000.00
Jan. 22–25	Bing Crosby Pro-Am	Bert Yancey	278	$25,000.00	$125,000.00
Jan. 29– Feb. 1	Andy Williams– San Diego Open	Pete Brown	275	$30,000.00	$150,000.00
Feb. 4–8	Bob Hope Desert Classic	Bruce Devlin	339	$25,000.00	$125,000.00
Feb. 12–15	Tucson Open	Lee Trevino	275	$20,000.00	$100,000.00
Feb. 19–22	San Antonio–Texas Open	Ron Cerrudo	273	$20,000.00	$100,000.00
Feb. 26– Mar. 1	Doral–Eastern Open	Mike Hill	279	$30,000.00	$150,000.00
Mar. 3–6	Florida Citrus Open	Bob Stone	278	$ 5,000.00	$ 35,000.00
Mar. 5–8	Florida Citrus	Bob Lunn	271	$30,000.00	$150,000.00
Mar. 12–15	Monsanto Open	Dick Lotz	275	$30,000.00	$150,000.00
Mar. 19–22	Greater Jacksonville Open	Don January	279	$20,000.00	$100,000.00
Mar. 26–29	National Airlines Open	Lee Trevino	274	$40,000.00	$200,000.00
Apr. 2–5	Greater Greensboro Open	Gary Player	271	$36,000.00	$180,000.00
Apr. 9–12	Masters	Billy Casper, Jr.	279	$25,000.00	$203,801.00
Apr. 9–12	Magnolia Classic	Chris Blocker	271	$ 5,000.00	$ 35,000.00
Apr. 16–19	Greater New Orleans Open	Miller Barber	278	$25,000.00	$125,000.00
Apr. 23–26	Tournament of Champions	Frank Beard	273	$30,000.00	$150,000.00
Apr. 23–26	Tallahassee Open	Harold Henning	277	$10,000.00	$ 50,000.00
Apr. 30– May 3	Byron Nelson Golf Classic	Jack Nicklaus	274	$20,000.00	$100,000.00
May 7–10	Houston/Champions International	Gibby Gilbert	282	$23,000.00	$115,000.00
May 14–17	Colonial National	Homero Blancas	278	$25,000.00	$125,000.00
May 21–24	Atlanta Classic	Tommy Aaron	275	$25,000.00	$125,000.00
May 28–31	Danny Thomas– Memphis Classic	Dave Hill	267	$30,000.00	$150,000.00

Date	Event	Winner	Score	1st Place Money	Total Purse
June 4–7	Kemper Open	Dick Lotz	278	$30,000.00	$150,000.00
June 4–7	Kiwanis Peninsula Open	Jerry Barrier	281	$ 5,000.00	$ 25,000.00
June 11–14	Western Open	Hugh Royer, Jr.	273	$26,000.00	$130,000.00
June 18–21	U.S. Open Championship	Tony Jacklin	281	$30,000.00	$203,500.00
June 25–28	Cleveland Open	Bruce Devlin	268	$30,000.00	$150,000.00
July 2–5	Canadian Open	Kermit Zarley	279	$25,000.00	$125,000.00
July 9–12	Greater Milwaukee Open	Deane Beman	276	$22,000.00	$110,000.00
July 16–19	IVB-Philadelphia Golf Classic	Billy Casper, Jr.	274	$30,000.00	$150,000.00
July 23–26	National Four-Ball Championship	Jack Nicklaus– Arnold Palmer	259	$20,000.00	$200,000.00
July 30– Aug. 2	Westchester Classic	Bruce Crampton	273	$50,000.00	$250,000.00
Aug. 6–9	American Golf Classic	Frank Beard	276	$30,000.00	$150,000.00
Aug. 13–16	PGA Championship	Dave Stockton	279	$40,000.00	$200,000.00
Aug. 20–23	AVCO Classic	Billy Casper, Jr.	277	$32,000.00	$160,000.00
Aug. 27–30	Dow Jones Open	Bobby Nichols	276	$60,000.00	$300,000.00
Sept. 4–7	Greater Hartford Open	Bob Murphy	267	$20,000.00	$100,000.00
Sept. 17–20	Robinson Open Golf Classic	George Knudson	268	$20,000.00	$100,000.00
Sept. 24–27	Green Island Open	Mason Rudolph	274	$12,000.00	$ 60,000.00
Oct. 1–4	Azalea Open	Cesar Sanudo	269	$12,000.00	$ 60,000.00
Oct. 22–25	Kaiser International Open	Ken Still	278	$30,000.00	$150,000.00
Oct. 29– Nov. 1	Sahara Invitational	Babe Hiskey	276	$20,000.00	$100,000.00
Nov. 26–29	Heritage Golf Classic	Bob Goalby	280	$20,000.00	$100,000.00
Nov. 26–28	Sea Pines Open	Larry Wood	282	$ 6,000.00	$ 30,000.00
Dec. 3–6	Coral Springs Open	Bill Garrett	272	$25,000.00	$125,000.00
Dec. 10–13	Bahama Islands Open	Doug Sanders	272	$26,000.00	$130,000.00
	1971 Tour				
Jan. 7–10	Glen Campbell– Los Angeles Open	Bob Lunn	274	$22,000.00	$110,000.00
Jan. 14–17	Bing Crosby Pro-Am	Tom Shaw	278	$27,000.00	$135,000.00
Jan. 21–24	Phoenix Open	Miller Barber	261	$25,000.00	$125,000.00
Jan. 28–31	Andy Williams– San Diego Open	George Archer	272	$30,000.00	$150,000.00
Feb. 4–7	Hawaiian Open	Tom Shaw	273	$40,000.00	$200,000.00
Feb. 10–14	Bob Hope Desert Classic	Arnold Palmer	342	$28,000.00	$140,000.00
Feb. 18–21	Tucson Open	J. C. Snead	273	$22,000.00	$110,000.00
Feb. 24–28	PGA Championship	Jack Nicklaus	281	$40,000.00	$200,000.00
Mar. 4–7	Doral–Eastern Open	J. C. Snead	275	$30,000.00	$150,000.00
Mar. 11–14	Florida Citrus Invitational	Arnold Palmer	270	$30,000.00	$150,000.00
Mar. 18–21	Greater Jacksonville Open	Gary Player	281	$25,000.00	$125,000.00
Mar. 25–28	National Airlines Open	Gary Player	274	$40,000.00	$200,000.00
Apr. 1–4	Greater Greensboro Open	Brian Allin	275	$38,000.00	$190,000.00
Apr. 8–11	Masters	Charles Coody	279	$25,000.00	$197,976.00
Apr. 15–18	Monsanto Open	Gene Littler	276	$30,000.00	$150,000.00
Apr. 22–25	Tournament of Champions	Jack Nicklaus	279	$33,000.00	$165,000.00
Apr. 22–25	Tallahassee Open	Lee Trevino	273	$12,000.00	$ 60,000.00
Apr. 29– May 2	Greater New Orleans Open	Frank Beard	276	$25,000.00	$125,000.00
May 6–9	Byron Nelson Golf Classic	Jack Nicklaus	274	$25,000.00	$125,000.00
May 13–16	Houston/Champions International	Hubert Green	280	$25,000.00	$125,000.00
May 27–30	Danny Thomas– Memphis Classic	Lee Trevino	268	$35,000.00	$175,000.00
June 3–6	Atlanta Classic	G. Dickinson	275	$25,000.00	$125,000.00
June 10–13	Kemper Open	Tom Weiskopf	277	$30,000.00	$150,000.00
June 17–20	U.S. Open	Lee Trevino	280	$30,000.00	$200,000.00
June 24–27	Cleveland Open	B. Mitchell	262	$30,000.00	$150,000.00

Date	Event	Winner	Score	1st Place Money	Total Purse
July 1–4	Canadian Open	Lee Trevino	275	$30,000.00	$150,000.00
July 8–11	Greater Milwaukee Open	D. Eichelberger	270	$25,000.00	$125,000.00
July 15–18	Western Open	Bruce Crampton	279	$30,000.00	$150,000.00
July 22–25	Westchester Classic	Arnold Palmer	270	$50,000.00	$250,000.00
Aug. 5–8	American Golf Classic	Jerry Heard	275	$30,000.00	$150,000.00
Aug. 12–15	Massachusetts Classic	Dave Stockton	275	$33,000.00	$165,000.00
July 29– Aug. 1	National Team Championship	Arnold Palmer– Jack Nicklaus	257	$20,000.00	$200,000.00
Aug. 19–22	IVB–Philadelphia Golf Classic	Tom Weiskopf	274	$30,000.00	$150,000.00
Aug. 25–29	U.S. Professional Match Play Championship	DeWitt Weaver d. Phil Rodger	71–77	$35,000.00	$200,000.00
Sept. 3–6	Greater Hartford Open	George Archer	268	$22,000.00	$110,000.00
Sept. 9–12	Southern Open	John Miller	267	$20,000.00	$100,000.00
Sept. 23–26	Robinson Open Golf Classic	L. Harris, Jr.	274	$20,000.00	$100,000.00
Oct. 21–24	Kaiser International Open	Billy Casper, Jr.	269	$30,000.00	$150,000.00
Oct. 28–31	Sahara Invitational	Lee Trevino	280	$27,000.00	$135,000.00
Nov. 18–21	Azalea Open	G. Johnson	274	$ 7,000.00	$ 35,000.00
Nov. 25–28	Sea Pines– Heritage Classic	Hale Irwin	279	$22,000.00	$110,000.00
Dec. 2–6	Walt Disney World Open	Jack Nicklaus	273	$30,000.00	$150,000.00
Dec. 9–12	Bahamas National Open	Bob Goalby	275	$26,000.00	$130,000.00

1972 Tour

Date	Event	Winner	Score	1st Place Money	Total Purse
Jan. 6–9	Glen Campbell– Los Angeles Open	George Archer	270	$25,000.00	$125,000.00
Jan. 13–16	Bing Crosby Pro-Am	Jack Nicklaus	284	$28,000.00	$140,000.00
Jan. 20–23	Dean Martin–Tucson Open	Miller Barber	273	$30,000.00	$150,000.00
Jan. 27–30	Andy Williams– San Diego Open	Paul Harney	275	$30,000.00	$150,000.00
Feb. 3–6	Hawaiian Open	Grier Jones	274	$40,000.00	$200,000.00
Feb. 9–13	Bob Hope Desert Classic	Bob Rosburg	344	$29,000.00	$145,000.00
Feb. 17–20	Phoenix Open	Homero Blancas	273	$25,000.00	$125,000.00
Feb. 24–27	Jackie Gleason– Inverrary Classic	Tom Weiskopf	278	$52,000.00	$260,000.00
Mar. 2–5	Doral–Eastern Open	Jack Nicklaus	276	$30,000.00	$150,000.00
Mar. 9–12	Florida Citrus Open	Jerry Heard	276	$30,000.00	$150,000.00
Mar. 16–19	Greater Jacksonville Open	Tony Jacklin	283	$25,000.00	$125,000.00
Mar. 23–26	Greater New Orleans Open	Gary Player	279	$25,000.00	$125,000.00
Mar. 30– Apr. 2	Greater Greensboro Open	George Archer	272	$40,000.00	$200,000.00
Apr. 6–9	Masters	Jack Nicklaus	286	$25,000.00	$204,649.00
Apr. 13–16	Monsanto Open	Dave Hill	271	$30,000.00	$150,000.00
Apr. 20–23	Tournament of Champions	Bobby Mitchell	280	$33,000.00	$165,000.00
Apr. 20–23	Tallahassee Open	Bob Shaw	273	$15,000.00	$ 75,000.00
Apr. 27–30	Byron Nelson Golf Classic	Juan Rodriguez	273	$25,000.00	$125,000.00
May 4–7	Houston Open	Bruce Devlin	278	$25,000.00	$125,000.00
May 11–14	Colonial National Invitational	Jerry Heard	275	$25,000.00	$125,000.00
May 18–21	Danny Thomas– Memphis Classic	Lee Trevino	281	$35,000.00	$175,000.00
May 25–28	Atlanta Classic	Bob Lunn	275	$26,000.00	$130,000.00
June 1–4	Kemper Open	Doug Sanders	275	$35,000.00	$175,000.00
June 8–11	IVB–Philadelphia Golf Classic	J. C. Snead	282	$30,000.00	$150,000.00
June 15–18	U.S. Open	Jack Nicklaus	290	$30,000.00	$200,000.00
June 22–25	Western Open	Jim Jamieson	271	$30,000.00	$150,000.00
June 29– July 2	Cleveland Open	David Graham	278	$30,000.00	$150,000.00
July 6–9	Canadian Open	Gay Brewer	275	$30,000.00	$150,000.00
July 13–16	Greater Milwaukee Open	Jim Colbert	271	$25,000.00	$125,000.00

Date	Event	Winner	Score	1st Place Money	Total Purse
July 20–23	American Golf Classic	Bert Yancey	276	$30,000.00	$150,000.00
July 27–30	National PGA Team Championship	Babe Hiskey Kermit Zarley	262	$20,000.00 (each)	$200,000.00
Aug. 3–6	PGA Championship	Gary Player	281	$45,000.00	$225,000.00
Aug. 10–13	Westchester Classic	Jack Nicklaus	270	$50,000.00	$250,000.00
Aug. 17–20	USI Classic	Bruce Devlin	275	$40,000.00	$200,000.00
Aug. 24–27	Liggett & Myers Open	Lou Graham	285	$20,000.00	$100,000.00
Aug. 24–27	U.S. Professional Match Play Championship	Jack Nicklaus d. Frank Beard	2 & 1	$40,000.00	$150,000.00
Sept. 1–4	Greater Hartford Open	Lee Trevino	269	$25,000.00	$125,000.00
Sept. 7–10	Southern Open	DeWitt Weaver	276	$20,000.00	$100,000.00
Sept. 14–17	Greater St. Louis Golf Classic	Lee Trevino	269	$30,000.00	$150,000.00
Sept. 21–24	Robinson's Fall Golf Classic	Grier Jones	273	$20,000.00	$100,000.00
Sept. 28– Oct. 1	Quad Cities Open	Deane Beman	279	$20,000.00	$100,000.00
Oct. 19–22	Kaiser International Open	George Knudson	271	$30,000.00	$150,000.00
Oct. 26–29	Sahara Invitational	Lanny Wadkins	273	$27,000.00	$135,000.00
Nov. 2–5	San Antonio Texas Open	Mike Hill	273	$25,000.00	$125,000.00
Nov. 23–26	Heritage Golf Classic	Johnny Miller	281	$25,000.00	$125,000.00
Nov. 30– Dec. 3	Walt Disney World Open	Jack Nicklaus	267	$30,000.00	$150,000.00

1973 Tour

Date	Event	Winner	Score	1st Place Money	Total Purse
Jan. 4–7	Los Angeles Open	Rod Funseth	276	$ 27,000.00	$135,000.00
Jan. 11–14	Phoenix Open	Bruce Crampton	268	$ 30,000.00	$150,000.00
Jan. 18–22	Dean Martin–Tucson Open	Bruce Crampton	277	$ 30,000.00	$150,000.00
Jan. 25–28	Bing Crosby Pro-Am	Jack Nicklaus	282	$ 36,000.00	$180,000.00
Feb. 1–4	Hawaiian Open	John Schlee	273	$ 40,000.00	$200,000.00
Feb. 7–11	Bob Hope Desert Classic	Arnold Palmer	343	$ 32,000.00	$160,000.00
Feb. 13–18	Andy Williams–San Diego Open	Bob Dickson	278	$ 34,000.00	$170,000.00
Feb. 22–25	Jackie Gleason–Inverrary Classic	Lee Trevino	279	$ 52,000.00	$260,000.00
Mar. 1–9	Florida Citrus Open	Brian Allin	265	$ 30,000.00	$150,000.00
Mar. 8–11	Doral–Eastern Open	Lee Trevino	276	$ 30,000.00	$150,000.00
Mar. 15–18	Greater Jacksonville Open	Jim Colbert	279	$ 26,000.00	$130,000.00
Mar. 22–25	Greater New Orleans Open	Jack Nicklaus	280	$ 25,000.00	$125,000.00
Mar. 24– Apr.1	Greater Greensboro Open	Chi Chi Rodriguez	267	$ 42,000.00	$210,000.00
Apr. 5–8	Masters	Tommy Aaron	283	$ 30,000.00	$204,000.00
Apr. 12–15	Monsanto Open	Homero Blancas	277	$ 30,000.00	$150,000.00
Apr. 19–22	Tournament of Champions	Jack Nicklaus	276	$ 40,000.00	$200,000.00
Apr. 19–22	Tallahassee Open	Hubert Green	277	$ 15,000.00	$ 75,000.00
Apr. 26–29	Byron Nelson Classic	Lanny Wadkins	277	$ 30,000.00	$150,000.00
May 3–6	Houston Open	Bruce Crampton	277	$ 41,000.00	$205,000.00
May 10–13	Colonial National Invitational	Tom Weiskopf	276	$ 30,000.00	$150,000.00
May 17–20	Danny Thomas–Memphis Classic	Dave Hill	283	$ 35,000.00	$175,000.00
May 24–27	Atlanta Classic	Jack Nicklaus	272	$ 30,000.00	$150,000.00
May 31– June 3	Kemper Open	Tom Weiskopf	271	$ 40,000.00	$200,000.00
June 7–10	IVB–Philadelphia Golf Classic	Tom Weiskopf	274	$ 30,045.00	$150,000.00
June 14–17	U.S. Open	Johnny Miller	279	$ 35,000.00	$200,000.00
June 21–24	American Golf Classic	Bruce Crampton	273	$ 32,000.00	$160,000.00
June 28– July 1	Western Open	Billy Casper, Jr.	272	$ 35,000.00	$175,000.00
July 5–8	Greater Milwaukee Open	Dave Stockton	276	$ 26,000.00	$130,000.00

Date	Event	Winner	Score	1st Place Money	Total Purse
July 12–15	Shrine Robinson Classic	Deane Beman	271	$ 25,000.00	$125,000.00
July 19–22	St. Louis Classic	Gene Littler	268	$ 42,000.00	$210,000.00
July 26–29	Canadian Open	Tom Weiskopf	278	$ 35,000.00	$175,000.00
Aug. 2–5	Westchester Classic	Bobby Nichols	272	$ 50,000.00	$250,000.00
Aug. 9–12	PGA Championship	Jack Nicklaus	277	$ 45,000.00	$225,000.00
Aug. 16–19	USI Classic	Lanny Wadkins	279	$ 40,000.00	$200,000.00
Aug. 23–26	U.S. Professional Match Play Championships	John Schroeder		$ 40,000.00	$100,000.00
Aug. 25–26	Liggett & Myers Open	Bert Greene	278	$ 20,000.00	$150,000.00
Aug. 31–Sept. 3	Sammy Davis, Jr. Greater Hartford Open	Billy Casper, Jr.	264	$ 40,000.00	$200,000.00
Sept. 6–9	Southern Open	Gary Player	270	$ 20,030.00	$100,000.00
Sept. 13–16	Heritage Classic	Hale Irwin	272	$ 30,000.00	$150,000.00
Sept. 20–23	B.C. Open	Hubert Green	266	$ 20,000.00	$100,000.00
Sept. 27–30	Quad Cities Open	Sam Adams	268	$ 20,000.00	$100,000.00
Oct. 4–7	Ohio Kings Island Open	Jack Nicklaus	271	$ 25,000.00	$125,000.00
Oct. 18–21	Kaiser International Open	Ed Sneed	275	$ 30,091.00	$150,000.00
Oct. 25–28	Sahara Invitational	John Mahaffey	271	$ 27,000.00	$135,000.00
Nov. 1–4	San Antonio–Texas Open	Ben Crenshaw	270	$ 25,000.00	$125,000.00
Nov. 9–12	World Open Golf Championship	Miller Barber	270	$100,000.00	$500,000.00
Nov. 29–Dec. 2	Walt Disney World Open	Jack Nicklaus	275	$ 30,000.00	$150,000.00

1974 Tour

Date	Event	Winner	Score	1st Place Money	Total Purse
Jan. 3–6	Bing Crosby Pro-Am	Johnny Miller	208	$ 27,750.00	$185,000.00
Jan. 10–13	Phoenix Open	Johnny Miller	271	$ 30,000.00	$150,000.00
Jan. 17–20	Dean Martin–Tucson Open	Johnny Miller	272	$ 30,000.00	$150,000.00
Jan. 31–Feb. 3	Andy Williams–San Diego Open	Bobby Nichols	275	$ 34,000.00	$170,000.00
Feb. 6–10	Hawaiian Open	Jack Nicklaus	271	$ 44,000.00	$220,000.00
Feb. 14–17	Bob Hope Desert Classic	Hubert Green	341	$ 32,048.00	$160,000.00
Feb. 21–24	Glen Campbell–Los Angeles Open	Dave Stockton	276	$ 30,000.00	$150,000.00
Feb. 29–Mar. 3	Jackie Gleason–Inverrary Classic	Leonard Thompson	278	$ 52,000.00	$260,000.00
Mar. 7–10	Florida Citrus Open	Jerry Heard	273	$ 30,000.00	$150,000.00
Mar. 14–17	Doral–Eastern Open	Brian Allin	272	$ 30,000.00	$150,000.00
Mar. 21–24	Greater Jacksonville Open	Hubert Green	276	$ 30,000.00	$150,000.00
Mar. 28–31	Heritage Classic	Johnny Miller	276	$ 40,000.00	$200,000.00
Apr. 4–7	Greater New Orleans Open	Lee Trevino	267	$ 30,000.00	$140,000.00
Apr. 11–14	Greater Greensboro Open	Bob Charles	270	$ 44,066.00	$220,000.00
Apr. 18–21	Masters	Gary Player	278	$ 35,000.00	$229,549.00
Apr. 25–28	Monsanto Open	Lee Elder	274	$ 30,045.00	$150,000.00
Apr. 25–28	Tournament of Champions	Johnny Miller	280	$ 40,000.00	$200,000.00
May 2–5	Tallahassee Open	Allen Miller	274	$ 18,000.00	$ 90,000.00
May 9–12	Byron Nelson Golf Classic	Brian Allin	269	$ 30,045.00	$150,000.00
May 16–19	Houston Open	Dave Hill	276	$ 30,000.00	$150,000.00
May 23–26	Colonial National Invitational	Rod Curl	276	$ 50,000.00	$150,000.00
May 29–June 2	Danny Thomas–Memphis Classic	Gary Player	273	$ 35,000.00	$175,000.00
June 6–9	Kemper Open	Bob Menne	270	$ 50,000.00	$200,000.00
June 13–16	IVB–Philadelphia Golf Classic	Hubert Green	271	$ 30,000.00	$150,000.00
June 20–23	U.S. Open	Hale Irwin	287	$ 35,000.00	$219,900.00
June 27–30	American Golf Classic	Jim Colbert	281	$ 34,000.00	$160,000.00
July 3–6	Western Open	Tom Watson	287	$ 40,000.00	$200,000.00
July 11–14	Greater Milwaukee Open	Ed Sneed	276	$ 26,000.00	$130,000.00
July 25–28	Quad Cities Open	Dave Stockton	271	$ 20,000.00	$100,000.00
July 25–28	B.C. Open	Richie Karl	273	$ 30,000.00	$100,000.00

Date	Event	Winner	Score	1st Place Money	Total Purse
Aug. 1–4	Canadian Open	Bobby Nichols	270	$ 40,000.00	$200,000.00
Aug. 8–11	Pleasant Valley Classic	Victor Regalado	278	$ 40,000.00	$200,000.00
Aug. 15–18	PGA Championship	Lee Trevino	276	$ 45,000.00	$225,000.00
Aug. 22–25	Sammy Davis, Jr.–Greater Hartford Open	Dave Stockton	268	$ 40,000.00	$200,000.00
Aug. 30– Sept. 2	Westchester Classic	Johnny Miller	269	$ 50,000.00	$250,000.00
Sept. 5–8	Tournament Players Championship	Jack Nicklaus	272	$ 50,000.00	$250,000.00
Sept. 7–8	Southern Open	Forrest Fezler	271	$ 20,000.00	$100,000.00
	World Series of Golf	Lee Trevino	139	$ 50,000.00	$ 77,500.00
Sept. 12–15	World Open	Johnny Miller	281	$ 60,000.00	$325,000.00
Sept. 19–22	Ohio Kings Island Open	Miller Barber	277	$ 30,000.00	$125,000.00
Sept. 26–29	Kaiser International Open	Johnny Miller	271	$ 30,000.00	$150,000.00
Oct. 3–8	Sahara Invitational	Al Geiberger	273	$ 27,000.00	$135,000.00
Oct. 17–20	San Antonio–Texas Open	Terry Diehl	269	$ 25,000.00	$125,000.00
Oct. 31– Nov. 3	Disney World Team Championship	Hubert Green B. R. McLendon	255	$ 25,000.00 each	$250,000.00

1975 Tour

Date	Event	Winner	Score	1st Place Money	Total Purse
Jan. 9–12	Phoenix Open	Johnny Miller	260	$ 30,000.00	$150,000.00
Jan. 16–19	Dean Martin–Tucson Open	Johnny Miller	263	$ 40,000.00	$200,000.00
Jan. 23–28	Bing Crosby Pro-Am	Gene Littler	280	$ 37,000.00	$185,000.00
Jan. 30– Feb. 2	Hawaiian Open	Gary Groh	274	$ 44,000.00	$220,000.00
Feb. 5–9	Bob Hope Desert Classic	Johnny Miller	339	$ 32,000.00	$160,000.00
Feb. 13–16	Andy Williams–San Diego Open	J. C. Snead	279	$ 34,000.00	$170,000.00
Feb. 20–23	Glen Campbell–Los Angeles Open	Pat Fitzsimons	275	$ 30,000.00	$150,000.00
Feb. 27– Mar. 2	Jackie Gleason–Inverrary Classic	Bob Murphy	273	$ 52,000.00	$260,000.00
Mar. 6–9	Florida Citrus Open	Lee Trevino	276	$ 40,000.00	$200,000.00
Mar. 13–16	Doral–Eastern Open	Jack Nicklaus	276	$ 30,000.00	$150,000.00
Mar. 20–23	Greater Jacksonville Open	Larry Ziegler	276	$ 30,000.00	$150,000.00
Mar. 27–30	Heritage Classic	Jack Nicklaus	271	$ 40,000.00	$200,000.00
Apr. 3–6	Greater Greensboro Open	Tom Weiskopf	275	$ 45,000.00	$225,000.00
Apr. 10–13	Masters	Jack Nicklaus	276	$ 40,000.00	$242,750.00
Apr. 17–20	Pensacola Open	Jerry McGee	271	$ 25,000.00	$125,000.00
Apr. 24–27	Mony Tournament of Champions	Al Geiberger	277	$ 40,000.00	$200,000.00
Apr. 24–27	Tallahassee Open	Rik Massengale	274	$ 12,000.00	$ 60,000.00
May 1–4	Houston Open	Bruce Crampton	273	$ 30,000.00	$150,000.00
May 8–11	Byron Nelson Golf Classic	Tom Watson	269	$ 35,000.00	$175,000.00
May 15–18	Greater New Orleans Open	Billy Casper, Jr.	271	$ 30,000.00	$150,000.00
May 22–25	Danny Thomas–Memphis Classic	Gene Littler	270	$ 35,000.00	$175,000.00
May 29– June 1	Atlanta Classic	Hale Irwin	271	$ 45,000.00	$225,000.00
June 5–8	Kemper Open	Ray Floyd	278	$ 50,000.00	$250,000.00
June 12–15	IVB–Philadelphia Golf Classic	Tom Jenkins	275	$ 30,000.00	$150,000.00
June 19–22	U.S. Open	Lou Graham	287	$ 40,000.00	$236,200.00
June 26–29	Western Open	Hale Irwin	283	$ 40,000.00	$200,000.00
July 2–5	Greater Milwaukee Open	Art Wall	271	$ 26,000.00	$130,000.00
July 10–13	Quad Cities Open	Roger Maltbie	275	$ 15,000.00	$125,000.00
July 17–20	Pleasant Valley Classic	Roger Maltbie	276	$ 40,000.00	$200,000.00
July 24–27	Canadian Open	Tom Weiskopf	274	$ 40,000.00	$200,000.00
July 31– Aug. 3	Westchester Classic	Gene Littler	271	$ 50,000.00	$250,000.00

Date	Event	Winner	Score	1st Place Money	Total Purse
Aug. 7–10	PGA Championship	Jack Nicklaus	276	$ 45,000.00	$225,000.00
Aug. 14–17	Sammy Davis, Jr.–Greater Hartford Open	Don Bies	267	$ 40,000.00	$200,000.00
Aug. 21–24	Tournament Players Championship	Al Geiberger	270	$ 50,000.00	$250,000.00
Aug. 29– Sept. 1	B.C. Open	Don Iverson	274	$ 35,000.00	$175,000.00
Sept. 4–7	Southern Open	Hubert Green	264	$ 20,000.00	$100,000.00
Sept. 6–7	World Series of Golf	Tom Watson	140	$ 50,000.00	$ 77,500.00
Sept. 11–14	World Open	Jack Nicklaus	280	$ 40,000.00	$200,000.00
Sept. 25–28	Sahara Invitational	Dave Hill	270	$ 27,000.00	$135,000.00
Oct. 2–5	Kaiser International Open	Johnny Miller	272	$ 35,000.00	$175,000.00
Oct. 16–19	San Antonio–Texas Open	Don January	275	$ 25,000.00	$125,000.00
Oct. 23–26	Disney World Team Championship	Jim Colbert Dean Refram	252	$ 20,000.00 each	$200,000.00

1976 Tour

Date	Event	Winner	Score	1st Place Money	Total Purse
Jan. 8–11	NBC–Tucson Open	Johnny Miller	274	$ 40,000.00	$200,000.00
Jan. 15–18	Phoenix Open	Bob Gilder	268	$ 40,000.00	$200,000.00
Jan. 22–25	Bing Crosby Pro-Am	Ben Crenshaw	281	$ 37,000.00	$185,000.00
Jan. 29– Feb. 1	Hawaiian Open	Ben Crenshaw	270	$ 46,000.00	$230,000.00
Feb. 4–8	Bob Hope Desert Classic	Johnny Miller	344	$ 36,000.00	$180,000.00
Feb. 12–15	Andy Williams–San Diego Open	J. C. Snead	272	$ 36,000.00	$180,000.00
Feb. 19–22	Glen Campbell–Los Angeles Open	Hale Irwin	272	$ 37,000.00	$185,000.00
Feb. 26– Mar. 1	Tournament Players Championship	Jack Nicklaus	269	$ 60,000.00	$300,000.00
Mar. 4–7	Florida Citrus Open	Hale Irwin	270	$ 40,000.00	$200,000.00
Mar. 11–14	Doral–Eastern Open	Hubert Green	270	$ 40,000.00	$200,000.00
Mar. 18–21	Greater Jacksonville Open	Hubert Green	276	$ 35,000.00	$175,000.00
Mar. 25–28	Sea Pines Heritage Classic	Hubert Green	274	$ 43,000.00	$215,000.00
Apr. 1–4	Greater Greensboro Open	Al Geiberger	268	$ 46,000.00	$230,000.00
Apr. 8–11	Masters	Raymond Floyd	271	$ 40,000.00	$254,852.00
Apr. 15–18	Mony Tournament of Champions	Don January	277	$ 45,000.00	$225,000.00
Apr. 15–18	Tallahassee Open	Gary Koch	277	$ 16,000.00	$ 80,000.00
Apr. 22–25	NBC–New Orleans Open	Larry Ziegler	274	$ 35,000.00	$175,000.00
Apr. 29– May 2	Houston Open	Lee Elder	278	$ 40,000.00	$200,000.00
May 6–9	Byron Nelson Golf Classic	Mark Hayes	273	$ 40,000.00	$200,000.00
May 13–16	Colonial National Invitational	Lee Trevino	273	$ 40,000.00	$200,000.00
May 20–23	Danny Thomas–Memphis Classic	Gibby Gilbert	273	$ 40,000.00	$200,000.00
May 27–30	Memorial Tournament	Roger Maltbie	288	$ 40,000.00	$200,000.00
June 3–6	IVB–Bicentennial Classic	Tom Kite	277	$ 40,000.00	$200,000.00
June 10–13	Kemper Open	Joe Inman	277	$ 50,000.00	$250,000.00
June 14–20	U.S. Open	Jerry Pate	277	$ 42,000.00	$268,000.00
June 24–27	Western Open	Al Geiberger	288	$ 40,000.00	$200,000.00
July 1–4	Greater Milwaukee Open	Dave Hill	270	$ 26,000.00	$130,000.00
July 8–11	Ed McMahon–Quad Cities Open	John Lister	268	$ 20,000.00	$100,000.00
July 15–18	American Express Westchester Classic	David Graham	272	$ 60,000.00	$300,000.00
July 22–25	Canadian Open	Jerry Pate	267	$ 40,000.00	$200,000.00
July 29– Aug. 1	Pleasant Valley Classic	Bud Allin	277	$ 40,000.00	$200,000.00

Date	Event	Winner	Score	1st Place Money	Total Purse
Aug. 5–8	B.C. Open	Bob Wynn	271	$ 40,000.00	$200,000.00
Aug. 12–15	PGA Championship	Dave Stockton	281	$ 45,000.00	$250,000.00
Aug. 19–22	Sammy Davis, Jr.–Greater Hartford Open	Rik Massengale	266	$ 42,000.00	$210,000.00
Aug. 26–29	American Golf Classic	David Graham	274	$ 40,000.00	$200,000.00
Sept. 2–5	World Series of Golf	Jack Nicklaus	275	$100,000.00	$300,000.00
Sept. 9–12	World Open	Ray Floyd	274	$ 40,000.00	$200,000.00
Sept. 16–19	Ohio Kings Island Open	Ben Crenshaw	271	$ 30,000.00	$150,000.00
Sept. 23–26	Kaiser International Open	J. C. Snead	274	$ 35,000.00	$175,000.00
Sept. 20–Oct. 3	Sahara Invitational	George Archer	271	$ 27,000.00	$135,000.00
Oct. 14–17	San Antonio–Texas Open	Butch Baird	273	$ 25,000.00	$125,000.00
Oct. 21–24	Southern Open	B. R. McLendon	274	$ 25,000.00	$125,000.00
Oct. 28–Nov. 1	Pensacola Open	Mark Hayes	275	$ 25,000.00	$125,000.00
Nov. 4–7	Disney World Team Championship	Woody Blackburn Bill Kratzert	260	$ 20,000.00 each	$200,000.00

1977 Tour

Date	Event	Winner	Score	1st Place Money	Total Purse
Jan. 6–9	Phoenix Open	Jerry Pate	277	$ 40,000.00	$200,000.00
Jan. 13–16	Joe Garagiola–Tucson Open	Bruce Lietzke	275	$ 40,000.00	$200,000.00
Jan. 20–23	Bing Crosby Pro-Am	Tom Watson	273	$ 40,000.00	$200,000.00
Jan. 27–30	Andy Williams–San Diego Open	Tom Watson	269	$ 36,000.00	$180,000.00
Feb. 3–6	Hawaiian Open	Bruce Lietzke	273	$ 48,000.00	$240,000.00
Feb. 9–13	Bob Hope Desert Classic	Rik Massengale	337	$ 40,000.00	$200,000.00
Feb. 17–20	Glen Campbell–Los Angeles Open	Tom Purtzer	273	$ 40,000.00	$200,000.00
Feb. 24–27	Jackie Gleason–Inverrary Classic	Jack Nicklaus	275	$ 50,000.00	$250,000.00
Mar. 3–6	Florida Citrus Open	Gary Koch	274	$ 40,000.00	$200,000.00
Mar. 10–13	Doral–Eastern	Andy Bean	277	$ 40,000.00	$200,000.00
Mar. 17–20	Tournament Players Championship	Mark Hayes	289	$ 60,000.00	$300,000.00
Mar. 24–27	Heritage Classic	Graham Marsh	273	$ 45,000.00	$225,000.00
Mar. 31–Apr. 3	Greater Greensboro Open	Danny Edwards	276	$ 47,000.00	$235,000.00
Apr. 7–10	Masters	Tom Watson	276	$ 40,000.00	$254,000.00
Apr. 14–17	Tournament of Champions	Jack Nicklaus	281	$ 45,000.00	$225,000.00
Apr. 14–17	Tallahassee Open	Ed Sneed	276	$ 16,000.00	$ 80,000.00
Apr. 21–24	NBC–New Orleans Open	Jim Simons	273	$ 35,000.00	$175,000.00
Apr. 28–May 1	Houston Open	Gene Littler	276	$ 40,000.00	$200,000.00
May 5–8	Byron Nelson Golf Classic	Raymond Floyd	276	$ 40,000.00	$200,000.00
May 12–15	Colonial National Invitational	Ben Crenshaw	272	$ 40,000.00	$200,000.00
May 19–22	Memorial Tournament	Jack Nicklaus	281	$ 45,000.00	$225,000.00
May 26–29	Atlanta Classic	Hale Irwin	273	$ 40,000.00	$200,000.00
June 2–5	Kemper Open	Tom Weiskopf	277	$ 50,000.00	$250,000.00
June 9–12	Memphis Classic	Al Geiberger	273	$ 40,000.00	$200,000.00
June 16–19	U.S. Open	Hubert Green	278	$ 45,000.00	$250,000.00
June 23–26	Western Open	Tom Watson	283	$ 40,000.00	$200,000.00
June 30–July 3	Greater Milwaukee Open	Dave Eichelberger	278	$ 26,000.00	$130,000.00
July 7–10	Quad Cities Open	Mike Morley	267	$ 25,000.00	$125,000.00
July 14–17	Pleasant Valley Classic	Raymond Floyd	271	$ 50,000.00	$250,000.00
July 21–24	Canadian Open	Lee Trevino	280	$ 45,000.00	$225,000.00
July 28–31	IVB–Philadelphia Golf Classic	Jerry McGee	272	$ 40,000.00	$200,000.00

Date	Event	Winner	Score	1st Place Money	Total Purse
Aug. 4–7	Greater Hartford Open	Bill Kratzert	265	$ 42,000.00	$210,000.00
Aug. 11–14	PGA Championship	Lanny Wadkins	282	$ 45,000.00	$250,000.00
Aug. 18–21	Westchester Classic	Andy North	272	$ 60,000.00	$300,000.00
Aug. 25–28	Colgate–Hall of Fame	Hale Irwin	264	$ 50,000.00	$250,000.00
Sept. 2–5	World Series of Golf	Lanny Wadkins	267	$100,000.00	$300,000.00
Sept. 1–4	Buick Open	Bobby Cole	271	$ 20,000.00	$100,000.00
Sept. 8–11	B.C. Open	Gil Morgan	270	$ 40,000.00	$200,000.00
Sept. 22–25	Kings Island Open	Mike Hill	269	$ 30,000.00	$150,000.00
Sept. 29–Oct. 2	Anheuser-Busch	Miller Barber	272	$ 40,000.00	$200,000.00
Oct. 13–16	San Antonio–Texas Open	Hale Irwin	266	$ 30,000.00	$150,000.00
Oct. 20–23	Southern Open	Jerry Pate	266	$ 25,000.00	$125,000.00
Oct. 27–30	Pensacola Open	Leonard Thompson	268	$ 25,000.00	$125,000.00
Nov. 3–6	Disney World Team Championship	Gibby Gilbert Grier Jones	253	$ 20,000.00 each	$200,000.00

* Event reduced to two rounds because of weather and under PGA regulations purse was cut in half.

Masters Tournament

The Masters, held annually at the Augusta National Golf Club, is strictly an invitation golf tournament based on past achievement. The field of players presently eligible to play include the following: all previous winners of the Masters; the past five years' winners of the United States and British Opens and the PGA Championship; the past two years' winners of the United States and British Amateur Championships; the United States Ryder Cup team of the last holding of this international event; the United States Walker Cup (even years) or the United States World Amateur (odd years) team; the first twenty-four, including ties, of the previous Masters Tournament; the first sixteen, including ties, of the previous United States National Open; the first eight, including ties, of the previous PGA Championship; the semi-finalists of the previous United States Amateur Championship; winners of co-sponsored PGA Tour events from the finish of the last Masters to the tournament preceding the current Masters. In addition, several foreign players receive special invitations based on their play in international events.

The field, which at the start usually numbers about ninety, is cut down to forty-four for the last two rounds. Previous winners of the Masters Tournament are as follows:

Betty Jameson (right) won the 1940 Trans-Mississippi Women's Championship by defeating Patty Berg 2 up. Miss Berg was the defending champion.

Year	Winner	Score	Runner-Up	Score
1934	Horton Smith	284	Craig Wood	285
1935	Gene Sarazen (144)[a]	282	Craig Wood (149)	282
1936	Horton Smith	285	Harry Cooper	286
1937	Byron Nelson	283	Ralph Guldahl	285

Year	Winner	Score	Runner-Up	Score
1938	Henry Picard	285	Ralph Guldahl	287
1939	Ralph Guldahl	279	Sam Snead	280
1940	Jimmy Demaret	280	Lloyd Mangrum	284
1941	Craig Wood	280	Byron Nelson	283
1942	Byron Nelson (69)[a]	280	Ben Hogan (70)	280
1943–1945	Not played			
1946	Herman Keiser	282	Ben Hogan	283
1947	Jimmy Demaret	281	Byron Nelson	283
1948	Claude Harmon	279	Cary Middlecoff	284
1949	Sam Snead	282	Lloyd Mangrum	285
			Johnny Bulla	285
1950	Jimmy Demaret	283	Jim Ferrier	285
1951	Ben Hogan	280	Robert Riegel[b]	282
1952	Sam Snead	286	Jack Burke, Jr.	290
1953	Ben Hogan	274	Ed Oliver	279
1954	Sam Snead (70)[a]	289	Ben Hogan (71)	289
1955	Cary Middlecoff	279	Ben Hogan	286
1956	Jack Burke, Jr.	289	Ken Venturi[b]	290
1957	Doug Ford	283	Sam Snead	286
1958	Arnold Palmer	284	Doug Ford	285
1959	Art Wall, Jr.	284	Fred Hawkins	285
1960	Arnold Palmer	282	Ken Venturi	283
1961	Gary Player	280	Arnold Palmer	281
			Charles Coe[b]	281
1962	Arnold Palmer (68)[a]	280	Gary Player (71)	280
			Dow Finsterwald (77)	280
1963	Jack Nicklaus	286	Tony Lema	287
1964	Arnold Palmer	276	Dave Marr	282
			Jack Nicklaus	282
1965	Jack Nicklaus	271	Arnold Palmer	280
			Gary Player	280
1966	Jack Nicklaus (70)[a]	288	Tommy Jacobs (72)	288
			Gay Brewer, Jr. (78)	288
1967	Gay Brewer, Jr.	280	Bob Nichols	281
1968	Bob Goalby	277	Roberto DeVicenzo	278
1969	George Archer	281	Billy Casper, Jr.	282
			George Knudson	282
			Tom Weiskopf	282
1970	Billy Casper, Jr. (69)[a]	279	Gene Littler (74)	279
1971	Charles Coody	279	Johnny Miller	281
			Jack Nicklaus	281
1972	Jack Nicklaus	286	Bruce Crampton	289
			Tom Weiskopf	289
			Bobby Mitchell	289
1973	Tommy Aaron	283	J. C. Snead	284
1974	Gary Player	278	Tom Weiskopf, Dave Stockton	280
1975	Jack Nicklaus	276	Johnny Miller, Tom Weiskopf	277
1976	Ray Floyd	271	Ben Crenshaw	279
1977	Tom Watson	276	Jack Nicklaus	278

[a] Winner in play-off. Figures in parentheses represent
scores in play-off.
[b] Amateur.

LPGA COMPETITIONS

The Ladies' Professional Golf Association of America is the women's equivalent to the men's PGA. It conducts its own LPGA championship, plus a full tour program.

LPGA Championship

Year	Winner	Runner-Up	Site
1955	Beverly Hanson (220—4 & 3)[a]	Louise Suggs (223)	Orchard Ridge CC Fort Wayne, Ind.
1956	Marlene Hagge[b] (291)	Patty Berg (291)	Forest Lake CC Detroit, Mich.
1957	Louise Suggs (285)	Wiffi Smith (288)	Churchill Valley CC Pittsburgh, Pa.
1958	Mickey Wright (288)	Fay Crocker (294)	Churchill Valley CC Pittsburgh, Pa.
1959	Betsy Rawls (288)	Patty Berg (289)	Sheraton Hotel CC French Lick, Ind.
1960	Mickey Wright (292)	Louise Suggs (295)	Sheraton Hotel CC French Lick, Ind.
1961	Mickey Wright (287)	Louise Suggs (296)	Stardust CC Las Vegas, Nev.
1962	Judy Kimball (282)	Shirley Spork (286)	Stardust CC Las Vegas, Nev.
1963	Mickey Wright (294)	Mary Lena Faulk Mary Mills Louise Suggs (296)	Stardust CC Las Vegas, Nev.
1964	Mary Mills (278)[c]	Mickey Wright (280)	Stardust CC Las Vegas, Nev.
1965	Sandra Haynie (279)	Clifford Ann Creed (280)	Stardust CC Las Vegas, Nev.
1966	Gloria Ehret (282)	Mickey Wright (285)	Stardust CC Las Vegas, Nev.
1967	Kathy Whitworth (284)	Shirley Englehorn (285)	Pleasant Valley CC Sutton, Mass.
1968	Sandra Post[d] (294)	Kathy Whitworth (294)	Pleasant Valley CC Sutton, Mass.
1969	Betsy Rawls (293)	Susie Berning Carol Mann (297)	Concord GC Kiamesha Lake, N.Y.
1970	Shirley Englehorn[e] (285)	Kathy Whitworth (285)	Pleasant Valley CC Sutton, Mass.

Frank Strafaci (left) congratulates Frank Stranahan (right) on winning the 1952 North and South Amateur title. Stranahan scored a smashing 8 and 7 victory over Strafaci to take the title for a third time. Strafaci was a two-time former winner of the title.

Gary Player eyes the PGA Championship Trophy which he won in 1972. Only Jack Nicklaus, Gene Sarazen and Player have won all the titles—U.S. Open, British Open, PGA Championship, and Masters—of the Professional Golf Grand Slam. None however, has won them all in the same year.

Year	Winner	Runner-Up	Site
1971	Kathy Whitworth (288)	Kathy Ahern (292)	Pleasant Valley CC Sutton, Mass.
1972	Kathy Ahern (293)	Jane Blalock (299)	Pleasant Valley CC Sutton, Mass.
1973	Mary Mills (288)	Betty Burfeindt (289)	Pleasant Valley CC Sutton, Mass.
1974	Sandra Haynie (288)	JoAnne Carner (290)	Pleasant Valley CC Sutton, Mass.
1975	Kathy Whitworth (288)	Sandra Haynie (289)	Pine Ridge CC Baltimore, Md.
1976	Betty Burfeindt (287)	Judy Rankin (288)	Pine Ridge CC Baltimore, Md.
1977	Chako Higuchi (279)	Pat Bradley, Judy Rankin, Sandra Post (282)	Bay Tree CC North Myrtle Beach, S.C.

a At the end of 54 holes, the two low scorers played a 36-hole match to determine winner.
b Won in Sudden Death play-off.
c Tournament record.
d Won play-off—68–75.
e Won play-off—74–78.

LPGA Tour

The play of LPGA tour is similar to that of the men's. Most events, however, are limited to 54 holes, although the number of 72-hole events is growing. Unfortunately, the women's prize money has not kept pace with the men's; but with women's golf on the increase, the women's purses, too, should continue to increase. Here are the recent official LPGA tour winners:

Date	Event	Winner	Score	1st Place Money	Total Purse
	1970 Tour				
Feb. 17–19	Burdine's Invitational	Carol Mann	216	$6,000.00	$40,000.00
Mar. 20–22	Orange Blossom Classic	Kathy Whitworth	216	$2,775.00	$18,000.00
Mar. 17–19	Raleigh Ladies Invitational	Sandra Haynie	212	$2,475.00	$15,000.00
May 1–3	Shreveport Kiwanis Invitational	Sandra Haynie	214	$2,250.00	$15,000.00
May 8–10	Dallas Civitan Open	Betsy Rawls	214	$3,750.00	$25,000.00
May 14–17	Londoff Chevrolet Invitational	Shirley Englehorn	216	$3,000.00	$20,000.00
May 22–24	Bluegrass Invitational	Donna Caponi	214	$3,000.00	$20,000.00
May 29–31	O'Sullivan Open	Shirley Englehorn	210	$2,250.00	$15,000.00
June 5–7	Lady Carling Open	Shirley Englehorn	210	$3,375.00	$22,000.00
June 11–14	LPGA Championship	Shirley Englehorn	285	$4,500.00	$30,000.00
June 19–21	George Washington Classic	Judy Rankin	212	$3,750.00	$25,000.00
June 26–28	Len Immke Buick Open	Mary Mills	216	$3,000.00	$30,000.00
July 2–5	USGA Women's Open	Donna Caponi	287	$5,000.00	$31,000.00
July 16–19	Springfield Jaycee Open	Judy Rankin	209	$3,000.00	$20,000.00
Aug. 6–9	Lady Carling Open	Jane Blalock	221	$3,000.00	$20,000.00
Aug. 13–16	Cincinnati Open	Betsy Rawls	210	$3,000.00	$20,000.00
Aug. 20–23	Southgate Ladies Open	Kathy Ahern	211	$3,000.00	$20,000.00
Sept. 10–13	Wendell West Open	JoAnne Carner	214	$6,000.00	$40,000.00
Sept. 24–27	Lincoln-Mercury Open	Judy Rankin	217	$3,450.00	$23,000.00
Oct. 15–18	Quality Chekd Classic	Kathy Whitworth	205	$2,250.00	$15,000.00
Oct. 22–25	Women's Charity Open	Marilynn Smith	214	$2,625.00	$17,500.00
	1971 Tour				
Feb. 18–21	Sears Women's World Classic of St. Lucie	Ruth Jessen	220	$10,000.00	$60,000.00
Mar. 18–21	Orange Blossom Classic	Jan Ferraris	218	$3,000.00	$20,000.00

Date	Event	Winner	Score	1st Place Money	Total Purse
Apr. 15–18	Raleigh Ladies Golf Classic	Kathy Whitworth	212	$3,000.00	$20,000.00
Apr. 22–25	Burdine's Invitational	Sandra Haynie	219	$4,500.00	$30,000.00
Apr. 29– May 2	Dallas Civitan Open	Sandra Haynie	201	$4,725.00	$31,500.00
May 6–9	San Antonio Open	Sandra Haynie	206	$3,000.00	$20,000.00
May 13–16	Sealy LPGA Classic	Sandra Palmer	289	$10,000.00	$50,000.00
May 20–23	Suzuki Golf International	Kathy Whitworth	217	$5,700.00	$38,000.00
June 4–6	Lady Carling Open	Kathy Whitworth	210	$3,750.00	$25,000.00
June 10–13	Eve–LPGA Championship	Kathy Whitworth	288	$7,950.00	$53,000.00
June 18–20	Heritage Open	Sandra Palmer	211	$3,750.00	$25,000.00
June 24–27	U.S. Women's Open	JoAnne Carner	288	$5,000.00	$31,000.00
July 9–11	George Washington Classic	Jane Blalock	208	$3,750.00	$25,000.00
July 15–17	LPGA Four-Ball Championship	Kathy Whitworth	206	$1,600.00	$20,000.00
July 23–25	O'Sullivan Ladies Open	Judy Kimball	211	$3,000.00	$20,000.00
July 30– Aug. 1	Bluegrass Invitational	JoAnne Carner	210	$3,750.00	$25,000.00
Aug. 5–8	Lady Pepsi Open	Jane Blalock	214	$3,000.00	$20,000.00
Aug. 13–15	Len Immke Buick Open	Sandra Haynie	206	$3,750.00	$25,000.00
Aug. 20–22	Southgate Open	Pam Barnett	210	$3,000.00	$20,000.00
Sept. 24–26	Lincoln-Mercury Open	Pam Higgins	215	$3,750.00	$25,000.00
Oct. 15–17	Quality-First Classic	Judy Rankin	214	$3,000.00	$20,000.00

1972 Tour

Date	Event	Winner	Score	1st Place Money	Total Purse
Jan. 7–9	Burdine's Invitational	Marlene Hagge	211	$4,500.00	$30,000.00
Mar. 10–12	Lady Eve Open	Judy Rankin	210	$3,750.00	$25,000.00
Mar. 17–19	Orange Blossom Classic	Carol Mann	213	$3,000.00	$20,000.00
Mar. 24–26	Sears Women's World Classic	Betsy Cullen	72	$12,000.00	$85,000.00
Apr. 14–16	Colgate–Dinah Shore Winners' Circle	Jane Blalock	213	$20,000.00	$110,000.00
Apr. 21–23	Birmingham Centennial Open	Betty Burfeindt	212	$4,500.00	$30,000.00
Apr. 28–30	Alamo Ladies Open	Kathy Whitworth	209	$3,750.00	$25,000.00
May 4–7	Sealy-LPGA Classic	Betty Burfeindt	282	$10,000.00	$50,000.00
May 12–14	Suzuki Golf International	Jane Blalock	208	$5,700.00	$38,000.00
May 19–21	Bluegrass Invitational	Kathy Cornelius	211	$3,750.00	$25,000.00
May 26–29	Titleholders Championship	Sandra Palmer	283	$3,000.00	$20,000.00
June 2–4	Lady Carling Open	Carol Mann	210	$4,500.00	$30,000.00
June 8–11	LPGA Championship	Kathy Ahern	293	$7,500.00	$50,000.00
June 29– July 2	USGA Women's Open	Susie Berning	299	$6,000.00	$38,350.00
July 7–9	George Washington Classic	Kathy Ahern	213	$4,500.00	$30,000.00
July 13–15	Angelo's LPGA Four-Ball Championship	Jane Blalock Sandra Palmer	130	$1,600.00 (each)	$20,000.00
July 21–23	Raleigh Golf Classic	Kathy Whitworth	212	$3,000.00	$20,000.00
July 28–30	Lady Pepsi Open	Jan Ferraris	221	$3,750.00	$25,000.00
Aug. 4–6	Knoxville Ladies Open	Kathy Whitworth	210	$3,750.00	$25,000.00
Aug. 11–13	Columbus Ladies Open	Marilynn Smith	210	$4,500.00	$30,000.00
Aug. 18–20	Southgate Ladies Open	Kathy Whitworth	216	$3,000.00	$20,000.00
Aug. 25–27	National Jewish Hospital Open	Sandra Haynie	207	$3,750.00	$25,000.00
Sept. 8–10	Dallas Civitan Open	Jane Blalock	211	$4,950.00	$33,000.00
Sept. 15–17	Waco Quality-First Classic	Sandra Haynie	206	$3,000.00	$20,000.00
Sept. 22–24	Lincoln-Mercury Open	Sandra Haynie	215	$4,200.00	$30,000.00
Sept. 29– Oct. 1	Portland Classic	Kathy Whitworth	212	$3,750.00	$25,000.00
Oct. 5–9	Heritage Village Open	Judy Rankin	212	$3,750.00	$25,000.00
Oct. 20–22	GAC Classic	Betsy Rawls	141	$4,500.00	$30,000.00
Oct. 27–29	Corpus Christi Civitan	JoAnn Prentice	210	$3,000.00	$20,000.00
Nov. 3–5	Lady Errol Open	Jane Blalock	214	$4,500.00	$30,000.00

Date	Event	Winner	Score	1st Place Money	Total Purse
		1973 Tour			
Jan. 5–7	Burdine's Invitational	JoAnn Prentice	212	$ 4,500.00	$ 30,000.00
Feb. 9–11	Naples-Lely Classic	Kathy Whitworth	219	$ 3,750.00	$ 25,000.00
Feb. 16–18	Pompano Beach Open	Sandra Palmer	215	$ 5,250.00	$ 35,000.00
Mar. 9–11	S&H Green Stamp Classic	Kathy Whitworth	214	$20,000.00	$100,000.00
Mar. 16–18	Orange Blossom Classic	Sandra Haynie	216	$ 3,750.00	$ 25,000.00
Mar. 23–25	Sears Women's Classic	Carol Mann	68*	$15,000.00	$100,000.00
Mar. 30–Apr. 1	Alamo Ladies Open	Betsy Cullen	218	$ 4,500.00	$ 30,000.00
Apr. 12–15	Colgate–Dinah Shore Winners' Circle	Mickey Wright	284	$25,000.00	$135,000.00
Apr. 27–29	Birmingham Classic	Gloria Ehret	217	$ 4,950.00	$ 33,000.00
May 4–6	America Defender–Raleigh Classic	Judy Rankin	217	$ 4,500.00	$ 30,000.00
May 11–13	Lady Carling Open	Judy Rankin	215	$ 4,500.00	$ 30,000.00
May 24–27	Bluegrass Open	Donna Young	216	$ 4,500.00	$ 30,000.00
May 31–June 3	Sealy-Fabergé	Kathy Cornelius	217	$25,000.00	$100,000.00
June 7–10	LPGA Championship	Mary Mills	288	$ 5,250.00	$ 50,000.00
June 14–17	La Canadienne Championship	Jocelyne Bourassa	214	$10,000.00	$ 50,000.00
June 22–24	Heritage Village Open	Susie Berning	207	$ 4,500.00	$ 50,000.00
June 29–July 1	Lady Tara Classic	Mary Mills	217	$ 4,500.00	$ 50,000.00
July 6–8	Marc Equity Classic	Mary Lou Crocker	210	$ 5,250.00	$ 35,000.00
July 13–15	George Washington Classic	Carole Jo Skala	214	$ 4,500.00	$ 30,000.00
July 19–22	U.S. Women's Open	Susie Berning	290	$ 6,000.00	$ 60,000.00
July 26–28	Angelo's LPGA Four-Ball Championship	Jane Blalock Sandra Palmer	206	$ 2,400.00 $ 2,400.00	$ 30,000.00
Aug. 3–5	Columbus Ladies Open	Judy Rankin	212	$ 5,250.00	$ 30,000.00
Aug. 10–12	Child and Family Service Open	Betty Burfeindt	212	$ 4,500.00	$ 30,000.00
Aug. 17–19	St. Paul Open	Sandra Palmer	209	$ 4,500.00	$ 30,000.00
Aug. 24–26	National Jewish Hospital Open	Sandra Palmer	210	$ 4,500.00	$ 30,000.00
Aug. 31–Sept. 2	Charity Golf Classic	Sandra Haynie	208	$ 4,500.00	$ 30,000.00
Sept. 7–9	Dallas Civitan Open	Kathy Whitworth	213	$ 4,950.00	$ 30,000.00
Sept. 14–16	Southgate Ladies Open	Kathy Whitworth	142	$ 3,750.00	$ 25,000.00

U.S. Women's Amateur Championship winners (left to right): Mrs. C. H. Vanderbeck (1915), Virginia Van Wie (1932, 1933, and 1934), Mrs. D. R. Carner (1957, 1960, 1962, 1966, and 1968), and Barbara McIntire (1959 and 1964).

Date	Event	Winner	Score	1st Place Money	Total Purse
Sept. 21–23	Portland Classic	Kathy Whitworth	144	$ 4,500.00	$ 30,000.00
Sept. 28–30	Cameron Park Open	Sandra Palmer	212	$ 4,500.00	$ 30,000.00
Oct. 5–7	Lincoln-Mercury Open	Sandra Haynie	212	$ 4,500.00	$ 30,000.00
Oct. 12–14	GAC Classic	Judy Rankin	215	$ 5,250.00	$ 30,000.00
Oct. 19–21	Waco Open	Kathy Whitworth	209	$ 3,750.00	$ 25,000.00
Oct. 26–28	Corpus Christi Civitan	Sharon Miller	210	$ 3,750.00	$ 25,000.00
Nov. 2–4	Lady Errol Open	Kathy Whitworth	213	$ 3,750.00	$ 25,000.00
	1974 Tour				
Feb. 1–3	Burdine's Invitational	Sandra Palmer	215	$ 4,950.00	$ 33,000.00
Feb. 8–10	Sears Women's Classic	Gail Denenberg	71*	$15,000.00	$100,000.00
Feb. 15–17	Naples-Lely Classic	Carol Mann	209	$ 5,400.00	$ 35,000.00
Mar. 1–3	Orange Blossom Classic	Kathy Whitworth	209	$ 4,250.00	$ 30,000.00
Mar. 8–10	S&H Green Stamp Classic	Carol Mann	219	$20,000.00	$100,000.00
Mar. 15–17	Bing Crosby International	Jane Blalock	215	$ 4,250.00	$ 30,000.00
Apr. 18–21	Colgate–Dinah Shore Winners' Circle	JoAnn Prentice	289	$32,000.00	$100,000.00
Apr. 26–28	Birmingham Classic	Jane Blalock	211	$ 5,000.00	$ 35,000.00
May 3–5	Lady Tara Classic	Sandra Spuzich	219	$ 5,000.00	$ 35,000.00
May 10–12	American Defender–Raleigh Classic	JoAnn Prentice	137	$ 5,000.00	$ 35,000.00
May 17–19	Bluegrass Invitational	JoAnne Carner	215	$ 5,000.00	$ 35,000.00
May 24–26	Hoosier Classic	JoAnne Carner	213	$ 5,000.00	$ 35,000.00
May 31– June 2	Baltimore Championship	Judy Rankin	144	$ 5,700.00	$ 40,000.00
June 6–9	Desert Inn Classic	JoAnne Carner	284	$20,000.00	$100,000.00
June 14–16	Medina Open	Sandra Haynie	215	$ 5,700.00	$ 40,000.00
June 20–23	LPGA Championship	Sandra Haynie	288	$ 7,000.00	$ 50,000.00
June 28–30	Peter Jackson Classic	Carole Jo Skala	208	$12,000.00	$ 60,000.00
July 5–7	Niagara Frontier Classic	Sue Roberts	213	$ 5,000.00	$ 35,000.00
July 12–13	Borden Classic	Sharon Miller	211	$ 5,700.00	$ 40,000.00
July 18–21	U.S. Women's Open	Sandra Haynie	295	$ 6,073.00	$ 40,000.00
July 26–28	Wheeling Classic	Carole Jo Skala	212	$ 5,000.00	$ 35,000.00
Aug. 2–4	George Washington Classic	Sandra Haynie	213	$ 5,700.00	$ 40,000.00
Aug. 8–10	Colgate-European Open	Judy Rankin	218	$10,000.00	$ 50,000.00
Aug. 16–18	St. Paul Open	JoAnne Carner	212	$ 5,000.00	$ 35,000.00
Aug. 23–25	National Jewish Hospital Open	Sandra Haynie	213	$ 5,000.00	$ 35,000.00
Aug. 30– Sept. 1	Southgate Ladies Open	Jane Blalock	142	$ 4,375.00	$ 35,000.00
Sept. 6–8	Dallas Civitan Open	Sue Roberts	142	$ 4,375.00	$ 40,000.00
Sept. 13–15	Charity Golf Classic	JoAnne Carner	217	$ 5,700.00	$ 40,000.00
Sept. 27–29	Portland Classic	Sandra Haynie	208	$ 5,700.00	$ 40,000.00
Oct. 4–6	Sacramento Union Classic	JoAnne Carner	211	$ 5,000.00	$ 35,000.00
Oct. 18–20	Cubic Classic	Carole Jo Skala	213	$ 5,000.00	$ 35,000.00
Nov. 22–24	Bill Branch Classic	Sandra Palmer	215	$ 5,000.00	$ 35,000.00
Nov. 29– Dec. 1	Lady Errol Open	Bonnie Bryant	209	$ 5,700.00	$ 40,000.00
	Japanese Classic	Jane Blalock	215	$ 5,000.00	$ 35,000.00
Dec. 6–8	Colgate–Far East Championship	Chako Higuchi	218	$15,000.00	$100,000.00
		Sandra Post	218	$13,330.00	$ 72,000.00
	1975 Tour				
Jan. 18–19	Colgate Triple Crown	Kathy Whitworth	144	$15,000.00	$ 50,000.00
Jan. 31– Feb. 2	Burdine's Invitational	Donna Young	208	$ 5,700.00	$ 40,000.00
Feb. 7–9	Naples-Lely Classic	Sandra Haynie	211	$ 5,700.00	$ 40,000.00
Feb. 21–23	Orange Blossom Classic	Amy Alcott	207	$ 5,000.00	$ 35,000.00
Mar. 21–23	Bing Crosby International	Sue Roberts	214	$ 6,400.00	$ 45,000.00

* Preceded by match play.

Date	Event	Winner	Score	1st Place Money	Total Purse
Mar. 27–29	Karsten Ping Classic	Jane Blalock	209	$10,000.00	$ 70,000.00
Apr. 18–21	Colgate–Dinah Shore Winners' Circle	Sandra Palmer	283	$32,000.00	$180,000.00
Apr. 25–27	Charity Golf Classic	Sandra Haynie	212	$ 6,400.00	$ 45,000.00
May 2–4	Birmingham Classic	Maria Astrologies	210	$ 5,700.00	$ 40,000.00
May 9–11	Lady Tara Classic	Donna Young	214	$ 5,700.00	$ 40,000.00
May 23–25	American Defender Classic	JoAnne Carner	206	$ 5,700.00	$ 40,000.00
May 30– June 1	LPGA Championship	Kathy Whitworth	288	$ 8,000.00	$ 55,000.00
June 6–8	Girl Talk Classic	JoAnne Carner	213	$ 7,000.00	$ 50,000.00
June 13–15	Lawson's LPGA Classic	Carol Mann	217	$ 7,000.00	$ 50,000.00
June 20–22	Hoosier Classic	Betsy Cullen	215	$ 5,700.00	$ 40,000.00
June 27–29	Peter Jackson Classic	JoAnne Carner	214	$12,000.00	$ 60,000.00
July 4–6	Wheeling Classic	Sue McAllister	212	$ 5,700.00	$ 40,000.00
July 11–13	Borden Classic	Carol Mann	209	$ 9,200.00	$ 65,000.00
July 17–20	U.S. Women's Open	Sandra Palmer	295	$ 8,044.00	$ 55,000.00
July 25–27	George Washington Classic	Carol Mann	206	$ 5,700.00	$ 40,000.00
Aug. 2–3	Lady Keystone Open	Susie B. Maxwell	142	$ 4,200.00	$ 30,000.00
Aug. 7–9	Colgate–European Open	Donna Young	283	$11,700.00	$ 72,000.00
Aug. 15–17	Patty Berg Classic	JoAnn Washam	206	$ 6,400.00	$ 45,000.00
Aug. 22–24	National Jewish Hospital Open	Judy Rankin	207	$ 5,700.00	$ 40,000.00
Sept. 5–7	Dallas Civitan Open	Carol Mann	208	$ 6,200.00	$ 43,000.00
Sept. 12–14	Southgate Ladies' Open	Kathy Whitworth	213	$ 5,700.00	$ 40,000.00
Sept. 19–21	Portland Classic	JoAnn Washam	215	$ 5,700.00	$ 40,000.00
Oct. 17–19	Japan Classic*	Shelley Hamlin	218	$15,000.00	$100,000.00
Oct. 23–26	Golf Inns of America	Mary Bea Porter	287	$ 5,700.00	$ 40,000.00
Nov. 14–16	Jacksonville Open	Sandra Haynie	223	$ 7,000.00	$ 50,000.00
Nov. 21–23	Greater Fort Myers Classic	Sandra Haynie	210	$ 5,700.00	$ 40,000.00
Dec. 5–7	Colgate Far East Open*	Pat Bradley	216	$12,560.00	$ 75,000.00
Dec. 13–14	Colgate Triple Crown*	Jane Blalock	142	$15,000.00	$ 50,000.00

* Unofficial event.

1976 Tour

Date	Event	Winner	Score	1st Place Money	Total Purse
Jan. 30– Feb. 1	Burdine's Invitational	Judy Rankin	213	$ 5,700.00	$ 40,000.00
Feb. 6–8	Sarah Coventry–Naples Classic	Jan Stephenson	218	$ 8,500.00	$ 60,000.00
Feb. 13–15	Orange Blossom Classic	JoAnne Carner	209	$ 6,400.00	$ 45,000.00
Feb. 20–22	Bent Tree Classic	Kathy Whitworth	209	$ 8,500.00	$ 60,000.00
Apr. 1–4	Colgate–Dinah Shore Winners' Circle	Judy Rankin	285	$32,000.00	$185,000.00
Apr. 15–17	Karsten-Ping Open	Judy Rankin	205	$14,000.00	$ 80,000.00
Apr. 23–25	Birmingham Classic	Jan Stephenson	203	$ 5,700.00	$ 40,000.00
Apr. 30– May 2	Lady Tara Classic	JoAnne Carner	209	$ 7,000.00	$ 50,000.00
May 6–9	Ladies Masters at Moss Creek	Sally Little	281	$10,000.00	$ 70,000.00
May 14–16	American Defender Classic	Sue Roberts	211	$ 6,400.00	$ 45,000.00
May 21–23	'76 LPGA Classic	Amy Alcott	209	$14,000.00	$ 76,000.00
May 27–30	LPGA Championship	Betty Burfeindt	287	$ 8,000.00	$ 55,000.00
June 4–6	Girl Talk Classic	Pat Bradley	217	$14,000.00	$ 76,000.00
June 11–13	Peter Jackson Classic	Donna C. Young	212	$12,000.00	$ 60,000.00
June 18–20	Hoosier Classic	JoAnne Carner	210	$ 7,000.00	$ 50,000.00
June 24–27	Babe Zaharias Invitational	Judy Rankin	287	$15,000.00	$100,000.00
July 2–4	Bloomington Bicentennial Classic	Sandra Palmer	209	$ 7,000.00	$ 50,000.00
July 8–11	U.S. Open	JoAnne Carner	292	$ 9,054.00	$ 60,000.00
July 16–18	Borden Classic	Judy Rankin	205	$10,000.00	$ 70,000.00
July 23–25	Lady Keystone Open	Susie Berning	215	$ 7,000.00	$ 50,000.00

Date	Event	Winner	Score	1st Place Money	Total Purse
Aug. 4–7	Colgate–European Open	Chako Higuchie	284	$15,000.00	$100,000.00
Aug. 13–15	Wheeling Classic	Jane Blalock	217	$ 7,000.00	$ 50,000.00
Aug. 20–22	Patty Berg Classic	Kathy Whitworth	212	$ 8,000.00	$ 55,000.00
Aug. 27–29	National Jewish Hospital Open	Sandra Palmer	206	$ 7,000.00	$ 50,000.00
Sept. 3–5	Jerry Lewis Muscular Dystrophy Classic	Sandra Palmer	213	$15,000.00	$100,000.00
Sept. 10–12	Dallas Civitan Open	Jane Blalock	205	$ 7,000.00	$ 50,000.00
Sept. 17–19	Portland Classic	Donna C. Young	217	$ 6,400.00	$ 45,000.00
Oct. 1–3	Carlton	Donna C. Young	282	$35,000.00	$205,000.00
Nov. 1–3	LPGA/Japan Mizuno	Donna C. Young	217	$15,000.00	$100,000.00
Nov. 18–20	Colgate–Hong Kong Open	Judy Rankin	216	$10,000.00	$ 50,000.00
Nov. 25–27	Colgate–Far East Championship	Amy Alcott	211	$15,000.00	$100,000.00
Dec. 17–19	Pepsi-Cola Mixed Team Championship*	Jo Ann Washam/ Chi Chi Rodriguez	275	$40,000.00	$200,000.00

* Unofficial event.

1977 Tour

Date	Event	Winner	Score	1st Place Money	Total Purse
Feb. 11–13	Cancer Society Classic	Pam Higgins	212	$ 7,500.00	$ 50,000.00
Feb. 18–20	Orange Blossom Classic	Judy Rankin	208	$ 7,500.00	$ 50,000.00
Feb. 25–28	Bent Tree Classic	Judy Rankin	209	$15,000.00	$100,000.00
Mar. 24–27	Honda Civic Classic	Sandra Palmer	281	$22,500.00	$150,000.00
Mar. 31– Apr. 3	Colgate–Dinah Shore Winners' Circle	Kathy Whitworth	289	$36,000.00	$240,000.00
Apr. 14–17	Women's International	Sandra Palmer	281	$12,000.00	$ 80,000.00
Apr. 22–24	American Defender Classic	Kathy Whitworth	206	$ 7,500.00	$ 50,000.00
Apr. 29– May 1	Birmingham Classic	Debbie Austin	207	$ 9,000.00	$ 60,000.00
May 6–8	Lady Tara Classic	Hollis Stacy	209	$ 7,500.00	$ 50,000.00
May 13–15	Baltimore Classic	Jane Blalock	209	$ 8,250.00	$ 55,000.00
May 20–22	Coca-Cola Classic	Kathy Whitworth	202	$11,500.00	$ 77,000.00
May 27–29	Keystone Classic	Sandra Spuzich	201	$ 7,500.00	$ 50,000.00
June 2–5	Talk Tournament	JoAnne Carner	284	$15,000.00	$100,000.00
June 9–12	LPGA Championship	Chako Higuchi	279	$22,500.00	$150,000.00
June 17–19	Mayflower Classic	Judy Rankin	212	$ 7,500.00	$ 50,000.00
June 25–27	Hoosier Classic	Debbie Austin	207	$ 7,500.00	$ 50,000.00
July 1–3	Peter Jackson Classic	Judy Rankin	212	$12,000.00	$ 80,000.00
July 8–10	Bankers Trust Classic	Pat Bradley	213	$11,000.00	$ 75,000.00
July 15–17	Borden Classic	JoAnne Carner	207	$12,000.00	$ 80,000.00
July 21–24	U.S. Women's Open	Hollis Stacy	292	$11,040.00	$ 80,000.00
July 29–31	Pocono Northeast Classic	Debbie Austin	213	$11,000.00	$ 80,000.00
Aug. 3–6	Colgate–European Open	Judy Rankin	281	$15,000.00	$100,000.00
Aug. 11–14	Long Island	Debbie Austin	279	$15,000.00	$100,000.00
Aug. 19–21	Wheeling Classic	Debbie Austin	209	$ 7,500.00	$ 50,000.00
Aug. 26–28	Patty Berg Classic	Bonnie Lauer	212	$ 8,250.00	$ 55,000.00
Sept. 2–4	Springfield Classic	Hollis Stacy	271	$15,000.00	$100,000.00
Sept. 9–11	National Jewish Hospital Open	JoAnne Carner	210	$ 7,500.00	$ 50,000.00
Sept. 16–18	LPGA Team Championship	Judy Rankin JoAnne Carner	202	$12,000.00	$ 60,000.00
Sept. 22–25	Sarah Coventry	Jane Blalock	282	$15,000.00	$100,000.00
Sept. 30– Oct. 2	Dallas Civitan Open	Vivian Brownlee	217	$ 7,500.00	$ 50,000.00
Oct. 7–9	Houston Exchange Clubs Classic	Amy Alcott	208	$ 7,500.00	$ 50,000.00
Nov. 1–3	Mizuno Classic	Debbie Massey	220	$15,000.00	$100,000.00

OTHER MAJOR UNITED STATES CHAMPIONSHIPS

There are many interesting tournaments held each year in the United States. For instance, the states of the Union each hold their own amateur championship, both for men and women, and the various regional golf associations—the Metropolitan, the Pacific Northwest, the Eastern, the Middle Atlantic, and so on—have amateur events of varying interest.

National Collegiate Athletic Association (NCAA) Championship

What United States golf tournament has been played more times than any other? If you said the U.S. Open, you are wrong, because although the Open, U.S. Amateur, and Women's Amateur were all begun in 1895, they were interrupted during both World Wars. The National Collegiate Athletic Association Championship was started in 1897, and except for three years (1900 and 1917–1918) has been held every year since. Many of the illustrious names of golf found their first prominence in this championship.

Year	Individual Champion	Team Champion
1897	Louis P. Bayard, Jr. (Princeton)	Yale
1898	John Reid, Jr. (Yale)—Spring	Harvard
	James F. Curtis (Harvard)—Fall	Yale
1899	Percy Pyne II (Princeton)	Harvard
1900	Not played	
1901	H. Lindsley (Harvard)	Harvard
1902	Charles Hitchcock, Jr. (Yale)—Spring	Yale
	H. Chandler Egan (Harvard)—Fall	Harvard
1903	F. O. Reinhart (Princeton)	Harvard
1904	A. L. White (Harvard)	Harvard
1905	Robert Abbott (Yale)	Yale
1906	W. E. Clow (Yale)	Yale
1907	Ellis Knowles (Yale)	Yale
1908	H. H. Wilder (Harvard)	Yale
1909	Albert Seckel (Princeton)	Yale
1910	Robert E. Hunter (Yale)	Yale
1911	George C. Stanley (Yale)	Yale
1912	F. C. Davidson (Harvard)	Yale
1913	Nathaniel Wheeler (Yale)	Yale
1914	Edward P. Allis III (Harvard)	Princeton
1915	Francis R. Blossom (Yale)	Yale
1916	J. W. Hubbell (Harvard)	Princeton
1917–1918	Not played	
1919	A. L. Walker, Jr. (Columbia)	Princeton
1920	Jess W. Sweetser (Yale)	Princeton
1921	J. Simpson Dean (Princeton)	Dartmouth
1922	Pollock Boyd (Dartmouth)	Princeton
1923	Dexter Cummings (Yale)	Princeton
1924	Dexter Cummings (Yale)	Yale
1925	G. Fred Lamprecht (Tulane)	Yale
1926	G. Fred Lamprecht (Tulane)	Yale
1927	Watts Gunn (Georgia Tech)	Princeton
1928	Maurice J. McCarthy, Jr. (Georgetown)	Princeton
1929	Tom Aycock (Yale)	Princeton
1930	George T. Dunlap, Jr. (Princeton)	Princeton
1931	George T. Dunlap, Jr. (Princeton)	Yale
1932	John W. Fischer, Jr. (Michigan)	Yale
1933	Walter Emery (Oklahoma)	Yale
1934	Charles R. Yates (Georgia Tech)	Michigan
1935	Ed White (Texas)	Michigan
1936	Charles Kocsis (Michigan)	Yale
1937	Fred Haas, Jr. (Louisiana State)	Princeton

Year	Individual Champion	Team Champion
1938	John P. Burke (Georgetown)	Stanford
1939	Vincent D'Antoni (Tulane)	Stanford
1940	F. Dixon Brooke (Virginia)	Princeton & LSU
1941	Earl Stewart (Louisiana State)	Stanford
1942	Frank Tatum, Jr. (Stanford)	Stanford & LSU
1943	Wallace Ulrich (Carleton)	Yale
1944	Louis Lick (Minnesota)	Notre Dame
1945	John Lorms (Ohio State)	Ohio State
1946	George Hamer (Georgia)	Stanford
1947	Dave Barclay (Michigan)	Louisiana State
1948	Bob Harris (San Jose State)	San Jose State
1949	Harvie Ward (North Carolina)	North Texas State
1950	Fred Wampler (Purdue)	North Texas State
1951	Tom Nieporte (Ohio State)	North Texas State
1952	Jim Vickers (Oklahoma)	North Texas State
1953	Earl Moeller (Oklahoma A&M)	Stanford
1954	Hillman Robbins (Memphis State)	Southern Methodist
1955	Joe Campbell (Purdue)	Louisiana State
1956	Rick Jones (Ohio State)	Houston
1957	Rex Baxter, Jr. (Houston)	Houston
1958	Phil Rodgers (Houston)	Houston
1959	Dick Crawford (Houston)	Houston
1960	Dick Crawford (Houston)	Houston
1961	Jack Nicklaus (Ohio State)	Purdue
1962	Kermit Zarley (Houston)	Houston
1963	R. H. Sikes (Arkansas)	Oklahoma State
1964	Terry Small (San Jose State)	Houston
1965	Marty Fleckman (Houston)	Houston
1966	Bob Murphy (Florida)	Houston
1967	Hale Irwin (University of Colorado)	Houston
1968	Grier Jones (Oklahoma State)	University of Florida
1969	Bob Clark (California State at Los Angeles)	Houston
1970	**Jack Mahaffey (Houston)**	**Houston**
1971	**Ben Crenshaw (Texas)**	**Texas**
1972	**Ben Crenshaw (Texas) Tom Kite (Texas)–tie**	**Texas**
1973	Ben Crenshaw (Texas)	Florida
1974	Curtis Strange (Wake Forest)	Wake Forest
1975	Jay Haas (Wake Forest)	Wake Forest
1976	Scott Simpson (Southern California)	Oklahoma State
1977	Scott Simpson (Southern California)	Houston

All-American Collegiate Team. Like other collegiate sports, golf also has its "All-American" team. Started in 1965, here are selections:

1965: Marty Fleckman, Houston; Randy Petri, Houston; Bob Dickson, Oklahoma State; Sherman Finger, University of Southern California; Bob Hammer, Florida; James Wiechers, Santa Clara.

1966: Bob Murphy, Florida; Sherman Finger, University of Southern California; Bob Dickson, Oklahoma State; Vinnie Giles, Georgia; George Boutell, Arizona State; Arne Dokka, California State.

1967: Bunky Henry, Georgia; Hale Irwin, Colorado; John Miller, Brigham Young; B. R. McLendon, Louisiana State; Hal Underwood, Houston; Ross Randall, San Jose State.

1968: Hal Underwood, Houston; Grier Jones, Oklahoma State; Bern Kern, New Mexico; Jack Lewis, Jr., Wake Forest; Steve Melnyk, Florida; Mike Morley, Arizona State; Kemp Richardson, University of Southern California; Bill Brask, Minnesota.

1969: Bob Clark, California State; Joe Inman, Jr., Wake Forest; Drue Johnson, Arizona; Jack Lewis, Jr., Wake Forest; John Mahaffey, Houston; Wayne McDonald, Indiana; Steve Melnyk, Florida; Gary Sanders, University of Southern California.

1970: Bob Clark, California State at Los Angeles; Joe Inman, Jr., Wake Forest; John Mahaffey, Houston; Wayne McDonald, Indiana; Howard Twitty, Arizona State; Tom Valentine, Georgia; Mark Haynes, Oklahoma State; Bruce Ashworth, Houston; Lanny Wadkins, Wake Forest.

1971: Ben Crenshaw, Texas; Jim Simons, Wake

Forest; Lanny Wadkins, Wake Forest; Mark Haynes, Oklahoma State; Bill Hoffer, Purdue; Ray Leach, Brigham Young; John Mills, Houston; Andy North, Florida State; Gary Sanders, University of Southern California.

1972: Ben Crenshaw, Texas; Tom Kite, Texas; Danny Edwards, Oklahoma State; Craig Greswold, Oregon; Steve Groves, Ohio State; Gary Koch, Florida; Howard Twitty, Arizona State; Jim Simons, Wake Forest.

1973: Ben Crenshaw, Texas; Tom Kite, Texas; Jimmy Ellis, Georgia Southern; Steve Groves, Ohio State; Gary Koch, Florida; Craig Stadler, University of Southern California; Lance Suzuki, Brigham Young; Bill Rogers, Houston.

1974: Keith Fergus, Houston; John Harris, Minnesota; Tom Jones, Oklahoma State; Gary Koch, Florida; Bill Kratzert, Georgia; Mike Reid, Brigham Young; Craig Stadler, University of Southern California; Curtis Strange, Wake Forest.

1975: Andy Bean, Florida; Keith Fergus, Houston; Jaime Gonzalez, Oklahoma; Jay Haas, Wake Forest; Mark Lye, San Jose; Mike Reid, Brigham Young; Phil Hancock, Florida; Jerry Pate, Alabama; Kelly Roberts, Indiana; Curtis Strange, Wake Forest.

1976: Michael Brannan, Brigham Young; Keith Fergus, Houston; Ralph Guarasci, Ohio State; Jay Haas, Wake Forest; Phil Hancock, Florida; Lindy Miller, Oklahoma State; Scott Simpson, University of Southern California; Curtis Strange, Wake Forest.

1977: David Edwards, Oklahoma State; Ed Fiori, Houston; Buddy Gardner, Auburn; Gary Hallberg, Wake Forest; Lee Mikles, Arizona State; Lindy Miller, Oklahoma State; Scott Simpson, University of Southern California; Chip Beck, Georgia; John Cook, Ohio State.

Women's National Intercollegiate Championship

Champions since its start in 1941 are as follows:

Year	Winner
1941	Eleanor Dudley (Alabama)
1942–1945	Not played
1946	Phyllis Otto (Northwestern)
1947	Shirley Spork (Michigan State)
1948	Grace Lenczyk (Stetson)
1949	Marilynn Smith (Kansas)
1950	Betty Rowland (Rollins)
1951	Barbara Bruning (Wellesley)
1952	Mary Ann Villegas (Ohio State)
1953	Pat Lesser (Seattle)
1954	Nancy Reed (George Peabody)
1955	Jackie Yates (Redlands)
1956	Marlene Stewart (Rollins)
1957	Meriam Bailey (Northwestern)
1958	Carol Ann Pushing (Carleton)
1959	Judy Eller (Miami)

Year	Winner
1960	JoAnne Gunderson (Arizona State)
1961	Judy Hoetmer (Miami)
1962	Carol Soreson (Washington)
1963	Claudia Lindor (Arizona State)
1964	Patti Shook (Valparaiso)
1965	Roberta Albers (Western Washington State)
1966	Joyce Kazmierski (Michigan State)
1967	Martha Wilkinson (California State)
1968	Gail Sykes (Odessa)
1969	Jane Bastanchury (Arizona State)
1970	Cathy Gaughan (Arizona State)
1971	Shelley Hamlin (Stanford)
1972	Ann Laughlin (Miami)
1973	Bonnie Laver (Michigan State)
1974	Mary Budke (Oregon State)
1975	Barbara Barrow (San Diego State)
1976	Nancy Lopez (Tulsa)
1977	Cathy Morse (Miami)

Porter Cup Tournament

This major prize among amateur men players is held each year at the Niagara Falls Country Club, Lewiston, New York. Since its start in 1959, winners are:

Year	Winner
1959	John Konsek III
1960	Ward Wettlaufer
1961	John Konsek III
1962	Ed Tutwiler
1963	Bill Harvey
1964	Deane Beman
1965	Ward Wettlaufer
1966	Robert Smith
1967	Robert Smith
1968	Randy Wolff
1969	Gary Cowan
1970	Howard Twitty
1971	Ronnie Quinn
1972	Ben Crenshaw
1973	Vinny Giles
1974	George Burns III
1975	Jay Siegal
1976	Scott Simpson
1977	Vance Heafner

Sunnehanna Amateur Championship

Another important trophy in which amateur men players compete is held each year at the Sunnehanna Country Club, Johnstown, Pennsylvania. Winners are as follows:

Year	Winner
1954	Don Cherry
1955	Hillman Robbins, Jr.
1956	Gene Dahlbender
1957	Joe Campbell

Year	Winner
1958	William Hyndman III
1959	Tommy Aaron
1960	Gene Dahlbender
1961	Dick Siderowf
1962	Dr. E. Updegraff
1963	Roger McManus
1964	Gary Cowan
1965	Bobby Greenwood
1966	Jack Lewis, Jr.
1967	William Hyndman III
1968	Bobby Greenwood
1969	Len Thompson
1970	Howard Twitty
1971	Bob Zender
1972	Mark Hayes
1973	Ben Crenshaw
1974	David Strawn
1975	Jaime Gonzalez
1976	Jay Siegel
1977	John Cook

Doherty Tournament

This is a major event for women amateurs. Previous winners are as follows:

Year	Winner
1933	Mrs. O. S. Hill
1934	Maureen Orcutt
1935	Jean Bauer
1936	Patty Berg
1937	Patty Berg
1938	Patty Berg
1939	Patty Berg
1940	Patty Berg
1941	Betty Hicks
1942	Georgia Tainter
1943	Billie Harting
1944	Marjorie Row
1945	Louise Suggs
1946	Louise Suggs
1947	Mrs. G. Zaharias
1948	Louise Suggs
1949	Dorothy Kirby
1950	Polly Riley
1951	Claire Doran
1952	Mary Lena Faulk
1953	Mary Lena Faulk
1954	Grace Smith
1955	Pat Lesser
1956	Joanne Goodwin
1957	Anne Quast
1958	May Ann Downing
1959	Mrs. J. B. Streit
1960	Mrs. J. B. Streit
1961	Mrs. J. B. Streit
1962	Phyllis Preuss
1963	Nancy Roth
1964	Nancy Roth
1965	Mrs. J. B. Streit
1966	Mrs. N. R. Syms[a]
1967	Mrs. P. Dye, Jr.

Year	Winner
1968	Mrs. D. R. Carner
1969	Barbara McIntire
1970	Martha Wilkinson
1971	Phyllis Preuss
1972	Mrs. M. Booth
1973	Jane Booth
1974	Debbie Massey
1975	Cindy Hill
1976	Tish Preuss
1977	Lancy Smith

[a] Mrs. Syms is the former Nancy Roth.

U.S. Seniors' Championship

This championship is the oldest senior (men over fifty-five years of age) event in the United States. The amateur tournament, over 36 holes of stroke play, is held at Apawamis Country Club, Rye, New York.

Year	Winner
1905	J. D. Foot
1906	J. D. Foot
1907	Dr. C. E. Martin
1908	J. D. Foot
1909	J. D. Foot
1910	F. A. Wright
1911	J. D. Foot
1912	J. A. Tyng
1913	W. Fairbanks
1914	F. A. Wright
1915	J. A. Tyng
1916	C. G. Waldo
1917	W. E. Truesdale
1918	W. E. Truesdale
1919	William Clark
1920	Hugh Halsell
1921	M. J. Condon
1922	F. Snare
1923	Hugh Halsell
1924	Claude M. Hart
1925	F. Snare
1926	F. H. Hoyt
1927	Hugh Halsell
1928	Dr. C. H. Walter
1929	Dr. G. T. Gregg
1930	Dr. G. T. Gregg
1931	J. D. Chapman
1932	F. S. Douglas
1933	Raleigh W. Lee
1934	C. H. Jennings
1935	C. W. Deibel
1936	R. H. Doughty
1937	Raleigh W. Lee
1938	Raleigh W. Lee
1939	C. H. Jennings
1940	C. H. Jennings
1941	A. H. Pierce
1942	J. E. Knowles
1943	J. E. Knowles

Year	Winner
1944	J. E. Knowles
1945	J. E. Knowles
1946	J. E. Knowles
1947	Col. M. S. Lindgrove
1948	J. F. Riddel
1949	Joseph M. Wells
1950	Alfred C. Ulmer
1951	T. C. Robbins
1952	T. C. Robbins
1953	Frank D. Ross
1954	J. E. Knowles
1955	John W. Roberts
1956	F. G. Clement
1957	F. G. Clement
1958	J. W. Dawson
1959	J. W. Dawson
1960	J. W. Dawson
1961	John Merrill
1962	George Dawson
1963	Jack Westland
1964	J. W. Brown
1965	Fred Brand
1966	George Haggarty
1967	Robert Kiersky
1968	Curtis Person
1969	William Scott, Jr.
1970	David Goldman
1971	James B. Knowles
1972	David Goldman
1973	Bob Kiersky
1974	James B. Knowles
1975	Dale Morey
1976	Dale Morey
1977	Dale Morey

U.S. National Senior Open

This tournament is a senior men's event which is open to both amateurs and professionals. Here are the winners over the years:

Year	Winner
1957	Fred Wood
1958	Willie Goggin
1959	Willie Goggin
1960	Charles Congdon
1961	Dutch Harrison
1962	Dutch Harrison
1963	Dutch Harrison
1964	Dutch Harrison
1965	Chandler Harper
1966	Dutch Harrison
1967	Pete Fleming
1968	Tommy Bolt
1969	Tommy Bolt
1970	Tommy Bolt
1971	Tommy Bolt
1972	Tommy Bolt
1973	Manuel de la Torre
1974	Willie Barber
1975	Willie Barber
1976	Willie Barber
1977	George Pottle

Western Amateur

The history of the Western Golf Association championships provides one of tournament golf's most colorful chapters. Tournaments were among the initial plans when the Association was founded in 1899. The Western Amateur and Open events quickly grew to top stature among the prestige tournaments of the country and now are traditional on the annual golf calendar for every leading amateur and professional golfer. The only other national events staged by WGA are the Western Junior and Junior Girls'. The Amateur is match play, while the Open is stroke play.

Year	Winner
1899	David R. Forgan
1900	William Waller
1901	P. B. Hoyt
1902	H. C. Egan
1903	Walter E. Egan
1904	H. C. Egan
1905	H. C. Egan
1906	D. E. Sawyer
1907	H. C. Egan
1908	Mason Phelps
1909	Charles Evans, Jr.
1910	Mason Phelps
1911	Albert Seckel
1912	Charles Evans, Jr.
1913	Warren K. Wood
1914	Charles Evans, Jr.
1915	Charles Evans, Jr.
1916	H. Schmidt
1917	Francis Ouimet
1918	Not played
1919	Harry G. Legg
1920	Charles Evans, Jr.
1921	Charles Evans, Jr.
1922	Charles Evans, Jr.
1923	Charles Evans, Jr.
1924	H. R. Johnston
1925	Keefe Carter
1926	Frank Dolp
1927	Bon Stein
1928	Frank Dolp
1929	Don Moe
1930	J. E. Lehman
1931	Don Moe
1932	Gus Moreland
1933	Jack Westland
1934	Zell Eaton
1935	Charles Yates
1936	Paul Leslie
1937	Wilford Wehrle
1938	Robert Babbish
1939	Harry Todd
1940	Marvin Ward
1941	Marvin Ward
1942	Buell Abbott
1943–1945	Not played

Year	Winner
1946	Frank Stranahan
1947	Marvin Ward
1948	Robert Riegel
1949	Frank Stranahan
1950	Charles R. Coe
1951	Frank Stranahan
1952	Frank Stranahan
1953	Dale Morey
1954	Bruce Cudd
1955	Edward Merrins
1956	Mason Rudolph
1957	Dr. E. Updegraff
1958	James Key
1959	Dr. E. Updegraff
1960	Tommy Aaron
1961	Jack Nicklaus
1962	Art Hudnutt
1963	Tom Weiskopf
1964	Steve Oppermann
1965	Bob Smith
1966	Jim Wiechers
1967	Bob Smith
1968	R. G. Massengale
1969	Steve Melnyk
1970	Lanny Wadkins
1971	Andy North
1972	Gary Sanders
1973	Ben Crenshaw
1974	Curtis Strange
1975	Andy Bean
1976	John Stark
1977	Jim Nelford

Western Open

Year	Winner	Score
1899	William Smith (74)[a]	156
	Lawrence Auchterlonie (84)	156
1900	Not played	
1901	Lawrence Auchterlonie	160
1902	Willie Anderson	299
1903	Alex Smith	318
1904	Willie Anderson	304
1905	Arthur Smith	278
1906	Alex Smith	306
1907	Robert Simpson	307
1908	Willie Anderson	299
1909	Willie Anderson	288
1910	Charles Evans, Jr.[b]	6 & 5
1911	Robert Simpson	2 & 1
1912	MacDonald Smith	299
1913	John J. McDermott	295
1914	James M. Barnes	293
1915	Tom McNamara	304
1916	Walter Hagen	286
1917	James M. Barnes	283
1918	Not played	
1919	James M. Barnes	283
1920	Jock Hutchison	296
1921	Walter Hagen	287
1922	Mike J. Brady	291

Year	Winner	Score
1923	Jock Hutchison	281
1924	William Mehlhorn	293
1925	MacDonald Smith	281
1926	Walter Hagen	279
1927	Walter Hagen	281
1928	Al Espinosa	291
1929	Tommy Armour	273
1930	Gene Sarazen	278
1931	Ed Dudley	280
1932	Walter Hagen	287
1933	MacDonald Smith	282
1934	Harry Cooper (67, 67)	274
	Ky Laffoon (67, 69)	274
1935	John Revolta	290
1936	Ralph Guldahl	274
1937	Ralph Guldahl (72)	288
	Horton Smith (76)	288
1938	Ralph Guldahl	279
1939	Byron Nelson	281
1940	Jimmy Demaret (70)	293
	Tony Penna (73)	293
1941	Ed Oliver	275
1942	Herman Barron	276
1943–1945	Not played	
1946	Ben Hogan	271
1947	Johnny Palmer	270
1948	Ben Hogan (64)	281
	Ed Oliver (72)	281
1949	Sam Snead	268
1950	Sam Snead	282
1951	Marty Furgol	270
1952	Lloyd Mangrum	274
1953	E. J. Harrison	278
1954	Lloyd Mangrum[c]	277
	Ted Kroll	277
1955	Cary Middlecoff	272
1956	Mike Fetchick (66)	284
	Jay Hebert (71)	284
	Don January (72)	284
	Doug Ford (75)	284
1957	Doug Ford[d]	279
	George Bayer	279
	Gene Littler	279
	Billy Maxwell	279
1958	Doug Sanders	275
1959	Mike Souchak	272
1960	Stan Leonard[e]	278
	Art Wall, Jr.	278
1961	Arnold Palmer	271
1962	Jacky Cupit	281
1963	Arnold Palmer (70)	280
	Julius Boros (71)	280
	Jack Nicklaus (73)	280
1964	Juan Rodriguez	268
1965	Billy Casper, Jr.	270
1966	Billy Casper, Jr.	283

[a] Numbers in parentheses represent play-off.
[b] Amateur.
[c] Mangrum won 1954 play-off on first Sudden Death hole.
[d] Ford won Sudden Death play-off on third extra hole.
[e] Leonard won Sudden Death play-off on first extra hole.

Year	Winner	Score
1967	Jack Nicklaus	274
1968	Jack Nicklaus	273
1969	Billy Casper, Jr.	276
1970	Hugh Royer	273
1971	Bruce Crampton	279
1972	Jim Jamieson	271
1973	Billy Casper, Jr.	272
1974	Tom Watson	287
1975	Hale Irwin	283
1976	Al Geiberger	288
1977	Tom Watson	283

Western Junior

For boys (amateur) who have not reached their twentieth birthday.

Year	Winner
1914	Charles Grimes
1915	DeWitt Balch
1916	John Simpson
1917	F. Wright
1918	Not played
1919	H. Sassman
1920	Harold Martin
1921	B. Mudge, Jr.
1922	K. Hisert
1923	Ira Couch
1924	E. Robinson
1925	E. Carey, Jr.
1926	Sam Alpert
1927	Albert Hakes
1928	R. Mullin
1929	Fred Lyon
1930	C. K. Collins
1931	Robert Cochran
1932	John Banks
1933	Frank Bredall
1934	Fred Haas, Jr.
1935	Fred Haas, Jr.
1936	S. Richardson
1937	J. Holmstrom
1938	Charles Betcher
1939	Sam Kocsis
1940	Ben Downing
1941	Ben Downing
1942	W. Witzleb
1943–1945	Not played
1946	Mac Hunter
1947	Tom Veech
1948	Gene Coulter
1949	Dean Lind
1950	Dean Lind
1951	Hillman Robbins, Jr.
1952	Don Nichols
1953	Henry Loeb
1954	Hebert Klontz
1955	G. McFerren
1956	Richard Foote
1957	Don Essig, III
1958	Jack Rule

Year	Winner
1959	Steve Spray
1960	Labron Harris, Jr.
1961	Phil Marston
1962	G. Shortridge
1963	George Boutell
1964	Jim Wiechers
1965	John Richart
1966	Ross Edler
1967	Mike Goodart
1968	Don Hawkins
1969	Jim Simons
1970	Jeff Reaume
1971	Richard Brooke
1972	Dennis Sullivan
1973	Tommy Jones
1974	Win Fisher
1975	Britt Harrison
1976	Gary Hallberg
1977	Gary Wilks

Western Women's Amateur

Year	Winner
1901	Bessie Anthony
1902	Bessie Anthony
1903	Bessie Anthony
1904	Frances Everett
1905	Mrs. C. L. Deering
1906	Mrs. C. L. Deering
1907	Lillian French
1908	Mrs. W. F. Anderson
1909	Vida Llewellyn
1910	Mrs. T. Harris
1911	Caroline Painter
1912	Caroline Painter
1913	Myra B. Helmer
1914	Mrs. H. D. Hammond
1915	Elaine V. Rosenthal
1916	Mrs. F. C. Letts, Jr.
1917	Mrs. F. C. Letts, Jr.
1918	Elaine V. Rosenthal
1919	Mrs. P. W. Fiske
1920	Mrs. F. C. Letts, Jr.
1921	Mrs. M. Jones
1922	Mrs. D. C. Gaut
1923	Miriam Burns
1924	Edith Cummings
1925	Mrs. S. L. Reinhardt
1926	Dorothy Page
1927	Mrs. H. Pessler
1928	Mrs. H. Pessler
1929	Mrs. O. S. Hill
1930	Mrs. O. S. Hill
1931	Mrs. O. S. Hill
1932	Mrs. O. S. Hill
1933	Lucille Robinson
1934	Mrs. L. D. Cheney
1935	Marion Miley
1936	Dorothy Traung
1937	Marion Miley
1938	Patty Berg

Year	Winner
1939	Edith Estabrooks
1940	Betty Jameson
1941	Mrs. R. Mann
1942	Betty Jameson
1943	Dorothy Germain
1944	Dorothy Germain
1945	Phyllis Otto
1946	Louise Suggs
1947	Louise Suggs
1948	Dorothy Kielty
1949	Helen Sigel
1950	Polly Riley
1951	Marjorie Lindsay
1952	Polly Riley
1953	Claire Doran
1954	Claire Doran
1955	Pat Lesser
1956	Anne Quast
1957	Meriam Bailey
1958	Barbara McIntire
1959	JoAnne Gunderson
1960	Mrs. A. C. Johnstone
1961	Anne Q. Decker[a]
1962	Carol Sorenson
1963	Barbara McIntire
1964	Barbara Fay White
1965	Barbara Fay White
1966	Peggy Conley
1967	Mrs. M. Porter
1968	Catherine Lacoste
1969	Jane Bastanchury
1970	**Jane Bastanchury**
1971	**Beth Barry**
1972	**Debbie Massey**
1973	Kathy Falk
1974	Lancy Smith
1975	Debbie Massey
1976	Nancy Lopez
1977	Lauren Howe

[a] Mrs. Decker is the former Anne Quast.

Western Junior Girls'

Year	Winner
1920	Mercedes Bush
1921	Katherine Bryant
1922	Mercedes Bush
1923	Josephine Morse
1924	Dorothy Page
1925	Virginia Van Wie
1926	Mildred Hackl
1927	Jean Armstrong
1928	Rena Nelson
1929	Ariel Vilas
1930	Priscilla Carver, III
1931	Dorothy Foster
1932	Janet Humphreys
1933	Alice A. Anderson
1934	Shirley Johnson
1935	Eleanor Dudley

Year	Winner
1936	Edith Estabrooks
1937	Muriel Veatch
1938	Jane Goodsill
1939	Mary Wilder
1940	Georgia Tainter
1941	Jeanne Cline
1942–1948	Not played
1949	Marlene Bauer
1950	Pat Lesser
1951	Virginia Dennehy
1952	Barbara McIntire
1953	Anne Richardson
1954	Anne Quast
1955	JoAnne Gunderson
1956	Clifford Ann Creed
1957	Sherry Wheeler
1958	Carol Mann
1959	Carol Sorenson
1960	Sharon Flados
1961	Ann Baker
1962	Mary Lou Daniel
1963	Janis Ferraris
1964	Janis Ferraris
1965	Jane Bastanchury
1966	Kathy Ahern
1967	Candace Michaeloff
1968	Jane Fassinger
1969	Jane Fassinger
1970	**Mary Budke**
1971	**Mary Budke**
1972	**Nancy Lopez**
1973	Nancy Lopez
1974	Nancy Lopez
1975	Connie Chillemi
1976	Lauren Howe
1977	Mari McDougall

Men's North and South Amateur

Year	Winner
1901	G. C. Dutton
1902	C. B. Corey
1903	T. S. Beckwith
1904	Walter J. Travis
1905	Dr. L. L. Harban
1906	Warren K. Wood
1907	Allan Lard
1908	Allan Lard
1909	J. D. Standish, Jr.
1910	Walter J. Travis
1911	Charles Evans, Jr.
1912	Walter J. Travis
1913	H. J. Topping
1914	R. S. Worthington
1915	F. K. Robeson
1916	P. V. G. Carter
1917	N. H. Maxwell
1918	I. S. Robeson
1919	Edward Beall
1920	Francis Ouimet
1921	B. P. Merriman

Year	Winner
1922	H. J. Topping
1923	Frank C. Newton
1924	F. W. Knight
1925	Arthur Yates
1926	Page Hufty
1927	George Voigt
1928	George Voigt
1929	George Voigt
1930	Eugene Homans
1931	G. T. Dunlap, Jr.
1932	M. P. Warner
1933	G. T. Dunlap, Jr.
1934	G. T. Dunlap, Jr.
1935	G. T. Dunlap, Jr.
1936	G. T. Dunlap, Jr.
1937	R. Dunkelberger
1938	Frank Strafaci
1939	Frank Strafaci
1940	G. T. Dunlap, Jr.
1941	Skip Alexander
1942	G. T. Dunlap, Jr.
1943	H. Offwitt
1944	Mal Galetta
1945	Ed Furgol
1946	Frank Stranahan
1947	Charles B. Dudley
1948	Harvie Ward, Jr.
1949	Frank Stranahan
1950	William C. Campbell
1951	Hobart Manley
1952	Frank Stranahan
1953	William C. Campbell
1954	William J. Patton
1955	Don Bisplinghoff
1956	Hillman Robbins, Jr.
1957	William C. Campbell
1958	Richard D. Chapman
1959	Jack Nicklaus
1960	Charlie Smith
1961	William Hyndman, III
1962	William J. Patton
1963	William J. Patton
1964	Dale Morey
1965	Tom Draper
1966	Ward Wettlaufer
1967	William C. Campbell
1968	Jack Lewis
1969	Joe Inman
1970	**Gary Cowan**
1971	**Eddie Pearce**
1972	**Danny Edwards**
1973	Mike Ford
1974	George Burns III
1975	Curtis Strange
1976	Curtis Strange
1977	Gary Hallberg

Women's North and South Amateur

Year	Winner
1903	Mrs. M. D. Paterson
1904	Mrs. M. D. Paterson

Year	Winner
1905	Mary H. Dutton
1906	Mrs. M. D. Paterson
1907	Molly B. Adams
1908	Julia Mix
1909	Mary Fownes
1910	Mrs. C. H. Vanderbeck
1911	Louise Elkins
1912	Mrs. J. R. Price
1913	Lillian Hyde
1914	Florence Harvey
1915	Mrs. R. H. Barlow
1916	Mrs. R. H. Barlow
1917	Elaine Rosenthal
1918	Mrs. J. V. Hurd
1919	Mrs. R. H. Barlow
1920	Mrs. J. V. Hurd
1921	Mrs. J. V. Hurd
1922	Glenna Collett
1923	Glenna Collett
1924	Glenna Collett
1925	Mrs. M. Jones
1926	Louise Fordyce
1927	Glenna Collett
1928	Mrs. O. S. Hill
1929	Glenna Collett
1930	Glenna Collett
1931	Maureen Orcutt
1932	Maureen Orcutt
1933	Maureen Orcutt
1934	Charlotte Glutting
1935	Estelle Lawson
1936	Deborah Verry
1937	Mrs. E. L. Page[a]
1938	Jane Cothran
1939	Mrs. E. L. Page
1940	Mrs. E. L. Page
1941	Mrs. E. L. Page
1942	Louise Suggs
1943	Dorothy Kirby
1944	Mrs. E. L. Page
1945	Mrs. E. L. Page
1946	Louise Suggs
1947	Mrs. G. Zaharias
1948	Louise Suggs
1949	Peggy Kirk
1950	Pat O'Sullivan
1951	Pat O'Sullivan
1952	Barbara Romack
1953	Pat O'Sullivan
1954	Joyce Ziske
1955	Wiffi Smith
1956	Marlene Stewart
1957	Barbara McIntire
1958	Mrs. P. Cudone
1959	Mrs. A. C. Johnstone
1960	Barbara McIntire
1961	Barbara McIntire
1962	Clifford Ann Creed
1963	Nancy Roth
1964	Phyllis Preuss
1965	Barbara McIntire
1966	Mrs. N. R. Syms[b]

Year	Winner
1967	Phyllis Preuss
1968	Mrs. P. Dye, Jr.
1969	Barbara McIntire
1970	**Hollis Stacy**
1971	**Barbara McIntire**
1972	**Mrs. M. Booth**
1973	Beth Barry
1974	Marlene Streit
1975	Cynthia Hill
1976	Carol Semple
1977	Marcia Dolan

a Mrs. Page is the former Estelle Lawson.
b Mrs. Syms is the former Nancy Roth.

North and South Seniors'

Like all other North and South events, this championship event is held at Pinehurst Country Club in North Carolina and like other senior tournaments is open to men over fifty-five years of age.

Year	Winner
1952	Judd Brumley
1953	O. V. Russell
1954	S. S. Overton
1955	B. K. Kraffert
1956	Tom Robbins
1957	J. W. Platt
1958	J. W. Brown
1959	Walter Pease
1960	Tom Robbins
1961	Robert Bell
1962	W. K. Lanman
1963	James McAlvin
1964	James McAlvin
1965	David Goldman
1966	Curtis Person
1967	Robert Cochran
1968	Curtis Person
1969	Curtis Person
1970	**Robert Cochran**
1971	**David Goldman**
1972	**William Hyndman III**
1973	Ray Palmer
1974	David Goldman
1975	Harry Welch
1976	Paul Severin
1977	George Pottle

Trans-Mississippi Amateur

This event, sponsored by the Trans-Mississippi Golf Association, was one of the earlier amateurs held in the United States and is match play. The Association comprises over sixty-five clubs and covers over fourteen states.

Year	Winner
1901	John Stuart
1902	R. R. Kimball
1903	John R. Maxwell
1904	H. P. Bend
1905	Warren Dickinson
1906	C. T. Jaffray
1907	Strague Abbot
1908	E. H. Seaver
1909	Harry G. Legg
1910	Harry G. Legg
1911	Harry G. Legg
1912	Harry G. Legg
1913	Steward Stickney
1914	J. D. Cady
1915	Allen B. Swift
1916	Harry G. Legg
1917	S. W. Reynolds
1918	G. L. Conley
1919	Nelson Whitney
1920	Robert McKee
1921	George Von Elm
1922	R. E. Knepper
1923	Eddie Held
1924	James Manion
1925	C. L. Wolff
1926	Eddie Held
1927	John Goodman
1928	Arthur L. Bartlett
1929	Robert McCrary
1930	Robert McCrary
1931	John Goodman
1932	Gus Moreland
1933	Gus Moreland
1934	Leland Hamman
1935	John Goodman
1936	John Dawson
1937	Don Schumacher
1938	Vene Savage
1939	Melvin Harbert
1940	A. L. Doering
1941	Frank Stranahan
1942	John Kraft
1943–1945	Not played
1946	Robert Riegel
1947	Charles R. Coe
1948	Robert Riegel
1949	Charles R. Coe
1950	James English
1951	L. M. Crannell, Jr.
1952	Charles R. Coe
1953	Joe Conrad
1954	James Jackson
1955	James Jackson
1956	Charles R. Coe
1957	Rex Baxter, Jr.
1958	Jack Nicklaus
1959	Jack Nicklaus
1960	Deane Beman
1961	Herb Durham
1962	Frank Ryan
1963	George Archer
1964	Wright Garrett

Year	Winner
1965	George Boutell
1966	James Wiechers
1967	Hal Underwood
1968	William Hyndman III
1969	Allen Miller
1970	**Allen Miller**
1971	**Allen Miller**
1972	**Ben Crenshaw**
1973	Gary Koch
1974	Tom Jones
1975	Tim Wilson
1976	Doug Clarke
1977	John Faught

Women's Trans-National Amateur

Year	Winner
1927	Mrs. M. B. Horn
1928	Mrs. O. S. Hill
1929	Mrs. O. S. Hill
1930	Mrs. H. S. Clarke
1931	Mrs. O. S. Hill
1932	Mrs. J. W. Beyer
1933	Phyllis Buchanan
1934	Mrs. O. S. Hill
1935	Marion Miley
1936	Marion Miley
1937	Betty Jameson
1938	Patty Berg
1939	Patty Berg
1940	Betty Jameson
1941	Mrs. R. C. Mann
1942–1945	Not played
1946	Mrs. G. Zaharias
1947	Polly Riley
1948	Polly Riley
1949	Betsy Rawls
1950	Marjorie Lindsay
1951	Mary Ann Downey
1952	Mrs. L. Bowman
1953	Mrs. E. Ihlanfeldt
1954	Vonnie Colby
1955	Polly Riley
1956	Wiffi Smith
1957	Mrs. J. Ferrie
1958	Marjorie Lindsay
1959	Mrs. A. C. Johnstone
1960	Sandra Haynie
1961	JoAnne Gunderson
1962	Jean Thompson
1963	Judy Bell
1964	Carol Sorenson
1965	Sharon Miller
1966	Roberta Albers
1967	Jane Bastanchury
1968	Mrs. M. Skala
1969	Jane Bastanchury
1970	**Martha Wilkinson**
1971	**Jane Bastanchury**
1972	**Michelle Walker**
1973	Liana Zambresky

Year	Winner
1974	Barbara Barrow
1975	Beverly Davis
1976	Nancy Lopez
1977	Cathy Reynolds

Southern Amateur

This championship, which dates back to 1902, has been won by many outstanding amateur men players, including the great Bobby Jones. Incidentally, Jones first played in this event at the age of thirteen.

Year	Winner
1902	A. F. Schwartz
1903	A. W. Gaines
1904	Andrew Manson
1905	Andrew Manson
1906	Leigh Carroll
1907	Nelson Whitney
1908	Nelson Whitney
1909	J. P. Edrington
1910	F. G. Byrd
1911	W. P. Steward
1912	W. P. Steward
1913	Nelson Whitney
1914	Nelson Whitney
1915	C. L. Dexter
1916	R. G. Bush
1917	Robert T. Jones, Jr.
1918	Not played
1919	Nelson Whitney
1920	Robert T. Jones, Jr.
1921	Perry Adair
1922	Robert T. Jones, Jr.
1923	Perry Adair
1924	Jack Wenzler
1925	Glenn Cressman
1926	R. E. Spicer
1927	Harry Ehle
1928	Watts Gunn
1929	Sam Perry
1930	R. E. Spicer
1931	C. Harris
1932	Sam Perry
1933	Jack Redmond
1934	Fred Haas, Jr.
1935	Robert Riegel
1936	Jack Munger
1937	Fred Haas, Jr.
1938	Carl Dann
1939	R. Dunkelberger
1940	Neil White
1941	Sam Perry
1942–1945	Not played
1946	George Hamer
1947	Tommy Barnes
1948	G. Dahlbender, Jr.
1949	Tommy Barnes
1950	Dale Morey

Year	Winner
1951	Arnold Blum
1952	Gay Brewer, Jr.
1953	Joe Conrad
1954	Joe Conrad
1955	Charles Harrison
1956	Arnold Blum
1957	Ed Brantley
1958	Hugh Royer, Jr.
1959	Dick Crawford
1960	Charles Smith
1961	William J. Patton
1962	Bunky Henry
1963	Mike Malarkey
1964	Dale Morey
1965	William J. Patton
1966	Herbert Green
1967	Marvin M. Gilles III
1968	Lanny Wadkins
1969	Herbert Green
1970	Lanny Wadkins
1971	Ben Crenshaw
1972	Bill Rogers
1973	Ben Crenshaw
1974	Danny Yates
1975	Vinny Giles
1976	Tim Simpson
1977	Lindy Miller

Women's Southern Amateur

Year	Winner
1911	Mrs. R. Smith
1912	Mrs. F. G. Jones
1913	Mrs. E. W. Daley
1914	Mrs. F. G. Jones
1915	Alexa Stirling
1916	Alexa Stirling
1917	Mrs. K. G. Duffield
1918	Not played
1919	Alexa Stirling
1920	Mrs. D. C. Gaut
1921	Mrs. D. C. Gaut
1922	Mrs. D. Lowndes
1923	Mrs. D. C. Gaut
1924	Mrs. D. Lowndes
1925	Mrs. J. Armstrong
1926	Marion Turpie
1927	Mrs. D. Reymond
1928	Marion Turpie
1929	Margaret Maddox
1930	Mrs. D. C. Gaut
1931	Mrs. M. Lake[a]
1932	Mrs. B. FitzHugh
1933	Angela Gorczyca
1934	Betty Jameson
1935	Mary Rogers
1936	Mrs. M. McGarry
1937	Dorothy Kirby
1938	Marion Miley
1939	Marion Miley
1940	Mrs. F. Goldthwaite

Year	Winner
1941	Louise Suggs
1942–1945	Not played
1946	Mrs. E. L. Page
1947	Louise Suggs
1948	Polly Riley
1949	Margaret Gunther
1950	Polly Riley
1951	Polly Riley
1952	Kathy McKinnon
1953	Polly Riley
1954	Polly Riley
1955	Mrs. S. Probasco, Jr.
1956	Mary Ann Downey
1957	Clifford Ann Creed
1958	Mrs. M. A. Reynolds
1959	Judy Eller
1960	Judy Eller
1961	Polly Riley
1962	Clifford Ann Creed
1963	Mrs. P. Hendrix
1964	Nancy Roth
1965	Phyllis Preuss
1966	Mrs. N. R. Syms[b]
1967	Mrs. T. Boddie
1968	Phyllis Preuss
1969	Mrs. J. Rathmell
1970	Kathy Hite
1971	Beth Barry
1972	Beth Barry
1973	Beth Barry
1974	Marth Jones
1975	Beth Barry
1976	Brenda Goldsmith
1977	Ceil MacLaurin

[a] Mrs. Lake is the former Marion Turpie.
[b] Mrs. Syms is the former Nancy Roth.

Jack Nicklaus playing out of the rough on the 6th fairway of Muirfield in the 1966 British Open Championship, which he won. He won it again in 1970 and 1978, and was runner-up six times.

MAJOR INTERNATIONAL GOLF EVENTS

British Open

The British Open, inaugurated in 1860, was "open" only to professional golfers in its first year of operation. The following year it was opened to amateurs. At first, the prize was a belt made of rich Morocco leather and decorated with silver ornaments. In 1863, prize money was offered. In 1870, Tom Morris, Jr., won the belt (three straight victories) as a permanent possession, and a new trophy, "The Cup," was offered in 1872 in addition to prize money. In 1892, the Championship was extended from 36 to 72 holes.

Golf's oldest championship is still a severe test of a golfer's skill and from 1927 through 1962, the British Open format was the most strenuous stroke play competition in all golf, consisting of a 36-hole qualifying round and the 72-hole championship, for which even the defending champion had to qualify. In 1963, a new table of exemptions spared a number of established players the necessity of qualifying for the event proper, whose field is now reduced to an even 120 players. Champions since the beginning of British Open are:

Year	Site	Winner	Runner-Up	Winning Score
1860	Prestwick, Scotland	Willie Park, Sr.	Tom Morris, Sr.	174
1861	Prestwick, Scotland	Tom Morris, Sr.	Willie Park, Sr.	163
1862	Prestwick, Scotland	Tom Morris, Sr.	Willie Park, Sr.	163
1863	Prestwick, Scotland	Willie Park, Sr.	Tom Morris, Sr.	168
1864	Prestwick, Scotland	Tom Morris, Sr.	Andrew Strath	167
1865	Prestwick, Scotland	Andrew Strath	Willie Park, Sr.	162
1866	Prestwick, Scotland	Willie Park, Sr.	David Park	169
1867	Prestwick, Scotland	Tom Morris, Sr.	Willie Park, Sr.	170
1868	Prestwick, Scotland	Tom Morris, Jr.	Tom Morris, Sr.	170
1869	Prestwick, Scotland	Tom Morris, Jr.	Tom Morris, Sr.	157
1870	Prestwick, Scotland	Tom Morris, Jr.	David Strath, Robert Kirk	149
1871	Not played			
1872	Prestwick, Scotland	Tom Morris, Jr.	David Strath	166
1873	St. Andrews, Scotland	Tom Kipp		179
1874	Musselburgh, Scotland	Mungo Park		159
1875	Prestwick, Scotland	Willie Park, Sr.	Robert Martin	166
1876	St. Andrews, Scotland	Robert Martin	David Strath (refused play-off)	176
1877	Musselburgh, Scotland	Jamie Anderson	R. Pringle	160
1878	Prestwick, Scotland	Jamie Anderson	Robert Kirk	157
1879	St. Andrews, Scotland	Jamie Anderson	Andrew Kirkaldy, J. Allan	170
1880	Musselburgh, Scotland	Robert Ferguson		162
1881	Prestwick, Scotland	Robert Ferguson	Jamie Anderson	170
1882	St. Andrews, Scotland	Robert Ferguson	Willie Fernie	171
1883	Musselburgh, Scotland	Willie Fernie [a]	Robert Ferguson	159
1884	Prestwick, Scotland	Jack Simpson	Douglas Rolland, Willie Fernie	160
1885	St. Andrews, Scotland	Robert Martin	Archie Simpson	171
1886	Musselburgh, Scotland	David Brown	Willie Campbell	157
1887	Prestwick, Scotland	Willie Park, Jr.	Robert Martin	161
1888	St. Andrews, Scotland	Jack Burns	B. Sayers, D. Anderson	171
1889	Musselburgh, Scotland	Willie Park, Jr.	Andrew Kirkaldy	155
1890	Prestwick, Scotland	John Ball [b]	Willie Fernie, Archie Simpson	164
1891	St. Andrews, Scotland	Hugh Kirkaldy	Andrew Kirkaldy, Willie Fernie	166
1892	Muirfield, Scotland	Harold H. Hilton [b]	John Ball, [b] Hugh Kirkaldy, Alexander Herd	305
1893	Prestwick, Scotland	William Auchterlonie	John Laidlay [b]	322
1894	Sandwich, England	John H. Taylor	Douglas Rolland	326
1895	St. Andrews, Scotland	John H. Taylor	Alexander Herd	322
1896	Muirfield, Scotland	Harry Vardon [a]	John H. Taylor	316
1897	Hoylake, England	Harold H. Hilton [b]	James Braid	314
1898	Prestwick, Scotland	Harry Vardon	Willie Park, Jr.	307

Richard Chapman holds the British Amateur trophy after defeating Charles Coe in 1951.

The participants in 1965 World Series of Golf (left to right): Jack Nicklaus, Peter Thomson, Dave Marr, and Gary Player.

Year	Site	Winner	Runner-Up	Winning Score
1899	Sandwich, England	Harry Vardon	Jack White	310
1900	St. Andrews, Scotland	John H. Taylor	Harry Vardon	309
1901	Muirfield, Scotland	James Braid	Harry Vardon	309
1902	Hoylake, England	Alexander Herd	Harry Vardon	307
1903	Prestwick, Scotland	Harry Vardon	Tom Vardon	300
1904	Sandwich, England	Jack White	John H. Taylor, James Braid	296
1905	St. Andrews, Scotland	James Braid	John H. Taylor, Rolland Jones	318
1906	Muirfield, Scotland	James Braid	John H. Taylor	300
1907	Hoylake, England	Arnaud Massy	John H. Taylor	312
1908	Prestwick, Scotland	James Braid	Tom Ball	291
1909	Deal, England	John H. Taylor	James Braid, Tom Ball	295
1910	St. Andrews, Scotland	James Braid	Alexander Herd	299
1911	Sandwich, England	Harry Vardon[a]	Arnaud Massy	303
1912	Muirfield, Scotland	Edward Ray	Harry Vardon	295
1913	Hoylake, England	John H. Taylor	Edward Ray	304
1914	Prestwick, Scotland	Harry Vardon	John H. Taylor	306
1915–1919 Not played				
1920	Deal, England	George Duncan	Alexander Herd	303
1921	St. Andrews, Scotland	Jock Hutchison[a]	Roger Wethered[b]	296
1922	Sandwich, England	Walter Hagen	George Duncan, James Barnes	300
1923	Troon, Scotland	Arthur Havers	Walter Hagen	295
1924	Hoylake, England	Walter Hagen	Ernest Whitcombe	301
1925	Prestwick, Scotland	James Barnes	Archie Compston, Edward Ray	300
1926	Royal Lytham and St. Anne's, England	Robert T. Jones, Jr.[b]	Al Watrous	291
1927	St. Andrews, Scotland	Robert T. Jones, Jr.[b]	Aubrey Boomer	285
1928	Sandwich, England	Walter Hagen	Gene Sarazen	292
1929	Muirfield, Scotland	Walter Hagen	Johnny Farrell	292
1930	Hoylake, England	Robert T. Jones, Jr.[b]	Macdonald Smith, Leo Diegel	291
1931	Carnoustie, Scotland	Tommy Armour	J. Jurado	296
1932	Princes, England	Gene Sarazen	Macdonald Smith	283
1933	St. Andrews, Scotland	Denny Shute[a]	Craig Wood	292
1934	Sandwich, England	T. Henry Cotton	S. F. Brews	283
1935	Muirfield, Scotland	Alfred Perry	Alfred Padgham	283
1936	Hoylake, England	Alfred Padgham	James Adams	287
1937	Carnoustie, Scotland	T. Henry Cotton	R. A. Whitcombe	290
1938	Sandwich, England	R. A. Whitcombe	James Adams	295
1939	St. Andrews, Scotland	Richard Burton	Johnny Bulla	290
1940–1945 Not played				
1946	St. Andrews, Scotland	Sam Snead	A. D. Locke, Johnny Bulla	290

Year	Site	Winner	Runner-Up	Winning Score
1947	Hoylake, England	Fred Daly	R. W. Horne, Frank Stranahan[b]	293
1948	Muirfield, Scotland	T. Henry Cotton	Fred Daly	284
1949	Sandwich, England	A. D. Locke[a]	Harry Bradshaw	283
1950	Troon, Scotland	A. D. Locke	Roberto DeVicenzo	279
1951	Portrush, Northern Ireland	Max Faulkner	A. Cerda	285
1952	Royal Lytham and St. Anne's, England	A. D. Locke	Peter W. Thomson	287
1953	Carnoustie, Scotland	Ben Hogan	Frank Stranahan,[b] Dai Rees, Peter W. Thomson, A. Cerda	282
1954	Royal Birkdale, England	Peter W. Thomson	S. S. Scott, Dai Rees, A. D. Locke	283
1955	St. Andrews, Scotland	Peter W. Thomson	John Fallon	281
1956	Hoylake, England	Peter W. Thomson	Flory VanDonck	286
1957	St. Andrews, Scotland	A. D. Locke	Peter W. Thomson	279
1958	Royal Lytham and St. Anne's, England	Peter W. Thomson[a]	Dave Thomas	278
1959	Muirfield, Scotland	Gary Player	Flory VanDonck	284
1960	St. Andrews, Scotland	K. D. G. Nagle	Arnold Palmer	278
1961	Royal Birkdale, England	Arnold Palmer	Dai Rees	284
1962	Troon, Scotland	Arnold Palmer	K. D. G. Nagle	276
1963	Royal Lytham and St. Anne's, England	Robert J. Charles[a] 36 holes (140)	Phil Rodgers (148)	277
1964	St. Andrews, Scotland	Tony Lema	Jack Nicklaus	279
1965	Southport, England	Peter W. Thomson	B. G. C. Huggett, Chris O'Connor	285
1966	Muirfield, Scotland	Jack Nicklaus	Doug Sanders, Dave Thomas	282
1967	Hoylake, England	Robert DeVicenzo	Jack Nicklaus	278
1968	Carnoustie, Scotland	Gary Player	Jack Nicklaus, Robert J. Charles	289
1969	Royal Lytham and St. Anne's, England	Tony Jacklin	Robert J. Charles	280
1970	St. Andrews, Scotland	Jack Nicklaus[a]	Doug Sanders	283
1971	Southport, England	Lee Trevino	Lu Liang Huan	278
1972	Muirfield, Scotland	Lee Trevino	Jack Nicklaus	278
1973	Troon, Scotland	Tom Weiskopf	Johnny Miller	276
1974	Royal Lytham and St. Anne's, England	Gary Player	Peter Oosterhuis	282
1975	Carnoustie, Scotland	Tom Watson[a] (71)	Jack Newton (72)	279
1976	Royal Birkdale, England	Johnny Miller	Jack Nicklaus, S. Ballesteros	279
1977	Turnberry, Scotland	Tom Watson	Jack Nicklaus	268[c]

[a] Won in play-off.
[b] Amateur.
[c] Record.

British Amateur

The first British Amateur Championship was conducted by the Royal Liverpool Club at Hoylake, England, with an informal competition in the summer of 1885. The success of this initial event moved the host club to petition the Royal and Ancient Club at St. Andrews to conduct an annual Amateur Championship. The format of the championship has always been match play, but until 1896, all matches were decided over 18 holes. That year the final was extended to 36 holes.

Now the quarter- and semi-finals are also decided over 36 holes.

After Walter J. Travis, an Australian native who made his home in the United States, became the first foreigner to win the British Amateur, no American reached the final until 1920 when Robert Gardner lost a 37-hole match to Cyril Tolley. Jesse Sweetser was the first native-born American to win the title, scoring in 1926. Four years later, Bob Jones won his only British Amateur title on his way toward the 1930 Grand Slam. Winners of the British Amateur Championship are:

Year	Site	Winner	Runner-Up	Score
1885	Hoylake, England	A. F. MacFie	H. G. Hutchinson	7 & 6
1886	St. Andrews, Scotland	H. G. Hutchinson	Henry Lamb	7 & 6

Year	Site	Winner	Runner-Up	Score
1887	Hoylake, England	H. G. Hutchinson	John Ball	1 up
1888	Prestwick, Scotland	John Ball	J. E. Laidlay	5 & 4
1889	St. Andrews, Scotland	J. E. Laidlay	L. M. B. Melville	2 & 1
1890	Hoylake, England	John Ball	J. E. Laidlay	4 & 3
1891	St. Andrews, Scotland	J. E. Laidlay	H. H. Hilton	20th hole
1892	Sandwich, England	John Ball	H. H. Hilton	3 & 1
1893	Prestwick, Scotland	Peter Anderson	J. E. Laidlay	1 up
1894	Hoylake, England	John Ball	S. M. Fergusson	1 up
1895	St. Andrews, Scotland	L. M. B. Melville	John Ball	19th hole
1896	Sandwich, England	F. G. Tait	H. H. Hilton	8 & 9
1897	Muirfield, Scotland	A. J. T. Allan	James Robb	4 & 2
1898	Hoylake, England	F. G. Tait	S. M. Fergusson	7 & 5
1899	Prestwick, Scotland	John Ball	F. G. Tait	37th hole
1900	Sandwich, England	H. H. Hilton	James Robb	8 & 7
1901	St. Andrews, Scotland	H. H. Hilton	J. L. Low	1 up
1902	Hoylake, England	C. Hutchings	S. H. Fry	1 up
1903	Muirfield, Scotland	R. Maxwell	H. G. Hutchinson	7 & 5
1904	Sandwich, England	W. J. Travis	Edward Blackwell	4 & 3
1905	Prestwick, Scotland	A. G. Barry	O. Scott	3 & 2
1906	Hoylake, England	James Robb	C. C. Lingen	4 & 3
1907	St. Andrews, Scotland	John Ball	C. A. Palmer	6 & 4
1908	Sandwich, England	E. A. Lassen	H. E. Taylor	7 & 6
1909	Muirfield, Scotland	R. Maxwell	Capt. C. K. Hutchinson	1 up
1910	Hoylake, England	John Ball	C. Aylmer	10 & 9
1911	Prestwick, Scotland	H. H. Hilton	E. A. Lassen	4 & 3
1912	Westward Ho!, England	John Ball	Abe Mitchell	38th hole
1913	St. Andrews, Scotland	H. H. Hilton	R. Harris	6 & 5
1914	Sandwich, England	J. L. C. Jenkins	C. O. Hezlet	3 & 2
1915–1919 Not played				
1920	Muirfield, Scotland	C. J. H. Tolley	R. A. Gardner	37th hole
1921	Hoylake, England	W. I. Hunter	A. J. Graham	12 & 11
1922	Prestwick, Scotland	E. W. E. Holderness	J. Caven	1 up
1923	Deal, England	R. H. Wethered	R. Harris	7 & 6
1924	St. Andrews, Scotland	E. W. E. Holderness	E. F. Storey	3 & 2
1925	Westward Ho!, England	R. Harris	K. F. Fradgley	13 & 12
1926	Muirfield, Scotland	Jesse Sweetser	A. F. Simpson	6 & 5
1927	Hoylake, England	Dr. W. Tweddell	D. E. Landale	7 & 6
1928	Prestwick, Scotland	T. P. Perkins	R. H. Wethered	6 & 4
1929	Sandwich, England	C. J. H. Tolley	J. N. Smith	4 & 3
1930	St. Andrews, Scotland	Robert T. Jones, Jr.	R. H. Wethered	7 & 6
1931	Westward Ho!, England	E. Martin Smith	J. DeForest	1 up
1932	Muirfield, Scotland	J. DeForest	E. W. Fiddian	3 & 1
1933	Hoylake, England	M. Scott	T. A. Bourn	4 & 3
1934	Prestwick, Scotland	W. Lawson Little	J. Wallace	14 & 13
1935	Royal Lytham and St. Anne's, England	W. Lawson Little	Dr. W. Tweddell	1 up
1936	St. Andrews, Scotland	H. Thomson	J. Ferrier	2 up
1937	Sandwich, England	R. Sweeny, Jr.	L. O. Munn	3 & 2
1938	Troon, Scotland	C. R. Yates	R. C. Ewing	3 & 2
1939	Hoylake, England	A. T. Kyle	A. A. Duncan	2 & 1
1940–1945 Not played				
1946	Royal Birkdale, England	J. Bruen	R. Sweeny, Jr.	4 & 3
1947	Carnoustie, Scotland	Willie D. Turnesa	R. D. Chapman	3 & 2
1948	Sandwich, England	Frank R. Stranahan	C. Stowe	5 & 4
1949	Portmarnock, Ireland	S. M. McCready	W. P. Turnesa	2 & 1
1950	St. Andrews, Scotland	Frank R. Stranahan	R. D. Chapman	8 & 6
1951	Porthcawl, South Wales	Richard D. Chapman	C. R. Coe	5 & 4
1952	Prestwick, Scotland	E. H. Ward	F. R. Stranahan	6 & 5
1953	Hoylake, England	J. B. Carr	E. Harvie Ward	2 up
1954	Muirfield, Scotland	D. W. Bachli	W. C. Campbell	2 & 1
1955	Royal Lytham and St. Anne's, England	J. W. Conrad	A. Slater	3 & 2
1956	Troon, Scotland	J. C. Beharrel	L. G. Taylor	5 & 4

Year	Site	Winner	Runner-Up	Score
1957	Formby, England	R. Reid Jack	H. B. Ridgley	2 & 1
1958	St. Andrews, Scotland	J. B. Carr	A. Thirlwell	3 & 2
1959	Sandwich, England	Deane Beman	William Hyndman III	3 & 2
1960	Portrush, Northern Ireland	J. B. Carr	R. Cochran	7 & 6
1961	Turnberry, Scotland	M. Bonallack	J. Walker	6 & 4
1962	Hoylake, England	R. Davies	J. Powell	1 up
1963	St. Andrews, Scotland	M. Lunt	J. Blackwell	2 & 1
1964	Ganton, England	C. Clark	M. Lunt	1 up (39)
1965	Porthcawl, South Wales	M. Bonallack	C. Clark	2 & 1
1966	Carnoustie, Scotland	C. R. Cole	R. Shade	3 & 2
1967	Formby, England	R. Dickson	R. Cerrudo	2 & 1
1968	Troon, Scotland	M. Bonallack	J. B. Carr	7 & 6
1969	Hoylake, England	M. Bonallack	William Hyndman III	3 & 2
1970	Hoylake, England	M. Bonallack	William Hyndman III	8 & 7
1971	Newcastle Co. Down, North Ireland	Steve Melnyk	Jim Simons	3 & 2
1972	Sandwich, England	Trevor Homer	Alan Thirlwell	4 & 3
1973	Porthcawl, South Wales	Dick Siderowf	Peter Moody	5 & 3
1974	Muirfield, Scotland	Trevor Homer	Jim Gabrielson	2 up
1975	Royal Liverpool, England	Vinny Giles	Mark James	8 & 7
1976	St. Andrews, Scotland	Dick Siderowf	John Davies	1 up (37)
1977	Ganton, England	Peter McEvoy	Hugh Campbell	5 & 4

British Ladies' Amateur

The first annual British Ladies' Golf Championship took place June 13, 1893, at the short links of Lytham at St. Anne's, where thirty-eight contestants were entered. Today it is the major women's event of Europe and is a match play tournament. Here are the winners over the years:

Year	Winner
1893	Lady Margaret Scott
1894	Lady Margaret Scott
1895	Lady Margaret Scott
1896	A. B. Pascoe
1897	E. C. Orr
1898	L. Thomson
1899	May Hezlet
1900	Rhona K. Adair
1901	Molly A. Graham
1902	May Hezlet
1903	Rhona K. Adair
1904	Lottie Dod
1905	B. Thompson
1906	Mrs. W. Kennion
1907	May Hezlet
1908	M. Titterton
1909	Dorothy Campbell
1910	G. Suttie
1911	Dorothy Campbell
1912	Gladys Ravenscroft
1913	Muriel Dodd
1914	Cecil Leitch
1915–1919	Not played
1920	Cecil Leitch
1921	Cecil Leitch
1922	Joyce Wethered

Year	Winner
1923	Doris Chambers
1924	Joyce Wethered
1925	Joyce Wethered
1926	Cecil Leitch
1927	Thion de la Chaume
1928	Nanette LeBlan
1929	Joyce Wethered
1930	Diana Fishwick
1931	Enid Wilson
1932	Enid Wilson
1933	Enid Wilson
1934	Mrs. A. M. Holm
1935	Wanda Morgan
1936	Pamela Barton
1937	Jessie Anderson
1938	Mrs. A. M. Holm
1939	Pamela Barton
1940–1945	Not played
1946	Mrs. G. W. Hetherington
1947	Mrs. George Zaharias
1948	Louise Suggs
1949	Frances Stephens
1950	Vicomtesse de Saint Sauveue
1951	Mrs. P. G. Maccann
1952	Moira Paterson
1953	Marlene Stewart
1954	Frances Stephens
1955	Mrs. G. Valentine
1956	Wiffi Smith
1957	Philomena Garvey
1958	Mrs. G. Valentine
1959	Elizabeth Price
1960	Barbara McIntire
1961	Mrs. A. D. Spearman
1962	Mrs. A. D. Spearman

Two of the more famous British Ladies' champions: Cecil Leitch (left) and Diana Fishwick (right).

Year	Winner
1963	Brigette Varangot
1964	Carol Sorenson
1965	Brigette Varangot
1966	E. Chadwick
1967	E. Chadwick
1968	Brigette Varangot
1969	Catherine Lacoste
1970	**Dinah Oxley**
1971	**Michelle Walker**
1972	**Michelle Walker**
1973	Ann Irvin
1974	Ann Irvin
1975	Julia Greenhalgh
1976	Cathy Panton
1977	Angela Uzielli

Argentine Open

Year	Winner
1905	Mungo Park
1906	J. C. Avery Wright
1907	Mungo Park
1908	F. A. Sutton
1909	Raul Castillo
1910	A. Philp
1911	Rodolfo Castillo
1912	Mungo Park
1913	A. Philp
1914	Raul Castillo

Year	Winner
1915	L. Gonzalez
1916	L. Gonzalez
1917	L. Gonzalez
1918	J. A. Eustace
1919	Raul Castillo
1920	J. Jurado
1921	A. Perez
1922	A. Perez
1923	A. Perez
1924	J. Jurado
1925	J. Jurado
1926	M. Churio
1927	J. Jurado
1928	J. Jurado
1929	J. Jurado
1930	T. Genta
1931	J. Jurado
1932	A. Perez
1933	M. Pose
1934	M. Churio
1935	J. I. Cruickshank
1936	J. I. Cruickshank
1937	Henry Picard
1938	Paul Runyan
1939	M. Pose
1940	Mario Gonzalez
1941	Jimmy Demaret
1942	M. Martin
1943	M. Churio
1944	R. DeVicenzo

Year	Winner
1945	Not played
1946	Lloyd Mangrum
1947	E. Bertolino
1948	A. Cerda
1949	R. DeVicenzo
1950	M. Pose
1951	R. DeVicenzo
1952	R. DeVicenzo
1953	Mario Gonzalez
1954	F. DeLuca
1955	E. Bertolino
1956	A. Cerda
1957	L. Ruiz
1958	R. DeVicenzo
1959	L. Ruiz
1960	F. DeLuca
1961	F. DeLuca
1962	A. Miguel
1963	J. Ledesma
1964	E. Nari
1965	R. DeVicenzo
1966	J. Castillo
1967	R. DeVicenzo
1968	V. Fernandez
1969	**V. Fernandez**
1970	**R. DeVicenzo**
1971	**F. Molina**
1972	**R. DeVIcenzo**
1973	Florentino Molina
1974	Roberto DiVicenzo
1975	Florentino Molina
1976	Florentino Molina
1977	Florentino Molina

Australian Open

Year	Winner
1904	Michael Scott
1905	D. Soutar
1906	Carnegie Clark
1907	Michael Scott
1908	Clyde Pearce
1909	C. Felstead
1910	Carnegie Clark
1911	Carnegie Clark
1912	Ivo Whitton
1913	Ivo Whitton
1914–1919	Not played
1920	J. H. Kirkwood
1921	A. LeFavre
1922	C. Campbell
1923	T. E. Howard
1924	A. Russell
1925	F. Popplewell
1926	Ivo Whitton
1927	R. Stewart
1928	F. Popplewell
1929	Ivo Whitton
1930	F. P. Eyre
1931	Ivo Whitton
1932	M. J. Ryan

Year	Winner
1933	M. L. Kelly
1934	W. J. Bolger
1935	F. McMahon
1936	Gene Sarazen
1937	G. Naismith
1938	Jim Ferrier
1939	Jim Ferrier
1940–1945	Not played
1946	H. O. Pickworth
1947	H. O. Pickworth
1948	H. O. Pickworth
1949	E. Cremin
1950	N. G. Von Nida
1951	Peter W. Thomson
1952	N. G. Von Nida
1953	N. G. Von Nida
1954	H. O. Pickworth
1955	A. D. Locke
1956	Bruce Crampton
1957	F. Phillips
1958	Gary Player
1959	K. D. G. Nagle
1960	Bruce Devlin
1961	F. Phillips
1962	Gary Player
1963	Gary Player
1964	Jack Nicklaus
1965	Gary Player
1966	Arnold Palmer
1967	Peter W. Thomson
1968	Jack Nicklaus
1969	Gary Player
1970	**Gary Player**
1971	**Jack Nicklaus**
1972	**Peter W. Thomson**
1973	Peter W. Thomson
1974	J. C. Snead
1975	Gary Player
1976	Jack Nicklaus
1977	David Graham

Brazilian Open

Year	Winner
1945	M. Pose
1946	Mario Gonzalez
1947	Not played
1948	Mario Gonzalez
1949	Mario Gonzalez
1950	Mario Gonzalez
1951	Mario Gonzalez
1952	Sam Snead
1953	Mario Gonzalez
1954	R. DeVicenzo
1955	Mario Gonzalez
1956	F. DeLuca
1957	R. DeVicenzo
1958	Billy Casper, Jr.
1959	Billy Casper, Jr.
1960	R. DeVicenzo
1961	P. Alliss

Year	Winner
1962	B. J. Hunt
1963	R. DeVicenzo
1964	R. DeVicenzo
1965	Not played
1966	Rex Baxter
1967	Not played
1968	T. Kono
1969	Manuel Gonzalez
1970	**Bert Greene**
1971	**Bruce Fleisher**
1972	**Gary Player**
1973	Robert DeVicenzo
1974	Gary Player
1975	Priscillo Gonzales Diniz
1976	P. Gonzalez
1977	Juan Quinteros

Canadian Open

Year	Winner
1904	J. H. Oke
1905	George Cumming
1906	C. R. Murray
1907	Percy Barrett
1908	Albert Murray
1909	Karl Keffer
1910	D. Kenny
1911	C. R. Murray
1912	George Sargent
1913	Albert Murray
1914	Karl Keffer
1915–1918	Not played
1919	J. Douglas Edgar
1920	J. Douglas Edgar
1921	William Trovinger
1922	Al Watrous
1923	Clarence Hackney
1924	Leo Diegel
1925	Leo Diegel
1926	Macdonald Smith
1927	Tommy Armour
1928	Leo Diegel
1929	Leo Diegel
1930	Tommy Armour
1931	Walter Hagen
1932	Harry Cooper
1933	Joe Kirkwood
1934	Tommy Armour
1935	G. Kunes
1936	W. Lawson Little
1937	Harry Cooper
1938	Sam Snead
1939	Harold McSpaden
1940	Sam Snead
1941	Sam Snead
1942	Craig Wood
1943–1944	Not played
1945	Byron Nelson
1946	George Fazio
1947	A. D. Locke
1948	C. Congdon

Year	Winner
1949	E. J. Harrison
1950	Jim Ferrier
1951	Jim Ferrier
1952	John Palmer
1953	Dave Douglas
1954	Pat Fletcher
1955	Arnold Palmer
1956	Doug Sanders
1957	George Bayer
1958	Wes Ellis, Jr.
1959	Doug Ford
1960	Art Wall, Jr.
1961	Jack Cupit
1962	Ted Kroll
1963	Doug Ford
1964	K. D. G. Nagle
1965	Gene Littler
1966	Don Massengale
1967	Billy Casper, Jr.
1968	R. J. Charles
1969	Tommy Aaron
1970	**Kermit Zarley**
1971	**Lee Trevino**
1972	**Gay Brewer**
1973	Tom Weiskopf
1974	Bobby Nichols
1975	Tom Weiskopf
1976	Jerry Pate
1977	Lee Trevino

Canadian Amateur

Year	Winner
1895	T. H. Harley
1896	Stewart Gillespie
1897	W. A. H. Kerr
1898	George S. Lyon
1899	Vere C. Brown
1900	George S. Lyon
1901	W. A. H. Kerr
1902	F. R. Martin
1903	George S. Lyon
1904	Percy Taylor
1905	George S. Lyon
1906	George S. Lyon
1907	George S. Lyon
1908	Alex Wilson, Jr.
1909	E. Legge
1910	Fritz Martin
1911	G. H. Hutton
1912	George S. Lyon
1913	G. H. Turpin
1914	George S. Lyon
1915–1918	Not played
1919	William McLuckie
1920	C. B. Grier
1921	Frank Thompson
1922	C. C. Fraser
1923	W. J. Thompson
1924	Frank Thompson
1925	Donald D. Carrick

Year	Winner
1926	C. Ross Somerville
1927	Donald D. Carrick
1928	C. Ross Somerville
1929	Eddie Held.
1930	C. Ross Somerville
1931	C. Ross Somerville
1932	Gordon Taylor
1933	Albert W. Campbell
1934	Albert W. Campbell
1935	C. Ross Somerville
1936	Fred Haas, Jr.
1937	C. Ross Somerville
1938	Ted Adams
1939	Kenneth Black
1940–1945	Not played
1946	Henry Martell
1947	Frank Stranahan
1948	Frank Stranahan
1949	Richard Chapman
1950	William Mawhinney
1951	Walter McElroy
1952	Larry Bouchey
1953	Don Cherry
1954	J. Harvie Ward, Jr.
1955	Moe Norman
1956	Moe Norman
1957	Nick Weslock
1958	Bruce Castator
1959	John Johnston
1960	R. K. Alexander
1961	Gary Cowan
1962	Reg Taylor
1963	Nick Weslock
1964	Nick Weslock
1965	Bunky Henry
1966	Nick Weslock
1967	S. Jones
1968	Jim Doyle
1969	Wayne McDonald
1970	**Allen Miller**
1971	Dick Siderowf
1972	**Doug Roxburgh**
1973	George Burns III
1974	Doug Roxburgh
1975	Jim Nelford
1976	Jim Nelford
1977	Rod Spittle

Women's Canadian Open Amateur

Year	Winner
1901	L. Young
1902	M. Thomson
1903	F. Harvey
1904	F. Harvey
1905	M. Thomson
1906	M. Thomson
1907	M. Thomson
1908	M. Thomson
1909	V. H. Anderson
1910	Dorothy Campbell
1911	Dorothy Campbell

Year	Winner
1912	Dorothy Campbell
1913	M. Todd
1914–1918	Not played
1919	Ada Mackenzie
1920	Alexa Stirling
1921	Cecil Leitch
1922	Mrs. W. A. Gavin
1923	Glenna Collett
1924	Glenna Collett
1925	Ada Mackenzie
1926	Ada Mackenzie
1927	Helen Payson
1928	Virginia Wilson
1929	Helen Hicks
1930	Maureen Orcutt
1931	Maureen Orcutt
1932	Margery Kirkham
1933	Ada Mackenzie
1934	Mrs. W. G. Fraser[a]
1935	Ada Mackenzie
1936	Mrs. A. B. Darling
1937	Mrs. J. Rogers
1938	Mrs. F. J. Mulqueen
1939–1946	Not played
1947	Grace Lenczyk
1948	Grace Lenczyk
1949	Grace DeMoss
1950	Dorothy Kielty
1951	Marlene Stewart
1952	Edean Anderson
1953	Barbara Romack
1954	Marlene Stewart
1955	Marlene Stewart
1956	Marlene Stewart
1957	Betty Stanhope
1958	Mrs. J. D. Streit[b]
1959	Mrs. J. D. Streit
1960	Judy Darling
1961	Judy Darling
1962	Gayle Hitchens
1963	Mrs. J. D. Streit
1964	Margaret Masters
1965	Jocelyn Bourassa
1966	Hélène Gagnon
1967	Bridget Jackson
1968	Mrs. J. D. Streit
1969	Mrs. J. D. Streit
1970	**Mrs. G. H. Moore**
1971	**Jocelyn Bourassa**
1972	**Mrs. J. D. Streit**
1973	Mrs. J. D. Streit
1974	Debbie Massey
1975	Debbie Massey
1976	Debbie Massey
1977	Mrs. Cathy Sherk

[a] Mrs. Fraser is the former Alexa Stirling.
[b] Mrs. Streit is the former Marlene Stewart.

Dutch Open

Year	Winner
1919	D. Oosterveer

Year	Winner
1920	H. Burrows
1921	H. Burrows
1922	Geo. Pannell
1923	H. Burrows
1924	Aubrey Boomer
1925	Aubrey Boomer
1926	Aubrey Boomer
1927	Percy Boomer
1928	E. R. Whitcombe
1929	J. J. Taylor
1930	J. Oosterveer
1931	F. Dyer
1932	A. Boyer
1933	M. Dallemagne
1934	S. F. Brews
1935	S. F. Brews
1936	F. Van Donck
1937	F. Van Donck
1938	A. H. Padgham
1939	A. D. Locke
1940–1947	Not played
1948	Cecil Denny
1949	J. Adams
1950	R. DeVicenzo
1951	F. Van Donck
1952	Cecil Denny
1953	F. Van Donck
1954	Ugo Grappasonni
1955	A. Angelini
1956	A. Cerda
1957	J. Jacobs
1958	D. Thomas
1959	S. Sewgolum
1960	S. Sewgolum
1961	B. B. S. Wilkes
1962	B. G. C. Huggett
1963	R. Waltman
1964	S. Sewgolum
1965	A. Miguel
1966	R. Sota
1967	P. Townsend
1968	J. Cockin
1969	Guy Wolstenholme
1970	**Vicente Fernandez**
1971	Ramon Sota
1972	**Jack Newton**
1973	Jack Newton
1974	Doug McClelland
1975	Brian Barnes
1976	Severiano Ballesteros
1977	Bob Byman

French Open

Year	Winner
1906	A. Massy
1907	A. Massy
1908	J. H. Taylor
1909	J. H. Taylor
1910	James Braid
1911	A. Massy
1912	Jean Gassiat

Year	Winner
1913	George Duncan
1914	J. Douglas Edgar
1915–1919	Not played
1920	Walter Hagen
1921	Aubrey Boomer
1922	Aubrey Boomer
1923	Jas. Ockenden
1924	C. J. H. Tolley
1925	A. Massy
1926	Aubrey Boomer
1927	George Duncan
1928	C. J. H. Tolley
1929	Aubrey Boomer
1930	E. R. Whitcombe
1931	Aubrey Boomer
1932	A. J. Lacey
1933	B. Gadd
1934	S. F. Brews
1935	S. F. Brews
1936	M. Dallemagne
1937	M. Dallemagne
1938	M. Dallemagne
1939	M. Pose
1940–1945	Not played
1946	T. Henry Cotton
1947	T. Henry Cotton
1948	F. Cavalo
1949	U. Grapposonni
1950	R. DeVicenzo
1951	H. Hassanein
1952	A. D. Locke
1953	A. D. Locke
1954	F. Van Donck
1955	Byron Nelson
1956	A. Miguel
1957	F. Van Donck
1958	F. Van Donck
1959	D. C. Thomas
1960	R. DeVicenzo
1961	K. D. G. Nagle
1962	A. Murray
1963	B. Devlin
1964	R. DeVicenzo
1965	R. Sota
1966	D. J. Hutchinson
1967	B. J. Hunt
1968	P. J. Butler
1969	J. Garialde
1970	**David Graham**
1971	Lu Liang Huan
1972	**Barry Jaeckel**
1973	Barry Jaeckel
1974	Peter Oosterhuis
1975	Peter Oosterhuis
1976	Vincent Tshabalala
1977	Severiano Ballesteros

German Open

Year	Winner
1911	Harry Vardon
1912	John H. Taylor

Year	Winner
1913–1925	Not played
1926	P. Alliss
1927	P. Alliss
1928	P. Alliss
1929	P. Alliss
1930	A. Boyer
1931	R. Golias
1932	A. Boyer
1933	P. Alliss
1934	A. H. Padgham
1935	A. Boyer
1936	A. Boyer
1937	T. Henry Cotton
1938	T. Henry Cotton
1939	T. Henry Cotton
1940–1950	Not played
1951	A. Cerda
1952	A. Cerda
1953	F. Van Donck
1954	A. D. Locke
1955	K. Bousfield
1956	F. Van Donck
1957	H. Weetman
1958	F. DeLuca
1959	K. Bousfield
1960	Peter W. Thomson
1961	B. J. Hunt
1962	F. R. Verwey
1963	B. G. C. Huggett
1964	R. DeVicenzo
1965	H. R. Henning
1966	R. Stanton
1967	D. Swaelens
1968	B. Franklin
1969	J. Garialde
1970	J. Garialde
1971	Neil Coles
1972	Graham Marsh
1973	Graham Marsh
1974	Francisco Abreu
1975	Simon Owen
1976	Simon Hobday
1977	Tienie Britz

Hong Kong Open

Year	Winner
1959	Lu Liang Huan
1960	Peter W. Thomson
1961	K. D. G. Nagle
1962	Len Woodward
1963	Hsieh Yung Yo
1964	Hsieh Yung Yo
1965	Peter W. Thomson
1966	Frank Phillips
1967	Peter W. Thomson
1968	R. Vines
1969	Teruo Sugihara
1970	Isao Katsumata
1971	Orville Moody
1972	Walter Godfrey

Year	Winner
1973	Walter Godfrey
1974	Frank Phillips
1975	Lu Liang Huan
1976	Ho Ming-chung
1977	Hsieh Min-nan

India Open

Year	Winner
1965	P. G. Sethi[a]
1966	Peter W. Thomson
1967	K. Hosoishi
1968	K. Hosoishi
1969	B. Arda
1970	Chen Chien Chin
1971	Graham Marsh
1972	Brian Jones
1973	Brian Jones
1974	Graham Marsh
1975	Kuo Chi Hsiung
1976	Peter W. Thomson
1977	Brian Jones

[a] Amateur.

Italian Open

Year	Winner
1925	F. Pasquali
1926	A. Boyer
1927	Percy Allis
1928	A. Boyer
1929	R. Golias
1930	A. Boyer
1931	A. Boyer
1932	A. Boomer
1933	not played
1934	N. Nutley
1935	Percy Alliss
1936	T. H. Cotton
1937	M. Dallemagne
1938	F. Van Donck
1939–46	not played
1947	F. Van Donck
1948	A. Casera
1949	H. Hassanein
1950	U. Grappasonni
1951	J. Adams
1952	E. C. Brown
1953	F. Van Donck
1954	U. Grappasonni
1955	F. Van Donck
1956	A. Cerda
1957	H. Henning
1958	Peter Alliss
1959	Peter W. Thomson
1960	B. B. S. Wilkes
1961–70	not played
1971	R. Sota
1972	N. Wood
1973	Norman Wood

Year	Winner
1974	Tony Jacklin
1975	Peter Oosterhuis
1976	Baldovino Dassu
1977	Angel Gallardo

Japanese Open

Year	Winner
1927	R. Akahoshi
1928	R. Asami
1929	T. Miyamoto
1930	T. Miyamoto
1931	R. Asami
1932	T. Miyamoto
1933	K. Nakamura
1934	Not played
1935	T. Miyamoto
1936	T. Miyamoto
1937	Chin Sei Sui
1938	R. M. Fuku
1939	T. Toda
1940	T. Miyamoto
1941	En Toku Shun
1942–1949	Not played
1950	Y. Hayashi
1951	Son Shi Kin
1952	T. Nakamura
1953	Son Shi Kin
1954	Y. Hayashi
1955	K. Ono
1956	T. Nakamura
1957	H. Kobari
1958	T. Nakamura
1959	Chen Ching-Po
1960	H. Kobari
1961	K. Hosoishi
1962	T. Sugihara
1963	T. Toda
1964	H. Sugimoto
1965	T. Kitta
1966	S. Sato
1967	T. Kitta
1968	T. Kono
1969	H. Sugimoto
1970	M. Kitta
1971	Y. Fujii
1972	Hahn Chang Sang
1973	Hahn Chang Sang
1974	Ben Arda
1975	Masashi Ozaki
1976	Kosaku Shimada
1977	Severiano Ballesteros

Korea Open

Year	Winner
1970	Hahn Chang Sang
1971	Hahn Chang Sang
1972	Hahn Chang Sang
1973	Hahn Chang Sang
1974	Kim Seung Hak

Year	Winner
1975	Cho Tae Wong
1976	Kazunari Takahashi
1977	Ho Min-chung

Malaysian Open

Year	Winner
1963	W. Dunk
1964	T. Ishii
1965	T. Ishii
1966	H. R. Henning
1967	I. Legaspi
1968	K. Hosoishi
1969	K. Hosoishi
1970	B. Arda
1971	Takaaki Kono
1972	Takashi Murakami
1973	Takashi Murakami
1974	Hideyo Sugimoto
1975	Graham Marsh
1976	Hsu Sheng-san
1977	Stewart Ginn

New Zealand Open

Year	Winner
1907	A. D. S. Duncan
1908	J. A. Clements
1909	J. A. Clements
1910	A. D. S. Duncan
1911	A. D. S. Duncan
1912	J. A. Clements
1913	E. S. Douglas
1914	E. S. Douglas
1915–1918	Not played
1919	E. S. Douglas
1920	J. H. Kirkwood
1921	E. S. Douglas
1922	A. Brooks
1923	A. Brooks
1924	E. J. Moss
1925	E. M. Macfarlane
1926	A. J. Shaw
1927	E. J. Moss
1928	S. Morpeth
1929	A. J. Shaw
1930	A. J. Shaw
1931	A. J. Shaw
1932	A. J. Shaw
1933	E. J. Moss
1934	A. J. Shaw
1935	A. Murray
1936	A. J. Shaw
1937	J. P. Hornabrook
1938	A. D. Locke
1939	J. P. Hornabrook
1940–1945	Not played
1946	R. H. Glading
1947	R. H. Glading
1948	A. Murray
1949	James Galloway

Year	Winner
1950	Peter W. Thomson
1951	Peter W. Thomson
1952	A. Murray
1953	Peter W. Thomson
1954	R. J. Charles
1955	Peter W. Thomson
1956	K. W. Berwick
1957	K. D. G. Nagle
1958	K. D. G. Nagle
1959	Peter W. Thomson
1960	Peter W. Thomson
1961	Peter W. Thomson
1962	K. D. G. Nagle
1963	B. W. Devlin
1964	K. D. G. Nagle
1965	Peter W. Thomson
1966	R. J. Charles
1967	K. D. G. Nagle
1968	K. D. G. Nagle
1969	K. D. G. Nagle
1970	R. J. Charles
1971	Peter W. Thomson
1972	W. Dunk
1973	W. Dunk
1974	Bob Charles
1975	Bob Gilder
1976	Simon Owen
1977	Bob Byman

Philippine Open

Year	Winner
1962	C. Tugot
1963	B. Arda
1964	Peter W. Thomson
1965	Lu Liang Huan
1966	L. Silverio
1967	Hsu Sheng San[a]
1968	Hsu Sheng San[a]
1969	Haruo Yasuda[a]
1970	Hsieh Yung Yo
1971	Chen Chien-Chung
1972	Hideyo Sugimoto
1973	Hideyo Sugimoto
1974	Kim Seung Hak
1975	Lu Liang Huan
1976	Quintin Mancao
1977	Hsieh Yung Yo

[a] Amateur.

Portuguese Open

Year	Winner
1953	E. C. Brown
1954	A. Miguel
1955	F. Van Donck
1956	A. Miguel
1957	Not played
1958	P. Alliss
1959	S. Miguel
1960	K. Bousfield

Year	Winner
1961	K. Bousfield
1962	A. Angelini
1963	R. Sota
1964	A. Miguel
1965	Not played
1966	A. Angelini
1967	A. Gallardo
1968	Max Faulkner
1969	B. Hunt
1970	R. Sota
1971	L. Platts
1972	G. Garrido
1973	G. Garrido
1974	Jaime Benito
1975	Brian Huggett
1976	Salvador Balbuena
1977	Manuel Ramos

Singapore Open

Year	Winner
1957	H. Knaggs
1958	D. W. McMullen
1959	R. C. W. Stokes
1960	Not played
1961	F. Phillips
1962	Brian Wilkes
1963	A. Brookes
1964	T. Ball
1965	F. Phillips
1966	R. Newdick
1967	B. Arda
1968	Hsieh Yung Yo
1969	Tomio Kamata
1970	Hsieh Yung Yo
1971	Haruo Yasuda
1972	Takaaki Kono
1973	Takaaki Kono
1974	B. Arda
1975	Eleuterio Nival
1976	Kensahiko Uchida
1977	Hsu Chi-san

South African Open

Year	Winner
1905	A. G. Gray
1906	A. G. Gray
1907	L. B. Waters
1908	G. Fotheringham
1909	J. Fotheringham
1910	G. Fotheringham
1911	G. Fotheringham
1912	G. Fotheringham
1913	J. A. W. Prentice
1914	G. Fotheringham
1915–1918	Not played
1919	H. G. Stewart
1920	L. B. Waters
1921	J. Brews
1922	F. Jangle

Year	Winner
1923	J. Brews
1924	B. H. Elkin
1925	S. F. Brews
1926	J. Brews
1927	S. F. Brews
1928	J. Brews
1929	A. Tosh
1930	S. F. Brews
1931	S. F. Brews
1932	C. McIlvenny
1933	S. F. Brews
1934	S. F. Brews
1935	A. D. Locke
1936	C. E. Olander
1937	A. D. Locke
1938	A. D. Locke
1939	A. D. Locke
1940	A. D. Locke
1941–1945	Not played
1946	A. D. Locke
1947	R. W. Glennie
1948	M. Janks
1949	S. F. Brews
1950	A. D. Locke
1951	A. D. Locke
1952	S. F. Brews
1953	J. R. Boyd
1954	R. C. Taylor
1955	A. D. Locke
1956	Gary Player
1957	H. R. Henning
1958	A. A. Stewart
1959	D. J. Hutchinson
1960	Gary Player
1961	R. Waltman
1962	H. R. Henning
1963	R. Waltman
1964	Alan Henning
1965	Gary Player
1966	Gary Player
1967	Gary Player
1968	Gary Player
1969	Gary Player
1970	**T. Horton**
1971	**Simon Hobday**
1972	**Gary Player**
1973	Gary Player
1974	Bob Charles
1975	Bobby Cole
1976	Dale Hayes
1977	Gary Player

Year	Winner
1920	Not played
1921	E. Laffitte
1922	Not played
1923	A. de la Torre
1924	Not played
1925	A. de la Torre
1926	F. Bernardino
1927	A. Massy
1928	A. Massy
1929	E. Laffitte
1930	J. Bernardino
1931	Not played
1932	G. Gonzalez
1933	G. Gonzalez
1934	M. Provencio
1935	T. Cayarga
1936–1940	Not played
1941	M. Provencio
1942	G. Gonzalez
1943	M. Provencio
1944	Don Luis I. Arana
1945	C. Celles
1946	M. Morcillo
1947	Don M. Gonzalez
1948	M. Morcillo
1949	M. Morcillo
1950	A. Cerda
1951	M. Provencio
1952	Max Faulkner
1953	Max Faulkner
1954	Sebastian Miguel
1955	H. de Lamaze
1956	P. Alliss
1957	Max Faulkner
1958	P. Alliss
1959	Peter W. Thomson
1960	S. Miguel
1961	A. Miguel
1963	R. Sota
1964	A. Miguel
1965	A. M. Gutierrez
1966	R. DeVicenzo
1967	S. Miguel
1968	R. Shaw
1969	J. Geraialde
1970	**A. Gallardo**
1971	**Dale Hayes**
1972	**A. Garrido**
1973	A. Garrido
1974	Neil Coles
1975	Jerry Heard
1976	Eddie Polland
1977	Bernard Gallacher

Spanish Open

Year	Winner
1912	A. Massy
1913–1915	Not played
1916	A. de la Torre
1917	A. de la Torre
1918	Not played
1919	A. de la Torre

Swiss Open

Year	Winner
1923	Aleck Ross
1924	Percy Boomer
1925	Aleck Ross
1926	Aleck Ross

Year	Winner
1927–1928	Not played
1929	A. Wilson
1930	A. Boyer
1931	M. Dallemagne
1932–1933	Not played
1934	A. Boyer
1935	A. Boyer
1936	F. Francis
1937	M. Dallemagne
1938	J. Saubaber
1939	F. Cavalo
1940–1947	Not played
1948	U. Grappasonni
1949	M. Dallemagne
1950	A. Casera
1951	E. C. Brown
1952	U. Grappasonni
1953	F. Van Donck
1954	A. D. Locke
1955	F. Van Donck
1956	D. J. Rees
1957	A. Angelini
1958	K. Bousfield
1959	D. J. Rees
1960	H. R. Henning
1961	K. D. G. Nagle
1962	R. J. Charles
1963	D. J. Rees
1964	H. R. Henning
1965	H. R. Henning
1966	A. Angelini
1967	R. Vines
1968	R. Bernardini
1969	R. Bernardini
1970	**Graham Marsh**
1971	**Peter Townsend**
1972	**Graham Marsh**
1973	Graham Marsh
1974	Hugh Baiocchi
1975	Bob Charles
1976	Manuel Pinero
1977	Severiano Ballesteros

Taiwan (China) Open

Year	Winner
1969	Hideyo Sugimoto

Year	Winner
1970	Chang Chung Fa
1971	Chang Chung Fa
1972	**Haruo Yasuda**
1973	Haruo Yasuda
1974	Eleuterio Nival
1975	Kuo Chi Hsiung
1976	Hsu Chi-san
1977	Hsieh Min-nan

Thailand Open

Year	Winner
1970	**David Graham**
1971	Liang Huan-Lu
1972	**Hsieh Min-nan**
1973	Hsieh Min-nan
1974	Graham Marsh
1975	Toshihiro Hitomi
1976	Ben Arda
1977	Yurio Akitomi

World Senior Amateur Championship

Year	Winner
1960	Harry Strasburger (U.S.)
1961	Howard Creel (U.S.)
1962	Howard Creel (U.S.)
1963	George Haggarty (U.S.)
1964	Dorsey Nevergall (U.S.)
1965	Jack Barkel (Australia)
1966	Cecil Dee (U.S.)
1967	Cecil Dee (U.S.)
1968	David Goodman (U.S.)
1969	David Goodman (U.S.)
1970	Merrill Carlsmith (U.S.)
1971	Jude Poynter (U.S.)
1972	Howard Everitt (U.S.)
1973	W. F. Colm (U.S.)
1974	Larry Pendleton (U.S.)
1975	Truman Connell (U.S.)
1976	Robert Willits (U.S.)
1977	Earl Burt (U.S.)

World Series of Golf (Men)

This event involved the winners of the Big Four Tournaments (United States Open and PGA, Masters, and British Open) in the original format.

It was altered in 1976 to include a true world field, and was designed to be the climax of the PGA Tour schedule. From the beginning it was played at the Firestone Country Club, Akron, Ohio.

Year	Winner	Score	Runner-Up	Score
1962	Jack Nicklaus	135	Arnold Palmer	139
			Gary Player	139
1963	Jack Nicklaus	140	Julius Boros	141

Year	Winner	Score	Runner-Up	Score
1964	Tony Lema	138	Ken Venturi	143
1965	Gary Player	139	Jack Nicklaus	142
1966	Gene Littler[a]	143	Jack Nicklaus	143
1967	Jack Nicklaus	144	Gay Brewer, Jr.	145
1968	Gary Player[b]	143	Bob Goalby	143
1969	Orville Moody	141	George Archer	143
1970	Jack Nicklaus	136	Billy Casper, Jr.	139
			Dave Stockton	139
1971	Charles Coody	141	Jack Nicklaus	142
1972	Gary Player	142	Jack Nicklaus	144
			Lee Trevino	144
1973	Tom Weiskopf	137		
1974	Lee Trevino	139		
1975	Tom Watson	140		
1976[c]	Jack Nicklaus	275		
1977	Lanny Wadkins	267		

[a] Littler won play-off on first extra hole.
[b] Player won play-off on fourth extra hole.
[c] Changed to 72 holes.

World Match Play Championship

This tournament was originated by Mark H. McCormack, business representative for some of the leading golfers of the world and was called the Piccadilly World Match Play Championship. It consisted of 36-hole match play elimination among the top eight golfers of the year, including the defending tournament champion and the winners of the Masters, U.S. Open, British Open, and British PGA Match Play. In 1977, it was taken over by the Colgate-Palmolive Company and the field was expanded to sixteen players. Since its beginning the tournament has been played at the Wentworth Club in England.

Year	Winner	Runner-Up	Score
1964	Arnold Palmer	Neil Coles	2 & 1
1965	Gary Player	Peter Thomson	3 & 2
1966	Gary Player	Jack Nicklaus	6 & 4
1967	Arnold Palmer	Peter Thomson	2 up
1968	Gary Player	Robert J. Charles	1 up
1969	Robert J. Charles	Gene Littler	1 up (37 holes)
1970	Jack Nicklaus	Lee Trevino	2 & 1
1971	Gary Player	Jack Nicklaus	5 & 4
1972	Tom Weiskopf	Lee Trevino	4 & 3
1973	Gary Player	Graham Marsh	at 40th
1974	Hale Irwin	Gary Player	2 & 1
1975	Hale Irwin	Al Geiberger	4 & 2
1976	David Graham	Hale Irwin	at 38th
1977	Graham Marsh	Raymond Floyd	5 & 3

INTERNATIONAL TEAM MATCHES

The Walker Cup Match

The Walker Cup is played for by teams of men amateur golfers selected from clubs under the jurisdiction of the United States Golf Association on the one side and from England, Scotland, Wales, Northern Ireland, and the Republic of Ireland on the other. The teams consist of not more than ten players (eight players and two alternates) and a captain. The United States team is selected by the United States Golf Association, and the British team by the Royal and Ancient Golf Club of St. Andrews, Scotland.

The teams play four 18-hole foursomes in the morning and eight 18-hole singles in the afternoon on each of the two days. Prior to 1963, the schedule comprised four 36-hole foursomes the first day and eight 36-hole singles the second day. Victory in a match scores one point. When a match goes the full distance without a decision, it is not played to a conclusion in extra holes and no score is made by either side. This scoring system has always prevailed.

A Walker Cup Match is held every two years, alternately in the United States and Great Britain. Either the larger United States ball or the smaller British ball is permissible in an international match. The country winning the Cup takes custody of it for the ensuing two years. In case of a tie, each country holds the Cup for one year. Incidentally, the Cup is named in honor of George H. Walker, President of USGA in the 1920's, who nurtured the program through its formative years.

The matches are scheduled to precede or follow the amateur championships of the host country, so players may compete in both the cup matches and the amateur championship.

Year	Winner/Loser	Site
1922	United States, 8	National Golf Links of America
	Great Britain, 4	Southampton, N.Y.
1923	United States, 6	St. Andrews, Scotland
	Great Britain, 5,	
	one match halved	
1924	United States, 9	Garden City Golf Club
	Great Britain, 3	Garden City, N.Y.
1926	United States, 6	St. Andrews, Scotland
	Great Britain, 5,	
	one match halved	
1928	United States, 11	Chicago Golf Club
	Great Britain, 1	Wheaton, Ill.
1930	United States, 10	Royal St. Georges GC
	Great Britain, 2	Sandwich, England
1932	United States, 8	The Country Club
	Great Britain, 1,	Brookline, Mass.
	three matches halved	
1934	United States, 9	St. Andrews, Scotland
	Great Britain, 2,	
	one match halved	
1936	United States, 9	Pine Valley Golf Club
	Great Britain, 0,	Clementon, N.J.
	three matches halved	
1938	Great Britain, 7	St. Andrews, Scotland
	United States, 4,	
	one match halved	
1947	United States, 8	St. Andrews, Scotland
	Great Britain, 4	
1949	United States, 10	Winged Foot GC
	Great Britain, 2	Mamaroneck, N.Y.
1951	United States, 6	Royal Birkdale Golf Club
	Great Britain, 3,	Southport, England
	three matches halved	
1953	United States, 9	Kittansett Club
	Great Britain, 3	Marion, Mass.
1955	United States, 10	St. Andrews, Scotland
	Great Britain, 2	
1957	United States, 8	Minikahda Club
	Great Britain, 3,	Minneapolis, Minn.
	one match halved	
1959	United States, 9	Honourable Company of Edinburgh Golfers
	Great Britain, 3	Muirfield, Scotland
1961	United States, 11	Seattle Golf Club
	Great Britain, 1	Seattle, Wash.

Year	Winner/Loser	Site
1963	United States, 12	Ailsa Course
	Great Britain, 8,	Turnberry, Scotland
	four matches halved	
1965	United States, 11	Baltimore CC
	Great Britain, 11	Five Farms, Baltimore, Md.
	two matches halved	
1967	United States, 13	Royal St. Georges GC
	Great Britain, 7,	Sandwich, England
	four matches halved	
1969	United States, 10	Milwaukee CC
	Great Britain, 8	Milwaukee, Wis.
	six matches halved	
1971	**Great Britain, 12**	St. Andrews, Scotland
	United States, 10	
	two matches halved	
1973	United States, 14	The Country Club
	Great Britain, 7	Brookline, Mass.
1975	United States, 15	St. Andrews, Scotland
	Great Britain, 8	
	one match halved	
1977	United States, 16	Shinnecock Hills GC
	Great Britain, 8	Southampton, N.Y.

The Curtis Cup Match

The Curtis Cup is played for by teams of women amateur golfers representing England, Scotland, Wales, Northern Ireland, and the Republic of Ireland on the one side and the United States on the other. The teams consist of not more than eight players (six players and usually two alternates) and a captain. The United States Team is selected by the United States Golf Association, and the British Team by the Ladies Golf Union. Players must be citizens of the country they represent.

Beginning in 1964, the teams played three 18-hole foursomes on the morning of each day and six 18-hole singles in the afternoon of each day. Previously, there were three 36-hole foursomes the first day and six 36-hole singles the second day. Victory in a match scores one point. When a match goes the full distance without a decision, it is not played to a conclusion in extra holes, and a half-point is awarded to each team. This scoring system has always prevailed.

The Curtis Cup Match is held biennially in the United States and the British Isles alternately. Either the larger United States ball or the smaller British ball is permissible in an international match. The country winning the Cup takes custody of it for the ensuing two years. In the event of a tie, the holder retains the Cup. The Cup was donated by Misses Harriot and Margaret Curtis, both former holders of the U.S. Amateur title.

Year	Winner/Loser	Site
1932	United States, 5½	Wentworth Golf Club
	Great Britain, 3½	Wentworth, England
1934	United States, 6½	Chevy Chase Club
	Great Britain, 2½	Chevy Chase, Md.
1936	United States, 4½	King's Course
	Great Britain, 4½	Gleneagles, Scotland
1938	United States, 5½	Essex Country Club
	Great Britain, 3½	Manchester, Mass.
1948	United States, 6½	Royal Birkdale Golf Club
	Great Britain, 2½	Southport, England
1950	United States, 7½	CC of Buffalo
	Great Britain, 1½	Williamsville, N.Y.

A smiling Lee Trevino shows off *The* Cup, on his winning of 1971 British Open. In the background is the second-place finisher, Lu Liang-Huan of Taiwan. Trevino also won The Cup in 1972.

Billy Casper watches Gay Brewer drive off during the play-off for the Alcan Golfer of the Year trophy at the Old Course at St. Andrews in 1967. Brewer won the play-off. This famous international event was discontinued in 1971.

The Curtis Cup was donated by Harriot Curtis (left), the 1906 U.S. Amateur Champion, and Margaret Curtis (right), the U.S. Amateur Champion in 1907, 1911, and 1912.

Year	Winner/Loser	Site
1952	Great Britain, 5	Honourable Company of
	United States, 4	Edinburgh Golfers
		Muirfield, Scotland
1954	United States, 6	Merion GC (East Course)
	Great Britain, 3	Ardmore, Pa.
1956	Great Britain, 5	Prince's GC
	United States, 4	Sandwich Bay, England
1958	Great Britain, 4½	Brae Burn CC
	United States, 4½	West Newton, Mass.
1960	United States, 6½	Lindrick GC
	Great Britain, 2½	Workshop, England
1962	United States, 8	Broadmoor GC (East Course)
	Great Britain, 1	Colorado Springs, Colo.
1964	United States, 10½	Royal Porthcawl GC
	Great Britain, 7½	Porthcawl, South Wales
1966	United States, 13	Virginia Hot Springs Golf & Tennis Club
	Great Britain, 5	(Cascades Course)
		Hot Springs, Va.
1968	United States, 10½	Royal County Downs GC
	Great Britain, 7½	Newcastle, North Ireland
1970	United States, 11½	Brae Burn CC
	Great Britain, 6½	West Newton, Mass.
1972	United States, 10	Western Gailes GC
	Great Britain, 8	Scotland
1974	United States, 10	San Francisco GC
	Great Britain, 4	San Francisco, Calif.
1976	United States, 11½	Royal Lytham and St. Anne's GC
	Great Britain, 6½	St.-Anne's-on-the-Sea, England

World Amateur Team Championship

The World Amateur Team Championship is sponsored by the World Amateur Golf Council, which comprises national governing bodies of golf in fifty-five countries. The council had only thirty-two member countries in its inaugural year of 1958.

The Championship consists of 72 holes, stroke play, with 18 holes played on each of four days. Each country's team may have three or four players, as may be preferred. In each 18-hole round the total of the three lowest scores by players from each team constitutes the team score for that round. The four-day total of these daily three-player team scores is the team's score for the Championship. If there is a tie, an 18-hole play-off between the tying teams determines the winner.

Players must be amateur golfers under the Rules of Amateur Status of either the Royal and Ancient Golf Club of St. Andrews, Scotland, or the United States Golf Association. Players must be citizens of the country represented, except that in cases where a team of citizens would be impracticable, players nor-

mally resident in the country concerned may be included. The Championship is rotated biennially among these geographical zones —European-African, American, and Australasian—in that order. The first match, played

The 1964 United States team that captured the Curtis Cup gather round their captain Mrs. Theodore Hawes, holding the trophy. The American amateur women golfers are (left to right): (front row) Nancy Roth, Mrs. Hawes, Peggy Conley; (behind Mrs. Hawes) Phillis Ann Preuss; (back row) Barbara McIntire, Barbara Fay White, Carol Sorenson, and Joanne Gunderson.

at St. Andrews in Scotland, drew players from twenty-nine different countries; ten years later, at Melbourne Golf Club, there were thirty-five.

In selecting the players for the World Amateur Team Championship, as well as the other *amateur* team matches such as Americas Cup, Walker Cup, and so on, there is no point system or any hard and fast rule. The USGA names the players on the basis of previous performance, with most of the emphasis on how they fared in recent United States and British Amateurs, the Trans-Mississippi, the Western Amateur, and the North and South Amateur, as well as in Open competition. The winning team receives a silver replica of the Eisenhower Trophy and custody of the Trophy for the ensuing two years. Members of the winning team receive gold medals; members of the second-place team, silver medals; members of the third-place team, bronze medals. The second- and third-place teams also receive replicas of the Eisenhower Trophy.

Year	Site	Champion	Runner-Up
1958	St. Andrews Golf Club, Scotland	Australia[a]	United States
1960	Merion Country Club, United States	United States	Australia
1962	Fuji Golf Club, Japan	United States	Canada
1964	Olgiata Golf Club, Italy	Great Britain & Ireland	Canada
1966	Club de Golf Mexico, Mexico	Australia	United States
1968	Royal Melbourne Golf Club, Australia	United States	Great Britain & Ireland
1970	Real Club de la Puerta de Hierro, Spain	United States	New Zealand
1972	Olivos Golf Club, Argentina	United States	Australia
1974	La Romana Club, Dominican Republic	United States	Japan
1976	Penina Golf Club, Algarve, Portugal	Great Britain & Ireland	Japan

[a] Australia won the play-off.

Women's World Amateur Team Championship

The first Women's World Amateur Team Championship was conducted by the French Golf Federation. Subsequent holdings, beginning in 1966, have been sponsored by the World Amateur Golf Council. Teams from twenty-five countries competed in 1964, while only seventeen took part in the 1968 event.

The Championship consists of 72 holes, stroke play, with 18 holes played on each of four days. Each country's team may have two or three players, as may be preferred.

In each 18-hole round the total of the two lowest scores by players from each team constitutes the team total for that round. The four-day aggregate of these daily two-player team scores is the team's score for the Championship. If there is a tie, an 18-hole play-off between the tying teams determines the winner. Players must be amateur golfers under the Rules of Amateur Status of either the Royal and Ancient Golf Club of St. Andrews, Scotland, or the United States Golf Association. Players must be citizens of the country represented, except that in cases where a team of citizens would be impracticable, players normally resident in the country concerned may be included.

The Championship is rotated biennially among three geographical zones—European-African, American, and Australasian—in that order. The winning team receives custody of the Espirito Santo Trophy for the ensuing two years.

Year	Site	Champion	Runner-Up
1964	St. Germain Golf Club, France	France	United States
1966	Mexico City Country Club, Mexico	United States	Canada
1968	Victoria Golf Club, Australia	United States	Australia
1970	Club de Campo, Spain	United States	France
1972	Hindu Country Club, Argentina	United States	France
1974	La Romana Club, Dominican Republic	United States	Great Britain & Ireland
1976	Vilamoura Golf Club, Algarve, Portugal	United States	France

The Ryder Cup Match

The Ryder Cup Matches were the end result of a match played between representatives of the American and British Professional Golfers' Associations in England in 1926, which, incidentally, was won by the British 13½ to 1½ on their native shores. Following this highly successful exhibition, Samuel A. Ryder, a wealthy British seed merchant, offered to donate a solid gold trophy bearing his name to be competed for in a series of matches between professionals of these two nations.

In placing the Ryder Cup in competition, the donor set forth certain terms which have to be observed by the parties concerned so long as the matches are conducted. Included among these stipulations are the following: (1) the matches will be played every other year on a home-and-home basis; (2) while both parties must mutually agree on the specific dates for each match, the host team may select the site and will be responsible for such arrangements and details as are normally the function of a sponsoring group; (3) the matches shall consist of two days of play with the first being devoted to foursomes and the second to singles matches; and (4) each member of the competing teams must be a member of his country's PGA and a native-born citizen of that country. Puerto Rican golfers are considered "native-born" citizens of the United States.

The matches were first officially played for the Ryder Cup in 1927 in the United States. They have been held continuously every other year except for the period from 1938 through 1946, when the exigencies of World War II forced their suspension.

In 1978, after the series had become heavily one-sided because of United States' domination, a radical change in the structure was agreed on. Under the new rules, players born in Europe, as well as in Britain and Ireland, will be eligible to play against the United States. Selection of the team will be based on the British–European Tournament Players Order of Merit, and the new structure was to go into effect for the 1979 matches in the United States.

The American team selection is based on a point system for performance in professional events on the U.S. tour.

Year	Site		Outcome		
1927	Worcester CC, Worcester, Mass.	U.S.	9½	G.B.	2½
1929	Moortown, England	G.B.	7	U.S.	5
1931	Scioto CC, Columbus, Ohio	U.S.	9	G.B.	3
1933	Royal Birkdale GC, Southport, England	G.B.	6½	U.S.	5½
1935	Ridgewood CC, Ridgewood, N.J.	U.S.	9	G.B.	3
1937	Royal Birkdale GC, Southport, England	U.S.	8	G.B.	4

The first Ryder Cup team to win on foreign soil (United States 8–Great Britain 4). The United States team that played at Southport, England, in 1937 included (left to right) (seated) Byron Nelson, Tony Manero, Ralph Guldahl, Denny Shute, and Johnny Revolta; (standing) Walter Hagen (captain), Ed Dudley, Henry Picard, Gene Sarazen, Sam Snead, Horton Smith, and Fred Corcoran (manager).

Year	Site	Outcome			
1947	Portland GC, Portland, Ore.	U.S.	11	G.B.	1
1949	Ganton GC, Scarborough, England	U.S.	7	G.B.	5
1951	Pinehurst CC, Pinehurst, N.C.	U.S.	9½	G.B.	2½
1953	Wentworth Club, Wentworth, England	U.S.	6½	G.B.	5½
1955	Thunderbird Ranch & CC, Palm Springs, Calif.	U.S.	8	G.B.	4
1957	Lindrick GC, Yorkshire, England	G.B.	7½	U.S.	4½
1959	Eldorado CC, Palm Desert, Calif.	U.S.	8½	G.B.	3½
1961	Royal Lytham and St. Anne's GC, St.-Anne's-on-the-Sea. England	U.S.	14½	G.B.	9½
1963	East Lake CC, Atlanta, Ga.	U.S.	23	G.B.	9
1965	Royal Birkdale GC, Southport, England	U.S.	19½	G.B.	12½
1967	Champion GC, Houston, Texas	U.S.	23½	G.B.	8½
1969	Royal Birkdale GC, Southport, England	U.S.	16	G.B.	16
1971	Old Warson CC St. Louis, Mo.	U.S.	18½	G.B.	13½
1973	Muirfield, Scotland	U.S.	18	G.B.	13
1975	Laurel Valley GC Ligonier, Pa.	U.S.	21	G.B.	11
1977	Royal Lytham and St. Anne's GC, St.-Anne's-on-the-Sea, England	U.S.	12½	G.B.	7½

The victorious 1961 Ryder Cup Team (left to right): (seated) Jerry Barber (captain), Jay Hebert, Arnold Palmer, and Mike Souchak; (standing) Bill Collins, Doug Ford, Dow Finsterwald, Art Wall, Jr., Billy Casper, Jr., and Gene Littler.

The World Cup Match

Originated in 1953 by John Jay Hopkins, a Canadian industrialist, to stimulate international golf competition and to develop outstanding professionals throughout the world, the World Cup (called the Canada Cup until 1967) is contested annually by two-man teams of professionals from more than forty countries. (Seven countries participated in the inaugural event.) The qualifications for playing in the World Cup vary in different countries. In the United States, the U.S. Open and PGA Championship win-

ners are selected, unless players have other commitments.

While the first World Cup's event was contested over 36 holes, it is now based on 72 holes.

The World Cup is sponsored by the International Golf Association, a nonprofit organization dedicated to creating international goodwill through golf. The finest golfers in the modern era have taken part in the event, although only token prize money is awarded.

Year	Site	Winner	Runner-Up
1953	Beaconsfield Golf Club Montreal	Argentina, 287 Antonio Cerda Roberto DeVicenzo	Canada, 297 Stan Leonard Bill Kerr
1954	Laval-sur-le-Lac Montreal	Australia, 556 Peter W. Thomson K. D. G. Nagle	Argentina, 560 Antonio Cerda Roberto DeVicenzo
1955	Columbia Country Club Washington, D.C.	United States, 560 Ed Furgol Chick Harbert	Australia, 569 Peter W. Thomson K. D. G. Nagle

Year	Site	Winner	Runner-Up
1956	Wentworth Club, Wentworth, England	United States, 567 Ben Hogan Sam Snead	South Africa, 581 A. D. Locke Gary Player
1957	Kasumigaseki Golf Club Tokyo	Japan, 557 Torakichi Nakamura Koichi Ono	United States, 566 Sam Snead Jimmy Demaret
1958	Club de Golf Mexico Mexico City	Ireland, 579 Harry Bradshaw Christy O'Connor	Spain, 582 Angel Miguel Sebastian Miguel
1959	Royal Melbourne Golf Club Melbourne	Australia, 563 Peter W. Thomson K. D. G. Nagle	United States, 573 Sam Snead Cary Middlecoff
1960	Portmarnock Golf Club Dublin	United States, 565 Sam Snead Arnold Palmer	England, 573 Harry Weetman Bernard Hunt
1961	Dorado Golf Club Puerto Rico	United States, 560 Sam Snead Jimmy Demaret	Australia, 572 Peter Thomson K. D. G. Nagle
1962	Jockey Golf Club of San Isidro Buenos Aires	United States, 557 Arnold Palmer Sam Snead	Argentina, 559 Roberto DeVincenzo Fidel DeLuca
1963	Saint Nom la Breteche Club Versailles	United States, 482[a] Jack Nicklaus Arnold Palmer	Spain, 485 Sebastian Miguel Ramon Sota
1964	Royal Kaanapali Golf Course Maui, Hawaii	United States, 554 Jack Nicklaus Arnold Palmer	Argentina, 564 Roberto DeVicenzo L. Ruiz
1965	Club de Campo Madrid	South Africa, 571 Gary Player Harold R. Henning	Spain, 579 Angel Miguel Ramon Sota
1966	Yomiuri Country Club Tokyo	United States, 548 Arnold Palmer Jack Nicklaus	South Africa, 553 Gary Player Harold R. Henning
1967	Club de Golf Mexico Mexico City	United States, 557 Arnold Palmer Jack Nicklaus	New Zealand, 570 Robert J. Charles Walter Godfrey
1968	Circolo Golf Olgiata Rome	Canada, 569 Al Balding George Knudson	United States, 571 Julius Boros Lee Trevino
1969	Singapore Island Country Club Singapore	United States, 552 Orville Moody Lee Trevino	Japan, 560 T. Kono H. Yasuda
1970	Jockey Golf Club of San Isidro Buenos Aires	Australia, 545 David Graham Bruce Devlin	Argentina, 555 Robert DeVicenzo V. Fernandez
1971	PGA National GC Palm Beach Gardens	United States, 555 Jack Nicklaus Lee Trevino	South Africa, 567 Gary Player Harold Henning
1972	Royal Melbourne GC Melbourne	Taiwan, 438[b] Hsieh Min-nan Lu Liang Huan	Japan, 444 Takaaki Kono Takashi Murakami
1973	Nueva Andalucia Marbella, Spain	United States, 558 Johnny Miller Jack Nicklaus	South Africa, 564
1974	Lagunita CC Caracas, Venezuela	South Africa, 554 Bobby Cole Dale Hayes	Japan, 559
1975	Navatanee GC Bangkok, Thailand	United States, 554 Johnny Miller Lou Graham	Taiwan, 564

Year	Site	Winner	Runner-Up
1976	Mission Hills CC Palm Springs, Calif.	Spain, 574 Severiano Ballesteros Manuel Pinero	United States, 576
1977	Wack Wack G & CC Manila, Philippines	Spain, 591 Severiano Ballesteros Antonio Garrido	Philippines, 594

[a] Play was restricted to 63 holes because of fog.

[b] Play 54 holes only.

The International Trophy. This trophy, inaugurated in 1954, is awarded to the player with the lowest individual score during the 72-hole World Cup Matches. In 1953, when the Trophy was not awarded, Antonio Cerda of Argentina had the best individual score of 140 over 36 holes. Winners of the International are as follows:

Year	Winner	Score
1954	Stan Leonard, Canada	275
1955	Ed Furgol, United States	279
1956	Ben Hogan, United States	277
1957	Torakichi Nakamura, Japan	274
1958	Angel Miguel, Spain	286
1959	Stan Leonard, Canada	275
1960	Flory Van Donck, Belgium	279
1961	Sam Snead, United States	272
1962	Roberto DeVicenzo, Argentina	276
1963	Jack Nicklaus, United States	237[a]
1964	Jack Nicklaus, United States	276
1965	Gary Player, South Africa	281

Year	Winner	Score
1966	George Knudson, Canada	272
1967	Arnold Palmer, United States	276
1968	Al Balding, Canada	274
1969	Lee Trevino, United States	275
1970	Roberto DeVicenzo, Argentina	269
1971	Jack Nicklaus, United States	271
1972	Hsieh Min-nan, Taiwan	217[b]
1973	Johnny Miller, United States	277
1974	Bobby Cole, South Africa	271
1975	Johnny Miller, United States	275
1976	Ernesto Acosta, Mexico	282
1977	Gary Player, South Africa	289

[a] Play was restricted to 63 holes because of fog.

[b] Play 54 holes only.

SECTION III

Golfdom's Who's Who

Golf has been played now for more than half a millennium that we know of and at present is played rather religiously by over fifteen millions on every continent in the world on which grass will grow. From all these golfers who have taken part in the sport, of course, many have arisen as "greats" of golf. In this book we have divided these players into "Great Golfers of All Time" and "Present-Day Touring Professionals—Men and Women."

GREAT GOLFERS OF ALL TIME

ANDERSON, WILLIE. Born in North Berwick, Scotland, in May, 1880. Died in 1910. He was among the first of the Scottish professionals to come to this country, arriving in the mid-1890's with his father, Tom, and his brother, Tom, Jr. He won the U.S. Open in 1901 and then put together three straight victories in 1903, 1904, and 1905 to become the first of the three men who have won four Open titles. He was runner-up in 1897 and finished in the top five on six other occasions: a remarkable record. He also scored four triumphs in the Western Open, which ranked second only to the U.S. Open in those days.

Anderson was the first great player to emerge in this country, but no one is sure just how great, since balls, clubs, and the condition of courses were far below today's standards. He hit the ball with a smooth, deliberate swing and was a good putter who never became rattled. Anderson was a dour man who attended strictly to business and displayed little sense of humor on the course,

but he was a mixer off the course and was popular with his fellow golfers. He was pro at ten clubs in fourteen years, and in 1906 and 1910 he moved to the club that was to be host to the next Open championship, so he obviously cared a great deal about adding another title to his list.

A friend of Anderson's said that although Willie was not a glad-hander, "he went the route with his friends and probably his convivial habits had much to do with undermining his health and hastened his end." He died in 1910 of arteriosclerosis, and his death came as a shock because he presented the outward appearance of perfect health right up to the end. In fact, he played three 36-hole matches during the week preceding his death.

ARMOUR, THOMAS DICKSON. Born in Edinburgh, Scotland, September 24, 1895. Died September 13, 1968. One of the most colorful and legendary figures in the history of golf. There was never anything small about Armour's reputation. At one time or another

WILLIE ANDERSON

THOMAS DICKSON ARMOUR

he was known as the greatest iron player, the greatest raconteur, the greatest drinker, and the greatest and most expensive teacher in golf. He definitely was a great player, while the rest of his reputation, like most legends, contains much picturesque exaggeration. Not long after his playing career came to a close, the prematurely gray hair, the Scottish background, the tournament record, and the legend in general merged to give him an elder-statesmanlike quality, and he typified golf—or what golf was thought to be—to many Americans.

During World War I Armour was a machine gunner in the tank corps and quickly rose to the rank of major. He was wounded and lost the sight of one eye, and while convalescing, he decided to make a career in golf. He won the French Amateur in 1920 and a couple of years later decided to take up residence in the United States. After a few amateur successes Armour turned pro, and by 1927 he was at the top. In that year he won six tournaments, including the U.S. Open and the Canadian Open. He won four more events in 1928 and a couple in 1929, including the Western Open with what was then a record score of 273. Having proved himself to be a great stroke player, Armour beat Gene

Sarazen in the final to win the 1930 PGA on Sarazen's home course, demonstrating he could win matches, too. He completed his collection of major titles by winning the 1931 British Open. He was a contender through 1935, when he lost to Johnny Revolta in the final of the PGA, but after that he played in tournaments less often and less effectively.

As a teacher, which he then became almost exclusively, he was respected by everybody, and top players from Lawson Little to Babe Didrikson went to him for assistance. At one time he collected the highest teaching fees in golf while sitting under an umbrella at Boca Raton. Armour always enjoyed conversation (it was said he was the only man who could rival Hagen in oratory), and as he passed his seventieth birthday he could still be found in Florida in the winter and at Winged Foot in New York in the summer drinking coffee and holding court in the clubhouse.

Tournament Record: 1920: Winner of French Amateur, Gleneagles Amateur, and Shawnee Invitation. 1925: Winner of Florida West Coast Open. 1927: Winner of U.S. Open, Canadian Open, Oregon Open, El Paso Open, Long Beach Open, and Miami Four-ball. 1928: Winner of Metropolitan

Open, Philadelphia Open, Pennsylvania Open, and National Golf Links Invitational. 1929: Winner of Western Open and Sacramento Open. 1930: Winner of PGA, Canadian Open, and St. Louis Open. 1931: Winner of British Open. 1932: Winner of Miami Open and Miami Four-ball. 1934: Winner of Canadian Open. 1935: Winner of Miami Open; runner-up in PGA.

BALL, JOHN. Born in Hoylake, England, December 24, 1861. Died in December, 1940. He was England's greatest amateur and ranks among the best in the history of the game. Ball grew up on the Hoylake course and by the age of fifteen was good enough to finish sixth in the British Open. He won the British Open in 1890, the first amateur to do so.

Ball won the British Amateur a record eight times between 1888 and 1912 and was still able to reach the sixth round in 1921—at the age of sixty! The British Amateur was not begun until 1885, nearly ten years after Ball reached championship caliber, and most

historians agree he would have won more than eight titles had the tournament been founded a decade earlier.

BARNES, JAMES M. Born in Lelant, Cornwall, England, in 1887. Died May 24, 1966. He was a caddie and apprentice club maker before coming to the United States in 1906. He stood 6 feet 3 inches and weighed about 170 and, not surprisingly, became known as Long Jim. Little was known of him until he popped up in second place in the Canadian Open of 1912. When he tied for fourth behind Vardon, Ray, and Ouimet in the 1913 U.S. Open, people began to take notice. Barnes won the Western Open in 1914 and then broke through with a victory in the 1916 PGA, the first time the event was held. He repeated in 1919 and then won the U.S. Open, by nine strokes, in 1921. Although he continued to win occasional tournaments for several years, his victory in the 1925 British Open came as something of a surprise because it was felt his best years were behind him. Although he lived in the United States, he remained British at heart, and through those years he steadfastly refused to relinquish his British citizenship.

Tournament Record: 1913: Winner of Pacific-Northwest Open. 1914: Winner of Western Open. 1915: Winner of Connecticut Open. 1916: Winner of PGA, North and South Open, Connecticut Open, New York Newspaper Open. 1917: Winner of Western Open and Philadelphia Open. 1919: Winner of PGA, North and South Open, Western Open, Shawnee Open, and Southern Open. 1920: Winner of Shawnee Open. 1921: Winner of U.S. Open; runner-up in PGA. 1922: Winner of California Open. 1923: Winner of Corpus Christi Open. 1924: Runner-up in PGA. 1925: Winner of British Open. 1930: Winner of Cape Cod Open. 1937: Winner of Long Island Open.

any golfer in history. She was runner-up in the U.S. Amateur when only seventeen years of age, just three years after taking up the game. She was second again in 1937 and won the title in 1938. She turned professional in 1940 and during her career won more than eighty tournaments, including the U.S. Open in 1946 and the Titleholders championship seven times. She shot a 64 in the 1952 Richmond (California) Open for a women's professional record.

BERG, PATRICIA JANE. Born in Minneapolis, Minnesota, February 13, 1918. One of America's pioneer women professionals as well as one of its all-time top players. Miss Berg not only gave the professional game a boost in this country by means of her skill but took the game to people everywhere and is reputed to have staged more clinics than

BOROS, JULIUS NICHOLAS. Born in Fairfield, Connecticut, March 3, 1920. Until he won his second U.S. Open championship in 1963, Boros was probably the most underrated golfer playing in the country. He had won the Open in 1952 and had followed that with two victories in George May's rich "World" tournament, but through all those years he seemed to be the forgotten man to the general public, and it always came as something of a surprise when he finished near the top in the Open each year. Nevertheless, from 1950, when he was ninth, through his

1963 triumph, Boros was in the top ten of the Open nine times, a record second only to Ben Hogan's since World War II.

Boros, who had been an accountant, turned pro late in 1949 after a successful amateur career. Although he won a couple of minor events, the 1952 Open was actually his first victory of consequence. From that point, however, he consistently was at his best in the prestige events. As he moved into his late forties, Boros seemed to get better. He was consistently winning over $100,000 a year, and he captured the PGA Championship in 1968 at the age of forty-eight.

In 1977, he tied for 59th place in the Pleasant Valley Classic and brought his career earnings to $1 million.

Tournament Record: 1948: Winner of Shore Line Open. 1951: Winner of Massachusetts Open. 1952: Winner of U.S. Open and World Championship. 1954: Winner of Carling Open and Ardmore Open. 1955: Winner of World Championship. 1958: Winner of Carling Open and Arlington Open. 1959: Winner of Dallas Open. 1960: Winner of Colonial Invitation. 1963: Winner of Colonial Invitational, Buick Open and U.S. Open. 1964: Winner of Greensboro Open and West Palm Beach Open. 1967: Winner of Buick Open, Phoenix Open, and Florida Citrus Open. 1968: Winner of PGA and Westchester Classic. 1971: Winner of PGA Seniors.

BRADY, MICHAEL JOSEPH. Born in Brighton, Massachusetts, April 15, 1887. Died December 3, 1972. He was one of the first of the American homebred professionals to become a championship player. Unfortunately, Brady is often best remembered for the championships he did not win. In 1911, carrying only six clubs, he tied Johnny McDermott and George Simpson for the U.S. Open title, but lost in a play-off. In 1912 he had a four-stroke lead, but closed with an 80 and tied for third. In 1915 he trailed Jerry Travers by a stroke going into the last round, but again had a final 80 and finished sixth. His most famous failure was in 1919, when he led by five strokes after three rounds and again closed with an 80. Walter Hagen tied him with a 75 and won the play-off the next day by a stroke. Despite these unfortunate mishaps, Brady was a very fine golfer.

In 1917 he broke 100 for 27 holes, and on

MICHAEL JOSEPH BRADY

Labor Day of the same year he made two holes in one during a single round. In 1922 he shot 291 and won the Western Open by ten strokes.

Tournament Record: 1911: Runner-up in U.S. Open. 1914: Winner of Massachusetts Open. 1916: Winner of Massachusetts Open. 1917: Winner of North and South Open. 1919: Runner-up in U.S. Open. 1922: Winner of Western Open. 1923: Winner of Massachusetts Open. 1924: Winner of Metropolitan Open. 1925: Winner of Westchester Open.

BRAID, JAMES. Born in Elie, Scotland, February 6, 1870. Died November 27, 1950. His is one of the most revered names in golf. Braid, along with Harry Vardon and J. H. Taylor, formed the "triumvirate" that dominated golf for twenty years prior to World War I. He was the first man to win the British Open five times, and he also won the British match play tournament four times and the French Open once. His record in the British Open is remarkable in that he won his five championships and was second three times all

JAMES BRAID

JACK BURKE, JR.

in the space of ten years. Braid was a tall, quiet man who hit the ball great distances, yet never appeared ruffled no matter how he was playing. It was once said of him that no one could be as wise as James Braid looked. He was one of the founding members of the British PGA and in his later years designed many courses.

BURKE, JACK, JR. Born in Fort Worth, Texas, January 29, 1923. One of America's top postwar golfers. He won four tournaments in a row, was runner-up in the Masters, and won the Vardon Trophy, all in 1952, and then was named golfer of the year in 1956 after winning the PGA and Masters. Although his closing 71 was a fine round under the prevailing conditions, his 1956 Masters victory unfortunately is remembered as the one Ken Venturi lost. Burke also had to come from behind to win the PGA. He was five down to Ed Furgol after 14 holes and three down to Ted Kroll after 19 in his last two matches. Burke, a fine putter, was a member of four Ryder Cup teams and won seven of eight matches. He won the 1952 Texas Open with a score of 260 (67–65–64–64).

He began playing at the age of seven under the tutelage of his father and was a good player by the time he reached his teens. He joined the tour in 1950 and won three tournaments in his first year. A wrist injury kept Burke out of the 1957 U.S. Open, and chronic trouble with his hand curtailed his play somewhat from then on.

Tournament Record: 1949: Winner of Metropolitan Open. 1950: Winner of Rio Grande Valley Open, Bing Crosby Pro-Am, St. Petersburg Open, and Sioux City Open. 1951: Winner of Piping Rock Pro-Am. 1952: Winner of St. Petersburg Open, Texas Open, Houston Open, Baton Rouge Open, and Miami Open; runner-up in Masters. 1953: Winner of Inverness Invitational. 1956: Winner of Masters and PGA. 1958: Winner of Insurance City Open. 1959: Winner of Houston Classic. 1961: Winner of Buick Open. 1963: Winner of Lucky International Open, Texas State Open, and St. Paul Open.

CARNER, JoANNE GUNDERSON. Born in Kirkland, Washington, April 4, 1939. Started golf at the age of ten, and compiled a brilliant amateur record before joining the pro tour. Graduated from Arizona State University with a B.A. in Physical Education and did not turn professional until nine years

JOANNE CARNER

later. Few women have ever brought such impressive credentials into the pro ranks.

She won the U.S. Amateur five times, the National Collegiate title, and just about every other important amateur championship at least once. She also played on four U.S. Curtis Cup teams.

As a professional, she has won 20 tournaments between 1970 and 1977, including the U.S. Open in 1971 and 1976. A tall woman, she is one of the longest hitters in women's golf history and plays best on the more difficult courses. She was named the LPGA Player of the Year in 1974, after she won six events. She is married to Don Carner, who helps manage her career.

Tournament Record: 1957: Winner of U.S. Amateur. 1958: Winner of Pacific Northwest Amateur. 1959: Winner of Western Amateur and Pacific Northwest Amateur. 1960: Winner of U.S. Amateur, the Southwest Amateur, and the NCAA. 1961: Winner of Trans-Mississippi Amateur. 1962: Winner of U.S. Amateur. 1966: Winner of U.S. Amateur. 1967: Winner of Northwest Amateur. 1968: Winner of U.S. Amateur and Eastern Amateur. 1970: Winner of Wendell West Open. 1971: Winner of U.S. Open and Bluegrass Invitational. 1974: Winner of Bluegrass In-

vitational, Hoosier LPGA Classic, Desert Inn Classic, St. Paul Open, Dallas Civitan Open, and Portland Ladies Class. 1975: Winner of American Defender, Girl Talk Classic, Peter Jackson Classic. 1976: Winner of U.S. Open, Orange Blossom Classic, Lady Tara Classic, and Hoosier Classic. 1977: Winner of Talk Tournament, Borden Classic, Jewish Hospital Open, and LPGA Team Championship (with Judy Rankin).

CASPER, WILLIAM EARL, JR. Born in San Diego, California, June 24, 1931. The 1959 and 1966 U.S. Open champion and one of the most consistent players—and money winners —in all golf. In his early years, Casper had unusual appeal in that he was overweight and would rather go fishing than practice, a combination that had to be popular with duffers everywhere. Despite this rather unathletic approach, he was a big winner almost from the start of his pro career. After gradually moving up the financial scale, Casper reached the big money in 1958 when he won four tournaments, was runner-up in the PGA Championship, and finished No. 2 on the money-winning list. The next year, he won five tournaments, including the biggest one of all, the U.S. Open. It was there, at Winged Foot, that his reputation as a putter was made. He needed only 114 putts for the 72 holes, and his performance soon had golfers the world over emulating his style on the greens. The praise he got for his putting prowess, although justified, always bothered Casper a little, because he felt his considerable skill with the other clubs was being overlooked.

As Casper started his second decade on the tour his appearance, if not his golf, underwent a change. After consulting an allergist, he began to avoid certain foods late in 1964 and by mid-1965 had lost forty pounds, changing his wardrobe three times to cope with his shrinking waist, and was so slender as to be almost unrecognizable.

Tournament Record: 1949: Winner of Southern California Interscholastic. 1950: Winner of San Diego Amateur. 1953: Winner of San Diego County Open. 1954: Winner of San Diego County Open and 11th Naval District Tourney. 1956: Winner of Labatt Open. 1957: Winner of Phoenix Open and Kentucky Derby Open. 1958: Winner of Bing Crosby National, New Orleans Open, Buick Open, and Havana Invitational; runner-up in PGA. 1959: Winner of U.S. Open, Portland Open, Lafayette Open, Mobile Open, and Brazil Open. 1960: Winner of Portland Open, Hesperia Open, and Orange County Open. 1961: Winner of Portland Open. 1962: Winner of Doral Open, Greensboro Open, 500 Festival Open, and Bakersfield Open. 1963: Winner of Bing Crosby National and Insurance City Open. 1964: Winner of Doral Open, Colonial Invitational, Seattle Open, and Almaden Open. 1965: Winner of Bob Hope Classic, Western Open, Sahara Invitational, and Insurance City Open. 1966: Winner of U.S. Open, San Diego Open, 500 Festival Open, and Western Open. 1967: Winner of Canadian Open and Carling World Open. 1968: Winner of Southern California Open, Los Angeles Open, Greensboro Open, Colonial Invitational, 500 Festival Open, Greater Hartford Open, and Lucky International Open. 1969: Winner of Bob Hope Desert Classic, Western Open, and Alcan Golfer of the Year Championship. 1970: Winner of Los Angeles Open, Masters, IVB-Philadelphia Classic, and AVCO Classic. 1971: Winner of Kaiser International Open and Miki Gold Cup. 1973: Winner of Western Open and Sammy Davis, Jr.–Greater Hartford Open. 1975: Winner of New Orleans Open.

COLLETT, GLENNA (MRS. EDWIN H. VARE). Born in New Haven, Connecticut,

GLENNA COLLETT

June 20, 1903. The greatest amateur player the United States ever produced. She won the U.S. women's championship a record six times in addition to being runner-up twice and a semifinalist twice, all in the space of fourteen years. Glenna also won the North and South and the Eastern six times each in the course of dominating American women's golf during the 1920's. However, she had the misfortune to come on the scene at the same time as Joyce Wethered, the incomparable British star, who defeated Glenna in a great British final in 1929 at St. Andrews. Glenna also gained the British final in 1930 at Formby, but lost to Diana Fishwick. She had been beaten in the third round by Miss Wethered in 1925. Glenna took up the game at the age of fourteen and was a pupil of Alex Smith, the U.S. Open champion who also tutored Jerry Travers.

COOPER, HARRY E. Born in Leatherhead, England, August 4, 1904. He was rated one of the best tee-to-green players of all time and was the winner of many tournaments, but, despite his great skills, Cooper was destined never to win a major championship. He began playing in England, but his game developed in Texas, where he moved with his parents when

HARRY E. COOPER

still quite young. After considerable local success, he burst on the national scene in 1926 by winning the Los Angeles and Del Monte Opens. He was in good position to win the 1927 U.S. Open, but three-putted the last green, was tied by Tommy Armour, and lost in a play-off. Over the next decade, Cooper won many tournaments and in 1937 was the leading money winner and took the Vardon Trophy. He seemed certain to win the Open at last in 1936 when he finished at 284, a tournament record, but Tony Manero came out of nowhere to win with 282. Cooper continued at the top until the advent of World War II. Since then he has been a respected club pro in the New York area and has remained good enough to win various senior titles.

Tournament Record: 1923, 1924: Winner of Texas PGA. 1926: Winner of Los Angeles Open and Del Monte Open. 1927: Winner of Oklahoma City Open; runner-up in U.S. Open. 1929: Winner of Oklahoma Open, Shawnee Open, Medinah Open, and Western New York PGA. 1930: Winner of Pasadena Open, St. Paul Open, Salt Lake City Open, and Medinah Open. 1931: Winner of Pasadena Open. 1932: Winner of Canadian Open and Tri-State Open. 1933: Winner of Illinois Open. 1934: Winner of Western Open, Illinois Open, and Illinois PGA. 1935: Winner of St. Paul Open, Medinah Open, and Illinois Open. 1936: Winner of Florida West Coast Open and St. Paul Open; runner-up in U.S. Open and Masters. 1937: Winner of Canadian Open, True Temper Open, Los Angeles Open, Houston Open, St. Petersburg Open, Oakland Open, and Oklahoma City Four-ball. 1939: Winner of Goodall Round Robin and Connecticut Open. 1942: Winner of Minnesota Open and Bing Crosby Pro-Am. 1955: Winner of PGA Quarter Century Club Tourney. 1962: Winner of Atlantic City Senior Open.

COTTON, THOMAS HENRY. Born in Holmes Chapel, England, January 26, 1907. He was one of England's greatest players and just about its only one of world stature in the

1930's and 1940's. Although Cotton won the British Open three times and captured many titles on the Continent, he had little success in his occasional trips to the United States, with the result that Americans always slightly underrated him. Besides his abilities as a player, Cotton was an effective teacher who authored several fine books of golf instruction. In later years he turned to course architecture and was the designer of several layouts in England, France, and Portugal. Cotton was a member of three Ryder Cup teams and was captain twice. He also is a golf correspondent for two British publications.

Tournament Record: 1926, 1927: Winner of Kent Professional. 1928: Winner of Kent Professional and Croydon and District Professional. 1929: Winner of Kent Professional. 1930: Winner of Belgian Open, Mar-del-Plata Open, and Kent Professional. 1931: Winner of Dunlop-Southport Tourney. 1932: Winner of *News of the World* Tourney and Dunlop-Southport Tourney. 1934: Winner of British Open and Belgian Open. 1935: Winner of Yorkshire *Evening News* Tourney and Leeds Tourney. 1936: Winner of Italian Open and Dunlop Metropolitan Tourney. 1937: Winner of German Open, British Open, Czechoslovak Open, and Silver King Tourney. 1938: Winner of German Open, Czechoslovak Open, and Belgian Open. 1939: Winner of German Open and *Daily Mail* Tourney. 1940: Winner of *News of the World* Tourney. 1945: Winner of *News Chronicle* Tourney. 1946: Winner of French Open, *News of the World* Tourney, Star Tourney, and Vichy Open. 1947: Winner of French Open, Spalding Tourney, and Yorkshire *Evening News* Tourney. 1948: Winner of British Open and White Sulphur Springs Invitational. 1953: Winner of Dunlop Tourney. 1954: Winner of Penfold Tourney.

CRUICKSHANK, ROBERT ALLAN. Born in Grantown-on-Spey, Scotland, November 16, 1894. Died August 27, 1975. Wee Bobby was one of the world's best players in the 1920's, was still a threat in every championship in the 1930's, was good enough to finish twenty-fifth in the U.S. Open at the age of fifty-five, and was still winning at the age of sixty. He finished fourth or better in the Open five times in fifteen years and twice reached the PGA semifinals, but never won

ROBERT ALLAN CRUICKSHANK

a major title. In the 1923 Open at Inwood Country Club, he tied Bobby Jones on the 72nd hole but lost in a play-off. In 1932 at Fresh Meadow he finished 69, 68, but Gene Sarazen was playing the last 28 holes in 100 strokes and again Bobby was second.

Cruickshank began playing at the age of four and was a golfing rival of Tommy Armour in school. After heroic service in World War I, during which he was taken prisoner, he turned to golf for a living and moved to the United States in 1921. Almost immediately he was a consistent winner, and he captured many titles over the next three decades.

Tournament Record: 1919, 1920: Winner of Edinburgh Coronation Trophy. 1921: Winner of New York Open and St. Joseph Open. 1922: Winner of Spalding Tourney and Wykagyl Tourney. 1923: Runner-up in U.S. Open. 1924: Winner of Colorado Open and Mid-Continent Open. 1925: Winner of Miami Four-ball and Oklahoma City Open. 1926: Winner of North and South Open, Westchester Open, and Mid-South Amateur-Pro; tied for first in Florida Open. 1927: Winner of North and South Open, Texas Open, Hot Springs Open, Miami Four-ball, Los Angeles Open, and South Central Open. 1928: Winner of

Maryland Open. 1929: Winner of Westchester Open; tied for first in Hot Springs Open. 1932: Tied for second in U.S. Open. 1933: Winner of Virginia Open. 1934: Winner of Virginia Open, National Capital City Open, and Nassau Open. 1935: Winner of Virginia Open, British Colonial Open, and Sarasota Open. 1936, 1937, 1939: Winner of Virginia Open. 1943: Winner of North and South Open. 1949, 1950: Winner of Tri-State PGA. 1954: Winner of Erie Open.

DEMARET, JAMES NEWTON. Born in Houston, Texas, May 25, 1910. He was one of the game's most colorful personalities and an outstanding player for three decades. Demaret became the first man to win three Masters titles (1940, 1947, 1950), was semifinalist in the PGA four times, finished fourth or better in the U.S. Open three times, was undefeated in six Ryder Cup matches, won

the Vardon Trophy, and was a member of the winning U.S. team in the Canada Cup competition. The Texas native has been identified with golf all his life, although he had a short career as a singer with a band in night clubs. He was one of nine children of a carpenter, and two of his brothers are professionals. After several years of local success, which included winning the Texas PGA five straight times, Demaret joined the pro circuit full time in 1938 and quickly won the San Francisco Match Play tournament. He won the Los Angeles Open in 1939 and by 1940 he was one of the best. That year he won seven tournaments, including the Masters. Demaret is one of Ben Hogan's closest friends, and in 1941 the two won the Inverness Four-ball, the first of six titles they were to win as partners. Many years later, Demaret wrote a book with Jimmy Breslin called *My Partner, Ben Hogan*. Demaret, a warmhearted man, parlayed his engaging personality with an eye-catching wardrobe to become a bona fide gate attraction after World War II. In later years he became a partner in the Champions Golf Club in Houston, vice-president of a club manufacturing company, and commentator on a TV golf series.

Tournament Record: 1934, 1935, 1936, 1937: Winner of Texas PGA. 1938: Winner of San Francisco Match Play and Texas PGA. 1939: Winner of Los Angeles Open. 1940: Winner of Masters, San Francisco Match Play, Western Open, New Orleans Open, St. Petersburg Open, Oakland Open, and Seminole Pro-Am. 1941: Winner of Inverness Four-ball, Connecticut Open, and Argentine Open. 1943: Winner of Michigan PGA and Golden Valley Four-ball. 1945: Winner of Texas PGA. 1946: Winner of Miami Four-ball, Inverness Four-ball, and Tucson Open. 1947: Winner of Masters, Miami Four-ball, Inverness Four-ball, Miami Open. St. Petersburg Open, and Tucson Open. 1948: Winner of Albuquerque Open, Inverness Four-ball, and St. Paul Open; runner-up in U.S. Open. 1949: Winner of Phoenix Open. 1950: Winner of Masters, Ben Hogan Open, and North Fulton Open. 1951: Winner of Havana Pro-Am. 1952: Winner of Bing Crosby National and National Celebrities Tourney. 1953: Winner of Seminole Pro-Am. 1956: Winner of Palm

Springs Invitational. 1957: Winner of Thunderbird Invitational, Baton Rouge Open, and Arlington Hotel Open.

DIEGEL, LEO. Born in Detroit, Michigan, April 27, 1899. Died in 1951. One of the greatest, and at the same time most tragic, figures in the history of golf. It has been said that in his inspired moments Diegel was the equal of any player who ever lived, but in the end, all he had to show for it was two PGA Championships, four Canadian Open titles, and an assortment of lesser tournament victories. That list is impressive enough, but it represents nothing like what Diegel seemed capable of doing. He was eighth or better eleven times in the British and U.S. Opens and was fourth or better on seven of those occasions. Eight times he was in position to win right down to the closing holes. His temperament was his undoing, and none of the many remedies he tried had any lasting effect. By nature he was an impatient player and a worrier. He would bound forward after each

shot, unable to walk down the fairway at a normal gait. Often, while waiting for another player to drive, Diegel would jump into the air or climb on a tee box in order to see from what lie he would be playing his next shot. The best-known, and most extreme, cure he tried was his famous spread-eagle putting stance in which he bent over with his chin almost touching the handle of the putter and stuck his elbows out in a fashion that looked like a car with both doors open. As early as 1922 he set a record for that time by winning the Shreveport Open with a 275. Later, Canadians called him "Eagle Diegel" after he won the Canadian Open with a 274 that included a 65. Once, at Columbia, he shot nine holes in 29 after betting he could break 30. Willie MacFarlane said he thought Diegel, given a week, could break the record at any course in the country. Often he broke 75 by hitting his shots while standing on one leg. Bernard Darwin once said Diegel was "in a way the greatest golfing genius I have ever seen."

Tournament Record: 1916: Winner of Michigan Open. 1920: Winner of Pinehurst Amateur-Pro; tied for second in U.S. Open. 1922: Winner of Shreveport Open; tied for first in Louisiana Open. 1924: Winner of Canadian Open, Shawnee Open, and Illinois Open. 1925: Winner of Canadian Open, Middle Atlantic Open, Mid-South Amateur-Pro, and Florida Open. 1926: Winner of Middle Atlantic Open and Maryland Open; runner-up in PGA. 1927: Winner of San Diego Open and Middle Atlantic Open. 1928: Winner of PGA, Canadian Open, and Massachusetts Open; tied for first in Long Beach Open. 1929: Winner of PGA, Canadian Open, San Diego Open, and Miami Four-ball. 1930: Winner of Oregon Open, San Francisco Match Play, and Southern California Open; tied for second in British Open. 1933: Winner of Timber Point Open, Southern California Open, and California Open. 1934: Winner of Walter Hagen Tourney and New England PGA Open.

DUDLEY, EDWARD BISHOP. Born in Brunswick, Georgia, February 10, 1901. Died October 25, 1963. Dudley was a big man with a relaxed swing that was one of the smoothest in golf. Henry Cotton once called Dudley's swing the most beautiful he had ever seen,

EDWARD BISHOP DUDLEY

and Chick Evans said Dudley was the only man whose swing could be compared to Harry Vardon's. Dudley was a consistent tournament winner for nearly two decades, but he never captured a major title. He led the 1937 U.S. Open after three rounds, but finished with a 76 and dropped to fifth. In 1928 he had moved into contention with a third-round 68 only to post a closing 75 that tied him for sixth. Six times he reached the quarter-finals of the PGA, but only once did he get as far as the semifinals. Dudley was active in the councils of the PGA for many years, and he served as national president from 1942 to 1948. He won more than twenty tournaments and was a member of three Ryder Cup teams.

Tournament Record: 1925, 1926: Winner of Oklahoma Open. 1928: Winner of Southern California PGA. 1929: Winner of Pennsylvania Open, Philadelphia Open, California Open, and California PGA. 1930: Winner of Shawnee Open and Pennsylvania Open. 1931: Winner of Los Angeles Open, Western Open, and Philadelphia PGA. 1932: Winner of Miami Four-ball, Pennsylvania Open, and Philadelphia Open. 1933: Winner of Hershey Open. 1935: Winner of True Temper Open. 1936: Winner of Philadelphia Open and Shawnee Open. 1937: Winner of Sacramento Open. 1939: Winner of Walter Hagen Tourney. 1940: Winner of Philadelphia Open. 1942: Winner of Utah Open.

DUTRA, OLIN. Born in Monterey, California, January 17, 1901. Dutra won the PGA in 1932 and the U.S. Open in 1934, along with several lesser titles, and was a member of two Ryder Cup teams. He worked in a hardware store in his teens and for several years practiced his golf by getting up at 4 A.M. three days a week. After turning pro he continued to get up at such an unlikely hour in order to hold two club jobs simultaneously. He became known as an indefatigable teacher, but still found time to hone a game that was one of the best in the early 1930's. In his Open victory, at Merion, Dutra, despite being ill, shot closing rounds of 71 and 72 to overtake Gene Sarazen, who met disaster at the 11th hole and finished with a 76. Dutra was still good enough in 1961, at the age of sixty, to shoot a 61 over the Jurupa Hills course where he was professional.

Tournament Record: 1922: Winner of Del Monte Match Play. 1928, 1929, 1930: Winner of Southern California PGA. 1931: Winner of Southern California PGA, Southwest Open, California State Match Play, and Pacific Southwest PGA. 1932: Winner of PGA, Metropolitan Open, North Shore Open, St. Paul Open, and Southern California Open. 1933: Winner of Southern California PGA. 1934: Winner of U.S. Open and Miami Biltmore Open. 1935: Winner of Sunset Fields Open and Santa Monica Open. 1936: Winner of True Temper Open. 1937: Winner of Sunset Fields Open. 1940: Winner of California Open.

EVANS, CHARLES (CHICK), JR. Born in Indianapolis, Indiana, July 18, 1890. One of America's great amateur golfers and a player whose competitive career spanned more than sixty years. After almost a decade of winning

everything but championships, Evans took both the U.S. Open and Amateur in 1916, and his 286 in the Open was a record that stood for twenty years. Although no one had ever before taken both championships in a single year, Evans' feat evoked little surprise because experts had recognized for years that he was a player of infinite promise. Since his first tournament victory in 1907, at the age of seventeen, Evans had won more than twenty events, including the French Amateur and so many Western Amateurs that it appeared he held the franchise. After playing dozens of Red Cross exhibitions during World War I, he won the Amateur for the second time in 1920, and, since he was only thirty, it appeared as if he might win it several more times. But although he was in the fight for another decade, during which he was runner-up twice, he never won again. Evans competed in the Amateur for more than fifty years, and it was unfortunate that he eventually began to meet players who never saw him during his prime. Evans was active in senior affairs for the rest of his career and was responsible for setting up the Evans Scholarship Foundation for caddies.

Tournament Record: 1907: Winner of Chicago Amateur, Western Junior, and Western Interscholastic. 1908: Winner of Chicago Amateur and Western Interscholastic. 1909: Winner of Western Amateur. 1910: Winner of Western Open. 1911: Winner of French Amateur, North and South Amateur, and Chicago Amateur. 1912: Winner of Western Amateur; runner-up in U.S. Amateur. 1914: Winner of Western Amateur and Chicago District Amateur; runner-up in U.S. Open. 1915: Winner of Western Amateur. 1916: Winner of U.S. Open and U.S. Amateur. 1920: Winner of U.S. Amateur and Western Amateur. 1921: Winner of Western Amateur. 1922: Winner of Western Amateur; runner-up in U.S. Amateur. 1923: Winner of Western Amateur. 1925: Winner of Kansas City Open. 1927: Runner-up in U.S. Amateur.

FARRELL, JOHN J. Born in White Plains, New York, April 1, 1901. The U.S. Open champion in 1928 and one of the most colorful and most competent players during the 1920's and early 1930's. In addition to winning the Open, Farrell was in the top five on three other occasions, was runner-up in the

JOHN J. FARRELL

sachusetts Open, Wheeling Open, Eastern Open, and Chicago Open. 1928: Winner of U.S. Open, LaGorce Open, Miami Open, and Miami Four-ball. 1929: Runner-up in British Open; runner-up in PGA. 1930: Winner of Pensacola Open and New York Open. 1931: Winner of Pensacola Open. 1936: Winner of New Jersey Open. 1940, 1941: Winner of Rhode Island Open.

British Open, and played on three Ryder Cup teams. In the PGA Championship from 1922 through 1937, he was runner-up once, a semi-finalist twice, and a quarter-finalist five times. Farrell started as a caddie in the Westchester area of New York and made his decision to stick with golf after watching the pros play in the first PGA tournament at Siwanoy in 1916. He burst on the scene in 1922 by winning the Shawnee Open, gaining the quarter-finals of the PGA and tying for eleventh in the U.S. Open as the playing partner of the equally unknown Gene Sarazen, who won the event. From that point Farrell was winning tournaments and knocking at the door of championships for more than a decade. During that time he gained the reputation of being the best-dressed pro in an era of snappy dressers, and he often won prizes for his dapper ensembles.

Tournament Record: 1922: Winner of Shawnee Open. 1925: Winner of Philadelphia Open and Miami Four-ball. 1926: Winner of Shawnee Open, Westchester Open, Florida Open, Central Florida Open, Miami Four-ball, and Mid-South Pro Best-ball. 1927: Winner of Shawnee Open, Philadelphia Open, Metropolitan Open, Pennsylvania Open, Mas-

FINSTERWALD, Dow. Born in Akron, Ohio, September 6, 1929. One of the most consistent money winners in golf during the late 1950's and early 1960's. Although he went on to win a lot of tournaments, Finsterwald was given a "bridesmaid" label during his early years on the tour because he finished second so often. In the major tournaments—the Open, PGA, and Masters—his combined record shows nine finishes in the top five, and he was almost that close several other times. His most notable achievement was winning the 1958 PGA after having been runner-up the year before. He also tied for third in the 1960 U.S. Open and tied for first in the 1962 Masters, only to finish third in the play-off the next day. At the pay window, the smooth-swinging Finsterwald finished second, third, fourth, third, and third from 1956 through 1960 in a display of coin-collecting consistency second only to that of the Internal Revenue Service. Although he gained the reputation of being a conservative player, Finsterwald actually was something of a scrambler and gained many of those pars through superior putting.

Tournament Record: 1955: Winner of Fort Wayne Open and Columbia Open. 1956: Winner of Carling Open. 1957: Winner of Tucson Open; runner-up in PGA. 1958: Winner of PGA and Utah Open. 1959: Winner of Greensboro Open, Carling Open, and Kansas City Open. 1960: Winner of Los Angeles Open and New Orleans Open. 1963: Winner of 500 Festival Open.

FORD, DOUGLAS. Born in West Haven, Connecticut, August 6, 1922. One of the fastest and most consistent players in golf after World War II. Ford won the 1955 PGA, the 1957 Masters, played on four Ryder Cup teams, and banked more than a third of a million dollars during his career. He was the No. 2 money winner twice and was never out of the top twenty during his first dozen years on the circuit. Ford, a member of a golfing family whose name originally was Fortunato, has been described as "the guy who looks as if he is playing through the group he is playing with." Ford relied on a strong short game to offset the big hitters on the tour.

Tournament Record: 1940: Winner of New York Junior. 1941: Winner of Westchester Junior. 1942: Winner of New York Junior. 1947: Winner of Westchester Ama-

teur. 1948: Winner of Houston Invitational. 1952: Winner of Jacksonville Open. 1953: Winner of Virginia Beach Open, LaBatt Open, and Miami Open. 1954: Winner of Greensboro Open and Fort Wayne Open. 1955: Winner of PGA, Carling Open, and All-America Open. 1957: Winner of Masters, Los Angeles Open, Western Open and Metropolitan PGA. 1958: Winner of Pensacola Open; tied for second in Masters. 1959: Winner of Canadian Open and Metropolitan PGA. 1960: Winner of 500 Festival Open and Metropolitan PGA. 1961: Winner of 500 Festival Open, Westchester Open, and Westchester PGA. 1962: Winner of Bing Crosby National and Eastern Open. 1963: Winner of Canadian Open and Metropolitan PGA.

GHEZZI, VICTOR. Born in Rumson, New Jersey, October 19, 1911. Died May 30, 1976. The PGA champion in 1941 and a prominent player from 1935, when he first attracted national attention by winning the Los Angeles Open. He tied Lloyd Mangrum and Byron Nelson for first place in the U.S. Open at Canterbury in 1946, and he and Nelson finished a stroke behind Mangrum in a play-off that went 36 holes. The next year he finished with a 69 to tie for sixth at St. Louis. In winning the PGA, he beat Mangrum, 1 up, in the semifinals and beat Nelson on the 38th hole of the final. He also reached the PGA semifinals on another occasion and was a quarterfinalist twice. Ghezzi was named to the Ryder Cup team in 1939 and 1941, but the matches were not held either year because of World War II.

Tournament Record: 1935: Winner of Los Angeles Open, Calvert Open, and Maryland Open. 1936: Winner of Hollywood Open. 1937: Winner of Lake Placid Open and New Jersey Open. 1938: Winner of North and South Open, Hershey Four-ball, and Inverness Four-ball. 1941: Winner of PGA. 1942: Winner of Spring Lake Invitational. 1943: Winner of New Jersey Open and Spring Lake Invitational. 1946: Tied for second in U.S. Open. 1947: Winner of Greensboro Open and Spring Lake Invitational. 1948: Winner of Dapper Dan Open and Alcoma Tournament.

GULDAHL, RALPH. Born in Dallas, Texas, November 22, 1911. Guldahl was a great stroke player who became one of the

few to win consecutive U.S. Open championships when he triumphed in 1937 and 1938. However, his years at the top were few, and the story of his ups and downs is a strange one. He joined the tour in the early 1930's, won one tournament, and was runner-up in the Open when his game suddenly fell apart. He finally became so discouraged he quit golf completely in 1935. A few months later he tried again after making some revisions in his swing and putting in countless hours of practice. This time the effort bore fruit, and in the next five years he won ten tournaments, including the two Opens and the Masters of 1939. These also included three straight Western Opens, an event that ranked only behind the Open, PGA, and Masters in those days. Then, again, his skills left him, virtually overnight, and no one has ever been able to fathom the reason, least of all Guldahl. Dozens of players watched him hit practice balls; he had slow-motion movies taken of his swing and compared with earlier films; and people everywhere came up with theories and remedies—but nobody found the right answer. Guldahl left the tour in 1942 and, except for a brief return in 1949, never played the circuit again.

Tournament Record: 1932: Winner of Phoenix Open. 1933: Runner-up in U.S. Open. 1936: Winner of Western Open, Augusta Open, and Miami-Biltmore Open. 1937: Winner of U.S. Open and Western Open; runner-up in Masters. 1938: Winner of U.S. Open and Western Open; runner-up in Masters. 1939: Winner of Masters, Miami Four-ball, Greensboro Open, and Dapper Dan Open. 1940: Winner of Milwaukee Open and Inverness Four-ball.

HAGEN, WALTER CHARLES. Born in Rochester, New York, December 21, 1892. Died October 6, 1969. The most colorful personality in the history of golf and one of its greatest players. His record of winning eleven major championships (second only to Bobby Jones's thirteen) would be more than enough to insure his lasting fame, but Hagen did far more than that. Because of his refusal to go second-class, he led the way in breaking down the social barrier between amateurs and professionals; he was the fashion plate everyone copied; he demanded—and got—large sums for exhibitions and tours, thus helping to raise

WALTER CHARLES HAGEN

considerably the prize money available to professionals; and above all, with his all-night parties just before a crucial match, his chauffeur-driven limousine, his sartorial splendor, his superior gamesmanship—plus his skill as a player—he imbued golf with a dash and color that put it increasingly in the public eye and gave it and him more newspaper space than it had won in all the years before he came on the scene.

Hagen was not a classic swinger, and he seldom had the consistency necessary to put four good rounds together. But he was a very good player, a great putter, and a man who had the almost uncanny ability to hit "impossible" recovery shots to the green, then sink a birdie putt to beat an opponent who was never out of the fairway. He also was a master of psychology and showmanship, and he used these tools along with his great ability as a scrambler to unnerve and defeat many a foe, even on days when his own game was not particularly sharp. The Haig won two U.S. Opens, four British Opens, and five PGA Championships—the last four in

succession—plus dozens of lesser titles. His total of career victories is estimated anywhere between 60 and 83, and he won hundreds of exhibitions during his many tours. Some of these were more or less formal ones, with Joe Kirkwood and others; and some consisted of a caravan of three limousines and an entourage that included chauffer, manager, personal caddie, and suitcases full of money collected at previous stops. The money was always something to be got rid of as quickly as possible, and Sir Walter used to take pride in saying he was the first golfer to make a million dollars and spend two.

Hagen's ability as a player and his contributions to the popularity and success of golf in general cannot be overestimated. As Bernard Darwin once wrote: "This difference, as there is so often between Hagen and the other man, is that Hagen just won and the other man just did not." Or, as A. C. M. Croome put it: "He makes more bad shots in a single season than Harry Vardon did from 1890 to 1914, but he beats more immaculate golfers because 'three of those and one of them' counts 4 and he knows it." And Gene Sarazen once wrote: "All the professionals who have a chance to go after the big money today should say a silent thanks to Walter Hagen each time they stretch a check between their fingers. It was Walter who made professional golf what it is."

Tournament Record: 1914: Winner of U.S. Open and Pinehurst Amateur-Pro. 1915: Winner of Massachusetts Open and Panama Exposition Open. 1916: Winner of Western Open, Shawnee Open, and Metropolitan Open. 1918: Winner of North and South Open. 1919: Winner of U.S. Open and Metropolitan Open. 1920: Winner of French Open, Metropolitan Open, and Bellevue Open. 1921: Winner of PGA, Western Open, Michigan Open, and Florida West Coast Open; tied for second in U.S. Open. 1922: Winner of British Open, New York Open, Deland Open, White Sulphur Springs Open, and Florida West Coast Open. 1923: Winner of North and South Open, Texas Open, Long Beach Open, Florida West Coast Open, and Asheville Open; tied for first in Wichita Open; runner-up in PGA; runner-up in British Open. 1924: Winner of PGA, British Open, Belgian Open, North and South Open, and Rockaway PGA. 1925: Winner of PGA. 1926: Winner of PGA, Western Open, and Eastern Open. 1927: Winner of PGA and Western Open. 1928: Winner of British Open. 1929: Winner of British Open, Great Lakes Open, Miami Four-ball, Long Beach Open, and Virginia Beach Open. 1930: Winner of Coral Gables Open and Michigan PGA. 1931: Winner of Canadian Open and Michigan PGA; tied for first in Coral Gables Open. 1932: Winner of Western Open and St. Louis Open. 1935: Winner of Gasparilla Open. 1936: Winner of Inverness Four-ball.

HARBERT, MELVIN R. (CHICK). Born in Dayton, Ohio, February 20, 1915. He was a long driver who was a good stroke player and an outstanding match player. Harbert reached the final of the PGA three times, winning in 1954. He first attracted notice in 1937, when, as an amateur, he won the Michigan Open with an impressive score of 268. He also won the Trans-Mississippi and gained the quarter-finals of the U.S. Amateur before turning pro. He won three tourna-

ments in his first two years on the tour, then spent four years in the Air Corps. During the next decade, Harbert won several more tournaments, played on two Ryder Cup teams, and served as chairman of the PGA tournament committee.

Tournament Record: 1937: Winner of Michigan Open. 1939: Winner of Trans-Mississippi Amateur. 1941: Winner of Beaumont Open. 1942: Winner of Texas Open, St. Paul Open, and Michigan Open. 1946: Winner of Michigan PGA. 1947: Winner of Michigan PGA; runner-up in PGA. 1948: Winner of Jacksonville Open, Charlotte Open, and Michigan Open. 1949: Winner of Inverness Four-ball. 1952: Runner-up in PGA. 1953: Winner of Michigan Open. 1954: Winner of PGA. 1958: Winner of LaFayette Open.

HARPER, CHANDLER. Born March 10, 1914, at Portsmouth, Virginia. After a decade of winning amateur and open tournaments in his home state, Harper emerged after World War II as one of the better players on the pro tour. He won the PGA Championship in 1950 and continued to win tournaments on the circuit until past the age of forty. Despite his victories, he is perhaps best remembered as the man who had George May's "World" title apparently won until Lew Worsham's famous wedge shot for an eagle on the last hole snatched the $25,000 first prize from his grasp. Harper was capable of very hot streaks, and he set a PGA record of 259 in winning the 1954 Texas Open with rounds of 70–63–63–63. He once used only 20 putts in a round at Tucson in 1950.

Tournament Record: 1930: Winner of Virginia Amateur. 1932: Winner of Virginia Open. 1933, 1934: Winner of Virginia Amateur. 1938, 1940, 1941: Winner of Virginia Open. 1942: Winner of Miami Four-ball. 1950: Winner of PGA and Tucson Open. 1952: Winner of Virginia Open. 1953: Winner of El Paso Open. 1954: Winner of Texas Open. 1955: Winner of Colonial Invitational and Virginia Beach Open. 1960: Winner of Virginia Open and Virginia PGA. 1965: Winner of National Senior Open. 1968: Winner of PGA Senior.

HARRISON, ERNEST JOE (DUTCH). Born in Conway, Arkansas, March 29, 1910. Although he never won a major championship, Harrison won many tournaments over a period of almost four decades and was considered one of America's finest players. Harrison won the Vardon Trophy for low scoring average in 1954 and was still good enough to tie for third in the U.S. Open in 1960 and to play all 72 holes in the 1968 Open at the age of fifty-eight. He started as a left-hander

in Little Rock and won a local tournament before switching to right-handed golf. He served at various clubs during the 1930's and survived on the tour mostly by his wits. Harrison finally began to win just before World War II and after that was a regular winner for fifteen years. After reaching the age of fifty he won the National Seniors Open five times in six years.

Tournament Record: 1937: Winner of Arkansas Open, Tupelo Open, and Jackson Open. 1939: Winner of Bing Crosby National and Texas Open. 1940: Winner of Mississippi Open and Illinois PGA. 1944: Winner of Charlotte Open and Miami Open. 1945: Winner of St. Paul Open. 1947: Winner of Delaware Open, Reno Open, Reading Open, and Hawaiian Open. 1948: Winner of Richmond Open. 1949: Winner of Canadian Open. 1950: Winner of Azalea Open, California Open, and Wilmington Open. 1951: Winner of Texas Open. 1952: Winner of Havana Invitational and Reno Open. 1953: Winner of St. Petersburg Open, Western Open, and Columbia Open. 1954: Winner of Bing Crosby Pro-Am. 1956: Winner of All-America Open. 1958: Winner of Tijuana Open. 1961: Winner of Montana Open. 1962, 1963, 1964, 1965, 1967: Winner of National Seniors Open.

HOGAN, WILLIAM BENJAMIN. Born in Dublin, Texas, August 13, 1912. Ranks with Vardon and Jones among history's greatest golfers and is considered by many to be the best of all. Hogan won four United States Opens, two PGA Championships, two Masters, and a British Open and came close to doubling that figure, at least. From 1940 through 1960, he was never out of the top ten in the U.S. Open. He was Masters runner-up four times and was never worse than seventh from 1941 through 1956. He won the British Open on his only attempt and broke the course record at Carnoustie in the process. He set the scoring record in the U.S. Open and Masters. He was undefeated in Ryder Cup play. He was PGA player of the year four times. He won the Vardon Trophy four times. Impressive as all this was and is, Hogan doubtless would have done even better had it not been for the automobile accident in 1949 that nearly cost him his life. Everyone knows that Ben came back to win

WILLIAM BENJAMIN HOGAN

hotel room at night and hit shots for hours before and after a round. After returning from World War II service, he immediately picked up where he left off, winning everything in sight in 1946, 1947, and 1948. By this time, his swing was so precise that someone described it as being like a machine stamping out bottle caps. One got the feeling, not without some justification, that he could put the ball where he wanted. After the accident he was, if anything, a better player than ever, but he had to limit his schedule drastically because of physical limitations. At about this time also, he became a little less sour—off the course, at least—and people began to say he had mellowed. Whether he had or not did not affect his golf game, which remained in a class by itself as long as his ailments permitted him to play. In the 1967 Masters, for example, Hogan set a record by shooting the back nine in 30 strokes, one of the most dramatic and heart-warming performances of his career.

six of his nine major titles after the accident, but most persons feel he would have surpassed that had he been in top physical condition. They point to the many times he came down to the closing holes limping and visibly exhausted, finishing on guts and pride alone. Guts he had in abundance, and he needed every bit of it he could muster before becoming the great player everyone today remembers.

Hogan started out swinging left-handed as a youngster, but soon switched and became a promising young player. He turned pro while still in his teens, but attracted no national notice for almost a decade. Meanwhile, he probably hit more practice balls than anyone in history in the process of trying to cure a bad hook and become a winner on the pro tour. Ben began to win in 1940, and in the next three years he won three Vardon Trophies and was leading money winner three times. This success did not surprise those who had watched his hard work over the years, but it did not necessarily please all of them, either, for Ben was not the most popular player around. He was a grim competitor who had little to say on the course and whose determination to succeed was so great that he practiced putting in his

Tournament Record: 1938: Winner of Hershey Four-ball. 1940: Winner of North and South Open, Greensboro Open, Asheville Open, Goodall Round Robin, and Westchester Open. 1941: Winner of Miami Four-ball, Asheville Open, Inverness Four-ball, Chicago Open, and Hershey Open. 1942: Winner of Los Angeles Open, San Francisco Open, Hale America Open, North and South Open, Asheville Open, and Rochester Open; runner-up in Masters. 1945: Winner of Nashville Open, Portland Open, Richmond Open, Montgomery Open, and Orlando Open. 1946: Winner of PGA, Phoenix Open, San Antonio Open, St. Petersburg Open, Miami Four-ball, Colonial Invitational, Western Open, Goodall Round Robin, Inverness Four-ball, Winnipeg Open, Golden State Open, Dallas Invitational, and North and South Open; runner-up in Masters. 1947: Winner of Los Angeles Open, Phoenix Open, Miami-Four-ball, Colonial Invitational, Chicago Open, Inverness Four-ball, International Invitational, and Seminole Pro-Amateur. 1948: Winner of U.S. Open, PGA, Los Angeles Open, Motor City Open, Western Open, Inverness Four-ball, Reading Open, Denver Open, Reno Open, Glendale Open. 1949: Winner of Bing Crosby Invitational and Long Beach Open. 1950: Winner of U.S. Open and Greenbrier Pro-Am. 1951: Winner of U.S. Open, Masters, World Championship. 1952: Winner of Colonial Invitational. 1953: Winner of U.S. Open, Masters, British Open, Colonial Invitational, and Pan-American Open. 1954: Runner-up in Masters. 1955: Runner-up in U.S. Open and Masters. 1956: Winner of Canada Cup; tied for second in U.S. Open. 1959: Winner of Colonial Invitational.

HUTCHISON, Jock. Born in St. Andrews, Scotland, June 6, 1884. Died October 18, 1977. An outstanding player who was surpassed only by Walter Hagen and Jim Barnes in the years just after World War I. Hutchison won the PGA, the British Open, and many lesser tournaments, and in the U.S. Open he was runner-up once, tied for second once, and was third twice. He was a nervous, talkative player who was capable of great scoring bursts and whose skills were so enduring that he was able to shoot a 66 at the age of sixty-five. Following the example of dozens of his countrymen, Hutchison came to the United States from Scotland in the early years of the century and settled in the Pittsburgh area. After several years of local successes, he came into prominence in 1916 by finishing second in both the Open and the PGA. He won the PGA in 1920 and the British Open in 1921 at his native St. Andrews. About this time it became a tradition for Hutchison and Fred McLeod to be the first twosome off the tee in the Masters each year.
Tournament Record: 1909, 1910, 1913, 1914, 1915: Winner of Western Pennsylvania Open. 1916: Winner of Florida Open and Western Pennsylvania Open; runner-up in U.S. Open; runner-up in PGA. 1918: Winner of Patriotic Open. 1920: Winner of PGA and Western Open; tied for second in U.S. Open. 1921: Winner of British Open and North and South Open. 1922: Winner of Columbia Open and Northern California Open. 1923: Winner of Western Open. 1928: Winner of Belleair Open. 1946: Tied for first in PGA Senior. 1947: Winner of PGA Senior.

JAMESON, Betty. Born in Norman, Oklahoma, May 9, 1919. The Jameson golf career is dotted with major tournament victories, the first of which was recorded at the tender age of fifteen, when she took down the

JOCK HUTCHISON

Southern Amateur Championship. The next year, 1935, Betty won the first of four consecutive Texas State championships. She won the Trans-Mississippi in 1937 and 1940, the Texas Open in 1938, as an amateur, and again in 1949, as a professional, the USGA Amateur Championship in 1939 and 1940 and the Western Amateur in 1940 and 1942. Betty also won the Western Open in 1942, as an amateur, and again in 1954, as a professional. She became the first woman player to win the Western Ladies Open and Western Amateur in the same year—1942. After turning professional in 1945, Betty Jameson won the National Open in 1947 with a score of 295 and became the first woman player to score lower than 300 for a 72-hole tournament. She was elected to the Ladies Golf Hall of Fame in 1951 and won the World Championship in 1952.

JONES, Robert Tyre, Jr. Born in Atlanta, Georgia, March 17, 1902. Died December 18, 1971. One of the two or three greatest golfers in history and considered by many to be the greatest of all. Jones won 13 major championships—more than any other golfer—and climaxed his career with the Grand Slam in 1930, which consisted of winning the U.S. Open, British Open, U.S. Amateur, and British Amateur in a single season. George Trevor called it the "impregnable quadrilateral," and that is what it was. Aside from the record itself, which is remarkable, there are two things that make Jones's achievements all the more impressive. First, he was an amateur, and, unlike the pros, played in only a few tournaments each year. Second, he had compiled his amazing record and retired by the age of twenty-eight, an age when many other champions were just getting started. In all, Jones won four U.S. Opens (a feat per-

BETTY JAMESON

ROBERT TYRE JONES, JR.

formed earlier by Willie Anderson and later by Ben Hogan), five U.S. Amateurs, three British Opens, and one British Amateur.

Bob Jones was a child prodigy, having taken up the game early and patterned his swing more or less along the lines of Stewart Maiden, the Scottish pro who served at East Lake, Jones's course in Atlanta. By the time he reached his teens, Jones was outstanding: good enough, in fact, to play in the 1916 U.S. Amateur at the tender age of fourteen. This first appearance in a championship began what O. B. Keeler, his biographer, called the "seven lean years." During this period, Jones established himself as a great player and one who was overdue to win a major title. The lean years ended in 1923, and the seven years of plenty began when Jones won the United States Open at Inwood. From that point it was Jones against the field, with Jones usually prevailing. His dominance is best understood by reviewing his record in the U.S. Open. After finishing eighth in 1920 and fifth in 1921, he embarked on a nine-year streak that saw him win the title four times, finish second three times, and tie for second once. Only in 1927, when he tied for eleventh, was he worse than second. Finally, the strain of getting keyed up for the championships proved not to be worth the effort, and Jones retired. Subsequently, he began a long association with Spalding, made a pioneering series of movie shorts on instruction, and conceived and helped design the Augusta National course in Augusta, Georgia. Jones and Clifford Roberts began the Masters tournament there in 1934 and saw it grow over a relatively short time into one of the world's most cherished titles. The Masters was Jones's only tournament appearance for many years. He had to quit after two rounds

in 1947 because of what was diagnosed as bursitis in his shoulders. Later, the trouble was found to be a spinal ailment. Surgery failed to help, and his condition gradually deteriorated to such an extent that he was confined to a wheel chair. In later years, new young fans knew Jones as the gracious host of the Masters on television, and it was hard to realize that here was the man who was the hero of the Golden Age of sport. He had everything: wealth, good looks, tremendous talent, and the proper measure of both confidence and modesty. In short, Bobby Jones was the ideal All-American.

Tournament Record: 1916: Winner of Georgia Amateur. 1917: Winner of Southern Amateur. 1919: Runner-up in U.S. Amateur. 1920: Winner of Southern Amateur. 1922: Winner of Southern Amateur; tied for second in U.S. Open. 1923: Winner of U.S. Open. 1924: Winner of U.S. Amateur and Georgia-Alabama Open; runner-up in U.S. Open. 1925: Winner of U.S. Amateur; runner-up in U.S. Open. 1926: Winner of U.S. Open and British Open; runner-up in U.S. Amateur. 1927: Winner of U.S. Amateur, British Open, Southern Open, and Atlanta Open. 1928: Winner of U.S. Amateur; runner-up in U.S. Open. 1929: Winner of U.S. Open. 1930: Winner of U.S. Open, British Open, U.S. Amateur, British Amateur, and Augusta Open.

WILLIAM LAWSON LITTLE, JR.

LITTLE, WILLIAM LAWSON, JR. Born in Fort Adams, Newport, Rhode Island, June 23, 1910. Died February 1, 1968. One of America's greatest amateurs and probably the greatest between the retirement of Bobby Jones and the advent of Jack Nicklaus. Little won the U.S. and British Amateurs in 1934, then won the same two events the next year in a feat that deserves to be ranked close to Jones's Grand Slam of 1930 and Ben Hogan's sweep of 1953. Although he turned professional in 1936 and later won the U.S. Open, Little's fame rests on that string of 31 consecutive match victories. Little first attracted real attention in the 1933 U.S. Amateur when he reached the semifinals, although he had created a stir back in 1929 when, as a teen-ager, he had beaten Johnny Goodman right after Goodman upset Jones in the first round at Pebble Beach. His performance in the 1933 Amateur earned Little a berth on the Walker Cup Team, and it was in those matches, against the British at St. Andrews in 1934, that his great streak began. He turned pro in 1936 amid great fanfare, but, although he was to win several tournaments, including the Open, he never really lived up to expectations.

Tournament Record: 1928, 1930: Winner of Northern California Amateur. 1932: Winner of Broadmoor Invitational. 1933: Winner of Colorado Closed Amateur. 1934:

Winner of U.S. Amateur and British Amateur. 1935: Winner of U.S. Amateur and British Amateur. 1936: Winner of Canadian Open. 1937: Winner of Shawnee Open and San Francisco Match Play. 1940: Winner of U.S. Open and Los Angeles Open. 1941: Winner of Texas Open. 1942: Winner of Inverness Four-ball. 1948: Winner of St. Petersburg Open.

LITTLER, GENE ALEC. Born July 21, 1930, at San Diego, California. The winner of both the U.S. Amateur and National Open and one of the smoothest swingers in golf. Littler turned pro early in 1954 and over the next 15 years won more than 20 tournaments and well over a half-million dollars. So fluid was his swing that when he won the San Diego Open in his first pro start, people were predicting Littler would be the game's next superstar. When he finished second in the U.S. Open that year, then won five tournaments in 1955, the experts seemed justified in their prognostications. Littler continued to win in 1956, but he was tapering off; and in 1957 and 1958, he fell into a slump that was broken only by his third straight victory in the Tournament of Champions. During this period he had begun to tinker with his swing and, in the course of struggling to regain his old consistency, received a spate of varied and confusing advice. However, it all came back in 1959 and Littler won five tournaments and finished the year as second money winner. Since then he has been one of the tour's steadiest money winners. In fact, in 1969, he jumped off to a phenomenal start with two victories and more than $100,000 in prize money in the first four months.

In the spring of 1972, Littler underwent surgery for cancer of the lymph glands, and it was feared his career was over. He rejoined the tour six months later and had won five tour events from then through 1977.

He was awarded the Ben Hogan Trophy for his courageous comeback in 1973.

Tournament Record: 1948: Winner of U.S. Jaycee Junior. 1953: Winner of U.S. Amateur, California Open, and California Amateur. 1954: Winner of San Diego Open; runner-up in U.S. Open. 1955: Winner of Los Angeles Open, Pan-American Open,

GENE ALEC LITTLER

ARTHUR D'ARCY LOCKE

Phoenix Open, Tournament of Champions, and LaBatt Open. 1956: Winner of Texas Open, Tournament of Champions, Palm Beach Round Robin, and Arizona Open. 1957: Winner of Tournament of Champions. 1959: Winner of Phoenix Open, Tucson Open, Arlington Hotel Open, Insurance City Open, and Miller Open. 1960: Winner of Oklahoma City Open and Eastern Open. 1961: Winner of U.S. Open. 1962: Winner of Lucky International Open and Thunderbird Invitational. 1964: Winner of Southern California Open. 1965: Winner of Canadian Open. 1966: Winner of World Series of Golf. 1969: Winner of Phoenix Open and Greater Greensboro Open. 1971: Winner of Monsanto Open and Colonial National Invitional. 1973: Winner of St. Louis Classic. 1975: Winner of Bing Crosby National Pro-Am, Danny Thomas–Memphis Classic, and Westchester Classic. 1977: Winner of Houston Open.

LOCKE, ARTHUR D'ARCY (BOBBY). Born in Germiston, Transvaal, South Africa, November 20, 1917. A four-time winner of the British Open and the first foreign player to become a consistent winner in the United States. Locke, the son of a successful sports outfitter in South Africa, took to the game early and was a champion while still in his teens. Then, after flying more than a hundred Liberator missions during World War II,

he returned to golf and quickly became a player of world stature. He hit the United States circuit in 1947 and proceeded to win seven tournaments and finish second on the money-winning list. He made several subsequent appearances in the States and was in the top five in the U.S. Open five times. Locke was not a stylish player, but he had a fine short game and was a great putter. In appearance he was the very antithesis of the postwar professional. He wore knickers, a white shirt, and tie and displayed a swing that could hardly be said to compare with Vardon's. All this made his appearance on the American scene a refreshing one, but he soon discovered that the important thing on the United States tour was money, and his attitude changed to a more businesslike one.

Tournament Record: 1931: Winner of South Africa Boys. 1935: Winner of South

Africa Open, South Africa Amateur, Natal Open, Natal Amateur, and Transvaal Amateur. 1936: Winner of Natal Open, Natal Amateur, and Lucifer Empire Trophy. 1937: Winner of South Africa Open, South Africa Amateur, Transvaal Amateur, and Orange Free State Amateur. 1938: Winner of South Africa Open, Irish Open, New Zealand Open, South Africa Professional, and Transvaal Open. 1939: Winner of South Africa Open, Dutch Open, South Africa Professional, and Transvaal Open. 1940: Winner of South Africa Open, Transvaal Open, and South Africa Professional. 1946: Winner of South Africa Open, South Africa Professional, Transvaal Open, Yorkshire *Evening News* Tournament, Dunlop Masters, and Brand Lochryn Tournament; runner-up in British Open. 1947: Winner of Canadian Open, Houston Invitational, Philadelphia *Inquirer* Open, All-America Open, Columbus Open, Goodall Round Robin, Carolinas PGA, and South Africa Dunlop Tournament. 1948: Winner of Phoenix Open, Chicago Victory Open, and Carolinas Open. 1949: Winner of British Open, Transvaal Open, Cavalier Invitational, Goodall Round Robin, and Greenbrier Pro-Am. 1950: Winner of British Open, South Africa Open, South Africa Professional, Transvaal Open, Dunlop Tournament, Spalding Tournament, All-America Open, and North British Tournament. 1951: Winner of South Africa Open, Transvaal Open, and South Africa Professional. 1952: Winner of British Open, French Open, Mexican Open, and Lotus Tournament. 1953: Winner of French Open, and Natal Open. 1954: Winner of Egyptian Open, German Open, Swiss Open, Dunlop Tournament, Dunlop Masters, Egyptian Match Play, Transvaal Open, and Swallow-Harrogate Tournament; tied for second in British Open. 1955: Winner of Australian Open, Transvaal Open, South Africa Open, and South Africa Professional. 1957: Winner of British Open, Daks Tournament, and Bowmaker Amateur-Professional. 1958: Winner of Transvaal Open.

MANGRUM, LLOYD EUGENE. Born in Trenton, Texas, August 1, 1914. Died November 17, 1973. One of the most succesful campaigners in postwar American golf. Mangrum won the U.S. Open in 1946 and tied for

LLOYD EUGENE MANGRUM

first in 1950, losing in a play-off. He also finished in the top five on four other occasions. In the Masters he was fourth or better seven times, and in the PGA he was a semifinalist twice and a quarter-finalist twice. In a career that covered more than two decades, he won over 50 tournaments, played on three Ryder Cup Teams, and twice won the Vardon Trophy for low scoring average.

Mangrum grew up in Texas, where he learned the game along with such heroes as Ben Hogan, Byron Nelson, Ralph Guldahl, and Jimmy Demaret. He turned pro in 1929 at the age of fifteen and played in his first PGA-sponsored tournament at nineteen. The 1930's were lean years for him, like everyone else, but near the end of the decade he began to display the skills that were to make him one of the game's top all-time money winners. Mangrum began to follow the tour in earnest in 1939, and by 1940 he had arrived. That season he won the Thomasville Open, finished second in the Masters after opening with a course-record 64, and ran fifth in the U.S.

Open. He was seventh money winner in 1941 and advanced to fourth in 1942 before entering the Army, where he attained the rank of staff sergeant. He was wounded twice in the Battle of the Bulge and spent part of his convalescent period at St. Andrews, where he won a GI tournament in 1945. Mangrum rejoined the tournament circuit in 1946 and launched a nine-year run during which he won 35 tournaments and never was out of the top 10 money winners. With his thin mustache and with black hair parted in the middle, he had the look of a river-boat gambler, and this, plus his obvious skills, quickly made him a gallery favorite.

Tournament Record: 1938: Winner of Pennsylvania Open. 1940: Winner of Thomasville Open; runner-up in Masters. 1941: Winner of Atlantic City Open. 1942: Winner of New Orleans Open, Inverness Fourball, and Seminole Pro-Amateur. 1945: Winner of Army Victory Tournament and GI Tournament. 1946: Winner of U.S. Open and Argentine Open. 1947: Winner of National Capital Open, Albuquerque Open, and Montebello Open. 1948: Winner of Bing Crosby Invitational, Rio Grande Valley Open, Greensboro Open, Columbus Open, All-American Open, World Tournament, Utah Open and Zooligans Open. 1949: Winner of Los Angeles Open, Tucson Open, and All-American Open; tied for first in Motor City Open. 1950: Winner of Eastern Open, Fort Wayne Open, Kansas City Open, Motor City Open, and runner-up in U.S. Open. 1951: Winner of Los Angeles Open, Tucson Open, Seminole Pro-Amateur, Azalea Open, and St. Paul Open. 1952: Winner of Phoenix Open, Pan-American Open, Western Open, California Open, and Montebello Open. 1953: Winner of Los Angeles Open, Phoenix Open, Bing Crosby Invitational, and All-American Open. 1954: Winner of Western Open. 1956: Winner of Los Angeles Open. 1960: Winner of Southern California Open.

McDERMOTT, JOHN J. Born in Philadelphia, August 12, 1891. Died August 1, 1971. America's first great homebred professional, a man who came virtually out of nowhere to win two straight U.S. National Opens, then disappeared from the scene almost as rapidly. McDermott tied for first in the 1910 Open,

JOHN J. McDERMOTT

lost the play-off, then won the next two years. Three years later, however, he was out of golf, the victim of mental illness. He was full of ego and determination, feared no one, and let everybody know it. He was bitterly disappointed at losing the 1910 play-off to Alex Smith, and he told Alex the situation would be corrected the following year. It was. He also played in two British Opens because he wanted to convince the British he was no accident. So bright was the flame within McDermott that many said he simply burned himself out in his unparalleled drive to be better than everyone else. At any rate, he raised himself from a run-of-the-mill player to the championship class in only one season.

Tournament Record: 1910: Runner-up in U.S. Open. 1911, 1912: Winner of U.S. Open. 1913: Winner of Western Open, Shawnee Open, and Philadelphia Open.

DR. CARY MIDDLECOFF

McLEOD, FREDERICK ROBERTSON. Born in North Berwick, Scotland, April 25, 1882. Died May 8, 1976. The 1908 U.S. Open champion and one of the game's most respected figures for more than half a century. McLeod came to the United States from Scotland in 1903 and succeeded despite his small size. In winning the 1908 Open, McLeod lost ten pounds, from 118 to 108. Over the years he played in 20 Opens and finished in the top ten eight times. He was runner-up in the 1919 PGA. McLeod won the PGA Senior in 1938 and was still able to shoot a 66 at the age of sixty-six. In later years he and Jock Hutchison became fixtures at Augusta each April when they traditionally were the first twosome off the tee in the Masters.

Tournament Record: 1898, 1903: Winner of Hope Challenge Medal. 1905: Winner of Riverside Open and Western PGA. 1907: Winner of Western PGA. 1908: Winner of U.S. Open. 1909: Winner of North and South Open. 1912: Winner of Shawnee Open. 1919: Runner-up in PGA. 1920: Winner of North and South Open. 1921: Tied for second in U.S. Open. 1924: Winner of St. Petersburg Open. 1927: Winner of Maryland Open. 1938: Winner of PGA Senior.

MIDDLECOFF, DR. CARY. Born in Halls, Tennessee, January 6, 1921. Winner of two U.S. Open titles and the biggest money winner in American golf in the fifteen years following World War II. Middlecoff also lost in a play-off for the Open and, in addition, won one Masters and was runner-up twice. Although he had a fine amateur record, Middlecoff did not attract widespread notice until 1945, when he defeated the pros in the North and South Open. At the time he was an officer in the Army Medical Corps, having followed his father into the practice of dentistry. After his discharge, he gained the quarterfinals of the 1946 U.S. Amateur and was named to the Walker Cup Team, but withdrew in order to turn professional. He won one tourney in 1947 and the next year won twice and was runner-up in the Masters. In 1949, he won the Open and five other tournaments, and a new star had emerged. Over the next seven years he won at least one tournament a year—and sometimes as many as six—and was never lower than sixth on the money list. Although he drew criticism for his excruciatingly slow play, no one denied Middlecoff's talent. He was a great striker of the ball, was very long off the tee, and did an excellent job around the greens.

Tournament Record: 1937: Winner of Tennessee High School title. 1938, 1939: Winner of Memphis Amateur. 1940: Winner of Tennessee Amateur and West Kentucky Open. 1941: Winner of Tennessee Amateur, West Kentucky Open, and Southeastern Intercollegiate. 1942, 1943: Winner of Tennessee Amateur. 1945: Winner of North and South Open. 1947: Winner of Charlotte Open. 1948: Winner of Miami Four-ball and Hawaiian Open; runner-up in Masters. 1949: Winner of U.S. Open, Rio Grande Valley Open, Miami Four-ball, Reading Open, Jacksonville Open, and Greenbrier Invitational; tied for first in Motor City Open. 1950: Winner of Houston Open, Seminole Pro-Amateur, Jacksonville Open, and St. Louis Open. 1951: Winner of Lakewood Park Open, Colonial Invitational, All-American Open, Eastern Open, St. Louis Open, and Kansas City Open. 1952: Winner of El Paso Open, Motor City Open, St. Paul Open, and Kansas City Open. 1953: Winner of Houston Open, Palm Beach Round Robin, and Carling Open. 1954: Winner of Motor City Open. 1955: Winner of Masters, Bing Crosby Invitational, Western Open, Miller Open, and Cavalcade of Golf. 1956: Winner of U.S. Open, Bing Crosby Invitational, and Phoenix Open. 1957: Runner-up in U.S. Open and winner of Bing Crosby Pro-Am. 1958: Winner of Miller Open. 1959: Winner of St. Petersburg Open; runner-up in Masters. 1961: Winner of Memphis Open.

MILLER, JOHN. Born in San Francisco, California, April 29, 1947. He received his degree in Physical Education at Brigham Young University in 1969, where he played varsity golf. He turned pro immediately. He had attracted attention initially in the 1966 U.S. Open, in which he was supposed to caddie. A last-minute dropout gave him a place in the field and he wound up the low amateur—at only nineteen years of age.

In his second year on the tour he began to show positive signs of being a comer. The next year he jumped to No. 18 on the money list. And then, in 1973, he startled the golf world with an incredible 63 in the final round to win the U.S. Open. He surpassed this feat in 1974, when he won eight tour events and set a new all-time money record of $353,021.

JOHNNY MILLER

He won the British Open in 1976, was runner-up twice in the Masters, and won two World Cup titles. He was the Player of the Year in 1974.

Tournament Record: 1971: ˊWinner of Southern Open. 1972: Winner of Heritage Classic. 1973: Winner of U.S. Open. 1974: Winner of Bing Crosby National Pro-Am, Phoenix Open, Dean Martin–Tucson Open, Heritage Classic, Tournament of Champions, Westchester Classic, World Open, Kaiser International. 1975: Winner of Phoenix Open, Dean Martin–Tucson Open, Bob Hope Desert Classic, Kaiser International. 1976: Winner of NBC Tucson Open, Bob Hope Desert Classic.

MORRIS, THOMAS (OLD TOM). Born in St. Andrews, Scotland, June 26, 1821. Died May 27, 1908. A leading figure in Scottish golf for more than half a century and the first four-time winner of the British Open. Morris was apprenticed at the age of eighteen to Allan Robertson, the leading player of the

THOMAS MORRIS, SR. AND JR.

day, in the ball-making trade. He was employed at Prestwick from 1851 to 1865, then returned to St. Andrews as greenskeeper, a post he held until 1904. Morris teamed with Robertson to win many great matches, and later he and his son, Tom, Jr., were virtually invincible. At his death, Morris was possibly the most revered man in the game. His British Open victories came in 1861, 1862, 1864, and 1867.

MORRIS, THOMAS, JR. (YOUNG TOM). Born in St. Andrews, Scotland, in 1850. Died December 25, 1875. The greatest player in the early recorded history of the game. Young Tom was a championship player at the age of sixteen, and by the time he was eighteen he won the first of his four British Open titles, all of which came in succession. By winning in 1868, 1869, and 1870, he gained permanent possession of the championship belt. The tournament was then held in abeyance for a year, and when the present cup was put up for competition in 1872, Morris won again. He and his father formed

a formidable combination on the links, and it was during their match with Willie and Mungo Park that Young Tom received news of the sudden death of his wife. He never recovered from the shock and died a few months later, at the age of twenty-five.

NELSON, JOHN BYRON, JR. Born in Fort Worth, Texas, February 4, 1912. One of the greatest players in the history of golf, a man whose true greatness can never accurately be gauged because of the circumstances that prevailed when he was at his peak. Nelson proved his ability by winning the U.S. Open, the Masters, and two PGA Championships and finishing second in two other PGA's between 1937 and 1942. But it was in 1944 and 1945, with most of the top players off to war (Nelson had been rejected because of hemophilia), that he really hit his stride. In 1944 he won seven tournaments, was the leading money winner, averaged 69.67 strokes for 85 rounds, and was voted the athlete of the year. Even that record paled before his performance in 1945, when he won 19 tournaments (11 in succession), was leading money winner, averaged an incredible 68.33 strokes for 120 rounds, and again was named athlete of the year. By the end of that span he had finished in the money in 113 consecutive tournaments and, at Seattle in 1945, had tied an 18-hole record of 62 and had set a 72-hole record of 259. During those years— and since—the argument raged: was he the greatest player who ever lived or were his records to be discounted because he set them when there was no competition?

At any rate, Nelson retired during the 1946 season because, like Bobby Jones before him, he was simply worn out from the strain of constant competition; it was getting to be too much of an effort to gear up emotionally to meet the challenge week after week.

Tournament Record: 1930: Winner of Southwest Amateur. 1935: Winner of New Jersey Open. 1936: Winner of Metropolitan Open. 1937: Winner of Masters, Belmont Open, Thomasville Open, and Central Pennsylvania Open. 1938: Winner of Thomasville Open and Hollywood Open. 1939: Winner of U.S. Open, Western Open, North and South Open, Phoenix Open, and Massachusetts Open; runner-up in PGA. 1940: Winner of PGA, Texas Open, Miami Open, and Ohio Open. 1941: Winner of Miami Open, Greensboro Open, Ohio Open, All-American Open, and Seminole Pro-Amateur; runner-up in PGA and Masters. 1942: Winner of Masters, All-American Open, Oakland Open, Ohio Open, and Charles River Invitational. 1943: Winner of Kentucky Open. 1944: Winner of All-American Open, San Francisco Open, Knoxville Open, Red Cross Open, Golden Valley Open, Beverly Hills Open, and Nashville Open; runner-up in PGA. 1945: Winner of PGA, Canadian Open, Canadian PGA, All-American Open, San Antonio Open, Phoenix Open, Corpus Christi Open, New Orleans Open, Miami Four-ball, Charlotte Open, Greensboro Open, Durham Open, Atlanta Open, Philadelphia *Inquirer* Open, Spring Lake Invitational, Chicago Victory Open, Knoxville Open, Esmeralda Open, Spokane Open, Seattle Open, and Fort Worth Open. 1946: Winner of Los Angeles Open, San Francisco Open, New Orleans Open, Houston Invitational, Columbus Invitational and Chicago Victory Open; tied for second in U.S. Open. 1947: Tied for second in Masters. 1948: Winner of Texas PGA. 1951: Winner of Bing Crosby Invitational. 1955: Winner of French Open.

NICKLAUS, Jack William. Born in Columbus, Ohio, January 21, 1940. An awesome golfer who, many persons believe, is the greatest player in the history of the sport. He already has won five Masters, three U.S. Opens, two British Opens, four PGA Championships, and two U.S. Amateurs. At the age of thirty-eight he is the all-time money winner on the PGA circuit. Nicklaus was good enough to win the Ohio Open at sixteen, win the U.S. Amateur at nineteen, and finish second in the U.S. Open at twenty, by which time he was driving the ball prodigious distances and had become the most talked-about amateur since Bobby Jones. After winning his second U.S. Amateur, in 1961, he turned pro, and in 1962 he defeated Arnold Palmer in a play-off to win the Open at Oakmont. From that moment he shared the limelight, if not the popularity, with Palmer, and the two began to be mentioned in the same breath as America's best. Nicklaus convinced the few who were present by beating Charlie Coe in a classic U.S. Amateur final at Broadmoor in 1959. Then, in the World Amateur team championship at Merion, in 1960, he convinced everybody else by scoring 269 for 72 holes over one of the game's greatest layouts. Hogan had won there in 1950 with a 287. He subsequently invited further comparison with Hogan by lowering the Ice Mon's record for both the Masters and U.S. Open.

Tournament Record: 1956: Winner of Ohio Open. 1957: Winner of Jaycee Junior. 1958: Winner of Trans-Mississippi Amateur and Queen City Open. 1959: Winner of U.S. Amateur, Trans-Mississippi Amateur, and North and South Amateur. 1960: Winner of World Amateur, International Four-ball, Colonial Invitational Amateur; runner-up in U.S. Open. 1961: Winner of U.S. Amateur, Western Amateur, and U.S. Intercollegiate. 1962: Winner of U.S. Open, World Series, Seattle Open, and Portland Open. 1963: Winner of World Series, Masters, PGA, Sahara Invitational, Palm Springs Classic, and Tournament of Champions. 1964: Winner of Phoenix Open, Portland Open, Whitemarsh Open, Tournament of Champions, and Australian Open; runner-up in British Open. 1965: Winner of Masters, Portland Open, Memphis Open, Thunderbird Classic, and Philadelphia Classic. 1966: Winner of Masters, British Open, Sahara Invitational, and PGA National Team Championship. 1967: Winner of U.S. Open, Bing Crosby Invitational, Western Open, Sahara Invitational, World Series, and Westchester Classic. 1968: Winner of Western Open and American Golf Classic. 1969: Winner of Andy Williams–San Diego Open, Sahara Invitational, and Kaiser International Open. 1970: Winner of Byron Nelson Classic, British Open, Piccadilly World Match Play Championship, World Series of Golf, and National Four-ball Championship with Arnold Palmer. 1971: Winner of PGA Championship, Tournament of Champions, Byron Nelson Classic, Walt Disney World Open, and National Team Championship with Arnold Palmer. 1972: Winner of Bing Crosby National Pro-Am, Doral-Eastern Open, Masters, USGA Open Championship, Westchester Classic, U.S. Professional Match Play Championship, Australian Open, and Walt Disney World Open. 1973: Winner of Bing Crosby National Pro-Am, New Orleans Open, Tournament of Champions, Atlanta Classic, PGA Championship, Ohio Kings Island Open, and Disney Team Championship.* 1974: Winner of Hawaiian Open and Tournament Players Championship. 1975: Winner of Doral-Eastern Open. 1976: Winner of Tournament Players Championship and World Series of Golf. 1977: Winner of Jackie Gleason–Inverrary Classic, Tournament of Champions, and Memorial Tournament.

OUIMET, FRANCIS DESALES. Born in Brookline, Massachusetts, May 8, 1893. Died September 2, 1967. America's first real golfing hero, the man who defeated Harry Vardon and Ted Ray in a play-off for the U.S. Open title in 1913 and thereby removed whatever stigma there might have been against golf being a game for the common man. Ouimet was a former caddie and the son of a man of modest means, and after his stunning victory, Americans no longer regarded golf as a game for the idle rich. Although Ouimet went on to win two U.S. Amateurs and many other tournaments and to build an impeccable reputation at home and abroad, he will always be remembered as the man who stopped the British with the shots heard round the golfing world. Ouimet followed his historic victory by winning the U.S. Amateur in 1914. Then came the war, and then came Bobby Jones, and it was 1931 before he won the Amateur again, although he was a semifinalist many times. Ouimet was player or captain of every

*Team event.

team America sent against Britain from 1921 through 1949, with the result that he became a very respected figure overseas. The British showed their opinion of him in 1951 when they made him captain of the Royal and Ancient Golf Club at St. Andrews, the first American to receive the honor.

Tournament Record: 1909: Winner of Boston Interscholastic. 1913: Winner of U.S. Open and Massachusetts Amateur. 1914: Winner of U.S. Amateur, French Amateur, and Massachusetts Amateur. 1915: Winner of Massachusetts Amateur. 1917: Winner of Western Amateur. 1919: Winner of Massachusetts Amateur. 1920: Winner of North and South Amateur; runner-up in U.S. Amateur. 1922: Winner of Massachusetts Amateur and Houston Invitational. 1923: Winner of St. George's Challenge Cup. 1924: Winner of Crump Memorial. 1925: Winner of Massachusetts Amateur and Gold Mashie Tournament. 1927: Winner of Crump Memorial. 1931: Winner of U.S. Amateur. 1932: Winner of Massachusetts Open.

PALMER, ARNOLD DANIEL. Born in Latrobe, Pennsylvania, September 10, 1929. One of the most dynamic and popular individuals in all the history of sport, a man who almost singlehandedly raised golf to its present level of popularity. From his earliest amateur days, Palmer was a go-for-broke player, and this style, coupled with his great ability, quickly produced victories on the pro tour and attracted fans by the thousands. Other players had hitched up their trousers and knocked in 50-foot putts, but none had done so quite like Palmer. His emotions were plain to see, after good shots and bad, and his Army suffered with him, in person or through the medium of television. His galleries finally became so huge it was a definite handicap to his playing partners, many of whom felt they had been trampled in the rush. With all this color, Palmer also provided skill. He won four Masters, one U.S. Open, and two British Opens in addition to the U.S. Amateur and dozens more. All this netted him more money than anyone ever made playing golf—over a million dollars by 1968—plus countless more dollars through a variety of businesses set up for him by his friend and manager, Mark McCormack. Much of this activity was

ARNOLD DANIEL PALMER

grouped under the heading of Arnold Palmer Enterprises and was sold to RCA for several millions of dollars in the mid-1960's. All this did not help his golf game, and it was a virtually unanimous feeling among observers of the sport that his widespread interests left him without enough time to hone his skill. Certainly as he passed the age of thirty-five his play became a little less forceful and he ceased making every putt he looked at. Meanwhile, he was flitting about the world in his private jet airplane, attending to business, playing exhibitions, appearing at various functions—and trying to squeeze in some tournament golf when possible. Despite his failure to win a major championship after 1964, his galleries remained the largest on the course and his supporters continued to greet every birdie with a cry of "Charge," even when he obviously was not in contention. The adulation of his fans was so great that the slightest injury or indisposition became of national concern. There were many who no doubt felt he could walk on water if the situation demanded it, and there had been a time when it seemed he almost could. That was in 1960 when his reputation as a "charger" was established. In the Masters that year he birdied the last two holes to win by a stroke, and in the U.S. Open at Cherry Hills he went out the last round and shot the front nine in 30 strokes, finishing with a 65 for what had seemed an impossible victory. Palmer was voted in 1970 the Associated Press Athlete of the Decade as well as winning the Golfer of the Decade poll.

Tournament Record: 1947: Winner of Western Pennsylvania Amateur. 1953: Winner of Ohio Amateur. 1954: Winner of U.S. Amateur and Ohio Amateur. 1955: Winner of Canadian Open. 1956: Winner of Insurance City Open and Eastern Open. 1957: Winner of Azalea Open, Houston Open, San Diego Open, Rubber City Open, and Western Pennsylvania Open. 1958: Winner of Masters, St. Petersburg Open, and Pepsi Open. 1959: Winner of West Palm Beach Open, Thunderbird Invitational, and Oklahoma City Open. 1960: Winner of U.S. Open, Masters, Palm Springs Classic, Texas Open, Baton Rouge Open, Pensacola Open, Insurance City Open, and Mobile Open; runner-up in British Open. 1961: Winner of British Open, San Diego Open, Phoenix Open, Baton Rouge Open, Seminole Pro-Amateur, Texas Open, and Western Open; tied for second in Masters. 1962: Winner of British Open, Masters, Palm Springs Classic, Phoenix Open, Texas Open, Tournament of Champions, American Golf Classic, and Colonial Invitational; runner-up in U.S. Open. 1963: Winner of Los Angeles Open, Phoenix Open, Pensacola Open, Thunderbird Classic, Cleveland Open, Western Open, and Whitemarsh Open; tied for second in U.S. Open. 1964: Winner of Masters and Oklahoma City Open; tied for second in PGA. 1965: Winner of Tournament of Champions; tied for second in Masters. 1966: Winner of Los Angeles Open, Tournament of Champions, Houston Champions International, and PGA National Team Championship; runner-up in U.S. Open. 1967: Winner of Los Angeles Open, Tucson Open, American Golf Classic, and Thunderbird Classic; runner-up in U.S. Open. 1968: Winner of Bob Hope Classic and Kemper Open; tied for second in PGA. 1969: Winner of Heritage Classic and Danny Thomas-Diplomat Classic. 1970: Winner of National Four-

ball Championship with Jack Nicklaus. 1971: Winner of Bob Hope Desert Classic, Florida Citrus Invitational, Westchester Classic, French Lancome, and National Team Championship with Jack Nicklaus. 1973: Winner of Bob Hope Desert Classic.

PICARD, HENRY G. Born in Plymouth, Massachusetts, November 28, 1907. Winner of the 1938 Masters and 1939 PGA Championship, Picard possessed one of the finest swings in golf and ranked high among the stars of the 1930's. Picard's first victory of consequence came in the 1934 North and South Open. In 1935 he became professional at Hershey, Pennsylvania, and almost immediately he moved to the fore among the touring pros. That season, labeled The Chocolate Soldier by writers after his move to Hershey, he won six tournaments. Although at his peak, Picard began to curtail his tournament play as early as 1940. He made only a few token appearances after World War II and thus was a disappointment to his many followers, who felt he could have stayed at the top for many more years.

Tournament Record: 1925, 1926, 1932, 1933: Winner of Carolina Open and Charleston Open. 1934: Winner of North and South Open. 1935: Winner of Atlanta Open, Agua Caliente Open, Charleston Open, Metropolitan Open, Miami Four-ball, and Inverness Four-ball. 1936: Winner of North and South Open, Hershey Open, Miami Four-ball, and Charleston Open. 1937: Winner of Miami Four-ball, Hershey Open, Argentine Open, and Charleston Open. 1938: Winner of Mas-

ters and Pasadena Open. 1939: Winner of
PGA, New Orleans Open, Thomasville Open,
Inverness Four-ball, Scranton Open, and
Metropolitan Open. 1941: Winner of New
Orleans Open and Harlingen Open. 1945:
Winner of Miami Open.

PLAYER, GARY JIM. Born in Johannes-
burg, South Africa, November 1, 1935. One
of only four men ever to win the four major
championships of golf, an intense, dedicated
young man who became one of the game's
Big Three with Palmer and Nicklaus despite
his small stature. Player finished fourth in the
British Open at the age of twenty, and to
prove he was really that good, he defeated his
fellow South African, Bobby Locke, in a
special 108-hole match the next year. This
established him as a player of talent, and he
never again had to prove anything to anybody.
Probably no one short of Hogan ever worked
any harder to achieve success. Aside from the
hours of practice, Player became a serious
physical fitness advocate and credited his con-
ditioning program with giving him added
strength, plus length off the tee.

Player won many friends when he gave
away his entire purse of $25,000 for winning
the 1965 U.S. Open. A portion was set aside
for medical research, and the rest went to the
USGA to further junior golf.

Tournament Record: 1956: Winner of

South African Open. 1958: Winner of Aus-
tralian Open and Kentucky Derby Open;
runner-up in U.S. Open. 1959: Winner of
British Open, South Africa Match Play, and
Transvaal Open. 1960: Winner of South Afri-
can Open, Transvaal Open, and South Africa
Dunlop Tournament. 1961: Winner of Mas-
ters, Lucky International Open, and Sunshine
Open. 1962: Winner of PGA, Australian
Open, and Transvaal Open; runner-up in
Masters. 1963: Winner of Australian Open
and San Diego Open. 1964: Winner of Pen-
sacola Open and 500 Festival Open. 1965:
Winner of U.S. Open, Australian Open, and
South African Open; tied for second in Mas-
ters. 1966: Winner of South African Open,
South African Dunlop Tournament, Natal
Open, and Transvaal Open. 1967: Winner of
South African Open. 1968: Winner of British
Open, World Series, Piccadilly Match Play,
South African Open, Natal Open, Western
Province Open, and Wills Masters. 1969:
Winner of South African Open, Australian
Open, and Tournament of Champions. 1970:
Winner of Greater Greensboro Open. 1971:
Winner of Greater Jacksonville Open, Aus-
tralian Open, Piccadilly Match Play Cham-
pionship, and National Airlines Open. 1972:
Winner of Greater New Orleans Open, South
African Open, International Japan Airlines
Open, PGA Championship, World Series of
Golf, and Brazilian Open. 1972: Winner of
New Orleans Open, PGA Championship;
World Series of Golf, and South African
Open. 1973: Winner of Southern Open, Pic-
cadilly Match Play. 1974: Winner of Masters,
British Open, Australian Open, Brazilian
Open, and Danny Thomas–Memphis Open.
1975: Winner of South African Open.

RANKIN, JUDITH TORLUEMKE. Born February 18, 1945, in St. Louis, Missouri.
Started to play golf at the age of six under her
father's tutelage, and by the time she was
eight she had won a string of four St. Louis
PeeWee titles. At fourteen, she was the
youngest ever to win a Missouri State championship. She was low amateur in the 1960
U.S. Open, when she was fifteen, and was a
semifinalist in the U.S. Girls' Junior. And
she was only seventeen when she joined the
professional ranks—one of the youngest ever.
Success didn't come easily as a pro, how-

JUDITH RANKIN

of National Jewish Hospital Open. 1976: Winner of Burdine's Invitational, Colgate–Dinah Shore Winners Circle, Karsten-Ping Open, Babe Zaharias Invitational, Borden Classic, and Colgate–Hong Kong Open. 1977: Winner of Orange Blossom Classic, Bent Tree Classic, Mayflower Classic, Peter Jackson Classic, Colgate–European Open, and LPGA Team Championship (with JoAnne Carner).

RAWLS, ELIZABETH EARLE (BETSY). Born May 4, 1928, at Spartanburg, South Carolina. A four-time winner of the U.S. Women's Open and one of the biggest money winners in the history of the LPGA tour. Betsy did not start playing golf until she was seventeen, but within four years she was good enough to win the Trans-Mississippi and the Texas Women's Amateur. The next year, 1950, she was again winning tournaments and was able to finish second in the U.S. Open as an amateur. In 1951, by now a Phi Beta Kappa graduate in physics from the University of Texas, she turned professional and immediately won the first of her four Open championships. Over the next two decades, Betsy won more than 50 tournaments and accumulated almost a quarter-million dollars in prize money. In July, 1975, she retired as an active player and became Tournament Director of the LPGA Tour.

ever. She had six years of waiting for her first tour victory in 1968. And her next one didn't come until 1970. But then she was on her way. She won three that year and through 1977 she had scored a total of 26 victories. She was also the first woman to exceed more than $100,000 in prize money in one season, achieving this in 1976.

She is one of the tiniest players on the women's tour, but one of the most consistent performers. She was named the LPGA's Player of the Year in 1976 and was elected president of LPGA that same year. She is married to Walter Rankin, and they have a son.

Tournament Record: 1968: Winner of Corpus Christi Civitan Open. 1970: Winner of George Washington Classic, Springfield Jaycee Open, Lincoln-Mercury Open. 1971: Winner of Quality-First Classic. 1972: Winner of Lady Eve Open and Heritage Village Open. 1973: Winner of Raleigh Open, Lady Carling Open, Columbus Open, and GAC Classic. 1974: Winner of Colgate-European Open and Baltimore Classic. 1975: Winner

RAY, EDWARD (TED). Born in Jersey, England, March 28, 1877. Died July 1970. Ray won the U.S. Open championship at Inverness in 1920, but is best remembered by Americans for the 1913 Open in which he and Harry Vardon were beaten by the then unknown Francis Ouimet. Ray also won the British Open in 1912 and was in the top ten on eleven

EDWARD RAY

JOHN REVOLTA

other occasions. Ray was a big man who wore a large mustache, always played in a hat instead of the traditional cap, and usually smoked a pipe on the course. He was one of the longest hitters of his day.

Tournament Record: 1899: Winner of Hampshire Amateur-Professional. 1903: Winner of Leeds Challenge Cup. 1906: Winner of Northern Section Tournament. 1910: Winner of Leeds Challenge Cup. 1911: Winner of Leeds Challenge Cup, Cruden Bay Tournament, and Northern Section Tournament; runner-up in French Open. 1912: Winner of British Open and Cramond Brig Tournament; runner-up in Belgian Open and German Open. 1913: Winner of Tooting Bec Cup; runner-up in British Open; tied for second in U.S. Open. 1919, 1922: Winner of Herts Open. 1923: Winner of *Daily Mail* Tournament and Herts Open. 1924: Winner of Herts Open. 1925: Tied for second in British Open. 1928, 1930, 1931, 1933, 1935: Winner of Herts Open.

REVOLTA, JOHN. Born in St. Louis, Missouri, April 5, 1911. The PGA champion and leading money winner in 1935 and one of the most successful players on the pro tour throughout the 1930's. Revolta began to caddie at the age of twelve and won the Wisconsin state caddie title two years later. He turned pro in 1929 and quickly established himself as one of the best players in the area. In the early 1930's, he beat the best ball of Gene Sarazen and Tommy Armour, who were touring the area, and friends encouraged him to try his luck on the tournament circuit. He won the Miami Open in 1933 and for the next decade was one of the game's most consistent winners. It was in the 1935 PGA that Revolta gained the reputation of being a fine trap player and putter. In beating medalist Walter Hagen in the first round and in other matches, including the 5 and 4 victory over Armour in the final, Revolta displayed a short game that was phenomenal. He continued to win tournaments until World War II interrupted the tour, and when it ended he chose to devote most of his time to his club job.

Tournament Record: 1925: Winner of Wisconsin Caddie Tournament. 1927: Winner of St. Petersburg Match Play. 1930: Winner of Wisconsin Open. 1931: Winner of Wisconsin Open and Minnesota Open. 1933: Winner of Miami Open. 1934: Winner of St. Paul Open, Queen City Open, Wisconsin Open, and Cincinnati Open. 1935: Winner of PGA, Western Open, Wisconsin Open, Miami Four-ball, and Inverness Four-ball. 1936: Winner of Thomasville Open, Miami Four-ball, Sarasota Open, and Illinois PGA. 1937: Winner of Miami Four-ball, Miami Biltmore Open, and Illinois PGA. 1938: Winner of St. Paul Open, Sacramento Open, St. Petersburg Open, Columbia Open, and Illinois PGA. 1939: Winner of Bing Crosby Invitational, Inverness Four-ball, and Seminole Pro-Amateur. 1941: Winner of San Francisco Match Play and Illinois PGA. 1942: Winner of Illinois PGA. 1944: Winner of Texas Open. 1947: Winner of Illinois PGA and Chicago Pro-Am. 1957: Winner of Mississippi Open.

ROBERTSON, ALLAN. Born in St. Andrews, Scotland, in 1815. Died September, 1858. An almost legendary golfer who supposedly was never beaten in an individual stake match. He was a ball maker by trade, and it was he to whom Tom Morris was apprenticed in 1839. These two titans apparently never faced each other in a significant match, so there is no basis for comparing them. It is recorded, however, that they were never beaten as a team. They seem to have come to the parting of the ways in a dispute over the new gutta-percha ball. Robertson fought the new innovation, seeing it as a threat to his trade in the feather-stuffed ball. Morris chose to adopt the new ball. Robertson died of an attack of jaundice in 1858, just two years before the first British Open. His fame rests on his feat of playing 36 holes at St. Andrews in 147 strokes, an incredible score in those days.

SARAZEN (SARACENI), GENE. Born in Harrison, New York, February 27, 1902. One of America's greatest players during the 1920's and 1930's, and a man who went from grade school dropout to world renown during his more than fifty years in the game. Sarazen was one of four men to win the four major titles open to professionals, and his record shows two U.S. Opens, three PGA's, a Masters, and a British Open in addition to membership on six Ryder Cup Teams and victory in dozens of lesser tournaments. Sarazen was a brash young man who had plenty of confidence—and the skill to back it up. He won the U.S. Open when he was only twenty, and a year later he had beaten the mighty Hagen in the final of the PGA. Only a few years earlier he had been forced to leave school to help support the family and had turned to caddying. He and Ed Sullivan were among the caddies at Apawamis in 1913 when Francis Ouimet beat the British and became the idol of all youngsters. Sarazen later became known as much for his longevity as for his skill, because he was still playing in all four major championships decades after his contemporaries had passed from the scene. Then he moved into a new career as television commentator on Shell's "Wonderful World of Golf," which led him to remark that more people saw him in one hour on television than watched him play in all his decades as a tournament player.

Sarazen was something of a come-from-behind player, and some of his feats will be remembered as long as the game is played. In 1922 he closed with a 68 to win the U.S. Open. In 1932 he played the last 28 holes in 100 strokes to come from nowhere and win the Open again. In 1935 he made his famed double-eagle in the Masters to make up a three-shot deficit on Craig Wood, whom he defeated in a play-off the next day. Sarazen also was an idea man who was always good "copy" for writers. His best idea was the sand wedge, which he produced after a series of experiments in his Florida garage around 1930. Such is the popularity of the wedge today that Sarazen could well consider its invention as his most notable achievement.

Tournament Record: 1922: Winner of U.S. Open, PGA, and New Orleans Open. 1923: Winner of PGA and North of England Professional. 1925: Winner of Metropolitan Open. 1927: Winner of Metropolitan PGA, Long Island Open, Miami Open, and Miami Beach Open. 1928: Winner of Miami Open, Miami Four-ball, Metropolitan PGA, Miami Beach Open, and Bahamas Open; runner-up in British Open. 1929: Winner of Miami Open, Agua Caliente Open, Miami Beach Open, and Sands Point Invitational. 1930: Winner of Western Open, Miami Open, and Middle Atlantic Open; runner-up in PGA. 1931: Winner of Florida West Coast Open, New Orleans Open, and Lannin Memorial. 1932: Winner of U.S. Open and British Open. 1933: Winner of PGA. 1934: Runner-up in U.S. Open. 1935: Winner of Masters and Massachusetts Open. 1936: Winner of Australian Open and St. Augustine Pro-Amateur. 1937: Winner of Florida West Coast Open and Chicago Open. 1938: Winner of Lake Placid Open. 1939: Winner of Metropolitan PGA. 1940: Runner-up in U.S. Open. 1941: Winner of Miami Four-ball. 1953: Runner-up in PGA Senior. 1954, 1958: Winner of PGA Senior.

SHUTE, HERMAN DENSMORE. Born in Cleveland, Ohio, October 25, 1904. Died May 13, 1974. One of the finest players in the world during the 1930's, when he won the British Open and two PGA Championships, was also runner-up in both the PGA and the U.S. Open, and played on four Ryder Cup Teams. Shute was a fine player in all departments, but never quite caught the fancy of the public. One reason was that he did not play the tour as regularly as some of the others and, as a result, did not get as much public exposure. But beyond that, he was a reserved person who had little color. He simply went his own steady way which, more often than not, put him at or near the top in the championships. Shute turned pro in 1928 and within three years had been a strong contender in two U.S. Opens, had won two tour tournaments, and had been named to the Ryder Cup Team. This set the tone for the next decade, during which Shute was winning, or almost winning, a title every year. Like most of the stars of the 1930's, Shute played little competitive golf after the war.

Tournament Record: 1923, 1925: Winner of West Virginia Amateur. 1927: Winner of Ohio Amateur. 1929: Winner of Ohio Open and Ohio PGA. 1930: Winner of Los Angeles Open, Texas Open, and Ohio Open. 1931: Winner of Ohio Open; runner-up in PGA. 1932: Winner of Miami Biltmore Open, Glens Falls Open, and Akron Open. 1933: Winner of British Open and Gasparilla Open. 1934: Winner of Miami Four-ball. 1936: Winner of PGA an Tropical Open. 1937: Winner of PGA. _)39: Winner of Glens

Falls Open and St. Augustine Pro-Amateur. 1941: Runner-up in U.S. Open. 1950: Winner of Ohio Open. 1956: Winner of Akron Open.

SMITH, ALEX. Born in Carnoustie, Scotland, in 1872. Died April 20, 1930. One of five brothers who came to the United States in the mid-1890's and were destined to have a great impact on American golf. Alex was in many ways the complete professional. Not only was he an experienced club-maker and greenskeeper; he was good enough to win the U.S. Open twice and he later taught Jerry Travers and Glenna Collett, who won 11 U.S. titles between them. Alex came to the United States in 1898 and took a job as assistant to Fred Herd in Washington Park in Chicago. Later that year, Herd won the U.S. Open and Alex was second. He was able to tie for fifth twenty-three years later, giving him a U.S. Open record of two wins, three seconds, three thirds, a fourth, and a fifth.

Alex was a convivial man and a very fast one on the golf course, where his motto was "miss 'em quick." His brother Willie also won the U.S. Open, and the youngest of the family, Macdonald, was an outstanding player for three decades.

Tournament Record: 1898, 1901: Runner-up in U.S. Open. 1903: Winner of Western Open. 1905: Winner of Metropolitan Open; runner-up in U.S. Open. 1906: Winner of U.S. Open and Western Open. 1909: Winner of Metropolitan Open. 1910: Winner of U.S. Open and Metropolitan Open. 1913: Winner of Metropolitan Open.

SMITH, HORTON. Born in Springfield, Missouri, May 22, 1908. Died October 13, 1963. A player of infinite promise who burst on the tournament scene in the winter of 1928–1929 to capture eight tournaments and become the year's leading money winner. Smith went on to win other tournaments, including the Masters twice, but he never again matched that first, glorious burst. In fairness to Smith it should be said that it would be almost impossible to duplicate his rookie season. However, he did tamper with his fine swing through constant experimentation, and later he turned more to rules and administration, and his duties as a PGA officer did not help his game. He was a member of the PGA tournament committee as early as 1932, and he worked his way up until he became national president in 1952. Later, he was president of the PGA Seniors. Smith was stricken with Hodgkin's disease in 1957 and underwent several operations over the next few years. However, he continued on the job despite his ailments and was given the Ben Hogan Award in 1961 for carrying on despite a physical handicap.

Tournament Record: 1928: Winner of Oklahoma City Open and Catalina Open. 1929: Winner of French Open, LaGorce Open, Jacksonville Open, North and South Open, Pasadena Open, Pensacola Open, and Fort Myers Open; runner-up in German Open. 1930: Winner of Savannah Open, Oregon Open, Berkeley Open, and Orlando Open. 1931: Winner of St. Paul Open. 1932: Winner of Capital City Open, Tri-State Open, and Michigan City Open. 1933: Winner of Miami Four-ball. 1934: Winner of Masters and Louisville Open. 1935: Winner of Miami Biltmore Open, Palm Springs Open, and Pasadena Open. 1936: Winner of Masters and Victoria Open. 1937: Winner of North and South Open, Inverness Four-ball, and Oklahoma City Four-ball. 1940: Winner of St. Augustine Pro-Amateur, Colorado Open, and Massachusetts Open. 1941: Winner of Belleair Open and St. Paul Open. 1948, 1954: Winner of Michigan PGA.

SMITH, MACDONALD. Born in Carnoustie, Scotland, 1892. Died in 1949. Youngest brother of Alex and Willie Smith and considered by many to be the best golfer in the family, although he never won a major championship. Mac Smith, often called the greatest player who never won an Open, had a beautiful swing and a game good enough to win him dozens of tournaments, but no big ones. From 1910, when he tied his brother Alex and Johnny McDermott for the U.S. Open title,

MacDONALD SMITH

until 1936, when he was fourth in the same event, Mac was within three strokes of winning the U.S. or British Open a staggering twelve times. However, he always seemed to be throwing away a sure thing on the last round or else turning in a fantastic closing score that left him just short of winning. At any rate, he was a magnificent player, and it was generally conceded that he deserved more than three Western Opens and a Canadian Open beside his name. Smith worked in a shipyard during World War I and did not return to tournament golf until 1923.

Tournament Record: 1910: Winner of Claremont Open, Presidio Open, and California Open; tied for first in U.S. Open. 1912: Winner of Western Open. 1914: Winner of Metropolitan Open and Pennsylvania Open. 1916: Winner of Florida West Coast Open. 1924: Winner of Miami Four-ball, Northern California Open, and California Open. 1925: Winner of Western Open, North and South Open, Long Island Open, and California Open. 1926: Winner of Canadian Open, Miami Four-ball, Metropolitan Open, Texas Open, Dallas Open, and Chicago District Open. 1927: Winner of Chicago District Open. 1928: Winner of Los Angeles Open, South Central Open, and Palos Verdes Open. 1929: Winner of Los Angeles Open and Long Island Open. 1930: Winner of Long Island Open; runner-up in U.S. Open; tied for second in British Open. 1931: Winner of Metropolitan Open and Long Island Open. 1932:

Winner of Los Angeles Open; runner-up in British Open. 1933: Winner of Western Open. 1934: Winner of Los Angeles Open. 1935: Winner of Oakmont Open and Oakmont-Nassau Tournament. 1936: Winner of Seattle Open.

SNEAD, SAMUEL JACKSON. Born in Hot Springs, Virginia, May 27, 1912. The greatest natural player in the history of golf, a man who won well over a hundred tournaments in his career, only to be best remembered for his failure to win the U.S. Open. Snead won the PGA three times, the Masters three times, and the British Open once—a remarkable record; but for years he struggled in vain to win the biggest one of all. He was second in 1937, the first year he ever competed in the Open, and everyone figured he was bound to win it, probably more than once. Then, in 1939, he came to the last hole needing a 5 to win and took an awful 8. That failure stuck with him for the remainder of his career. In 1947 he tied Lew Worsham for the title, but lost the play-off, and he was also second in 1949 and 1953. Sam also won the Vardon

Trophy four times, was leading money winner three times, was a member of eight Ryder Cup Teams and captain once, and won two PGA Senior Championships. Snead came out of the West Virginia mountains in 1937 and was totally unknown. When he startled the golf world by winning the Oakland Open in early 1937, people (including the official tournament scorer) did not even know how to spell his name. Although Snead was no fool and soon displayed a great talent for making—and keeping—money, he was known for years as a hillbilly type who always had a vast storehouse of pungent jokes. He made no effort to disprove the claim that he had all his money buried in tin cans somewhere on his property in West Virginia. His smooth, graceful swing became a legend, and rightly so, because for more than thirty years it was held up as a model of how the club should be handled. Although Snead developed severe putting troubles and eventually adopted croquet and, later, sidesaddle putting techniques, **his swing was as powerful and effortless as ever.**

Tournament Record: 1936: Winner of West Virginia Closed Pro. 1937: Winner of Oakland Open, Bing Crosby Invitational, St. Paul Open, Nassau Open, and Miami Open; runner-up in U.S. Open. 1938: Winner of Bing Crosby Invitational, Greensboro Open, Inverness Four-ball, Goodall Round Robin, Chicago Open, Canadian Open, Westchester Open, and White Sulphur Springs Open; runner-up in PGA. 1939: Winner of St. Petersburg Open, Miami Four-ball, Miami Open, and Ontario Open; runner-up in Masters. 1940: Winner of Canadian Open, Inverness Four-ball, and Anthracite Open; runner-up in PGA. 1941: Winner of Bing Crosby Invitational, St. Petersburg Open, North and South Open, Rochester Open, Henry Hurst Invitational, and Canadian Open. 1942: Winner of PGA, St. Petersburg Open, and Corduba Open. 1944: Winner of Richmond Open and Portland Open. 1945: Winner of Los Angeles Open, Gulfport Open, Pensacola Open, Jacksonville Open, Dallas Open, and Tulsa Open. 1946: Winner of British Open, Jacksonville Open, Greensboro Open, Viriginia Open, Miami Open, and World Championship. 1947: Winner of Tulsa Invitational, Bing Crosby Pro-Am; runner-up in U.S. Open.

1948: Winner of Texas Open, Seminole Pro-Amateur, West Virginia PGA, Havana Invitational, and West Virginia Open. 1949: Winner of Masters, PGA, Greensboro Open, Washington *Star* Open, Dapper Dan Open, National Celebrities Invitational, Western Open, and Decatur Open; tied for second in U.S. Open. 1950: Winner of Los Angeles Open, Texas Open, Miami Beach Open, Greensboro Open, Western Open, Colonial Invitational, Inverness Four-ball, Reading Open, North and South Open, and Miami Open. 1951: Winner of PGA, Greenbrier Invitational, and Miami Open. 1952: Winner of Masters, Seminole Pro-Amateur, Greenbrier Invitational, Goodall Round Robin, Inverness Four-ball, All-American Open, Eastern Open, and Julius Boros Invitational. 1953: Winner of Orlando Two-ball, Baton Rouge Open, and Greenbrier Invitational; runner-up in U.S. Open. 1954: Winner of Masters, Panama Open, and Palm Beach Round Robin. 1955: Winner of Bayshore Open, Greensboro Open, Palm Beach Round Robin, Insurance City Open, and Miami Open. 1956: Winner of Greensboro Open. 1957: Winner of Dallas Open, West Virginia Open, and Palm Beach Round Robin; runner-up in Masters. 1958: Winner of Greenbrier Invitational and Dallas Open. 1959: Winner of Sam Snead Festival. 1960: Winner of DeSoto Open, Greensboro Open, and West Virginia Open. 1961: Winner of Tournament of Champions and Sam Snead Festival. 1964: Winner of Haig and Haig Foursome Invitational and PGA Senior. 1965: Winner of PGA Senior and Greensboro Open. 1968: Winner of West Virginia Open. 1970: Winner of PGA Seniors Championship. 1971: Winner of PGA Club Pro's Championship. Winner of the PGA Seniors Championship in 1964, 1965, 1967, 1970, 1972, and 1973. Winner of World Series Championship in 1964, 1965, 1970, 1972, and 1973.

SUGGS. LOUISE. Born in Atlanta, Georgia, September 7, 1923. Winner of fifty tournaments on the Ladies' PGA tour following a successful amateur career that included victories in both the United States and British championships. Louise Suggs turned professional in 1948 and subsequently won the U.S. Open twice and the LPGA Championship once. Her record also included being the

LOUISE SUGGS

tour's leading money winner twice. She first played golf at the age of ten under the tutelage of her father and went on to develop one of the smoothest swings in the game. Her best year was 1953, when she won eight tournaments and collected almost $20,-000, an unusually large sum on the women's tour in those days.

TAYLOR, JOHN HENRY. Born in Northam, North Devon, England, March 19, 1871. Died in February, 1963. A five-time winner of the British Open Championship and, with Braid and Vardon, a member of the game's famed "triumvirate." J.H., as he was generally known, won the Open in 1894, 1895, 1900, 1909, and 1913. He also was second five times and third once. He accompanied Vardon to the United States in 1900 and was second to the Great Man in the U.S. Open that year. He also won the French Open twice and the German Open once and captured the British PGA title in 1904 and 1908. Taylor represented England against Scotland nine times and frequently partnered Vardon or Braid in matches on which a large sum was at stake.

THOMSON, PETER. Born in Melbourne, Australia, August 23, 1929. Winner of the British Open five times, a player who com-

JOHN HENRY TAYLOR

PETER THOMSON

manded great respect throughout the international golfing world, but was always badly underestimated by Americans. Thomson played in the U.S. on several occasions, but he finally began to make his visits few and far between. Americans never seemed to take to him, and the reverse was also true. He had a game that was ideally suited to seaside courses and to places that required improvisation and a certain finesse. On American courses, which were lush and well watered and demanded great accuracy with the pitching wedge, Thomson was never at home. Thus it was difficult for Americans to understand how he could win the British Open five times and still fail to win over here. Thomson could hit the low hook and get great distance on hard, wind-swept links, while the same shot left him far short on lush terrain. Nevertheless, his great record outside the United States, made on a wide variety of courses under all conditions, is evidence of his right to be classed among the great players. Thomson won the Texas Open and was fourth in the U.S. Open and in the 1956 and 1957 Masters. In the British Open, he had the almost unbelievable record of finishing either first or second for seven straight years from 1952 through 1958.

Tournament Record: 1950: Winner of New Zealand Open. 1951: Winner of Australian Open and New Zealand Open. 1952: Runner-up in British Open. 1953: Winner of New Zealand Open and New Zealand Professional; tied for second in British Open. 1954: Winner of British Open, Ampol Tournament, and *News of the World* Tournament. 1955: Winner of British Open and New Zealand Open. 1956: Winner of British Open and Texas Open. 1957: Runner-up in British Open. 1958: Winner of British Open and Dunlop Professional; tied for first in Daks Tournament. 1959: Winner of New Zealand Open, Italian Open, and Spanish Open. 1960: Winner of German Open, South China Open, Hong Kong Open, New Zealand Open, and Daks Tournament. 1961: Winner of New Zealand Open, Dunlop Masters, and *News of the World* Tournament; tied for first in Esso Golden Tournament. 1962: Winner of Martini International and Piccadilly Tournament. 1963: Winner of India Open. 1964: Winner of Philippine Open. 1965: Winner of British Open, New Zealand Open, Hong Kong Open, and Daks Tournament. 1966: Winner of *News of the World* Tournament and India Open. 1967: Winner of Australian Open, Alcan International, Australian Professional, Hong Kong Open, and *News of the World* Tournament. 1968: Winner of Dunlop Masters, Victoria Open, and South Australian Open. 1971: Winner of International Japan Airlines Open, New Zealand Open, International Dunlop, and Tournament Wizard Championship (Japan). 1972: Australian Open. 1973: Winner of Australian Open.

Nassau Invitational. 1906: Winner of Metropolitan Amateur and Eastern Scholastic. 1907: Winner of U.S. Amateur, Metropolitan Amateur, and New Jersey Amateur. 1908: Winner of U.S. Amateur and New Jersey Amateur. 1911: Winner of Metropolitan Amateur and New Jersey Amateur. 1912: Winner of U.S. Amateur and Metropolitan Amateur. 1913: Winner of U.S. Amateur, Metropolitan Amateur, and New Jersey Amateur. 1914: Runner-up in U.S. Amateur. 1915: Winner of U.S. Open.

TRAVERS, JEROME DUNSTAN. Born in New York, New York, May 19, 1887. Died in 1951. The only man besides Bobby Jones to win as many as five U.S. Amateur titles and one of only five amateurs ever to win the U.S. National Open. Travers was the son of a rich man and was able to devote all the time necessary to developing a good game. His teacher was Alex Smith, who once said he thought Travers' golf temperament was even superior to that of Walter Hagen. Travers was a great putter, and his short game and competitive spirit more than offset any trouble he might have with his driver. His greatest demonstration of ability probably came in the 1915 U.S. Open, which he won despite severe driving problems. Prior to that victory he had done little at stroke play, and people were of the opinion he was strictly a match player. Travers ran into financial troubles in later years and eventually turned professional, although he never competed as a pro.

Tournament Record: 1904: Winner of

TRAVIS, WALTER J. Born in Maldon, Victoria, Australia, January 10, 1862. Died in 1927. One of the most remarkable figures in golf in that he did not take up the game until his mid-thirties, yet became a championship player within two years. Travis won his first U.S. Amateur at the age of thirty-eight, then went on to win two more of them, plus the British Amateur and dozens more. He was still good enough to win the tough Metropolitan Amateur at the age of fifty-three. After Travis had won three U.S. Amateurs in four years, he decided to take a crack at the British championship, and he almost caused an international incident. He was a taciturn man on the course and a stickler for the rules, and, for whatever reason, he quickly alienated the British. He won the tournament, mainly on the strength of his work with the Schenectady putter, and the British never forgave him. They banned the putter, accused Travis of surly behavior, and otherwise made clear their feelings. For his part, Travis thought he had been treated shabbily, and if he was responsible for his treatment by his own brusque manner, he could never make himself believe it. In later years Travis turned to course architecture and also was the editor of the magazine *American Golfer* for many years.

Tournament Record: 1900: Winner of U.S. Amateur and Metropolitan Amateur. 1901: Winner of U.S. Amateur. 1902: Winner of Metropolitan Amateur; tied for second in U.S. Open. 1903: Winner of U.S. Amateur. 1904: Winner of British Amateur and North and South Amateur. 1906: Winner of Florida Open. 1909: Winner of Metropolitan Amateur. 1910, 1912: Winner of North and South Amateur. 1913, 1914: Winner of Cuban Amateur. 1915: Winner of Metropolitan Amateur and Southern Florida Amateur. 1916: Winner of Southern Florida Amateur.

TREVINO, Lee B. Born in Dallas, Texas, December 1, 1939. An incredible aspect of Lee Trevino's rags-to-riches saga is that he attained fame only a few years after he was polishing clubs and shining shoes as an assis-

tant in Texas. In the spring of 1967, his wife sent his entry to the local qualifier for the U.S. Open. They could ill afford the $20 fee. Lee went all the way, finished fifth at Baltusrol, won $6,000. In subsequent years he did everything but walk across the water.

Raised near Dallas by his grandfather, a grave-digger, Lee went as far as the eighth grade before he had to work. He became a handyman at a pitch-and-putt course and also learned to play. But it was during a four-year hitch in the Marines that his game developed. After the Marines, it was back to a $30-a-week assistant's post in El Paso, where he played in some local events and finally, a fateful entry for the 1967 Open. If the golf world wondered about Trevino at Baltusrol, all the questions were answered when he won the 1968 U.S. Open.

In 1971, Trevino won many top awards both inside and outside golfing circles. In the latter group was the Hichok Pro Athlete of the Year and the coveted Associated Press Athlete of the Year Award. The latter had been particularly difficult for a male golfer to win. A poll of the nation's sports writers settled the issue and since its inception in 1934 only Byron Nelson (twice), Ben Hogan, and Arnold Palmer were golfing winners.

Tournament Record: 1968: Winner of U.S. Open and Hawaiian Open. 1969: Winner of Tucson Open. 1970: Winner of Tucson Open and National Airlines Open. 1971: Winner of Tallahassee Open, Danny Thomas–Memphis Classic, U.S. Open, Canadian Open, British Open, and Sahara Invitational. 1972: Winner of Danny Thomas–Memphis Classic, British Open, Greater Hartford Open, and Greater St. Louis Golf Classic. 1973: Winner of Jackie Gleason–Inverrary Classic, Doral-Eastern Open. 1974: Winner of PGA Championship, New Orleans Open. 1975: Winner of Florida Citrus Open. 1976: Winner of Colonial Invitational. 1977: Winner of Canadian Open.

VARDON, Harry. Born in Grouville, Isle of Jersey, England, May 7, 1870. Died March 20, 1937. The chief figure of Britain's famed "triumvirate" and considered by many to be the greatest player who ever lived. Vardon won six British Opens (a record), was runner-up four times, and was in the top five on

HARRY VARDON

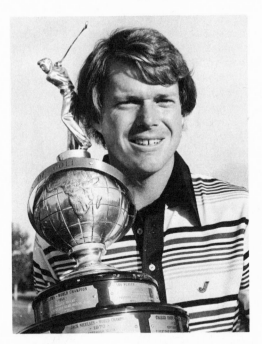

TOM WATSON

six other occasions—sixteen times in the top five over a span of twenty-one years. He was just as impressive in America, which he toured on several occasions. He won the U.S. Open in 1900, tied for first and lost the play-off in 1913, and tied for second in 1920 at the age of fifty. He also won the British PGA in 1912 and the German Open in 1911 with a score of 279. The overlapping grip was first used by Vardon in the 1890's and was named for him, although J. H. Taylor is said to have employed it first. Vardon was a master fairway wood player, and historians without exception dwell at length on his ability to hit full brassie shots stiff to the pin. Certainly he had as graceful a swing as could be imagined, and for later generations of golfers, the highest compliment was to have one's swing compared to Vardon's.

WATSON, THOMAS. Born in Kansas City, Missouri, September 4, 1949. After playing collegiate golf at Stanford University, where he earned his B.A. in Psychology in 1971, he immediately became a professional. His rookie season on the tour, 1972, was hardly spectacular, although he came within a stroke of winning the Quad Cities Open. In 1973, he had victory within his grasp twice but let it get away, and this began to be his reputation. In 1974, he led the U.S. Open for three rounds but closed with a 79 and lost it. But he came charging back the next week to score his first pro victory in the tough Western Open, making up six shots in the closing round.

His big breakthrough came in 1975, when he won the British Open at Carnoustie and finished in the top ten in the other events that make up the Big Four. Three strokes off the lead on the final days, he rallied to gain a tie with Jack Newton. He won the play-off the next day. He was in seventh place on the money list with $153,795, and observers agreed that he was on his way.

He didn't win in 1976, although he finished in the top ten in eleven events and earned over $138,000. In 1977, he became the game's best player. He beat Jack Nicklaus in the

Masters and the British Open with spectacular play and won three other events. He exceeded $300,000 in prize money and was the PGA Player of the Year.

Tournament Record: 1974: Winner of Western Open. 1975: Winner of British Open and Byron Nelson Classic. 1977: Winner of Masters, British Open, Western Open, Bing Crosby National Pro-Am, and San Diego Open.

had her fill of competition at an early age, but the lure of St. Andrews brought her back one more time, in 1929, and she defeated Glenna Collett in the final. Thereafter, she limited her tournament play to an annual appearance in the foursomes at Worplesdon, which she won eight times in fifteen years. Her brother Roger was one of Britain's finest amateurs during the 1920's.

WETHERED, JOYCE (LADY HEATHCOAT-AMORY). Born November 17, 1901. Rated for many years as being without question the greatest female golfer in the history of the game. Despite the rise of women's golf and the large number of outstanding players being developed, she still is rated as no worse than equal with Babe Didrikson Zaharias and Mickey Wright. Miss Wethered came on the tournament scene in 1920 and was virtually unbeatable from the start. She won the English Ladies championship five straight times beginning in 1920, and in the British women's championship, the premier event of its day, she played six times, winning four, being runner-up once and semifinalist once. As a matter of fact, she retired after 1925, having

WHITWORTH, KATHRYNNE ANN (KATHY). Born in Jal, New Mexico, September 22, 1939. The all-time leading money winner on the LPGA circuit, winner of almost every tournament on record except the USGA Women's Open, Miss Whitworth started in golf at age fifteen and began touring in 1958. She was named Associated Press Woman Athlete of the Year in 1965 and 1966. She won the Eve Challenge Cup in its inaugural year (1971). At age thirty-eight, Miss Whitworth had one of her best seasons in 1977, when she won more than $108,000, and three tournaments, including the Colgate–Dinah Shore Winners Circle.

WOOD, CRAIG RALPH. Born in Lake Placid, New York, November 18, 1901. Died

CRAIG RALPH WOOD

May 8, 1968. A long-hitting, extremely popular player who finally got a well-deserved championship to his credit when he won both the 1941 U.S. Open and Masters at the age of thirty-nine. Wood had begun to win tournaments on the winter tour as early as 1928, but it was thirteen years before he would take a major title. In between, he was runner-up in the Masters twice and in the U.S. Open, PGA, and British Open. On the first hole at St. Andrews, Wood drove the ball into the Swilcan Burn, a belt of more than 350 yards. Wood operated an automobile agency for many years after World War II, then returned to golf in the early 1960's as pro at the Lucayan Beach Club on Grand Bahama Island, a position he held at his death.

Tournament Record: 1925: Winner of Kentucky Open. 1926: Winner of Kentucky PGA. 1928: Winner of Pasadena Open and New Jersey PGA. 1929: Winner of Oklahoma City Open, Hawaiian Open, and New Jersey PGA. 1930: Winner of Harlingen Open,

Reddy Tee Tournament, and New Jersey PGA. 1932: Winner of Pasadena Open, San Francisco Match Play, Radium Springs Open, and New Jersey PGA. 1933: Winner of Los Angeles Open; runner-up in British Open. 1934: Winner of Galveston Open and New Jersey Open; runner-up in Masters and PGA. 1935: Runner-up in Masters. 1936: Winner of General Brock Open. 1939: Winner of Augusta Open; runner-up in U.S. Open. 1940: Winner of Miami Four-ball and Metropolitan Open. 1941: Winner of U.S. Open and Masters. 1942: Winner of Canadian Open and Metropolitan PGA. 1943: Winner of Golden Valley Four-ball. 1944: Winner of Durham Open.

WRIGHT, MARY KATHRYN (MICKEY). Born in San Diego, California, February 14, 1935. Generally ranked with Joyce Wethered and Babe Didrikson Zaharias at the head of any list of great women golfers. Miss Wright's domination of the LPGA tour in the early 1960's was complete, and from 1960 through 1964 she was leading money winner four times and Vare Trophy winner five times. She won 13 tournaments in 1963 to set a record, and in two other years she won 10 tournaments each. Her career total of nearly 80 pro victories includes four U.S. Opens and four LPGA Championships. Like many great players before her, Miss Wright began to find the grind too much for her in the mid-1960's, and she announced her retirement to enter college at Southern Methodist University. However, she was back in action next season, although she never again played the entire schedule.

ZAHARIAS, MILDRED DIDRIKSON (BABE). Born in Port Arthur, Texas, June 26, 1914. Died September 27, 1956. Voted the greatest woman athlete of all time in every poll ever taken. Besides her golf exploits, she was the

star of the 1932 Olympic Games and excelled at virtually every sport she tried, including baseball. At golf, Zaharias became so proficient as to be mentioned in the same breath as Joyce Wethered. She climaxed a fine amateur career by winning the U.S. women's championship in 1946 and the British title a year later, becoming the first American to win the British championship. The Babe dominated the budding women's tour almost as soon as she left the amateur ranks, and she was the leading money winner in each of her first four years as a professional. She also won three U.S. Opens and captured the Vare Trophy in 1954. The Babe, who was married to George Zaharias, was the first woman to hold the post of head professional at a golf club, was voted Woman Athlete of the Half Century (1949) by the Associated Press, and was voted Woman Athlete of the Year by AP ballot in 1932, 1945, 1946, 1947, and 1950. None of her accomplishments stirred the public as did her fight against cancer, for which she first underwent surgery in 1953. She supposedly was not going to be able to play again, but she came back to win the 1954 U.S. Open by a record 12 strokes. She won four other events that year and two more in 1955 before her condition deteriorated to a degree her courage and determination could not overcome.

Current Touring Professionals (Men)

Player	Date of Birth	Birthplace	Turned Pro
Aaron, Tommy	Feb. 22, 1937	Gainesville, Ga.	1960
Adams, Sam	May 9, 1946	Boone, N.C.	1969
Allin, Brian	Oct. 13, 1944	Bremerton, Wash.	1970
Archer, George	Oct. 1, 1939	San Francisco, Calif.	1963
Armstrong, Wally	June 19, 1945	New London, Conn.	1970
Baird, Butch	July 20, 1936	Chicago, Ill.	1959
Barbarossa, Robert	Sept. 8, 1947	St. Cloud, Minn.	1970
Barber, Miller	March 31, 1931	Shreveport, La.	1958
Bean, Andy	March 13, 1953	Lafayette, Ga.	1975
Beard, Frank	May 1, 1939	Dallas, Texas	1962
Bies, Don	Dec. 10, 1937	Cottonwood, Idaho	1957
Blackburn, Woody	July 26, 1951	Pikeville, Ky.	1974
Blancas, Homero	March 7, 1938	Houston, Texas	1965
Boros, Julius	March 3, 1920	Fairfield, Conn.	1949
Brask, Bill, Jr.	Dec. 18, 1946	Annapolis, Md.	1969
Brewer, Gay, Jr.	March 19, 1932	Middletown, Ohio	1956
Brown, Pete	Feb. 2, 1935	Port Gibson, Miss.	1954
Burns, George III	July 29, 1949	Brooklyn, N.Y.	1975

Player	Date of Birth	Birthplace	Turned Pro
Cadle, George	May 9, 1948	Pineville, Ky.	1971
Casper, Billy, Jr.	June 24, 1931	San Diego, Calif.	1954
Cerrudo, Ron	Feb. 4, 1945	Palo Alto, Calif.	1967
Colbert, Jim, Jr.	March 9, 1931	Elizabeth, N.J.	1965
Cole, Robert	May 11, 1958	Springs, South Africa	1967
Coody, Charles	July 13, 1937	Stamford, Texas	1963
Courtney, Chuck	Oct. 11, 1940	Minneapolis, Minn.	1963
Crawford, Richard	June 28, 1939	El Dorado, Ark.	1962
Crenshaw, Ben	Jan. 11, 1952	Austin, Tex.	1973
Dent, James	May 11, 1942	Augusta, Ga.	1970
Devlin, Bruce	Oct. 10, 1937	Armidah, New South Wales, Australia	1961
Dickinson, Gardner, Jr.	Sept. 14. 1927	Dothan, Ala.	1952
Diehl, Terry	Nov. 9, 1949	Rochester, N.Y.	1972
Dill, Terry	April 13, 1939	Fort Worth, Texas	1962
Dougherty, Ed	Nov. 4, 1947	Chester, Pa.	1969
Douglass, Dale	March 5, 1936	Wewoka, Okla.	1960
Edwards, Danny	June 14, 1951	Ketchikan, Alaska	1973
Eichelberger, Dave	Sept. 3, 1943	Waco, Texas	1966
Elder, Lee R.	July 14, 1934	Washington, D.C.	1967
Ewing, Jack	May 21, 1944	Los Angeles, Calif.	1970
Fezler, Forrest	Sept. 23, 1949	Hayward, Calif.	1969
Finger, Sherman	Feb. 2, 1944	Evanston, Ill.	1966
Fitzsimons, Pat	Dec. 15, 1950	Coos Bay, Ore.	1971
Fleckman, Marty	April 23, 1944	Port Arthur, Texas	1967
Fleisher, Bruce	Oct. 16, 1948	Union City, Tenn.	1971
Floyd, Raymond	Sept. 4, 1942	Fort Bragg, N.C.	1961
Ford, Doug	Aug. 6, 1922	West Haven, Conn.	1949
Funseth, Rod	April 3, 1933	Spokane, Wash.	1955
Geiberger, Al	Sept. 1, 1937	Red Bluff, Calif.	1959
Gilbert, Gibby	Jan. 14, 1941	Chattanooga, Tenn.	1962
Gilder, Bob	Dec. 31, 1950	Corvallis, Ore.	1973
Goalby, Bob	March 14, 1931	Belleville, Ill.	1957
Graham, David	May 23, 1946	Windsor, Australia	1962
Graham, Lou	Jan. 7, 1938	Nashville, Tenn.	1962
Green, Hubert	Dec. 28, 1946	Birmingham, Ala.	1970
Groh, Gary	Oct. 11, 1944	Chicago, Ill.	1971
Hayes, Dale	Jan. 7, 1952	Pretoria, South Africa	1971
Hayes, Mark	July 12, 1949	Stillwater, Okla.	1973
Hayes, Ted	Aug. 3, 1940	Atlanta, Ga.	1963
Heard, Jerry	May 1, 1947	Visalia, Calif.	1968
Hill, Dave	May 20, 1937	Jackson, Mich.	1958
Hill, Mike	Jan. 27, 1939	Jackson, Mich.	1963
Hinson, Larry	Aug. 5, 1944	Gastonia, N.C.	1968
Hiskey, Babe	Nov. 21, 1938	Burley, Idaho	1962
Inman, Joe	Nov. 29, 1947	Indianapolis, Ind.	1972
Irwin, Hale	June 3, 1945	Joplin, Mo.	1968
Iverson, Don	Oct. 28, 1945	LaCrosse, Wis.	1971
Jacklin, Tony	July 7, 1944	Scunthorpe, England	1962
Jacobs, Tommy	Feb. 13, 1935	Denver, Colo.	1956
Jaeckel, Barry	Feb. 14, 1949	Los Angeles, Calif.	1971
Jamieson, Jim	April 21, 1943	Kalamazoo, Mich.	1971
January, Don	Nov. 20, 1929	Plainview, Texas	1955
Jenkins, Tom	Dec. 14, 1947	Houston, Tex.	1971
Johnson, George	Dec. 8, 1938	Columbus, Ga.	1964
Johnson, Howie	Sept. 8, 1925	St. Paul, Minn.	1956
Jones, Grier	May 6, 1946	Wichita, Kan.	1971
Kaser, Monty	Sept. 24, 1941	Wichita, Kan.	1966
Kite, Tom	Dec. 9, 1949	Austin, Tex.	1972
Koch, Gary	Nov. 21, 1952	Baton Rouge, La.	1975
Knudson, George	June 28, 1937	Winnipeg, Manitoba, Canada	1958
Kratzert, Bill	June 29, 1952	Quantico, Va.	1974
Lewis, Jack	June 21, 1947	Florence, S.C.	1971

Player	Date of Birth	Birthplace	Turned Pro
Lietzke, Bruce	July 18, 1951	Kansas City, Kan.	1974
Lister, John	Sept. 3, 1947	Temuka, New Zealand	1971
Littler, Gene	July 21, 1930	San Diego, Calif.	1954
Lott, Lyn	April 9, 1950	Douglas, Ga.	1973
Lotz, Dick	Oct. 15, 1942	Oakland, Calif.	1963
Mahaffey, John	May 9, 1948	Kerryville, Texas	1971
Maltbie, Roger	June 20, 1951	Modesto, Calif.	1973
Marr, Dave	Dec. 27, 1933	Houston, Texas	1953
Marti, Fred	Nov. 15, 1940	Houston, Texas	1964
Massengale, Rik	Feb. 6, 1947	Jacksboro, Texas	1969
McCullough, Mike	March 21, 1945	Coshocton, Ohio	1972
McGee, Jerry	July 21, 1943	New Lexington, Ohio	1966
McLendon, B. R.	Aug. 10, 1945	Atlanta, Ga.	1968
Melnyk, Steve	Feb. 26, 1947	Brunswick, Ga.	1971
Menne, Bob	Feb. 19, 1942	Gardner, Mass.	1965
Miller, Allen	Aug. 10, 1948	San Diego, Calif.	1971
Miller, Johnny	April 29, 1947	San Francisco, Calif.	1969
Mitchell, Bobby	Feb. 23, 1943	Chatham, Va.	1959
Moody, Orville	Dec. 9, 1933	Chickasha, Okla.	1957
Morgan, Gil	Sept. 25, 1946	Wewoka, Okla.	1972
Morley, Michael	June 17, 1946	Morris, Minn.	1971
Murphy, Bob	Feb. 14, 1943	Brooklyn, N.Y.	1967
Nelson, Larry	Sept. 10, 1947	Fort Payne, Ala.	1971
Nevil, Dwight D.	Aug. 26, 1944	Altus, Okla.	1971
Nichols, Bobby	April 14, 1936	Louisville, Ky.	1959
Nicklaus, Jack	Jan. 21, 1940	Columbus, Ohio	1961
North, Andy	March 9, 1950	Thorp, Wis.	1972
Oosterhuis, Peter	May 3, 1948	London, England	1968
Owens, Charles	Feb. 22, 1937	Winter Haven, Fla.	1971
Pace, Roy	June 21, 1941	Runge, Texas	1964
Palmer, Arnold	Sept. 10, 1929	Latrobe, Pa.	1954
Pate, Jerry	Sept. 16, 1953	Macon, Ga.	1975
Payne, Bob	Nov. 29, 1943	Bluford, Ill.	1971
Pearce, Eddie	March 16, 1952	Fort Myers, Fla.	1972
Player, Gary	Nov. 1, 1935	Johannesburg, South Africa	1953
Porter, Joe	June 5, 1945	Pasadena, Calif.	1971
Reasor, Mike	Dec. 4, 1941	Seattle, Wash.	1971
Refram, Dean	Nov. 8, 1936	Miami, Fla.	1957
Regalado, Victor	April 15, 1948	San Diego, Calif.	1971
Rodgers, Phil	April 3, 1938	San Diego, Calif.	1960
Rodriquez, Juan	Oct. 23, 1935	Bayamon, Puerto Rico	1960
Rogers, Bill	Sept. 10, 1951	Waco, Tex.	1973
Rudolph, Mason, Jr.	May 23, 1934	Clarksville, Tenn.	1958
Sanders, Doug	July 24, 1933	Cedartown, Ga.	1956
Sanudo, Cesar	Oct. 26, 1943	Navajoa, Mexico	1966
Schlee, John	June 2, 1939	Kramling, Colo.	1964
Schroeder, John	Nov. 12, 1945	Great Barrington, Mass.	1971
Shaw, Tom	Dec. 13, 1938	Wichita, Kans.	1963
Sifford, Charles	June 2, 1923	Charlotte, N.C.	1947
Sifford, Curtis	May 6, 1942	Charlotte, N.C.	1967
Sikes, Dan	Dec. 7, 1930	Wildwood, Fla.	1960
Sikes, R. H.	March 6, 1940	Paris, Ark.	1964
Simons, Jim	May 15, 1950	Pittsburgh, Pa.	1972
Smith, Bob E.	Dec. 2, 1942	Sacramento, Calif.	1967
Snead, J. C.	Oct. 14, 1941	Hot Springs, Va.	1964
Snead, Sam	May 27, 1912	Hot Springs, Va.	1934
Sneed, Ed	Aug. 6, 1944	Columbus, Ohio	1971
Starks, Nate	June 20, 1940	Brownwood, Ga.	1973
Still, Ken	Feb. 12, 1935	Tacoma, Wash.	1953
Stockton, Dave	Nov. 2, 1941	San Bernardino, Calif.	1964
Thompson, Leonard	Jan. 1, 1947	Laurinburg, N.C.	1970
Trevino, Lee	Dec. 1, 1939	Dallas, Texas	1962

Player	Date of Birth	Birthplace	Turned Pro
Twitty, Howard	Jan. 15, 1949	Phoenix, Ariz.	1973
Venturi, Ken	May 15, 1931	San Francisco, Calif.	1956
Wadkins, Bobby	July 26, 1951	Richmond, Va.	1973
Wadkins, Lanny	Dec. 5, 1949	Richmond, Va.	1971
Wall, Art, Jr.	Nov. 25, 1923	Honesdale, Pa.	1949
Watson, Tom	Sept. 4, 1949	Kansas City, Mo.	1971
Weaver, DeWitt	Sept. 4, 1939	Danville, Ky.	1963
Weiskopf, Tom	Nov. 9, 1942	Massilon, Ohio	1964
Wiechers, Jim	Aug. 7, 1944	Oakland, Calif.	1969
Wood, Larry	June 30, 1939	Centralia, Ill.	1962
Wynn, Bob	Jan. 27, 1940	Lancaster, Ky.	1959
Zarley, Kermit	Sept. 29, 1941	Seattle, Wash.	1962
Zender, Bob	June 22, 1943	Chicago, Ill.	1971
Ziegler, Larry	August 12, 1939	St. Louis, Mo.	1959
Zoeller, Fuzzy	Nov. 11, 1951	New Albany, Ind.	1973

Current Touring Professionals (Women)

Player	Date of Birth	Birthplace	Turned Pro
Ahern, Kathy	May 7, 1949	Pittsburgh, Pa.	1966
Alcott, Amy	Feb. 22, 1956	Kansas City, Mo.	1975
Astrologes, Maria	Aug. 10, 1951	Valparaiso, Ind.	1973
Austin, Debbie	Feb. 1, 1948	Oneida, N.Y.	1968
Barnett, Pam	March 2, 1944	Charlotte, N.C.	1966
Baugh, Laura	May 31, 1955	Gainesville, Fla.	1973
Benson, Joyce	July 14, 1949	Santa Monica, Calif.	1972
Berg, Patty	Feb. 13, 1918	Minneapolis, Minn.	1940
Berning, Susie Maxwell	June 22, 1941	Pasadena, Calif.	1964
Bertolaccini, Silvia	Jan. 30, 1950	Rafaeka, Argentina	1975
Blalock, Jane	Sept. 19, 1945	Portsmouth, N.H.	1969
Bourossa, Jocelyne	May 30, 1947	Shawinigan, South Quebec, Canada	1972
Boykin, Gerda Whalen	Feb. 20, 1938	Baden-Baden, Germany	1955
Bradley, Pat	March 24, 1951	Arlington, Mass.	1974
Breer, Maurie Lindstrom	Jan. 20, 1939	St. Petersburg, Fla.	1957
Britz, Jerilyn	Jan. 1, 1943	Luverne, Minn.	1973
Brownlee, Vivian	Jan. 24, 1947	Linwood, N.J.	1972
Bruce, Louise	Nov. 26, 1953	Toronto, Canada	1972
Bryant, Bonnie	Oct. 5, 1943	Tulare, Calif.	1972
Burfeindt, Betty	July 20, 1945	New York, N.Y.	1969
Carner, JoAnne Gunderson	March 4, 1939	Kirkland, Wash.	1972
Cornelius, Katharine (Kathy)	Oct. 27, 1932	Boston, Mass.	1953
Creed, Clifford Ann	Sept. 23, 1938	Alexandria, La.	1962
Crocker, Mary Lou Daniel	Sept. 17, 1944	Louisville, Ky.	1966
Cullen, Mary Elizabeth (Betsy)	Aug. 14, 1938	Tulsa, Okla.	1963
Denenberg, Gail	Jan. 17, 1947	New York City, N.Y.	1969
Duggan, Catherine	Oct. 7, 1949	Evergreen Park, Ill.	1969
Ehret, Gloria Jean	Aug. 23, 1941	Allentown, Pa.	1965
Englehorn, Shirley Ruth	Dec. 12, 1940	Caldwell, Idaho	1959
Farrer, Kathy	May 20, 1944	Detroit, Mich.	1968
Ferraris, Jan	June 2, 1947	San Francisco, Calif.	1966
Floyd, Marlene	April 2, 1944	Fayetteville, N.C.	1976
Germain, Dot	May 21, 1947	Atlantic, Iowa	1973
Gibson, Althea	Aug. 25, 1927	Silver, S.C.	1963
Hagge, Marlene Bauer	Feb. 16, 1934	Eureka, S.D.	1950
Hamlin, Shelley	May 28, 1949	San Mateo, Calif.	1972
Haynie, Sandra	June 4, 1943	Fort Worth, Texas	1960
Higgins, Pam	Dec. 5, 1945	Columbus, Ohio	1969
Higuchi, Hisago (Chako)	Oct. 13, 1945	Tokyo, Japan	1970
Hite, Kathy	Sept. 8, 1948	Florence, S.C.	1974
Horner, Mary	July 20, 1948	San Francisco, Calif.	1971

Player	Date of Birth	Birthplace	Turned Pro
Jessen, Ruth	Nov. 12, 1936	Seattle, Wash.	1956
Kazmierski, Joyce	Aug. 14, 1945	Pontiac, Mich.	1968
Kimball, Judy	June 17, 1938	Sioux City, Iowa	1960
Lauer, Bonnie	Feb. 20, 1951	Detroit, Mich.	1975
LePera, Janet Caponi	July 29, 1947	Detroit, Mich.	1968
Little, Sally	Oct. 12, 1951	South Africa	1971
Mann, Carol	Feb. 3, 1941	Buffalo, N.Y.	1960
Martin, Kathy	Feb. 9, 1945	Berwyn, Ill.	1972
Masters, Margie	Oct. 24, 1934	Swan Hill, Australia	1965
McAllister, Mary H. (Susie)	Aug. 27, 1947	Beaumont, Texas	1971
McMullen, Kathy	Nov. 4, 1949	Bradenton, Fla.	1970
Meister, Judy	July 26, 1947	Erie, Pa.	1973
Miller, Sharon	Jan. 13, 1941	Marshall, Mich.	1966
Mills, Mary	Jan. 19, 1940	Laurel, Miss.	1962
Moran, Sharron	Oct. 28, 1942	Chicago, Ill.	1967
Owens, Norma Diane (Dede)		St. Petersburg, Fla.	1969
Palmer, Sandra Jean (Sandy)	March 10, 1941	Ft. Worth, Texas	1964
Patterson, Diane	Nov. 15, 1947	Longview, Tex.	1971
Porter, Mary Bea	Dec. 4, 1949	Everett, Wash.	1973
Post, Sandra	June 4, 1948	Ontario, Canada	1968
Postlewait, Kathy	Nov. 11, 1949	Norfolk, Va.	1972
Powell, Renee	May 4, 1946	Canton, Ohio	1967
Prentice, JoAnn (Fry)	Feb. 9, 1933	Birmingham, Ala.	1956
Pulz, Penny	Feb. 2, 1952	Melbourne, Australia	1973
Rankin, Judy Torluemke	Feb. 18, 1945	St. Louis, Mo.	1962
Roberts, Sue	June 22, 1948	Oak Park, Ill.	1969
Skala, Carole Jo	June 13, 1938	Eugene, Ore.	1970
Smith, M. J.	May 14, 1952	Huttm, New Zealand	1973
Smith, Marilynn Louise (Smitty)	April 13, 1929	Topeka, Kansas	1949
Spuzich, Sandra Ann (Spuz)	April 3, 1937	Indianapolis, Ind.	1962
Stacy, Hollis	March 16, 1954	Savannah, Ga.	1974
Stephenson, Jan	Dec. 22, 1951	Sydney, Australia	1973
Stone, Beth	May 15, 1940	Harlingen, Texas	1961
Suggs, Louise	Sept. 7, 1923	Atlanta, Ga.	1948
Tu, Ai-Yu	Sept. 29, 1954	Taipei, Taiwan	1976
Walker, Michelle	Sept. 17, 1952	Alwoodley, England	1973
Washam, Jo Ann	May 24, 1950	Auburn, Wash.	1973
Whitworth, Kathrynne Ann (Kathy)	Sept. 22, 1939	Monahans, Texas	1958
Wilkins, Mardell	Nov. 20, 1947	San Pedro, Calif.	1971
Wilson, Peggy Joyce (Peg)	Dec. 28, 1934	Lauderdale, Miss.	1962
Wright, Mickey	Feb. 14, 1935	San Diego, Calif.	1954
Young, Donna Caponi	Jan. 29, 1945	Detroit, Mich.	1965

Recent PGA Tournament Winners

1956

Besselink, Al	Havana Invitational
Burke, Jack	Masters; PGA Championship
Casper, Billy	Labatt Open
Demaret, Jimmy	Thunderbird Invitational
Dickinson, Gardner	Miami Beach Open
Fairfield, Don	Pensacola Open
Fetchick, Mike	St. Petersburg Open; Western Open; Mayfair Inn Open
Finsterwald, Dow	Carling Open
Furgol, Ed	Miller Open; Rubber City Open
Harrison, E. J.	All-American
Hawkins, Fred	Oklahoma City Open
Kroll, Ted	Tucson Open; Houston Open; World Championship
Littler, Gene	Texas Open; Tournament of Champions
Mangrum, Lloyd	Los Angeles Open
Maxwell, Billy	Arlington Hotel Open
Mayer, Dick	Philadelphia *Daily News* Open
Mayfield, Shelly	Baton Rouge Open
Middlecoff, Cary	Bing Crosby Pro-Am; Phoenix Open; USGA Open
O'Leary, Paul	Imperial Valley Open
Palmer, Arnold	Insurance City Open; Eastern Open
Rosburg, Bob	Motor City Open; San Diego Open
Sanders, Doug	Canadian Open
Snead, Sam	Greensboro Open

Souchak, Mike	Caliente Open; Azalea Open; Colonial National Invitational; St. Paul Open
Thomson, Peter	Texas Open
Wall, Art	Fort Wayne Open
Wininger, Bo	Kansas City Open

1957

Balding, Al	Miami Beach Open; West Palm Beach Open; Havana Invitational
Bayer, George	Canadian Open
Besselink, Al	Kansas City Open; Caracas Open
Bolt, Tommy	Eastern Open
Burkemo, Walter	Mayfair Inn Open
Casper, Billy	Phoenix Open; Kentucky Derby Open
Cooper, Pete	St. Petersburg Open
Demaret, Jimmy	Thunderbird Invitational; Baton Rouge Open; Arlington Hotel Open
DeVicenzo, Roberto	Colonial National Invitational; All-American
Dickinson, Gardner	Insurance City Open
Ellis, Wes	Piping Rock Pro-Am
Ferree, Jim	Concord International Pro-Am
Finsterwald, Dow	Tucson Open
Ford, Doug	Los Angeles Open; Masters; Western Open
Furgol, Ed	Caliente Open
Harney, Paul	Carling Open; Labatt Open
Harrison, E. J.	Greenbrier Invitational
Hebert, Jay	Texas Open; Bing Crosby Pro-Am
Hebert, Lionel	PGA Championship
Inman, Bob	Denver Open
Lema, Tony	Imperial Valley Open
Leonard, Stan	Greater Greensboro Open
Littler, Gene	Tournament of Champions
Maxwell, Billy	Hesperia Open
Mayer, Dick	U.S. Open; World Championship
Middlecoff, Cary	Bing Crosby Pro-Am
O'Leary, Paul	Erie Open
Palmer, Arnold	Houston Open; Azalea Open; Rubber City Open; San Diego Open
Sifford, Charles	Long Beach Open
Snead, Sam	Palm Beach Invitational; Dallas Open
Venturi, Ken	St. Paul Open; Miller Open
Wall, Art	Pensacola Open

1958

Bayer, George	Havana Invitational; Mayfair Inn Open
Bolt, Tommy	Colonial National Invitational; U.S. Open
Boros, Julius	Arlington Hotel Open; Carling Open
Burke, Jack	Insurance City Open
Casper, Billy	Bing Crosby Pro-Am; Greater New Orleans Open; Buick Open; Havana International

Cooper, Pete	West Palm Beach Open
Ellis, Wes	Canadian Open
Ferree, Jim	Vancouver Open
Finsterwald, Dow	PGA Championship; Utah Open
Ford, Doug	Pensacola Open
Goalby, Bob	Greater Greensboro Open
Harney, Paul	Dorado Beach Invitational
Harrison, E. J.	Tijuana Open
Hawkins, Fred	Jackson Open
Hebert, Jay	Bing Crosby Pan-Am; Lafayette Open
Hebert, Lionel	Tucson Open
Jacobs, Tommy	Denver Open
Johnson, Howie	Azalea Open
Johnston, Bill	Texas Open
Leonard, Stan	Tournament of Champions
Maxwell, Billy	Memphis Invitational
McMullin, John	Hesperia Open
Middlecoff, Cary	Miller Open
Oliver, Ed	Houston Invitational
Palmer, Arnold	St. Petersburg Open; Masters; Pepsi Open
Player, Gary	Kentucky Derby Open
Sanders, Doug	Western Open
Snead, Sam	Greenbrier Invitational; Dallas Open
Souchak, Mike	St. Paul Open
Stranahan, Frank	Los Angeles Open
Venturi, Ken	Thunderbird Invitational; Phoenix Open; Baton Rouge Open; Gleneagles–Chicago Open
Vossler, Ernie	Kansas City Open
Wall, Art	Rubber City Open; Eastern Open

1959

Boros, Julius	Dallas Open
Burke, Jack	Houston Classic
Casper, Billy	USGA Open; Portland Open; Lafayette Open; Mobile Open
Collins, Bill	New Orleans Open
Ellis, Wes	Texas Open
Finsterwald, Dow	Greensboro Open; Carling Open; Kansas City Open
Ford, Doug	Canadian Open
Furgol, Marty	San Diego Open; El Paso Open
Harney, Paul	Pensacola Open
Hebert, Jay	Orange County Open
Hogan, Ben	Colonial National
Johnson, Howie	Baton Rouge Open
Littler, Gene	Phoenix Open; Tucson Open; Arlington Hotel Open; Insurance City Open; Miller Open
Middlecoff, Cary	St. Petersburg Open
Monti, Eric	Hesperia Open
Nieporte, Tom	Rubber City Open
Palmer, Arnold	Thunderbird Invitational; Oklahoma City Open; West Palm Beach Open
Ragan, Dave	Eastern Open
Rosburg, Bob	PGA Championship
Rudolph, Mason	Golden Gate Open

Sanders, Doug	Coral Gables Open
Snead, Sam	Sam Snead Festival
Souchak, Mike	Tournament of Champions; Western Open; Motor City Open
Venturi, Ken	Los Angeles Open; Gleneagles–Chicago Open
Vossler, Ernie	Tijuana Open
Wall, Art	Bing Crosby National; Azalea Open; Masters; Buick Open
Whitt, Don	Memphis Open; Kentucky Open

1960

Barber, Jerry	Tournament of Champions; Yorba Linda Open
Bayer, George	St. Petersburg Open
Bolt, Tommy	Memphis Open
Boros, Julius	Colonial National
Casper, Billy	Portland Open; Hesperia Open; Orange County Open
Collins, Bill	Houston Classic; Hot Springs Open
Fairfield, Don	St. Paul Open
Finsterwald, Dow	Los Angeles Open; Greater New Orleans Open
Fleck, Jack	Phoenix Open
Ford, Doug	"500" Festival Open
Goalby, Bob	Coral Gables Open
Hebert, Jay	PGA Championship
Hebert, Lionel	Cajun Classic
January, Don	Tucson Open
Johnston, Bill	Utah Open
Leonard, Stan	Western Open
Littler, Gene	Oklahoma City Open; Eastern Open
Marr, Dave	Sam Snead Festival
Nieporte, Tom	Azalea Open
Palmer, Arnold	Palm Springs Golf Classic; Texas Open; Baton Rouge Open; Pensacola Open; Masters; USGA Open; Insurance City Open; Mobile Open
Pott, Johnny	Dallas Open; West Palm Beach Open
Snead, Sam	DeSoto Open; Greensboro Open
Souchak, Mike	San Diego Open; Buick Open
Venturi, Ken	Bing Crosby National; Milwaukee Open
Vossler, Ernie	Carling Open; Panama Open
Wall, Art	Canadian Open

1961

Barber, Jerry	Azalea Invitational; PGA Championship
Bolt, Tommy	Pensacola Open
Brewer, Gay	Carling Open; Mobile Open; West Palm Beach Open
Burke, Jack	Buick Open
Campbell, Joe	Beaumont Open
Casper, Billy	Portland Open
Crampton, Bruce	Milwaukee Open
Cupit, Jacky	Canadian Open

Ferrier, Jim	Almaden Open
Fleck, Jack	Bakersfield Open
Ford, Doug	"500" Festival Open
Goalby, Bob	Los Angeles Open; St. Petersburg Open
Hebert, Jay	Houston Classic; American Classic
Hill, Dave	Denver Open; Tucson Open
January, Don	St. Paul Open
Knudson, George	Coral Gables Open
Lema, Tony	Hesperia Open
Littler, Gene	U.S. Open
Marr, Dave	Greater Seattle Open
Maxwell, Billy	Palm Springs Classic; Insurance City Open
McCallister, Bob	Orange County Open
Middlecoff, Cary	Memphis Open
Monti, Eric	Ontario Open
Palmer, Arnold	Phoenix Open; Baton Rouge Open; Texas Open; Western Open; San Diego Open
Player, Gary	Lucky International; Sunshine Open; Masters
Rosburg, Bob	Bing Crosby National
Sanders, Doug	New Orleans Open; Colonial National; Hot Springs Open; Eastern Open; Cajun Classic
Snead, Sam	Tournament of Champions, Sam Snead Festival
Souchak, Mike	Greensboro Open
Stewart, Earl	Dallas Open
Whitt, Don	Caracas Open

1962

Barnum, John	Cajun Classic
Campbell, Joe	Baton Rouge Open
Casper, Billy	Doral Open; Greensboro Open; "500" Festival Open; Bakersfield Open
Collins, Billy	Buick Open
Crampton, Bruce	Motor City Open
Cupit, Jacky	Western Open
Dickinson, Gardner	Coral Gables Open
Ford, Doug	Bing Crosby National; Eastern Open
Geiberger, Al	Caracas Open; Ontario Open
Goalby, Bob	Insurance City Open; Denver Open
Hebert, Lionel	Memphis Open
Jacobs, Tommy	San Diego Open
Johnson, Al	Hot Springs Open
Kroll, Ted	Canadian Open
Lema, Tony	Sahara Invitational; Orange County Open; Mobile Open
Littler, Gene	Lucky International; Thunderbird Classic
Marr, Dave	Azalea Open
Maxwell, Billy	Dallas Open
Nichols, Bobby	St. Petersburg Open; Houston Classic
Nicklaus, Jack	U.S. Open; Portland Open; Seattle Open

Palmer, Arnold	Palm Springs Classic; Phoenix Open; Masters; Texas Open; Tournament of Champions; Colonial National; American Classic	Boros, Julius	Greater Greensboro Open
		Brown, Pete	Waco Turner Open
		Casper, Billy	Colonial National; Greater Seattle Open; Almaden Open; Doral Open
Player, Gary	PGA Championship	Coody, Charles	Dallas Open
Pott, Johnny	Waco Turner Open	Courtney, Chuck	St. Paul Open
Ragan, Dave	Beaumont Open; West Palm Beach Open	Crampton, Bruce	Texas Open
		Cupit, Jacky	Tucson Open
Rodgers, Phil	Tucson Open; Los Angeles Open	Devlin, Bruce	St. Petersburg Open
		Harney, Paul	Los Angeles Open
Sanders, Doug	Pensacola Open; St. Paul Open; Oklahoma City Open	Jacobs, Tommy	Palm Springs Classic
		Knudson, George	Caracas Open; Fresno Open
Wininger, Bo	New Orleans Open; Carling Open	Lema, Tony	Bing Crosby National; Thunderbird Classic; Buick Open; Cleveland Open

1963

		McCallister, Bob	Sunset-Camellia Open
Barber, Jerry	Azalea Open	McGowan, Jack	Mt. View Open
Baxter, Rex	Cajun Classic	Nagle, Kel	Canadian Open
Beard, Frank	Frank Sinatra Open	Nichols, Bobby	PGA Championship; Carling Open
Boros, Julius	Colonial National; Buick Open; USGA Open		
Brewer, Gay	Waco Turner Open	Nicklaus, Jack	Phoenix Open; Tournament of Champions; Whitemarsh Open; Portland Open
Burke, Jack	Lucky International; St. Paul Open		
		Palmer, Arnold	Masters; Oklahoma City Open
Casper, Billy	Bing Crosby National; Insurance City Open	Player, Gary	Pensacola Open; "500" Festival Open
Charles, R. J. "Bob"	Houston Classic	Rodriguez, Juan	Lucky International; Western Open
Fairfield, Don	Oklahoma City Open		
Finsterwald, Dow	"500" Festival Open	Rudolph, Mason	Greater New Orleans Open
Floyd, Ray	St. Petersburg Open	Sikes, R. H.	Sahara Invitational
Ford, Doug	Canadian Open	Souchak, Mike	Houston Classic; Memphis Open
Geiberger, Al	Almaden Open		
Hill, Dave	Hot Springs Open	Venturi, Ken	U.S. Open; Insurance City Open; American Classic
Jacobs, Tommy	Utah Open		
January, Don	Tucson Open	Wall, Art	San Diego Open
Knudson, George	Portland Open		
Lema, Tony	Memphis Open		
Nichols, Bobby	Seattle Open		**1965**
Nicklaus, Jack	Palm Springs Classic; Masters; Tournament of Champions; PGA Championship; Sahara Invitational		
		Archer, George	Lucky International
		Baird, Butch	PGA National Four-ball with Gay Brewer
Palmer, Arnold	Los Angeles Open; Phoenix Open; Pensacola Open; Thunderbird Classic; Cleveland Open; Western Open; Whitemarsh Open	Beard, Frank	Texas Open
		Besselink, Al	Caracas Open
		Blancas, Homero	Mexican Open
		Brewer, Gay	Greater Seattle Open; Hawaiian Open; PGA National Four-ball with Butch Baird
Player, Gary	San Diego Open		
Pott, Johnny	American Classic	Casper, Billy	Bob Hope Classic; Western Open; Insurance City Open; Sahara Invitational
Rodgers, Phil	Texas Open		
Rodriguez, Juan	Denver Open		
Rudolph, Mason	Fig Garden Open	Charles, R. J. "Bob"	Tucson Open
Rule, Jack	St. Paul Open	Crampton, Bruce	Bing Crosby National; Colonial National; "500" Festival
Sanders, Doug	Greensboro Open		
Sikes, Dan	Doral Open	Ellis, Wes	San Diego Open
Wall, Art	Caracas Open	Floyd, Ray	St. Paul Open
Wininger, Bo	Greater New Orleans Open	Funseth, Rod	Phoenix Open
		Geiberger, Al	American Classic
		Harney, Paul	Los Angeles Open
	1964	Hart, Dick	Azalea Open
		Hiskey, Babe	Cajun Classic
Barber, Miller	Cajun Classic	Lema, Tony	Buick Open; Carling Open
Besselink, Al	Azalea Open	Littler, Gene	Canadian Open

Marr, Dave	PGA Championship
Mayer, Dick	Greater New Orleans Open
Nichols, Bobby	Houston Classic
Nicklaus, Jack	Masters; Memphis Open; Thunderbird Classic; Philadelphia Classic; Portland Open
Palmer, Arnold	Tournament of Champions
Player, Gary	U.S. Open
Rule, Jack	Oklahoma City Open
Sanders, Doug	Pensacola Open; Doral Open
Sikes, Dan	Cleveland Open
Snead, Sam	Greensboro Open
Verwey, F. R. "Bob"	Almaden Open
Weaver, Bert	Jacksonville Open

1966

Beard, Frank	New Orleans Open
Blancas, Homero	Seattle–Everett Open
Brewer, Gay	Pensacola Open
Campbell, Joe	Tucson Open
Casper, Billy	**San Diego Open; U.S. Open; Western Open; "500" Festival Open**
Cupit, Jacky	Cajun Classic
DeVicenzo, Roberto	Dallas Open
Devlin, Bruce	**Colonial National; Carling Open**
Geiberger, Al	PGA Championship
Hebert, Lionel	Citrus Open
Henning, Harold	Texas Open
January, Don	Philadelphia Classic
Lema, Tony	Oklahoma City Open
Makalena, Ted	Hawaiian Open
Massengale, Don	Bing Crosby National; Canadian Open
McCallister, Bob	Mexico Open
Nichols, Bobby	Minnesota Classic
Nicklaus, Jack	Masters; Sahara Invitational; PGA National Team Championship with Arnold Palmer
Palmer, Arnold	Los Angeles Open; **Tournament of Champions; Houston Inter**national; PGA National Team Championship with Jack Nicklaus
Rodgers, Phil	Doral Open; Buick Open
Rudolph, Mason	Thunderbird Classic
Sanders, Doug	Bob Hope Classic; Jacksonville Open; **Greater Greensboro Open**
Sikes, R. H.	Cleveland Open
Venturi, Ken	Lucky Invitational
Wall, Art	Insurance City Open; Caracas Open
Wysong, Dudley	Phoenix Open
Yancey, Bert	Azalea Open; **Memphis Open; Portland Open**

1967

Archer, George	Greater Greensboro Open
Barber, Miller	Oklahoma City Open

Beard, Frank	Tournament of Champions; Houston International; "500" Festival Open
Boros, Julius	Citrus Open; Phoenix Open; Buick Open
Brewer, Gay	Pensacola Open; Masters
Casper, Billy	Canadian Open; Carling Open
Charles, R. J. "Bob"	Atlanta Classic
Dickinson, Gardner	Cleveland Open
Fleckman, Marty	Cajun Classic
Glover, Randy	Azalea Open
Goalby, Bob	San Diego Open
Graham, Lou	Minnesota Classic
Hill, Dave	Memphis Open
January, Don	PGA Championship
Knudson, George	Greater New Orleans Open
Nicklaus, Jack	Bing Crosby National; U.S. Open; Western Open; Westchester Classic; Sahara Invitational
Nieporte, Tom	Bob Hope Classic
Palmer, Arnold	Los Angeles Open; Tucson Open; American Classic; Thunderbird Classic
Rodriguez, Juan	Texas Open
Sanders, Doug	Doral Open
Sifford, Charlie	Insurance City Open
Sikes, Dan	Jacksonville Open; Philadelphia Classic
Stockton, Dave	Colonial National Invitational
Wysong, Dudley	Hawaiian Open
Yancey, Bert	Greater Dallas Open

1968

Archer, George	Pensacola Open; Greater New Orleans Open; PGA Team **Championship***
Baird, Butch	Panama Open
Barber, Miller	Byron Nelson Classic
Boros, Julius	PGA Championship; Westchester Classic
Casper, Billy	Los Angeles Open; Greater Greensboro Open; Colonial National; "500" Festival Open; Greater Hartford Open; Lucky International
Cerrudo, Ron	Cajun Classic
Charles, R. J. "Bob"	Canadian Open
Crampton, Bruce	West End Classic
DeVicenzo, Roberto	Houston International
Dickinson, Gardner	Doral Open
Dickson, Bob	Haig Open
Goalby, Bob	Masters
Jacklin, Tony	Jacksonville Open
January, Don	Tournament of Champions
Knudson, George	Phoenix Open; Tucson Open
Lunn, Bob	Memphis Open; Atlanta Classic
McLendon, B. R.	Magnolia State Classic
Mowry, Larry	Rebel Yell Open
Murphy, Bob	Philadelphia Classic; **Thunder**bird Classic
Nichols, Bobby	**PGA Team Championship***

Nicklaus, Jack	Western Open; American Classic
Palmer, Arnold	Bob Hope Classic; Kemper Open
Pott, Johnny	Bing Crosby National
Refram, Dean	Robinson Open
Reid, Steve	Azalea Open
Rodriguez, Juan	Sahara Invitational
Sikes, Dan	Citrus Open; Minnesota Classic
Stockton, Dave	Cleveland Open; Greater Milwaukee Open
Trevino, Lee	U.S. Open; Hawaiian Open
Weiskopf, Tom	San Diego Open; Buick Open
Zarley, Kermit	Kaiser International Open

1969

Archer, George	Bing Crosby Pro-Am; Masters
Barber, Miller	Kaiser International Open
Beard, Frank	Minnesota Classic; Westchester Classic
Beman, Deane	Texas Open
Casper, Billy	Bob Hope Desert Classic; Western Open
Colbert, Jim	Monsanto Open
Coody, Charles	Cleveland Open
Courtney, Chuck	Tallahassee Open
Crampton, Bruce	Hawaiian Open
Devlin, Bruce	Byron Nelson Classic
Dickinson, Gardner	Colonial National Invitational
Douglass, Dale	Azalea Open; Kemper Open
Floyd, Ray	Greater Jacksonville Open; American Classic; PGA Championship
Goalby, Bob	Robinson Open
Henry, Bunky	National Airlines Open
Hill, Dave	Memphis Open; Buick Open; Philadelphia Classic
Hinson, Larry	Greater New Orleans Open
Kaser, Monty	Indian Ridge Hospital Open
Littler, Gene	Phoenix Open; Greater Greensboro Open
Lotz, Dick	Alameda Open
Lunn, Bob	Greater Hartford Open
Moody, Orville	USGA Open
Mowry, Larry	Magnolia Classic
Nicklaus, Jack	Andy Williams–San Diego Open; Sahara Invitational; Kaiser International Open
Palmer, Arnold	Heritage Classic; Danny Thomas–Diplomat Classic
Player, Gary	Tournament of Champions
Shaw, Tom	Doral Open; AVCO Classic
Sifford, Charles	Los Angeles Open
Spray, Steve	Lucky International Open
Still, Ken	Florida Citrus Open; Greater Milwaukee Open
Trevino, Lee	Tucson Open
Yancey, Bert	Atlanta Classic
Ziegler, Larry	Michigan Classic

1970

Aaron, Tommy	Atlanta Classic

Barber, Miller	Greater New Orleans Open
Barrier, Jerry	Kiwanis Peninsula Open
Beard, Frank	Tournament of Champions; American Golf Classic
Beman, Deane,	Greater Milwaukee Open
Blancas, Romero	Colonial National Invitational
Blocker, Chris	Magnolia Classic
Brown, Pete	Andy Williams–San Diego Open
Casper, Billy	Los Angeles Open; Masters; IVB-Philadelphia Classic; AVCO Classic
Cerrudo, Ron	San Antonio Open
Crampton, Bruce	Westchester Classic
Devlin, Bruce	Bob Hope Desert Classic, Cleveland Open
Douglass, Dale	Phoenix Open
Garrett, Bill	Coral Springs Open
Gilbert, Gibby	Houston/Champions International
Goalby, Bob	Heritage Golf Classic
Henning, Harold	Tallahassee Open
Hill, Dave	Danny Thomas–Memphis Classic
Hill, Mike	Doral Open
Hiskey, Babe	Sahara Invitational
Jacklin, Tony	USGA Open
January, Don	Greater Jacksonville Open
Knudson, George	Robinson Open
Lotz, Dick	Monsanto Open; Kemper Open
Lunn, Bob	Citrus Invitational
Murphy, Bob	Greater Hartford Open
Nichols, Bobby	Dow Jones Open
Nicklaus, Jack	Byron Nelson Classic; National Four-Ball Championship*
Palmer, Arnold	National Four-Ball Championship*
Player, Gary	Greater Greensboro Open
Royer, Hugh	Western Open
Rudolph, Mason	Green Island Open
Sanders, Doug	Bahama Islands Open
Sanudo, Cesar	Azalea Open
Still, Ken	Kaiser International Open
Stockton, Dave	PGA Championship
Stone, Bob	Citrus Open
Trevino, Lee	Tucson Open; National Airlines Open
Wood, Larry	Sea Pines Open
Yancey, Bert	Bing Crosby National Pro-Am
Zarley, Kermit	Canadian Open

1971

Allin, Brian	Greater Greensboro Open
Archer, George	Andy Williams–San Diego Open; Greater Hartford Open
Barber, Miller	Phoenix Open
Beard, Frank	Greater New Orleans Open
Casper, Billy	Kaiser International Open
Coody, Charles	Masters
Crampton, Bruce	Western Open
Dickinson, Gardner	Atlanta Golf Classic
Eichelberger, Dave	Greater Milwaukee Open
Goalby, Bob	Bahamas National Open

Green, Hubert	Houston/Champions International
Harris, Labron, Jr.	Robinson Open Golf Classic
Heard, Jerry	American Golf Classic
Irwin, Hale	Sea Pines-Heritage Classic
Littler, Gene	Monsanto Open; Colonial National Invitational
Lunn, Bob	Glen Campbell–Los Angeles Open
Miller, Johnny	Southern Open
Mitchell, Bobby	Cleveland Open
Nicklaus, Jack	PGA Championship; Tournament of Champions; Byron Nelson Golf Classic; National Team Championship*; Walt Disney World Open
Palmer, Arnold	Bob Hope Desert Classic; Florida Citrus Invitational; Westchester Classic; National Team Championship*
Player, Gary	Greater Jacksonville Open; National Airlines Open
Shaw, Tom	Bing Crosby National Pro-Am; Hawaiian Open
Snead, J. C.	Tucson Open; Doral-Eastern Open
Stockton, Dave	Massachusetts Classic
Trevino, Lee	Tallahassee Open; Danny Thomas–Memphis Classic; USGA Open; Canadian Open; Sahara Invitational
Weiskopf, Tom	Kemper Open; Philadelphia Classic
Weaver, DeWitt	U.S. Professional Match Play Championship

1972

Archer, George	Glen Campbell–Los Angeles Open; Greater Greensboro Open
Barber, Miller	Dean Martin–Tucson Open
Beman, Deane	Quad Cities Open
Blancas, Homero	Phoenix Open
Brewer, Gay	Canadian Open
Colbert, Jim	Greater Milwaukee Open
Devlin, Bruce	USI Classic; Houston Open
Graham, Dave	Cleveland Open
Graham, Lou	Liggett & Myers Open
Harney, Paul	Andy Williams–San Diego Open
Heard, Jerry	Florida Citrus Open; Colonial National Invitational
Hill, Dave	Monsanto Open
Hill, Mike	San Antonio–Texas Open
Hiskey, Babe	National Team Championship*
Jacklin, Tony	Greater Jacksonville Open
Jamieson, Jim	Western Open
Jones, Grier	Hawaiian Open; Robinson's Fall Golf Classic
Knudson, George	Kaiser International Open
Lunn, Bob	Atlanta Golf Classic
Miller, Johnny	Heritage Golf Classic
Mitchell, Bobby	Tournament of Champions

Nicklaus, Jack	Bing Crosby National Pro-Am; Doral-Eastern Open; Masters; USGA Open Championship; Westchester Classic; U.S. Professional Match Play Championship; Walt Disney World Open
Player, Gary	Greater New Orleans Open; PGA Championship
Rodriguez, Juan	Byron Nelson Golf Classic
Rosburg, Bob	Bob Hope Desert Classic
Sanders, Doug	Kemper Open
Shaw, Bob	Tallahassee Open
Snead, J. C.	IVB-Philadelphia Golf Classic
Trevino, Lee	Danny Thomas–Memphis Classic; Greater Hartford Open; Greater St. Louis Golf Classic
Wadkins, Lanny	Sahara Invitational
Weaver, DeWitt	Southern Open
Weiskopf, Tom	Jackie Gleason–Inverrary Classic
Yancey, Bert	American Golf Classic
Zarley, Kermit	National Team Championship*

1973

Aaron, Tommy	Masters
Adams, Sam	Quad Cities Open
Allin, Buddy	Florida Citrus Open
Barber, Miller	World Open
Beman, Deane	Shrine Robinson Classic
Blancas, Homero	Monsanto Open
Casper, Billy	Western Open; Sammy Davis, Jr.–Greater Hartford Open
Colbert, Jim	Greater Jacksonville Open
Crampton, Bruce	Phoenix Open; Dean Martin–Tucson Open; Houston Open; American Golf Classic
Crenshaw, Ben	San Antonio–Texas Open
Dickson, Bob	Andy Williams–San Diego Open
Funseth, Rod	Los Angeles Open
Green, Hubert	Tallahassee Open; B.C. Open
Greene, Bert	Liggett & Myers Open
Hill, Dave	Danny Thomas–Memphis Open
Irwin, Hale	Heritage Classic
Littler, Gene	St. Louis Classic
Mahaffey, John	Sahara Invitational
Miller, Johnny	U.S. Open
Nichols, Bobby	Westchester Classic
Nicklaus, Jack	Bing Crosby National Pro-Am; Greater New Orleans Open; Tournament of Champions; Atlanta Classic; PGA Championship; Ohio Kings Island Open; Walt Disney Golf Classic
Palmer, Arnold	Bob Hope Desert Classic
Player, Gary	Southern Open
Rodriguez, Chi Chi	Greater Greensboro Open
Schlee, John	Hawaiian Open
Schroeder, John	U.S. Match Play
Sneed, Ed	Kaiser International

* Team event.

Stockton, Dave	Greater Milwaukee Open
Trevino, Lee	Jackie Gleason–Inverrary Classic; Doral-Eastern Open
Wadkins, Lanny	Byron Nelson Classic; US! Classic
Weiskopf, Tom	Colonial National Invitational; Kemper Open, IVB-Philadelphia Classic; Canadian Open

1974

Allin, Buddy	Doral-Eastern Open; Byron Nelson Classic
Barber, Miller	Ohio Kings Island Open
Charles, Bob	Greater Greensboro Open
Colbert, Jim	American Golf Classic
Curl, Rod	Colonial National Invitational
Diehl, Terry	San Antonio–Texas Open
Elder, Lee	Monsanto Open
Fezler, Forrest	Southern Open
Geiberger, Al	Sahara Invitational
Green, Hubert	Bob Hope Desert Classic; Greater Jacksonville Open; IVB-Philadelphia Classic; Disney Team Championship*
Heard, Jerry	Florida Citrus Open
Hill, Dave	Houston Open
Irwin, Hale	U.S. Open
Karl, Richie	B.C. Open
McLendon, B. R.	Disney Team Championship*
Menne, Bob	Kemper Open
Mlller, Allen	Tallahassee Open
Miller, Johnny	Bing Crosby National Pro-Am; Phoenix Open; Dean Martin–Tucson Open; Heritage Classic; Tournament of Champions; Westchester Classic; World Open; Kaiser International
Nichols, Bobby	Andy Williams–San Diego Open; Canadian Open
Nicklaus, Jack	Hawaiian Open; Tournament Players Championship
Player, Gary	Masters; Danny Thomas–Memphis Open
Regalado, Victor	Pleasant Valley Classic
Sneed, Ed	Greater Milwaukee Open
Stockton, Dave	Glen Campbell Los Angeles Open; Quad Cities Open; Sammy Davis, Jr.–Greater Hartford Open
Thompson, Leonard	Jackie Gleason–Inverrary Classic
Trevino, Lee	Greater New Orleans Open; PGA Championship; World Series of Golf
Watson, Tom	Western Open

1975

Bies, Don	Sammy Davis, Jr.–Greater Hartford Open
Casper, Billy	New Orleans Open

Colbert, Jim	Disney Team Championship*
Crampton, Bruce	Houston Open
Fitzsimons, Pat	Glen Campbell–Los Angeles Open
Floyd, Ray	Kemper Open
Geiberger, Al	Tournament of Champions; Tournament Players Championship
Graham, Lou	U.S. Open
Green, Hubert	Southern Open
Groh, Gary	Hawaiian Open
Hill, Dave	Sahara Invitational
Irwin, Hale	Atlanta Classic; Western Open
Iverson, Don	B.C. Open
January, Don	San Antonio Texas Open
Jenkins, Tom	IVB-Philadelphia Classic
Littler, Gene	Bing Crosby National Pro-Am; Danny Thomas–Memphis Open; Westchester Classic
Maltbie, Roger	Quad Cities Open; Pleasant Valley Classic
McGee, Jerry	Pensacola Open
Miller, Johnny	Phoenix Open; Dean Martin–Tucson Open; Bob Hope Desert Classic; Kaiser International
Murphy, Bob	Jackie Gleason–Inverrary Classic
Nicklaus, Jack	Doral-Eastern Open; Heritage Classic; Masters; PGA Championship; World Open
Refram, Dean	Disney Team Championship*
Snead, J. C.	Andy Williams–San Diego Open
Trevino, Lee	Florida Citrus Open
Wall, Art	Greater Milwaukee Open
Watson, Tom	Byron Nelson Classic; World Series of Golf
Weiskopf, Tom	Greater Greensboro Open; Canadian Open

1976

Allin, Buddy	Pleasant Valley Open
Archer, George	Sahara Invitational
Baird, Butch	San Antonio–Texas Open
Blackburn, Woody	Disney Team Championship*
Crenshaw, Ben	Bing Crosby National Pro-Am; Hawaiian Open; Ohio Kings Island Open
Elder, Lee	Houston Open
Floyd, Ray	Masters; World Open
Green, Hubert	Doral-Eastern Open; Greater Jacksonville Open; Heritage Classic
Geiberger, Al	Greater Greensboro Open; Western Open
Gilbert, Gibby	Danny Thomas–Memphis Open
Gilder, Bob	Phoenix Open
Graham, David	Westchester Classic; American Golf Classic
Hayes, Mark	Byron Nelson Classic; Pensacola Open
Hill, Dave	Greater Milwaukee Open

Inman, Joe	Kemper Open
Irwin, Hale	Glen Campbell–Los Angeles Open; Florida Citrus Open
January, Don	Tournament of Champions
Kite, Tom	IVB-Philadelphia Classic
Koch, Gary	Tallahassee Open
Kratzert, Bill	Disney Team Championship*
Lister, John	Quad Cities Open
Maltbie, Roger	Memorial Tournament
Massengale, Rik	Sammy Davis, Jr.–Greater Hartford Open
McLendon, Mac	Southern Open
Miller, Johnny	Tucson National Open; Bob Hope Desert Classic
Nicklaus, Jack	Tournament Players Championship; World Series of Golf
Pate, Jerry	U.S. Open; Canadian Open
Snead, J. C.	Andy Williams–San Diego Open; Kaiser International
Stockton, Dave	PGA Championship
Trevino, Lee	Colonial National Invitational
Wynn, Bob	B.C. Open
Ziegler, Jerry	NBC New Orleans Open

1977

Barber, Miller	Anheuser-Busch Open
Bean, Andy	Doral-Eastern Open
Cole, Bobby	Buick Open
Crenshaw, Ben	Colonial National Invitational
Edwards, Danny	Greater Greensboro Open
Eichelberger, Dave	Greater Milwaukee Open
Floyd, Ray	Byron Nelson Classic; Pleasant Valley Classic
Geiberger, Al	Memphis Classic
Gilbert, Gibby	Disney Team Championship*
Green, Hubert	U.S. Open
Hayes, Mark	Tournament Players Championship
Hill, Mark	Ohio Kings Island Open
Irwin, Hale	Atlanta Classic; Colgate Hall of Fame; San Antonio–Texas Open
Jones, Grier	Disney Team Championship*
Koch, Gary	Florida Citrus Open
Kratzert, Bill	Sammy Davis, Jr.–Greater Hartford Open
Lietzke, Bruce	Garagiola-Tucson Open; Hawaiian Open
Littler, Gene	Houston Open
Marsh, Graham	Heritage Classic
Massengale, Rik	Bob Hope Desert Classic
McGee, Jerry	IVB-Philadelphia Classic
Morgan, Gil	B.C. Open
Morley, Mike	Quad Cities Open
Nicklaus, Jack	Jackie Gleason–Inverrary Classic; Tournament of Champions; Memorial Tournament
North, Andy	Westchester Classic
Pate, Jerry	Phoenix Open; Southern Open
Purtzer, Tom	Glen Campbell–Los Angeles Open
Simons, Jim	NBC–New Orleans Open
Sneed, Ed	Tallahassee Open

Thompson, Leonard	Pensacola Open
Trevino, Lee	Canadian Open
Wadkins, Lanny	PGA Championship; World Series of Golf
Watson, Tom	Bing Crosby National Pro-Am; Andy Williams–San Diego Open; Masters; Western Open
Weiskopf, Tom	Kemper Open

Recent LPGA Tournament Winners

1955

Berg, Patty	Titleholders Championship; Women's Western Open; All-American Open; World Championship; St. Petersburg Open; Clock Open
Crocker, Fay	Serbin Open; USGA Women's Open; Wolverine Open
Hanson, Bev	LPGA Championship; Battle Creek Open
Jameson, Betty	Sarasota Open; Babe Zaharias Open; White Mountains Open; Richmond Open
Pung, Jackie	Sea Island Open; Jacksonville Open
Rawls, Betsy	Carrollton Open
Smith, Marilynn	Heart of America Open; Mile High Open
Suggs, Louise	Los Angeles Open; Oklahoma City Open; Eastern Open; Triangle Round Robin; St. Louis Open
Zaharias, Babe	Tampa Open; Serbin Diamond Golf Ball

1956

Berg, Patty	Dallas Open; Arkansas Open
Cornelius, Kathy	St. Petersburg Open; USGA Women's Open
Crocker, Fay	Serbin Open; St. Louis Open
Dodd, Betty	Lawton Open
Faulk, Mary Lena	Kansas City Open
Hagge, Marlene Bauer	Sea Island Open; Clock Open; Babe Zaharias Open; Denver Open; Pittsburgh Open; LPGA Championship; World Championship; Triangle Round Robin
Hanson, Bev	Women's Western Open
Rawls, Betsy	Tampa Open; Peach Blossom Open; Sarasota Open
Suggs, Louise	Titleholders Championship; Havana Open; All-American Open
Wright, Mickey	Jacksonville Open
Ziske, Joyce	Syracuse Open

1957

Berg Patty	Titleholders Championship; Women's Western Open; All-American Open; World Championship; Havana Open
Crocker, Fay	Serbin Open; Triangle Round Robin
Dodd, Betty	Colonial Open
Faulk, Mary Lena	St. Petersburg Open
Hagge, Marlene Bauer	Babe Zaharias Open; Lawton Open
Hanson, Bev	Smokey Open; Land of Sky Open
Rawls, Betsy	USGA Women's Open; Tampa Open; Lake Worth Open; Peach Blossom Open; Reno Open
Smith, Wiffi	Dallas Open; San Francisco Open
Suggs, Louise	LPGA Championship; Heart of America Invitational
Wright, Mickey	Sea Island Open; Jacksonville Open; Wolverine Open

1958

Berg, Patty	Women's Western Open; American Women's Open
Crocker, Fay	Havana Biltmore Invitational; Waterloo Open
Faulk, Mary Lena	Macktown Open
Hagge, Marlene Bauer	Lake Worth Open; Land of Sky Open
Hanson, Bev	Titleholders Championship; Lawton Open
Hoffmann, Bonnie	Kansas City Open
Pung, Jackie	Jackson Open
Rawls, Betsy	Tampa Open; St. Petersburg Open
Smith, Marilynn	Jacksonville Open
Smith, Wiffi	Peach Blossom Open
Suggs, Louise	Babe Zaharias Open; Gatlinburg Open; French Lick Sheraton Open; Triangle Round Robin
Wright, Mickey	Sea Island Open; Opie Turner Open; Dallas Civitan Open; LPGA Championship; USGA Women's Open

1959

Cornelius, Kathy	Cosmopolitan Open
Hagge, Marlene Bauer	Mayfair Open; Hoosier Celebrity Open
Hanson, Bev	American Women's Open; Spokane Open; Links Inc. Invitational Open
Jessen, Ruth	Tampa Women's Open
Rawls, Betsy	LPGA Championship; Lake Worth Open; Royal Crown Open; Babe Zaharias Open; Land of Sky Open; Mt. Prospect Open; Women's Western

	Open; Crown Open; Babe Zaharias Open; Land of Sky Open; Waterloo Open; Opie Turner Open; Triangle Round Robin
Smith, Marilynn	Memphis Open
Smith, Wiffi	Peach Blossom Open; Miami Triangle Open
Spork, Shirley	California Derby Open
Suggs, Louise	Titleholders Championship; St. Petersburg Open; Dallas Civitan Open
Wright, Mickey	Jacksonville Open; Cavalier Open; Alliance Machine International Open; USGA Women's Open
Ziske, Joyce	Howard Johnson Invitational Open

1960

Berg, Patty	American Women's Open
Crocker, Fay	Lake Worth Open; Titleholders Championship
Hanson, Bev	St. Petersburg Open
Rawls, Betsy	USGA Women's Open; Babe Zaharias Open; Cosmopolitan Open; Asheville Open
Smith, Wiffi	Royal Crown Open; Peach Blossom Open; Waterloo Open
Suggs, Louise	Dallas Civitan Open; Triangle Round Robin; Youngstown Kitchens Open; San Antonio Civitan Open
Wright, Mickey	Sea Island Open; Tampa Open; Grossinger Open; Eastern Open; Memphis Open; LPGA Championship
Ziske, Joyce	Women's Western Open; Wolverine Open

1961

Cornelius, Kathy	Tippecanoe Open
Faulk, Mary Lena	Triangle Round Robin; Babe Zaharias Open; Eastern Open; Women's Western Open
Jessen, Ruth	Peach Blossom Open
Kimball, Judy	American Women's Open
Rawls, Betsy	Cosmopolitan Open; Bill Brannin's Swing Parade
Suggs, Louise	Sea Island Invitational; DeSoto Lakes Open; Dallas Civitan Open; Kansas City Open; San Antonio Civitan Open
Wright, Mickey	St. Petersburg Open; Miami Open; Columbus Open; Waterloo Open; Spokane Open; Sacramento Valley Open; USGA Women's Open; LPGA Championship; Titleholders Championship; Mickey Wright Invitational

1962

Berg, Patty	Muskogee Civitan Open

Englehorn, Shirley	Carling Eastern Open; Eugene Women's Open
Cornelius, Kathy	Babe Zaharias Open*a*
Faulk, Mary Lena	Peach Blossom Open; Visalia Country Club Ladies' Open
Haynie, Sandra	Austin Civitan Open; Cosmopolitan Open
Jessen, Ruth	Dallas Civitan Open; Sacramento Valley Open
Kimball, Judy	LPGA Championship
Lindstrom, Maurle MacKenzie	USGA Women's Open; San Antonio Civitan Open
Rawls, Betsy	J. E. McAuliffe Memorial; Babe Zaharias Open*a*
Smith, Marilynn	Sunshine Women's Open; Waterloo Women's Open
Suggs, Louise	**St. Petersburg Open**
Whitworth, Kathy	Phoenix Thunderbird Ladies Open; Kelly Girl Open
Wright, Mickey	Sea Island Invitational; Titleholders Championship; Women's Western Open; Milwaukee Jaycee Open; Heart of America Invitational; Albuquerque Swing Parade; Salt Lake City Open; Spokane Women's Open; San Diego Ladies Open; Carlsbad Cavern City Open

a Co-winners.

1963

Englehorn, Shirley	Lady Carling Eastern Open
Hagge, Marlene Bauer	Sight Open
Haynie, Sandra	Phoenix Thunderbird Ladies' Open
Jessen, Ruth	Cosmopolitan Open
Mills, Mary	USGA Women's Open
Rawls, Betsy	Sunshine Women's Open
Romack, Barbara	Rock City Ladies' Open
Smith, Marilynn	Titleholders Championship; Peach Blossom Open; Eugene Ladies' Open; Cavern City Open
Whitworth, Kathy	Carvel Ladies' Open; Wolverine Open; Milwaukee Jaycee Open; Ogden Ladies' Open; Spokane Women's Open; Hillside Open; San Antonio Civitan Open; Mary Mills Mississippi Gulf Coast Invitational
Wright, Mickey	Sea Island Invitational; St. Petersburg Women's Open; Alpine Civitan Open; Muskogee Civitan Open; Dallas Civitan Open; Babe Zaharias Open; Women's Western Open; Waterloo Women's Open Invitational; Albuquerque Swing Parade; Idaho Centennial Ladies' Open; Visalia Ladies' Open; Mickey Wright Invita-

	tional; LPGA Championship; Haig and Haig Invitational

1964

Creed, Clifford Ann	Lady Carling Open; Cosmopolitan Open; Riverside Ladies' Open
Englehorn, Shirley	Waterloo Women's Open Invitational; Haig and Haig Invitational
Faulk, Mary Lena	St. Petersburg Women's Open Invitational
Hagge, Marlene Bauer	Mickey Wright Invitational
Haynie, Sandra	Baton Rouge Ladies Open Invitational; Las Cruces Ladies' Open
Jessen, Ruth	Babe Zaharias Open Invitational; Yankee Women's Open; Omaha Jaycee Open Invitational; Hillside House Ladies' Open; Phoenix Thunderbird Ladies' Open
Mann, Carol	Women's Western Open
Mills, Mary	Eugene Open; LPGA Championship
Rawls, Betsy	Dallas Civitan Open; Vahalla Open
Smith, Marilynn	Titleholders Championship; Albuquerque Professional–Amateur
Whitworth, Kathy	San Antonio Civitan Open
Wright, Mickey	Peach Blossom Invitational; Alexandria Ladies' Open Invitational; Squirt Ladies' Open Invitational; Muskogee Civitan Open Invitational; Lady Carling Eastern Open; Waldemar Open; USGA Women's Open; Milwaukee Jaycee Open; Visalia Ladies' Open; Tall City Open; Mary Mills Mississippi Gulf Coast Invitational

1965

Creed, Clifford Ann	Omaha Jaycee Open; Visalia Ladies' Open Invitational; Las Cruces Ladies' Open
Hagge, Marlene Bauer	Babe Zaharias Open; Milwaukee Jaycee Open; Phoenix Thunderbird Ladies' Open; Tall City Open; Alamo Open
Haynie, Sandra	Cosmopolitan Open; LPGA Championship
Jessen, Ruth	Haig and Haig Invitational
Mann, Carol	Lady Carling Open; USGA Women's Open
Maxwell, Susie	Muskogee Civitan Invitational; Women's Western Open
Mills, Mary	St. Louis Invitational; Pacific Ladies' Classic
Prentice, Jo Ann	Allstate Ladies' Invitational
Rawls, Betsy	Pensacola Ladies' Invitational;

	Waterloo Women's Open Invitational
Smith, Marilynn	Peach Blossom Invitational
Whitworth, Kathy	St. Petersburg Women's Invitational; Shreveport Kiwanis Club Invitational; Bluegrass Ladies' Invitational; Lady Carling Midwest Open; Yankee Women's Open; Buckeye Savings Invitational; Mickey Wright Invitational; Titleholders Championship
Wright, Mickey	Baton Rouge Ladies' Invitational; Dallas Civitan Open

1966

Creed, Clifford Ann	Dallas Civitan Open; Lady Carling Open (Columbus); Success Open
Ehret, Gloria	LPGA Championship
Englehorn, Shirley	Babe Zaharias Open
Haynie, Sandra	Buckeye Savings Invitational; Glass City Classic; Alamo Ladies' Open; Pensacola Ladies' Invitational
Mann, Carol	Raleigh Ladies' Invitational; Peach Blossom Invitational; Baton Rouge Ladies' Invitational; Waterloo Women's Open Invitational
Smith, Marilynn	St. Petersburg Women's Open; Louise Suggs Delray Beach Invitational
Spuzich, Sandra	USGA Women's Open; Haig and Haig Invitational
Whitworth, Kathy	Tall City Open; Clayton Federal Invitational; Milwaukee Jaycee Open; Supertest Ladies' Open; Lady Carling Open (Sutton); Lady Carling Open (Baltimore); Las Cruces Ladies' Open; Amarillo Ladies' Open; Titleholders Championship
Wright, Mickey	Venice Ladies' Open; Shreveport Kiwanis Club Invitational; Bluegrass Invitational; Women's Western Open; Pacific Ladies' Classic; Shirley Englehorn Invitational; Mickey Wright Invitational

1967

Creed, Clifford Ann	Pacific Golf Classic; Corpus Christi Civitan Open
Englehorn, Shirley	Shirley Englehorn Invitational
Haynie, Sandra	Amarillo Ladies' Open; Mickey Wright Invitational
Lindstrom, Murle MacKenzie	Carlsbad Jaycee Open
Mann, Carol	Tall City Open; Buckeye Savings Invitational; Supertest Ladies' Open

Masters, Margie	Quality Chekd Classic
Maxwell, Susie	Louise Suggs Invitational; Milwaukee Jaycee Open
Prentice, Jo Ann	Dallas Civitan Open
Smith, Marilynn	St. Petersburg Orange Classic; Babe Zaharias Open
Whitworth, Kathy	Venice Ladies' Open; Raleigh Ladies' Invitational; St. Louis Women's Invitational; LPGA Championship; Lady Carling Open (Columbus); Women's Western Open; Ladies' Los Angeles Open; Alamo Ladies Open
Wright, Mickey	Shreveport Kiwanis Club Invitational; Bluegrass Invitational; Lady Carling Open (Baltimore); Pensacola Ladies' Invitational

1968

Berning, Susie Maxwell	USGA Women's Open
Englehorn, Shirley	Concord Open
Haynie, Sandra	Pacific Ladies' Classic
Mann, Carol	Lady Carling Open; Raleigh Ladies' Invitational; Shreveport Kiwanis Club Invitational; Bluegrass Invitational; Pabst Classic; Buckeye Savings Invitational; Willow Park Ladies' Invitational
Masters, Margie	Quality Chekd Classic
Post, Sandra	LPGA Championship
Rankin, Judy	Corpus Christi Civitan Open
Rawls, Betsy	Mickey Wright Invitational
Smith, Marilynn	O'Sullivan Ladies' Open
Whitworth, Kathy	Orange Blossom Classic; Dallas Civitan Open; Lady Carling Open (Baltimore); Gino Paoli Open; Holiday Inn Classic; Kings River Open; River Plantation Women's Open; Canyon Ladies Classic; Pensacola Ladies' Invitational; Louise Suggs Invitational
Wilson, Peggy	Hollywood Lakes Open
Wright, Mickey	Port Malabar Invitational; Palm Beach County Open; Tall City Open; "500" Ladies' Classic

1969

Berning, Susie	Lady Carling Open
Caponi, Donna	USGA Women's Open; Lincoln-Mercury Open
Hagge, Marlene Bauer	Strohs–WBLY Open
Haynie, Sandra	Shreveport Kiwanis Invitational; St. Louis Open; Supertest Open
Lindstrom, Murle MacKenzie	O'Sullivan Open

Mann, Carol	Raleigh Invitational; Dallas Civitan Open; Lady Carling Open; Southgate Open; Tournament of Champions; Molson's Canadian Open; Mickey Wright Invitational; Corpus Christi Civitan Open
Mills, Mary	Quality Chekd Classic
Rawls, Betsy	LPGA Championship
Spuzich, Sandra	Buckeye Savings Invitational
Whitworth, Kathy	Orange Blossom Open; Port Charlotte Invitational; Port Malabar Invitational; Lady Carling Open; Pabst Classic; Wendell-West Open; River Plantation Open
Wright, Mickey	Bluegrass Invitational

1970

Ahern, Kathy	Southgate Ladies Open
Blalock, Jane	Lady Carling Open (Atlanta)
Caponi, Donna	Bluegrass Invitational; USGA Women's Open
Carner, JoAnne	Wendell West Open
Englehorn, Shirley	Londoff Chevrolet Invitational; O'Sullivan Ladies Open; Lady Carling Open (Baltimore); LPGA Championship
Haynie, Sandra	Raleigh Ladies Invitational; Shreveport Kiwanis Invitational
Mann, Carol	Burdine's Invitational
Mills, Mary	Len Immke Buick Open
Rankin, Judy	George Washington Classic; Springfield Jaycee Open; Lincoln-Mercury Open
Rawls, Betsy	Dallas Civitan Open; Cincinnati Open
Smith, Marilynn	Women's Golf Charities Open
Whitworth, Kathy	Orange Blossom Classic; Quality Chekd Classic

1971

Barnett, Pam	Southgate Open
Blalock, Jane	George Washington Classic; Lady Pepsi Open
Carner, JoAnne	USGA Women's Open; Bluegrass Invitational
Ferraris, Jan	Orange Blossom Classic
Haynie, Sandra	Burdine's Invitational; Dallas Civitan Open; San Antonio Alamo Open; Len Immke Buick Open
Higgins, Pam	Lincoln-Mercury Open
Jessen, Judy	Sears Women's World Classic
Kimball, Judy	O'Sullivan Ladies Open; LPGA Four-Ball Championship
Palmer, Sandra	Sealy-LPGA Classic; Heritage Open
Rankin, Judy	Quality-First Classic
Whitworth, Kathy	Raleigh Golf Classic, Suzuki Golf Internationale; Lady Carling Open; LPGA Championship; LPGA Four-Ball Championship

1972

Ahern, Kathy	George Washington Classic
Berning, Susie	USGA Women's Open
Blalock, Jane	Colgate–Dinah Shore Winners' Circle; Suzuki Golf Internationale; LPGA Four-Ball Championship, Dallas Civitan Open; Lady Errol Classic
Burfeindt, Betty	Birmingham Centennial Open; Sealy-LPGA Classic
Cornelius, Kathy	Bluegrass Invitational
Cullen, Betsy	Sears Women's World Classic
Ferraris, Jan	Lady Pepsi Open
Hagge, Marlene	Burdine's Invitational
Haynie, Sandra	National Jewish Hospital Open; Waco Quality-First Classic; Lincoln-Mercury Open
Mann, Carol	Orange Blossom Classic; Lady Carling Open
Palmer, Sandra	Titleholders Championship; LPGA Four-Ball Championship
Prentice, JoAnn	Corpus Christi Civitan
Rankin, Judy	Lady Eve Open; Heritage Village Open
Rawls, Betsy	GAC Classic
Smith, Marilynn	Columbus Ladies Open
Whitworth, Kathy	Alamo Ladies Open; Raleigh Golf Classic; Knoxville Ladies Open; Southgate Ladies Open; Portland Classic

1973

Berning, Sue	Heritage Village Open; USGA Women's Open
Bourassa, Jocelyne	La Canadienne Golf Championship
Burfeindt, Betty	Child and Family Services Open
Cornelius, Kathy	Sealy-Fabergé Classic
Crocker, Mary Lou	Marc Equity Classic
Cullen, Betsy	Alamo Ladies Classic
Ehret, Gloria	Birmingham Classic
Ferraris, Jan	Japan-LPGA Classic
Haynie, Sandra	Orange Blossom Classic; Charity Golf Classic; Lincoln-Mercury Classic
Mann, Carol	Sears Women's Classic
Miller, Sharon	Corpus Christi Civitan Open
Mills, Mary	LPGA Championship; Lady Tara Classic
Palmer, Sandra	Pompano Beach Classic; St. Paul Open; National Jewish Hospital Open; Cameron Park Open
Prentice, JoAnn	Burdine's Invitational
Rankin, Judy	American Defender–Raleigh Classic; Lady Carling Open; Pabst Ladies Classic; GAC Classic
Skala, Carole Jo	George Washington Classic

Whitworth, Kathy	Naples-Lely Classic; S&H Green Stamp Classic; Dallas Civitan Open; Southgate Ladies' Open; Portland Ladies' Open; Waco *Tribune Herald* Ladies' Classic; Lady Errol Classic
Wright, Mickey	Colgate–Dinah Shore Winners' Circle
Young, Donna Caponi	Bluegrass Invitational

1974

Blalock, Jane	Bing Crosby International Classic; Birmingham Classic; Southgate Ladies' Open; Lady Errol Classic
Bryant, Bonnie	Bill Branch LPGA Classic
Carner, JoAnne	Bluegrass Invitational; Hoosier LPGA Classic; Desert Inn Classic; St. Paul Open; Dallas Civitan Open; Portland Ladies' Classic
Deneberg, Gail	Sear's Women's Classic
Haynie, Sandra	Lawson's LPGA Open; LPGA Championship; U.S. Women's Open; George Washington Classic; National Jewish Hospital Open; Charity Golf Classic
Higuchi, Chako	Japan LPGA Golf Classic
Mann, Carol	Naples-Lely Classic; S&H Green Stamp Classic
Miller, Sharon	LPGA Borden's Classic
Palmer, Sandra	Burdine's Invitational; Cubic Corporation Classic
Post, Sandra	Colgate–Far East Open
Prentice, JoAnn	Colgate–Dinah Shore Winners' Circle; American Defender–Raleigh Classic
Rankin, Judy	Baltimore Golf Championship; Colgate-European Open
Roberts, Sue	Niagara Frontier Classic; Southgate Ladies' Open
Skala, Carole Jo	Peter Jackson Ladies' Classic; Wheeling Ladies' Classic; Sacramento Union Ladies' Classic
Spuzich, Sandra	Lady Tara Classic
Whitworth, Kathy	Orange Blossom Classic

1975

Alcott, Amy	Orange Blossom Classic
Astrologes, Maria	Birmingham Golf Classic
Berning, Sue	Lady Keystone Open
Blalock, Jane	Karsten-Ping Open; Colgate Triple Crown
Bradley, Pat	Colgate–Far East Open
Carner, JoAnne	American Defender Classic; All-American Sports Classic; Peter Jackson Classic

Cullen, Betsy	Hoosier Classic
Hamlin, Shelley	Japan LPGA Classic
Haynie, Sandra	Naples-Lely Classic; Charity Golf Classic; Jacksonville Ladies Open; Greater Ft. Myers Open
McAllister, Susie	Wheeling Ladies' Classic
Mann, Carol	Lawson's LPGA Classic; Borden Classic; George Washington Ladies' Classic; Dallas Civitan Open
Palmer, Sandra	U.S. Women's Open; Colgate–Dinah Shore Winners' Circle
Porter, Mary Bea	Golf Inns of America
Rankin, Judy	National Jewish Hospital Open
Roberts, Sue	Bing Crosby International Classic
Washam, JoAnn	Patty Berg Golf Classic; Portland Ladies' Classic
Whitworth, Kathy	Colgate Triple Crown; Baltimore-LPGA Championship; Southgate Ladies' Open
Young, Donna Caponi	Burdine's Invitational; Lady Tara Classic; Colgate-European Open

1976

Alcott, Amy	LPGA Classic, Colgate–Far East Championship
Berning, Susie	Lady Keystone Open
Blalock, Jane	Wheeling Classic; Dallas Civitan Open
Bradley, Pat	Girl Talk Classic
Burfeindt, Betty	LPGA Championship
Carner, JoAnne	Orange Blossom Classic; Lady Tara Classic; Hoosier Classic; U.S. Women's Open
Higuchi, Chako	Colgate-European Open
Little, Sally	Ladies Masters at Moss Creek
Palmer, Sandra	Bloomington Bicentennial Classic; National Jewish Hospital Open; Jerry Lewis Muscular Dystrophy Classic
Rankin, Judy	Burdine's Invitational; Colgate–Dinah Shore Winners' Circle; Karsten-Ping Open; Babe Zaharias Invitational; Borden Classic; Colgate–Hong Kong Open
Roberts, Sue	American Defender Classic
Stephenson, Jan	Sarah Coventry-Naples Classic; Birmingham Classic
Whitworth, Kathy	Bent Tree Classic; Patty Berg Classic
Young, Donna Caponi	Peter Jackson Classic; Portland Classic; The Carlton; LPGA/Mizuno Japan Classic

1977

Austin, Debbie	Birmingham Classic; Hoosier Classic; Pocono Northeast

	Classic; Long Island Classic; Wheeling Classic
Blalock, Jane	Baltimore Classic; Sarah Coventry
Bradley, Pat	Bankers Trust Classic
Carner, JoAnne	Talk Tournament; Borden Classic; National Jewish Hospital Open
Higgins, Pam	Cancer Society Classic
Higuchi, Chako	LPGA Championship
Lauer, Bonnie	Patty Berg Classic
Palmer, Sandra	Honda Civic Classic; Women's International
Rankin, Judy	Orange Blossom Classic; Bent Tree Classic; Mayflower Classic; Peter Jackson Classic; Colgate-European Open
Spuzich, Sandra	Keystone Classic
Stacy, Hollis	Lady Tara Classic; U.S. Open; Springfield Classic
Whitworth, Kathy	Colgate–Dinah Shore Winners' Circle; American Defender Classic; Coca-Cola Classic

MONEY-WINNING RECORDS

Money prizes are what the professional touring golfer plays for. Over the years, like playing equipment and course design, prize money in golf has greatly improved. The first prize award in the U.S. Open when started in 1895 was $150. During the 1930's a tournament winner received on an average of $1,500. The $10,000 of the 1940's was a major step toward better winnings, and in the early 1950's, when George S. May presented the $100,000 All-American and World Championship at Tam O'Shanter, golf was on its way to the big money era. Below is a listing of men's tournament prize money, in tour events only, in the modern era of golf:

Year	Events	Total Purses	Average Purse
1950	33	$ 459,950	$13,938
1951	30	460,200	15,340
1952	32	498,016	15,563
1953	32	562,704	17,585
1954	26	600,819	23,108
1955	36	782,010	21,723
1956	36	847,070	23,530
1957	32	820,360	25,636
1958	39	1,005,800	25,789
1959	43	1,187,340	27,613
1960	41	1,187,340	28,959
1961	45	1,461,830	32,485
1962	49	1,790,320	36,537
1963	43	2,044,900	47,497
1964	41	2,301,063	56,123
1965	36	2,848,515	79,403
1966	36	3,074,445	85,401
1967	37	$ 3,979,162	$ 108,356
1968	45	5,077,600	112,835
1969	47	5,465,875	116,295
1970	47	6,259,501	126,689
1971	52	6,587,976	112,968
1972	46	6,954,649	151,188

Year	Events	Total Purses	Average Purse
1973	75	$8,657,225	
1974	57	8,165,941	
1975	51	7,895,450	
1976	49	9,157,522	
1977	45	9,090,000	

Modern-Era Leading Money Winners (Men)
(In Regular PGA Tour Events)

1955

	Player	Money
1.	Julius Boros	$63,121
2.	Cary Middlecoff	39,567
3.	Doug Ford	33,503
4.	Mike Souchak	29,462
5.	Gene Littler	28,974
6.	Ted Kroll	25,117
7.	Sam Snead	23,464
8.	Tommy Bolt	22,585
9.	Fred Haas, Jr.	22,372
10.	Jerry Barber	18,865

1956

	Player	Money
1.	Ted Kroll	$72,835
2.	Dow Finsterwald	29,513
3.	Cary Middlecoff	$ 27,352
4.	Fred Hawkins	24,805
5.	Jack Burke, Jr.	24,085
6.	Gene Littler	23,833
7.	Ed Furgol	23,125
8.	Mike Souchak	21,486
9.	Peter Thomson	20,413
10.	Doug Ford	19,389

1957

	Player	Money
1.	Dick Mayer	$65,835

	Player	Money
2.	Doug Ford	45,378
3.	Dow Finsterwald	32,872
4.	Sam Snead	28,260
5.	Arnold Palmer	27,802
6.	Paul Harney	21,735
7.	Art Wall, Jr.	20,831
8.	Al Balding	20,824
9.	Billy Casper, Jr.	20,807
10.	Ken Venturi	18,761

1958

	Player	Money
1.	Arnold Palmer	$42,607
2.	Billy Casper, Jr.	41,323
3.	Ken Venturi	36,267
4.	Dow Finsterwald	35,393
5.	Art Wall, Jr.	29,841
6.	Julius Boros	29,817
7.	Tommy Bolt	26,940
8.	Jay Hebert	26,834
9.	Bob Rosburg	25,170
10.	Doug Ford	21,874

1959

	Player	Money
1.	Art Wall, Jr.	$53,167
2.	Gene Littler	38,296
3.	Dow Finsterwald	33,906
4.	Billy Casper, Jr.	33,899
5.	Arnold Palmer	32,461
6.	Mike Souchak	31,807
7.	Bob Rosburg	31,676
8.	Doug Ford	31,009
9.	Jay Hebert	26,034
10.	Ken Venturi	25,886

1960

	Player	Money
1.	Arnold Palmer	$75,262
2.	Ken Venturi	41,230
3.	Dow Finsterwald	38,541
4.	Billy Casper, Jr.	31,060
5.	Jay Hebert	29,748
6.	Mike Souchak	28,903
7.	Doug Ford	28,411
8.	Gene Littler	26,837
9.	Bill Collins	26,496
10.	Doug Sanders	26,470

1961

	Player	Money
1.	Gary Player	$64,450
2.	Arnold Palmer	61,191
3.	Doug Sanders	57,428
4.	Billy Casper, Jr.	37,776
5.	Jay Hebert	35,583
6.	Johnny Pott	32,267
7.	Gay Brewer, Jr.	31,149
8.	Bob Goalby	30,918

	Player	Money
9.	Gene Littler	29,245
10.	Billy Maxwell	28,335

1962

	Player	Money
1.	Arnold Palmer	$81,448
2.	Gene Littler	66,200
3.	Jack Nicklaus	61,868
4.	Billy Casper, Jr.	61,842
5.	Bob Goalby	46,240
6.	Gary Player	45,838
7.	Doug Sanders	43,385
8.	Dave Ragan, Jr.	37,327
9.	Bobby Nichols	34,311
10.	Dow Finsterwald	33,619

1963

	Player	Money
1.	Arnold Palmer	$128,230
2.	Jack Nicklaus	100,040
3.	Julius Boros	77,356
4.	Tony Lema	67,112
5.	Gary Player	55,455
6.	Dow Finsterwald	49,862
7.	Mason Rudolph, Jr.	39,120
8.	Al Geiberger	34,126
9.	Don January	33,754
10.	Bobby Nichols	33,604

1964

	Player	Money
1.	Jack Nicklaus	$113,284
2.	Arnold Palmer	113,203
3.	Billy Casper, Jr.	90,653
4.	Tony Lema	74,130
5.	Bobby Nichols	74,012
6.	Ken Venturi	62,465
7.	Gary Player	61,449
8.	Mason Rudolph, Jr.	52,568
9.	Juan Rodriguez	48,338
10.	Mike Souchak	39,559

1965

	Player	Money
1.	Jack Nicklaus	$140,752
2.	Tony Lema	101,816
3.	Billy Casper, Jr.	99,931
4.	Doug Sanders	72,182
5.	Gary Player	69,964
6.	Bruce Devlin	67,657
7.	Dave Marr	63,375
8.	Al Geiberger	$ 59,699
9.	Gene Littler	58,898
10.	Arnold Palmer	57,770

1966

	Player	Money
1.	Billy Casper, Jr.	$121,944
2.	Jack Nicklaus	111,419

	Player	Money
3.	Arnold Palmer	110,467
4.	Doug Sanders	80,096
5.	Gay Brewer, Jr.	75,687
6.	Phil Rodgers	68,360
7.	Gene Littler	68,345
8.	R. H. Sikes	67,348
9.	Frank Beard	66,041
10.	Al Geiberger	63,220

1967

	Player	Money
1.	Jack Nicklaus	$188,988
2.	Arnold Palmer	184,065
3.	Billy Casper, Jr.	129,423
4.	Julius Boros	126,785
5.	Dan Sikes, Jr.	111,508
6.	Doug Sanders	109,455
7.	Frank Beard	105,778
8.	George Archer	84,344
9.	Gay Brewer, Jr.	78,548
10.	Bob Goalby	77,106

1968

	Player	Money
1.	Billy Casper, Jr.	$205,168
2.	Jack Nicklaus	155,285
3.	Tom Weiskopf	152,946
4.	George Archer	150,972
5.	Julius Boros	148,310
6.	Lee Trevino	132,127
7.	Arnold Palmer	114,602
8.	Dan Sikes, Jr.	108,330
9.	Miller Barber	105,845
10.	Bob Murphy	105,595

1969

	Player	Money
1.	Frank Beard	$175,224
2.	Dave Hill	156,423
3.	Jack Nicklaus	140,167
4.	Gary Player	123,898
5.	Bruce Crampton	118,956
6.	Gene Littler	112,737
7.	Lee Trevino	112,418
8.	Ray Floyd	109,957
9.	Arnold Palmer	105,128
10.	Billy Casper, Jr.	104,689

1970

	Player	Money
1.	Lee Trevino	$157,037
2.	Billy Casper, Jr.	147,372
3.	Bruce Crampton	$142,609
4.	Jack Nicklaus	142,149
5.	Arnold Palmer	128,853
6.	Frank Beard	124,690
7.	Dick Lotz	124,539
8.	Larry Hinson	120,897
9.	Bob Murphy	120,639
10.	Dave Hill	118,415

1971

	Player	Money
1.	Jack Nicklaus	$244,490
2.	Lee Trevino	231,202
3.	Arnold Palmer	209,603
4.	George Archer	147,769
5.	Gary Player	120,016
6.	Miller Barber	117,359
7.	Jerry Heard	112,389
8.	Frank Beard	112,337
9.	Dave Eichelberger	108,312
10.	Billy Casper, Jr.	107,276

1972

	Player	Money
1.	Jack Nicklaus	$320,942
2.	Lee Trevino	214,805
3.	George Archer	145,027
4.	Grier Jones	140,177
5.	Jerry Heard	137,198
6.	Tom Weiskopf	129,422
7.	Gary Player	120,719
8.	Bruce Devlin	119,768
9.	Tommy Aaron	118,924
10.	Lanny Wadkins	116,616

1973

	Player	Money
1.	Jack Nicklaus	$308,362
2.	Bruce Crampton	274,266
3.	Tom Weiskopf	245,463
4.	Lee Trevino	210,017
5.	Lanny Wadkins	200,455
6.	Miller Barber	184,014
7.	Hale Irwin	130,388
8.	Billy Casper, Jr.	129,474
9.	Johnny Miller	127,833
10.	John Schlee	118,017

1974

	Player	Money
1.	Johnny Miller	$353,021
2.	Jack Nicklaus	238,178
3.	Hubert Green	211,709
4.	Lee Trevino	203,422
5.	J. C. Snead	164,486
6.	Dave Stockton	155,105
7.	Hale Irwin	152,520
8.	Jerry Heard	145,788
9.	Brian Allin	137,950
10.	Tom Watson	135,474

1975

	Player	Money
1.	Jack Nicklaus	$298,149
2.	Johnny Miller	226,118
3.	Tom Weiskopf	219,140
4.	Hale Irwin	205,380

5.	Gene Littler	182,883
6.	Al Geiberger	175,693
7.	Tom Watson	153,795
8.	John Mahaffey	141,475
9.	Lee Trevino	134,206
10.	Bruce Crampton	132,532

1976

	Player	Money
1.	Jack Nicklaus	$266,438
2.	Ben Crenshaw	257,759
3.	Hale Irwin	252,718
4.	Hubert Green	228,031
5.	Al Geiberger	194,821
6.	J. C. Snead	192,645
7.	Ray Floyd	178,318
8.	David Graham	176,174
9.	Don January	163,622
10.	Jerry Pate	153,102

1977

	Player	Money
1.	Tom Watson	$310,653
2.	Jack Nicklaus	284,509
3.	Lanny Wadkins	244,882
4.	Hale Irwin	221,456
5.	Bruce Lietzke	202,156
6.	Tom Weiskopf	197,639
7.	Ray Floyd	163,261
8.	Miller Barber	148,320
9.	Hubert Green	140,255
10.	Bill Kratzert	134,758

Leading Money Winners (Men)
Prior to 1955

(Yearly Record)

Year	Player	Money
1934	Paul Runyan	$ 6,767
1935	Johnny Revolta	9,543
1936	Horton Smith	7,682
1937	Harry Cooper	14,138
1938	Sam Snead	19,543
1939	Henry Picard	10,303
1940	Ben Hogan	10,655
1941	Ben Hogan	18,358
1942	Ben Hogan	13,143
1943	No statistics compiled	
1944	Byron Nelson	37,967
1945	Byron Nelson	63,335
1946	Ben Hogan	42,556
1947	Jim Demaret	27,936
1948	Ben Hogan	32,112
1949	Sam Snead	31,593
1950	Sam Snead	35,758
1951	Lloyd Mangrum	26,088
1952	Julius Boros	37,032
1953	Lew Worsham	34,002
1954	Bob Toski	65,819

All-Time Leading Money Winners (Men)
(In Official PGA Tour Events, through 1977)

	Player	From Year	Total Winnings
1.	Jack Nicklaus	1962	$3,092,721
2.	Arnold Palmer	1955	1,762,082
3.	Billy Casper, Jr.	1955	1,658,458
4.	Lee Trevino	1966	1,620,723
5.	Tom Weiskopf	1965	1,553,826
6.	Gene Littler	1954	1,383,772
7.	Bruce Crampton	1957	1,374,294
8.	Gary Player	1957	1,329,307
9.	Miller Barber	1959	1,249,864
10.	Hale Irwin	1968	1,234,230
11.	Johnny Miller	1969	1,144,065
12.	Al Geiberger	1960	1,077,972
13.	Dave Hill	1959	1,055,896
14.	Ray Floyd	1963	1,039,168
15.	Julius Boros	1950	1,000,642
16.	Frank Beard	1962	983,317
17.	Dave Stockton	1964	967,785
18.	George Archer	1964	967,449
19.	Bobby Nichols	1960	925,353
20.	Hubert Green	1970	895,696
21.	Don January	1955	892,528
22.	Lou Graham	1964	853,528
23.	Tom Watson	1972	838,692
24.	J. C. Snead	1968	824,771
25.	Charles Coody	1963	822,878

Leading Money Winners (Women)
(In Regular LPGA Tour Events)

Year	Player	Money
1950	Babe Zaharias	$14,800
	Patty Berg	5,442
1951	Babe Zaharias	15,087
	Patty Berg	13,237
1952	Betsy Rawls	14,505
	Betty Jameson	12,660
1953	Louise Suggs	19,816
	Patty Berg	18,623
1954	Patty Berg	16,011
	Babe Zaharias	14,452
1955	Patty Berg	16,497
	Louise Suggs	13,729
1956	Marlene Hagge	20,235
	Patty Berg	12,560
1957	Patty Berg	16,272
	Fay Crocker	12,019
1958	Bev Hanson	12,639
	Marlene Hagge	11,890
1959	Betsy Rawls	26,774
	Mickey Wright	18,182
1960	Louise Suggs	16,892
	Mickey Wright	16,380
1961	Mickey Wright	22,236
	Betsy Rawls	15,672

Year	Player	Money
1962	Mickey Wright	21,641
	Kathy Whitworth	17,044
1963	Mickey Wright	$ 31,269
	Kathy Whitworth	26,858
1964	Mickey Wright	29,800
	Ruth Jessen	23,431
1965	Kathy Whitworth	28,658
	Marlene Hagge	21,532
1966	Kathy Whitworth	33,517
	Sandra Haynie	30,157
1967	Kathy Whitworth	32,937
	Sandra Haynie	26,543
1968	Kathy Whitworth	48,379
	Carol Mann	45,921
1969	Carol Mann	49,152
	Kathy Whitworth	48,171
1970	Kathy Whitworth	30,235
	Sandra Haynie	26,606
1971	Kathy Whitworth	41,182
	Sandra Haynie	36,219
1972	Kathy Whitworth	65,063
	Jane Blalock	57,323
1973	Kathy Whitworth	82,864
	Judy Rankin	72,989
1974	JoAnne Carner	87,570
	Jane Blalock	87,266
1975	Sandra Palmer	76,374
	JoAnne Carner	64,842

Year	Player	Money
1976	Judy Rankin	150,734
	Donna Caponi Young	106,553
1977	Judy Rankin	122,890
	JoAnne Carner	113,711

All-Time Leading Money Winners (Women) (In Official Tour Events, through 1977)

	Player	From Year	Total Winnings
1.	Kathy Whitworth	1959	$745,359.44
2.	Judy Rankin	1962	600,789.49
3.	Sandra Palmer	1964	500,631.00
4.	Sandra Haynie	1961	490,337.32
5.	Carol Mann	1961	481,970.12
6.	Jane Blalock	1969	475,942.16
7.	JoAnne Carner	1970	443,668.51
8.	Donna Caponi Young	1965	381,322.47
9.	Mickey Wright	1955	349,638.99
10.	Marlene Hagge	1950	329,602.42
11.	JoAnn Prentice	1956	315,295.57
12.	Betsy Rawls	1951	302,664.38
13.	Marilynn Smith	1949	293,102.33
14.	Mary Mills	1962	277,374.29
15.	Sandra Post	1968	254,200.48

ALL-TIME RECORDS

Professional

All-time PGA Scoring Records (Official Tournaments Only)

72 Holes. 257 (60–68–64–65), by Mike Souchak, at Brackenridge Park Golf Course, San Antonio, Texas, in 1955 Texas Open.

54 Holes. 189 (63–63–63), by Chandler Harper, at Brackenridge Park Golf Course, San Antonio, Texas, in last three rounds of 1954 Texas Open.

36 Holes. 126 (62–64), by Johnny Palmer, at El Rio Country Club, Tucson, Ariz., in third and fourth rounds of 1948 Tucson Open. 126 (63–63), by Sam Snead, at Brackenridge Park Golf Course, San Antonio, Texas, in third and fourth rounds of 1950 Texas Open. 126 (63–63), by Chandler Harper, at Brackenridge Park Golf Course, San Antonio, Texas, in second and third rounds of 1954 Texas Open. 126 (63–63), by Chandler Harper, at Brackenridge Park Golf Course, San Antonio, Texas, in third and fourth rounds of 1954 Texas Open. 126

(64–62), by Tommy Bolt, at Cavalier Yacht and Country Club, Virginia Beach, Va., in first and second rounds of 1954 Virginia Beach Open. 126 (60–66), by Sam Snead, at Glen Lakes Country Club, Dallas, Texas, in second and third rounds of 1957 Dallas Open. 126 (61–65), by Jack Rule, Jr., at Keller Golf Club, St. Paul, Minn., in second and third rounds of 1963 St. Paul Open.

18 Holes. 59, by Al Geiberger at Colonial Country Club, Memphis, Tenn. in second round of 1977 Danny Thomas–Memphis Classic.

9 Holes. 27, by Mike Souchak, at Brackenridge Park Golf Course, San Antonio, Texas, on second nine of first round in 1955 Texas Open. 27, by Andy North at En-Joie Golf Club, Endicott, N.Y., on par 34 second nine of first round of 1975 B.C. Open.

Consecutive Birdies. 8, by Bob Goalby in the fourth round of the 1961 St. Petersburg Open.

Fewest Putts. 19, by Bill Nary, in 1952 El

Paso Open; by Bob Rosburg, in 1959 Pensacola Open; by Randy Glover, in 1965 St. Paul Open; by Deane Beman, in 1968 Haig National Open; and by Dave Stockton, in 1971 Monsanto Open.

Fewest putts (72 holes). 99, by Bob Menne, at Sawgrass Golf Club, Ponte Vedra Beach, Fla., in 1977 Tournament Players Championship.

Miscellaneous Records for the PGA Tour (Official Tournaments Only)

Most Consecutive Wins. 11, by Byron Nelson, from Miami Four-ball, March 8–11, 1945, through Canadian Open, August 2–4, 1945.

Most Tournaments Won in One Calendar Year. 18, by Byron Nelson, in 1945.

Most Consecutive Tournaments in the Money. 113, by Byron Nelson, during the 1940's.

Longest Drive. Longest known drive in major competition was made by American pro Craig Wood in the 1933 British Open at St. Andrews, Scotland. Wood cranked out a 430-yarder on the fifth hole. The course was dry, and there was a strong following wind.

Consecutive Major Championship. 4, Walter Hagen, PGA Championship (1924–1927).

Youngest Tournament Winner. Gene Sarazen, twenty, when he won the 1922 U.S. Open, is the youngest professional winner of an official tournament since the PGA was formed in 1917.

Oldest Tournament Winner. Sam Snead was fifty-two years, ten months, and seven days old when he won the 1965 Greensboro (North Carolina) Open.

All-Time LPGA Scoring Records (Official Tournaments Only)

72 Holes. 273 (68–71–69–65), by Kathy Whitworth, at Tuckaway Country Club, Milwaukee, Wis., in 1966 Milwaukee Jaycee Open.

54 Holes. 200 (66–66–68), by Carol Mann, at Canongate Country Club, Palmetto, Ga., in 1968 Lady Carling Open. 200 (69–65–64), by Ruth Jessen, in 1964 Omaha Jaycee Open, Omaha, Neb.

36 Holes. 132 (66–66), by Carol Mann, at Cannongate Country Club, Palmetto, Ga., in 1968 Lady Carling Open.

18 Holes. 62, by Mickey Wright, at Hogan Park Golf Club, Midland, Texas, in final round of 1964 Tall City Open.

9 Holes. 29, by Marlene Hagge, on first nine in first round of 1971 Len Immke Buick Open at Raymond Memorial Golf Course in Columbus, Ohio. 29, by Carol Mann at Riviera Country Club on first nine of first round of 1975 Borden Classic.

Most Birdies in Round. 9, by Mickey Wright in 1964, Tall City Open.

Fewest Putts in Round. 20, by Judy Kimball, at Sunset Golf Club, St. Petersburg, Fla., in first round of 1963 St. Petersburg Women's Open; and by Cynthia Sullivan, at Amarillo Country Club, Amarillo, Texas, in third round of 1967 Amarillo Ladies Open.

Miscellaneous Records for the LPGA Tour (Official Tournaments Only)

Most Consecutive Victories. 4 by Mickey Wright (twice, in 1962 and 1963); Kathy Whitworth in 1969; and Shirley Englehorn in 1970.

Most Wins in Single Season. 13, by Mickey Wright in 1963.

Youngest Winner. Marlene Hagge, eighteen when she won 1952 Sarasota Open.

Oldest Winner. Patty Berg, forty-four when she won 1962 Muskogee Open.

Hall of Fame (PGA)

The great sports writer Grantland Rice suggested a Hall of Fame for golfers through his nationally syndicated sports columns. Today there are three recognized Halls of Fame; one established by the PGA, one by the LPGA, plus the World Golf Hall of Fame at Pinehurst, N.C.

Golf's Hall of Fame was established by the Professional Golf Association of America in 1940 to honor those who by their lifetime playing ability have made outstanding contributions to the game. A special committee selected the original group of twelve men for the Hall of Fame. Included in the twelve were four amateurs.

No additions were made to the Hall of Fame until 1953, when, at the request of the PGA of America, the Golf Writers Association of America chose three more members. In 1954, the PGA established a new format for Hall of Fame selections. Under this plan one player was chosen each year, that player to be at least fifty years of age and retired from active national competition. Each year the PGA's local sections were asked to nominate candidates for the Hall of Fame. The one player to be inducted each year was then decided by a vote of the PGA membership and those on the PGA press list. That system remained in effect through 1958. Then the PGA Special Awards Committee recommended and the PGA Executive Committee approved certain modifications.

In 1959, for the first time in six years, three players were elected to the Hall of Fame in a nationwide vote restricted to PGA members. In 1960, two players were elected by the 1959 system. Subsequently, a third player was elected by a vote of those already in the Hall of Fame. The same system was used in the selection of three new members in 1961. In 1962, one player was chosen in a nationwide poll of PGA members, and a second was chosen, subsequently, by a vote of those already in the Hall of Fame. The same method of selection was used in 1963 and 1964. In 1965, the format was changed, whereby only one new member was elected to the PGA Hall of Fame. The new member was elected by the present living members of the PGA Hall of Fame. Today, the players are elected to the Hall by the PGA Executive Committee, after nominations by a select committee. Players elected to the PGA's Golf Hall of Fame are:

Year	Player
1940	Willie Anderson
	Tommy Armour
	Jim Barnes
	Chick Evans[a]
	Walter Hagen
	Bob Jones[a]
	John McDermott
	Francis Ouimet[a]
	Gene Sarazen
	Alex Smith
	Jerry Travers[a]
	Walter Travis
1953	Ben Hogan
	Byron Nelson
	Sam Snead
1954	Macdonald Smith
1955	Leo Diegel
1956	Craig Wood
1957	Denny Shute
1958	Horton Smith

Year	Player
1959	Harry Cooper
	Jock Hutchison, Sr.
	Paul Runyan
1960	Mike Brady
	Jimmy Demaret
	Fred McLeod
1961	Johnny Farrell
	W. Lawson Little
	Henry Picard
1962	E. J. Harrison
	Olin Dutra
1963	Ralph Guidahl
	Johnny Revolta
1964	Lloyd Mangrum
	Ed Dudley
1965	Vic Ghezzi
1966	Billy Burke
1967	Bobby Cruikshank
1968	M. R. "Chick" Harbert
1969	Chandler Harper
1974	Julius Boros
	Cary Middlecoff
1975	Jack Burke, Jr.
	Doug Ford
1976	Babe Zaharias

[a] Amateur.

Hall of Fame (LPGA)

At the 1967 annual meeting of the Ladies' Professional Golf Association, in Corpus Christi, Texas, it was decided to establish a Ladies PGA Hall of Fame for its members only. The members who had previously been elected to the Hall of Fame established in Augusta, Georgia, in 1950 were automatically inducted into this new Hall of Fame. Definite criteria must be met in order to be considered for election to this new honor. In 1977, the LPGA Hall of Fame became a part of the World Golf Hall of Fame at Pinehurst, N.C. Members elected to the Ladies' PGA Hall of Fame are:

Year	Player
1950	Joyce Wethered Amory
	Margaret Curtis
	Alexa Stirling Fraser
	Beatrix Hoyt
	Dorothy Campbell Hurd
	Virginia Van Wie
	Glenna Collett Vare
1951	Patty Berg
	Betty Jameson
	Louise Suggs
	Mildred (Babe) Didrikson Zaharias
1960	Betsy Rawls

1964	Mickey Wright
1974	Kathy Whitworth
1977	Carol Mann
	Sandra Haynie

World Golf Hall of Fame

The World Golf Hall of Fame, standing on the rim of the famous Pinehurst No. 2 course, where so much golf history has been made, was dedicated by President Gerald R. Ford on September 11, 1974. On that day the original thirteen enshrinees were formally inducted into the Hall of Fame, with all eight living members in attendance.

The Hall is a handsome edifice built at the cost of $2.5 million by the Diamondhead Corporation, operators of the North Carolina golf resort. Diamondhead later turned over the Hall to a nonprofit foundation, which now operates it.

The Golf Writers Association of America has the responsibility for nominating and electing deserving golfers and contributors to the growth of the game to the Hall.

The thirteen enshrinees in 1974 were:

Patty Berg	Gary Player
Walter Hagen	Gene Sarazen
Ben Hogan	Sam Snead
Robert T. Jones, Jr.	Harry Vardon
Byron Nelson	Mildred (Babe) Zaharias
Jack Nicklaus	
Francis Ouimet	
Arnold Palmer	

1975:

Willie Anderson	Thomas Morris, Jr.
Fred Corcoran*	John H. Taylor
Joseph C. Dey*	Glenna Collett Vare
Charles (Chick) Evans	Joyce Wethered

1976:

Tommy Armour	Mickey Wright
Jerome Travers	Thomas Morris, Sr.
James Braid	

1977:

John Ball, Jr.	Bobby Locke
Herb Graffis*	Donald Ross*

* For distinguished service.

TROPHY AND AWARD WINNERS

In addition to prize money, professional golfers take great pride in winning the various awards and trophies given annually. Here are major trophies and awards:

The PGA Vardon Trophy. The PGA Vardon Trophy, named in honor of the internationally famous British golfer Harry Vardon, was placed in competition among American professionals in 1937 as a successor to the Harry E. Radix Trophy, which, prior to that time, had been awarded annually to the professional having the finest tournament record in competitive play in this country.

Today, the Vardon Trophy, a bronze-colored plaque measuring 39 by 27 inches, is awarded each year to the member of the PGA of America maintaining the finest playing average in those events cosponsored or so designated by the PGA.

As of January 1, 1962, the minimum number of official tournament rounds required for consideration for the Vardon Trophy was increased to eighty in any one year. The Vardon Trophy has not always been awarded on a basis of seasonal playing average. From 1937 through 1941, the winner was decided on a point basis. Under this system, the leading players in each event received a predetermined number of points, and at the end of the year, the player with the greatest number of points was named the winner.

Year	Winner	Average
1934	Ky Laffoon[a]	
1935	Paul Runyan[a]	
1936	Ralph Guldahl[a]	
1937	Harry Cooper	500
1938	Sam Snead	520
1939	Byron Nelson	473
1940	Ben Hogan	423
1941	Ben Hogan	494
1942	Ben Hogan[a]	
1943–1944	Not played	
1945	Byron Nelson[a]	
1946	Ben Hogan[a]	
1947	Jimmy Demaret	69.90
1948	Ben Hogan	69.30
1949	Sam Snead	69.37
1950	Sam Snead	69.23

1951	Lloyd Mangrum	70.05
1952	Jack Burke, Jr.	70.54
1953	Lloyd Mangrum	70.22
1954	Dutch Harrison	70.41
1955	Sam Snead	69.86
1956	Cary Middlecoff	70.35
1957	Dow Finsterwald	70.30
1958	Bob Rosburg	70.11
1959	Art Wall, Jr.	70.35
1960	Billy Casper, Jr.	69.95
1961	Arnold Palmer	69.85
1962	Arnold Palmer	70.27
1963	Billy Casper, Jr.	70.58
1964	Arnold Palmer	70.01
1965	Billy Casper, Jr.	70.58
1966	Billy Casper, Jr.	70.27
1967	Arnold Palmer	70.18
1968	Billy Casper, Jr.	69.82
1969	Dave Hill	70.34
1970	Lee Trevino	70.64
1971	Lee Trevino	70.28
1972	Lee Trevino	70.89
1973	Bruce Crampton	70.57
1974	Lee Trevino	70.53
1975	Bruce Crampton	70.51
1976	Don January	70.89
1977	Tom Watson	70.32

a Radix Trophy awarded.

The LPGA Vare Trophy. The Vare Trophy was presented to the Ladies' Professional Golf Association by Betty Jameson in 1952 in honor of the great American player Glenna Collett Vare. Miss Jameson requested that this trophy be awarded to the player with the lowest scoring average at the end of each year. Vare Trophy scoring averages are computed on the basis of a player's total yearly score in official rounds she played during the year. A further requirement is that a player must compete in seventy official rounds of tournament competition during the LPGA tour year.

Year	Winner	Average
1953	Patty Berg	75.00
1954	Babe Zaharias	75.48
1955	Patty Berg	74.47
1956	Patty Berg	74.57
1957	Louise Suggs	74.64
1958	Bev Hanson	74.92
1959	Betsy Rawls	74.03
1960	Mickey Wright	73.25
1961	Mickey Wright	73.55
1962	Mickey Wright	73.67
1963	Mickey Wright	72.81
1964	Mickey Wright	72.46

1965	Kathy Whitworth	72.61
1966	Kathy Whitworth	72.60
1967	Kathy Whitworth	72.74
1968	Carol Mann	72.04
1969	Kathy Whitworth	72.38
1970	Kathy Whitworth	72.26
1971	Kathy Whitworth	72.88
1972	Kathy Whitworth	72.38
1973	Judy Rankin	73.08
1974	JoAnne Carner	72.87
1975	JoAnne Carner	72.40
1976	Judy Rankin	72.25
1977	Judy Rankin	72.16

PGA Player-of-the-Year Award. Each year the PGA of America honors America's leading professional player by presenting him the PGA Player-of-the-Year Award. This award is made on the basis of the playing record for the year, including such things as money winnings, Vardon Trophy scoring average, Ryder Cup points, and an over-all evaluation of playing achievements.

Selection of the PGA Player of the Year is made each year by a vote of the PGA membership and the individuals on the PGA National Press List. The winner receives a plaque at the President's Dinner during the PGA annual meeting.

Year	Winner	Year	Winner
1948	Ben Hogan	1963	Julius Boros
1949	Sam Snead	1964	Ken Venturi
1950	Ben Hogan	1965	Dave Marr
1951	Ben Hogan	1966	Billy Casper, Jr.
1952	Julius Boros	1967	Jack Nicklaus
1953	Ben Hogan	1968	No winner
1954	Ed Furgol	1969	Orville Moody
1955	Doug Ford	1970	Billy Casper, Jr.
1956	Jack Burke, Jr.	1971	Lee Trevino
1957	Dick Mayer	1972	Jack Nicklaus
1958	Dow Finsterwald	1973	Jack Nicklaus
1959	Art Wall, Jr.	1974	Johnny Miller
1960	Arnold Palmer	1975	Jack Nicklaus
1961	Jerry Barber	1976	Jack Nicklaus
1962	Arnold Palmer	1977	Tom Watson

LPGA Player of the Year Award. Virginia C. Lord, a long-time booster of women's golf and the Ladies' PGA, established in 1966 the $500 Virginia C. Lord Award for the LPGA Player-of-the-Year. This award was established to recognize the player who, during a current tour year, has the most consistent and outstanding record. Points are awarded only to those players finishing in the first five positions in official LPGA cosponsored or approved events. LPGA Player-of-the-Year Award winners are:

Year	Winner	Year	Winner
1966	Kathy Whitworth	1972	Kathy Whitworth
1967	Kathy Whitworth	1973	Kathy Whitworth
1968	Kathy Whitworth	1974	JoAnne Carner
1969	Kathy Whitworth	1975	Sandra Palmer
1970	Sandra Haynie	1976	Judy Rankin
1971	Kathy Whitworth	1977	Judy Rankin

PGA Golf Professional-of-the-Year Award. Awarded annually by the PGA of America, the PGA Golf Professional-of-the Year Award was established in 1955. This unique award, originally suggested by Richard S. Tufts of Pinehurst, North Carolina, former President of the United States Golf Association, was established to honor PGA club professionals for outstanding achievements. Among the things considered in the selection are promotion of junior golf, encouragement of ladies' golf service to the club, devotion to the game of golf itself, promotion of public relations, interest in caddie welfare, service to the community, and so on.

Each of the PGA's local sections chooses its own Golf Professional of the Year. Until 1966, the names of section winners, along with complete information as to the basis for their selection, went to an anonymous National Committee. This committee, made up entirely of outstanding individuals in amateur golf, made the final selection of the national winner.

In 1966, the names of section winners, along with complete information as to the basis for their selections, went to members of the PGA Executive Committee. The PGA Executive Committee, with the assistance of the PGA Advisory Committee, made the final selection of the national winner.

Year	Winner
1955	Bill Gordon, Tam O'Shanter Country Club, Niles, Ill.
1956	Harry Shepherd, Mark Twain Country Club, Elmira, N.Y.
1957	Dugan Aycock, Lexington (N.C.) Country Club
1958	Harry Pezzullo, Mission Hills Golf Club, Northbrook, Ill.
1959	Eddie Duino, San Jose (Calif.) Country Club
1960	Warren Orlick, Tam O'Shanter Country Club, Orchard Lake, Mich.
1961	Don Padgett, Green Hills Golf and Country Club, Selma, Ind.
1962	Tom LoPresti Haggin, Oakes Golf Course, Sacramento, Calif.
1963	Bruce Herd, Flossmer (Ill.) Country Club
1964	Lyle Wehrman, Merced (Calif.) Golf and Country Club
1965	Hubby Habjan, Onwentsia Club, Lake Forest, Ill.
1966	Bill Strausbaugh, Jr., Turf Valley Country Club, Ellicott City, Md.
1967	Ernie Vossler, Quail Creek Golf and Country Club, Oklahoma City, Okla.
1968	Hardy Loudermilk, Oak Hills Country Club, San Antonio, Texas
1969	Wally Mund, Midland Hill Country Club, St. Paul, Minn.; A. Hubert Smith, Jr., Arnold Center Golf Club, Tallahoma, Tenn.
1970	Grady C. Shumate, Tanglewood Golf Club, Clemmons, S.C.
1971	Ross T. Collins, Dallas Athletic Club, Dallas, Texas
1972	Howard Morrette, Twin Lakes Country Club, Kent, Ohio
1973	Warren Smith, Cherry Hills Country Club, Englewood, Colo.
1974	Paul Harvey, Paul Harvey's Golf Club, Hatchville, Mass.
1975	Walker Inman, Jr., Scioto Country Club, Columbus, Ohio
1976	Ron Letellier, Cold Spring Harbor Country Club, Cold Spring Harbor, N.Y.
1977	Don Soper, Royal Oak Golf Club, Royal Oak, Mich.

LPGA Teacher-of-the-Year Award. In 1958, the Ladies' Professional Golf Association established the Teacher-of-the-Year Award. Since that time, this award has been made annually to the woman professional who has most exemplified her profession during the year. Qualifications for this award are that the recipient be a Class A member of the Teaching Division in good standing; she must presently be engaged in the teaching of golf at a country club, golf club, or approved driving range; she must have shown exceptional leadership and dedication to the game of golf; she must have contributed to the promotion of golf by encouraging junior golf, by supervising tournaments on local and state levels, by teaching individual and group lessons, and by having shop management experience.

In 1963, nominees for the award were recommended by the LPGA Teaching Committee and were voted on by the membership at the Annual Meeting of the Association. Since 1964, nominations for the award have been submitted by LPGA members. The nominations are then screened by the Teaching Committee, and the names are submitted for final vote of the general membership at the annual meeting.

Year	Winner	Year	Winner
1958	Helen Dettweiler	1968	Gloria Fecht
1959	Shirley Spork	1969	Joann Winter
1960	Barbara Rotvig	1970	Gloria Armstrong
1961	Peggy Kirk Bell	1971	Jeannette Rector
1962	Ellen Griffin	1972	Lee Spencer
1963	Vonnie Colby	1973	Penny Zavichas
1964	Sally Doyle	1974	Mary Dagraedt
1965	Goldie Bateson	1975	Carol Johnson
1966	Ann Johnstone	1976	Marge Burns
1967	Jackie Pung	1977	De De Owens

Horton Smith Trophy. In 1964, the Horton Smith Trophy was donated to the PGA National Advisory Committee. It was the function of the Executive Committee in cooperation with the Special Awards Committee to determine an award for the presentation of the Horton Smith Trophy. At the 1965 annual meeting of the Professional Golfers' Association of America held in Palm Beach, Florida, it was decided that the Horton Smith Trophy should be awarded to a golf professional who has made outstanding contributions in the field of golf professional education.

Year	Winner
1965	Emil Beck, Port Huron, Mich.
1966	Gene C. Mason, Portland, Ore.
1967	Donald E. Fischesser, Evansville, Ind.
1968	R. William Clarke, Phoenix, Md.
1969	Paul Walser, Oklahoma City, Okla.
1970	Joe Walser, Oklahoma City, Okla.
1971	Irv Schloss, Dunedin, Fla.
1972	John Budd, New Port Richey, Fla.
1973	George Aulbach, San Antonio, Texas
1974	Bill Hardy, Chevy Chase, Md.
1975	John Henrich, Clarence, N.Y.
1976	Jim Bailey, Brighton, Colo.
1977	Paul Runyan, Denver, Colo.

Ben Hogan Trophy. Given annually by Golf Writers Association of America to the individual who has continued to be active in golf despite a physical handicap.

Year	Winner
1954	Babe Zaharias
1955	Ed Furgol
1956	Dwight Eisenhower
1957	Clint Russell
1958	Dale Bourisseau
1959	Charlie Boswell
1960	Skip Alexander
1961	Horton Smith
1962	Jimmy Nichols
1963	Bobby Nichols
1964	Bob Morgan
1965	Ernest Jones
1966	Ken Venturi
1967	Warren Pease
1968	Shirley Englehorn
1969	Curtis Person
1970	Joe Lazaro
1971	Larry Hinson
1972	Ruth Jessen
1973	Gene Littler
1974	Gay Brewer, Jr.
1975	Patty Berg
1976	Paul Hahn
1977	Desmond Sullivan

The William D. Richardson Trophy. Given annually by Golf Writers' Association of America to the individual who has made consistently outstanding contributions to golf.

Year	Winner
1948	Robert A. Hudson
1949	Scotty Fessenden
1950	Bing Crosby
1951	Richard S. Tufts
1952	Chick Evans
1953	Bob Hope
1954	Babe Zaharias
1955	Dwight Eisenhower
1956	George S. May
1957	Francis Ouimet
1958	Bob Jones
1959	Patty Berg
1960	Fred Corcoran
1961	Joseph C. Dey, Jr.
1962	Walter Hagen
1963	Herb and Joe Graffis
1964	Clifford Roberts
1965	Gene Sarazen
1966	Robert E. Harlow
1967	Max Elbin
1968	Charles Bartlett
1969	Arnold Palmer
1970	Roberto DeVincenzo
1971	Lincoln Werden
1972	Leo Fraser
1973	Ben Hogan
1974	Byron Nelson
1975	Gary Player
1976	Herbert Warren Wind
1977	Mark Cox

Charles Bartlett Award. Given annually by the Golf Writers' Association of America to a playing professional for unselfish contribution to the betterment of society.

Year	Winner
1971	Billy Casper, Jr.
1972	Lee Trevino
1973	Gary Player
1974	Chi Chi Rodriguez
1975	Gene Littler
1976	Arnold Palmer
1977	Lee Elder

Player of the Year (Men). Given annually by the Golf Writers' Association of America.

Year	Winner
1968	Billy Casper, Jr.
1969	Orville Moody
1970	Billy Casper, Jr.
1971	Lee Trevino
1972	Jack Nicklaus
1973	Tom Weiskopf
1974	Johnny Miller
1975	Jack Nicklaus
1976	Jerry Pate and Jack Nicklaus
1977	Tom Watson

Player of the Year (Women).

Year	Winner
1972	Kathy Whitworth
1973	Kathy Whitworth
1974	JoAnne Carner
1975	Sandra Palmer
1976	Judy Rankin
1977	Judy Rankin

Bobby Jones Award. Given annually by the United States Golf Association for distinguished sportsmanship in golf.

Year	Winner
1955	Francis Ouimet
1956	William C. Campbell
1957	Babe Zaharias
1958	Margaret Curtis
1959	Findlay S. Douglas
1960	Charles Evans, Jr.
1961	Joe Carr
1962	Horton Smith
1963	Patty Berg
1964	Charles R. Coe
1965	Mrs. Glenna Collett Vare
1966	Gary Player
1967	Richard S. Tufts
1968	Robert B. Dickson

Year	Winner
1969	Gerald H. Micklem
1970	Roberto DeVicenzo
1971	Arnold Palmer
1972	Michael F. Bonallack
1973	Gene Littler
1974	Byron Nelson
1975	Jack Nicklaus
1976	Ben Hogan
1977	Bing Crosby
	Bob Hope

Golf's Player-of-the-Year Award. An annual award given by *Golf* Magazine to the PGA touring pro voted by his fellow golfers to be the most outstanding player of the year. This vote is in conjunction with the All-America team selections.

Year	Player	Year	Player
1969	Frank Beard	1974	Johnny Miller
1970	Billy Casper, Jr.	1975	Jack Nicklaus
1971	Lee Trevino	1976	Raymond Floyd
1972	Jack Nicklaus	1977	Tom Watson
1973	Tom Weiskopf		

College Golfer-of-the-Year Award. An annual award given by *Golf* Magazine to the most outstanding college golfer of the year.

Year	Player	Year	Player
1971	Jim Simons	1975	Jay Haas
1972	Ben Crenshaw	1976	Scott Simpson
1973	Ben Crenshaw	1977	Scott Simpson
1974	Curtis Strange		

Golf Writers' Association of America Brunswick–MacGregor Charles Bartlett Award. Awarded annually by Brunswick-MacGregor. Entries are collected by the Golf Writers' Association of America and judged by the journalism department of the University of Illinois.

Year	Winners
1957	News: Gene Gregston, Fort Worth (Texas) *Star Telegram*
	Feature: Dan Jenkins, Fort Worth (Texas) *Press*
1958	News: Dana Mozley, New York *Daily News*
	Feature: Tom Davison, Houston *Post*
1959	News: Wally Wallis, Oklahoma City (Okla.) *Daily Oklahoman*
	Feature: Gary Cartwright, Dallas *Times Herald*

1960 News: Dana Mozley, New York *Daily News*
Feature: Ray Haywood, Oakland (Calif.) *Tribune*

1961 News: Charles Bartlett, Chicago *Tribune*
Feature: Ray Haywood, Oakland (Calif.) *Tribune*

1962 News: Irwin Smallwood, Greensboro (N.C.) *News*
Feature: Dan Jenkins, Dallas (Texas), *Times Herald*

1963 News: Irwin Smallwood, Greensboro (N.C.) *News*
Feature: Jack Murphy, San Diego (Calif.) *Union*

1964 News: Irwin Smallwood, Greensboro (N.C.) *News*
Feature: Frank Hannigan, U.S. Golf Association *Journal*

1965 News: Bruce Phillips, Raleigh (N.C.) *Times*
Feature: Jerry Izenberg, Newark (N.J.) *Star-Ledger*

1966 News: Sam Blair, Dallas (Texas) *Morning News*
Feature: Phil Taylor, Seattle (Wash.) *Post Intelligencer*
Magazine: Gwilym S. Brown, *Sports Illustrated*

1967 News: Art Spander, San Francisco *Chronicle*
Feature: Joe Schwendeman, Philadelphia *Evening Bulletin*
Magazine: Herbert Warren Wind, *Golf Digest*

1968 News: Jim Trinkle, Fort Worth *Star*
Feature: Jack Patterson, Akron *Beacon-Journal*
Magazine: Cal Brown, *Golf Digest*

1969 News: Gene Roswell, New York *Post* (afternoon); Jim Trinkle, Fort Worth (Texas) *Star-Telegram* (morning)
Feature: Doug Mintline, Flint (Mich.) *Journal*
Magazine: Dan Jenkins, *Sports Illustrated*

1970 News: Blackie Sherrod, Dallas *Times-Herald*
(afternoon); Art Spander, San Francisco *Chronicle* (morning)
Feature: Sam Blair, Dallas *Morning News*
Magazine: Dan Jenkins, *Sports Illustrated*

1971 News: Jack Patterson, Akron (Ohio) *Beacon-Journal* (afternoon); Phil Taylor, Seattle *Post*
Feature: Maury White, Des Moines *Register*
Magazine: Dan Jenkins, *Sports Illustrated*

1972 News: Fred Russell, Nashville *Banner* (afternoon); D. L. Stewart, Dayton *Herald-Journal* (morning)
Feature: Bill Beck, St. Louis *Post-Dispatch*
Magazine: Lee Mueller, *Golf* Magazine

1973 News: Blackie Sherrod, Dallas *Times-Herald* (afternoon) D. L. Stewart, Dayton *Herald-Journal* (morning)
Feature: Dave Nightingale, Chicago *Daily News*
Magazine: Jim Trinkle, *Golf* Magazine

1974 News: Bill Beck, St. Louis *Post-Dispatch* (afternoon); Mary Moss, Montreal *Gazette* (morning)
Feature: Blackie Sherrod, Dallas *Times-Herald*
Magazine: Ross Goodner, *Golf* Magazine

1975 News: Gary Nuhn, Dayton *Daily News* (afternoon); Marino Parascenzo, Pittsburgh *Post-Gazette* (morning)
Feature: Ronald Green, Charlotte (N.C.) *News*
Magazine: Jolee Edmundson, *Golf* Magazine

1976 News: Gary Nuhn, Dayton *Daily News*
Feature: Bob Green, Associated Press
Magazine: Dick Taylor, *Golf World*
Column: Larry Bush, Palm Beach *Times*

1977 News: Bruce Phillips, Raleigh *Times*
Features: Tim Horgan, Boston *Herald-American*
Column: Ronald Green, Charlotte *Times*
Magazine: Charles Price, *Golf* Magazine

The Golf Magazine All-America Team.

An annual selection by *Golf* Magazine originally designed to select eight professionals most proficient with a particular club or group of clubs. In 1970, the system was changed so that touring pros were voted by their fellow professionals to be the most outstanding players of the year on the strength of their overall play. But in 1973, at the request of the players, the selection reverted to the original format. In 1973 *Golf* Magazine also presented a women's All-America for the first time, based on balloting by members of the LPGA.

Men's All-America

	1964	1965	1966	1967	1968	1969
Driver	Jack Nicklaus	Jack Nicklaus	Jack Nicklaus	Arnold Palmer	Arnold Palmer	Orville Moody
Fairway Woods	Gary Player	Gary Player	Al Geiberger	Gary Player	Gary Player	Gary Player
Long Irons	Arnold Palmer	Arnold Palmer	Arnold Palmer	Jack Nicklaus	Jack Nicklaus	Ray Floyd
Middle Irons	Gene Littler	Gene Littler	Doug Sanders	Dan Sikes, Jr.	Dan Sikes, Jr.	Frank Beard
Short Irons	Ken Venturi	Tony Lema	Gene Littler	Doug Sanders	Billy Casper, Jr.	Gene Littler
Pitching Wedge	Tony Lema	Dave Marr	Gay Brewer, Jr.	Billy Casper, Jr.	Lee Trevino	Billy Casper, Jr.
Sand Wedge	Julius Boros	Sam Snead	Julius Boros	Julius Boros	Julius Boros	Julius Boros
Putter	Billy Casper, Jr.	Billy Casper, Jr.	Billy Casper, Jr.	Frank Beard	George Archer	George Archer

1970 Billy Casper, Jr., Jack Nicklaus, Lee Trevino, Frank Beard, Dave Hill, Larry Hinson, Bruce Crampton, Bob Lotz.

1971 Lee Trevino, Jack Nicklaus, Arnold Palmer, Gene Littler, Gary Player, Charles Coody, Dave Eichelberger, Bobby Nichols.

1972 Jack Nicklaus, Lee Trevino, Gary Player, Bruce Crampton, George Archer, Jerry Heard, Sam Snead, Jim Jamieson.

	1973	1974	1975	1976	1977
Driver	Lanny Wadkins	Lee Trevino	Johnny Miller	Hale Irwin	Tom Watson*
Fairway Woods	Deane Beman	Hubert Green	Hale Irwin	Ray Floyd*	Hale Irwin
Long Irons	Tom Weiskopf*	Jack Nicklaus	Tom Weiskopf	Jack Nicklaus	Tom Weiskopf
Middle Irons	Johnny Miller	Johnny Miller*	Gene Littler	Johnny Miller	Lanny Wadkins
Short Game	Bruce Crampton	Hale Irwin	Al Geiberger	Jerry Pate	Hubert Green
Sand Play	Gary Player	Gary Player	Gary Player	Hubert Green	Gary Player
Trouble Play	Lee Trevino	Bobby Nichols	Tom Watson	Dave Stockton	Jack Nicklaus
Putter	Jack Nicklaus	Dave Stockton	Jack Nicklaus*	Ben Crenshaw	Ben Crenshaw

Ladies All-America

	1973	1974	1975	1976	1977
Driver	Betty Burfeindt	JoAnne Carner*	JoAnn Washam	JoAnne Carner	Debbie Austin*
Fairway Woods	Judy Rankin*	Judy Rankin	Judy Rankin	Sandra Palmer	Judy Rankin
Long Irons	Sandra Haynie	Sue Roberts	Sandra Haynie	Pat Bradley	Pat Bradley
Middle Irons	Jane Blalock	Jane Blalock	Donna Young	Jane Blalock	Jane Blalock
Short Game	JoAnn Prentice	JoAnn Prentice	Sandra Palmer	Jan Stephenson	Sandra Palmer
Sand Play	Sandra Palmer	Sandra Palmer	JoAnne Carner	Sally Little	JoAnne Carner
Trouble Play	Betsy Rawls	Kathy Whitworth	Kathy Whitworth	Kathy Whitworth	Kathy Whitworth
Putter	Kathy Whitworth	Sandra Haynie	Carol Mann	Judy Rankin*	Hollis Stacy

* Player of the Year.

SECTION IV

Golf Equipment

THE EVOLUTION OF GOLF EQUIPMENT

One reason you see better golf scores today than ever before in the history of the game is the better equipment, for there is simply no comparison between today's golf clubs and the old hickory-shafted ones—woods with heads the size of sledge hammers and irons forged by blacksmiths—that were in use as late as the early thirties. But a look back at the evolution of golf equipment really reveals how the game has progressed into the popular sport it is today.

The Golf Ball

The golf ball has dictated the design of the other golf equipment. Actually, as was stated in Section I, modern golf time is divided into periods based on the type of ball that was in use.

The Feather-Ball Period. Golf, as we know it, was originally played with a leather-covered ball stuffed with feathers, and the principles of the present *Rules of Golf* were developed in this era. The feather ball remained the standard missile for at least four centuries, until about 1848. Featheries undoubtedly were in use far longer than that, but the details of golf's origin are lost in antiquity. It is known, however, that in 1681 King James VI granted to James Melvill, a golf ball maker of that period, a monopoly

for 21 years for making and selling golf balls in Scotland, and also a monopoly of importing and selling foreign balls, chiefly from Holland.

The making of feather balls was a tedious and wearisome task, and most ball makers could produce only four to six top-quality ones a day. In the making, the leather was softened with alum and water and cut into four, three, or two pieces. These were stitched together with waxed threads outside in and reversed when the stitching was nearly completed. A small hole was left for the insertion of boiled goose feathers. The ball maker held the leather cover in his hand, in a recessed ball holder, and pushed the first feathers through the hole with a stuffing rod, a tapering piece of wrought iron sixteen to twenty inches long and fitted with a wooden crosspiece to be braced against the ball maker's chest. When the stuffing iron failed, an awl was brought into play, and a volume of feathers which would fill the crown of a beaver hat eventually was inserted into the leather cover. The hole was then stitched up, and the ball was hammered hard and round and given three coats of paint.

Feather balls were seldom exactly round. In wet weather, they tended to become sodden and fly apart. They were easily cut on the seams. A player was fortunate if his ball endured through two rounds. The best balls sold for up to five shillings apiece; in bulk, rarely less than one pound for a dozen.

Originally, there appear to have been ball makers in each golfing community, but in the middle of the eighteenth century the Gourlay family, of Leith and Musselburgh, Scotland, became pre-eminent, and a "Gourlay" was accepted as the best and most expensive of all the feather balls on the market. The patriarch of the family was Douglas Gourlay, at Leith, but it was his son, at Musselburgh, who brought the family name its greatest renown. Their principal competitor was Allan Robertson of St. Andrews.

The Gutta-Percha Ball Period. The first gutta-percha ball is believed to have been made in 1845 by the Rev. Dr. Robert Adams Paterson from the gutta-percha which had been used as packing around a black marble statue of Vishnu which had been sent from India. The statue is now at St. Andrews University, in St. Andrews, Scotland.

The earliest balls were produced under the name "Paterson's Patent." They were brown in color and were made with the hand by rolling the gutta-percha on a flat board. They had smooth surfaces, lined to simulate the seaming of a feather ball, and then ducked quickly in flight until they had been marked and cut in play. Thus they were not introduced into the game generally until 1848, by which time the makers had learned to apply effective permanent markings to the surface so that they would fly properly.

The introduction of the gutta ball occasioned one of the great rejuvenations in the history of the game. Its lower cost, longer life, improved flight, and truer run on the greens and the fact that it did not fall apart in the rain attracted an enormous number of new players, and the feathery was quickly replaced, despite the best propaganda efforts of its makers to protect their livelihood.

The influx of new players, in turn, forced the conversion of the Old Course at St. Andrews to a full eighteen holes. Until the gutta ball was developed, golfers played "out" along what is now known as the left-hand course, until they reached the End Hole. There they turned around and played "in" to the same holes. If two groups approached a green

simultaneously, preference was given to those playing "out." However, as golfers multiplied with the advent of the gutta ball, the links proved too narrow to accommodate them, and about 1857 it was widened sufficiently to turn the greens into double ones so that eighteen holes could be cut instead of nine.

Gutta balls were generally as large as, if not larger than, the modern United States ball of diameter not less than 1.68 inches. They were marked 26, 26½, 27, 27½, 28, 28½, or 29 to designate their weight. These numbers probably referred to pennyweights in the troy weight scale. In this scale, 20 pennyweights equals an ounce.

Gutta balls were far easier to make than featheries, since they consisted solely of the single lump of gutta-percha, properly molded. Gutta-percha is a concrete juice produced by various trees and has the property of becoming soft and impressible at the temperature of boiling water and of retaining its shape when cooled. It is not affected by water except at boiling temperature.

Gutta-percha was procured from overseas in long, round rods about an inch and one-half in diameter. Sufficient gutta-percha was cut from this rod, with the aid of a gauge, to make a ball of the desired size and weight. This piece was softened in hot water. At first it was shaped and rolled by hand and nicked with the thin end of a hammer. Later iron molds, or ball presses, were introduced, first with plain molding surfaces and subsequently with indented surfaces to create markings on the ball. When first painted, gutta balls were given several coats, until it was noticed that this tended to fill the indentations of the markings. The number of coats was then reduced to two. It became customary, after applying the first coat, to let the balls season on racks for weeks before finishing them off.

The best-known balls were the hand-marked private brands of the club makers, such as the Auchterlonies, Old Tom Morris, and Robert Forgan, and the bramble and patent brands, such as the *Eureka, Melfort, White Melfort* (of white gutta-percha), *White Brand, Henley, O.K., Ocobo, Silvertown No. 4, A.1, Clan, Thornton, Park's Special,* and *Agrippa.* The *Agrippa,* with bramble marking, became a great favorite. The *A.1* floated, but guttas in general did not.

In the earlier part of this period, there was a rival to the gutta ball, commonly called the putty ball to distinguish it from the "gutta." It was named the *Eclipse* and was made of undisclosed ingredients, possibly including India rubber and cork fillings. It had a shorter carry, but longer run and better wearing qualities. Gradually in the nineties it lost favor.

The Rubber-Ball Period. The rubber ball was the invention of Coburn Haskell, a Cleveland golfer, in association with Bertram G. Work, of the B. F. Goodrich Company, at Akron, Ohio. In 1898 Haskell adapted the art of winding rubber thread produced by Goodrich under tension on a solid rubber core to produce a ball far livelier than the gutta. Actually, the earliest covers were of black gutta-percha, lightly lined by hand. Paint tended to fill the indentations, causing the balls to duck in flight just as had the first, smooth gutta balls. Dave Foulis, a Chicago professional, put one in an *Agrippa* mold and produced the bramble marking which was common to both the late gutta and early rubber balls.

Haskell balls were placed on the market by Goodrich in 1899 and became known as "bounding billies." It is estimated that they could be hit about 25 yards farther than the gutta, just as the gutta was about 25 yards longer than the feathery. The consensus at first, however, was that the distance a player gained did not offset the difficulty of controlling the lively ball on the green. As a matter of fact, Walter J. Travis, considered the best putter of his day, resolved this debate by using a Haskell ball from an *Agrippa* mold in winning the USGA Amateur Championship in September, 1901. The gutta thereafter became a relic of the past, and the game was again revolutionized and popularized as it had been with the advent of the gutta.

The day of the ball made by hand in the professional's shop was then ending. A. G. Spalding & Brothers., at Chicopee, Massachusetts, a manufacturer of sporting goods, had undertaken production of the first gutta ball in the United States, the *Vardon Flyer,* in

1898 and obtained a license to produce its first rubber ball, the *Spalding Wizard,* in 1903. Soon thereafter the balata cover was developed for Spalding, and its improved adhering qualities made it an important innovation. In 1905 Spalding also introduced the first "true" white golf balls. All former golf ball covers were black and they showed ugly dark patches when the white paint was nicked. The white did away with these patches by offering a cover of approximately the same color as the paint.

Earliest experiments with the rubber ball concerned the core. It was determined that the best cores, for resilience, were mobile cores which offered least resistance to distortion of the ball caused by club-head impact. Operating on this theory, the Kempshall Golf Ball Company produced the Kempshall Water Core, in which a small sac of water was substituted for solid rubber. The competition to produce a longer ball was under way. Manufacturers tried lead in solution, in an effort to combine weight with a mobile core, but lead proved injurious to curious children and animals. Zinc oxide was substituted, but the pigment tended to settle and unbalance the ball. In the twenties, true solutions involving glue, glycerin, and water were developed for first-line balls.

More telling improvements have been made in winding, the critical factor in the modern ball. Machines replaced men and were constantly improved for this process. The race was to him who could obtain the greatest tension—to him who could most closely approach the breaking point of rubber thread. The earliest thread was of wild rubber from the Amazon River Basin; development of plantation rubber greatly improved the quality of thread for this race.

Early rubber balls were made with the bramble and reverse mesh markings of the gutta ball, but experiments developed improvements as they revealed the best relationship of both depth and area of indentation to the ball's total surface. William Taylor, in England, reversed the markings on his molds to produce the dimple, in contrast to the bramble, in 1908. The mesh, in contrast to the original reverse mesh, was a natural aftermath.

Relative sizes of the British ball (left) and the American ball.

Haskell balls at first were light and large, about 1.55 ounces in weight and 1.71 inches in diameter, and they floated. In the absence of regulations governing size or weight, manufacturers pursued one another's leads in the quest for the most efficient combination. Heavy solutions in the core increased the weight to about 1.72 ounces in the first decade. Then both size and weight underwent a gradual reduction to 1.62 ounces by 1.63 inches about the time the Haskell patent expired in 1915.

Expiration of this patent increased the competition, which had tended to make courses obsolete. Therefore, in 1920 the USGA and the Royal and Ancient Golf Club of St. Andrews, Scotland, agreed jointly that (1) after May 1, 1921, balls used in their championships must weigh not more than 1.62 ounces and measure not less than 1.62 inches and (2) the two organizations would take whatever steps they deemed necessary in the future to limit the power of the ball. The ball actually was unchanged by this regulation; it continued to measure 1.63 inches, .01 inch above the minimum.

In 1923, the USGA decided that the power should be reduced. A series of experiments under William C. Fownes, Jr., and Herbert Jaques, Jr., led to introduction in the United States in 1930 of the so-called "balloon ball," weighing not more than 1.55 ounces and measuring not less than 1.68 inches. This ball, with no regulation of its velocity, became standard in the United States on January 1, 1931, and was the first deviation from the British ball. It proved too light to hold on line in flight in a wind or on a green as it lost momentum, and it survived only one year.

The present slightly heavier ball, weighing not more than 1.62 ounces and measuring not less than 1.68 inches, became standard in the United States on January 1, 1932. The velocity of this ball was not regulated, however, until the USGA completed a satisfactory testing machine in 1941. Since January 1, 1942, the USGA has required that the velocity of the ball be not greater than 250 feet per second when measured on the Association's machine under specified conditions. Since that time, the ball has remained substantially the same, thanks to USGA standardization.

A few years ago there was a strong move to get the R & A and the USGA to adopt a uniform ball, thus achieving a universal standard for the game. But these efforts were not successful. However, in the professional side of the game, there appears to be a movement toward standardizing on the American-sized ball. The British professional Tour events have made the "big" ball mandatory for some years, as has the British Open. And in the Ryder Cup matches, the professional golfers' association of Britain and the U.S.A. have agreed to the use of the American ball only. On the amateur side, the situation is different. The British ball is illegal in the U.S. because USGA rules state the size, "must not be less than 1.68 inches in diameter." But the American ball can be used in countries who abide by R & A rules because they, too, deal in minimums. R & A rules state the ball must not be less than 1.62 inches in diameter —there's nothing to say it cannot be more. In amateur international matches, such as the Walker Cup, players are given the option of using either ball. Usually they pick the British ball for its greater distance.

Rather closely related to the history of the golf ball is the *tee*. In the early days, the tees were sand tees. Golfers had to go to a box filled with sand, located on every tee, take out a hearty pinch to make a proper-size mound and tee their ball on top of it. Sometimes this sand was already dampened, other times a pail of water was placed conveniently nearby and the golfer would dip hand and sand into the liquid before getting ready to build his own tee.

It made for sloppy golf, of course, and this chore fell to the caddie, who would be directed where to pile the sand by the tapping of the driver on the precise spot. This, we must add, was a European custom, practiced by the more pompous gentlemen. When it was first tried in the United States, so one story goes, the American caddies saw fit to refuse "to bow down to the foreigners," and there were a few embarrassing moments until the "stand-off" was amicably settled. Later, someone fashioned a mold resembling an elongated thimble that removed much of the guesswork as to size of the sand mound and the making of a tee became a do-it-yourself science, for everyone.

Originally, the use of the word "tee" did not refer to the implement as we now know it but to the teeing ground—and even the teeing ground was not then as we now know it. When the Regulations for the Game of Golf were adopted by the St. Andrews Society of Golfers at their meeting on Friday, May 1, 1812, Rule 1 stated: "The ball must be teed not nearer the hole than two club lengths, not farther from it than four." This meant the golfers of that time were hitting their drives from within 8 to 15 feet of the cup. Naturally, this did the putting surface no good at all, and it was not long before they designated another spot for the purpose of "teeing off."

The origin of the wooden tee is a bit vague. A forerunner was the rubber tee advertised by A. G. Spalding as far back as 1893. A patent for a tee with a wooden stem and a flexible tubular head was granted to a man named Grant in 1899. But the first marketable all-wooden tee was the *Reddy Tee* invented in 1920 by a dental surgeon named William Lowell. Its popularity was abetted by a huge order from the powerful F. W. Woolworth chain, and its adoption by the playing golfers and pros was spurred on by none other than Walter Hagen, who would place one conspicuously behind his ear and walk down the fairway in full view of the gallery.

Today, the *wooden* tee is made in an astounding variety of shapes, sizes, and materials, and a check of your own supply will undoubtedly expose them in many colors, lengths, and head dimensions. You will probably find tall tees, for those who like to hit up on the ball, or for use on courses with lush grass in the tee-off area; short tees to help correct a tendency to hook or for use on hard tees with little grass; or tees with large cavities, called by many "hurricane tees," so the ball will not be easily blown off by the high winds common to seaside courses, or links.

The Golf Club

The history of the golf club is *very* closely integrated with the history of the ball. In fact, the club evolved in response to new developments in the ball, and thus its history is divided into the same three periods of golf "time."

The Feather-Ball Period. The full, free style which has come to be known as the "St. Andrews swing" developed out of the feather-ball period. The clubs, which were at first rudimentary, tended toward the end of the period to be long, thin, and graceful; and the feathery was swept from the ground with a full swing which also tended to be long and graceful. The shafts were whippy and the grips thick. There was a considerable elegance to these clubs. The foremost club makers, Hugh Philp and Douglas McEwan, have become known as the Chippendale and Hepplewhite of club making.

The earliest known club maker was William Mayne, of Edinburgh, who received a Royal Warrant as club maker and spear maker from James VI in 1603. An old notebook records payments for the repair of "play clubis," "bonker clubis," and an "irone club." There are no known examples of these clubs, although some were pictured in the art of the times, showing their rudimentary nature.

Among the oldest known clubs is a set of six woods and two irons preserved in a case in the Big Room at the Troon Golf Club, Troon, Scotland. These were found in a walled-up closet of a house at Hull, England, with a copy of a Yorkshire paper dated 1741. It is possible that they are of Stuart times. All six woods and two irons are shafted with ash. Only one wood and one iron have grips. The woods are leaded and boned, the lead extending from near the toe two-thirds of the way to the heel. Although the stamp is too worn for identification, they could have been made by Andrew Dickson, of Leith, or Henry Mill, of St. Andrews, who were well-known club makers of the Stuart era and next in our line of knowledge after Mayne.

Club making reached its zenith in the last century of the feather-ball era, with the advent of the real artists: Simon Cossar of Leith; the successive generations of McEwans, James, Peter, and Douglas, of Leith and Musselburgh; Hugh Philp, of St. Andrews, and his assistant, James Wilson; and Harold White of St. Andrews. Cossar, Philp, Wilson, and the McEwans were noted for their woods; Cossar, Wilson, and White for cleeks and irons. White is credited with giving Allan Robertson and Young Tom Morris such refined irons that they were able to introduce a wide range of new strokes into the game.

Douglas McEwan made his club heads from small cuts of hedgethorne which had been planted horizontally on sloping banks so that the stems grew at an angle at the root and created a natural bend for the neck. The shafts, spliced onto the heads, were made of split ash.

By the first half of the nineteenth century, clubs had come to be divided into four classes: drivers, spoons, irons, and putters. Drivers were distinguished by their long, tapering, and flexible shafts and their small, raking heads. They comprised "play clubs," which had little loft and were designed for use over safe ground only, and "grassed drivers," which had more loft and were designed to lift a ball from a heavy or downhill lie or over a hazard.

Spoons were of four types: long spoons, middle spoons, short spoons, and baffing spoons, the distinctions being in the degree of loft. For a time there was also a fifth spoon, the niblick, a well-lofted club with a small head designed to drive a ball out of a wagon-wheel rut or similar man-made hazard.

Irons were three in number: driving irons, cleek, and bunker irons. There were two types of putters: driving putters, for approach work over unencumbered terrain, and green putters, for use on putting greens. With these sets, players negotiated their feather balls over holes measuring 80 to 400 yards.

The Gutta-Percha Ball Period. The gutta-percha ball was harder than the feather ball and put a considerable strain on the slender clubs with which feather balls had been stroked. Thus wooden heads gradually became shorter and squatter in shape. Hard thorn was discarded for the softer apple, pear, and beech in the heads, and leather inserts appeared in the faces. Hickory, which for golf originally came from Russia and later from Tennessee, replaced ash in the making of shafts.

Iron clubs increased in both number and variety and became vastly more refined. The superlative play of Young Tom Morris at St. Andrews is credited with popularizing the iron clubs he used so deftly. A full range of clubs at the zenith of the gutta ball period consisted of seven woods (driver, bulger driver, long spoon, brassie, middle spoon, short spoon, and putter) and six irons (cleek, midiron, lofting iron, mashie, niblick, and cleek putter). From these the golfer usually selected about eight. The range of clubs which Willie Park, Jr., had in winning the British Open Championships of 1887 and 1889 was bulger driver, straight-faced driver, spoon, brassie niblick, wooden putter, cleek, iron, mashie, iron niblick, and Parks Patent putter. The increase in the number of clubs brought about another innovation in the early nineties, that of a simple sailcloth bag in which to carry them. Previously, the few clubs a player might need had been carried loose under the arm. Thus, the golf bag got its start in the gutta-percha era.

The introduction of the gutta ball did not change the club makers; it simply required them to develop new designs and materials. Douglas McEwan lived until 1896 and bridged both the feathery and the gutta periods. His son Peter in his turn became a club maker and was followed by his four sons, who constituted the fifth generation of club-making McEwans. James Wilson, who had made clubs for the feather ball under Hugh Philp, set up his own shop at St. Andrews in 1852, and Philp then took in his nephew, Robert Forgan. Forgan and his son Thomas continued the business under their own name after Philp's death and achieved their own fame.

Robert Forgan was the first to appreciate

the merit of hickory shafts after bolts of the wood had come up the Clyde to Glasgow for conversion to handles for pick, shovel, rake, hoe, and ax. Thomas Forgan produced the bulger driver and the ebony putter. Old Tom Morris, the Andersons, and the Auchterlonies were other noted club makers at St. Andrews, and there were Ben Sayers at North Berwick, Willie Park of Musselburgh, the Simpsons of Carnoustie, and many more.

In March, 1891, Willie Dunn, son of Willie of the famed Dunn twins of Scotland, arrived in the United States to lay out the course at Southampton, New York, for the Shinnecock Hills Golf Club, and he remained in the U.S. to make clubs. Other Scottish professionals emigrated in the nineties and contributed to the establishment of the trade of American club making.

The trade itself was little changed. Wooden heads were cut out of a block, filed, spoke-shaved, chiseled, gouged, leaded, boned, glass-papered, sometimes stained, and treated with a hare's foot dipped in a mixture of oil and varnish. Where the club heads used by Allan Robertson were only $\frac{5}{16}$ of an inch deep, the depth gradually increased to 1 inch and, for a time, 2 inches.

Iron heads were hand-forged from a bar of mild iron, heated, hammered, tempered, emery-wheeled, and polished, and the socket was pierced for the rivet and nicked. Hickory shafts were seasoned, then cut, filed, planed, scraped, and glass-papered down to the required length, shape, and degree of whippiness, which was the real art. Shafts for wooden heads were finished in a splice, glued onto the heads, and whipped with tarred twine. Shafts for irons were finished with a prong to fit into the socket and holed for the iron cross rivet. Strips of untanned leather, shaped with a chisel, were nailed to the top of the shafts, wound on spirally over a cloth foundation similarly applied, rolled tight between two polished boards, and nailed at the bottom. Both ends of the grip were bound with tarred twine, and the whole grip was then varnished.

Caliber of play improved greatly with the advent of the gutta ball. Allan Robertson shattered all precedent by scoring a 79 at St. Andrews in 1858, and this record stood until Young Tom Morris made a 77 in 1869. The British Open Championship was instituted at Prestwick, Scotland, in 1860 and was played there through 1872. Willie Park, Sr., won the first Open with a score of 174 for 36 holes, and Young Tom Morris retired the belt, emblematic of the Championship, by winning his third successive Championship, with a score of 149, in 1870. The first golf in the United States was played with gutta balls, and the USGA Amateur, Open, and Women's Championships originated in 1895, three years before the invention of the rubber ball.

The Rubber-Ball Period. Golf was being overtaken by the Industrial Revolution when the rubber ball came into the game at the beginning of the twentieth century. These two factors wrought major changes in the clubs and the methods by which they were produced as craftsmanship moved out of the individual professional's shop and into the factory.

The harder rubber ball brought about the use of persimmon rather than dogwood, applewood, hickory, and beechwood, which were formerly employed. Later laminated club heads were also used. Hard insets appeared in the faces. Increased demand led to the adaptation of shoe-last machine tools for the fashioning of wooden club heads. Sockets were bored in the hosels, and shafts were inserted rather than spliced. Drop forging almost completely replaced hand forging in the fashioning of iron clubs, and faces were deepened to accommodate the livelier ball and were machine-lined to increase the spin on the ball in flight. Stainless steels replaced carbon steels. Seamless steel shafts took the place of hickory. Composition materials were developed as an alternative to leather in grips, and the grip foundations were molded in so many ways that they were regulated in 1947. Inventive minds created novel clubs, not only center-shafted and aluminum putters and the sand wedge but also types which were such radical departures from the traditional form and make that they could not be approved by the USGA or by the Royal and Ancient Golf Club of St. Andrews, Scotland.

These changes had their genesis in the United States when Julian W. Curtiss, of A. G. Spalding & Bros., purchased some clubs in London in 1892 for resale in his company's retail stores. Two years later, Spalding em-

The clubs shown here (except Calamity Jane I, shown at top) were used by Bobby Jones during the last six years (1924 to 1930) of his tournament career. He presented these hickory-shafted clubs to the Augusta National Golf Club. The remaining clubs of the complete set of sixteen (not shown here) are: a driver now at the Royal and Ancient Golf Club, St. Andrews, Scotland; a brassie now in the James River Museum, James River, Virginia; a run-up club, lost; and a sand wedge at the USGA. Calamity Jane II, which Jones used to win the Grand Slam, was the exact duplicate of Calamity Jane I. It is now in the USGA Museum in New York City.

ployed some Scottish club makers and began producing its own clubs.

Hand modeling of woods and hand forging of irons naturally did not long survive the demands of factory production. Within the first decade, the Crawford, McGregor & Canby Company in Dayton, Ohio, a maker of shoe lasts, was turning out wooden heads, foundries were converting drop-forging processes to iron heads, and Allan Lard, in Chicopee, Massachusetts, was experimenting with perforated steel rods for shafts.

A. W. Knight, of the General Electric Company, in Schenectady, New York, joined this inventive movement and produced an aluminum-headed putter with the shaft attached near the center, instead of at the heel. Walter J. Travis used this "Schenectady" putter in winning the British Amateur in 1904, and center-shafted clubs immediately were banned in Britain. It was not until 1933 that center-shafted putters were legalized.

During the twenty-nine years of its prohibition in England, the putter's popularity spread throughout the United States and brought forth an endorsement from William H. Taft, then President of the United States. President Taft sent a letter to Travis, telling how much he enjoyed using the Schenectady putter and that it had improved his game. So far as is known, this is the only time a President has lent endorsement to a golf club.

Seven years after he had patented the putter, Knight made his second contribution, the steel-shaft club. Again, that invention was brought about by Knight's desire to improve his own game. Seeking to get a greater "whip" to his driver, Knight reduced the diameter of his wooden shaft. But it made his driver unreliable for direction. It was then he began experimenting with steel. He found that the steel shaft produced the desired results and helped to improve his game.

The import of all these developments was

such that, in promulgating its revised code of rules in September, 1908, the Royal and Ancient Golf Club of St. Andrews appended the notation that it would not sanction any substantial departure from the traditional and accepted form and make of golf clubs. This principle has been invoked many times in an effort to preserve the original form of the game.

When Jock Hutchison won the British Open in 1921 with deeply slotted faces on his pitching clubs, the Royal and Ancient Golf Club immediately banned such faces, and the USGA concurred with a regulation governing markings which became effective in 1924. After Horton Smith had so effectively used a sand wedge with a concave face designed by E. M. MacClain, of Houston, Texas, the principle of concavity was banned in 1931. However, Gene Sarazen developed a straight-faced sand wedge and used it so well in winning the British and USGA Opens in 1932 that he completed the revolution of bunker play.

Experiments with steel shafts went through several phases. Lard's perforated steel rod was no substitute for hickory, and the locked-seam shaft of Knight proved not the answer, either, although the USGA approved such shafts in 1924. However, in 1924, the Union Hardware Company, of Torrington, Connecticut, drew a seamless shaft of high carbon steel which could be heat-treated and tempered. This came into the game in the late twenties, was approved by the Royal and Ancient Golf Club in 1929, and substantially replaced hickory in the early thirties. Importing its steel from Sweden, Union soon cornered almost the entire market, furnishing shafts to such old-line companies as Bristol, Kroydon, and Heddon and then and now to Spalding, Wilson, MacGregor, as well as to Hillerich & Bradsby, Northwestern, Dubow, and Professional Golf.

Improvement of the steel shaft was accompanied by the general introduction of numbered clubs, rather than named clubs, and by the merchandising of matched sets, rather than individual clubs; clubs had become more numerous and more finely manufactured to specifications for flexibility and point of flex. Where formerly a golfer seeking new clubs went through a rack of mashies until he found one that "felt right" and then tried to find

other clubs of similar feel, he now bought a whole set manufactured to impart the same feel. The merchandising aspect of this development was perhaps something more than a happy coincidence for the manufacturers. In any case, the merchandising opportunities inherent in the numbered and matched sets were carried to an extreme, and in 1938 the USGA limited to fourteen the number of clubs a player might use in a round. The Royal and Ancient Golf Club concurred in a similar edict the next year.

The superiority of the steel shaft went unchallenged until the fifties, with introduction of the glass shafts. The Fiberglas Wonder-Shaft produced by the Shakespeare Company, Kalamazoo, Michigan, received a great deal of attention and publicity (Fiberglas is a registered trademark of Owens-Corning Fiberglas Corporation), mostly through the successes of its chief proponent, Gary Player. He used this shaft in winning the 1965 U.S. Open, among other tournaments.

The Shakespeare Fiberglas shaft consisted of more than a half-million glass fibers bonded in parallel into a double-built tubular shaft, with the fibers running lengthwise on the shaft around a central spiral Fiberglas wall.

In the mid-1950's, Golfcraft Incorporated of Escondido, California, introduced its Glasshaft clubs, also made of Owens-Corning Fiberglas, but with a different concept. In Glasshaft, the fibers were laminated to a thin steel core.

Another glass shaft offered to the golfers was the patented filament-woven shaft developed by Plas/Steel Products of Walkerton, Indiana. Introduced under the name Plas/ Steel, it had better torque strength than did steel, according to its designers.

In 1965, after ten years of experimentation, an aluminum shaft more than 10 per cent stronger in tensile strength than steel alloy shafts but lighter by 30 per cent was brought onto the market. The first to learn of this highest-strength aluminum on the market were all the major golf manufacturers, to whom sample shafts were shipped by Le Fiell Products, Inc., of Sante Fe Springs, California. It caught their fancy from the start. Here was lightweight material strong enough to hold the club head in position in relation to the hands, without torque. Was this it, then? Was this the shaft of the future?

From the present perspective, more than ten years later, the answer has to be a decided no. At first, aluminum took off like a rocket. The great Arnold Palmer used an aluminum-shafted set early in 1968, and even won a tournament with them, which certainly didn't hurt sales. Also a factor were the distance claims made for the aluminum shaft. Since the shaft was about half an ounce lighter than the original or regular steel shaft, this meant, according to the manufacturer, that some of the weight saved in the shaft could be added to the club head, giving the golfer a club that weighed less over all but with a slightly heavier club head. Since the club head—the object being swung—was heavier, and the golfer could swing a slightly lighter over-all weight faster, more distance was assured. How much distance? Around one club stronger than steel, say, 10 yards longer per club.

What happened? After the dust settled, the following conclusions could be drawn: (1) The lighter over-all weight did suit seniors and women golfers, and many of these did in fact experience a slight distance bonus; (2) On the other hand, most average golfers found that the distance claims had been exaggerated, at least so far as they were concerned; (3) Aluminum gave a "softer" hit than steel. Some golfers liked it, but many more found it "dead" compared to the more lively impact feel they were used to in steel; (4) For better golfers, the softer feel of aluminum dulled feedback on a shot—with steel they knew if they had hit the ball well or badly, with aluminum, they did not; (5) Aluminum shafts put an end to any chance of

Fiberglas shafts dominating the market. Although Fiberglas had a nice, cushioned feel at impact, the shafts were heavy and this tended to reduce club-head feel in the swing. Worse, "heavy" shafts meant there were no glamorous distance claims to be made.

In 1973, the graphite shaft (graphite fibers bonded together by resin in similar fashion to Fiberglas) was introduced. Because a graphite shaft is 1½ to 2 ounces lighter than a regular steel shaft, and from 1 to 2 ounces lighter than aluminum or lightweight steel shafts, again much promotional hay was made in regard to distance. Highly exaggerated claims of 20 to 50 additional yards off the tee were made. Aluminum revisited, one might call it. And again, when the clubs got into the hands of average golfers, the distance bonus just wasn't there, except for seniors and women. Another problem was the price—a full set of graphite clubs retailed for $1,100 to $1,800. Although the cost of graphite clubs has since come off that high of about $125 per club, the average golfer today has usually done no more than dabble with a graphite driver.

Other developments in recent years have included titanium shafts (again, very light, but as expensive as graphite), stainless steel shafts (slightly lighter, but also slightly more expensive than regular steel), and graphite composite shafts (cheaper but heavier than graphite shafts). However, more interesting for the average golfer has been a succession of what might be described as "super lightweight" steel shafts. These shafts are up to an ounce lighter than regular steel at an affordable price.

What does the future hold? Only one thing is certain: change.

TYPES OF GOLF CLUBS

Golf clubs today are generally classified in two categories, namely, *woods* and *irons*. Clubs of each category are designed for a particular kind of stroke. Most clubs are named, but are more familiarly known by numbers.

The Woods

The club head of this type of club is made from wood; hence its name. As previously de-

tailed, most early clubs were made from wood. Today, woods are designed primarily for distance. This does not mean that a player should not try to be as accurate with them as he possibly can. But the average golfer cannot expect pin-point accuracy with them.

The distance range given for the various woods here is a guide to what can be accomplished by an average golfer rather than an expert. Adjust to your capacity and ability,

Normal Distance for Average Golfers

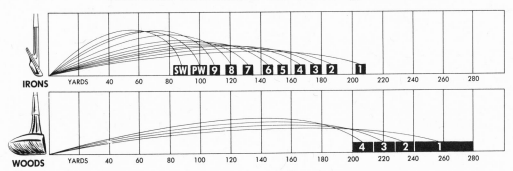

based on your own experience. In addition, remember that weather and course conditions can also have a great effect on distance that can be obtained from the various strokes.

No. 1 Wood or Driver. Used from the tee for maximum distance and rather flat trajectory. Has a large head and deep face which is almost vertical. For the average player, the driver's range from a tee is 210 yards and up.

No. 2 Wood or Brassie. Named because of the brass plate on the sole of the club. It has more loft to the face than a driver and hits the ball higher into the air. Its normal use is from the fairway, when the ball is sitting up well on fairway grass. Under certain circumstances, it is used in driving from the tee, even by expert players. Distance range: 200 to 235 yards.

No. 3 Wood or Spoon. Face has more of a loft than a brassie or driver. The club sometimes has a shorter shaft than the driver or brassie. It is used for rather long shots from poor lies in the fairway or off the tee when a high ball is desired to go long with a favorable wind. Distance range: 190 to 220 yards.

No. 4 Wood or Cleek. Smaller head, shallower face, and more loft than a spoon. Customary use is from bad lies in fairways where a rather long shot with fairly high arc of flight is desired. This club is sometimes called a No. 4 spoon or short spoon. Distance range: 180 to 210 yards.

No. 5 Wood or Baffy. This wood is a rather new addition to the wood family. It has more loft than the other woods mentioned and is used from the fairway and rough when the player is confronted with a poor lie. It gets the ball up into the air quickly. It is an excellent club for women golfers. The No. 5 wood, incidentally, is becoming an increasingly

popular club with all golfers, and the No. 2 wood seems to be obsolescent. Distance range: 160 to 200 yards.

No. 6 Wood. This is another new wood and is used much the same as No. 5 wood. It provides a little more loft on the ball. Distance range: 150 to 190 yards. A few club makers produce a No. 7 and No. 8 wood, but they are very seldom used. The range loft of No. 7 is greater and its distance is less than a No. 6 wood. The No. 8 wood has a very short range —about 100 yards.

The Irons

The iron clubs—so named because of drop-forged iron or steel club heads—are intended for shots where accuracy rather than distance is the prime consideration and for shots that are lying in grass or on sand where the face of the club must get down and hit the ball up with a rather quick rise. The irons fall into three general categories: long, medium, and short. The Nos. 1, 2, and 3 irons are classified as the long irons; the Nos. 4, 5, and 6 are regarded as medium irons; and the Nos. 7, 8, 9, and wedges rate as the short irons.

Iron clubs have shorter shafts than wood clubs and have the shafts joined to the club heads at more upright angles than in wood club design. Consequently, to play them correctly, the player must stand closer to the ball when playing an iron than when playing a wood. By making sure that the bottom (the sole) of the club is squarely on the ground when one is taking the stance for making the shot, the player will see from the location of the leather grip just where to stand in order to use the club in the manner for which it is designed. The distance that can be made with any particular club depends on the individual.

Again the ranges given here are representative of distances obtained by the average golfer.

No. 1 Iron or Driving Iron. A club seldom used or carried by the average golfer. (Most manufacturers no longer include the No. 1 iron in their standard matched sets.) The No. 4 wood has replaced this club to a large extent. It is a club with very little loft to its face and is used when a low ball is desired such as is required when hitting into the wind. Distance range: 190 to 210 yards.

No. 2 Iron or Midiron. An all-around club for long shots from the fairway, tee, and sometimes rough. However, the No. 2 iron is a rather difficult club for the beginner to master because of the little loft and the extra strength required to obtain the proper distance. This iron is being replaced in many golfers' bags by the No. 5 wood. Distance range: 165 to 190 yards.

No. 3 Iron or Mid Mashie. Has a greater loft than the No. 2 iron and is much easier to use. It is generally the longest iron that most beginning players can handle with any degree of certainty. Distance range: 150 to 175 yards.

No. 4 Iron or Mashie Iron. A useful iron for shots from the fairway, rough, or bad lies. Used off the tee on many par-3 holes. Distance range: 140 to 165 yards.

No. 5 Iron or Mashie. For fairly long, high shots from the fairway or rough and off the tee on some par-3 holes. A popular and relatively easy club to use in pitching the ball high to the green so it will stop after hitting the ground. Also may be used for pitch-and-run shots from 30 to 50 yards off the green when it is desired that the ball travel part way through the air and roll the rest of the distance to the objective. Distance range: 130 to 155 yards.

No. 6 Iron or Spade Mashie. For pitch-and-run shots to the green and for playing the ball from high grass or difficult lies. It is useful from a clean lie in the sand trap when some distance is needed. It is also employed from the fairway. It has greater loft than the No. 5 iron. Distance range: 100 to 145 yards.

No. 7 Iron or Mashie Niblick. More loft, less distance than spade mashie. Used for short pitch or chip shots onto the green and to get out of traps, over trees, and so on. Im-

parts plenty of backspin to the ball to hold the green. Distance range: 100 to 135 yards.

No. 8 Iron or Pitching Niblick. Used much the same as No. 7 iron. For pitch shots from the fairway, rough, or quick-rising pitches over hazards and bunkers. Distance range: 80 to 120 yards.

No. 9 Iron or Niblick. For sand shots from traps and some shots from bad rough. The face has a great deal of loft, and the head is heavy to carry it through long tough grass or heavy sand. Distance range: 80 to 110 yards.

Putter. A club with straight or nearly straight face for rolling ball on green. There are many styles of putters, and the one you select is a matter of preference.

Special Irons. Not all golf club manufacturers agree on the names and numbers of the 6, 7, 8, and 9 irons, offering slightly different clubs in their sets. But in practically all cases, the higher the number, the heavier and shorter the club and the more loft to the face. Special flanged or wedge-type niblicks, heavier than a No. 9 iron and with decided loft to get the ball into the air quickly and to drop with very little roll, are also made by different manufacturers. These irons, each bearing a manufacturer's number or copyrighted name, such as dual-purpose wedge, do-all wedge, sand wedge, pitching wedge, and the like, are made with a heavy flange to prevent the club head from digging too deeply into the sand or heavy turf and to assist it in following through after the ball. These clubs are also good to use on pitch shots. Distance range of wedges: maximum 100 yards.

The chipping iron, also known as the chipper, jigger, and run-up iron, is favored by some players on special chip-shot problems. This iron has the approximate loft of No. 4 iron, but has a short shaft. It is used for short pitch-and-run shots.

It is very important to remember that a total of fourteen clubs is the limit permitted by the USGA in tournament play. Select the fourteen clubs that are most suitable for your type of play, but do not go over this number for any particular round of play. This is a rule of golf and should not be deviated from, regardless of the informality of the game you are in. Only for strict practice should you carry more than the allotted number.

MANUFACTURE OF GOLF EQUIPMENT

In no other game or sport except golf is there quite the ignorance about the equipment with which it is played. In a sense, this is understandable. There are more than 200 operations that go into the making of a wood, more than 150 in an iron, several dozen in a ball. As a result, most golfers buy equipment on blind faith. To have some idea of what you are going to purchase, or of what you have already purchased, the following account may help to clarify· the manufacturing mysteries behind golf equipment.

The Golf Clubs

Possibly the most common misconception about club making is the notion that expensive clubs are handmade and that inexpensive clubs are manufactured by machine. All clubs, regardless of their price, are handmade. They are put together in a multistage process by craftsmen as skilled as surgeons. The difference, of course, comes in how much you want to spend for a set of clubs. Higher-priced custom-made sets get the individual treatment and styling of a tailor-made suit; lower-grade clubs are mass-produced on an assembly-line basis.

Woods. The business end of a wood is generally made from persimmon, a species known for its toughness. The heads are made from a solid block of wood. Steel, steel-wood combinations, and plastic are also used. In the latter type, a head is made from a metal mold which was cast originally from a wooden head. Wooden club heads are solid all the way through, except for the hollowed-out neck into which a metal or other type shaft is fitted.

Once the wooden heads are shaped, many club makers give them a bath in a specially produced wood pregnator that allows a moisture content of 8 to 10 per cent. This is important, for too much moisture will lead to eventual swelling and "popping" of the face insert. Too little, and the club will crash with the impact of a golf ball. After the pregnator bath, the clubs are ready to be assembled.

The first specific step in assembly is the drilling out of the face insert and sole plate and the facing. Face inserts (most commonly, Cycolac, but epoxy, aluminum, fiber, brass, nylon, steel, and graphite inserts are also used) are first glued and then, in some cases, screwed into the head. Next, they are soled by brass and aluminum plates. Incidentally, the driver generally has an aluminum sole plate, while the other woods have brass sole plates. (A few manufacturers break with tradition and use aluminum plates for their Nos. 1, 2, and 3 woods, while brass is employed on the other woods.)

In the making of custom-built woods, it is while the head is being honed and shaped to specification that dubious aids to a golfer's swing, such as a hook, can be achieved. To put a hook into a wood, the face is cut back toward the heel. Asking for a built-in hook (mostly to counterbalance a player's self-made slice) is a common request, though not necessarily a professional one. At this stage, the wood has not yet been fitted to a shaft; and before this occurs, more planing on the head of the club and shaping of the neck must be done. The wood also receives a facial: a rough sanding.

By the time a shaft is inserted in the neck of the wood, all the original excess weight has been trimmed off. When the shaft and head are put together, metal rings, called ferrules, are slipped around the neck to keep it from splitting. Once the ferrules are in place, a resilient nylon thread is wrapped by hand around the neck area of the club; the thread has a plastic coating which gives it a sheen and makes it smooth. (Some firms have changed from thread to a plastic-coated ferrule.) The club gets one step closer to completion when the grips are slipped over the top of the shaft. In clubs where leather grips are being wound on, underpacking is used as a base.

Sometimes, after the constant planing and whittling down of the head, the club's over-all weight is reduced too much to fit the original specifications of the golfer buying the club. In such instances, hot lead is poured into the head to make up for the deficit. For large

Making woods.

quantities, such as five-eighths of an ounce, a hole is cut into the back of the head and the lead is poured in. For smaller amounts, the lead is added under the plate. The weight of the club is measured on a scale in a process that would do credit to the Bureau of Standards. Once the weight is adjusted to specification, the wood is put through a series of staining and polishing. While varnish was formerly used, today most club makers use a pressure-impregnated material, such as a polyurethane sealer, as the final finish. Such a material is impervious to weather conditions and preserves and protects the wood against scratching and marring.

Irons. The various stages of putting an iron together closely parallel those in putting together a wood. The difference, of course, is in the head. Each company has its own dies for its iron heads, which are forged by a steel company. When the club is assembled, the irons are ground and polished and, of course, checked for weight every bit as carefully as the woods are. The relation of one club to another with regard to weight can be explained like this: As each iron gets one inch shorter, it must pick up a quarter-ounce more in weight in its head in order to arrive

at a correct balance. As a rule, the stainless steel heads are a little more expensive than the chrome-plated carbon steel ones, but are more durable and retain their shine longer.

In recent years, investment casting of irons has become increasingly important. The process has made possible the vast array of "cavity back" irons with heel/toe weighting, perimeter weighting or extreme sole weighting which make up at least half of most manufacturers' lines. However, the other half is still the forged iron, often promoted as a "player's" club or a club for the better golfer. It's improbable that investment cast irons will ever totally replace forged irons because forged irons are 10 to 20 per cent cheaper to produce.

The Golf Ball

No article of recreation is more abused, cursed, and dispatched to such inglorious reward than the innocent-looking, dimple-faced golf ball. In order to appreciate fully any factor of the golf ball or of its performance, it would be wise to consider the basic structure of the ball.

The center of the ball probably has experienced more change than any other part of the modern ball. Over the years such varied substances as steel, fiberglass, pills, glass, rubber, silicone, water, blood, iodine, mercury, tapioca, dry ice, gelatin, arsenic, and viscous pastes have been used in the center.

Today, to satisfy the demand for golf balls to be sold at various prices, there are four basic center, or core, constructions. The lowest in price is generally made with a solid rubber center 1¼ inches in diameter. The next better grade is made with solid rubber core 1⅛ inches in diameter, while the better grade of this group is made with a solid rubber center 1¹/₁₆ inches in diameter. (These balls are generally made with thread somewhat thicker than that used on the first-grade balls because it is less expensive and also because it can be wound faster and therefore makes the ball more economical to produce.) The top-grade golf balls are all made with cores approximately 1¹/₁₆ inches in diameter and have liquid centers. (One particular brand is made with centers filled with paste.)

Making golf balls.

In recent years, several top-grade brands have come onto the market containing centers approximately 1 1/16 inches in diameter but consisting of two solid rubber halves cemented around and enclosing a pellet of some type. These centers contain nylon pellets, steel pellets, fiberglass pellets, steel ball bearings, small oil-filled capsules, and what have you. These pellets are invariably approximately between 5/16 and 3/8 inch in diameter. Most of the pellets tend to give the ball a harder feel, and their principal advantage, aside from being a basis for advertising claims, is an economic one in that they are less expensive to produce. These pellet-containing centers are first molded into two hemispherical halves which contain a concave section to receive the pellet or capsule. After the halves have been molded, they are usually cemented around the pellet or capsule.

There are many reasons for the various types of centers used in the top-grade balls. Many manufacturers believe that a liquid-filled center gives a much sharper click or sound at impact. They also believe that a liquid is noncompressible and therefore makes the ball recover faster from its deformation when struck with a club, resulting in a faster getaway and a pleasing feel. A ball that does not get away fast feels heavy and is not as

satisfactory to the player. Those who use the other types of centers probably have their own reasons and ideas about them. Therefore, the first operation in making a golf ball is the manufacture of the center. In prior years, only natural rubber had been found completely satisfactory for this purpose. However, more recently synthetic rubbers with greater resiliency have been developed. The advantage of this greater resiliency can be used for best results only where a large percentage of the center is composed of rubber.

The liquid-filled or paste-filled centers require very accurate calendering of the stock. A pellet of the fluid medium can be frozen and the stock pressed around it and later cured, or hollow rubber balls may first be prepared and later filled with the liquid. In another process, two pieces of uncured stock are sealed together on the edges, forming a sort of rubber pillow case which is filled with the necessary liquid. This filled container is then punched out with dies forming individual, uncured, rubber balls which are placed in molds and vulcanized.

After the center has been made, it must be frozen to prepare it for winding. This is important because to wind a true sphere, the center must retain its shape until it is completely surrounded by the thread of the winding operation. It is necessary in the case of liquid-filled centers to have them completely full, with the air entirely eliminated. If there is any air present, the center will collapse when it thaws out and go off shape. This can result in erratic performance of the finished ball.

After the center has been made, it is wound with rubber thread into a core. This winding, which supplies the power, is considered by some to be the greatest achievement in ball manufacture. The thread has been greatly improved through modern technology, and the chemicals that have been added make this new isoprene thread more uniform in feel and resiliency. The prestretched winding may be put on in one operation or in two separate but related stages. As it is applied under tension, it stores up an abundance of energy. It has been said that there is enough energy in the thread to lift a 150-pound man two feet off the ground.

The center of the ball is placed under very high pressure by the winding. This effect can be illustrated by wrapping a rubber band around your finger. One turn and you can notice the pressure. If you build up several layers, it continues to get tighter and tighter. This is what happens to the golf ball center. The pressure on the center actually builds up to about 2,500 pounds per square inch. In other words, the center as a whole is sustaining a total pressure of from 7,000 to 8,000 pounds.

Golf ball thread is made of synthetic natural rubber (generally polyisoprene) and is vulcanized in the form of a sheet and then cut with slitters or rotary knives lubricated with water. Slit-cut thread has been used more and more in recent years and may eventually replace all the thread cut with rotary knives. The cut or slit thread, as it may be, is then wound on spools. The next step is to wind the thread around the frozen center. There are many types of machines available to do this with either of two basic patterns. One type of machine packs the thread around the center rather tightly. Another type winds the thread with a more open weave or pattern. It is desirable to put on as much thread as possible to get maximum resiliency or distance consistent with proper feel and quick getaway.

However, if the thread is packed too tightly, an outer layer of thread with a more open weave is required. If this is not done, the cover stock cannot penetrate properly in the molding operation. The outer layer controls the proper amalgamation of the cover stock to the wound ball.

All types of winding machines have automatic stops so that when a ball has been wound to its predetermined size the machine will shut off. However, this is not completely reliable, and after the balls have been wound they must be measured. This may be done by various means. The balls of proper size are then surrounded by two hemispherical cups and are ready for molding.

The cups of cover stock that are placed around the wound balls prior to molding are made either of a compound containing balata as its principal component or in recent years of Surlyn. The latter is being used more and more now because of its proven resistance to cutting.

There are several methods for molding the cups from the prepared stock, which is thermoplastic at this stage. In one of the methods, the heated stock is tubed into strips and cut into blanks of the proper size. The blanks are allowed to cool and are placed in cavities of a cold multiple-cavity cup-forming mold. The loaded mold is then heated, and sufficient hydraulic pressure is applied to cause the heated blanks to take the shape of the mold. After the stock has been heated and pressed out, the mold is chilled. This cools the formed cups, enabling the operator to remove them from the mold.

In another method, instead of using cold blanks, warm sheets or strips of stock are placed in a cold mold, hydraulic pressure is applied to cause the stock to take the shape of the mold, and then the mold is chilled and opened, permitting the removal of the formed cups. In some methods the cups are molded individually, while in others they are formed as a sheet. Therefore, it may or may not be necessary to die out or cut out these cups, depending on the method of molding used. In most cases, the flash or surplus stock can be reused.

After these balls have been properly prepared, they are subjected to some particular type of process in which the supplementary ingredients necessary to complete the vulcanization are introduced into the cover. The balls are then generally aged at a slightly elevated temperature for the desired time which is necessary for vulcanization to be completed.

After the covers on the balls have been vulcanized, they must be properly cleaned. In addition to this, they must be treated in preparation for painting. The balls are then painted on spray machines that are basically similar. Years ago, there was a variety of paints used on golf balls, depending on the selection by the manufacturer according to the way the balls were prepared. In recent years, practically all the golf ball manufacturers have progressively adopted the same basic type of paint, known as a polyurethane. The balls are generally sprayed with two or three coats of white polyurethane paint, at the choice of the individual manufacturer. The length of drying time between coats may also vary due to the conditions under which the painted balls are dried. The golf balls are then packaged for sale.

The method just described is the one most generally followed in the construction of conventional or three-part golf ball (so named because of its three main parts: the center core, the highly tensioned thread winding, and the outside cover). Recently, a so-called "solid ball" was introduced to golfing. This ball is a one-piece affair (or a variation with a cover), the one piece being injection molding of a polybutadiene/silica/monomer system. The two-piece solid ball has a core of 77 per cent of this material, covered by a Surlyn cover (Surlyn is a thermoplastic ionomer resin produced by Du Pont).

Many claims, including virtual indestructibility, truer flight, and less hook and slice, are made by manufacturers of solid balls. However, one thing seems certain. Average golfers have taken to the "solid" balls and Surlyn-covered wound balls in droves because of their long-wearing properties. Many golf industry experts forecast that soon only low-handicappers and pros will use balata-covered wound balls.

Incidentally, regardless of construction, the dimples on all balls, while distinctive, are not intended to be a mere attractive design. They generally number 336, and they affect the aerodynamics of the flight of the ball. From the impact and force of the tee shot, backspin is imparted on the ball, causing it to rotate at a rate of 4,000 to 5,000 revolutions per minute. As the ball backspins, the rotation causes air to pile under the ball while sucking it away from the top of the ball. This creates a pressure underneath and a vacuumlike condition above, similar to the vacuum over the wings of an airplane in flight. This condition causes the rise of the ball and keeps it airborne. The number, size, and depth of the dimples influence the lift and flight of the ball. More recently, there have been many experiments with number, depth, shape, and arrangement of dimples to give a better trajectory or to correct hooks and slices.

Such an analysis might appear to the uninitiated to be a belaboring of the task of making a little white ball. But this is hardly the case. Indeed, some of the procedures have been minimized for clarity in the foregoing description. One manufacturer claims that 85 separate steps are required in the production of his ball—a sobering thought for anyone who has teed up a new ball and neatly dispatched it to a watery grave.

The ball maker's burden, of course, is weighted considerably by the necessity of working within the restrictions imposed by the USGA. It would be quite simple to produce a ball that would travel 500 yards or more when properly hit. But Rule 2–3 of the *Rules of Golf* states that the velocity of a ball may not exceed 250 feet per second when tested on the USGA machine. Balls must also meet the newer USGA Distance Standard. The desire to fulfill the average golfer's demand for a ball that will travel far and handsome, while staying within the USGA's limitations, has presented the manufacturers with a challenge.

In fairness to the governing fathers of the game, it should be made clear that some measure of flexibility is extended to the ball makers. There is no rule that specifies what materials must be used or in what amounts. The ball simply must be no smaller than 1.680 inches in diameter and no heavier than 1.620 ounces (and, of course, pass the velocity and distance tests). Beyond these controls, the manufacturers are free to design any ball that will appeal to the golfer; and this is what they have been doing at a fast pace.

SELECTION OF GOLF EQUIPMENT

Anyone who has a real interest in becoming proficient in the sport of golf owes it to himself to obtain the best equipment he can afford. It is false economy to shop for bargains without giving very careful consideration to their suitability. The value of your time devoted to learning golf makes the purchase of correctly fitted equipment the cheapest part of your investment in learning the sport. This is particularly true with regard to the selection of your clubs—the most basic equipment items.

A Set of Clubs

The average golfer who goes out to buy a set of clubs usually winds up doing something like this: he goes to a pro shop or a sporting-goods store, waggles clubs from several different sets, and then buys the set most comfortable to his grip and pocketbook. That is like buying a new car in a dark room.

Before you go out to buy that next (or first) set of golf clubs, here are some questions to ask yourself: Should you get an S-shaft, or do you need the extra flex provided by an L-shaft? Do you know what your swing weight is? Should the head of your driver lie

in or lie out, and should it have a deep face or a shallow face? The foregoing are not just a lot of mumbo-jumbo terms trumped up by canny manufacturers who are after your dollar. They represent some of the characteristics that are built into every intelligently purchased golf club to fit your particular swing. There is much more to swinging a golf club than meets the eye. You must remember that the key to good golf is a grooved swing, and the only thing that will permit a grooved swing is a set of clubs that are matched within themselves and fit the person's playing requirements. There are several important factors in the selection of golf clubs for each player. Among them are:

1. Your physical specifications and aptitudes.
2. Your athletic and occupational background.
3. Your age.
4. Club shaft flexibility, length, weight, and so on.

These are factors that an experienced golf professional considers in prescribing clubs for your individual needs. He knows precisely the club specifications that most conform to your golf swing. Just like the doctor who makes a diagnosis and then writes out a medical prescription for your ailment, the golf professional does the same thing in the matter of prescribing the proper golf clubs most suitable for you. Still, it can be helpful to both you and your pro only if you are able to discuss your needs with him on a knowledgeable basis.

When purchasing golf clubs, you may select from standard matched sets or have a set of custom clubs made. By a matched set of clubs is meant that the woods and irons are of a specific swing weight, the shaft lengths are graduated, and there is uniformity in the flexibility of the shafts. This, in a general way, reduces the problem of selection for the ordinary golfer to knowing what swing weight, grip, shaft flex, and so on are right for him.

The difference, of course, between custom club makers and regular club manufacturers

NOMENCLATURE OF THE WOODS

1—Head
2—Sole
3—Heel
4—Lie
5—Whipping
6—Toe
7—Face
8—Corrugation
9—Insert
10—Neck
11—Shaft
12—Grip
13—Sole Plate
14—Loft
15—Face Progression

is that the former make clubs on order to fit certain specifications furnished by the buyer, through his professional, whereas the regular manufacturers turn out their clubs to certain standard specifications. There is also a difference in price. The standard sets are usually less expensive. But remember that the selection of good clubs is a long-time investment. They are long-lived, and, over a period of years that you will be using them, the amount of money saved at the time of purchase will dwindle into relative insignificance. Whether you decide on custom or standard clubs, however, keep the following basic specifications in mind when selecting them: shaft flexibility, shaft length, swing weight, grip size and type, loft and lie of the club head, and wood club facing.

Shaft Flexibility. Shaft flexibility, or flex, as it is often called, refers to the amount of stiffness built into a golf club shaft. Since the center of a golf shaft is hollow, flex variation between shafts is accomplished by making slight changes in the diameters of the hollow metal. Stiffer shafts have larger diameters than more flexible shafts.

The golf shaft is designed to do more than connect the grip end of the club to the hitting end: it is capable of power, of movement, of giving assistance to the hit, of getting the club head squarely into the ball. If

there is a magic wand in golf, it could well be the golf shaft itself.

The club shaft bends on both the backswing and the downswing. Just how much of this flexing will occur depends basically on two factors: (1) the stiffness of the shaft and (2) the speed of the swing. Actually, the speed of your swing dictates the type of shaft you should use. Generally, the fast swinger needs the stiffer shaft because he has the power to flex it properly. The slower swinger needs a more flexible shaft so that it can actually add controlled club-head speed at the moment of impact. The most pronounced flexing of the shaft occurs during the downswing. Usually the club head lags behind the hands until they approach the impact position. Then the shaft, like a spring, begins to straighten until the club head overtakes the hands and slams into the ball. To get maximum accuracy and power from your swing, the club head has to be slightly ahead of the shaft at impact.

A shaft that is too stiff for a player's swing will not deflect enough, and the needed spring effect will be lost. A shaft that is too soft will deflect too much, will not uncoil in time, and all control will be lost. Although shaft designations vary with different manufacturers, the majority of companies make clubs with the five following flexibilities:

Shaft Designation	Type of Player Most Likely to Use It
X or Extra Stiff	A very stiff shaft used by strong tournament professionals.
S, Stiff, or No. 1	A firm shaft used usually by golf professionals, low-handicap amateurs, and other strong players.
R, Medium, or No. 2	A medium-stiff shaft used by most men and stronger women golfers.
A, Flexible, Medium Soft, or No. 3	A shaft with medium flex used by senior men and strong women golfers.
L, Soft, or No. 4	A shaft with plenty of whip used principally by average women golfers.

How can you tell if the shafts on your present clubs are doing this job? If you are hitting them far and straight most of the time, do not worry. But, remember, if you constantly hook or slice, your shafts may be too flexible. Your swing may be too powerful for the shaft, which flexes excessively on the downswing. As a result, you may be losing control of the club head, which either is reaching the impact area too early with the club face "closed," causing a hook, or is arriving too late with the club face "open,"

causing a consistent push or slice.

Consistently straight shots require control of the club head at all times. A shaft that is too soft for your swing does not give proper control. If you feel that your shaft is not working for you, it may be because your swing is not strong enough to flex the shaft sufficiently. You may be losing the added distance that can be obtained from a properly controlled flexing of the shaft. In this connection, it is important to remember that a "stiff" shaft is not designed to give greater distance. Although most of the various shafts on the market are available in all five flexes, any one model of club may only be available in certain flexes.

Shaft Length. The shaft lengths of a set of clubs, although different from the short putter to the long driver, are "matched" to each other and to the specific function of each club. The proper method of club fitting for shaft length starts with determining your exact driver length requirement as the basis for determining the proper shaft length for every club in your set.

The length of club you use is dependent, not on your height, but on two other factors: the length of your arms and your strength. The average man who plays golf is 5 feet 11 inches and has a distance of approximately 27 inches from his fingertips to the ground while standing in a normal position. A shorter player with short arms, but with enough strength in them, can often gain extra arc in his swing by employing a longer shaft. Most tall golfers with long arms can generally

use standard-length clubs without any difficulty.

Here is a quick way to determine whether your present clubs are built with the right shaft length for you: place a golf ball on the floor and imagine that you are about to use your driver. Without a driver in your hands, get into position to hit the ball and be sure to take a position for a full swing. This will take some concentration, but you will be surprised how well you can do this even without having the driver in your hands.

After you have done this, keep your feet in position and have someone remove the golf ball after inconspicuously marking the spot on which it was placed. Now, take your driver, grip it where you normally would, and still without moving your feet, again get in position to hit a drive. When you have regained a comfortable—and natural—position, sole your driver and have the golf ball replaced on its original spot. If the golf ball now lines up too much with the toe of your club, your driver may be too short for you. If the ball lines up with the heel of the club, your driver may be too long for your most natural swing.

Your golf professional can analyze your swing and stance in more detail to determine the correct driver shaft length for you. In doing so, he will take stock of your physical make-up—the length of your arms, legs, and torso—and how you stand up to the ball, all of which determine the distance of your hands from the ground as you address the ball. Generally, the closer your hands are to the ground at address, the less shaft length you will need.

Your golf professional will also be interested in the plane of your swing to determine if it is upright, medium, or flat. If your swing is upright, you move the club head back on a plane which is relatively vertical. At the top of the backswing, your hands are positioned well above your right shoulder. As an upright swinger, you require less shaft length than the flat swinger because you stand closer to the ball when you address it. On the other hand, a golfer with a naturally flat swing moves the club head around his body in a more horizontal plane, and his hands do not get as high at the top of the backswing. A flat swing needs more shaft length than the

NOMENCLATURE OF THE IRONS

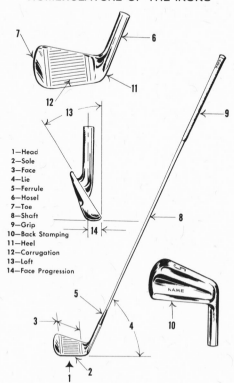

1—Head
2—Sole
3—Face
4—Lie
5—Ferrule
6—Hosel
7—Toe
8—Shaft
9—Grip
10—Back Stamping
11—Heel
12—Corrugation
13—Loft
14—Face Progression

upright swing in order for the club to reach out for the ball.

A medium swing, of course, falls between these two extremes. Once your driver length has been established, all other clubs in your set can be properly "matched" to this length. The chart below shows the "average" shaft lengths for the most popular golf clubs in a set. Club length corrections are made using these specifications as the base measurement.

Shaft Length Table (Inches)

Woods	Men's	Women's
No. 1	43	41½
No. 2	42¾	41¼
No. 3	42¼	40¾
No. 4	42	40½
No. 5	41½	40
No. 6	41	39¾

Irons	Men's	Women's
No. 1	39	38
No. 2	38½	37½
No. 3	38	37
No. 4	37½	36½
No. 5	37	36
No. 6	36½	35½
No. 7	36	35
No. 8	35½	34½
No. 9	35	34
Pitching and Sand Wedge	35	34
Putter	35	34

Swing Weight. There are two weights—swing weight and total weight—to consider when selecting golf clubs. The difference between the two can be explained as follows: *swing weight* is the weight which the golfer feels in the head of the club when he swings it as opposed to the *total weight* he would feel if he simply picked it up. That is, the swing weight indicates the distribution of the weight of a club. It is the proportion of the weight in the head compared to the shaft and grip, and it is measured on either of two different scales. One is called the official standard scale,

which is graded numerically. The other, which is more commonly employed, is the lorythmic scale, which is designated by letters A, B, C, D, and E and by ten numerical gradations in each letter designation, from 0 through 9. These designations are computed from the official swing weight scale.

A reading of, say, 20.05 on the official scale equals a reading of D-0 on the lorythmic scale. A swing weight of 21.75, or D-9, would be very strong and quite probably a club which could be handled only by someone such as a powerful professional golfer. A reading of 18.75 (C-0), on the other hand, would represent a weak club with plenty of whip and would be suitable only for a small woman. That is, A and B swing weights are exceptionally light and are seldom employed in standard clubs. C swing weights are those used by most women golfers, the average ranging between C-4 and C-7. Stronger women and men players employ clubs in the D range, the swing weight for most men falling in the D-1 to D-5 area. Incidentally, to get an idea how much head weight change is involved in a three-point adjustment, the weight of a quarter coin when added to the head of a No. 5 iron will increase the club's swing weight by three points.

The following chart indicates the most common swing weight nomenclatures which are designed for various types of players:

C-4 to C-7	For players hitting about 160 yards.
C-8 to D-1	For players hitting about 185 yards.
D-1 to D-3	For players hitting about 210 yards.
D-3 to D-5	For players hitting about 225 yards.
D-5 to E-0	For extra powerful hitters who average over 235 yards.

Stiffer-shafted clubs usually require slightly higher swing weights to achieve proper "head feel." Slight increases in head weight also improve the flex characteristics of these stronger shafts. The proper swing weight on a club

Typical Total Weight Range (in Ounces) For Carbon Steel Shafted Clubs

	No. 1 Shaft	No. 2 Shaft	No. 3 Shaft	No. 4 Shaft
Men's woods	13½ to 13⅞	13¼ to 13½	13 to 13⅜	
Men's irons	15 to 15⅜	14¾ to 15⅛	14⅜ to 14¾	
Women's woods		12⅞ to 13	12¾ to 13	12½ to 13
Women's irons		14¼ to 14½	14¼ to 14½	14 to 14½

with a No. 1 (stiff) shaft will therefore be proportionately heavier than a club with a No. 3 shaft. But remember that if you use a club with too stiff a shaft and too heavy a swing weight for your strength, not only will you tend to top or slice but also you will develop hitches in your swing. Too whippy a shaft and too light a swing weight will cause loss of distance and a tendency to hook the ball.

The total weight (or club weight) is not significant in itself. The over-all weight of a club must always be in proportion to the swing weight to give true feel. In other words, a heavy club will normally have a greater swing weight than a light club, although there would be an overlapping in swing weight for slight changes in over-all weight. Generally speaking, the heavier the club head, the more force it will impart to the ball at impact, assuming, of course, that the club head is moving at a fixed rate of speed. Balancing that is the fact that you can swing a lighter club head faster than you can a heavier one. (The principle there is that if two subjects are moved with equal force, the lighter one will be moved faster.) Actually, it is due to this that the lightweight shafts offer so much promise to the average player. That is, by using lighter shafts, the manufacturer has been able to decrease the over-all weight of the golf club, thereby allowing the golfer to generate greater club-head speed with the same amount of effort. Increased club-head speed means greater distance. Also, club-head weight has been increased, giving the golfer more weight where he can best use it, which also helps achieve more distance.

Manufacturers claim that most golfers will find they will be using one less club with lightweight shafts. In other words, where you would normally hit a No. 6 iron with a steel-shafted club, you should be able to accomplish the same thing with a No. 7 iron equipped with a lightweight shaft.

Lightweight shafts today come in a profusion of materials. Besides the lightweight steel shafts and newer super-lightweight steel shafts, there are graphite shafts, as well as those made from exotic materials such as titanium. For the purposes of comparison, here are the weights of more commonly available shafts (figures are for driver-length shafts; lower numbers represent more flexible shafts, higher numbers, stiffer shafts): Original steel shaft, 4¼ to 4½ oz.; lightweight steel shaft and aluminum shaft, 3¾ to 4 oz.; graphite shaft, 2¼ to 3¼ oz.; Zirtech titanium shaft, 2½ to 3½ oz.; True Temper Superlite shaft, 3⁷⁄₁₆ to 3¾ oz.; UCV 340 chrome vanadium shaft, 3¼ to 3½ oz.

Grip Size and Type. If the golf shot were not such a violent stroke, the size of the grips on your clubs might not be too important. But the stroke is a violent one, and if your grips are too small or too large for your hands, something in that connecting link is going to give at the precise moment everything should be firm. Keep in mind that the club head that is traveling 150 miles an hour or more at impact cannot be held delicately, or be allowed to slip from your grasp, or be so big there is no feel.

The grip of the club must fit your hands so that there is a firm bond between golfer and club. One that is too small will be hard to hold and will permit the club to twist during the hit. You will lose all control and feel of the shot. On the other hand, if the grip is too thick for your hands, you will be forced to hold the club in the meaty part of your hand; all feel is choked away, and circulation is cut off at the wrist. The arms then get tired, and the correct approach to the swing disappears.

How do you know if your grips really fit? Generally, if the fingers of the left hand dig into the heel of the palm, the grips are too thin. If there is a noticeable separation between the fingers and the palm, they are too thick. A perfect grip would find the finger tips *barely* touching the palm.

The right-size grip gives your hands that "feel" of your clubs that is essential to good club control. "Feel" in your hands is so sensitive that you can actually notice the difference when the diameter of your grip is changed by a mere ¹⁄₃₂ inch. For the record, the difference between the standard men's grip and the standard women's grip is only ¹⁄₁₆ inch.

By the way, manufacturers have a unique method of specifying the size of their grips. The standard men's grip measures ²⁸⁄₃₂ inch in diameter at a point 2½ inches from the top of the shaft and is tapered to $\frac{25}{32}$ inch at a point 5½ inches from the top. An undersize grip is described as "$\frac{1}{32}$ inch under," which means $\frac{1}{32}$ inch below standard. An oversize is "$\frac{1}{32}$ inch over," and a full oversize is "$\frac{1}{16}$ inch over."

There are a variety of styles of grips available. Whichever type you select, be sure that you are able to grip the club firmly with your fingers. You also need a grip with good traction, a grip that will not slip or turn in any weather. Moisture, whether from perspiration or the elements, must also be dispersed. On the cork and rubber grips, the golfer gets traction from the material itself and the surface design. Pockets or indentations in the grip displace moisture and prevent slipping, without the golfer's having to grip harder.

Leather grips rely on their tackiness to get traction, with an assist from the small round perforations made in the leather. These tiny holes help drain away sweat or moisture, which then evaporates in the atmosphere. The edges of the grips are skived (thinned) so that when they are wound on they form ridges or grooves down the grip which also help to stop slipping.

Through the years, manufacturers have come up with many shapes of grip other than those with circular cross sections. One reason for this was that the club twists during the swing, and this could turn the club in the hands. The other was that many golfers found it difficult, while swinging, to feel their hands were in the correct position. It is a fact that if you were to blindfold even an expert golfer and then hand him a club with a round grip, he could not square the club with the line of flight without first placing it on the ground. Today there are numerous specially shaped grips on the market to take care of this. Some have flattened sides; others have a flattening at the top of the grip; still others have a rib on the bottom or top and bottom of the grip. On putters you can now get an almost bewildering variety of shapes. There are even grips with forms which place the hands or fingers in more or less locked-in positions, but these are strictly training grips. USGA rules prevent their use in competition.

Perhaps you have wondered why most grips taper down from top to bottom. This has been the conventional shape for grips from time immemorial. The reason can be better understood by making this experiment. Stretch out your arms, with the hands together, as when holding a club. Your arms form a "V," and you will note that the opening in your hands—where the grip would be—is conically shaped and naturally fitting

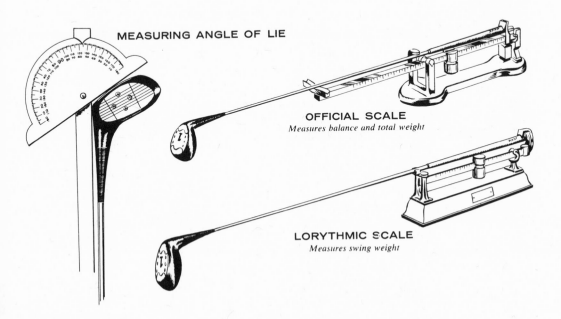

MEASURING ANGLE OF LIE

OFFICIAL SCALE
Measures balance and total weight

LORYTHMIC SCALE
Measures swing weight

the conventional grip. This conical grip, therefore, is designed to conform to the hands in action.

In choosing new clubs, or new grips for your clubs, remember this: your grips should feel good in your hands—at all times, in all climates. They should have a good, positive feel and not hurt your hands. They should enable you to grasp the club correctly, firmly, and easily to maintain control, power, and club-face alignment.

The Loft and Lie of a Club Head. The loft angle of a golf club is the angle between the face of the club and a vertical line from the sole of the club. It is the angle that gives elevation to a golf shot. The higher the number of the club, the more loft angle and, of course, the more elevation you can expect.

The difference in the loft of the same club number from one manufacturer to another may vary slightly. Also a few manufacturers put out half sizes; that is, they make a No. 2 wood with a loft of 13 degrees and No. 2½ wood (which is still called a brassie) with a 14½ degree loft. Most of the time, the manufacturer specifies the amount of loft of his various clubs in his catalogue. Therefore, if you have any difficulty in hitting the ball into the air, you may find it best to employ the style with the greater loft. But, with greater loft, the hitting range decreases.

Standard Loft Angles

Woods	Average Number of Degrees
No. 1	10–12
No. 2	13–15
No. 3	16–18
No. 4	19–21
No. 5	22–24
No. 6	24–26

Irons	Average Number of Degrees
No. 1	17–19
No. 2	20–21
No. 3	23–24
No. 4	27–28
No. 5	31–32
No. 6	35–36
No. 7	39–40
No. 8	43–44
No. 9	47–49
Pitching Wedge	54–55
Sand Wedge	58–59
Putter	2½–8

Players who have no trouble getting the ball into the air regardless of the iron they use may prefer a "strong" set of clubs. They have the clear option of specifying lofts that are one-half club less than standard. In other words, the No. 5 iron in such a set would have 30-degree loft, the No. 8 iron would have 42-degree loft, and so forth. This selection provides for a set of iron clubs from which each properly hit shot will deliver somewhat greater distance than can be obtained from a set with standard loft angles.

However, the margin for error in such a set is reduced, particularly on the long irons; and the set can be hard to handle, and mishit shots can often result.

Many times higher-handicap players are better served by a slightly "lofted" set in which each club has one-half club or more loft than standard. Such a set of clubs will be easier to handle, particularly for players who have trouble obtaining elevation on all their iron shots.

These options are also of particular interest to players who have some difficulty handling their long irons. In these cases, the player can have his three long irons specified with "lofted" angles and the rest of the clubs in the set made "standard."

The lie of a golf club is the angle between the center line of the shaft and the horizontal. It is important in the proper fit method because it is the correctness of this angle for your swing that allows you to bring the hitting surface of the club head square to the ball at the moment of impact. If the lie angle of the club is too flat—too little lie angle—the natural tendency will be for the toe of this club to dig into the ground with the heel up off the ground. Now look at the line of flight. The ball is being driven to the right in an obvious "push" or "slice" direction.

The opposite is true when the club is too "upright." The toe of the club is off the ground, and the hitting point of the club is cocked toward the left. The result is a "pulled" or "hooked" shot. These built-in equipment errors can be corrected by the player only through an unnatural adjustment of his stance or swing. Properly fitted clubs make this adjustment unnecessary.

The lie of the club should be such that the

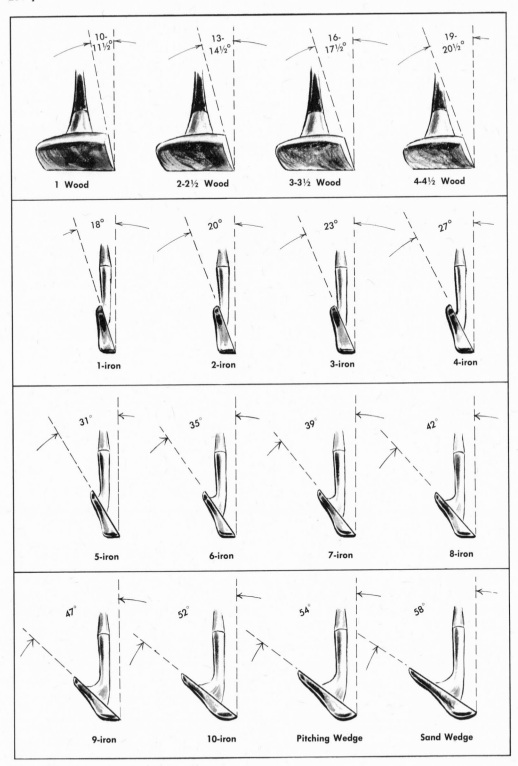

Loft angles of various popular clubs.

sole of the club can be placed flat on the ground or with the toe tilted up slightly at a normal address position. The lies of most standard clubs will be suitable for the person of average build. However, if you have either exceptionally long or short arms, you may need a lie other than standard. It is relatively easy to check the lie of your present clubs to see if it is right.

Find a floor-length mirror and take a stance with your No. 2 iron as if you were going to hit it into the glass. Pay no attention to the club head as you are setting up, except to get it square to the mirror and comfortable to your stance. Do not make the mistake of first setting your club flat on the ground and then taking your stance. If you do this, you are accommodating yourself to your clubs, and the test will reveal nothing. Now get settled and look in the mirror. If the toe of your club is up more than a fraction you need a "flatter" lie. If the heel of the club is up at all, you need a set of clubs with a more "upright" lie angle.

To determine just how much of an adjustment should be made in the lie of your new clubs, your golf professional will probably follow this simple procedure. Take a No. 2 iron of the proper length for you, grip it normally, and have someone wrap a strip of tape around the grip of the club at a point just below your right hand. Mark this strip "standard." Wrap additional strips of tape around the grip on both sides of the "standard" tape at intervals of every ¾ inch and mark the two strips of tape on each side of the "standard" tape with a No. 1, the next strips No. 2, and so on. Now take your stance in front of the mirror again and address the "ball." If the toe of your club is up, indicating the need for a "flatter" lie, gradually choke up on the club without changing the position of either your hands or your feet. The result of the action will be that the club head will move in toward your feet, and the toe of the club head will begin to drop. Keep doing this until the sole of the club becomes level, indicating a proper lie. When this position is reached, check your hand position to see what numbered tape is now just below your right hand. The No. 3 tape in this position indicates that you need your set made "3

clubs flat." The No. 2 tape indicates "2 clubs flat," and so on.

The reverse of this procedure can be used if it is determined that the standard No. 2 iron needs to be made "upright" to fit you. Instead of choking down the grip, allow the grip to slide through your hands, moving the club head away from your feet. Do not change the position of your hands or feet. As the club moves away from you, the heel of the club will begin to drop, and when the sole of the club has become level, the tape number just below your right hand will indicate how many clubs "upright" your set must be made.

In most of their conventional matched set lines, the major manufacturers offer iron sets with five variations in lie, which is the angle at which the club head joins the shaft. The variations are standard lie (54 degrees), flat lie (53 degrees), upright lie (57 degrees), medium lie (55 degrees), and medium upright lie (56 degrees). In general, players of short stature would prefer the flat or medium flat lie clubs, and taller players would be better accommodated with the upright or medium upright lie clubs. But the main consideration is whether your swing tends to be flat or upright. As noted, a professional is your best source of information on this and similar matters.

Wood Club Facing. The "facing" of a wood club refers to the angle between the club face and a line exactly perpendicular to the desired line of flight. If this angle is "zero," the club is said to be faced "straight." A right-handed club is said to be "open" when the club face looks slightly to the right. It is said to be "closed" when the club face looks slightly to the left. The true facing of a club is often difficult for most golfers to recognize because the club maker is dealing with slight but important angles when he faces the club.

To see just how important these slight angles can be, consider the fact that a 2-degree modification in face angle will affect the left-to-right position of a 200-yard drive by as much as 21 feet. This degree of error results from the off-line hit effect of an open or closed face at the moment of impact. It does not allow for the added slice or hook effect, which can be as much or greater, bringing the combined error close to 15 yards. How many times have you wished your ball was a little to the left or right on your drive? Proper club facing can help you keep the ball where it belongs: in the fairway.

The club maker "closes" the face of a club to compensate for a natural slicing tendency on the part of a player. Since the "average" golfer has the tendency to slice, most standard wood sets are made with slightly closed faces. This built-in hook in a standard set, no matter how slight, can be disastrous if the player happens to have a natural hook, for it only accentuates the problem. And it probably will not be sufficiently helpful to a natural slicer who usually needs more of a built-in hook than he happens to get in a standard set. Any reasonable degree of facing is possible with custom-made woods. The real problem is to find out how much of your hook or slice is natural and how much is caused by a faulty swing or other playing error. Your golf professional can help you correct basic swinging errors and prescribe how "open" or "closed" the faces of your woods should be. Bear in mind at all times that custom clubs are not intended to be a crutch to compensate for faults that should be corrected in the swing itself. Whether you finally favor open or closed, it is never wise to go to an extreme either way. Remember that in purchasing your custom clubs you have already introduced several variations that can have eliminated much of what caused your off-line shots in the first place. Be content to establish, with the help of your golf professional, what tendency your normal ball flight has; then be moderate in picking your particular club facing.

When selecting your clubs, be sure that you keep all the factors—shaft flexibility, length, swing weight, grip design, loft, and lie—in mind. Remember that no other sport is so exacting as golf in that so many specifications must be met to a precision fit of implement and player.

The Putter

Putters—the clubs, that is—are as individual as neckties. At most pro shops today, you get just as wide a choice. On the market there are literally dozens of types of putters, each as distinctly different to the eye as a polka dot is from a red stripe. At one time you were blissfully limited to a choice of six—Calamity Jane, Blade Type Mallet, Blue Goose, Mills, Schenectady, and Cash-in—but today the choice is maddeningly wider, although most of them are but subtle variations on these original six.

Actually, the selection of the putter can be one of the most important choices you make that can have an effect on the final outcome of your score. It is next to impossible for anyone to tell you what putter is best for you. Only you can make the final choice of what putter feels best. But to help you make your selection, keep these factors in mind: (1) feel in your hands, (2) proper balance, (3) lie and loft, (4) weight, (5) shaft length, and (6) shape of the head.

You should be able to tell if the putter has good feel and balance merely by swinging it back and forth a few times and hitting a

Some of the many styles of putters that are on the market today.

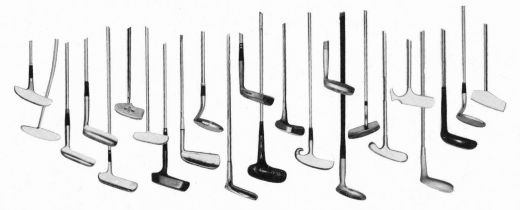

few balls with it on the practice green. Select a putter that is easy to line up and easy to look at. Although putting styles have changed little over the years, many new putters have been added to the golf equipment line. You should not have much trouble finding a putter to suit your particular needs and putting habits if you spend a little time looking over the various models.

The lie is the angle of inclination between the head and the shaft, measured with the sole (bottom) of the putter lying flat on a level surface. The average angle of inclination is about 65 degrees. A putter with that approximate angle between head and shaft would be said to have a medium lie. An angle of, say, 72 degrees would put the putter into the flat-lie classification, and an angle in the 55-degree range would give the putter an upright lie. Putters are, of course, available nowadays with any head-shaft angle you specify. But there is no real need to know about specific angles, or even about the three general classifications of lies, because a set of simple tests will tell you what you want to know. Make the first test standing on a level surface. Take the putter and stand to the ball as you normally would to putt, comfortably situated, with your eyes directly over the ball and your hands as you would usually place them. If the sole of the putter is approximately flush with the surface on which you are standing, the lie is basically right for you.

Just how much loft is a matter of controversy for experts, but most professionals agree that the most important factor is the type of greens on which you are playing. If the greens in your area are smooth and fast, you will need a putter with less loft. When the greens in your section of the country are slow and rather rough, you should use a more lofted putter. Four degrees of loft are considered average and are suitable for all types of greens. (Lofts of putters usually range from 2½ to 8 degrees.) Your club professional can be of great help on the subject of putter loft.

As to putter weight, the conventional amount is from 15 to 18 ounces, with the head accounting for not quite two-thirds of the over-all weight. Shaft lengths range from about 33 to 36 inches. Unless you are of highly exceptional build, the weight and length in the ranges specified above should be right for you. If you exceed these limits, you will understand that you are going against what years of experience have revealed to be essentially correct. Most professionals use a 35-inch shaft length and an over-all weight of 16 or 17 ounces.

Although the final decision on the weight of the putter is up to you, the golf course where you expect to do most of your playing should again enter into your consideration. If the greens are fast, the lightweight putter is probably best for you. But if the greens are particularly slow, a heavier putter may be best. Heavier putters cut down on your touch, while light ones can require almost too firm a "hit" even for short 3- or 4-footers. Medium-weight putters work equally well on fast and slow greens.

While there are many styles and types, most can be placed in one of two broad categories: the blade and mallet. Both major classes of putters come in two variations: a standard shaft connecting at the heel of the head and one connecting near the center of the head. Either shaft may be goosenecked just above where it reaches the club head. While individual preference is the most important criterion in the selection of a putter, many professionals state that the mallet type performs best on slow greens, while the blade types are more suitable for fast greens. But the important thing to remember is not to just walk into the pro shop, take the first putter you see, and buy it. Take two or three out on the putting green and practice with them until you find one that feels most comfortable. This is the putter best for you.

The Golf Ball

Golf balls vary in price to some extent, but you get what you pay for. Use the best brand and model consistent with your type of game.

Ball compression has been a somewhat magic word in ball setting. Some ball makers use it in their sales presentations, while others protest that it is a grossly exaggerated and misunderstood factor. Most ball makers will

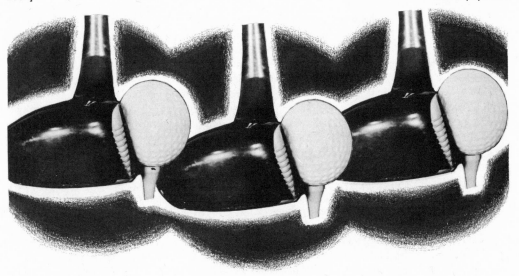

How a ball looks as it is hit.

point out, however, that compression—high, medium, or low—is a factor in the make-up of all golf balls and that it plays an important role in helping the golfer achieve the maximum performance from the ball. Such a statement is true, but it is far too general in its scope. Indeed, it is almost impossible to deal with ball compression in broad terms and apply it to specific golfers.

Technically, compression is a measure of a golf ball's resistance to deformation, or "flattening" when force is applied, which is what happens when the ball is struck by a club. When a golf ball is hit, it is flattened or compressed. The more power it takes to compress it, and also the higher the compression, the more it resists this so-called deformation. For this reason, high-compression balls are spoken of as being harder. This is true only in regard to "feel," and not to the durability of the ball's cover. A higher-compression ball will cut more easily than a lower-compression ball (if both have a balata cover), because the harder core of a high-compression ball will not "give" and absorb the force of a blow as much as the softer core of a low-compression ball.

In a wound golf ball, compression is determined by the rubber thread winding around the ball's center, which usually is either liquid, solid rubber, or steel. Approximately 30 yards of winding is used to make a wound ball, and the higher the compression, the more the thread is stretched. For a high-compression ball, the rubber winding is stretched more than eight times its relaxed length to a total of more than 240 yards.

For a golf ball to have "go" or distance, it must be compressed or "flattened" to a certain degree. Therefore, a soft, easy swinger would not benefit from using a higher-compression ball over a low-compression ball because of his inability to compress or "flatten" the higher-compression ball. In the same sense, a strong, powerful swinger will be able to hit a 90-compression ball farther than a 70-compression ball, assuming, of course, he has the strength to compress the higher-compression ball. To put it in easier terms, if you see yourself as the easy swinging type, do not play with a ball of 100 compression. In fact, there is only a small percentage of touring professionals who play with a 100-compression ball, so the average golfer can expect his best results using a ball in the 70- to 90-compression range. And, as pointed out earlier, the lower-compression ball will not cut as easily as the higher-compression ball.

Compression once was one of the properties commonly used to judge the quality of the ball and its performance. Today, without any doubt, compression is a property to determine feel and click of the ball at impact.

Yet this, too, is actually only a partial measurement, since initial velocity (see USGA Rule 2-3 in Section IV) and coefficient enter into it. (Coefficient is defined as the ratio of the velocity of the ball and the club after impact to their relative velocity before impact.)

Aside from the feel and the click, there is one more factor that must be considered: the ball's trajectory. The higher the compression rating, the less impact-area distortion the ball will have. As the area of distortion measured on the club face becomes greater, the trajectory of the ball will be higher. The touring professional, with his grooved, powerful, and accelerating swing, can flatten out a high-compression golf ball and get the trajectory, as well as the click and the feel, that he wants. But the amateur cannot. He needs a softer or lower-compression ball—a ball that, with his moderate impact force, will have the same feel, click, and trajectory that the professional gets from a ball of his choice. (*Note:* The number of dimples, their depths, and their diameters also can dictate the ball's trajectory. The deeper the dimples, the higher the ball will travel and the more sensitive it will be to hook and to slice. When the dimples are softened, the ball becomes less inclined to wayward shots and will travel lower.)

Weather is also a big factor when choosing the correct ball. A low-compression ball is better for everyone on cold days, because of the difficulty in flattening a hard ball when it is cold. That is why even most strong swingers would be better off teeing up with a lower-compression during those early rounds in the spring or late ones in the fall.

Most manufacturers label *high-compression* conventional balls (90 to 100) with black brand name and black numbers. Other markings are as follows: For *medium-compression* balls (70–90), black brand name and red number; for *low-compression* balls (70 and under), name and number all in red. Most solid construction golf balls have a compression rating of medium.

Remember that the amateur who uses the 70- or 80-compression ball can expect to get the same performance that the pros get from the balls they use, thanks to recent technical advances in the manufacturing. In other words, quality is not determined by com-

pression. The results with any ball will be proportional to the amount of skill the player has. In the final analysis, compression is not something of which the player should be either ashamed or proud. The important thing—the only important thing—is to find a ball that fits *your* swing and will do as much for *your* game as possible.

The Golf Bag

A bag to carry your clubs in can be very simple or very elaborate. Bags are made from leather, vinyl or nylon plastic, or canvas, or they can be a combination of two of these materials. They also come in a variety of shapes, colors, and prices. It is usually wise to purchase one large enough to hold all the extra items—rain gear, hand towel, Band-Aids, salt tablets, insect repellent, pencils, extra matches, extra glove, balls, and tees—that come in so handy. Thus, be sure the bag is of ample size. Too often a small bag is used, and the golfer has to jam his clubs into too small a space, raising havoc with the grips and endangering the shafts as well. Also, if you plan to carry the bag yourself, use a lighter basic bag, but one that still has room enough for the important accessories.

Golf Carts

The pull or "caddie" cart was invented in the late 1930's to answer the demand of golfers on public links who wanted to play but could not afford caddies. The pull cart was a cheap way to take the load off your back, and the influx of new players (combined with the financially debilitating effects of the Depression) created an instant market. The first pull carts were heavy, unwieldy, and nonfolding, but they sold. Manufacturers, convinced that they were onto a good thing, streamlined their carts after the war, making them lighter, folding, and easy to carry.

The pull-cart industry has even withstood the advent of the electric golf car and the concomitant resistance of some private clubs to allow pull carts on their courses. A fleet of golf cars is a virtual gold mine for any club, and many of them have forbidden the use of pull carts because they would cut

An electric golf car (left) and a golf cart (right).

into this certain income. A few clubs also feel that pull carts tend to give off the air of a "public links" course and are thus undesirable at a country club. But the dearth of caddies has offset the strictures of private clubs, and the rise in the median standard of living has cracked the rigid status system of golf, freed more people to play, built more public courses, and broken the captive market of the clubs with their stables of electric cars. There are new players and new courses —and new markets for pull carts. For the beginner, a pull cart is certainly preferable to the golf car because of its cost.

If you are familiar with the wheel, you should not need much instruction on the mechanical operation of a pull cart. But every beginning golfer should realize that pull carts are becoming a major source of concern for golf course superintendents and agronomists. Loaded down with a heavy bag, fourteen clubs, extra clothing, balls, and tees, and sometimes the player too (when the cart includes a fold-out seat to rest on), the pull cart is a mass of weight centered on two wheels. The wheels dig into the turf, cause ruts, and enrage greenskeepers. From the outset, manufacturers agreed to establish a minimum diameter for the wheels, setting the standard of 10 inches. The larger wheels spread the dead weight of the cart over a bigger area, reducing the tendency of the tires to plow channels in

the turf.

Electric or gasoline golf cars are fine for the senior golfers or ones who cannot take the rigors of the golf course walk. In selecting one of these mechanized vehicles, use the same care and techniques as you would in purchasing an automobile.

Golf Clothing and Golfing Accessories

Forty years ago or more knickers were considered the style for men playing golf. Today any sport clothes, such as slacks, sport shirts, and sweaters are acceptable. Many golf clubs even permit their players to wear shorts while on the course. But whatever clothes you wear, be sure that you are comfortable and have freedom of movement. It is a good idea to wear a bright-colored cap or hat. It helps other players to spot you.

Shoes with steel or tungsten spikes on the heel and sole are essential parts of your golfing equipment. They provide the necessary surer footing, thereby permitting you a more solid foundation from which to hit the ball. Without them, you will slip and slide when making your shots. If golf shoes fit properly, there should be no breaking-in period, blisters, and the like. On a properly fit blucher shoe, the two flaps at the top of the arch, when laced, should be approximately one-half inch apart. Be sure the ball of the foot rests in the correct location and that the heel fits snugly, but not tightly. A blucher-type shoe is easier to fit than a bal style because there is more room for adjustment across the top of the arch. It is suggested that a man with a high arch should avoid purchasing a bal shoe.

A look at the majority of top touring professionals would seem to rate a golf glove as an important piece of equipment. True, a fine glove can offer a sensitive feel of the club and more confidence in your grip. On the fashion side, golf gloves are becoming attractive accessories. With the growing range of hues avail-able, gloves now can provide bright color accents or be matched to a color-co-ordinated outfit for the total look.

There are many accessories that you will wish to have available in your golf bag. Rain gear of some type—at least a water-repellent jacket and hat—is advisable to have in your bag. A golf umbrella is also a good rain accessory. Club covers for woods are an accessory that pays dividends by keeping the clubs in good condition. Actually golf is a game of gimmicks and gadgetry. There is no limit to the accessories that you can acquire.

CARE OF GOLF EQUIPMENT

Undeniably, the golf equipment of today is the finest ever. A not surprising corollary to this statement is that it is also the most expensive. To protect your sizable investment, it makes good sense to take good care of it.

The Golf Clubs

Golf clubs, as previously described, have undergone a great evolution, even in recent years. Changes have taken place from end to end, although the nomenclature remains substantially the same. That is, a wood club still consists of head, insert, slug in sole, sole plate, screws, whipping, shaft with steps or gradations and a grip, while an iron consists of head or blade and hosel, shaft, either screwed in the hosel or held in place by a pin, shaft with steps or gradations, and grip.

While in play, you can save your clubs a lot of grief by just a little thought. For instance, never bang the club on the ground in a fit of temper. This shock and vibration will bend the shaft where it is not meant to be bent, and it will be incapable of flexing properly. Remember that an error of one degree at the outset can amount to as much as a 30-foot error at the target 200 yards away. This shattering experience to the club can also cause the inside wall of the shaft to flake off or to loosen some of the impregnated lead inside, making an audible noise as the club is taken from the bag and brought into address position. It has been known to crack heads.

Dirt and grime left on your clubs can have an effect on your game. For example, the addition of one-eighth of an ounce to the club head can change the swing weight one point. The wear of the grip can also change the swing weight. Therefore, replace any grip that has begun to wear out before it gets too thin. If you wait too long to replace a worn grip, the new one will not feel right to your hands, and it will be a long time before you regain your touch.

Do not attempt to repair any damage to any of the components, and do not tinker with sole plates, shafts, or heads. Major alterations are the job of skilled craftsmen qualified to handle the particular brand of club you are using. The repair of clubs has become so highly technical and demanding that at least one major manufacturer either trains its own men around the country or approves only those recommended by their district managers. And above all, do not attempt to drill the heads of the sole plate screws when they are not easily removed with a conventional screw driver.

Modern-day woods have a finish that rivals the top of a Carnegie Hall piano. This pressure-impregnated finish makes the woods practically impervious to moisture, eliminating the chances of swelling, shrinking, or warping as they were once wont to do. This, of course, is an important break-through: not only does the head's stability remain intact; its swing weight is not altered by conditions. And they are much easier to keep clean. Where once the job of refinishing heads kept the lights on in the pro shops until the wee hours of the morning, nowadays such extra work is just about nonexistent.

To restore the gleaming, piano-top luster on the woods, apply a coat of furniture polish that also contains ingredients that will remove marks or stains and follow with a good brushing with a soft cloth. If ball marks are or remain the problem, buff with the special rubbing compound of the type garage men use to rub down the finish of the exterior of cars, giving them their high protective sheen.

But no set of woods will look good long if the golfer feels that head covers are too much of a bother. Due to the different lengths of the woods, if they are left uncovered, the top of the longer ones will rub against the sole plate of each of the shorter ones, cutting ugly and permanent scratches into the varnish painstakingly put there by the manufacturers. Head covers represent very little money compared to what they are protecting; however, if they should get wet, remove them immediately, wipe off the woods, and replace the covers after they are thoroughly dry. Do not leave your clubs in the rear of your car over long periods of time, since the hot and damp weather may affect them.

Wash composition club grips occasionally with a soapy water solution and then rinse and dry. Clean leather grips with naptha, followed by two light applications of a good leather preservative.

The neck whippings on the woods play an important part in the clubs' strength, and some firms have changed from the thread to a plastic-coated ferrule. But in either case pay close attention to keep it in top condition, and if repair or replacement is necessary, have a qualified professional do the job.

You might appreciate the permanency, balance, and maintenance ease of your present woods a bit more by this review of what had to be done to refinish a head just a few years ago. For one thing, the old finish had to be completely removed. This was usually done by soaking the club head in a can of lacquer thinner, like acetone, and wiping off the finish as it peeled, continuing this operation until all the finish was cleaned off. Or if the job was really tough, the finish was scraped off with a hand scraper or piece of glass, sand-

paper, or steel wool. Imagine what this did to the club's swing weight and balance! This also lessened the club's stability, because more often than not the filler, a paste that filled in the pores of the wood, was gouged out. Filler then had to be reapplied and allowed to set for some 15 to 20 minutes until the gloss disappeared, then wiped off with burlap, first across the grain, then lightly with the grain. The filler next had to dry for about 48 hours before the surface could be sanded. (If you are still inclined to remove the finish from present-day clubs, do so with a leather wheel. The finish will disappear, but the filler will not; in fact, the leather wheel actually burnishes the old finish back into the pores.)

The choice of finishes in those days was shellac, then lacquer, followed by the spar varnish and plastic finishes of today. Note these directions to be followed after the application of varnish: Lay on two full coats, not thick enough to sag or ripple. Sand lightly with garnet paper between coats. Allow the final coat to dry for three days. Since dirt and mud will clean off more readily if the final coat is rubbed with pumice and linseed oil on a felt pad, it is advisable that you do so. Then rub with the grain, but do not press hard enough to burn the top coat. When the gloss is gone, wipe clean with a dry cloth. An occasional wiping with a silicone cloth of furniture polish will keep the club new-looking all season.

The irons have also undergone some changes, but the reasons for and the methods of keeping them clean remain the same. You cannot expect to play your best golf with clubs that are clogged with dirt or bits of grass; not only will the ball react crazily after being hit but the actual "feel" of the club will be altered. To control the shot and get proper backspin on the ball, keep the scoring free of dirt and the club face clean. To do this, first clean the corrugations in the club face with a toothpick or tee. Then give the clubs a thorough washing in a soap and water solution, rinse, and dry. That is all. Never use any harsh brushes, steel wool, or abrasives, else you will cut through the nickel-chrome plating, adding to the problem and ruining the club's appearance. This nickel-plating process is relatively new, having undergone extensive testing for ruggedness and corrosion resistance under the severest of conditions. It is comparable in thickness to that found on most automobile bumpers. Precisely 0.001-inch of nickel is electroplated over the carbon steel, followed by a chrome flash: the nickel to resist corrosion, the chrome flash for added appearance. All in all, one firm gives each iron a series of seven polishings, most of them to prepare the surface for the nickel coating, which lasts thirty minutes, and the chrome flash, which is given 7 minutes. If the head is too rusted or pitted, arrange to have it returned to the manufacturer for repair or reheading.

Grip adjustment, breakage of clubs, or bent shafts as pertaining to the woods apply to irons as well. Do not take any unnecessary chances: have a qualified professional do the repairing, or have the club sent back to the manufacturer.

The Golf Balls

Golf balls require very little care, but here are several tips to remember:

1. Always store balls in a dark, cool place, below room temperature if possible. Deterioration of golf balls is a chemical action, and such deterioration slows down in a cool, dark area.
2. When storing balls, wrap them in paper and keep away from solvents.
3. Keep all balls clean. Mud on a ball will directly affect its flight, since it may close up the dimpled surface.

The Golf Bag and Accessories

The care of the golf bag depends on the type of material it is made of. For example, duck and canvas bags are easy to wash. Just immerse them fully in soapy detergent. Rub with a brush if exceptionally dirty. Then rinse thoroughly and allow to dry.

Nylon and most other plastic bags can be washed with a good soapy detergent to get out mud, grass stains, and other spots. Rust marks are almost impossible to remove, but good, hard rubbing will improve them a lot. (Never clean a nylon bag with a dry-cleaning fluid, as it may dissolve the rubber backing which gives body to the nylon and waterproofs it.)

Leather bags should be cleaned with saddle soap or a good leather conditioner to prevent cracking and excessive wear and to add to the looks. Do not oil a leather bag, as it will pick up dirt and dust too easily.

Regardless of material, replace the strap when there is evidence of wear and prevent the inconvenience of a possible strap break in the middle of a round. Also check the condition of the zippers and avoid the expense of losing costly items. Do not allow anyone to sit on the bag and destroy the rings that give it its shape and strength, and be a little careful in inserting or removing clubs. Pulling them out or thrusting them in forcibly causes abrasions to the finish of both woods and irons.

Prolonging the Life of a Golf Umbrella. A golf umbrella is a handy addition to a golfer's complement of supplies. Remember to open it when it rains and again when it is time to dry. Do not pound it into the bag compartments. You will break the ribs and damage the fabric. Keep the umbrella in its sheath when possible.

Caring for the Golf Shoe. All golfers would agree that the right golf shoes can have a great effect on their game. Yet, most either neglect to or do not know how to properly care for these valuable items of equipment.

Remove grass and dirt from the spikes, or cleats, and soles before placing them in your locker, carryall bag, or car trunk. The temperature changes from outside to locker room and especially the variations in the trunk of the car would crack and stiffen any leather articles and tend to deteriorate rubber products. Keep the shoes treated and polished with a good leather conditioner, and always use good shoe trees to keep the shoes in shape.

Remember that mud and early morning dew are the greatest enemies of golf shoes. Continual exposure to this moisture, as well as an improper drying process, breaks down the fibers of the soles, and they will get out of shape eventually. Avoiding moisture is virtually impossible for the golfer. However, you can follow a simple procedure to protect your shoes. After golf shoes get wet, upon return to the clubhouse, immediately put well-ventilated wooden shoe trees in them, and dry at room temperature—never on a radiator or in a hot automobile trunk. When they are thoroughly dry, spray on a coat of silicone around the welts and polish with a good grade of shoe wax before wearing again.

It is important to use the proper methods of cleaning golf shoes, too. For leathers such as calfskin, for example, wash with a mild soap, dry them properly, and polish. For alligator and other reptile skins, wash with saddle soap. This type of soap keeps scales from cracking. For poromeric shoes, wash with soap and water and buff with a dry cloth. White poromeric material may require a bit more care in cleaning than darker colors. Since poromeric is porous, dirt can build up in the creases that naturally develop on the vamps of shoes. Therefore, according to shoe manufacturers, white poromeric shoes should be thoroughly cleaned in this area.

Check the golf shoes periodically for loose or missing spikes. Take measures to correct the situation. Also when the spikes on the metatarsal bone are worn half down, it is time to replace the entire set.

When storing during the winter months or for extended periods of time, the golf shoes should be dried on shoe trees, sprayed with a coat of silicone, polished, and stored in a dry area of normal room temperature. It is also a good idea to replace spikes and worn shoelaces at this time so the shoes are ready for wear the next season.

Prolonging the Life of a Golf Glove. Leather golf gloves should be handled with the same care given to any fine piece of apparel. A few simple rules will assure long service from any high-quality leather golf glove:

1. Slip glove on by gently pulling at the cuff from both the front and back alternately. Flexing the fingers helps work them into the glove. Then smooth each finger and the thumb, beginning at the finger tip and working the leather toward the palm.

2. Slip the glove off one finger at a time. Then smooth it out to help retain its shape and size, particularly if it is damp. Do not allow a damp glove to dry in excessive heat or sunlight, which could destroy its suppleness.

3. Leather golf gloves should be washed before they become too soiled. Use rich suds of mild, neutral soap or flakes in lukewarm water. Rinse thoroughly in clear, lukewarm water. Then use a very light suds rinse. This will help to keep the glove pliable and soft. Do not squeeze or wring. Roll the glove in a heavy towel to blot. Unroll at once and blow into the glove to shape it. Dry gradually again, avoiding excessive heat and sunshine. When the glove is slightly damp, work it between your fingers or on your hand to soften the leather. In fact, some manufacturers even suggest that you shampoo the glove while it is on your hand. To improve the leather's luster after the glove is dry, buff lightly with a soft cloth.

Caring for the Golf Cart. Clean your "caddie" golf cart the same as an iron club, and do not forget to oil or grease the axle. Use mineral oil, too, to help preserve the metal finish. If your cart is painted and becomes chipped, you can touch it up, of course, with a little paint of the same color.

Motor golf cars should be serviced and cared for as directed in the manufacturer's instruction booklet. Be sure to follow these instructions to the letter.

Taking everything into consideration, the initial cost of top-grade golf equipment is rather high, but with little care the investment can be one that lasts a lifetime. You will play better, receive more for your money, and enjoy the game to the fullest by getting the best and by keeping it in top-flight condition.

SECTION V

Principles of Golf

FUNDAMENTALS OF GOLF

There is no getting away from it: golf is a difficult game to play—to play well, that is. Most people, however, make the game a good deal tougher than it has to be simply because they do not take the trouble to learn the fundamentals of hitting the ball. They handicap themselves at the very beginning by not learning the proper grip, the most important part of the golf swing. They do not understand where their feet should be placed on the various shots, how the shoulders and hips should operate, or how to make use of their weight—or lack of it. As a result, they seldom improve, no matter how diligently they practice. They do not improve because, having failed to learn the fundamentals properly, they groove all their bad habits on the practice tee until every clumsy idiosyncrasy becomes second nature; until, in other words, they are beyond all help. Get the fundamentals straight in the beginning, and improvement will come as a matter of course.

There are three basic operations to every properly executed golf shot. First, there is *footwork*, which is needed to provide proper balance throughout the swing. Second, there is *body action*, which actually swings the club and determines and regulates the amount of power in the swing. Third, there is *hand action*, which enables the power generated by the body to reach the club. And as the hands apply this power to the club, they have the added duty not only of placing the club in the correct position but of keeping the club in that position throughout the swing. It is this position of the club that determines the style and character of the shot and, of course, the direction. But remember that using your hands effectively starts with a good grip.

The Grip

Teaching professionals agree that the primary concern in anyone's game should be the grip. A picture-book swing will make little difference in your score if you are holding the club incorrectly. Actually no other step in golf has as many parts to play as the grip, because it is the grip that is basically connected with every movement of the swing. Most professionals consider that the grip is about 75 per cent of the swing.

There are three basic grips in use today. Over 95 per cent of the touring professionals and leading amateurs use the *Vardon*, or overlapping, grip. A few, like Art Wall and Bob Rosburg, use the *full-finger*, or baseball, grip, while players like Jack Nicklaus and Gene Sarazen employ the *interlock* grip, but of different types. Regardless of the type of grip used, the most important factor is that it should be completely comfortable.

The Vardon Grip. The late, immortal British golf professional Harry Vardon popular-

The basic three golf grips (left to right): interlock, baseball, and overlap.

ized the overlapping grip in the 1900's, and since then this grip has been referred to as the Vardon grip. Here are the steps that should be taken in forming this popular grip:

1. With the club head on the ground in the normal golfing lie or position, place the extended left hand, with the thumb close to the fingers, slightly over the top of the shaft, with three knuckles visible. The shaft should now be diagonally across the base of the first and middle fingers and across the palm below the ring and little fingers, with the end of the club nestled comfortably in the heel of the left hand. This is a combination finger-and-palm grip, and greatest pressure will be exerted by the last three fingers. The heel supports the grip.

2. The left thumb is then placed on the top right side of the shaft. The V formed by the thumb and forefinger should point in the general direction of your chin, or slightly to the right of it. (With small hands, the V of your left hand is in a better position when it points toward the right shoulder.) Two knuckles should be visible on the left hand, or certainly no more than three. In placing the thumb on the shaft, make the knuckle concave. This permits the wrists to set properly at the top of the backswing.

3. Now place the right hand on the grip so that the little pocket in the heel caresses the left thumb. Make certain that the first thing the right hand touches is the left thumb. Cuddle this thumb with the pocket in the heel; then place the right hand over the left so that the "life line" of the right palm covers the left thumb. The little finger of the right hand should overlap the first finger of the left hand, resting there with no apparent pressure. As with the left hand, the V formed by the thumb and first finger should point toward the chin or slightly right of it. Actually, you can even move both hands still farther to the right— say, with the V's pointing to the right shoulder —until you start hitting solidly, as this position almost forces you to take the club back inside. If you start to hook too much, you can gradually move the hands back toward the top of the shaft. But remember: the thumb should nestle in the palm of the right hand throughout the swing. If this is done, the hands will remain together. This is particularly important at the top of the swing where a loose grip can lead to a hit from the top. By all means grip with the last three fingers and the palm of the left hand, and have a secure grip with the fingers of the right hand. But the link between the two hands is provided by the thumb of the left hand staying in the palm of the right hand. At impact your hit will be more solid.

The variations of the Vardon grip are, of course, endless. Just as no two persons' fingers and hands have precisely the same size and shape, so, too, no two persons have *exactly* the same style of the overlapping grip. But, to get a correct Vardon grip of the club, your hands should be about in the same place as they are when they hang naturally by your sides. The handle of the club will run diagonally across the upper part of your palm, extending from the inverted V formed by the left index finger as it bends around the club grip. The little finger of your right hand is placed on top of the index finger of your left hand. The handle of the club should fall into the fingers of your right hand. Do not think that there is only one proper place to grip the club. You should not be afraid to go up and down the handle of the club if you feel the shot calls for it. Let your emotions, rather than strict adherence to form, be the guide. Then the grip will feel natural to you, and the shot will have a better chance of succeeding than if tension had been caused by an uncomfortable position. For instance, by gripping a No. 3 iron low, you would take advantage of less loft for a short, under-the-branches type of shot. In other short shots around the green, both your determination and accuracy improve when your club is choked up, due to the added firmness.

As has already been stated, the right-hand grip is mainly a finger grip to prevent a tendency to clutch too tensely with your right hand. Such tension will slow your swing and tend to prevent a free, full, smooth application of power. Keep both your fingers and hands close together so that they can work as a single unit. This gives the left hand a better chance to control the usually stronger right. Actually, you should have a feeling of holding the club more firmly in the left hand than in the right. In the correct golf swing, the left hand should control the swing and the right should provide much of the power.

Grip so you have a feeling of controlling the club and of feeling the weight of the club head, but not so tightly that you are stiffening your forearms or making your body rigid. Such a tight grip causes the left wrist to lock and encourages picking the club up too abruptly on the backswing. Remember that there is a difference between firmness and stiffness in a grip. Do not stiffen your wrists or arms when gripping the club. Use just enough firmness to keep it under control. Be careful not to grip the club too tightly. A death grip causes the left wrist to lock and encourages picking the club up too abruptly on the backswing. Two important don'ts: don't loosen the grip at impact—and don't change the pressure of the grip during the swing.

The Vardon grip, which finds seven fingers placed directly on the handle of the club, may feel awkward at first, but this feeling should disappear with practice. There are, of course, fractional variations that can be made to suit the individual. But all too many times the correct grip is discarded in favor of gripping the club in a way which is most comfortable. Do not be complacent and assume that you're employing the proper grip just because it feels "right." If after a fair trial the overlapping grip still feels very clumsy, you may then, and only then, experiment with the other two golf club grips.

Interlocking Grip. In this grip, which is the second most popular one, the little finger of the right hand lies between the middle and forefingers of the left hand and is wrapped around the forefinger. The fingers and thumb of the left and right are otherwise the same as in the overlapping grip. That is, with the proper interlock, the correct grip is one in which the V's formed by the crease between the thumb and first finger of each hand point over the right shoulder and the thumb of the left hand rests in the life line of the right. Keep the hands and fingers close together, and grip the club firmly in the same manner as for the Vardon grip.

The interlock grip is recommended for players who have small hands. While this grip ensures that the hands are closely unified, it may not give the average player sufficient club control because it places only six fingers on the golf club handle.

Full-Finger Grip. Although this grip, also called two-handed or ten-finger grip, is the newest fad in grips, it is very similar to the baseball grip which was the original golf grip abandoned in the 1890's. The fingers in the two-handed grip do not overlap or interlock. The club is held approximately the same by both hands. Since this grip has all eight fingers on the handle, maximum club control is usually obtained, but it does not unify the hands as well as do the other grips. Thus, the success a player has with the full-finger grip depends greatly on how well his hands are functioning together. If you must employ this grip, here are some points to remember about it:

1. The first finger and thumb of the right hand, the first finger and thumb of the left, and the palm of the left hand should always keep an even pressure on the shaft. These are the points where you receive the "feel of the club."

2. The hands should not turn, or permit the shaft to turn, during the swing; yet the grip should not be too tight. The full-finger grip is more popular among women and with men or boys who have weak hands.

Regardless of the grip used, recheck it after your swing to see if you have changed or altered it unconsciously during the act of swinging. A firm grasp on the club grip with your fingers will keep the club from turning in your hands. The pressure in your fingers need not be extreme, but it needs to be sufficient to hold the club firmly. Proper grip pressure is necessary for club control and a smooth swing. Remember that a golf glove helps maintain the correct grip throughout the swing.

The Stance

Any athlete will prepare himself well before executing whatever he has to do. The approach to the golf ball is known as the address or stance. Once acquired, the stance is simple.

The first consideration is the width of the stance. The proper distance between the feet entails a compromise between two conflicting needs. The closer the stance, the easier it is to achieve smooth footwork for the weight shift and pivot. On the other hand, the wider the stance, the easier it is to maintain balance. Most golfers fail to reconcile these considerations in changing their stance for different shots. Since maintaining balance for a drive is more difficult than for a 50-yard pitch shot, the drive obviously requires a wider stance. Yet many golfers use nearly the same width of stance for every shot, when they should reduce the distance between the feet as the

length and arc width of the swing diminish. Proper width of stance for different golfers can vary considerably, but here is a good general rule: keep the stance as narrow as possible consistent with good balance.

To demonstrate the validity of this rule, try swinging a club first with your feet as close together as possible, then with your feet as far apart as possible. In the first position you will have maximum freedom of motion for weight shift and pivot, with knees free for easy movement. In the second position your knees will lock under the sheer structural necessity of functioning as the legs of a roughly equilateral triangle supporting the body. Your pivot and weight shift will be severely restricted. Moreover, your whole body will drop closer to the ground, flattening and therefore constricting the arc of the swing. Despite the problem of balance, most players find that they can swing harder with the feet-together stance than they can with the straddle-legged stance. Also remember that the spread of your feet gives the foundation so important for pivoting in the full golfing swing.

Next consideration in proper stance is the problem of how far to stand from the ball. Here the common error again entails a failure to adapt the stance to the club length and the arc of the swing. Too many golfers stand too far from the ball on a drive, and as the club length shortens, the magnitude of this error increases. Some golfers stand almost as far from the ball for a pitch shot as they do for a drive. This tenses the arms and upsets the co-ordinated thrust of the right arm which should brush close by the right hip as the club head enters the hitting zone. As the club length decreases with increasing loft, and the arc of the swing becomes tighter and more upright for short irons and pitch shots, you must obviously stand closer to the ball.

Standing too far from the ball ordinarily places too much weight on the toes and tension on the backs of the legs, which must then balance the golfer like a bent model of the leaning tower of Pisa. The leaning-tower golfer will often find himself hitting the ball on the heel of the club face and pitching forward during follow-through. This will usually cause a slice. Conversely, the golfer with his weight on both heels will probably find him-

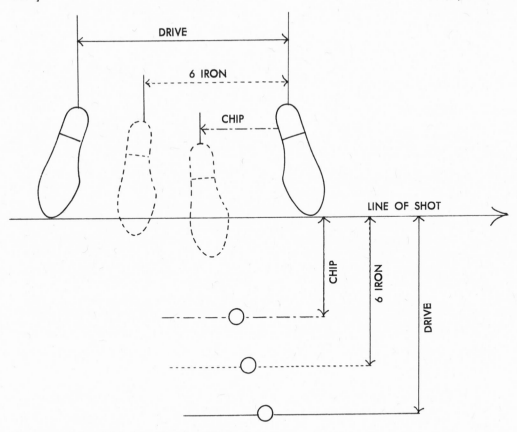

The stance varies slightly for each of the clubs used.

self hitting the ball on the toe and smother-hooking and falling backward. To compensate for standing too far away from the ball, the golfer bends over too much in an effort to get closer to it. Of course, if you are taller than average, standard equipment will not suit you. You should then acquire clubs from one-half inch to an inch longer than standard. The best way to solve poor-posture problems is to make sure that you straighten your back and crouch at the knees. Remember, bend the knees, not the back. The improved posture will allow you greater freedom of movement in the knees and lower body, and your weight will be thrown back on your heels where it belongs for power. In addition, the more upright stance permits better balance and an easier, freer, fuller shoulder turn on the backswing. That is, when addressing the ball, be sure to stand close enough to it so that your club head reaches it comfortably, with your arms hanging naturally from your shoulders. When

the sole of the club is flat on the ground, the position of the club handle determines how far from the ball you should stand. Keep your hands and arms comfortably close to your body. That makes it easier to groove your swing.

A finer point concerns the question of open, square, or closed stance. An "open" stance has the right foot placed across the line of the shot; a "square" stance has both feet parallel to this line; and a "closed" stance has the left foot placed across the line. The stance should open from a slightly closed or square stance for a drive to an open stance for wedge shots. Moreover, since for short shots there is no need to turn the right toe outward to facilitate the pivot, the right foot should turn progressively inward as the stance width and shot length decrease. For chip shots it should be aligned parallel to the left foot. This parallel alignment of the right foot, with the right knee bent inward, restricts the tendency toward superfluous swaying, a common error of those who take too wide a stance for short shots. More information on the employment of the different types of stances for the various golfing shots can be found in following portions of this section.

The position of the ball in relation to the feet also varies with the type of shot being made. When the ball is hit with a horizontal blow, maximum power and distance are obtained; for woods and long irons, the ball is most often played opposite the left heel. On medium irons, line the ball about equidistant between the feet. The feet should be closer together than on long shots. For short-iron shots, bring the feet closer together and play the ball farther back toward the right heel. Remember that more height and less roll result when the ball is placed near the right foot; therefore, as the range decreases the ball is moved back.

In the correct stance, your right shoulder should be slightly below the level of your left. To achieve this automatically when addressing the ball, grip the club with the right hand and set the blade behind the ball, placing the right foot as you do. Then put the left hand on the grip and the left foot in place. When you do this you will find that the right shoulder will be lower than the left at address. As a rule your head should be slightly behind the ball.

One common address error is to assume a stance facing squarely toward the ball, with the hips aligned parallel to the direction of the shot and both knees locked or bent in the same position. To see why such a stance is wrong, think of the body position at impact. Flinging the club through the ball requires a rather full hip turn to the left, with the right elbow brushing by the right hip and the flexed leg pouring in power. To smooth the path of the swing toward the correct position at impact, your stance at address must approach the position at impact. Aligning the hips parallel to the direction of the shot at address partly destroys the function of the backswing, which stores torsional energy later released as the body spring unwinds during the downswing.

For the proper position at address, turn your hips slightly counterclockwise; that is, turn your left hip slightly away from the ball, your right hip toward the ball. Though neither leg should be straight, this hip turn will naturally exaggerate the right-knee bend toward the ball. Note, however, that the proper position at address is a compromise between orienting the swing for the full hip turn at impact and an easy start for the backswing. Thus your counterclockwise hip turn at address is much less than the full hip turn at impact.

Maintaining balance in this proper position at address requires a different distribution of weight. Bear in mind four things:

1. Distribute weight about equally on each leg.
2. Stand with the toes pointed *slightly* outward.
3. Turn knees slightly inward so the weight bears somewhat on the inside edges of the feet.
4. To a considerable degree, distribute weight on the ball of the right foot; to a lesser degree, on the heel of the left foot. (Keeping the weight on the ball of the right foot keeps the right leg "alive," ready to pour power into the shot. Transferring the weight to the right heel during the backswing is death.)

The most difficult footwork action is the roll of the left foot. You must not lift the heel too far clear of the ground. A good golf swing has a compact stability in which the major body movements are lateral (weight shift) and torsional (pivot). Since it raises the whole body, allowing the left heel to rise an inch or two above the ground introduces into the swing a superfluous bobbing motion, destroying its smooth efficiency. It ruins one's chances of setting the left heel before starting the downswing, the key to efficient use of the swing's stored energy. By setting the left heel before starting the downswing, you can delay release of the swing's stored energy-dissipating action known as "hitting from the top."

The proper roll of the left foot accompanies a proper weight shift at the start of the backswing. Because of the old exaggerated taboo against swaying, many golfers fail to make the subtle hip shift and weight transfer required *before* pivoting. The weight transfer is essential to develop the swing's full potential power. At the start of the backswing, as the weight shifts to the right foot, the left knee should bend easily inward, and the left foot should merely roll about the inside edge of the ball of that foot. The heel should barely rise off the ground, even on a full swing. On short iron shots (say, No. 8 iron on up), the heel need not leave the ground at all.

This proper rolling action of the left foot is a compromise between two opposite extremes: the heel-raising rotating action about the toe, warned against earlier, and a lateral rolling about the inside edge of the *whole* foot. The latter action generally accompanies premature pivoting, in which the weight remains predominantly on the left foot and the left side buckles. This is commonly a fault of golfers who start the backswing from a tense, motionless position without a "forward press." The recoil from the forward press will generally accomplish the weight transfer to the right foot and facilitate the proper rolling action of the left foot about the *ball* of the foot.

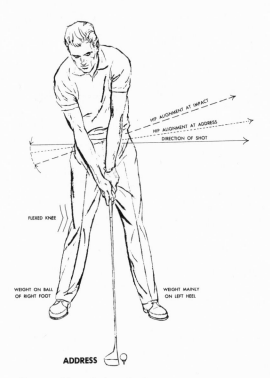

ADDRESS

Proper address is important.

Before starting the downswing, set the left heel and then let fly. With the start of the downswing, you have performed the last conscious act of the swing. If you find yourself falling forward or backward, with the symptoms mentioned earlier, look for sins committed elsewhere. To use a slightly mixed metaphor, if you start off on the wrong foot you cannot change stride in the middle of the swing. That is, many golfers, when addressing the ball, point their toes and flex their knees to the ball. This tightens the hips, restricts body turn, and forces a lateral sway or slide with weight on the toes during the backswing. Now, if the same golfers in addressing the ball were to take a square stance, then move the toes of their left foot slightly to the left and bend the right knee a bit sideways toward the left, the left hip would be turned back, thereby creating a relaxation on both hips. The player may now feel as if his stance is open, but if he checks he will find it remains square. He may also use a closed or open stance with the left hip procedure with the same results. By pulling the left hip back, the player should find himself in a natural forward press position with the hands slightly ahead of the ball and the right knee pointing to the ball. Relaxing the left side makes it easy to take the club back, the hands, left knee, hips, and shoulders performing in a solid, one-piece action. This creates a torque, a coiled rotation that takes the club back on the correct inside arc, thereby completing a full turn with most of the weight on the right foot. The golfer is now ready to swing into and through the ball.

To develop the feel of good footwork, assume a narrow stance (about 8 inches clear between heels) and swing the club easily and continuously, alternating full backswings and downswings. Concentrate on keeping that left heel close to the ground so you can easily set it before starting the downswing.

The Swing

The purpose of the swing is to move the club head in a controlled arc that will bring it against the ball at the most efficient striking angle and, where distance is an important consideration, at the greatest possible speed. Unfortunately, the true golf swing is a highly unnatural action and must be learned. Very few players have what can rightly be termed a natural swing.

A good golf swing is one continuous, in-

Bobby Jones' famous swing as caught by high speed camera.

divisible, free-flowing motion with a definite shape: a part of a circle, or an arc. When you create a swinging motion in the club, you get centrifugal force, the greatest force you can generate with your body. Now, the formula for force is speed squared times weight. In the golf club, most of the weight is in the club head. So the golfer's single object should be to swing the club head with gradually accelerating speed so that by the time of impact he is generating the greatest amount of force possible. (This speed of swing is personal, so that only by trial and error will the golfer learn how fast he can swing without destroying the swinging action.) Centrifugal force proceeds from a center to the outside. This center or zero point is somewhere in the body. But you cannot swing with zero, so you swing the club head with your hands. Your hands are the only part of the body in contact with the club. They are also the only medium through which the power of the body is

transmitted to the club head and the only place where you can "feel" the swing.

When you swing the club correctly, the centrifugal force sets up a constant outward pull in the club head. As you swing back and through, you can feel this outward pull in the hands. This "feel" of the club head in your hands is what keeps you in the groove; in fact, it *is* the groove. When you swing the club head, you do not have to think about the myriad "bits and pieces" of golf tips that most golfers worry about. As you swing, the outward pull of the club head will keep your left arm extended, cock your wrists, maintain your balance, delay the hit, and so on *automatically*. If your action is a swinging one, the body will respond to the swing of the club head naturally. It is when the body wants to get into the act too vigorously and too soon that all the damage is done. The larger muscles, those of the shoulders, arms, back, and legs, should be considered admirable followers of the hands, but disastrous leaders. Often, this problem is caused by fear, which creates tension in the hands. The hold on the club should be firm enough so you have control of the club, but light enough so you can feel what you are doing with it. If the golfer squeezes the club, feel vanishes, the wrists stiffen and cannot act freely as they should (like the hinges on a door), and the basic rule of the swing—freedom—is violated. All the golfer has left to hit with is the larger muscles, and the results are swaying, heaving, and chopping at the ball. Feel the club head in your hands, and then you can swing it.

A good golf swing, of course, presupposes a proper grip, which maintains correct club-head angle, and a correct stance, which helps to maintain body balance and control. The swing can be broken down into five basic phases or steps: the waggle, the forward press, the backswing, the downswing, and the follow-through.

The Waggle. This is the name given to the little series of preparatory movements made between the time you take your stand, or address the ball, and begin your swing. Actually the waggle is the swing in miniature. It has a tendency to keep you relaxed while at the same time giving you a feeling of the rhythm of the swing. The waggle consists merely of short, loose, back-and-forth movements of the club head. The club head is carried back 12 to 24 inches from the ball and returned to position immediately behind the ball. This procedure should be repeated two or three times. Some golfers even permit the club head to pass back and forth over the ball several times. Whatever feels most relaxing and comfortable for you should be employed. During the waggle, you obtain a better feel of the club and loosen the wrist tension. In addition, these brief preliminary swings permit you to feel the firmness of your grip and stance to ascertain that they are correct. Any semblance of a tight grip is also avoided, which in turn lessens the danger of a hurried backswing. Just before the swing is taken, the club head should come to rest on the ground in back of the ball.

The Forward Press. The forward action is a suggestion of a movement of the right knee, hip, and shoulder around to the left that moves the hands an inch or two in front of the ball so the shaft of the club is slanting forward. This movement is performed almost subconsciously with the forward movement of the hands, arms, and body. The value of the forward press is that it gets the body, hands, and arms in simultaneous action easily and smoothly. The forward press starts the swing movement. Immediately after it, reverse the action of the body twist and start the backswing. In other words, the backswing is actually started from the recoil of the forward press.

The Backswing. The initial movement of backswing should be a turning of the hips from left to right. The shoulders will turn as the hips turn, and the arms turn with the shoulders; it is all one smooth, co-ordinated motion. The club head is not picked up with the hands, but starts back from the ball due to the recoil of the forward press. Throughout the entire swing your left arm should remain straight. In this beginning of the swing, the hands should operate simply as extensions of your arms. There is no hand action in this initial movement. If the swing starts correctly, the club head starts low along the ground and follows the turn of your body. If this first movement is incorrect, and in a great percentage of players it is, it is almost impossible to get good results.

During this early stage of the backswing, your body weight will begin to shift to the inside of the right foot. The shift of weight from your left foot should find the weight that remains on the left side centering along the entire inner edge of the foot. This rolling action takes place with no lifting of your left heel during the entire first portion of the backswing.

Most professionals agree that the first few feet of the golf swing are the most important. If you get started on the right track, very probably you will stay there throughout the entire swing. However, if the first motion is not correct, anything can happen. How do we get the right groove on the backswing? First, take the club back until the shaft parallels the ground. Now, here is precisely where the check point is reached. Drop the club from the right hand and see if the right hand is not in a perfect handshaking position. If your club does not fall into this slot, you are probably troubled by a "flying" right elbow and a bad slice. Or else your elbow is jammed too tightly against the right side, restricting proper arm and shoulder movement. Try this check point. You will find the cure for these faults surprisingly easy if you practice this little handshaking position exercise a few minutes before playing.

Getting back to the backswing itself, your body should continue to turn, the hips and shoulders turning as a unit. Your arms will also follow the windup of your body. As the arms rise, the wrists should begin gradually to cock. (There should be no conscious cocking of the wrists at any time during the swing. The cocking of the wrists is gradual as you proceed with the backswing.) This cocking of your wrists is executed correctly when the wrist movement is that which occurs if the palms are placed together and in front of the body, the thumbs being brought toward the body.

The left arm is kept straight throughout the backswing. Although your right arm will bend at the elbow, it should remain quite close to your body. The loose or "flying" right elbow is a common fault among high-handicap golfers, and in good measure it is the reason for their poor performance. The right elbow should stay close to the side all the way through the backswing, and at the top of the swing the forearm and elbow should be pointing to the ground. However, in search for power, the tendency is to let it sway way out, resulting in bad position at the top and a loss in efficiency and control coming into the ball. When the elbow comes away from the body, it forces a turn that produces an outside-in swing. That is, the club face comes into the ball from outside the line, rather than from inside, where the power is. Keeping the right elbow close to the side may seem awkward at first, but it will pay off later in good length and control, especially on tee shots.

The length of your backswing need not remain constant. Actually, to be effective, it may even differ from one day to the next. For example, it would change if a round of golf were played in the morning when you might be more refreshed than if you were to play after a tiring day of work, or when you are fighting a heavy wind, or when playing a tight course where accuracy is a premium. The length of all backswings on tee shots

should fall between the point where the left arm is parallel to the ground (minimum) and where the club shaft is parallel to the ground (maximum). A good check point is to go back as far as you can to the maximum position without spraying the shot and without losing hand control of the club. Your immediate goal is timing. The proper change in the length of the backswing can rid one of a slice, hook, push, or scoop and at the same time increase total distance. Many professionals test their backswing on the practice tee before playing, solely to develop their timing for that day's play.

Keep the head steady all through the swing. Many golfers raise their left heel much too far off the ground, and as a result, when the heel returns to the ground during the downswing, it is perhaps as much as an inch away from the spot in which it had originally been. In terms of the club face meeting the ball, however, this error can be greatly magnified to the extent that it can cause a bad slice or hook. Care also must be taken not to permit your right foot to roll toward its outer edge or your right knee to sway out of play. The latter is the focal point of the pivot. It must stay in the same spot throughout the backswing. At the top of a full swing with a wood or a long iron, the only weight remaining on your left foot is on the outer edge of your big toe. On shorter clubs this transference of weight is not so pronounced.

Keep your grip on the club firm throughout. At the top of your backswing the club should be held just as firmly in both hands as it was when taking your stance. (At the top of the swing, however, there is more pressure on the last three fingers of your left hand than at any other place in your grip.) Any looseness in the grip at any time, of course, can cause trouble, but at this point in your swing, it can be disastrous.

The Downswing. While the proper swing is a fluid rhythmical motion, there should be a very *slight* pause at the top of the backswing before beginning the downswing. This pause permits the backswing to be completed before starting the club downward. Without this slight pause, the swing becomes too fast and jerky, and the proper action of the club head is made impossible.

The hips initiate the downswing, not the

hands. The hands merely "ride" into the hitting zone in a fully cocked position through the turning of your left hip to the left and a pulling down of the left arm. Your shoulders should follow your hips around. (If the hips follow the shoulders around you will find the club will travel from the outside in, which is wrong.) As the body uncoils, the weight should be largely shifted to the left leg. That is, in starting the downswing, the weight is shifted to the left side, and the left hip rotates in a counterclockwise motion. The weight shift lowers the hands when you get to the top of the backswing. During the lowering, the wrists remain cocked. The longer you can delay uncocking your wrists, the better. This way, you can generate more club-head speed in the hitting area. The hitting area is located from 6 to 8 inches behind the ball. During the downswing, the hips should continue to move counterclockwise and should be well out of the way until you finish, with your stomach facing the hole. During the swing, the head position should be exactly as it was at the address. A cautionary note: never let your hands move past the bulk of your weight at any time. Your hands move faster than your body. Consequently, you must start the downswing by first moving the hips. This creates the slight pause at the top of the backswing. The most important part of the swing is balance, and you get proper balance with the correct hip action. If you maintain good balance, you will have no trouble keeping the ball in play, whether you hit it solidly or not. As a result of proper weight shift, the hands are automatically pulled down into correct position, the right elbow close to the body. The head should remain absolutely steady.

As your hands enter the hitting area (the left hip will have turned well out of the way of the shot), the wrists still should be cocked; that is, the right hand has not yet begun to work. At this point, the wrists should be uncocked to bring the club again into alignment with your left arm, thus delivering a powerful blow through the ball. Do not make the mistake of forcing your hands ahead of the club past the hitting area, as some golfers do in a misguided effort to steer the shot. On every shot from a putt to a drive, you should consciously feel that the club head is leading from the instant of impact. Once the club

head catches up with the hands, it should never fall behind.

At the moment of impact, the wrists should be completely unwound and the left arm still straight. Do not spoil an otherwise sound swing by forcing the wrists to uncock early in the downswing in an attempt to throw the club head at the ball. This action is premature and gives the appearance of hacking or chopping at the ball. You will eliminate the early hit problem entirely if you get your hands pulling the club head through the ball and into the follow-through without strain. Remember that as you approach the bottom of the swing, you are only half through. You may have heard that the best way to eliminate casting (early breaking of the wrists) is to imagine you are trying to hit the ball with the butt of the club handle. While this advice is good, it does not go far enough. It has often been found that most golfers, when they think their hands have reached the "butt hand-to-ball" position and feel the club head dragging behind, will snap their wrists in a faulty effort to recoup. It is far better for the golfer not to think of snapping his wrists. Continuous pulling of the hands will automatically allow centrifugal force to uncock them, swinging the club head down, into, and through the ball. This pulling theory is demonstrated every day by the trick-shot artists who, with their hinged shafts, rubber-hose shafts, and chain shafts prove that centrifugal force must be the key to timing and club-head speed.

Lunging forward with your upper body and head must be avoided. If your swing is correct up to this point, the body from the hips down will move smoothly while the portion above the hips will remain behind the swing. All of the motion up to this point is designed to permit the hands to hit the ball. Here is a quick check to determine if there is proper co-ordination between the body and the swinging of the club. Have a friend place his hand in the hitting area where impact would be if you had a club in your hand. Then place your left hand beside your left hip. The feeling should be of hitting your friend's hand with your right hand at the same time your hip strikes your left hand. If the two are not simultaneous, your swing just is not grooved; and, after all, a grooved swing is what every golfer is looking for.

The Follow-Through. If the swing is properly executed, the club will follow the line to the hole until your wrists naturally begin to turn. The club must hit into and through the ball, with the club head held steady until the arms are fully extended in front of the ball. That is, the tenet about keeping your head down is one of the most common pieces of advice in the whole philosophy of golf. To a point, it is certainly sage advice. But only to a point. It is not wise to adhere to this thought throughout the whole swing. Somewhere in the course of the follow-through, you have to let the club head come up. After the ball has been hit, the hips, the shoulders, and the arms are still turning naturally. By trying to keep the head down at this point of the swing, you will restrict this natural turn. On the contrary, the head should turn easily and naturally with the shoulders on the follow-through because the restraint of holding the head down after the ball has been hit will also put restraint on the follow-through.

The finish of a full swing will find your hands well up above the shoulders, and the head should be turned toward the target area but at the same level as at the start; there should be *no* straightening up. At this point, your body weight will have been shifted completely to the left foot. All the tension will have left the right side, and the right toe will be the only part of the right foot that still remains on the ground.

One essential element of the golf stroke, regardless of what path it may take, is a smooth, even acceleration from the top of the swing to and through the ball. Anything that disturbs this smoothness and introduces a jerk into the swing is bound to upset the timing and destroy the accuracy of the blow. It is this picture of gradual acceleration that eludes the average player. Once reaching the top of the swing, he can see but one thing to be done: to hit as hard and as quickly as he can. He does not always realize that the appearance of ease is simply the result of leisurely and well-timed hitting. Rhythm and timing are the two things every golfer must have; yet no one knows how to teach either. The nearest approach to an accurate description of what they are is found in the expression of this conception of swinging. The golfer who hits at the ball rather than through it has no sense of rhythm. Similarly, the golfer who, after a short backswing, attempts to make up for lost space by initiating the downstroke with convulsive effort has no sense of rhythm. The only one who has a chance to achieve a rhythmic, well-timed stroke is the player who in spite of all else swings the club head.

WOOD SHOTS

To most amateurs, the woods are simply implements for gaining distance. To most professionals, they are subtle scoring devices. Contrary to what you might observe as a member of a gallery, distance to a pro is of only secondary importance in the woods. He knows that in the process of creating a par round he will have to take at least fourteen shots with the driver and five or six more shots with the fairway woods. Together, these shots will constitute more than one-quarter of all the shots he will take. Needless to say, therefore, he tries to use them as judiciously as possible.

Most golfers find that woods are easier to use than irons. For one thing, the standard woods—the driver, brassie, spoon, and No. 4 —are usually employed off the tee or only from good lies in the fairway. Also, a wood club has a wide, flat sole designed to right the club if it should be swung a little too deeply into the turf.

The popularity of woods can be seen by the introduction of the No. 5 and No. 6 woods. Many golfers, especially women and beginners, find that these woods are easier for them to use than the long irons. This is particularly true of the No. 5 wood as a substitute for the No. 2 iron. Many beginners find that they have difficulty in getting the ball up consistently with this long iron. On the other hand, the No. 5 wood, because of the slightly greater loft in its face, is an easy club for lifting. It gives the same or slightly more distance range than a No. 2 iron. To a lesser degree, the same relationship holds for the No. 3 iron and No. 6 wood.

There are, of course, many times when

woods cannot be used, even where distance is needed. Nine times out of ten, woods should not be employed when the ball is in the deep rough or in a close fairway lie. There are cases, too, when the distance you probably could obtain with a wood would only expose you to hazards that could be avoided by a shorter, but more controlled, iron shot. As you can see, golf is a game of many clubs: fourteen, to be exact.

The Tee Shot

Driving is the offensive part of golf. Nobody can score well who cannot drive well, who cannot drive accurately with all the distance of which he is physically capable. Actually, if you can consistently split the fairway with good distance from the tee, you will have a big psychological advantage over your opponent. On the other hand, a mis-hit tee shot puts you on the defense from the start. A good tee shot can mean pars and birdies.

The first step in the tee shot is to tee the ball up on a wooden or plastic tee. But teeing the ball is an individualistic affair and varies as each person's perspective varies. Golfers who have the feeling of hitting under and through or on a high trajectory like to see the ball well off the ground. The high tee, then, is recommended for those who stay behind the shot well or remain a little longer on the right side. They sweep through, as compared to those who prefer to look at a ball just off the ground because they hit through. If you can move to your left side smoothly, or if you tend to hit down on the ball (and get away with it), tee it low. Where does the slice come in? Low-ball hitters generally fade the ball, because they will open the face of the club at impact to conform to the terrain, as customarily happens when a driver is used from the fairway. Conversely, a ball that is teed high will encourage a hook. For those who feel that it helps to tilt the tee slightly when playing downwind, do so. Any idiosyncrasy is healthy as long as it is believed. But definitely use a tee on the par-3's. Your "lie" will always be good, the height can be adjusted to personal taste, and uniform contact can be made every time.

Whether a wood or an iron is used in a tee shot, a full-swing stroke is usually employed

and is accomplished in the same manner as the basic swing described earlier in this section. There are some points about that swing, however, that should be reviewed with special emphasis on the tee shots.

First, the stance most generally used is either square or slightly closed, with the right foot back from the desired line of flight of the ball. Line up your drive with the ball opposite your left heel and your shoulders at a right angle to the target. When lined up in this manner, you should be able to look over your shoulder down the fairway. Your weight should be evenly distributed on both feet at the address with the knees slightly bent or flexed. Grip the club firmly, but not tightly, with the left hand in full control.

As the backswing starts, let your body turn naturally and shift your weight to the right foot. About halfway back, your wrists will start their cocking action. At the top of the swing, the club should be back over your shoulders and approximately parallel with the ground. Do not allow it to dip below the horizontal.

One of the worst faults all too many beginning golfers have is to speed up their backswing whenever they are faced with the prospect of attempting for extra distance off the tee or, as a matter of fact, anywhere else on the course where added distance is desired. Slugging forces you to exceed your swing capabilities—forces you out of character, so to speak—and the distance you might get is just not worth the harm you will probably do to your timing. Timing is, of course, very important in golf. The hands must be timed with the hips, and you can't speed up hand action without also speeding up the hip turn. Swinging harder than normal makes this timing impossible and so defeats its own purpose, because distance is the direct result of this timing and not, as most people seem to think, the result of a harder swing. As a check point on swinging within yourself, you should feel that at the top of your backswing the shaft of your driver has not gone beyond a line parallel with the ground.

The hurrying or slugging action also throws you off balance. If you get your backswing started just right, so that it does not affect your balance or stance over the ball, you can control it more easily the rest of the way. You

Al Geiberger executing a drive from a tee.

should arrive at the end of your backswing in position to start the downswing with your hands together, and the whole action should be compact so that when you start down you are still in balance and still in good stance. Your chance of hitting the ball correctly is then extremely good. But the only way to achieve this satisfying sequence of events is to start exactly right. At the outset, there should be no excess motion or excess effort to impair the smoothness of the swing. If you begin nice and easy when your stance is relaxed, your balance will remain good. Consequently, you should have no trouble keeping this balance as well as the correct motion throughout the swing.

The downswing should begin with the unwinding of your hips, bringing the body weight onto the left foot. This action will bring the hands into the hitting area (about waist level) with the wrists still cocked. This is the point at which you begin to "unleash" the power in your wrists. But do not roll your wrists. Whip them through so that your hands return to the same position they were in at the address of the ball. The reason for this is to keep the club face square to the ball. One of the major faults of beginning golfers is to bring the hands (wrists) into play too soon, causing a definite loss of club-head speed. Remember that speed and timing produce distance; but most of the club-head speed is generated in the last 90 degrees of the hitting arc.

For the sake of control and consistency, it is just as important that the trunk of the body (from the hips to the head) remain at the same angle throughout the swing as it is at address. If the trunk is raised on the backswing, you top the ball; if it lowers on the way down, you hit behind the ball. Concentrate on keeping the trunk steady through the hitting zone. You can acquire this feeling by keeping your head as free of movement as you possibly can. Swing the club through the impact zone, riveting your head behind the spot where the ball was teed. As the club passes through this area, throw the club head out toward the target, allowing your hands to come to a high finish. This "hands high" action encourages an inside-out pattern in your swing. The steady trunk keeps the arc consistent, bringing the club along the same path on which it went back. Do this, and you will observe both finer control and greater distance on all your wood shots.

You have not completed your tee shot preparations until you have determined where you want your ball to stop and have checked on your alignment. This ritual should become a routine prerequisite to any shot, because only then will you begin to discipline yourself and your game. First, note the position of the flag and location of hazards or trouble. Then decide which will be the best approach to the green. Always select a target area or object in the background and hit toward it. Unless you are a *very* accurate driver, always leave yourself a safe margin for error in your tee shots. Do not aim too close to out-of-bounds lines, water hazards, and so on, even if it means getting into the best position for your second shot. Play it safe and keep the ball in play.

In selecting a target, be fair with yourself. Visualize an area at least the size of a green that is within your capabilities to reach. Remember that you can get just so much distance out of your clubs and no more. Once the target is chosen, align yourself properly. Many professionals recommend that you sight the line of flight by walking up to the ball from the rear, then position your feet so that an imaginary line drawn between your toes (or heels) is parallel to your intended direction. Guard against unknowingly aiming too much to the right, in what you may think is a desired closed stance. You may never become a top-rate golfer until you learn to swing the club from inside out; but aiming right is not the solution, because you risk blocking the left side, forcing you to pull your body and hands across the ball improperly. Before teeing off, pick out a target area, check your alignment, square your stance; and when you stay with the shot, the correct action follows.

The Fairway Shot

When playing fairway wood shots, you must swing your club even more skillfully to get the desired results than when hitting a teed ball. Such shots require the ultimate in a sound swing and sound thinking.

The number one trouble many golfers have with fairway wood shots is getting the ball into the air. Quite often this difficulty is due to the use of the wrong wood. For example, the fairway woods most golfers use are far too deep in the face. These woods may work

fine when you are playing under the so-called winter rules, but they will not enable you to get the ball out of the relatively tight lies you will find under the actual rules. A fairway wood should be shallow enough so that the top of the ball lies above the top of the face. In addition to not being shallow enough, most fairway woods do not have enough loft. A No. 3 wood, for example, should have about 17 degrees of loft. As a matter of fact, on most golf courses where you will play, you will find that the No. 3 wood is more effective from an average fairway lie, and it follows that you will get more lies of this type than the exceptional ones that require the No. 2 wood. (Many touring professionals do not carry a brassie any more, not only because of the fourteen-club limit but because they do not have the occasion to use it.) The No. 4 wood is usually employed when the lie is a little too close or a little too poor in the location of the ball to make the No. 3 a safe choice. This club can also be a great deal of help if you are in the not-too-deep rough and require length on your shot. Since it parts the grass rather than cutting it as the club head moves into the hitting area, the No. 4 wood will not lose as much club-head acceleration as an iron. Therefore, when hitting a fairway shot, just do not grab any wood and hit and hope. Instead, exercise your best possible judgment in selecting the proper wood under certain conditions and subscribe to the following philosophy: do not always try for maximum distance with fairway woods. Many times it is good to hit the ball "soft," as the pros say. By hitting the ball "soft," it is not meant that you hit the ball more easily than usual. To the contrary, you hit full out on the shot, because altering your timing is always dangerous business. Actually you shorten the length of the shot (without any loss in accuracy) by choking the shaft about 1 to 4 inches. Then, addressing the ball in your normal manner, you swing as you ordinarily would. While it sacrifices distance, choking up a little on the grip makes for a shorter swing, an easier swing, a more relaxed swing, and, as a consequence, greater accuracy and surer results from fairway woods.

The differences between wood shots from the tee and from the fairway are slight and amount only to the positioning of the ball. On tee shots, the ball was hit slightly on the upswing side of the stroke. This could be accomplished because the ball was teed up off the ground. But, in fairway shots where the ball is on the grass, the wood swing must be slightly more downward in nature so that the bottom of the arc is reached a slight bit sooner in the stroke. To be precise, with the fairway wood you want to catch the ball just a trifle before the club reaches the very bottom of the downswing. To put it simply, you want to hit down on the ball. Actually, although the club is traveling down, it is also traveling forward at great speed. Immediately after impact, you will reach the bottom of your swing arc and hit a fraction of an inch below the turf or at the exact spot where the ball has been resting. No power will be lost by hitting the ground then, because the ball is already on its way. Swinging this way, the angled club face will consistently send the ball climbing into the air.

To accomplish this, you must change the position of the ball in regard to your stance. On tee shots, the ball was played opposite the left heel. On fairway shots, the ball is played a half-inch to 2 inches back from the left heel so that the bottom of the swing arc is reached a trifle earlier. Actually, the distance back from the heel depends on the number of wood being used. For example, the No. 2 wood is played only about a half-inch back from the left heel, whereas the No. 3 wood usually is played about 1 inch back. The No. 4 wood may be played anywhere from 1 to 1½ inches away from the left heel. In playing

most fairway woods, the square stance should be used.

To prevent topping the fairway woods, you must maintain a constant hip level throughout the swing. You can do this by turning the hips smartly toward the left at the start of the downswing. This lateral action will keep your feet firmly planted on the ground throughout the swing. As a result, your weight will work across the instep of your right foot to the instep of your left foot. With proper hip action and footwork, you will soon develop a smooth release of hand and arm power. This, combined with the natural loft of the wood, will sail the ball well into the air.

The lie of the fairway also has an effect on where the ball should be played. On an uphill lie, for instance, play the ball nearer your left heel with a slightly closed stance and use a club with a little less loft: either a No. 2 or No. 3 wood. On a downhill lie, play the ball nearer your right heel with a slightly open stance and employ the club with the most loft: either a No. 4 or No. 5 wood. In other words, you do not want to get ahead of the ball on an uphill lie or behind it on a downhill position.

Another minor difference between a wood tee shot and one from a fairway is the position of the hands in respect to the ball. On tee shots the hands at address are located slightly behind the ball, whereas on the fairway variety the hands are above or slightly in front of the ball. Aside from these minor differences, the swing of a wood from a fairway is the same.

Common Wood-Shot Errors

Unfortunately, in golf, as in everything else in life, we make errors. But in golf these errors show up as slices, hooks, skying, topping, and the like. The following are some results and causes of some mental and physical errors that occur on wood shots, from both the tee and fairway, and ways to eliminate them.

Slices. As any competent teaching professional knows, the most common fault among golfers is, by all odds, the slice. Even when playing their best, fully 90 per cent of all golfers will have trouble with the slice at some point or another in their round. It is the mistake most golfers are most apt to make, particularly when the pressure of a match becomes intense.

What causes the slice? Obviously, left-to-right spin is being imparted to the ball. The club face is being left open and then permitted to cut across the ball from outside in instead of inside out, as it should. There are times when knowing how to slice is important. For instance, a good golfer can guard against hazards by fading away from the trouble.

To slice, take an exaggerated open stance, which is one with the left foot drawn back from the stance line (this line is parallel to flight line which points directly to the objective) and the right foot advanced forward over the line. This brings the club head into the ball from outside the line of flight to the inside and imparts cut to produce the spin of the ball in the flight required to accomplish a slice. The degree of slice may be controlled by gripping the club farther around to the left with the right hand more on top of the shaft and the left hand underneath. Aim to the left of the objective. Take the club back outside the flight line with a feeling of the left hand being firmly in control and retain that left-hand domination. The club head should be high at the top of the backswing and low at the finish.

Although sometimes a player can use a slice to his advantage, most of the time it is a problem. Many faults can creep into your swing to cause the ball to be hit in a frustrating, though graceful, arc into the rough or out of bounds at the right of the fairway. As already pointed out, the slice is caused by having the face of the club head drawn across the ball. To help you in detection and correction of an unwanted slice, the following check list gives the more common causes of this difficulty and ways to remedy them.

1. *Improper grip.* Be sure the V's formed by the thumb and first finger point toward the right shoulder.

2. *Incorrect stance.* Place a club on the ground touching both toes. It should point parallel with the intended line of flight. Check club-head position at address to be sure that the bottom line of the face is perpendicular to the line of flight.

3. *Opening left side too soon.* Caused when you are too anxious to get the shot off; the left hip moves too fast for the arms and shoulders. This will cause the club head to cut across the ball from the outside in. To correct, close your stance and keep the weight balanced properly.

4. *Falling back on right foot.* This is really an exaggeration of the "opening of the left side too soon"; as the left side pivots, the weight falls back on the right foot, forcing the club head across the ball from the outside in. To prevent this, keep your feet stationary. Bend forward more, close your stance, and keep the left side from opening too soon.

5. *Swaying.* When you sway your hips, like a hula dancer, during the backswing, the right leg bends to the right and too much weight shifts to the right foot. The proper hip-turning movement will prevent the right hip or leg from moving laterally toward the right.

6. *Overturning.* Although it may sound self-contradictory, overturning—too much hip action—can give the same results as those from the sway or lack of hip turn. Overturning causes the club to go too much around the body on the backswing and then to point to the right of the target on the top. A correct turn, on the other hand, will help you keep the club parallel to the flight line at the top of the backswing.

7. *Overswinging.* When your club head goes back too far, the left arm usually bends, causing loss of control; furthermore, there is a great tendency to lead too much with the body when the club is carried too far back. To cure, keep your left arm straight.

8. *Knees too stiff.* If your knees are too stiff, the shoulders will turn too soon on the downswing, causing the club head to be thrown outside the flight line.

9. *Improper hand action.* If the hands are too far ahead of the club head in the hitting area, a slice is bound to result. To correct, accelerate the club head on the downswing, especially the last 90 degrees of the hitting arc.

Hooks. There is a right way and a wrong way to hook a ball. The correct way permits you to play the ball with control; that is, to draw the ball.

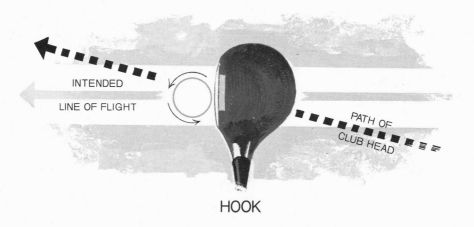

HOOK

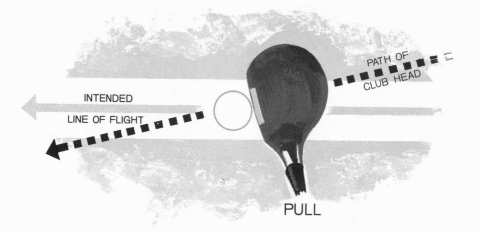

PULL

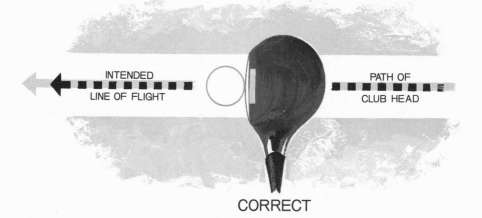

CORRECT

To play a controlled hook, or draw, the first and most important step is to assume the proper grip. This should be done with the left hand firm, so that it dominates in control of the club head. Actually, the degree of hook may be accentuated or controlled by gripping the club with hands rotated to the right on the grip with the right hand well underneath. Aim to the right of the target. Keep your right elbow close to the body and pivot well on the backswing. Hit from the inside out. In the hook the ball travels with overspin, giving it considerable roll after landing. (The draw, therefore, is not considered a good shot for use in getting to the green where the ball may roll off the putting surface.)

The second most important step in making a draw shot is to assume a closed stance, which means putting the left foot forward of the stance line and the right foot back of the stance line, with the ball placed almost opposite the heel of the right foot. But do not put too much faith in the closed stance alone to create the hook. Actually, it is only an expedient. It permits you to take the club back on a flatter plane. Thus, you are able to return the club head to the ball inside the intended line of flight, from which direction you will be able to swing up and over it and so impart that right-to-left spin which causes a hook.

The wrong way to hook a ball leaves you without any control over the shot; that is, you pull the ball or "smother-hook" it. Here are some of the common causes of hooking and how to remedy them.

1. *Improper grip.* The right hand too far under the shaft produces a hook. To correct, grip the club with your hands turned more to the left, holding the shaft more in your fingers. Also check the firmness of your grip. The right hand should never grip tighter than the left. Actually, the left hand should be a little firmer.

2. *Incorrect stance.* Reaching for the ball can cause a hook, but can be easily remedied by standing closer to the ball in a more upright posture. Be sure to line your feet, hips, and shoulders at right angles to the target.

3. *Rolling right hand over.* When the right hand operates independently of the left, there is danger of its rolling over. Keep your wrists firm throughout the swing.

4. *Loose left hand.* You encourage a hook by a loose left hand at the top of the backswing. To correct, firm up your grip with the left hand. Be sure that the right wrist is under the shaft, the left hand is strong, and the left wrist is straight at the top.

5. *Hitting too quickly.* When applying too much power (uncocking the wrists) too soon, your hands roll over before impact, and this error causes the hook. Power should be applied only in the last 90 degrees of the hitting arc.

Remember that the usual cause of a hook is too much hand action. Hand action is desirable in golf, but if overdone a hook may result.

Pushes. The pushed shot is one that travels in more or less a straight line, but to the right of the target. The push, though squarely met, goes right because the club head is moving from the inside to the outside, across the flight line, during impact. Common causes and cures of pushing are:

1. *Improper grip.* If a push persists, the V's formed by the thumbs and first fingers may be pointed to the right of the right shoulder.

2. *Incorrect stance.* If your stance is open too much, that alone can cause you to push, because the club will naturally come into the ball somewhat open. Also a push will result if the body is too far away from the ball. To correct, merely check your stance and square it off as it should be, playing the ball opposite the left heel.

3. *Swaying.* A body sway forward to the right from the ball can cause a push. Sometimes a sway to the right on the backswing can be compensated by swaying or moving the body laterally to the left on the downswing, but this is a rare occurrence. Most of the time the body and hands will get too far ahead of the ball and club head, causing a push or a slice. The best way to cure this difficulty is to rotate your body properly.

4. *Lifting left heel.* If the left heel is raised too far off the ground on the backswing and is not replaced exactly in the same position on the downswing, you will generally push your shot. To correct, raise the left heel just enough for proper body rotation.

5. *Moving head.* Any unnecessary move-

ment of your head can cause a push. The solution is, of course, to keep it still.

Pulls. The pull is the opposite of the push and differs from the hook in that the ball travels in a more or less straight line to the left of target, instead of curving. Any error that will produce an outside-in club-head movement may cause a pulled shot. Some of the more common errors and their corrections are:

1. *Improper grip.* If a pull persists, the V's of the thumbs and first fingers may be shifted to a point to the left of the right shoulder.

2. *Incorrect stance.* A pull will result if the feet are too close together and the ball is played too far off the left foot. As a result, the left arm becomes too relaxed, the right hand comes too far under the shaft, and the weight is concentrated too much on the left foot. The cure, obviously, is the correct stance.

3. *Lifting the club.* If you lift your club up with your hands as you come back, rather than swinging it back, this will cause outside-in movement that causes pulls. To correct, move your hands, arms, and club on the start of the backswing as a solid unit.

4. *Swaying.* Any movement of the body laterally to the right on the backswing can cause a pull. If you coil your body correctly on the backswing, swaying cannot occur.

5. *Top of backswing.* Check to be sure that the weight is shifted to the right foot, the shoulders are turned properly, the right wrist is under the shaft, and the shaft is parallel to the ground before starting the downswing.

6. *Hitting too quickly.* If you start to uncock your wrist at the beginning of the downswing, you will either hook or pull. To correct, just allow your wrists to uncock naturally into the ball.

Topping. Hitting the ball on its top is a very common error of most beginners, and unfortunately there are a multitude of contributing causes to a topped shot. Generally speaking, however, most people top the ball because they play it near or at the center of their stance, a position that places the ball too far back. When the ball is in this position, you cannot get your weight behind the ball nor swing the club head under it. The result

is that you swing the club head *over* the ball.

Too tight a grip will also contribute to the top. So will trying to hit the ball too hard, or inadequate use of the hands, or overuse of the arms.

Another mistake that can cause a top is to assume too wide a stance. This creates a false sense of security in your balance, with the result that you swing too hard at the ball by utilizing the muscles of the body from the waist up. This action causes you to overuse your arms and shoulders, forcing you to pull up and over the ball.

To cure the top, there are a number of check points you can use. First, examine your grip. Make sure that you are not gripping too tightly with either hand and that you are maintaining a lighter grip with the right than with the left hand. Check your stance to see that it is not too wide. When addressing the ball, play it to the left of center; that is, within line of the left foot for woods and long irons.

When swinging at the ball, avoid overpowering the club head with the arms. Let the hands do the work. They will help you to avoid hitting down on the ball. Instead of hitting down on the ball, you should have the sensation of hitting up on the ball, much in the manner in which you would swing at a low pitch in baseball. This feeling will help to eliminate the forcing of the right arm and hand.

The cause of a top may not be physiological at all, but psychological. That is to say, you simply have a fear of hitting behind the ball. If so, you should make a determined effort to hit the ground about 2 inches behind the ball. The psychology of this is that, actually, there is no way you can hit 2 inches behind the ball and still pull up through the swing.

In any event, do not put too much faith in keeping your head down as a cure for topping. It is impossible to keep your head down if your right side is forcing your right shoulder against your chin, which, in turn, forces your head to move up and forward. Actually, overemphasizing the advice to "keep your head down" can cause a top.

Smothering. To smother a shot, you must hit the ball with the club face turned over or "hooded." When you do this, the loft built into the club face is not only eliminated but actually reversed by the turning over of the club head. It is impossible, therefore, for the ball to get into the air.

There are two major causes for smothering shots: (1) an improper grip and (2) an incorrect position at the top of the backswing. The latter is caused mainly by the wrong position of the wrists and failure to shift the weight to the right foot. Once these two causes are corrected, you should not have any trouble avoiding smothered shots.

Skying. A skied shot in golf is analogous to a pop fly in baseball: both are the result of the ball's being hit too much from the under-side. In golf this is usually caused by teeing the ball too high, failing to transfer your body weight properly, lifting the club quickly on the backswing, dropping your right shoulder on the downswing, turning over the club head at impact, and employing a chopping swing. All these faults, except for teeing up the ball, can be corrected by using the proper swing.

If you are guilty of any of the errors that are given here, make the necessary correction. But if you cannot find the root of your trouble, then, to paraphrase the drug commercial, "if pain persists, see your club professional."

IRON SHOTS

Almost every hole on every golf course in the world demands good iron shots. If you can consistently lay the ball near the hole with your approach shots, you are going to get a good share of pars and birdies. If you get in trouble off the tee, a good iron recovery may salvage a par. A poor iron player has no chance. Remember that you measure accurate drives in yards, but accurate irons in feet.

The Long Irons

The No. 1, No. 2, and No. 3 irons are known as the long irons. When a shot calls for distance plus accuracy, the long irons are employed. These are clubs to use when the distances call for them and the lie on the fairway will not permit the use of the No. 3 or No. 4 woods. Also the long iron is a mighty handy club for playing a shot into a heavy wind. Under such conditions, it is recommended that you use a club at least one number stronger than you would on a calm day.

Consistency, confidence, timing: these are key words in hitting with any club, but especially the long irons. For many golfers, the long irons are by far the hardest clubs to hit. They have a tendency to make the long irons more difficult than they really are. Actually, these clubs are handled much the same way as the woods: (1) the grip is the same, except the club is held a little more firmly,

(2) the swing is unhurried, (3) the weight is focused on the inside of the heels, and (4) the divot taken is like the long sweeping motion of the fairway wood. There are, of course, a few differences, too. Let us take a look at them.

The best stance for most long irons is squared stance. Weight should be evenly distributed on both feet and slightly back on the heels. The head should be anchored over the ball and should remain there during the swing. The ball should be slightly inside the left heel at address. Assuming that a drive would be addressed opposite the left heel and that the No. 5 iron would be played opposite the middle of the stance, the long irons would be just about halfway between. Hands should be kept well ahead of the club head at address to induce a descending blow. Hit down and through the ball. Take a bit of turf, and finish your swing with your hands high. To ensure balance, be sure to roll your right foot and knee as you start the backswing. This action will ensure the proper turning of the hips and guard against a sway. On the downswing, shift the weight to the left side, the left hand now dominating the swing. On the follow-through, you should finish the shot on your right toe to complete the fluid turn of the body.

The long-iron shot must be a sharp hit, whereas a wood shot is swung and the ball swept off either the tee or the fairway. Since the length of the shaft of these clubs is shorter

The long Iron swing as caught by the high-speed camera.

than that on a wood and because the ball *must* be contacted on the *downswing,* the action of the hands and the body must be speeded up to some extent. The average player makes the mistake of trying to lift the ball with the club face when he hits a long iron. He is so afraid the ball will not get air-borne that he tries to pick or scoop it up with the club head. This, of course, leads to hitting from the top, to expending almost all power before impact, and also to hitting behind the ball or topping it. The basic principle to keep in mind in hitting a long-iron shot is to hit slightly down and through the ball. We say "slightly down" to caution a player against this scooping action so prevalent among high-handicappers.

While you are swinging more crisply, you should bring the long-iron backswing to the horizontal position. At first, you may have some difficulty doing this. In such a case, aim to check your backswing before the club reaches the horizontal level. Cut down on the body action on rotation; bring the hands and arms into freer play. When you are hitting the ball on target with ease, you can lengthen your backswing a bit at a time, until you reach the desired full swing.

The first movement in the downswing for the long irons is, just as it was with woods, the turning of your left hip to the left. When your hips are turned to the left there is enough lateral movement to put your weight on your left foot. The transference of the weight to the left side, however, must be faster on long-iron shots than it is on wood ones. This quicker shift of weight brings the lowest part of the swing in front of the ball, enabling you to hit down on the ball. On iron shots you must follow a more pronounced down-and-through swing pattern.

At impact, your hands should be slightly ahead of the club head. This aids in hitting down on the ball, adding punch to your long-iron shots. Remember to keep in good position with the head over the ball. Avoid any swaying of head or body. Do not try to hit the ball too hard. Even after impact, your hands should lead the club head. Be sure to keep the hands and wrists firm and deliberate as you take them away from the ball. The normal trajectory of a long-iron shot, of course, is low. But in the event an even lower than normal trajectory is desired—as, for example, when a player wants to keep a shot under the branches of a tree or low against the wind—choke up an inch or so on the shaft. In choking up, you reduce the arc of the swing, cutting the club-head velocity, and the ball does not carry so far.

Most professionals believe that the biggest problem in hitting the long irons is mostly a mental one. So if you use them with confidence, you can count on swinging with consistency, and the long irons will fit nicely into your game.

The Middle Irons

The middle, or medium, irons are those numbered 4, 5, and 6. For the average golfer the middle irons are easier to play than the long ones and are more versatile, offering a wide variety of shots. And you should be able to achieve a great deal more accuracy with the middle irons than with the long ones.

Compared to the long irons and the woods, the stance for the middle irons is narrower and more open. Actually, while playing all the various iron clubs in your bag, your stance varies. A simple rule for the amount of this variation is to remember that as the number of your irons increases, the width of your stance decreases and also opens.

The open stance, of course, keeps the arms closer to the body and reduces the tendency to allow too much body turn. On the backswing, the weight is on the inside of the right foot, with the knees flexed to allow a full

and correct turn. (Bend from the knees instead of the waist to prevent throwing your body forward too much.) Stiff knees will restrict the backswing and force the shoulders to remain level. At the top of the swing, the left shoulder must be lower than the right, and the shoulder turn should be greater than that of the hips.

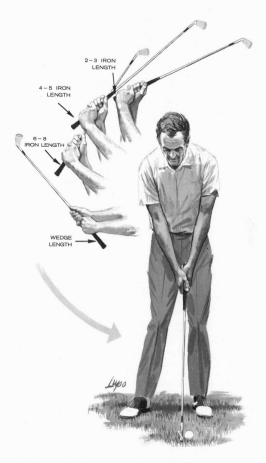

The backswing for the various iron shots.

In medium-range iron play, the backswing is shorter and more upright than with the long irons. This is especially true of the No. 5 and No. 6 irons. In their case, on backswing, the arms continue upward until the club head points to a 2 o'clock position above the left shoulder and the left arm points toward 11 o'clock. (With the wood swing, the club head points to 3 o'clock or directly toward the target. This would be approximately a three-quarter backswing when com-

Gene Littler making a middle iron shot.

pared with the basic full swing described for long irons. Actually, many beginners use the three-quarter swing with their long irons until consistency has been obtained, then employ the full swing.) The weight shift and pivot, of course, must be completed at this point in the swing.

The downswing is the same as for the long irons. That is, the grip is firm with the hands leading the take-away, moving the club back in one piece and returning it into and through the ball. Strike the ball first, and take a larger divot than with the long irons. Although there is more punch and less sweep to crisper, more compact middle-iron movement, it is still a swing, from start to finish, and must have the same smooth rhythm and timing of the full swing.

The Short Irons

The most important factor in playing the short irons—Nos. 7, 8, and 9, plus the pitching wedge—is accuracy. Distance is strictly incidental. Short-iron shots are rated very important because, when playing them, you are either in an excellent position for a low score on a par-4 hole after a good drive, or you're trying to recover after two comparatively poor shots on a par-4 hole or after a poor drive on a par-3 hole. A well-executed short-iron shot to the green very often will enable you to get a birdie or recover sufficiently from a bad shot to enable you to get your par. The short irons are also trouble clubs. They are the ones most generally employed to get out of deep rough or sand

The short iron shot as made by Tony Lema.

traps, over trees or bushes, and all other bad lies on the golf course.

For the short-iron shots, you move a little closer to the ball and have your feet closer together than for the middle-iron shots. The stance should be slightly more open, too. Position the ball equidistant between your feet, and have your weight evenly distributed on both feet at address. Have a little flex in the knees for balance and freedom of movement, and for better control grip the club about an inch or so down the shaft.

Your swing with the short irons is the three-quarter swing of the middle irons. Do not keep the club low to the ground on the backswing, and don't overswing. Allow the body to turn on the backswing without lifting the left heel off the ground. Remember that the greater the body turn, the greater the chance there is for error. With less motion, you will get more accuracy.

On the downswing, control it by keeping the left arm straight and be sure the entire left side moves first when you start. Allow your wrists to break early, and avoid any unnecessary hand action, or you will hit behind the ball. Co-ordinated action by the left side is the answer to a successful short shot. Like the other iron swings previously described, the secret of a short-iron shot is to hit the ball cleanly, taking turf after the ball has been hit. This indicates that the lowest point of the golf swing's arc is in front of and down on the ball.

The "half-shot" is roughly what the name implies: a stroke, usually with the middle or short irons, with which the ball travels perhaps 10 or 15 yards less than it would with the normal swing of the same club. It is a particularly valuable shot when playing into the wind. While it should not be any more difficult than the full and three-quarter shots, there are several things to remember in its execution. In the stance, the feet should be placed closer together. The club should be gripped from 1 inch to 1½ inches down the shaft, bringing your whole body closer to the ball. Then the elements of the backswing must be restricted: its length, the wrist break, and the weight shift. The wrist break should be no more than three-quarters of normal. What weight is shifted to the right side should never move fully onto the right foot, but only to the inside portion of it. The best check point here is to be sure the movement of the left heel off the ground is restricted. Coming back to the ball, keep the downswing flowing and—this is very important—do not quit on the shot. Continue to a full follow-through. Perhaps the most common error with players executing the "half-shot" is the tendency to get soft or sloppy with the hands in the grip and the wrist action. It is vital to maintain firmness throughout the swing. You will find on this shot that the ball will not sail as high because of the shorter distances being covered. But, because of the sharpness of the strike of the ball, you should get as much backspin and consequent "bite" as you do on a full shot with the same club. The important thing to remember about a part shot is that, although the backswing is restricted, the follow-through must not be.

Speaking of backspin, this is not the result of some secret trick which professionals use during their swings. Actually, to obtain it, all you have to do is to hit down on and through the ball, in a manner that any divot your club head takes is beyond the ball. This descending type of blow tends to pinch the ball against the turf, thus producing the desired backspin to hold the shot on line and make the ball bite in when it hits the green.

Chip and Pitch Shots

The chip and pitch shots are frequently employed around the greens and if properly executed will save you many strokes. But before going any further, it would be wise to define the differences between the so-called "chip" shot and the "pitch" shot. The former is generally regarded as a low-trajectory shot that can be expected to land on the green and roll toward the hole with little backspin retarding the ball's forward progress. The pitch shot, on the other hand, is hit with loft,

the ball landing hopefully near the pin and, because of the backspin applied, quickly coming to rest.

The chip, or pitch-and-run, shot is an extremely valuable shot in the professional's repertoire, and it should be developed by every golfer. When the ball is within 20 to 25 yards of the green and when the shot to it is open (there is not a bunker that must be negotiated), it is best generally to employ the chip shot. You may use any club from a No. 4 through a No. 8 iron. (Some players use a special club, such as a chipping iron, for this shot.) The exact club selection depends on several factors: the distance from the hole, the lie of the ball in the grass, the character of the green's turf, the amount of distance between the ball and the pin, the lie of ground between the ball and the hole, and even to some extent the velocity and direction of the wind.

As a rule of thumb, a No. 4 iron will hit the green and roll farther than a No. 5 iron that is hit with the same degree of force. The No. 5 iron runs farther than the No. 6 iron, and so on. When chipping with the wind rather than against (that is, of course, when there is sufficient wind to be a factor), it is generally wise to use a club one or two numbers less; that is, for example, a No. 5 or No. 6 iron rather than a No. 7 iron. When the grain of the green (the turf) is against you, take a slightly less lofted club than you would if the grain were with you.

There is less opportunity of scuffing behind the ball with a less lofted club than with the more lofted ones. For this reason, it is usually recommended to employ the least lofted club that will take the ball just onto the green in flight and still not let it roll past the pin. In other words, on a chip shot use as little loft and as much roll as possible. Chip the ball to the edge of the green, just on the putting surface, and allow the ball to run toward the hole.

Employ the same amount of thought that you used to select your club for the chip shot when choosing the spot for it to land on the green. Always try to pick out a place on the green beyond the fringe, and attempt to land the ball there. (This will generally preclude the possibility of getting a bad bounce from the often unpredictable fringe.)

The pitching wedge shot as made by Dave Marr.

The spot you select may be a dark or light patch of grass, a speck of dirt, a pebble, or something similar. Or it can be a purely mental spot. But your selection for the landing location of the ball should be guided by the terrain between it and the hole. To do this you should "read" the green (details on reading a green can be found on page 280) and allow for any slopes or rolls. If the green slopes to the left, for instance, you would naturally want your ball to land slightly to the right to play for the roll.

After selecting the landing spot, take a few practice strokes alongside your ball. Each time, try to visualize in your mind's eye the spot where the ball is to land, and try to swing the club with just enough force to put it there. Then repeat the same procedure with the actual shot, still seeing that spot in your mind. Remember that one of the keys to a successful chip shot is making sure that the ball lands on the green at the desired spot.

For the chip shot, you should use an open stance: the left foot back slightly from the line of the shot. The feet should be fairly close together—no more than 10 inches apart—and the ball should be kept in a line halfway between the feet. (Some golfers, when chipping, prefer to play the ball opposite the left heel.) Keep your weight on the left foot to facilitate hitting the ball first and then the turf. In taking your grip, choke well down on the club, gripping it about 2 to 3 inches above the point where the grip ends and the shaft begins. Be sure to keep your wrists firm and address the ball with hands slightly ahead of the ball. (The hands should remain in this position throughout the shot.) A chip shot is played almost entirely with the hands and arms. There is little or no wrist motion, and your over-all swing is rather pendulumlike since you keep the club very close to the ground throughout the entire swing. Bend or relax your knees slightly so that you feel an inclination to sit.

The backswing is quite short—the length of the backswing controls the distance the ball will travel and comes with experience—and your right elbow should be kept close to your right hip. Do not pick the club up on the backswing, but rather brush it away from the ball, keeping the wrists firm so that the stroke does not become wobbly. After a slight hesitation at the top of the backswing, bring the club head back down to the ball, trying to hit it at the bottom of the arc. Keep your hand in a firm position on the shaft, and get the right hand to do the work in hitting the ball. The right hand provides the power; the left guides the club. Make sure your tempo is smooth and easy, never jerky. Keep body motion or movement to a very minimum.

At impact you should feel yourself striking down and through the ball. This action may at first give you the sensation that you are closing the club head, but actually you are just giving yourself a chance to follow through in a straight line that follows the course of the ball. Try not to hurry, push, sweep, or poke at the ball, and don't try to lift the ball. The loft of the club head will do that for you.

If the shot is executed properly, the ball will shoot away· from the club head with a nice little click, flying a foot or two off the ground in a straight line to the spot on the green you selected for the ball to land and rolling on toward the pin. The backswing for the chip shot is short; therefore the follow-through is short. This should carry out until the club head is pointed right toward the pin.

Concerning the hit-and-run aspects of the chip shot, most professionals prefer to let the ball run about two-thirds of the way toward the cup after it lands on the green. Naturally there are times when this is not possible or not preferred. For example, when you happen to be about 15 feet off the green and the hole is only 10 feet from the apron, this certainly could not apply. In this situation, hitting the ball on the very edge of the green and letting it run all the way would be the best plan. Sometimes, you will run a ball only one-third of the way, letting the carry take up two-thirds of the distance. You do this when there is a rise in the green or rough spots to carry over.

On uphill chips, play the ball off the right foot, mainly because you want to hit the ball as solidly as possible. The change in tactics with this shot concerns the selection of the proper club. If you would use a No. 6 iron from a level lie, use a No. 5 when the chip is uphill. The incline will add loft to the ball to the extent that a No. 5 iron shot will behave like a No. 6 or even a No. 7 iron.

Downhill chip shots require the opposite approach on two counts. First, less club should be used than under normal conditions. You would use a No. 7 or No. 8 iron from a spot which would call for a No. 6 iron on a level lie. Second, play the ball off the left

The chip shot requires good thinking. How you choose to play it depends on your position around the green, the lie of the ball, and how much roll you can expect as well as how much you desire. Pin placement will also affect your choice. Only after such considerations can you select your club intelligently.

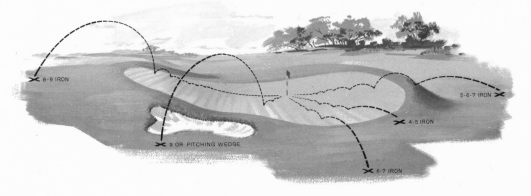

heel. Since the green is sloping downhill, you do not want to hit the ball firmly at all. Instead, you want to drop it onto the green softly.

A chip from the fringe of a green is usually handled like a long putt (see page 287). Use a club with little loft: a No. 2, 3, or 4 iron. (Many top golfers use their putter—referred to in such circumstances as a "Texas Wedge"—off the edge of the green.) Stand with your feet close together, and keep your weight on the left foot. Do not try to loft the ball, but rather give the ball a crisp running stroke, relying on your sense of distance (and experience, which you gain after practicing this stroke) to tell you how hard to hit the ball.

The pitch shot is used generally when the ball is beyond 20 to 25 yards from the putting green or when the ball must clear obstacles, such as bunkers, trees, or water hazards. Because of the latter, the accuracy of a pitch shot is more essential than the chip shot because the margin of error for a pitch shot is greater and if a shot is muffed, trouble usually follows because you usually wind up in the hazard you wanted to avoid. When the chip shot is dubbed, you still get closer to the hole, and the ensuing shot will generally be easier.

For the pitch shot, a well-lofted short iron —the No. 7 to No. 9 iron or the pitching wedge—is employed. The pitching wedge is an excellent club for this purpose since its extra weight and loft help to add height and backspin.

There are two basic types of pitching shots: the high, soft pitch and the low-running pitch. The soft pitch shot, hit with a more lofted club, flies high to the green, lands near the pin, and because of the backspin applied comes quickly to rest. This shot, often called the lofted pitch, is a "must" when you must hit over a trap or other hazard and stop the ball in a hurry. This type of shot is especially necessary when the green is hard or when the pin is set close to a trap or forward on the green. It is also valuable when the wind is behind you, when the lie of the ball is good, or when the green slopes away from your ball.

The pitch-and-run shot, though lofted, lands short on the green and runs a bit to the pin. This shot is generally employed where the opening to the green is wide and smooth, or where the flag is set on a plateau near the back and higher than the front of the green. It is also useful when hitting against the wind or when the lie of the ball is bad. When using the pitch-and-run shot, it is important to select the landing spot for the ball so that it will run properly toward the pin. Follow the same techniques described earlier for chip shots when determining the landing spot.

The stance for the pitch shot should be opened almost a full 45 degrees from the intended line of flight. The ball should be played midway between the feet. The grip should be "weakened," which is to say the left hand should be placed more to the left side of the shaft and the right hand more on top of the shaft to be kept in opposition to the left. About 60 per cent of your weight should be placed on the left foot. But the most important thing you can do in order to position yourself properly is to sit down to the ball, just as though you were about to sit on a chair. However, do not crouch over the ball; remain bent at the waist. The head should be almost directly over the ball and the knees slightly flexed. Grip the club 2 or 3 inches from the end of the shaft.

In the pitch shot, the hands and arms do most of the work and must be kept close to the body. Limit the backswing to a three-quarter backswing and use just enough hip and shoulder action to avoid strain. Keep the left arm straight and right elbow tight against the body. Be sure the wrists are fully cocked on the backswing. This will make your swing more upright and will produce greater backspin and height on the shot. Actually, except for the blast from a sand trap, this is the only time that an early wrist cock is recommended.

On the downswing, bring the club head down and through the ball. Keep the hands ahead of the ball and club face throughout the shot, and strive for a soft, rhythmic swing. Never chop or stab at the ball. The key to this shot is in the wrists. Keep them firm throughout, without any break. The firm wrists control the action of the shot, and too much wristiness usually results in hitting the ball too hard. Hit down on the ball with a smooth crispness, and at the finish of the swing, the club should be allowed to follow

The chip shot from the fringe of
the green properly performed by
Al Geiberger.

through to the same degree as the backswing.

When making a pitch shot, it is sometimes wise to punch-stroke. This is true when you have to fight either a cross wind or a wind blowing right into your face. The intention is to keep the ball low so the effect of the

The punch shot as made by Dave Marr.

wind will be kept to a minimum. The important characteristic of the shot is that the ball will "bite" when it hits the green. Therefore, it is very important that you judge the distance you want very carefully.

To achieve a well-hit punch shot you must make some adjustments in your stance. Put all your weight on your left foot. In fact, many golfers find that they are actually leaning toward the direction they want the ball to take. Keep your hands well ahead of the ball. Play the ball more toward your right foot than normal.

At impact you will feel that your hands are going through the ball lower than for the full short iron. Take your divot well after impact, keeping your left arm and wrists firm as the club meets the ball and turf. Your follow-through will finish low, with your club pointing in the direction of the target.

Another shot that you should consider is the cut stroke, which is exactly the opposite of the punch shot. The result is a high, soft shot that sits almost immediately when it hits the green. You will find this useful when the wind is at your back or when there are tall obstacles you must hit over.

For the cut shot, play the ball slightly· forward of the center of your stance. The key to getting the ball in the air is to open (lay back) the club face. Also, open your stance a little more than usual. This will cause the club head to move in an outside-in path, cutting under the ball and giving it a clockwise spin. To counteract the slicing tendency of the ball, aim a little to the left of the intended target. If the ball bounces once it hits the green, it will move from left to right. Your swing is identical to the full wedge shot except that the open stance will make your swing more upright and get you completely under the ball. One important thing to remember: use the cut shot only when your ball is lying high in grass. Do not use it when the grass is not plush or on any type of hard surface. The club will then bounce into the ball, causing a bad shot.

One common error that is often made on pitch shots is trying to loft the ball with some movement of the body or hands. Let the loft of the club pick the ball up. If you need more loft use a loftier club, but do not attempt to swing under the ball. Actually, you should make contact with the ball while the club head is still moving slightly downward. In other words, the club head should touch the ground after it has contacted the ball and in front of the original ball location. Strange as it may seem, the loft of club face will cause the ball to spin upward despite the fact that it makes contact with the ball on the downward portion of the pitch swing.

The Trouble Shots

It is virtually impossible for even the finest golfer to avoid trouble completely in any round of golf. The big difference, however, between the week-end player and the pro is the way they go about getting out. The pro refuses to panic and instead spends his time figuring the best possible shot he can reasonably expect to make. Remember that a good recovery from behind trees, bad lies in the fairway, and sand traps or bunkers should be made with the loss of only one stroke. In other words, when your shot has gone astray, be sure to select the proper club and the correct technique so that you will get out of your difficulty by using only one stroke rather than several, which could be the case if you do not teach yourself how to make the various trouble shots.

Shots from the Sand Trap. There is many a stroke in golf lost in trap and trouble shots. Many of these useless strokes are the result of a mental barrier which the player conjures up when he finds himself confronted with trouble. That is, the major problem with trap shots is tension and fear. The trap shot itself is really no more difficult than any other shot in golf. It is just that people think it is.

While the sand-trap shot can generally be accomplished with a No. 9 iron, the sand wedge is a better choice. With its heavy head and thick, rounded sole or flange on the bottom, this wedge readily slides under a ball in the sand without cutting too deep.

The *basic* swing of the sand-trap shot, often called the "explosion shot," is rather simple, and the basic rules you should bear in mind are:

1. Have the blade open at address.
2. Hit from 1 to 2 inches behind the ball.
3. Swing smoothly and easily.
4. Follow through fully.

Play the explosion shot with an open stance, the feet being slightly farther apart than in chipping. The stance also turns the shoulders toward the green, permitting a free follow-through. The ball is played about 2 inches inside the left heel, with the feet well planted in the sand. Keep about 60 per cent of your weight on your left foot, and flex your knees slightly.

Address the ball opposite or slightly inside the left, or forward, foot, and keep the hands well forward of the club head. As you address the ball, open the face of the club, or turn it to the right of the target. This allows the sole of the club to hit the sand first and prevents the club from digging into the sand. Aim an inch or two behind the ball, but make certain that you do not incur a two-stroke penalty by permitting the club head to touch the sand during the address or on the backswing (see Section VI for details of this rule).

When you take the club back, cock your

In the standard trap shot, the ball is played off the left heel at address, with the stance open and the heels no more than six inches apart. The right foot is at a right angle to the line of flight, and the left foot is turned out at a 45-degree angle. The hands and arms are close to the body. The right arm cocks early, and by the top of the swing, the left knee has moved forward and the weight shifted to the right foot. The right side, from hip to shoulder, has been drawn back while the cocking of the right arm has carried the club up in

wrists quickly and abruptly as you do on a lofted pitch shot. This enables you to hit down into the sand more effectively. (This abruptness in your backswing, of course, should be employed only on shorter trap shots. On longer recoveries from the sand, your backswing should be more like that of a normal short-iron shot described previously.) Also employ very little body movement: just enough to permit your hands and arms to perform freely and rhythmically. The length of the shot will determine the length of the backswing.

Start the club on its downswing in the same way as for other short-iron shots, being sure your hands lead the club head through the shot. Make certain not to allow the hands to turn or cross over. Hit the sand approximately an inch or two behind the ball in order to create a cushion of sand between the ball and club head. Do not stop the action, but hit through the ball. The follow-through need not be so high as the backswing, but you must get through the ball. Since you employ an open stance, the club

head cuts across the desired line of flight on the follow-through.

When blasting from a sand trap, it is a good idea to read the greens (see page 280) beforehand. If the green runs down and away from you, for example, allow for some roll. The slope takes much of the bite off the ball. If the green slopes upward, carry the ball as close to the pin as possible. The ball will not only hold the green but is liable to back up on you. Right and left breaks on a green should also be considered. On left-to-right breaks, remember that the normal spin on the ball will make it "kick" to the right, so play the shot more left than usual. On a right-to-left break, the slope will diminish the amount of spin to the right.

With a buried lie, the club face should be slightly closed since you want to take maximum advantage of the force of the club head. Closing the face assures a more pronounced explosion, while opening the face provides more of a cutting action. The buried lie is the only type of explosion shot that requires more sand to be taken behind the ball.

an upright plane to the correct position. On the downswing, the left hip pulls back as the right knee goes forward, shifting the weight back to the left foot. The downswing is dominated by the stretching of the left side, an action that contracts the left arm and pulls the club down into the hitting area. The right arm exerts the power that was stored in it by correct cocking on the backswing, then straightens out to apply the club head to the ball and continue the stroke to a smooth, balanced finish. Harry Obitz demonstrates.

Sometimes, it is wise to hit as much as 4 inches behind the ball so that the club head will be able to dig in and scoop the ball out of the depression it is in.

If the sand is moist or wet, there are two methods of recovery, each dictated by the lie of the ball. If the ball is buried in the sand, address the ball—as you should with all trap shots—with an open stance and with your weight distributed mainly toward the left side. The club head is lifted abruptly on the backswing and then stuck in the sand, without any conscious effort at following through, up to 4 inches behind the ball. Since the follow-through is restricted, this method will require some practice in order to get the feel of how hard to hit the ball, which will come out of the sand much faster than normally and with little or no backspin. If the ball is lying cleanly in the sand, on the other hand, your method of recovery will be dictated by the nature of the sand itself. If the sand is soggy, you should play the shot with your sand wedge. If, however, the sand is hard, use your pitching wedge, the

sharper blade of which will encourage digging; the flange on the sand wedge would simply bounce ineffectively. In either of these two cases—contrary to the method of exploding a ball—make a definite follow-through by accelerating the club head to the finish of your swing.

When you are playing out of powdery or "beach" sand, composed of rather fine particles, you can get good action (backspin) on the ball. Hit the sand about an inch behind the ball. On the other hand, coarse, gravelly sand demands different treatment. Hit closer to the ball, and expect the ball to have a certain amount of run. The reason for this is that the club face never gets close enough to the ball to put any action on it.

Sometimes, when you are placing your feet in the sand, you will find a layer of hard-packed sand, clay, or dirt below the top layer of sand. In this case, there is a danger that the wide flange of the sand wedge will "bounce" off the hard layer, causing a skulled shot. In this case, switch to a pitching wedge or even a No. 9 iron.

For any uphill lie in the sand, the key is to hit up and not into the bank itself, where the club will be buried. However, since the ball will jump higher with the open club face angled back, and since you will naturally take more sand with this shot, swing a little harder than normally.

On a downhill lie in a trap, employ the standard explosion shot, but the club head should enter the sand farther behind the ball —about a half-inch—than it would on a normal lie shot. This is necessary because the downhill slope affords less sand resistance between the ball and club. Also place a little more weight on your right foot to prevent swaying forward. As a rule, a shot from a downhill lie produces less loft than is normal. If you require loft, open the club face a few extra degrees and compensate for it by pulling your forward foot farther back from the line of flight.

A downhill lie from the back edge of a trap can be a difficult shot. Your left foot, in such cases, will be in the sand, your right on the ground and higher. Your stance still should be open, but not so much as in a normal lie. Make your address with the club face square to the target line or even slightly closed, and play the ball more toward the right foot. You should attempt to hit at least 2 inches behind the ball, or even more if there is enough room to do so. Use a longer backswing and full follow-through so that you get the ball into the air.

When playing an uphill lie in a trap, use the basic explosion technique except that the club head should enter the sand a little closer to the ball—approximately a half-inch—because the sand is deeper at the club's point of entry. Place more weight on your left or forward foot for this shot, and remember that the deeper sand will slow up the club head, necessitating a more deliberate follow-through.

An uphill lie from the front edge of a trap is a rather easy shot and is played as just described. If there is no overhanging lip on the trap and the side of the green is smooth, you can even get out with a putter. To do this, keep your weight on the left foot, and try to hit the ball without first contacting the sand. Make certain to hit the shot squarely, for if you contact the ball too much on top, it can bury the ball in the sand. This shot should not be attempted if the sand is powdery or soft.

You can chip a shot from a sand trap if the ball is completely exposed on flat sand and there is no high obstacle along the desired line of flight. When making this shot follow the same procedure described on page 264, making sure the club head strikes the ball before hitting the sand; otherwise it will be caught in and slowed down by the sand.

One of the most difficult trap shots is with the ball below the level of the feet, which is generally the case when the ball is in the sand and the feet are on the bank of the trap. Here you require an exaggerated knee bend to get the hands into hitting position. Hold the club on the end of the grip, and, to maintain balance, shorten the backswing. The reason for this is that the more body movement, the more you are likely to miss the shot.

Another demanding trap shot is one where you want to carry the ball some distance, say 20 to 30 yards. The problem here is judging how much sand to take. As a general rule, the longer the shot, the less sand you take, and vice versa. Square up the blade, consciously keep more weight on the left side than on the shorter bunker shot, and take a three-quarter swing. Try very hard not to lean forward or backward or sway during the swing. Because you are taking a fuller swing, you are apt to slide around in the sand. This could cause a skull or, worse, leave the ball in the trap. Do not stop the club head at impact, as this can be disastrous. Swing down and through to a high finish.

One of the hardest shots in golf to play, and one few golfers execute successfully, is the long trap shot to the green. This is a shot that must travel as much as 50 yards. It is a combination trap shot and cut shot and should be executed with a full swing, the sand iron striking the sand about 2 inches behind the ball. Most golfers have trouble with the long trap shot because they simply do not hit the ball far enough. The key to making this shot successfully is to restrict the action of the left hand. The feeling you should get is that the left hand goes only as far as the ball and then quits, enabling the right hand to take over and dominate the rest of the swing. This "left hand quitting and the right taking over" produces a cutting action that enables the player to hit the ball 50 yards or more. The long trap shot should be thrown right at the flag. It is not a pitch-and-run shot. Do not try to run the ball. Try to land it right in the hole. Do not worry; the ball will stop. After the left hand quits at the ball, it simply remains on the club in a passive capacity and is pulled

On a downhill lie, since you're forbidden to touch the sand on the backswing, simply take the club back more steeply and follow through to a full finish. Failure to do so will leave the club buried in the sand—and the ball as well. And, just as on the fairway, the ball is played off the highest foot—in this case, the right.

through the ball by the dominant right hand. Most golfers, when confronted by a long trap shot to the green, do one of two things, generally. They either leave the ball far short or try to pick the ball out of the trap and invariably succeed only in hitting the shot thin, or "skulling" it right over the green and into more trouble.

Where there is a good clean lie in a fairway bunker and distance is desired, it is often possible to use a long- or middle-iron shot or even a No. 3, 4, or 5 wood. The irons can be played in their normal manner except that the pivot should be slightly restricted and it is imperative that the club head contact the ball before it touches or enters the sand. If you hit the sand first, it will ruin your shot. Woods should also be played for a square club-ball contact. A good rule to follow in hitting fairway-bunker or sand-trap shots is to use a club one number higher than you would normally require, because on sand shots your pivot is slightly restricted.

Shots from the Water. You treat the water shot much as you do the basic explosion shot from the sand. However, keep your club face square to the intended line of flight and employ a square stance. Hit about 2 inches behind the ball, since the club head will skid forward in the water. It is not advisable to attempt a shot from water that is more than 2 inches deep. Actually, it is almost always safer to take the one-stroke penalty any time your ball is in the water and drop behind the hazard as prescribed by the *Rules of Golf* (see Section VI).

Shots from the Rough. When that fine-looking shot takes a bad bounce and ends up in the rough, do not push the panic button! Instead, handle this situation with the same planning and judgment that might go into the preparation of dinner. The key words are planning and judgment.

There is no specific rule that can be given as to what club is best to use in a rough. It is completely a matter of judgment, and you must decide for yourself in each given situation. As a *general* rule, however, the more lofted clubs—No. 5 to No. 9 irons—are best. The actual selection should be based on the height of the grass. High grass has a tendency to wrap itself around an iron club and squeeze in between the ball and the club face. This will minimize the loft of the club. For this reason, it is usually wise to open the club face slightly when addressing the ball. Then the club head can turn slightly as it cuts through the heavy grass on the downswing. By the time impact is made, the club head will have turned back to its normal square-faced position, and the shot will clear the rough with the desired loft and on a straight path. Tall grass also slows up the club and tends to hold it up. To help reduce this holding action,

do not sole the club when addressing the ball. Let the sole of the club rest about an inch behind the ball, barely touching the top of the grass. By not soling your club, you eliminate to a great extent the possibility of catching the heavy grass as the club head is taken back.

The swing you take depends on the type of rough. If the grass is very long, very heavy, and very green, use a high-loft club and employ a lofted pitch-shot swing. Remember that in executing an iron shot from the rough it is important to keep the left hand more firmly on the club so that it will not turn when it contacts the heavy grass. Also remember to make your backswing more upright. It even helps to take the club back very slightly outside the line and play the shot as a slight cut shot. Avoid sweeping the club back. It helps you take a more upright backswing if you employ a slightly open stance. The reason for using a more upright swing than usual is that this helps a player get under the ball better. And, most important, break your wrist since this will make your backswing more nearly vertical and will therefore restrict your pivot. This restriction will, in turn, afford you more control. By so restricting your pivot, you will be less apt to lose your swing, a common malady when you try to force a shot. In other words, concentrate on making the correct swing from the rough and not on

getting the ball out by sheer power.

In playing a shot to the green out of the rough, remember that your ball cannot be stopped quickly because it is almost next to impossible to apply backspin. Consequently, when playing a shot from this position, always try to figure on playing the ball to land much shorter than you normally do for either the pitch or chip stroke, and let it take its roll up to the pin. You can try all sorts of different things to impart spin to the ball, but few, if any, work. It is best to anticipate that the ball will roll, and if you properly plan it that way, your recovery shot will generally work out fine.

To play out of a short rough is not generally too difficult. Usually, a medium iron, often a long iron, can be played in normal manner if the lie is good. Sometimes it is even feasible to hit a No. 3, 4, or 5 wood from short rough, provided there is a decent lie. For this type of rough shot these woods have sufficient lift, and the grass does not wrap around them as it does an iron. When playing a wood from a short rough, play the ball on the upswing. But even if you can get to the fairway with a wood or less lofted iron, most times you will be better off by employing the safer lofted clubs out of almost any type of rough and depending on your next shot to the green to make up the necessary distance. In other words, it is far better to give up one

A wood shot from the sand requires a good lie and a low lip to the trap.

shot than to take a chance of losing two or more. And often it is possible to make up that one stroke by making a good approach shot from the fairway.

Shots from Various Trouble Lies. Playing a ball from a lie that is anything but level is a problem that you will have to face on most golf courses. Uneven lies usually fall into four categories: uphill, downhill, standing above the ball, and standing below the ball. Here is how each should be played:

Uphill Lie. This lie will give your shot more height, so use a less lofted club than you would normally on a flat surface. Place your weight downhill (on the right foot), and play the ball in the regular vicinity of your left foot; except on the steeper slopes, you should play the ball more forward (up to 6 inches to the left) so that it will be contacted later in your swing. Take a somewhat shorter grip, use a shorter backswing, and pivot a little less. Follow the slope down with your backswing and then up with your follow-through. Since the weight is on your rear foot, this shot has a tendency to hook, and therefore you should

aim to the right side of your target to compensate for it.

Downhill Lie. This lie generally offers more trouble. Since the downhill lie will give your shot less height, use a more lofted club in order to get the ball up into the air. But since the ball will be hit down upon, it will usually travel lower and more roll can be expected, thus making up for this reduction in club power to a degree. Place your weight downhill (on the left foot) and play the ball uphill. (The exact distance the ball should be played off the right foot will depend on the contour of the land.) Open your stance slightly, and flex your right knee. Again follow the slope up with your backswing, and then down with your follow-through. Since this shot has a tendency to fade or slice, you should aim to the left of your target to compensate for it.

Standing Below the Ball. On a sidehill lie with the ball above you, use the same club you normally would for the length of the shot involved. Play the ball opposite the center of a square stance, flex your knees slightly, and keep your weight forward on the balls of your feet. The ball, being higher, will be closer to you, so compensate by shortening your grip on the club so that the club head rests on the ground without the arms being bent more than for the normal shot. Since a hook is probable from this position, allow for it by aiming to the right of your target, and play the ball naturally.

Standing Above the Ball. On a sidehill lie with the ball below you, play the shot from the center of a square stance. However, the stance should be slightly wider than normal to help maintain your balance, and the knees must be bent more than usual, with the weight kept back on your heels. Stand closer to your ball, and stay low through the entire stroke. Do not take a full swing, but rather take a club one number lower (for example, No. 3 iron instead of a No. 4 iron) if the lie permits, and employ a three-quarter swing. This will give you better balance on this shot. Since a shot from this location will usually fade or slice, compensate for it by playing the ball to the left of target.

Shots Near Trees. Although trees add beauty to a golf course, they certainly spell trouble for the golfer's game. When you are confronted with trees, you have only three choices: go over, around, or under. To go over trees you can use an intentional hook or slice. To go under a tree, you must keep the ball low. To do this, play the shot with a straight-faced club, usually a No. 3 or No. 4 iron. Choke up on the club according to the distance you need, but never grip it full length. (If you swing too fully with a full grip, you cannot expect to keep the ball low.) The ball should be played slightly back of its normal long-iron shot position and the hands kept ahead of the ball on the address. The ball should be punched rather than hit, and, in order to accomplish this, use no more than a three-quarter swing with the right elbow close into the side and with little or no pivot, or wrist action. Be sure to hit down on the ball with the body weight well through on the left foot. Like the backswing, the follow-through should be kept to three-quarters that of the normal swing.

Bad Lies. Occasionally on a fairway, you may find your ball in a divot hole. To get the ball out, play it more off the right foot than normal and close the club face slightly. Hit down on the ball and through it with plenty of wrist action. If there is any doubt in your mind, use a more lofted club than a straight-faced one.

A heavy clover lie on the fairway can cause some trouble if not properly played. As most players know, a golf ball hit from a clover lie has a tendency to run after it lands because the clover gets between the club and the ball, eliminating backspin. "Flier lies," as the pros call a lie in clover or tufted grass, tend to make you hit the ball higher on the club face than normally. This gets the ball up in the air more and makes it harder to control. If a lie is so bad that you feel you cannot help but hit a flier, take one club less to allow for the additional run. Also, try to uncock the wrists sooner than usual, giving you almost the feeling that you are hitting from the top. This will enable you to avoid a cutting action and come into the ball at a shallower level.

As for hitting a shot from a bare lie or from hard ground, you should play it just as you would a fairway sand-trap or bunker shot, except do not take the extra club. On hard ground, because you can pivot normally, it is not necessary to use more club. Be sure to hit down on the ball. If you hit behind the ball with no turf there, your club is going to skid, and so will the ball.

Common Iron-Shot Errors

All iron shots can be sliced, hooked, pushed, pulled, or topped just as well as wood shots and for exactly the same reasons described on page 258. Although they can be smothered, thanks to the irons' greater lofts the effect usually is not as disastrous as with woods. Iron shots can also be skied, but it is generally for a different reason than with a wood. With irons, skying occurs when you hit them with a slightly open face and not with a descending blow.

Shanking. Although shanking can occur with woods, it seems more prevalent with irons. It is the fault of hitting the ball with the shank, or neck, of the club instead of with the club head. It produces the worst type of shot result. The ball goes off the club at almost a right angle to the target. The principal causes of the shanking are these:

1. Bringing the club head down in an out-

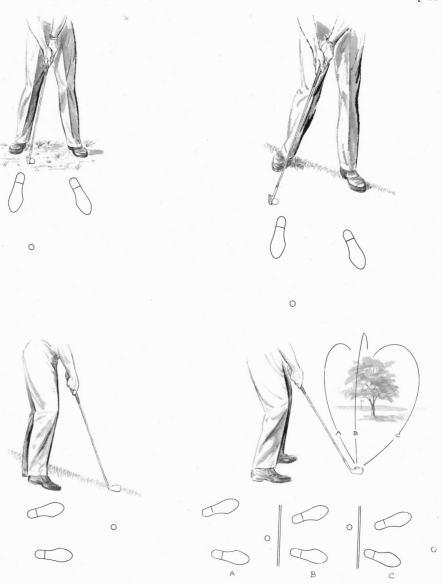

The proper position and method of playing shots from various trouble lies. Top (left to right): Tight lie and a downhill lie. Bottom (left to right): Side hill lie with the ball lower and a partial stymie. In the latter case, you can maneuver the ball without changing grip. (A) To slice, open stance, swing outside-in. (B) For quick loft, play ball well forward. (C) To hook, close stance, swing more from inside-out.

side-in path and cutting across and over the ball. At the same time, the shoulders and arms are pulling away from the ball and the hands and wrists are freezing all action.

2. Faulty body action that results in diving under the ball with hips and shoulders and jolting to a stop, with the hands and wrists flipping the club face up at impact.

3. Rolling the club open on the backswing and taking the club back too flat around the body, then returning to the ball in the same manner, with the body ahead of the hands, thus blocking the action.

4. Skywriting, especially at the top of the backswing of long irons, can also cause shanking, as well as a few other difficulties. (Skywriting receives its name from the fact that the club head describes or makes a loop

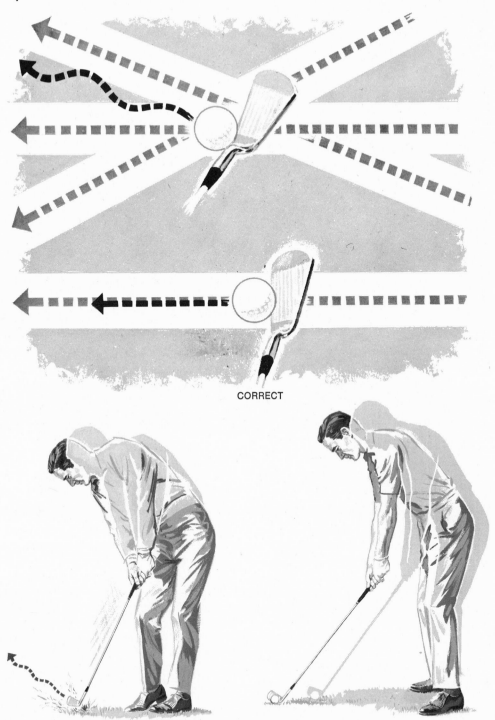

CORRECT

A shank can result from almost any kind of swing: outside-in, inside-out, or even straight-through. When a player stands too far from the ball at address, he puts himself in an awkward position—almost as if he were on a sidehill lie. His weight is on his toes, his body is leaning out of position, and he is rigid. The result (right) is that the player's body has pitched even farther forward during the swing itself, and he has rocked into such a position that the clubhead is beyond the ball and cannot hit it.

or a circle at the top.) Since skywriting makes for general club wildness, guard against changing the position of your hands at the top of the backswing—its principal cause.

Shanking a pitch or chip shot is caused by excess pivot. These short shots should be played with the feet fairly close together and the knees flexed in a sitting position. The lower the knees, the more upright the swing will be and the better the chances of avoiding undue twisting and breaking of the body. The body plays little part in the short shot. It should respond just enough to permit a proper swing. The golfer who uses the same body pivot on every shot, regardless of length, is inviting trouble.

If you are guilty of shanking, check anything and everything, from correct grip to correct position at top of backswing and correct movement of the downswing, that will cause the swing to go outside its normal arc.

Scuffing. To scuff a shot is to hit behind the ball. Instead of the club head's catching the ball cleanly at impact, it sort of stumbles over the ball, much in the way a child who is learning to walk might stumble over something because he has not yet learned to pick up his feet.

The scuff is a frequent fault among beginners because they have not yet learned to achieve balance in their swing, to take a proper stance, and to position the ball properly at the address. The tendency among beginners is to scuff the ball with the lofted irons and to hit over the ball with the longer irons. The more advanced player, on the other hand, has just the opposite tendency; he is more apt to scuff the long irons. In either event, the fault almost invariably lies in the same stance.

PUTTING

The average club golfer takes approximately 38 to 42 putts per round. Against a regulation 36 putts for 18 holes, this means he is taking at least two to six three-putt greens a round. A good professional, on the other hand, is taking two or three less than regulation. To win a tournament on the PGA tour today, you would probably have to average around 30 putts a round.

How come the massive difference between the club golfer's performance and that of the tournament winner? Confidence? Practice? Natural ability? Yes, all these are factors in the development of a successful putter. But what about those players who practice their putting from dawn till dark, yet cannot buy a putt? Actually, successful putting can be broken down into three interdependent elements: (1) reading greens; (2) judging distance and break; and (3) proper stroking of the ball.

Reading the Greens

The length and type of the grass, its dryness or wetness, and its level (downhill or up) are very important considerations when putting. Another factor, often overlooked by many golfers, is the direction of the grain on a putting green. It has a definite effect not only on how far a putt will roll but also on which direction it will bend. On some greens the grain can alter by as much as 25 per cent how hard a putt should be struck—the amount depending on whether you're putting with or against it.

It is, of course, illegal to roughen the grass on a green to find out which way the grass lies. Generally, however, the grass just off a green, on its fringe, will have the same grain as on the green itself. And it is legal to brush your putter across the fringe and thus determine the direction of the grain. But the safest method of determining the grain of a green is to look for its shine. When looking toward the hole, should you notice a shiny reflection of the sun on the green, you are usually looking with the grain, and thus your ball will roll a great deal more freely and much farther than you might normally expect. This sheen is caused by the mowers clipping the fibrous runners of the grass. Conversely, if the surface of the green appears dull from where you stand, you are looking against the grain, and you must hit the ball much harder than you might generally consider necessary.

Another way you can determine the grain is to study the growth around the edge of

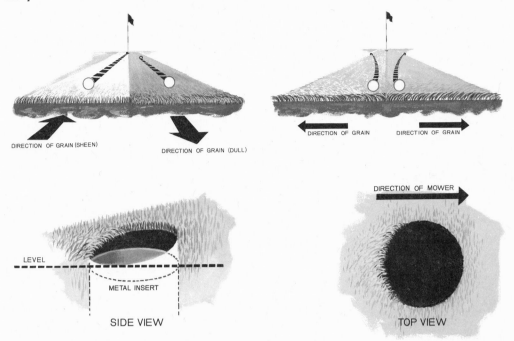

DIRECTION OF GRAIN (SHEEN)

DIRECTION OF GRAIN (DULL)

DIRECTION OF GRAIN   DIRECTION OF GRAIN

DIRECTION OF MOWER

LEVEL

METAL INSERT

SIDE VIEW

TOP VIEW

Top left: Putt against the grain must be hit harder or it will pull up short. Top right: Cross grain can cause a straight putt to swerve off line. Bottom left: Damage to the cup and a lower soil layer indicate the bottom side. Bottom right: Direction of mowing grain is disclosed by grass pulled into hole.

the hole. When you look closely at it, you notice that the grass around three-quarters of its circumference is sharp, distinct, and cleanly cut. On the remaining portion, the grass will be more ragged and inconsistent. This is because the grass on the side of the cup toward which the grass lies will readily die due to the fact that more of the root system is severed on the "down-grain" side of the hole when the green is cut. It means that when standing on the same side of the hole as the rough edge and looking across the cup, you will be looking into the grain. Should you have to putt over this rough edge, you are stroking against the grain and will have to hit harder.

When you putt with the grain, your ball meets little resistance from the grass, which already bends in the direction of the putt. Such a putt must be hit approximately 15 to 25 per cent more softly than a putt rolling against the grain. In like manner, the grain that runs directly across the line of your putt will have a similarly strong effect, and you must allow for some right or left roll even on an almost absolutely flat surface. For ex-

ample, a long putt breaking right on a green with its grain growing left to right would probably require you to allow for 2 or 3 more inches of break, depending on the amount of slope.

The type of grass employed on the green also has an effect on your putting. There are two basic types of grass used on golf courses: Bermuda and bent. There are almost infinite varieties of these two, but these are the fundamental strains. The easiest way to tell the two apart is to remember that bent grass does exactly what its name implies: it bends. Bent grass is allowed to grow longer than Bermuda, and the tops of the leaves curl over and lie flat, so that the length of the blade is bent almost double. Bermuda grass, on the other hand, looks like a crew cut. It is much shorter than bent, and it is bristly and stubby to touch. The two grasses have very different characteristics.

Bermuda grass is used mainly in the South and Southwest because it stands up well under hot, dry conditions. Bermuda is generally more grainy than bent, and the grain it does have is usually more consistent. The grain on some Bermuda greens is produced almost entirely by the cutting pattern of a lawn mower. Bermuda grass is thick, and its large, coarse leaf makes for a slow putting green. Bermuda greens have less break, too, because the heavy leaves keep the ball from sliding off. The grain on a Bermuda green, however, can radically affect the break or speed of a putt. Going with the grain, a 10-foot putt is equal to a 6-footer, and putting across the grain can double the amount of break, pulling a straight 10-footer a full 2 feet off line. Because Bermuda greens tend to be slow and bumpy, try to contact the ball at the bottom of your putting stroke in order to get the ball rolling smoothly. Also, make allowances for the grain. If you are putting with it, play the ball toward the center of your stance to avoid getting overspin, and play the ball more forward when going against the grain. Through the green, there are several things to keep in mind. Bermuda greens are closely cropped and are usually hard. You may have to land the ball in front of them and let it roll on. Because Bermuda is thick and full, it makes excellent fairways that yield perfect lies. But for the same reason, it becomes an impenetrable rough when left to grow. In tangled, matted grass, do not try for distance. Take what you need to get back to the fairway, and play it safe. Bermuda rough grabs the club head, and you may leave the ball right where you found it.

Bent grass is found mainly in the North, although a few southern courses (Augusta National and Pinehurst) use it. It is a cool-weather grass, and its fine leaf makes for a smooth, true, and slick putting surface. Bent grass can be very grainy, especially near mountains and water, and a good hint to remember is that the grain on such courses will grow toward the mountains and away from the water. Because bent greens are so fast, play the ball more toward the center of your stance as you would on a straight down-hill putt. Incidentally, bent fairways are not as easy to hit off as Bermuda. Because the grass is thin and soft, and the turf soft, too, there is a tendency for the player to hit every shot fat. And on some bent fairways, especially in the Midwest, patches of clover creep into the bent, producing flier lies. Confronted with his ball lying in clover, the player should

take one club less and try to pick the ball clean.

Judging Distance and Break

One of the first things you should do when your ball arrives on the green is inspect it carefully. The *Rules of Golf* permit you to pick up the ball and remove any foreign matter from it. The rules also allow you to repair ball marks on the green and to remove any loose impediments, such as leaves, either by picking them up or brushing them aside with your hand or club. Although the Rules permit you to repair ball marks, you cannot repair other imperfections in the putting surface. To do so, the USGA feels, would further slow down the game; golf is slow enough as it is without making it worse.

Study the grass around the edge of the hole very carefully for any footprints, spike scuffs, or ragged edges that could seriously impede the line of your putt. If there is more damage to the grass on one edge than on the other side, chances are good that your putt will roll to that side. Also your ball, because it will be traveling more slowly at the end of its stroke as it nears the hole, is more subject to the slightest imperfections on the green. Thus, when such imperfections are found, it is usually advisable to hit the ball more firmly so that it will be able to overcome these rough spots.

When putting on a green with a slope or slant, you must be able to judge the break of your ball as it comes toward the hole. Generally, you can determine this break by getting well away from the ball and taking a good over-all look at the entire green surface. If this does not answer your break question, examine the cup itself. If one side looks lower than the other, the green does slope toward that side. Judging the break of your ball and how to read slopes of a green comes only with experience and practice. But keep in mind that a putt which must break twice is going to break much more sharply off the second turn than the first. This is again due to the fact that your ball will have slowed down sufficiently so that it will be affected more by the contour of the green. For this same reason, a putt that has to roll across a slant at the near conclusion of its

Stand so that a straight line extends from your dominant eye to the ball and on to the hole, and cover the ball with the lower part of the shaft. Run your dominant eye up the shaft and sight the putt. The break will then appear as shown.

roll will break more sharply at that point than it would have if the slope were met shortly after the ball was stroked. In other words, on putts that must roll over several slopes, be sure to allow for more of a break nearer the cup than at the beginning of the stroke.

Wet greens are slower as a rule than dry ones; therefore you must stroke your ball more firmly. Remember that putts will not break as far as normal on a sloping green when it is wet; also, you are permitted to move your ball on a green if casual water impedes the line of your putt.

To line up a putt, try to picture in your

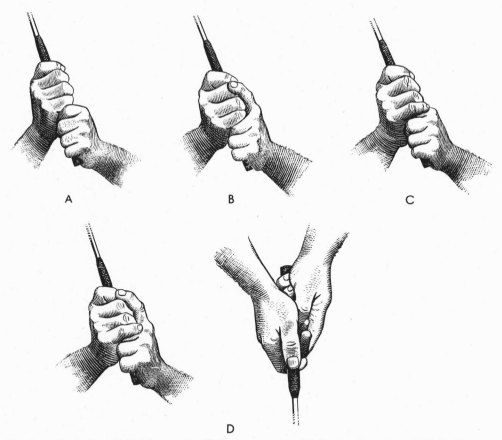

Popular putting grips: (A) Full-finger grip; (B) Reverse overlap; (C) Overlapping grip; and (D) Double reverse overlap, two views.

mind just where the ball is going to have to go to reach the hole and at what speed it is going to have to travel. Look over the ball position from all conceivable angles. This means not only from behind the ball but also from behind the cup and from the sides. You should note not only the grain of the grass and side roll but also the degree of downward or upward slant between your ball and the cup. The final judgment of the distance between the ball and the hole, its proper line, and the power needed to sink your putt comes, of course, with practice and experience. In this book, a long putt is referred to as one over 12 feet; a short putt as one from 2 to 12 feet; and a very short putt as one 2 feet or less.

The plumb-bob technique of lining up in which the player uses his putter in the manner of a surveyor's instrument is becoming more and more popular. In using the system, you must stand so that a straight line extends from your dominant eye to the ball and then on to the hole. The other eye must be kept closed. Your dominant eye is the eye which allows you to see one object superimposed over another in the same way both eyes can see the superimposition. The putter should be held perpendicularly at arm's length with the thumb and forefinger gripping it at the bottom of the grip. It is best to stand from 3 to 6 feet back of the ball when lining up. As a rule, the shorter the putt, the closer you stand to the ball. Cover the ball with the lower part of the putter shaft and then run your dominant eye up the shaft. If the shaft covers the hole, the putt is straight. If the shaft falls to the left of the hole, the putt will break from left to right. If the shaft falls to the right of the hole, the putt will break from right to left. The system works best on putts of 15 feet or less.

Putting Strokes

There is more controversy about the putting stroke than about any other phase of golf. You will see more different techniques on the putting green than colors in a kaleidoscope. Each has its ardent devotees, and each, apparently, enjoys a certain degree of success. There is, however, one basic principle that must always be followed: the putter must be firmly held with the left hand, but not so tightly as to restrict the movement. The ball is stroked with the right hand. In other words, the left hand guides and the right provides the power.

A correct putting grip for you is something you will have to decide for yourself. The five most popular putting grips are: (1) the normal Vardon grip, which allows the player to hold the club the same on every shot; (2) the cross-hand style, with the left hand below the right; (3) the reverse overlap grip, with the left index finger over the right little finger; (4) a variation of the reverse overlap, with the finger extended down the shaft; and (5) a separated grip, with the hands spread well apart. But, whatever grip you employ that feels most comfortable to you, be sure to hold the putter gently but firmly. One of the best ways to determine the proper pressure on the shaft is to consider it as an egg. In other words, if you squeeze the egg too firmly or hard, it will break; if you hold it too loosely, you will drop it. Give your putter the same treatment as you would the egg. Any unnecessary pressure on the club would set up tensions in the hands and arms that could cause a jerky stroke. Too loose a grip could cause a serious hitch in the stroke and a mis-hit ball. Also never change the pressure of your grip once the stroke has begun.

A really good putting stance is also one that is comfortable, yet permits proper balance. To achieve this, most good putters keep their feet close together (3 to 10 inches apart) and their weight evenly distributed back on the heels of both feet. Your feet should be at right angles to the hole. Although a great many players favor the square stance—toes parallel to the target or putting line—the position of your right foot is really a matter of personal comfort.

For a straight putt, play the ball on the inside of the left heel; if, however, there is a break in your line, the ball position should be properly altered. On a left-to-right break, play the ball off the left toe. This maneuver will encourage a strong stroking action that will hold the ball to the left and eliminate pushing off straight or to the right of the hole. And on a right-to-left break, position the ball off the right foot. This ball position prevents premature pulling of the ball to the left and promotes a firm putt on the break line. That is, this keeps your hands ahead of the ball so that the putt will not veer to the left at the start.

In putting, as in all golf shots, your hips must be in balance at all times and your knees should be flexed. Flexing the knees naturally lowers the hip position. This action lowers the center of gravity and thus improves your balance. Bending the hips is essential for the proper timing of your putt and also helps to relax the entire body. There are other factors which determine your hip position: the length of the putter, type of putter head, contour of the green, and so forth. Although these are all important, the basic requirement is that your hips should be in a comfortable position since your hands and arms must be permitted to come into the ball in the most efficient and comfortable manner. Keep a straight back, bending your head from the neck only.

Be sure your eyes are directly over the ball and the center of your putter's blade or club head is placed behind the ball, square to the putting line. If you look straight down at a point between the ball and your feet, you will know that you are standing too far away from your ball. On the other hand, should you look down on a spot ahead of your ball, you are standing too close to it. Your shoulders should be parallel to the putting line.

Be sure to keep your shoulders relaxed, because when they are tense, the result may be tension in your arms and hands. Your arms should hang in a completely relaxed and natural position. Do not force your elbows either in or out. Although it is true that some of the great putters seem to use their legs as a means to restrain their arms as the ball is stroked, in the final analysis the arms must

The putting technique of Doug Sanders.

have freedom to come into the ball. To sum-
marize, your eyes should be directly above
the club head, and your hands should be
just behind the ball, opposite the putter blade,
with your forearms barely touching or just
missing your pants.

The fundamental putting stroke can be
broken down into four steps: the waggle,
the backswing, the downswing, and the follow-through.

Your actual putting stroke begins with
the waggle, which helps to establish the "feel"
of the stroke, just as it was employed when
taking a full swing. Many golfers start their
waggle with the putter blade in front of the
ball and then square it in front of the ball
two or three times. This waggle method is
supposed to aid them in lining up the shot,
and by moving the putter in back and in
front of the ball, they can get their stroke
smoothly under way. Some players' waggle
is no more than a slight up-and-down tapping
motion of the club head behind the ball. Regardless of the waggle method employed,
use it to loosen your muscles and relieve tension.

The backswing must be a very smooth and
cohesive action. Start the motion back with
the left hand square to the putting line, and
use only the hands and forearms in bringing
the club back with its face square to the line
of the putt. Keeping the right elbow tight
against the right side helps hold the hands in
line. As you bring the putter back, keep it as
low to the ground as possible. The wrist
action should be a natural feeling. No effort
should be made to restrict—or overdo—the
wrist movement. With the longer putts there
will naturally be more wrist break than with
the shorter putts. However, even with the
shortest strokes, you will still feel a slight
suppleness in your wrists. Although length
of the backswing is determined to some degree by the length of the putt to be made, it
should be kept at a minimum. This reduces
the chance for possible error. On short putts
you generally have to take the club head
back only 4 or 5 inches, on long ones 2 feet
at the maximum. On very long ones it may
be necessary to take the club head back to a
point where the right forearm will slide back
2 or 3 inches. But otherwise this forearm
should move only very slightly. Also, although

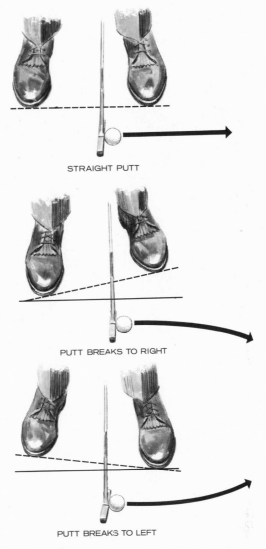

STRAIGHT PUTT

PUTT BREAKS TO RIGHT

PUTT BREAKS TO LEFT

While the square stance is ideal for straight putts,
it generally is wise to move the left foot either forward or back on greens with a sharp break.

the speed of the backswing is a matter of
personal preference, most golfers find the
deliberate backswing more effective than the
brisk one.

On the downswing your left hand does the
guiding and your right supplies the power.
After only a very slight pause at the top of the
backswing, the right hand takes over and
starts moving the club slowly down. As it
moves toward the ball, the acceleration
should be gradually increased. While the right

It is not the angle of the blade at address that determines the line the ball travels, but the path of the blade on the take-away and follow-through. Left, the blade is toed-in, but the clubhead travels directly away from and then directly toward the hole—and the ball goes in. Right, the blade is square to the hole, but a bad stroke will send the ball off line.

hand applies this increased force, the left should be guiding the club head through the ball by remaining square to the putting line.

The follow-through should be straight along the intended line of the putt with the club face still square to the hole. The length of the follow-through will vary with the distance of the putt. On short putts, the follow-through is short, too. The club head comes into the ball and stops quickly on the ground only 2 to 4 inches after impart. On putts of greater length you should make a complete, more natural follow-through. Actually, the length of follow-through, like that of your backswing, can be learned only by practice, and more practice.

During the entire putt, hold your body and head steady. By doing this you will restrict body movement to a very minimum. Do not move your head until reasonably sure the ball has dropped into the cup or ceased motion. In most cases, be sure to hit your putts crisply. Do not "baby" them. And remember: no putt that is short of the hole ever has a

chance to go in. But when you do give yourself a chance to hole the putt and may go past, be cautious and do not risk having a tricky downhill, sidehill putt coming back.

Make up your mind before you address your ball as to the amount of force you are going to apply and whether or not you are going to stroke firmly for the hole or just lag it up. There are some instances where it is better to have a putt fall short of a hole than overrun it. For example, most golfers would rather have a five-footer uphill than a three-footer downhill. But on long putts that you intend to play short, always attempt to leave your ball in a good position for your second putt. If you are going to stroke boldly toward the hole, it is not necessary to allow for as great a break as you would if you were lagging your shot. A ball stroked firmly tends to overcome the breaks and bumps more readily than a lagged putt.

The question of whether or not to have a flagstick or pin attended is generally a matter of personal preference. On long putts, most golfers usually prefer to have the pin attended. This gives them a background to hit at and often a place to aim. On short putts, it is generally best to have the pin removed since you will want as much room as possible for your ball in the cup, and leaving the flagstick in does not help matters. With downhill chips, unless they are very short, leave the flagstick in. It may slow a ball up that might otherwise go sailing past; sometimes the ball may even bounce right into the cup.

Do not freeze over your ball. Once you have the line, have made your judgment as to amount of force needed, and have taken your practice swing, step up to it confidently and stroke away. Many putts, especially short ones, are missed for one of two reasons: not taking enough time or taking too much. Actually, many golfers prefer the "tap" stroke on a short putt.

In the tap putt the stroke is executed with the hands only, using the wrists as hinges. The arms and the rest of the body remain still. This cuts down on the radius of the swing. On the long putt stroke it is from the shoulders to the club head. On the tap stroke it is only from the wrists to the club head. In it the forward action of the club head stops a few inches after the ball is struck. This cuts down on the arc of the swing, compared with the long putt stroke, which is more like the action of a pendulum with a follow-through similar in length to the backswing.

The two characteristics of the tap putt—the shorter radius of the swing and the shorter swing arc—cut down on the force you get compared with using the same amount of effort with the longer putt stroke. This means you can "tap" your short putts quite firmly and still only send the ball the short distance desired. Better yet, you can again feel the swing of the club head in your hands, so that there is no temptation to jerk or wrench the putt off line. A word of warning: there comes a point where the tap putt will not develop enough force to achieve the required distance and still stay on line. As a rule of thumb, therefore, do not attempt to use the tap stroke on putts of much more than 6 feet. Forcing the tap stroke is just as senseless as using the long putt stroke for short putts.

GOLF STRATEGY

Golf is largely a mental game—a game played mostly between your ears. For example, you should never just walk up to the ball and hit away. That is, every shot you make while out on the course should have a purpose. When you step up to the tee or come up to your ball elsewhere on the course, try to visualize the way the shot should be played and where you want to place your ball. Keep in mind that some holes and shots can be played aggressively; others should be played more conservatively. Weigh the risks and consequences against conditions, the situation, and your normal playing ability, and then make the shot accordingly. Often the longest hit is not the best hit; always consider the next shot. If you do not have the honor, carefully watch your partner and/or opponents shoot and see what happens to their shots. Consider especially the wind and terrain, and be aware of any hazards. Speaking of hazards, remember that they should always be approached with the positive-thinking psychology. That is, when you approach the shot with a sinking feeling in the pit of your stomach at the thought of an approaching obstacle, your ball always seems to be attracted to that hazard as if it had some sort of a strong magnet. To prevent this, concentrate on where you want to put the ball, not on where you do not want to hit it.

As you stand on the tee, remember that it is extremely important to control your drive position, because substantial error can affect all subsequent shots. In a fairway that is very narrow, for example, it often pays to tee the ball a little lower and not to swing too hard. This encourages you to stay down on the ball better and to hit through it. Also when hitting drives, employ the club in which you have the most confidence. There is a misconception among beginning players that they must use a driver from the tee. This is not true. Actually, if you are not hitting the No. 1 wood well, try the No. 3 wood. In this way, you will have a better chance to get the ball up into the air, and there is actually little difference in the resulting distance: about 15 to 30 yards between the two clubs. Remember that it is going to take at least two shots to get on the green anyway, so why not play safe and get on in two? It is wise to play the percentages; it usually pays.

On short par-3 holes, it is a good idea to use a tee, even if you are using an iron, because the ball will come off it the same way every time. If you play it from the turf on the tee, you will not have as predictable a shot as you have from a tee.

In addition to planning each shot carefully, be sure that its alignment is proper. Before addressing the ball, stand behind it and study the situation carefully. This will give you a better over-all perspective of the shot, a chance to formulate a plan and to draw an imaginary target line. Then, as you walk toward the ball, keep looking at your target. This will focus in your mind a clear mental picture of what you are going to attempt to do when you take your stroke. When you get to your ball, you will be able to take the proper stance and swing to carry out the desired plan for the shot. Actually, this deliberate lining-up procedure should be followed on all shots since it will aid greatly in carrying out your planned strategy.

Even when winter rules permit teeing up in the fairway, do not do it unless the lie is very bad. Play the ball where it lies, because when you tee the ball up this practice encourages a scooping action that is bad for your fairway game. If you are in the rough or must play out of trouble, play it safe and do not gamble recklessly. One stroke lost is not going to make too great a difference in your final score. So if you are in trouble, play a safety shot into the fairway and try to salvage a par from there. Many times, an 80-shooter will end up with a score of over 90 because he gambled on shots where the odds were totally against him. Play it safe, and eliminate those eights and nines.

When you get close to the green, keep in mind the flagstick position. But, on longer approach shots, it is still safer and generally a more effective course of action to play to the center of the green rather than the pin. On short pitches and chips to a sloping green, it is usually better to be on the low side of the

hole. Study putts carefully; then stroke decisively and give your ball a chance to drop in on a putt. Do not, however, be overbold; keep your putt moving, but dying, at the cup. Remember that three-putt greens should be avoided at all cost.

Most good golfers follow the old philosophy that it takes only one good shot a hole to get a par. An excellent drive to the green on a par-3 hole, for example, will place your ball on the green within two putts of par. A well-executed approach shot can make up for a poor drive. Sinking a long putt may erase the missed iron shot out on the fairway. So, if you do not become discouraged after a poor shot, but go after the next one to make up for it, you will often end with a par on the hole. But never become ruffled, stubborn, or angry. Although every player needs a little temper to keep him fired up, too many allow their tempers to get the better of them. The result, of course, is that they have trouble in visualizing their shots and just swing harder and harder. For this reason, keep your temper under control. Remember that next to a good swing, a cool head, coupled with good judgment, is the most valuable asset in golf.

"Playing within yourself" means you must know your own game and its limitations. In golf, there is no point in fooling yourself. If you are not a professional, you are an amateur; if you are an amateur, you are probably an average golfer. And an average golfer simply cannot be expected to play scratch golf. If you can admit that fact to yourself, you are on the way to knowing your game and playing in character.

One good method to genuine improvement and knowing your game is to estimate your own par before you step on the first tee this weekend. Par, for instance, for the 18-handicapper is not 72; it is 90. Most courses have four short holes (par-3), four long holes (par-5), and ten other holes of varying lengths over which the scratch player's par is four. Therefore, the sensible amateur must figure the numbers printed on the card so that they come within his own abilities. For example, a long par-4 will be a par-5 for him, and if he gets a four he has, in effect, made a personal birdie. The same applies, of course, to those difficult par-3 holes. They become par-4's for the average golfer. Now, using a little arithmetic on this imaginary game, you should reach the following conclusion. If you take fours at all the short holes, fives at all the long holes, and fives again on all the par-4's, your total will be 86. That's playing 14-handicap golf, and 14-handicap golf is a good deal better than average.

Be sure to select the club which will allow you to stay well within your swing's capabilities. Many players do not do this because they overrate their strength. This means they must swing too hard to get the full distance. It would be better to take one more club (for example, the No. 4 iron instead of No. 5 iron) to make the shot. By not swinging as hard, you will make more solid contact and, of course, have greater accuracy. Remember that it is better to sacrifice distance for accuracy. You will generally score better.

You must, of course, overclub with care, and there are cases where it is even unwise. For example, if there is an out-of-bounds, a water hazard, a big sand trap, or woods beyond a green, do not overclub. Here, it would be better to take the club that, if hit perfectly, will put you on the green. Should you take more club, in this instance, and hit the shot perfectly, you would be in deep trouble. On the other hand, if there is a big trap in front of the green and no trouble behind it, the opposite strategy would usually hold true. In this case, you should take ample club and, if you mis-hit the shot slightly, you will still reach the green or be hole-high. Even if you hit the shot perfectly and go over the green, you won't be in so much trouble as if you were short of the green. In other words, select the club that puts you in the best position for your next shot and that will keep you out of worse trouble.

There are certain shots for which location of the green will determine the amount of club to employ. For instance, when hitting from an elevated position to the green, use one club less than normal, whereas when hitting to elevated greens, take one more club. But, in normal situations, it is best to use ample club for your shot.

Always make the easiest possible shot. Do not try to show off and impress your partner or opponents. For example, do not take short cuts on dog-legs. It does not pay except in extraordinary situations. It is al-ways wise to play the hole as it is designed, and you will have a better angle from which to play your next shot. Although it may sound very elementary, play the shot the easiest possible way, and you will enjoy your round of golf a great deal more.

As you can see, attacking a golf course for the lowest possible score demands more than strength, timing, and a repeating golf swing. You must (1) know your own game, (2) know your limitations, (3) play within them, and (4) think! And you must never forget that the name of the game is "Keep the ball in play."

The Vardon Trophy is awarded each year by the PGA to the player with the lowest average score per round for a minimum of 80 rounds (see Section III). The difference between the top money winners and the player who is barely able to cover expenses is only one or two strokes per round. Actually, the differences in scores are so small on the average that it is difficult at times to distinguish the characteristics of the very best players from the others who are nearly as skillful. The following analysis of the performances of the best players in the last two U.S. Open Championships gives a fairly precise idea of how good you have to be at a variety of shots in order to rank among the best:

Driving. You have to drive a ball consistently between 250 and 275 yards, and land in a fairway less than 35 yards wide four out of five times.

Long Irons. You have to hit a ball over 200 yards and, on the average, be able to come within 36 feet of the pin or less than 6 per cent of the original distance.

Medium Irons. From a distance of from 150 to 175 yards, you have to land, on the average, within 26 feet of the target.

Long Putts. From 75 feet away, you have to putt to within 4 feet of the pin. On putts of less than 75 feet, you have to come proportionately closer. Thus a 40-foot putt should come only 2.4 feet away; and a 30-foot putt, only 1.8 feet away.

Short Putts. You have to sink all putts up to 2½ feet, half of the 6-footers, and one out of ten of the 20-footers. You have to do this on every variety of green and under all conditions of play.

Driving downwind.

Driving against the wind.

Chip Shots. You have to chip nearly as well as when putting. From 75 feet, the shot should get within 5 feet of the hole, on the average.

Recovery Shot. When a shot misses the green, the next one should come within 10 feet of the pin if it is taken from 75 feet out in deep grass, and within 12 feet from this same 75-foot distance if it is taken from a sand trap.

When you realize just how well the tournament players of today must play to win, you can only stand back and admire their performances.

The Weather Conditions

Golf is fast becoming a year-round sport, even in our northern states. In many areas, the only thing that stops the sport is a snowstorm. Actually, your golf strategy changes as the weather changes. In colder weather you must dress for comfort and freedom of movement, especially through the shoulders. It is also important to keep your hands and the golf ball warm. Most golf balls perform best at a temperature of approximately 85 degrees. As the ball becomes colder, it can lose 10 to 20 yards of distance on a shot. To keep both your hands and ball warm, use one of those small hand-warmers that are available and keep your hands and extra ball in your pockets. Change to the warm ball on each hole.

In hot weather, pace yourself so that you will not be tired out before the round is completed. Rest at every opportunity. Also be sure to keep your hands dry. If you wear a glove, carry a spare so that you can change it when the one you are using becomes wet. When the fairways are sun-baked, tee your ball a little lower so that you can take full advantage of the extra roll.

Wet-Weather Play

To best his worst weather enemy, rain, a golfer must have the ability to adapt his game to wet-weather conditions. Beating the rain depends largely on maintaining a firm grip and selecting the proper club. Unless consideration is given to these essentials, no effective shot, short of an accident, can be made.

A firm grip depends on keeping the hands and club dry. Wet hands, besides causing slippage, also promote a feeling of insecurity that could affect the rest of the swing. Before handling the grip, wipe it dry with a towel kept in the umbrella ribs for that purpose. Without wasting much time, address the ball and make your shot as fast as possible so that the rain doesn't have time to affect your grip. Immediately afterward, the club is replaced in the golf bag and a cover placed over the clubs. This cover should be kept over the clubs at all times to prevent water from dripping into the bag while moving from shot to shot. Once the grips become saturated, good golf is seriously hampered.

A person who plays with gloves cuts down the possibility of slippage. A handkerchief wrapped around the grip can accomplish the same purpose. Even when the handkerchief itself is soaked, it is helpful, because the wrinkles in the fabric form rough, grippable ridges. But do not worry about keeping the ball or the club head dry. It is just a waste of time and will only take your mind off the serious business of hitting the shot.

Before teeing the ball, select a firm spot to take your stance. It is important to have your feet set so that they will not slip during the swing. Check the spikes on your shoes occasionally and clean them if they become clogged with bits of grass and mud. This will ensure a firmer stance, which is necessary when playing in wet weather.

Hitting from a wet, slippery fairway is similar to playing out of a fairway sand trap: maintaining a firm footing should be your first concern. As in playing out of the sand, only an absolutely clean-hit shot will do, so concentrate on making a controlled swing. To keep from sliding, minimize footwork by keeping the left heel planted. Make the swing mostly with the upper part of your torso: the hands, arms, and shoulders. To facilitate a solid footing, use a slightly wider stance than you normally do. While this rain stance will feel stiff, it provides a sure foundation and will keep you from losing your balance on sloppy ground.

Another thing to keep in mind when playing in the rain or on wet fairways is that the course will play longer because the roll will be less than under normal conditions. Accept this fact, and hit your drives as you would normally. By trying to hit the ball higher or differently to get more distance, you will only get into more trouble and make more mistakes. The wetness of the grass has a tendency to keep the ball low when hit off the fairway. For this reason, avoid using the less lofted clubs. It is more difficult to use clubs like the No. 2 iron or No. 3 wood under these conditions. Most golfers prefer using a No. 4 wood off wet grass because it is easier to get the ball into the air than with a No. 2 or No. 3 wood.

Occasionally, the ball will come to rest in a patch of mud. When this happens, take a club with enough loft to get out in one shot. Mud on a ball will affect its flight. There is not much that you can do about it except to hit the ball as usual and hope for the best. If the Local Rule on embedded balls is in effect, a ball embedded in the turf can be lifted and wiped without penalty; so can a ball lying on a green, anytime. The exception is when the ball is embedded in a hazard. Then it must be played as it lies.

Should the ball land in casual water, not in a trap or other hazard, you are entitled to a free drop. The drop must be made to the closest point of relief, no nearer the hole. Whenever you have a free drop, take it. It is to your advantage, unless, of course, you have to drop behind a tree.

When the ball goes off line and into the rough, your main concern should be to get out in one stroke. This can be accomplished best by using a more lofted club, from a No. 4 iron up, depending on the texture of the grass. Generally the ball has to be hit harder than normally. There is a good reason for avoiding the less lofted clubs. They produce lower shots that will take water and be stopped by the grass. You have to have enough loft to get the ball into the air as quickly as possible.

(A) Playing a right-to-left wind. Always play the ball against the wind, regardless of its direction. With the wind blowing from right to left, therefore, you will have to align the shot well to the right of your intended target. How far to the right you align your stance will depend upon the velocity of the wind and your own discretion. Keep in mind that the ball will roll five or six yards more than usual after it alights, because a right-to-left wind puts overspin on the ball.

(B) Playing a left-to-right wind. Still following the rule of thumb of always playing the ball against the wind, you will have to align the shot well to the left of your target. Of course, how far to the left you align your stance will still depend upon the velocity of the wind and your own discretion.

(C) Playing against the wind or downwind. Align your stance so that the ball is played directly on target. Position the ball farther back than usual; the reasons for this will be discussed on the following pages. Your choice of clubs will be dictated, again, by wind velocity and your discretion.

Generally, short irons cause the most trouble. A club head striking a wet ball in wet grass will cause a "flier" in which the ball leaves the face without spin and travels farther than normal. Under such conditions, it is advisable to use less club.

Although there are disadvantages to playing over a wet course, they can be offset by the advantages of playing on the green and around it. Play around the green tends to be easier. You can strike right for the hole, because the ball does not bounce as badly or roll as far. Wet greens, of course, tend to slow the ball down, but not to any great extent. This allows you to stroke more boldly for the cup. Reading the greens for breaks is less of a chore because the wet grass tends to keep the ball on line better. So aim more directly for the hole. If you read too much into the green, you will find that the ball is more apt to roll to one side or the other instead of into the cup.

There are two points to remember if there is casual water on the green: (1) Coming off the apron, it is best to chip over the water because the ball stops rather quickly. If the ball must be putted, the stroke should be much firmer to get it through the water. (2) At no time are you required to stand in water or putt from water on the green. The casual-water rule applies on the green as well as on the fairway. So remember: do not hesitate to move the ball or yourself to a drier location, provided it is no nearer the hole.

The enjoyment of playing golf in the rain will be increased if you dress properly. There is nothing more annoying than playing in wet clothes. Besides, there is always the danger of wetting your hands on wet clothing. Golfers who wear glasses have the added problem of keeping them clear of water to maintain good vision. They will find it helpful to wear a long-billed cap. One other thing. Keep several towels in your bag as replacements for the one in your umbrella. They will come in handy if the going is really wet.

If you are caught out on the course during a thunder and lightning storm, seek shelter in a low spot or in a substantial building of some type. Never stand under a tree or on a high location. Also be sure to leave your golf clubs elsewhere since the metal in them could attract lightning. The adjustable hood on the golf bag will keep them dry.

Windy-Day Strategy

No matter on what golf course you play, sooner or later you will find yourself playing on a windy day. There are a few adjustments you must make in your strategy so that you can play well under wind conditions. For instance, when playing your irons against the wind, use a club with less loft than you normally would. If the shot calls for a No. 7 iron, take a No. 4 or No. 5 iron. Align your stance so that the ball is played directly on target, but address the ball a little more toward the right foot than you normally would. Choke up on the grip an inch or two and swing the club just a little more easily than you would for a usual full shot. The purpose of choking up on the grip is, of course, to reduce the arc of the swing. This permits you to use the less lofted club and to keep the ball lower against the wind. In making impact with the ball, the club head should hit into the ball with a decided descending blow. The follow-through should be restricted to the degree that when completed, your extended arms will point toward the green, with the back of your left hand pointing skyward.

On shots from the tee against the wind, position the ball at address slightly more toward the center of your stance than normal. The ball should also be teed lower than usual. A handy way to gauge the proper height of the tee is to plant the tee in the ground until it rests no higher from the turf than the thickness of your finger. In swinging, do not try to "kill" the ball; take an easy swing.

Although it may seem strange, you use the same strategy and stroke with irons downwind as against the wind. But the object is still the same: you must keep the ball from where the wind can get at it. It goes without saying that you should use less club going downwind. Furthermore, the shot should be played with less force. This should be accomplished by slowing the tempo of your swing.

On shots from the tee with the wind, the strategy of shot differs radically from that in using an iron. Instead of keeping the ball away from the wind, you want to take full advantage of it. To get the ball high into the air, therefore, you should tee the ball as high as the tee will allow and play the ball more toward the left foot than normally. In hitting the ball, you should again avoid the temptation to kill it.

When playing a cross wind, always play both woods and irons in the same manner as you do against the wind. If the wind is blowing from right to left, you should aim your shot well to the right of your intended target. When playing a left-to-right wind, you will have to aim your shot well to the left of your target. How far to the right or to the left you align your stance, of course, will depend on the velocity of the wind and your own discretion.

Wind can also affect your putting. When the ball nears the cup and is traveling at a very slow speed, a strong wind can easily move it to one side or the other of your putting line. Therefore, on long putts that you plan to lag up to the hole, take this into consideration.

Practice Strategy

The importance of a short practice session before a game of golf cannot be emphasized too strongly. Athletes in all other sports warm up before they start actual competition. Lack of warm-up is one reason why a golfer will find himself playing better on the back nine than on the opening nine. He actually spends the first nine holes warming up, although he is probably unaware of it. He loses valuable strokes, and he runs the danger of compounding his first simple mistakes in larger errors as the game progresses.

Arrive on the practice driving range about forty-five minutes before your golf game. Do not take friends or acquaintances along, because even their most well-meaning suggestions and comments are a distraction. Assume the attitude that you are about to give yourself a brief private review lesson in basic golf techniques. As you proceed through the warm-up, check yourself for a smooth swing; proper stance, balance, grip, and hand-and-arm action; straight drives, accurate putting, and sharp timing. It is important to remember that the warm-up is only a conditioner. It is not the occasion to experiment with new ideas, or an opportunity to practice difficult shots, or a chance to try blasting your way out of a sand trap. Your chief concern is to perfect the basic shots. You can spend time on these more difficult problems in your practice sessions during the week. Some courses have practice driving ranges; others do not. If your course does not have one, the best thing to do is stop off at one en route to the course.

Start warming up with the woods. To loosen your arm muscles and trim the waistline, pick two woods out of your bag and swing them easily at an imaginary ball for about two minutes. Then put one back in your bag and begin hitting balls from the tee. Aim for certain areas out on the fairway. After the ball falls short, or over, or to the left or right of those areas, adjust your subsequent drives accordingly. A good idea is to start driving with your highest-numbered wood and gradually work your way down to your driver. But do not swing hard.

After you have finished driving a few dozen balls, take out your irons. Start with the highest-numbered one and drive it easily from the tee. Then hit several balls from the grass with it. Repeat this procedure with the next highest-numbered iron, then the next, and so on. And again, do not swing hard. When you have finished in this manner with all your woods and irons, take out your driver and slam into a few balls as hard as you normally do. Do the same thing with each of your irons, starting from the highest-numbered.

In putting, begin 1 foot away from the cup. It is very important to practice short putts; but unfortunately, golfers do not seem to practice them often enough. Remember: the most important putts are the short ones. When you are sinking the one-footers regularly, try putting from 2 feet out; then 3, 4, 5, and so on. Continue this procedure until you are scoring from about 20 feet away and you are confident that you are putting accurately.

Follow your practice putts with brief exercises to strengthen arms. For example: (1) Hold a club straight out in your left hand and raise it up and down several times. (2) Take several hard swings with two woods at the same time. (3) Place a wood behind your back and wrap your arms around the shaft. Twist your trunk from left to right; loosen up your waist, your knees, your arms, and

your back. To conclude the practice, take the club which feels the most comfortable (maybe the No. 5 iron or No. 4 wood) and hit a few lusty drives with it. This will give you an added feeling of confidence in your ability and serve to brighten your mental outlook for the coming game.

Warming up may sound like a hard routine. Actually, it normally should take you about a half-hour to complete the entire practice. This would enable you to relax for about fifteen minutes prior to the match.

How to Take a Lesson

Much has been written about the art of teaching golf; however, the importance of the art of taking a lesson has been generally overlooked. While it does not require any physical skill, you must use a modicum of common sense.

First and foremost, be honest with your golf professional and tell him exactly what you are trying to accomplish. Do you want a complete picture of the golf swing, or do you just want to play for the exercise? Are you willing to practice, or don't you have the time? Is this lesson to be one of a series, or a one-shot deal? Having your objectives clear at the start and making them known to the instructor can save both of you a lot of grief. But being honest with the pro doesn't stop there. Reveal any physical handicaps you may have, however minor, that could affect the way you swing.

Another problem with many of the players is that they are not good listeners. Their one idea is to belt as many balls as they can in the allotted time. Remember, it is impossible to get your money's worth if you insist on hitting while the instructor is explaining something. Only by listening will you be able to absorb it. Also remember that listening to your golf professional entails carrying out what he is telling you—even if it does not feel comfortable for a time. When you do anything new, it is bound to feel strange at first. It means listening to *him*, not listening to well-meaning, but mostly uninformed, advice from your golf buddies.

A good listener also has patience. Do not expect miracles in five minutes or worry unduly just because you cannot hit each shot perfectly. Do not be impatient when your pro tells you he liked the swing, even when you missed! What he means is that you are that much nearer to really swinging the club. So keep at it, and, with hard work and patience, you will be surprised how good you can become.

Never be afraid to ask your pro a question. After all, that is what he is there for. This applies to any point he is making, not just golf language. If he knows you do not understand, he can usually find another way of putting it which will be clear to you.

Many people are too anxious when they go for a lesson. They tighten up and can hardly hit a shot. Remember that fear and the golf swing do not mix. Confidence, on the other hand, is one of the best tonics for a golf swing.

So next time you take a lesson:

1. Be honest with your pro and state your objectives.
2. Listen to him—and only him—and do what he tells you.
3. Be patient; the golf swing, like Rome, is not built in a day.
4. Be confident. Remember: fear will make a paralyzed rabbit out of anyone!
5. Ask your pro questions; he will not bite!

SECTION VI

Rules and Etiquette of Golf

Basically, golf is a simple game, but a thousand things may happen between tee and cup. To cover these irregular situations, the *Rules of Golf* are long and complicated.

THE

RULES

OF

GOLF

as approved by

THE UNITED STATES GOLF ASSOCIATION

and

THE ROYAL AND ANCIENT GOLF CLUB

OF ST. ANDREWS, SCOTLAND

Effective January 1, 1979

CONTENTS

SECTION I — ETIQUETTE
SECTION II — DEFINITIONS
SECTION III— THE RULES OF PLAY

Rule 1: The Game
Rule 2: The Club and the Ball
Rule 3: Maximum of Fourteen Clubs
Rule 4: Agreement to Waive Rules Prohibited
Rule 5: General Penalty
Rule 6: Match Play
Rule 7: Stroke Play
Rule 8: Practice
Rule 9: Advice and Assistance
Rule 10: Information as to Strokes Taken
Rule 11: Disputes, Decisions and Doubt as to Rights
Rule 12: The Honor
Rule 13: Playing Outside Teeing Ground
Rule 14: Ball Falling off Tee
Rule 15: Order of Play in Threesome or Foursome
Rule 16: Ball Played as It Lies
Rule 17: Improving Lie or Stance and Influencing Ball Prohibited
Rule 18: Loose Impediments
Rule 19: Striking at Ball
Rule 20: Ball Farther from the Hole Played First
Rule 21: Playing a Wrong Ball or from a Wrong Place
Rule 22: Lifting, Dropping and Placing
Rule 23: Identifying or Cleaning Ball
Rule 24: Ball Interfering with Play
Rule 25: A Moving Ball
Rule 26: Ball in Motion Stopped or Deflected
Rule 27: Ball at Rest Moved
Rule 28: Ball Unfit for Play
Rule 29: Ball Lost, Out of Bounds, or Unplayable
Rule 30: Provisional Ball
Rule 31: Obstructions
Rule 32: Casual Water, Ground Under Repair, Hole Made by Burrowing Animal
Rule 33: Hazards
Rule 34: The Flagstick
Rule 35: The Putting Green
Rule 36: The Committee
Rule 37: The Player
Rule 38: Scoring in Stroke Play
Rule 39: Bogey, Par or Stableford Competitions
Rule 40: Three-Ball, Best-Ball and Four-Ball Match Play
Rule 41: Four-Ball Stroke Play

APPENDIX I: LOCAL RULES
  Lifting an Embedded Ball
  Practice at Putting Green of Hole Played
  Marking Position of Lifted Ball
  Prohibition against Touching Line of Putt with Club
  Relief from Temporary Obstructions
  "Preferred Lies" and "Winter Rules"

APPENDIX II: DESIGN OF CLUBS

APPENDIX III: MARKINGS ON CLUBS

APPENDIX IV: MISCELLANEOUS
  How to Decide Ties in Handicap Events
  Pairings for Match Play
  Par Computation
  Flagstick Dimensions
  Protection of Persons against Lightning
  Rules of Amateur Status
  USGA Policy on Gambling

CHANGES SINCE 1978

THE RULES OF GOLF

Section I
ETIQUETTE

Courtesy on the Course

Consideration for Other Players

In the interest of all, players should play without delay.

No player should play until the players in front are out of range.

Players searching for a ball should signal the players behind them to pass as soon as it becomes apparent that the ball will not easily be found; they should not search for five minutes before doing so. They should not continue play until the players following them have passed and are out of range.

When the play of a hole has been completed, players should immediately leave the putting green.

Behavior During Play

No one should move, talk or stand close to or directly behind the ball or the hole when a player is addressing the ball or making a stroke.

The player who has the honor should be allowed to play before his opponent or fellow-competitor tees his ball.

Priority on the Course

In the absence of special rules, two-ball matches should have precedence of and be entitled to pass any three- or four-ball match.

A single player has no standing and should give way to a match of any kind.

Any match playing a whole round is entitled to pass a match playing a shorter round.

If a match fails to keep its place on the course and loses more than one clear hole on the players in front, it should allow the match following to pass.

Care of the Course

Holes in Bunkers

Before leaving a bunker, a player should carefully fill u and smooth over all holes and footprints made by him.

Restore Divots, Repair Ball-Marks and Damage by Spikes

Through the green, a player should ensure that any tu cut or displaced by him is replaced at once and pressed dow and that any damage to the putting green made by the ba is carefully repaired. Damage to the putting green caused b golf shoe spikes should be repaired *on completion of the ho*

Damage to Greens—Flagsticks, Bags, etc.

Players should insure that, when putting down bags, or th flagstick, no damage is done to the putting green, and tha neither they nor their caddies damage the hole by standin close to it, in handling the flagstick or in removing the ba from the hole. The flagstick should be properly replaced i the hole before the players leave the putting green.

Golf Carts

Local Notices regulating the movement of golf carts shoul be strictly observed.

Damage Through Practice Swings

In taking practice swings, players should avoid causin damage to the course, particularly the tees, by removing divo

Section II
DEFINITIONS

1. Addressing the Ball

A player has "addressed the ball" when he has taken hi stance and has also grounded his club, except that in a hazar a player has addressed the ball when he has taken his stanc

2. Advice

"Advice" is any counsel or suggestion which could influence a player in determining his play, the choice of a club, or th method of making a stroke.

Information on the Rules or Local Rules is not advice.

3. Ball Deemed to Move

A ball is deemed to have "moved" if it leave its positio and come to rest in any other place.

4. Ball Holed

A ball is "holed" when it lies within the circumference o the hole and all of it is below the level of the lip of the hol

5. Ball in Play, Provisional Ball, Wrong Ball

a. A ball is "in play" as soon as the player has made a strok on the teeing ground. It remains as his ball in play until hole out, except when it is out of bounds, lost or lifted, or anothe ball has been substituted under an applicable Rule or Loca Rule: a ball so substituted becomes the ball in play.

b. A "provisional ball" is a ball played under Rule 30 fo a ball which may be lost outside a water hazard or may b out of bounds. It ceases to be a provisional ball when the Rul provides *either* that the player continue play with it as th ball in play *or* that it be abandoned.

c. A "wrong ball" is any ball other than the ball in play o a provisional ball or, in stroke play, an alternate ball playe in accordance with Rule 11-5.

6. Ball Lost

A ball is "lost" if:

a. It be not found, or be not identified as his by the playe within five minutes after the player's side, or his or thei caddies have begun to search for it; *or*

b. The player has put another ball into play under the Rules, en though he may not have searched for the original ball; *or* c. The player has played any stroke with a provisional ball m a point beyond the place where the original ball is ely to be, whereupon the provisional ball becomes the ll in play.

Time spent in playing a wrong ball is not counted in the e minute period allowed for search.

Caddie, Forecaddie and Equipment

a. A "caddie" is one who carries or handles a player's clubs ring play and otherwise assists him in accordance with e Rules.

When one caddie is employed by more than one player, he always deemed to be the caddie of the player whose ball involved, and equipment carried by him is deemed to be at player's equipment, except when the caddie acts upon ecific directions of another player, in which case he is nsidered to be that other player's caddie.

Note: *In threesome, foursome, best-ball and four-ball play, addie carrying for more than one player should be assigned the members of one side.*

b. A "forecaddie" is one employed by the Committee to dicate to players the position of balls on the course, and is outside agency (Definition 22).

c. "Equipment" is anything used, worn or carried by or for e player except his ball in play. Equipment includes a golf rt. If such a cart is shared by more than one player, its tus under the Rules is the same as that of a caddie employed more than one player.

Casual Water

"Casual water" is any temporary accumulation of water ich is visible before or after the player takes his stance and ich is not a hazard of itself or is not in a water hazard. Snow d ice are either casual water or loose impediments, at the tion of the player.

Committee

The "Committee" is the committee in charge of the com- tition.

D. Competitor

A "competitor" is a player in a stroke competition. A "fellow- mpetitor" is any person with whom the competitor plays. either is partner of the other.

In stroke play foursome and four-ball competitions, where e context so admits, the word "competitor" or "fellow- mpetitor" shall be held to include his partner.

1. Course

The "course" is the whole area within which play is per- itted. It is the duty of the Committee to define its boun- aries accurately.

2. Flagstick

The "flagstick" is a movable straight indicator provided by e Committee, with or without bunting or other material tached, centered in the hole to show its position. It shall e circular in cross-section.

3. Ground Under Repair

"Ground under repair" is any portion of the course so arked by order of the committee concerned or so declared y its authorized representative. It includes material piled for emoval and a hole made by a greenkeeper, even if not so arked. Stakes and lines defining ground under repair are ot in such ground.

4. Hazards

A "hazard" is any bunker or water hazard. Bare patches, rapes, roads, tracks and paths are not hazards.

a. A "bunker" is an area of bare ground, often a depression,

which is usually covered with sand. Grass-covered ground bordering or within a bunker is *not* part of the hazard.

b. A "water hazard" is any sea, lake, pond, river, ditch, surface drainage ditch or other open water course (regardless of whether or not it contains water), and anything of a simi- lar nature.

All ground or water within the margin of a water hazard, whether or not it be covered with any growing substance, is part of the water hazard. The margin of a water hazard is deemed to extend vertically upwards.

c. A "lateral water hazard" is a water hazard or that part of a water hazard so situated that it is not possible or is deemed by the Committee to be impracticable to drop a ball behind the water hazard and keep the spot at which the ball last crossed the margin of the hazard between the player and the hole.

d. It is the duty of the Committee in charge of a course to define accurately the extent of the hazards and water hazards when there is any doubt. That part of a hazard to be played as a lateral water hazard should be distinctively marked. Stakes and lines defining the margins of hazards are not in the hazards.

15. Hole

The "hole" shall be 4-1/4 inches in diameter and at least 4 inches deep. If a lining be used, it shall be sunk at least 1 inch below the putting green surface unless the nature of the soil makes it impractical to do so; its outer diameter shall not exceed 4-1/4 inches.

16. Honor

The side which is entitled to play first from the teeing ground is said to have the "honor."

17. Loose Impediments

The term "loose impediments" denotes natural objects not fixed or growing and not adhering to the ball, and includes stones not solidly embedded, leaves, twigs, branches and the like, dung, worms and insects and casts or heaps made by them.

Snow and ice are either casual water or loose impediments, at the option of the player.

Sand and loose soil are loose impediments on the putting green, but not elsewhere on the course.

18. Marker

A "marker" is a scorer in stroke play who is appointed by the Committee to record a competitor's score. He may be a fellow-competitor. He is not a referee.

A marker should not lift a ball or mark its position unless authorized to do so by the competitor and, unless he is a fellow-competitor, should not attend the flagstick or stand at the hole or mark its position.

19. Observer

An "observer" is appointed by the Committee to assist a referee to decide questions of fact and to report to him any breach of a Rule or Local Rule. An observer should not attend the flagstick, stand at or mark the position of the hole, or lift the ball or mark its position.

20. Obstructions

An "obstruction" is anything artificial, whether erected, placed or left on the course, including the artificial surfaces and sides of roads and paths but excepting: —

a. Objects defining out of bounds, such as walls, fences, stakes and railings;

b. In water hazards, artificially surfaced banks or beds, in- cluding bridge supports when part of such a bank. Bridges and bridge supports which are not part of such a bank are ob- structions;

c. Any construction declared by the Committee to be an integral part of the course.

21. Out of Bounds

"Out of bounds" is ground on which play is prohibited.

When out of bounds is fixed by stakes or a fence, the out of bounds line is determined by the nearest inside points of the stakes or fence posts at ground level; the line is deemed to extend vertically upwards. When out of bounds is fixed by a line on the ground, the line itself is out of bounds.

A ball is out of bounds when all of it lies out of bounds.

22. Outside Agency

An "outside agency" is any agency not part of the match or, in stroke play, not part of a competitor's side, and includes a referee, a marker, an observer, or a forecaddie employed by the Committee. Neither wind nor water is an outside agency.

23. Partner

A "partner" is a player associated with another player on the same side.

In a threesome, foursome or a four-ball where the context so admits, the word "player" shall be held to include his partner.

24. Penalty Stroke

A "penalty stroke" is one added to the score of a side under certain Rules. It does not affect the order of play.

25. Putting Green

The "putting green" is all ground of the hole being played which is specially prepared for putting or otherwise defined as such by the Committee.

A ball is deemed to be on the putting green when any part of it touches the putting green.

26. Referee

A "referee" is a person who has been appointed by the Committee to accompany players to decide questions of fact and of golf law. He shall act on any breach of Rule or Local Rule which he may observe or which may be reported to him by an observer (Definition 19).

In stroke play the Committee may limit a referee's duties.

A referee should not attend the flagstick, stand at or mark the position of the hole, or lift the ball or mark its position.

27. Rub of the Green

A "rub of the green" occurs when a ball in motion is stopped or deflected by any outside agency.

28. Sides and Matches

SIDE: A player, or two or more players who are partners.

SINGLE: A match in which one plays against another.

THREESOME: A match in which one plays against two, and each side plays one ball.

FOURSOME: A match in which two play against two, and each side plays one ball.

THREE-BALL: A match in which three play against one another, each playing his own ball.

BEST-BALL: A match in which one plays against the better ball of two or the best ball of three players.

FOUR-BALL: A match in which two play their better ball against the better ball of two other players.

Note: *In a best-ball or four-ball match, if a partner be absent for reasons satisfactory to the Committee, the remaining member(s) of his side may represent the side.*

29. Stance

Taking the "stance" consists in a player placing his feet in position for and preparatory to making a stroke.

30. Stipulated Round

The "stipulated round" consists of playing the holes of the course in their correct sequence unless otherwise authorized by the Committee. The number of holes in a stipulated round is 18 unless a smaller number is authorized by the Committee.

In match play only, the Committee may, for the purpose of settling a tie, extend the stipulated round to as many holes as are required for a match to be won.

31. Stroke

A "stroke" is the forward movement of the club made wi■ the intention of fairly striking at and moving the ball.

32. Teeing

In "teeing," the ball may be placed on the ground or ■ sand or other substance in order to raise it off the grou■

33. Teeing Ground

The "teeing ground" is the starting place for the hole ■ be played. It is a rectangular area two club-lengths in dep■ the front and the sides of which are defined by the outsi■ limits of two tee-markers. A ball is outside the teeing grou■ when all of it lies outside the stipulated area.

When playing the first stroke with any ball (including ■ provisional ball) from the teeing ground, the tee-marke■ are immovable obstructions (Definition 20).

34. Terms Used in Reckoning in Match Play

In match play, the reckoning of holes is kept by the terms: ■ so many "holes up" or "all square," and so many "to pla■

A side is "dormie" when it is as many holes up as there a■ holes remaining to be played.

35. Through the Green

"Through the green" is the whole area of the cour■ except:—

a. Teeing ground and putting green of the hole being playe■

b. All hazards on the course.

36. Types of Club

There are three recognized types of golf club:—

An "iron" club is one with a head which usually is relative■ narrow from face to back, and usually is made of steel.

A "wood" club is one with a head relatively broad from fac■ to back, and usually is made of wood, plastic or a light met■

A "putter" is a club designed primarily for use on the puttir■ green — see Definition 25.

Section III
THE RULES OF PLAY

Rule 1
The Game

The Game of Golf consists in playing a ball from the teein■ ground into the hole by successive strokes in accordanc■ with the Rules.

PENALTY FOR BREACH OF RULE:
Match play—Loss of hole; Stroke play—Disqualification

Rule 2
The Club (Def. 36) and the Ball

The United States Golf Association and the Royal an■ Ancient Golf Club of St. Andrews reserve the right to chang■ the Rules and the interpretations regulating clubs and bal■ at any time.

1. Legal Clubs and Balls

The player's clubs, and the balls he uses, shall conform wit■ Clauses 2 and 3 of this Rule.

2. Form and Make of Clubs

a. GENERAL CHARACTERISTICS

The golf club shall be composed of a shaft and a head, an■ all of the various parts shall be fixed so that the club is on■

it; the club shall not be designed to be adjustable, except r weight.

Note: *Playing characteristics not to be changed during a und—Rule 2-2b.*

The club shall not be substantially different from the tra-tional and customary form and make, and shall conform ith the regulations governing the design of clubs at Appendix and the specifications for markings on clubs at Appendix III.

b. PLAYING CHARACTERISTICS NOT TO BE CHANGED

The playing characteristics of a club shall not be purposely hanged during a round; foreign material shall not be added the club face at any time.

Note: *Players in doubt as to the legality of clubs are advised consult the USGA. If a manufacturer is in doubt as to the gality of a club which he proposes to manufacture, he should bmit a sample to the USGA for a ruling, such sample to ecome the property of the USGA for reference purposes.*

The Ball

a. SPECIFICATIONS

The weight of the ball shall be *not greater* than 1.620 ounces oirdupois, and the size *not less* than 1.680 inches in diameter. The velocity of the ball shall be not greater than 250 feet per cond when measured on apparatus approved by the USGA: maximum tolerance of 2% will be allowed. The temperature the ball when so tested shall be 75 degrees Fahrenheit.

A brand of golf ball, when tested on apparatus approved by e USGA on the outdoor range at the USGA Headquarters

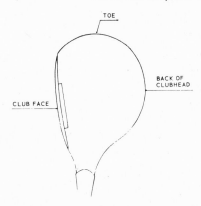

FIGURE B—TOP VIEW, WOOD CLUB

under the conditions set forth in the Overall Distance Standard for golf balls on file with the USGA, shall not cover an average distance in carry and roll exceeding 280 yards, plus a tolerance of 8%. (Note: The 8% tolerance will be reduced to a minimum of 4% as test techniques are improved.)

Exception:—In international team competitions, the size of the ball shall be *not less* than 1.620 inches in diameter and the Overall Distance Standard shall not apply.

Note: *The Rules of the Royal and Ancient Golf Club of St. Andrews, Scotland, provide that the weight of the ball shall be not greater than 1.620 ounces avoirdupois, the size not less than 1.620 inches in diameter and the velocity not greater than 250 feet per second (with 2% tolerance) when measured on apparatus approved by the Royal and Ancient Golf Club.*

b. FOREIGN MATERIAL PROHIBITED

Foreign material shall not be applied to a ball for the pur-pose of changing its playing characteristics.

PENALTY FOR BREACH OF RULE: *Disqualification.*

Rule 3
Maximum of Fourteen Clubs

1. Selection and Replacement of Clubs

The player shall start a stipulated round with not more than fourteen clubs. He is limited to the clubs thus selected for that round except that, without unduly delaying play, he may:—

a. If he started with fewer than fourteen, add as many as will bring his total to that number;

b. Replace, with any club, a club which becomes unfit for play in the normal course of play.

The addition or replacement of a club or clubs may not be made by borrowing from any other person playing on the course.

2. Side May Share Clubs

Partners may share clubs provided that the total number of clubs carried by the side does not exceed fourteen.

PENALTY FOR BREACH OF RULE 3-1 OR 3-2, REGARDLESS OF NUMBER OF WRONG CLUBS CARRIED:

Match play—Loss of one hole for each hole at which any violation occurred; maximum penalty per round: loss of two holes. The penalty shall be applied to the state of the match at the conclusion of the hole at which the violation is discovered, provided all players in the match have not left the putting green of the last hole of the match.

Stroke play—Two strokes for each hole at which any violation occurred; maximum penalty per round: four strokes.

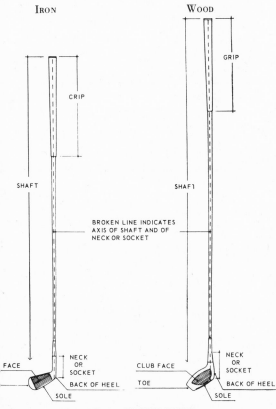

IRON   WOOD

FIGURE A—FRONT VIEW

Stableford Competitions—From total points scored for the round, deduction of two points for each hole at which any violation occurred; maximum deduction per round: four points.

Note: *A serious breach of this Rule should be dealt with by the Committee under Rule 1.*

3. Wrong Club Declared Out of Play

Any club carried or used in violation of this Rule shall be declared out of play by the player immediately upon discovery and thereafter shall not be used by the player during the round under *penalty of disqualification.*

Rule 4

Agreement to Waive Rules Prohibited

Players shall not agree to exclude the operation of any Rule or Local Rule or to waive any penalty incurred.

PENALTY FOR BREACH OF RULE:
Match play—Disqualification of both sides;
Stroke play—Disqualification of competitors concerned.

Rule 5

General Penalty

Except when otherwise provided for, the penalty for a breach of a Rule or Local Rule is:

Match play—Loss of hole;
Stroke play—Two strokes.

Rule 6
Match Play

1. Winner of Hole

In match play the game is played by holes.

Except as otherwise provided for in the Rules, a hole is won by the side which holes its ball in the fewer strokes. In a handicap match the lower net score wins the hole.

2. Halved Hole

A hole is halved if each side holes out in the same number of strokes.

When a player has holed out and his opponent has been left with a stroke for the half, nothing that the player who has holed out can do shall deprive him of the half which he has already gained; but if the player thereafter incur any penalty, the hole is halved.

3. Winner of Match

A match (which consists of a stipulated round, unless otherwise decreed by the Committee) is won by the side which is leading by a number of holes greater than the number of holes remaining to be played.

Rule 7
Stroke Play

1. General Rule

The Rules for match play, so far as they are not at variance with specific Rules for stroke play, shall apply to stroke competitions. The converse is not true.

2. Winner

The competitor who holes the stipulated round or rounds in the fewest strokes is the winner.

3. Failure to Hole Out

If a competitor fail to hole out at any hole before he has played a stroke from the next teeing ground, or, in the case of the last hole of the round, before he has left the putting green, *he shall be disqualified. (Ball purposely moved, touched or lifted—Rule 27-1c.)*

Rule 8
Practice

1. During Play of Hole

During the play of a hole, a player shall not play a practice stroke.

PENALTY FOR BREACH OF RULE 8-1:
Match play—Loss of hole; Stroke play—Two strokes.

2. Between Holes

Between the play of two holes, a player shall not play a practice stroke from any hazard, or on or to a putting green other than that of the hole last played.

PENALTY FOR BREACH OF RULE 8-2:
Match play—Loss of hole; Stroke play—Two strokes.
The penalty applies to the next hole.

3. Stroke Play

On any day of a stroke competition or play-off, a competitor shall not practice on the competition course before a round or play-off. When a competition extends over consecutive days, practice on the competition course between rounds is prohibited.

If a competition extending over consecutive days is to be played on more than one course, practice between rounds on any competition course remaining to be played is prohibited.

Note: *The Committee may, at its discretion, waive or modify these prohibitions in the conditions of the competition (Appendix I-12).*

PENALTY FOR BREACH OF RULE 8-3: *Disqualification.*
(Duty of Committee to define practice ground—Rule 36-4.)

Note 1: *A practice swing is not a practice stroke and may be taken at any place on the course provided the player does not violate the Rules.*

Note 2: *Unless otherwise decided by the Committee, there is no penalty for practice on the course on any day of a match play competition.*

Rule 9

Advice (Def. 2) and Assistance

1. Giving or Asking for Advice; Receiving Assistance

a. ADVICE

A player may give advice to, or ask for advice from, only his partner or either of their caddies.

b. ASSISTANCE

In making a stroke, a player shall not seek or accept physical assistance or protection from the elements.

2. Indicating Line of Play

Except on the putting green, a player may have the line of play indicated to him by anyone, but no mark shall be placed to indicate the line, nor shall anyone stand on or close to the line while the stroke is being played.

(Indicating line of play on putting green—Rule 35-1e.)
PENALTY FOR BREACH OF RULE:
Match play—Loss of hole; Stroke play—Two strokes.

Rule 10

Information as to Strokes Taken

1. General

A player who has incurred a penalty shall state the fact to his opponent or marker as soon as possible. The number of strokes a player has taken shall include any penalty strokes incurred.

2. Match Play

A player is entitled at any time during the play of a hole to ascertain from his opponent the number of strokes the lat s taken. If the opponent give wrong information as to the number of strokes he has taken and correct his mistake before e player has played his next stroke, he shall incur no penalty; he fail to do so, *he shall lose the hole.*

Rule 11

Disputes, Decisions and Doubt as to Rights

Claims and Penalties

a. MATCH PLAY

In match play, if a dispute or doubt arise between the players any point, in order that a claim may be considered it must made before any player in the match plays from the next eing ground, or, in the case of the last hole of the match, fore all players in the match leave the putting green. Any er claim based on newly discovered facts cannot be con- ered unless the player making the claim had been given rong information by an opponent.

b. STROKE PLAY

In stroke play no penalty shall be imposed after the com- tition is closed unless wrong information had been given by e competitor. A competition is deemed to have closed: —

In stroke play only—When the result of the competition officially announced;

In stroke play qualifying followed by match play—When e player has teed off in his first match.

Referee's Decision

If a referee has been appointed by the Committee, his ecision shall be final.

Committee's Decision

In the absence of a referee, the players shall refer any dis- ite to the Committee, whose decision shall be final.

If the Committee can not come to a decision, it shall refer e dispute to the USGA Rules of Golf Committee whose ecision shall be final.

If the point in dispute or doubt has not been referred to the ules of Golf Committee, the player or players have the right refer an agreed statement through the Secretary of the Club the Rules of Golf Committee for an opinion as to the orrectness of the decision given. The reply will be sent to e Secretary of the Club or Clubs concerned.

If play be conducted other than in accordance with the ules of Golf, the Rules of Golf Committee will not give a ecision on any question.

Decision by Equity

If any point in dispute be not covered by the Rules or Local ules, the decision shall be made in accordance with equity.

Stroke Play: Doubt as to Procedure

In stroke play only, when a competitor is doubtful of his ghts or procedure, he may play out the hole with both the riginal ball and, at the same time, an alternate ball in a manner at he believes may be proper under the Rules for the given tuation. The competitor's decision to invoke this Rule must e announced to his marker before the alternate ball is put to play and before any stroke is played with the original all from the doubtful situation.

The competitor must complete the hole with both balls and, n completing the round, report the facts immediately to the 'ommittee. If the Committee determine that the alternate all was put into play in accordance with the Rules, the score ith the alternate ball shall count.

Note 1: *If the original ball is not immediately recoverable, he first ball put into play shall be treated as the original ball.*

Note 2: *The sole purpose of this Rule is to enable a com- etitor to avoid disqualification when doubtful of his rights r procedure.*

Note 3: *The privilege of playing an alternate ball does not exist in match play. An alternate ball played under Rule 11-5 is not a provisional ball under Rule 30.*

PENALTY FOR BREACH OF RULE 11-5: *Two strokes.*

Note: *A serious breach of Rule 11-5 should be dealt with by the Committee under Rule 1.*

Rule 12

The Honor (Def. 16)

1. The Honor

a. MATCH PLAY

A match begins by each side playing a ball from the first teeing ground in the order of the draw. In the absence of a draw, the option of taking the honor shall be decided by lot.

The side which wins a hole shall take the honor at the next teeing ground. If a hole has been halved, the side which had the honor at the previous teeing ground shall retain it.

b. STROKE PLAY

The honor shall be taken as in match play.

2. Playing out of Turn

a. MATCH PLAY

If, on the teeing ground, a player play when his opponent should have played, the opponent may immediately require the player to abandon the ball so played and to play a ball in correct order, without penalty.

b. STROKE PLAY

If, on the teeing ground, a competitor by mistake play out of turn, no penalty shall be incurred and the ball shall be in play.

c. SECOND BALL FROM TEE

If a player play a second ball, including a provisional ball, from the tee, he should do so after the opponent or the fellow-competitor has played his first stroke. If a player play a second ball out of turn, the provisions of Clauses 2a and 2b of this Rule apply.

Rule 13

Playing Outside Teeing Ground (Def. 33)

1. Match Play

If a player, when starting a hole, play a ball from outside the teeing ground, the opponent may immediately require the player to replay the stroke, in which case the player shall tee a ball and play the stroke from within the teeing ground, without penalty.

2. Stroke Play

If a competitor, when starting a hole, play his first stroke from outside the teeing ground, he shall count that stroke and any subsequent stroke so played and then shall tee a ball and play from within the teeing ground, without penalty. If the competitor fail to rectify his mistake before making a stroke on the next teeing ground, or, in the case of the last hole of the round, before leaving the putting green, *he shall be disqualified.*

PENALTY FOR BREACH OF RULE 13-2: *Disqualification.*

Note: STANCE. *A player may take his stance outside the teeing ground to play a ball within it.*

Rule 14

Ball Falling Off Tee

If a ball, when not in play, fall off a tee or be knocked off a tee by the player in addressing it, it may be re-teed without penalty, but if a stroke be made at the ball in these circum- stances, whether the ball be moving or not, the stroke shall be counted but no penalty shall be incurred.

Rule 15

Order of Play in Threesome or Foursome

1. General

In a threesome or a foursome, the partners shall strike off alternately from the teeing grounds, and thereafter shall strike alternately during the play of each hole. Penalty strokes (Definition 24) do not affect the order of play.

2. Match Play

If a player play when his partner should have played, *his side shall lose the hole.* In a match comprising more than one stipulated round, the partners shall not change the order of striking from the teeing grounds after any stipulated round.

3. Stroke Play

If the partners play a stroke or strokes in incorrect order, such stroke or strokes shall be cancelled, and *the side shall be penalized two strokes.* A ball shall then be put in play as nearly as possible at the spot from which the side first played in incorrect order. This must be done before a stroke has been played from the next teeing ground, or, in the case of the last hole of the round, before the side has left the putting green. If they fail to do so, *they shall be disqualified.* If the first ball was played from the teeing ground, a ball may be teed anywhere within the teeing ground; if from through the green or a hazard, it shall be dropped; if on the putting green, it shall be placed.

Note: *As in stroke play a stipulated round cannot be more than 18 holes (Def. 30), the order of play between partners may be changed for a second or subsequent round, unless the conditions of the competition provide otherwise.*

Rule 16

Ball Played as It Lies

The ball shall be played as it lies, except as otherwise provided for in the Rules or Local Rules.
(Ball at Rest Moved by Player, Purposely—Rule 27-1c.)
(Ball at Rest Moved by Player, Accidentally—Rule 27-1d.)
(Ball at Rest Moving Accidentally after Address—Rule 27-1f.)

Rule 17

Improving Lie or Stance and Influencing Ball Prohibited

1. Improving Line of Play or Lie Prohibited

A player shall not improve, or allow to be improved, his line of play, the position or lie of his ball or the area of his intended swing by moving, bending or breaking anything fixed or growing, or by removing or pressing down sand, loose soil, cut turf placed in position or other irregularities of surface except:—

a. As may occur in the course of fairly taking his stance;

b. In making the stroke or the backward movement of his club for the stroke;

c. On the teeing ground a player may press down irregularities;

d. In repairing damage to the putting green under Rule 35-1c.

The club may be grounded only lightly and must not be pressed on the ground.
(Sand and loose soil on the putting green—Def. 17 and Rule 35-1b.)
(Removal of obstructions—Rule 31-1.)
Note: *Things fixed include objects defining out of bounds.*

2. Long Grass and Bushes

If a ball lie in long grass, rushes, bushes, whins, heather or the like, only so much thereof shall be touched as will enable the player to find and identify his ball; nothing shall be do which may in any way improve its lie.

The player is not of necessity entitled to see the ball wh playing a stroke.

3. Building of Stance Prohibited

A player is always entitled to place his feet firmly on t ground when taking his stance, but he is not allowed to bu a stance.

4. Exerting Influence on Ball

No player or caddie shall take any action to influence t position or the movement of a ball except in accordance wi the Rules.

PENALTY FOR BREACH OF RULE:
Match play—Loss of hole; Stroke play—Two strokes.
Note: *In the case of a serious breach of Rule 17-4. t Committee may impose a penalty of disqualification.*

Rule 18

Loose Impediments (Def. 17)

Any loose impediment may be removed without penal except when both the impediment and the ball lie in or tou a hazard. When a ball is in motion, a loose impediment sh not be removed.

PENALTY FOR BREACH OF RULE:
Match play—Loss of hole; Stroke play—Two strokes.
(Ball moving after loose impediment touched—Rule 27-1 (Finding ball in hazard—Rule 33-1e.)

Rule 19

Striking at Ball

1. Ball to be Fairly Struck at

The ball shall be fairly struck at with the head of the cl and must not be pushed, scraped or spooned.
PENALTY FOR BREACH OF RULE 19-1:
Match play—Loss of hole; Stroke play—Two strokes.

2. Striking Ball Twice

If a player strike the ball twice when making a stroke, I shall count the stroke and *add a penalty stroke,* making tw strokes in all.
(Playing a moving ball—Rule 25.)

Rule 20

Ball Farther from the Hole Played First

1. General

When the balls are in play, the ball farther from the ho shall be played first. If the balls are equidistant from the ho the option of playing first should be decided by lot.

A player or a competitor incurs no penalty if a ball is move in measuring to determine which ball is farther from the ho A ball so moved shall be replaced.

2. Match Play

Through the green or in a hazard, if a player play when h opponent should have done so, the opponent may immediate require the player to replay the stroke. In such a case, th player shall drop a ball as near as possible to the spot fro which his previous stroke was played, and play in correct ord without penalty.
PENALTY FOR BREACH OF RULE 20-2: *Loss of hole.*
(Playing out of turn on putting green—Rule 35-2b.)

3. Stroke Play

If a competitor play out of turn, no penalty shall be incurre The ball shall be played as it lies.

Rule 21

Playing a Wrong Ball (Def. 5) or from a Wrong Place

General

A player must hole out with the ball driven from the teeing
round unless a Rule or Local Rule permit him to substitute
other ball.

Match Play

1. WRONG BALL

If a player play a stroke with a wrong ball (Def. 5) except
a hazard, *he shall lose the hole.* There is no penalty if a
yer play any strokes in a hazard with a wrong ball provided
then play the correct ball; the strokes so played with a
ong ball do not count in the player's score.

If the wrong ball belong to another player, it shall be re-
ced where it originally lay.

When the player and the opponent exchange balls during
play of a hole, the first to play the wrong ball other than
m a hazard shall lose the hole; when this cannot be deter-
ned, the hole shall be played out with the balls exchanged.

b. BALL PLAYED FROM WRONG PLACE

If a player play a stroke with a ball which has been dropped
placed under an applicable Rule but in a wrong place, *he
ll lose the hole.*

Note: *For a ball played outside teeing ground, see Rule 13-1.*

Stroke Play

1. WRONG BALL

If a competitor play any strokes with a wrong ball (Def. 5)
cept in a hazard, *he shall add two penalty strokes* to his
ore for the hole and shall then play the correct ball. Strokes
yed by a competitor with a wrong ball do not count in his
ore. There is no penalty if a competitor play any strokes in
hazard with a wrong ball, provided he then play the correct
l.

If the wrong ball belong to another player, a ball shall be
ced where the original ball lay.

b. RECTIFICATION AFTER HOLING OUT

If a competitor hole out with a wrong ball, he may rectify
mistake by proceeding in accordance with Clause 3a of
s Rule, subject to the prescribed penalty, provided he has
made a stroke on the next teeing ground, or, in the case
the last hole of the round, has not left the putting green. *The
mpetitor shall be disqualified* if he does not so rectify his
stake.

c. BALL PLAYED FROM WRONG PLACE

If a competitor play a stroke with a ball which has been
opped or placed under an applicable Rule but in a wrong
ce, *he shall add two penalty strokes* to his score for the hole
d shall then play out the hole with that ball.

Note 1: *For a ball played outside teeing ground, see Rule
2.*

Note 2: *A serious breach of Rule 21-3c should be dealt with
the Committee under Rule 1.*

Rule 22

Lifting, Dropping and Placing

Lifting

A ball to be lifted under the Rules or Local Rules may be
ed by the owner, his partner or either of their caddies, or by
other person authorized by the owner. In any such case the
ner shall be responsible for any breach of the Rules or
cal Rules.

Note: *A referee or observer should not lift a ball or mark
position (Defs. 19 and 26).*

Dropping

a. HOW TO DROP

A ball to be dropped under the Rules or Local Rules shall
be dropped by the player himself. He shall face the hole, stand
erect, and drop the ball behind him over his shoulder. If a ball
be dropped in any other manner and remain the ball in play
(Definition 5), *the player shall incur a penalty stroke.*

If the ball touch the player before it strikes the ground, the
player shall re-drop without penalty. If the ball touch the
player after it strikes the ground, or if it come to rest against
the player and move when he then moves, there is no penalty,
and the ball shall be played as it lies.

b. WHERE TO DROP

When a ball is to be dropped, it shall be dropped as near as
possible to the spot where the ball lay, but not nearer the hole,
except when a Rule permits it to be dropped elsewhere or
placed. In a hazard, the ball must come to rest in that hazard; if
it roll out of the hazard, it must be re-dropped, without penalty.

c. ROLLING INTO HAZARD, OUT OF BOUNDS, TWO CLUB-
LENGTHS OR NEARER THE HOLE

If a dropped ball roll into a hazard, out of bounds, more
than two club-lengths from the point where it first struck the
ground, or come to rest nearer the hole than its original
position, it shall be re-dropped, without penalty. If the ball
again roll into such a position, it shall be placed where it first
struck the ground when re-dropped.

PENALTY FOR BREACH OF RULE 22-2:
Match play—Loss of hole; Stroke play—Two strokes.

3. Placing

a. HOW AND WHERE TO PLACE

A ball to be placed or replaced under the Rules or Local
Rules shall be placed by the player, his partner or either of
their caddies on the spot where the ball lay, except when a
Rule permits it to be placed elsewhere.

b. LIE OF BALL TO BE PLACED OR REPLACED ALTERED

If the original lie of a ball to be placed or replaced has been
altered, the ball shall be placed in the nearest lie most similar
to that which it originally occupied, not more than two club-
lengths from the original lie and not nearer the hole.

c. SPOT NOT DETERMINABLE

If it be impossible to determine the spot where the ball is to
be placed, through the green or in a hazard, the ball shall be
dropped, or on the putting green it shall be placed, as near as
possible to the place where it lay but not nearer the hole.

d. BALL MOVING

If a ball when placed fail to remain on the spot on which
it was placed, it shall be replaced without penalty. If it still
fail to remain on that spot, it shall be placed at the nearest
spot not nearer the hole where it can be placed at rest.

PENALTY FOR BREACH OF RULE 22-3:
Match play—Loss of hole; Stroke play—Two strokes.

4. Ball in Play when Dropped or Placed

A ball dropped or placed under a Rule governing the particular case is in play (Definition 5) and shall not be lifted or
re-dropped or replaced except as provided in the Rules.

5. Lifting Ball Wrongly Dropped or Placed

A ball dropped or placed but not played may be lifted
without penalty if:—

a. It was dropped or placed under a Rule governing the
particular case but not in the right place or otherwise not in
accordance with that Rule. The player shall then drop or
place the ball in accordance with the governing Rule.

b. It was dropped or placed under a Rule which does not
govern the particular case. The player shall then proceed
under a Rule which governs the case. However, in match play,
if, before the opponent plays his next stroke, the player fail
to inform him that the ball has been lifted, *the player shall
lose the hole.*

Note: *In stroke play a serious breach of Rule 22 should be
dealt with by the Committee under Rule 1.*

Rule 23

Identifying or Cleaning Ball

The responsibility for playing the proper ball rests with the player. Each player should put an identification mark on his ball.

1. Identifying Ball

Except in a hazard, the player may, without penalty, lift his ball in play for the purpose of identification and replace it on the spot from which it was lifted provided this is done in the presence of his opponent in match play or marker in stroke play.

(Touching grass, etc., for identification—Rule 17-2.)

2. Cleaning Ball

A ball may be cleaned when lifted as follows:—
From an unplayable lie under Rule 29-2;
For relief from an obstruction under Rule 31;
From casual water, ground under repair or otherwise under Rule 32;
From a water hazard under Rule 33-2 or 33-3;
On the putting green under Rule 35-1d or on a wrong putting green under Rule 35-1j.

Otherwise, during the play of a hole a player may not clean a ball, except to the extent necessary for identification or if permitted by Local Rule.

PENALTY FOR BREACH OF RULE:
Match play—Loss of hole; Stroke play—Two strokes.

Rule 24

Ball Interfering with Play

Through the green or in a hazard, a player may have any other ball lifted if he considers that it might interfere with his play. A ball so lifted shall be replaced after the player has played his stroke.

If a ball be accidentally moved in complying with this Rule, no penalty shall be incurred and the ball so moved shall be replaced.

(Lie of ball to be placed or replaced altered—Rule 22-3b.)
(Putting green—Rule 35-2a and 35-3a.)

PENALTY FOR BREACH OF RULE:
Match play—Loss of hole; Stroke play—Two strokes.

Rule 25

A Moving Ball

1. Playing Moving Ball Prohibited

A player shall not play while his ball is moving.

Exceptions:—
Ball falling off tee—Rule 14.
Striking ball twice—Rule 19-2.
As hereunder—Rule 25-2.

When the ball only begins to move after the player has begun the stroke or the backward movement of his club for the stroke, he shall incur no penalty under this Rule, but he is not exempted from the provisions for:—

Ball at Rest Moved by Player, Accidentally—Rule 27-1d.
Ball at Rest Moving after Loose Impediment Touched—Rule 27-1e.
Ball at Rest Moving Accidentally after Address—Rule 27-1f.

2. Ball Moving in Water

When a ball is in water in a water hazard, the player may, without penalty, make a stroke at it while it is moving, but he must not delay to make his stroke in order to allow the wind or current to better the position of the ball. A ball moving in

water in a water hazard may be lifted if the player elec[t] invoke Rule 33-2 or 33-3.

PENALTY FOR BREACH OF RULE:
Match play—Loss of hole; Stroke play—Two strokes.

Rule 26

Ball in Motion Stopped or Deflected

1. General

a. BY OUTSIDE AGENCY

If a ball in motion be accidentally stopped or deflected any outside agency, it is a rub of the green and the ball s be played as it lies, without penalty.

Exception:—On putting green—Rule 35-1h.

b. LODGING IN OUTSIDE AGENCY

If a ball lodge in any moving outside agency, the player s through the green or in a hazard, drop a ball, or on the putt green place a ball, as near as possible to the spot where object was when the ball lodged in it, without penalty.

Rule 26: What is happening here?

2. Match Play

a. BY PLAYER

If a player's ball be stopped or deflected by himself, partner or either of their caddies or equipment, *he sh lose the hole.*

b. BY OPPONENT

If a player's ball be stopped or deflected by an opponent, caddie or equipment, *the opponent's side shall lose the h*

(Ball striking opponent's ball—Rule 27-2b.)

Exception:—Ball striking person attending flagstic Rule 34-3b.

3. Stroke Play

a. BY COMPETITOR

If a competitor's ball be stopped or deflected by hims his partner or either of their caddies or equipment, *the c petitor shall incur a penalty of two strokes.* The ball shal played as it lies, except when it lodges in the competitor's, partner's or either of their caddies' clothes or equipment, which case the competitor shall, through the green or i hazard, drop the ball, or on the putting green place the b as near as possible to where the article was when the [b] lodged in it.

Rule 26–2a: Player hit by his own ball.

b. By Fellow-Competitor

If a competitor's ball be accidentally stopped or deflected by a fellow-competitor, his caddie, ball or equipment, it is a rub of the green and the ball shall be played as it lies.

Exceptions: —

Ball lodging in fellow-competitor's clothes, etc.—Clause b of this Rule.

On the putting green, ball striking fellow-competitor's ball in play—Rule 35-3c.

Ball played from putting green stopped or deflected by fellow-competitor, his caddie or equipment—Rule 35-1h.

Ball striking person attending flagstick—Rule 34-3b.

PENALTY FOR BREACH OF RULE:

Match play—Loss of hole; Stroke play—Two strokes.

Note: *If the referee or the Committee determine that a ball has been deliberately stopped or deflected by an outside agency, including a fellow-competitor or his caddie, further procedure should be prescribed in equity under Rule 11-4. On the putting green, Rule 35-1h applies.*

Rule 27

Ball at Rest Moved (Def. 3)

. **General**

a. By Outside Agency

If a ball at rest be moved by any outside agency, the player shall incur no penalty and shall replace the ball before playing another stroke.

(Opponent's ball moved by player's ball—Rule 27-2b.)

Note 1: *Neither wind nor water is an outside agency.*

Note 2: *If the ball moved is not immediately recoverable, another ball may be substituted.*

b. During Search

During search for a ball, if it be moved by an opponent, a fellow-competitor or the equipment or caddie of either, no penalty shall be incurred. The player shall replace the ball before playing another stroke.

c. By Player, Purposely

When a ball is in play, if a player, his partner or either of

their caddies purposely move, touch or lift it, except as provided for in the Rules or Local Rules, *the player shall incur a penalty stroke* and the ball shall be replaced. The player may, however, without penalty, touch the ball with his club in the act of addressing it, provided the ball does not move (Def. 3).

d. By Player, Accidentally

When a ball is in play, if a player, his partner, their equipment or either of their caddies accidentally move it, or by touching anything cause it to move, except as provided for in the Rules or Local Rules, *the player shall incur a penalty stroke* and the ball shall be replaced.

(Ball accidentally moved when measuring to determine which ball farther from the hole—Rule 20-1.)

(Ball accidentally moved in the process of marking—Rule 35-2a or 35-3a.)

e. Ball Moving after Loose Impediment Touched

Through the green, if the ball move before the player has addressed it but after any loose impediment lying within a club-length of it has been touched by the player, his partner or either of their caddies, the player shall be deemed to have caused the ball to move. *The penalty shall be one stroke,* and the ball shall be replaced.

(Loose impediment on putting green—Rule 35-1b.)

f. Ball Moving Accidentally after Address

If a ball in play move after the player has addressed it (Def. 1), he shall be deemed to have caused it to move and *shall incur a penalty stroke,* and the ball shall be played as it lies.

2. Match Play

a. By Opponent

If a player's ball be touched or moved by an opponent, his caddie or equipment (except as otherwise provided in the Rules), *the opponent shall incur a penalty stroke.* The player shall replace the ball before playing another stroke.

b. Opponent's Ball Moved by Player's Ball

If a player's ball move an opponent's ball, no penalty shall

Rule 27–1a: Doggone ball gone.

be incurred. The opponent may either play his ball as it lies or, before another stroke is played by either side, he may replace the ball.

If the player's ball stop on the spot formerly occupied by the opponent's ball and the opponent declare his intention to replace the ball, the player shall first play another stroke, after which the opponent shall replace his ball.
(Putting green—Rule 35-2c.)
(Three-Ball, Best-Ball and Four-Ball match play—Rule 40-1c.)

3. Stroke Play
BALL MOVED BY A FELLOW-COMPETITOR

If a competitor's ball be moved by a fellow-competitor, his caddie, ball or equipment, no penalty shall be incurred. The competitor shall replace his ball before playing another stroke.
Exception to penalty:—Ball striking fellow-competitor's ball on putting green—Rule 35-3c.

PENALTY FOR BREACH OF RULE:
*Match play—Loss of hole; *Stroke play—Two strokes.*
(Playing a wrong ball—Rule 21.)
Note 1: *If a player who is required to replace a ball fail to do so, the general penalty for a breach of this Rule will apply in addition to any other penalty incurred.*
***Note 2:** A serious breach of this Rule should be dealt with by the Committee under Rule 1.*

Rule 28

Ball Unfit for Play

If the ball become so damaged as to be unfit for play, the player may substitute another ball, placing it on the spot where the original ball lay. Substitution may only be made on the hole during the play of which the damage occurred and in the presence of the opponent in match play or the marker in stroke play.

If a ball break into pieces as a result of a stroke, the stroke shall be replayed, without penalty.

PENALTY FOR BREACH OF RULE:
Match play—Loss of hole; Stroke play—Two strokes.
(Ball unplayable—Rule 29-2.)
Note 1: *Mud or loose impediments adhering to the ball do not make it unfit for play.*
Note 2: *A player is not the sole judge as to whether his ball is unfit for play. If the opponent or the marker dispute a claim of unfitness, the Referee, if one is present, or the Committee shall settle the matter (Rule 11-2 or 11-3).*

Rule 29

Ball Lost (Def. 6), Out of Bounds (Def. 21), or Unplayable

1. Lost or Out of Bounds
a. PROCEDURE

If a ball be lost outside a water hazard or be out of bounds, the player shall play his next stroke as nearly as possible at the spot from which the original ball was played or moved by him, *adding a penalty stroke* to his score for the hole. If the original stroke was played from the teeing ground, a ball may be teed anywhere within the teeing ground; if from through the green or a hazard, it shall be dropped; if on the putting green, it shall be placed.
(Ball lost in casual water, ground under repair, etc.—Rule 32-3.)
b. ASCERTAINING LOCATION

A player has the right at any time of ascertaining whether his opponent's ball is out of bounds.

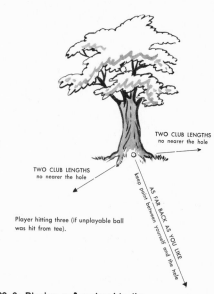

TWO CLUB LENGTHS
no nearer the hole

TWO CLUB LENGTHS
no nearer the hole

keep point between yourself and the hole

AS FAR BACK AS YOU LIKE

Player hitting three (if unplayable ball was hit from tee).

Rule 29-2: Playing an unplayable lie.

A person outside the match may point out the location of a ball for which search is being made.
c. STANDING OUT OF BOUNDS

A player may stand out of bounds to play a ball lying within bounds.

2. Unplayable
a. PLAYER SOLE JUDGE

The player is the sole judge as to whether his ball is unplayable. It may be declared unplayable at any place on the course except in a water hazard (Rule 33-2, -3).
b. PROCEDURE

If the player deem his ball to be unplayable, he shall either:
(i) Play his next stroke as provided in Clause 1a of this Rule *(stroke-and-distance penalty),*
or
(ii) Drop a ball, *under penalty of one stroke,* either (a) within two club-lengths of the point where the ball lay, but not nearer the hole, or (b) behind the point where the ball lay keeping that point between himself and the hole, with no limit to how far behind that point the ball may be dropped: if the ball lay in a bunker, a ball must be dropped in the bunker.
(Ball in casual water, etc.—Rule 32.)
(Ball unfit for play—Rule 28.)

PENALTY FOR BREACH OF RULE:
*Match play—Loss of hole; *Stroke play—Two strokes.*
***Note:** A serious breach of this Rule should be dealt with by the Committee under Rule 1.*

Rule 30

Provisional Ball (Def. 5)
Procedure

If a ball may be lost outside a water hazard or may be out bounds, to save time the player may play another ball proisionally as nearly as possible from the spot at which the ginal ball was played. If the original ball was played from e teeing ground, the provisional ball may be teed anywhere thin the teeing ground; if from through the green or a hazard, shall be dropped; if on the putting green, it shall be placed.

a. The player must inform his opponent or marker that he ends to play a provisional ball, and he must play it before or his partner goes forward to search for the original ball: he fail to do so, and play another ball, such ball is not a proional ball and becomes the ball in play *under penalty of oke and distance* (Rule 29-1); the original ball must be andoned.

b. Play of a provisional ball from the teeing ground does not fect the order in which the sides play (Rule 12-2).

c. A provisional ball is never an outside agency.

Play of a Provisional Ball

a. The player may play a provisional ball until he reaches e place where the original ball is likely to be. If he play any okes with the provisional ball from a point beyond that ace, the original ball is deemed to be lost (Def. 6c).

b. If the original ball be lost outside a water hazard or be t of bounds, the provisional ball becomes the ball in play, der penalty of stroke-and-distance (Rule 29-1).

c. If the original ball be neither lost outside a water hazard r out of bounds, the player shall abandon the provisional ll and continue play with the original ball. Should he fail do so, any further strokes played with the provisional ball all constitute playing a wrong ball and the provisions of Rule shall apply.

PENALTY FOR BREACH OF RULE:
Match play—Loss of hole; Stroke play—Two strokes.
Note: *If the original ball be unplayable or lie or be lost in water hazard, the player must proceed under Rule 29-2 or le 33-2 or 33-3, whichever is applicable.*

Rule 31

Obstructions (Def. 20)

. Movable Obstruction May Be Removed

Any movable obstruction may be removed. If the ball be oved in so doing, it shall be replaced on the exact spot from hich it was moved, without penalty. If it be impossible to etermine the spot or to replace the ball, the player shall roceed in accordance with Rule 22-3.

When a ball is in motion, an obstruction other than an atended flagstick and equipment of the players shall not be emoved.

. Interference by Immovable Obstruction

a. INTERFERENCE

Interference by an immovable obstruction occurs when the all lies in or on the obstruction, or so close to the obstruction hat the obstruction interferes with the player's stance or the rea of his intended swing. The fact that an immovable obtruction intervenes on the line of play is not, of itself, intererence under this Rule.

b. RELIEF

A player may obtain relief from interference by an immovble obstruction, without penalty, as follows:—

(i) *Through the Green:*

Through the green, the nearest point shall be determined without crossing over, through or under the obstruction) which (a) is not nearer the hole, (b) avoids interference as

Rule 31-1: Moveable obstruction may be moved.

defined in Clause 2a of this Rule, and (c) is not in a hazard or on a putting green. He shall lift the ball and drop it within two club-lengths of the point thus determined on ground which fulfils (a), (b) and (c) above.

Note: *The prohibition against crossing over, through or under the obstruction does not apply to the artificial surfaces and sides of roads and paths or when the ball lies in or on the obstruction.*

(ii) *In a Hazard:*

In a hazard, the player may lift and drop the ball in accordance with Clause (i) above, but the ball must be dropped in the hazard.

(iii) *On the Putting Green:*

On the putting green, the player may lift and place the ball in the nearest position to where it lay which affords relief from interference, but not nearer the hole.

c. RE-DROPPING

If a dropped ball roll into a position covered by this Rule, or nearer the hole than its original position, it shall be redropped without penalty. If it again roll into such a position, it shall be placed where it first struck the ground when redropped.

PENALTY FOR BREACH OF RULE:
Match play—Loss of hole; Stroke play—Two strokes.

Rule 32

Casual Water (Def. 8), Ground Under Repair (Def. 13), Hole Made by Burrowing Animal

1. Interference

Interference by casual water, ground under repair, or a hole, cast or runway made by a burrowing animal, a reptile or a

Rule 31–2: Interference by an Immovable obstruction.

c. *On the Putting Green*—On the putting green, or if su[c]
condition on the putting green intervene between a ball lyi[ng]
on the putting green and the hole, the player shall lift the b[all]
and place it without penalty in the nearest position to whe[re]
it lay which affords maximum relief from the condition, b[ut]
not nearer the hole nor in a hazard.

3. Ball Lost

a. *Outside a Hazard*—If a ball be lost under a conditi[on]
covered by this Rule, except in a hazard, the player may ta[ke]
relief as follows: the nearest point to the spot where the b[all]
last crossed the margin of the area shall be determined whi[ch]
(a) is not nearer the hole than where the ball last crossed th[e]
margin, (b) avoids interference by the condition, and (c) is n[ot]
in a hazard or on a putting green. He shall drop a ball witho[ut]
penalty within two club-lengths of the point thus determin[ed]
on ground which fulfils (a), (b) and (c) above.

b. *In a Hazard*—If a ball be lost in a hazard under a c[on]
dition covered by this Rule, the player may drop a ball either:

Without penalty, in the hazard, but not nearer the ho[le]
than the spot at which the ball last crossed the margin of t[he]
area, on ground which affords maximum relief from t[he]
condition;

or,

Under penalty of one stroke, outside the hazard, but n[ot]
nearer the hole, keeping the spot at which the ball last cross[ed]
the margin of the hazard between himself and the hole.

In order that a ball may be treated as lost under a co[n]
dition covered by this Rule, there must be reasonable eviden[ce]
to that effect.

4. Re-Dropping

If a dropped ball roll into the area from which relief w[as]
taken, or come to rest in such a position that that area st[ill]
affects the player's stance or the area of his intended swi[ng]
the ball shall be re-dropped, without penalty. If the ball aga[in]
roll into such a position, it shall be placed where it first stru[ck]
the ground when re-dropped.

PENALTY FOR BREACH OF RULE:
Match play—Loss of hole; Stroke play—Two strokes.

Rule 32–1: Hole made by burrowing animal in a hazard

Rule 33

Hazards (Def. 14)

1. Touching Hazard Prohibited

When a ball lies in or touches a hazard or a water hazar[d]

bird occurs when a ball lies in or touches any of these conditions or when the condition interferes with the player's
stance or the area of his intended swing. If interference exists,
the player may either play the ball as it lies or take relief as
provided in Clause 2 of this Rule.

2. Relief

If the player elect to take relief, he shall proceed as follows:—

a. *Through the Green*—Through the green, the nearest point
shall be determined which (a) is not nearer the hole, (b) avoids
interference by the condition, and (c) is not in a hazard or on
a putting green. The player shall lift the ball and drop it without penalty within two club-lengths of the point thus determined on ground which fulfils (a), (b) and (c) above.

b. *In a Hazard*—In a hazard, the player shall lift and drop
the ball either:—

Without penalty, in the hazard as near as possible to the
spot where the ball lay, but not nearer the hole, on ground
which affords maximum relief from the condition;

or,

Under penalty of one stroke, outside the hazard, but not
nearer the hole, keeping the spot where the ball lay between
himself and the hole.

thing shall be done which may in any way improve its lie.
...ore making a stroke, the player shall not touch the ground
...the hazard or water in the water hazard with a club or
...erwise, nor touch or move a loose impediment lying in
...touching the hazard, nor test the condition of the hazard
...of any similar hazard; subject to the following consid-
...tions:—

a. STANCE
The player may place his feet firmly in taking his stance.

b. TOUCHING FIXED OR GROWING OBJECT
...n addressing the ball or in the stroke or in the backward
...vement for the stroke, the club may touch any wooden or
...ne wall, paling or similar fixed object or any grass, bush,
...e, or other growing substance (but the club may not be
...ed in the hazard).

c. OBSTRUCTIONS
The player is entitled to relief from obstructions under the
...visions of Rule 31.

d. LOOSE IMPEDIMENT OUTSIDE HAZARD
Any loose impediment not in or touching the hazard may
...removed.

e. FINDING BALL
...f the ball be covered by sand, fallen leaves or the like, the
...yer may remove as much thereof as will enable him to
...the top of the ball. If the ball be moved in such removal, no
...nalty shall be incurred, and the ball shall be replaced.
...f the ball is believed to be lying in water in a water hazard,
...player may probe for it with a club or otherwise. If the
...l be moved in such search, no penalty shall be incurred;
...ball shall be replaced, unless the player elects to proceed
...der Clause 2 or 3 of this Rule.
The ball may not be lifted for identification.

f. PLACING CLUBS IN HAZARD
The player may, without penalty, place his clubs in the
...zard prior to making a stroke, provided nothing is done
...ich may improve the lie of the ball or constitute testing
...soil.

g. SMOOTHING IRREGULARITIES
There is no penalty should soil or sand in the hazard be
...oothed by the player after playing a stroke, or by his caddie
...any time without the authority of the player, provided
...thing is done that improves the lie of the ball or assists the
...yer in his subsequent play of the hole.

h. CASUAL WATER, GROUND UNDER REPAIR
The player is entitled to relief from casual water, ground
...der repair, and otherwise as provided for in Rule 32.

i. INTERFERENCE BY A BALL
The player is entitled to relief from interference by another
...ll under the provisions of Rule 24.

Ball in Water Hazard (Def. 14b)
...f a ball lie or be lost in a water hazard (whether the ball
...in water or not), the player may drop a ball *under penalty
one stroke,* either:—

a. Behind the water hazard, keeping the spot at which
...e ball last crossed the margin of the water hazard between
...mself and the hole, and with no limit to how far behind the
...ter hazard the ball may be dropped,

or

b. As near as possible to the spot from which the original
...ll was played; if the stroke was played from the teeing
...ound, the ball may be teed anywhere within the teeing ground.

Note: *If a ball has been played from within a water hazard
...d has not crossed any margin of the hazard, the player may
...op a ball behind the hazard under Rule 33-2a.*

Ball in Lateral Water Hazard (Def. 14c)
If a ball lie or be lost in a lateral water hazard, the player
...ay, *under penalty of one stroke,* either:—

a. Play his next stroke in accordance with Clause 2a or 2b
...f this Rule,

or

Rule 33–2a: Ball in water hazard.

b. Drop a ball outside the hazard within two club-lengths
of the point where the ball last crossed the margin of the
hazard or a point on the opposite margin of the hazard equidistant from the hole. The dropped ball must come to rest not
nearer the hole than the point where the original ball last
crossed the margin of the hazard.

Note: *If a ball has been played from within a lateral water
hazard and has not crossed any margin of the hazard, the
player may drop a ball outside the hazard under Rule 33-3b.*

PENALTY FOR BREACH OF RULE:

Match play—Loss of hole; *Stroke play—Two strokes.

*Note 1: *A serious breach of this Rule should be dealt
with by the Committee under Rule 1.*

Note 2: *It is a question of fact whether a ball lost after
having been struck toward a water hazard is lost inside or
outside the hazard. In order to treat the ball as lost in the
hazard, there must be reasonable evidence that the ball lodged
therein. In the absence of such evidence, the ball must be
treated as a lost ball and Rule 29-1 applies.*

Rule 34

The Flagstick (Def. 12)

1. Flagstick Attended, Removed or Held up

Before and during the stroke, the player may have the flagstick attended, removed or held up to indicate the position of
the hole. This may be done only on the authority of the player
before he plays his stroke. If the flagstick be attended or removed by an opponent, a fellow-competitor or the caddie of
either with the knowledge of the player and no objection is
made, the player shall be deemed to have authorized it.

If a player or a caddie attend or remove the flagstick or
stand near the hole while a stroke is being played, he shall be
deemed to attend the flagstick until the ball comes to rest.

If the flagstick be not attended before the stroke is played,
it shall not be attended or removed while the ball is in motion.

2. Unauthorized Attendance

a. MATCH PLAY

In match play, an opponent or his caddie shall not attend or remove the flagstick without the knowledge or authority of the player.

b. STROKE PLAY

In stroke play, if a fellow-competitor or his caddie attend or remove the flagstick without the knowledge or authority of the competitor, and if the ball strike the flagstick or the person attending it, it is a rub of the green, there is no penalty, and the ball shall be played as it lies.

PENALTY FOR BREACH OF RULE 34-1 AND -2:
Match play—Loss of hole; Stroke play—Two strokes.

3. Ball Striking Flagstick or Attendant

The player's ball shall not strike either:—

a. The flagstick when attended or removed by the player, his partner or either of their caddies, or by another person with the knowledge or authority of the player; or

b. The player's caddie, his partner or his partner's caddie when attending the flagstick, or another person attending the flagstick with the knowledge or authority of the player, or equipment carried by any such person; or

c. The flagstick in the hole, unattended, when the ball has been played from the putting green.

PENALTY FOR BREACH OF RULE 34-3:
Match play—Loss of hole; Stroke play—Two strokes, and the ball shall be played as it lies.

4. Ball Resting Against Flagstick

If the ball rest against the flagstick when it is in the hole, the player shall be entitled to have the flagstick removed, and if the ball fall into the hole the player shall be deemed to have holed out at his last stroke; otherwise, the ball shall be placed on the lip of the hole, without penalty.

Note: *A referee, observer, marker, steward, gallery marshal or other outside agency should not attend the flagstick.*

Rule 35

The Putting Green (Def. 25)

1. General

a. TOUCHING LINE OF PUTT

The line of the putt must not be touched except as provided in Clauses 1b, 1c and 1d of this Rule, or in measuring (Rule 20-1), but the player may place the club in front of the ball in addressing it without pressing anything down.

b. LOOSE IMPEDIMENTS

The player may move sand, loose soil or any loose impediments on the putting green by picking them up or brushing them aside with his hand or a club without pressing anything down. If the ball be moved, it shall be replaced, without penalty.

c. REPAIR OF BALL MARKS

The player may repair damage to the putting green caused by the impact of a ball. If the player's ball lie on the putting green, it may be lifted to permit repair and shall be replaced on the spot from which it was lifted; in match play the ball must be replaced immediately if the opponent so requests.

If a ball be moved during such repair, it shall be replaced, without penalty.

d. LIFTING AND CLEANING BALL

A ball lying on the putting green may be lifted, without penalty, cleaned if desired, and replaced on the spot from which it was lifted; in match play the ball must be replaced immediately if the opponent so requests.

e. DIRECTION FOR PUTTING

When the player's ball is on the putting green, the player's caddie, his partner or his partner's caddie may, before the stroke is played, point out a line for putting, but the line of the putt shall not be touched in front of, to the side of, or behind the hole.

While making the stroke, the player shall not allow his

caddie, his partner or his partner's caddie to position hims on or close to an extension of the line of putt behind the b

No mark shall be placed anywhere on the putting green indicate a line for putting.

f. TESTING SURFACE

During the play of a hole, a player shall not test the surf of the putting green by rolling a ball or roughening or scrap the surface.

g. OTHER BALL TO BE AT REST

While the player's ball is in motion after a stroke on putting green, an opponent's or a fellow-competitor's ball sh not be played or touched.

h. BALL IN MOTION STOPPED OR DEFLECTED

If a ball in motion after a stroke on the putting green stopped or deflected by any moving or animate outside agen the stroke shall be cancelled and the ball shall be replac

Note: *If the referee or the Committee determine that ball has been deliberately stopped or deflected by an outsi agency, including a fellow-competitor or his caddie, furth procedure should be prescibed in equity under Rule 11-4.*

i BALL OVERHANGING HOLE

When any part of the ball overhangs the edge of the ho the owner of the ball is not allowed more than a few secon to determine whether it is at rest. If by then the ball has n fallen into the hole, it is deemed to be at rest.

j. BALL ON A WRONG PUTTING GREEN

If a ball lie on a putting green other than that of the ho being played, the nearest point shall be determined which (is not nearer the hole and (b) is not in a hazard or on a putti green. The player shall lift the ball and drop it without penal within two club-lengths of the point thus determined on grou which fulfils (a) and (b) above.

Note: *Unless otherwise stipulated by the Committee, th term "a putting green other than that of the hole being playe includes a practice putting or pitching green lying within t boundaries of the course.*

k. BALL TO BE MARKED WHEN LIFTED

When a ball on the putting green is to be lifted, its positic shall be marked.

(Lifting and placing—Rule 22.)

Note: *The position of a lifted ball should be marked b placing a ball-marker or other small object on the puttin green, immediately behind the ball. If the marker interfer with the play, stance or stroke of another player, it should b placed one or more putterhead-lengths to one side.*

L. STANDING ASTRIDE OR ON LINE OF PUTT PROHIBITED

The player shall not make a stroke on the putting gree from a stance astride, or with either foot touching, the lir of the putt or an extension of that line behind the ball. Fc the purpose of Rule 35-1L only, the line of putt does not exten beyond the hole.

PENALTY FOR BREACH OF RULE 35-1:
Match play—Loss of hole; Stroke play—Two strokes.

Rule 35–1i: How long is too long?

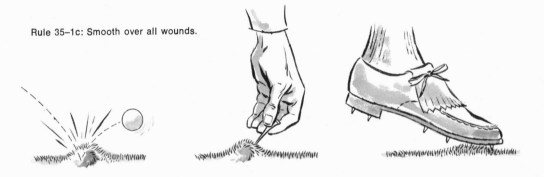

Rule 35–1c: Smooth over all wounds.

Match Play

a. Ball Interfering with Play

When the ball nearer the hole lies on the putting green, if the player consider that the opponent's ball might either be struck by his ball or interfere with his stance or stroke, the player may require the opponent to lift his ball. The opponent shall replace his ball after the player has played his stroke. If the player's ball stop on the spot formerly occupied by the lifted ball, the player shall first play another stroke before the lifted ball is replaced.

If a ball be accidentally moved in complying with this Rule, no penalty shall be incurred and the ball shall be replaced.

b. Playing Out of Turn

If a player play when his opponent should have done so, the opponent may immediately require the player to replay the stroke, in which case the player shall replace his ball and play in correct order, without penalty.

c. Opponent's Ball Displaced

If the player's ball knock the opponent's ball into the hole, the opponent shall be deemed to have holed out at his last stroke. If the player's ball move the opponent's ball, the opponent may replace it, but this must be done before another stroke is played by either side. If the player's ball stop on the spot formerly occupied by the opponent's ball, and the opponent declare his intention to replace his ball, the player shall first play another stroke, after which the opponent shall replace his ball.

(Three-Ball, Best-Ball and Four-Ball match play—Rule 40-1c.)

d. Conceding Opponent's Next Stroke

When the opponent's ball has come to rest, the player may concede the opponent to have holed out with his next stroke and may remove the opponent's ball with a club or otherwise.

If the player does not concede the opponent's next stroke and the opponent's ball fall into the hole, the opponent shall be deemed to have holed out with his last stroke.

If the opponent's next stroke has not been conceded, the opponent shall play without delay in correct order.

Penalty for breach of Rule 35-2: *Loss of hole.*

Stroke Play

Ball Interfering with Play

When the ball nearer the hole lies on the putting green, if the competitor consider that the fellow-competitor's ball might either be struck by his ball or interfere with his stance or stroke, the competitor may require the fellow-competitor to lift or play his ball, at the option of its owner, without penalty.

If a ball be accidentally moved in the process of marking, lifting or replacing, no penalty shall be incurred and the ball so moved shall be replaced.

If the owner of the ball refuse to comply with this Rule when required to do so, the competitor making the request may lift the ball, and *the owner of the ball shall be disqualified.*

Note: *It is recommended that the ball nearer the hole be played, rather than lifted, unless the subsequent play of a fellow-competitor is likely to be affected.*

b. Ball Assisting Play

If the fellow-competitor consider that his ball lying on the putting green might be of assistance to the competitor, the fellow-competitor may lift or play first, without penalty.

c. Ball Striking Fellow-Competitor's Ball

LESS THAN 20 YARDS

PLAYER

Rule 35-3c: Striking a competitor's ball.

When both balls lie on the putting green, if the competitor's ball strike a fellow-competitor's ball, the *competitor shall incur a penalty of two strokes* and shall play his ball as it lies. The fellow-competitor's ball shall be at once replaced.

d. BALL LIFTED BEFORE HOLED OUT

For ball lifted before holed out, see Rule 7-3 and Rule 27-1c.

Rule 36

The Committee (Def. 9)

1. Conditions

The Committee shall lay down the conditions under which a competition is to be played.

Certain special rules governing stroke play are so substantially different from those governing match play that combining the two forms of play is not practicable and is not permitted. The results of matches played and the scores returned in these circumstances shall not be accepted.

2. Order and Times of Starting

a. GENERAL

The Committee shall arrange the order and times of starting.

b. MATCH PLAY

When a competition is played over an extended period, the Committee shall lay down the limit of time within which each round shall be completed.

When players are allowed to arrange the date of their match within these limits, the Committee should announce that the match must be played at a stated hour on the last day of the period unless the players agree to a prior date.

c. STROKE PLAY

Competitors shall play in couples unless the Committee authorizes play by threes or fours. If there be a single competitor, the Committee shall provide him with a player who shall mark for him, or provide a marker and allow him to compete alone, or allow him to compete with another group.

3. Decision of Ties

The Committee shall announce the manner, day and time for the decision of a halved match or of a tie, whether played on level terms or under handicap.

A halved match shall not be decided by stroke play. A tie in stroke play shall not be decided by a match.

4. The Course

a. NEW HOLES

New holes should be made on the day on which a stroke competition begins, and at such other times as the Committee considers necessary, provided all competitors in a single round play with each hole cut in the same position.

b. PRACTICE GROUND

Where there is no practice ground available outside the area of a competition course, the Committee should lay down the area on which players may practice on any day of a competition, if it is practicable to do so. On any day of a stroke competition, the Committee should not normally permit practice on or to a putting green or from a hazard of the competition course.

c. COURSE UNPLAYABLE

If the Committee or its authorized representative consider that for any reason the course is not in a playable condition, or that there are circumstances which render the proper playing of the game impossible, it shall have the power in match and stroke play to order a temporary suspension of play, or in stroke play to declare play null and void and to cancel all scores for the round in question.

When a round is cancelled, all penalties incurred in that round are cancelled.

When play has been temporarily suspended, it shall be resumed from where it was discontinued, even though resumption occur on a subsequent day.

(Procedure in discontinuing play—Rule 37-6b.)

5. Modification of Penalty

The Committee has no power to waive a Rule of Golf. penalty of disqualification, however, may, in exceptional individual cases, be waived or be modified or be imposed under Rule 1 if the Committee consider such action warranted.

6. Defining Bounds and Margins

The Committee shall define accurately:—

a. The course and out of bounds.

b. The margins of hazards, water hazards, and later water hazards, where there is any doubt.

c. Ground under repair.

d. Obstructions.

7. Local Rules

a. POLICY

The Committee shall make and publish Local Rules for abnormal conditions, having regard to the policy of the Governing Authority of the country concerned as set forth in Appendix I attached to these Rules.

b. WAIVING PENALTY PROHIBITED

A penalty imposed by a Rule of Golf shall not be waived by a Local Rule.

Rule 37

The Player

1. Conditions

The player shall be responsible for acquainting himself with the conditions under which the competition is to be played.

2. Caddie and Forecaddie

For any breach of a Rule or Local Rule by his caddie, the player incurs the relative penalty.

The player may have only one caddie, *under penalty of disqualification.*

The player may send his own caddie forward to mark the position of any ball.

If a forecaddie be employed by the Committee, he is an outside agency (Definition 22).

3. Infringement Assisting Partner

If a player's infringement of a Rule or Local Rule assist his partner's play, *the partner incurs the relative penalty in addition to any penalty incurred by the player.*

4. Handicap

Before starting in a handicap competition, the player shall ensure that his current handicap is recorded correctly on the official list, if any, for the competition and on the card issued for him by the Committee. In the case of match play or bogey par or Stableford competitions, he shall inform himself of the holes at which strokes are given or taken.

If a player play off a higher handicap than his current one, *he shall be disqualified* from the handicap competition. If he play off a lower one, the score, or the result of the match shall stand.

5. Time and Order of Starting

The player shall start at the time and in the order arranged by the Committee.

PENALTY FOR BREACH OF RULE 37-5: *Disqualification.*

6. Discontinuance of Play

a. WHEN PERMITTED

The player shall not discontinue play on account of bad weather or for any other reason, unless:—

He considers that there be danger from lightning,

or

There be some other reason, such as sudden illness, which the Committee considers satisfactory.

If the player discontinue play without specific permission from the Committee, he shall report to the Committee as soon as possible.

General Exception:—Players discontinuing match play by agreement are not subject to disqualification unless by so doing the competition is delayed.

PENALTY FOR BREACH OF RULE 37-6a: *Disqualification.*

b. PROCEDURE
When play is discontinued in accordance with the Rules, it should, if feasible, be discontinued after the completion of the play of a hole. If this is not feasible, the player should lift his ball after marking the spot on which it lay; in such case he shall replace the ball on that spot when play is resumed.

PENALTY FOR BREACH OF RULE 37-6b:
*Match play—Loss of hole; *Stroke play—Two strokes.*
Note: *A serious breach of this Rule should be dealt with by the Committee under Rule 1.*

7. Undue Delay
The player shall at all times play without undue delay. Between the completion of a hole and driving off the next tee, the player may not delay play in any way.

PENALTY FOR BREACH OF RULE 37-7:
Match play—Loss of hole; Stroke play—Two strokes. For repeated offense—Disqualification.
If the player delay play between holes, he is delaying the play of the next hole, and the penalty applies to that hole.

8. Refusal to Comply with Rule
If a competitor in stroke play refuse to comply with a Rule affecting the rights of another competitor, *he shall be disqualified.*

9. Artificial Devices
Except as provided for under the Rules, the player shall not use any artificial device:—
a. Which might assist him in making a stroke or in his play;
b. For the purpose of gauging or measuring distance or conditions which might affect his play, or
c. Which, not being part of the grip (see Appendix IId), is designed to give him artificial aid in gripping the club.
(Exceptions to Rule 37-9c: Plain gloves and material or substance applied to the grip, such as tape, gauze or resin.)

PENALTY FOR BREACH OF RULE 37-9: *Disqualification.*

Rule 38
Scoring in Stroke Play

1. Recording Scores
The Committee shall issue for each competitor a score card containing the date and the competitor's name.
After each hole the marker shall check the score with the competitor. On completion of the round the marker shall sign the card and hand it to the competitor; should more than one marker record the scores, each shall sign the part for which he is responsible.

2. Checking Scores
The competitor shall check his score for each hole, settle any doubtful points with the Committee, ensure that the marker has signed the card, countersign the card himself, and return it to the Committee as soon as possible. The competitor is solely responsible for the correctness of the score recorded for each hole.

PENALTY FOR BREACH OF RULE 38-2: *Disqualification.*
The Committee is responsible for the addition of scores and application of the handicap recorded on the card.
Exception: Four-ball stroke play—Rule 41-1d.

3. No Alteration of Scores
No alteration may be made on a card after the competitor has returned it to the Committee.

If the competitor return a score for any hole lower than actually played, *he shall be disqualified.*
A score higher than actually played must stand as returned.
Exception:—Four-ball stroke play—Rule 41-8a.

Rule 39
Bogey, Par or Stableford Competitions

1. Conditions
A bogey, par or Stableford competition is a form of stroke competition in which play is against a fixed score at each hole of the stipulated round or rounds.
a. The reckoning for bogey or par competitions is made as in match play. The winner is the competitor who is most successful in the aggregate of holes.
b. The reckoning in Stableford competitions is made by points awarded in relation to a fixed score at each hole as follows:—

For hole done in one over fixed score	1 point
For hole done in fixed score	2 points
For hole done in one under fixed score	3 points
For hole done in two under fixed score	4 points
For hole done in three under fixed score	5 points

The winner is the competitor who scores the highest number of points.

2. Rules for Stroke Play Apply
The Rules for stroke play shall apply with the following modifications:—
a. NO RETURN AT ANY HOLE
Any hole for which a competitor makes no return shall be regarded as a loss in bogey and par competitions and as scoring no points in Stableford competitions.
b. SCORING CARDS
The holes at which strokes are to be given or taken shall be indicated on the card issued by the Committee.
c. RECORDING SCORES
In bogey and par competitions the marker shall be responsible for marking only the gross number of strokes for each hole where the competitor makes a net score equal to or less than the fixed score. In Stableford competitions the marker shall be responsible for marking only the gross number of strokes at each hole where the competitor's net score earns one or more points.
Note: *Maximum of 14 Clubs—see Rule 3-2 and Rule 41-7.*

3. Disqualification Penalties
a. FROM THE COMPETITION
A *competitor shall be disqualified* from the competition for a breach of any of the following:
Rule 2—The Club and the Ball.
Rule 4—Agreement to Waive Rules Prohibited.
Rule 8-3—Practice before Round.
Rule 35-3a—Putting Green: Stroke Play, Ball Interfering with Play.
Rule 37-2—Caddie and Forecaddie.
Rule 37-5—Time and Order of Starting.
Rule 37-6a—Discontinuance of Play.
Rule 37-7—Undue Delay (repeated offense).
Rule 37-8—Refusal to Comply with Rule.
Rule 37-9—Artificial Devices.
Rule 38-2—Checking Scores.
Rule 38-3—No Alteration of Scores, except that the competitor shall not be disqualified when a breach of this Rule does not affect the result of the hole.
b. FOR A HOLE
In all other cases where a breach of a Rule would entail disqualification, *the competitor shall be disqualified only for the hole at which the breach occurred.*
(Modification of penalty—Rule 36-5.)

Rule 40

Three-Ball, Best-Ball and Four-Ball Match Play

1. General

a. RULES OF GOLF APPLY

The Rules of Golf, so far as they are not at variance with the following special Rules, shall apply to all three-ball, best-ball and four-ball matches.

b. BALL INFLUENCING PLAY

Any player may have any ball (except the ball about to be played) lifted if he consider that it might interfere with or be of assistance to a player or side, but this may not be done while any ball in the match is in motion.

c. BALL MOVED BY ANOTHER BALL

There is no penalty if a player's ball move any other ball in the match. The owner of the moved ball shall replace his ball.

d. PLAYING OUT OF TURN

Through the green or in a hazard, a player shall incur no penalty if he play when an opponent should have done so. The stroke shall not be replayed.

On the putting green, if a player play when an opponent should have done so, the opponent may immediately require the player to replay the stroke in correct order, without penalty.

2. Three-Ball Match Play

In a three-ball match, each player is playing two distinct matches.

a. BALL STOPPED OR DEFLECTED BY AN OPPONENT

If a player's ball be stopped or deflected by an opponent, his caddie or equipment, *that opponent shall lose the hole in his match with the player.* The other opponent shall treat the occurrence as a rub of the green (Definition 27).

Exception: — Ball striking person attending flagstick — Rule 34-3b.

b. BALL AT REST MOVED BY AN OPPONENT

If the player's ball be touched or moved by an opponent, his caddie or equipment (except as otherwise provided in the Rules), Rule 27-2a applies. *That opponent shall incur a penalty stroke in his match with the player,* but not in his match with the other opponent.

3. Best-Ball and Four-Ball Match Play

a. ORDER OF PLAY

Balls belonging to the same side may be played in the order the side considers best.

b. BALL STOPPED BY PLAYER'S SIDE

If a player's ball be stopped or deflected by the player, his partner or either of their caddies or equipment, *the player is disqualified for the hole.* His partner incurs no penalty.

c. BALL STOPPED BY OPPONENT'S SIDE

If a player's ball be stopped or deflected by an opponent, his caddie or equipment, *the opponent's side shall lose the hole.*

Exception: — Ball striking person attending flagstick — Rule 34-3b.

d. WRONG BALL

If a player play a stroke with a wrong ball (Def. 5) except in a hazard, *he shall be disqualified for that hole,* but the penalty shall not apply to his partner. If the wrong ball be a ball in the match, its owner shall place a ball on the spot from which the wrong ball was played.

e. PARTNER'S BALL MOVED BY PLAYER ACCIDENTALLY

If a player, his partner, or either of their caddies accidentally move a ball owned by their side or by touching anything cause it to move (except as otherwise provided for in the Rules), *the owner of the ball shall incur a penalty stroke,* but the penalty shall not apply to his partner. The ball shall be replaced.

f. BALL MOVED BY OPPONENT'S SIDE

If a player's ball be touched or moved by an opponent, his caddie or equipment (except as otherwise provided for in the Rules), *that opponent shall incur a penalty stroke,* but the

penalty shall not apply to the other opponent. The player sha replace the ball, without penalty.

g. MAXIMUM OF FOURTEEN CLUBS

The side shall be penalized for a violation of Rule 3 by eithe partner.

h. DISQUALIFICATION PENALTIES

A player shall be disqualified from the match for a breac of Rule 37-5 (Time and Order of Starting), but, in the discretio of the Committee, the penalty shall not necessarily apply to hi partner (Definition 28 — Note).

A side shall be disqualified for a breach of any of th following: —

Rule 2 — The Club and the Ball.

Rule 4 — Agreement to Waive Rules Prohibited.

Rule 37-2 — Caddie and Forecaddie.

Rule 37-7 — Undue Delay (repeated offense).

Rule 37-9 — Artificial Devices.

A player shall be disqualified for the hole in question and from the remainder of the match for a breach of Rule 37-6a (Discontinuance of Play), but the penalty shall not apply to his partner.

(Modification of penalty — Rule 36-5.)

i. INFRINGEMENT ASSISTING PARTNER OR AFFECTING OPPONENT

If a player's infringement of a Rule or Local Rule assist his partner's play or adversely affect an opponent's play, *the partner incurs the relative penalty in addition to any penalty incurred by the player.*

j. PENALTY APPLIES TO PLAYER ONLY

In all other cases where, by the Rules of Golf, a player would incur a penalty, the penalty shall not apply to his partner

k. ANOTHER FORM OF MATCH PLAYED CONCURRENTLY

In a best-ball or a four-ball match when another form of match is played concurrently, the above special Rules shall apply.

Rule 41

Four-Ball Stroke Play

1. Conditions

a. The Rules of Golf, so far as they are not at variance with the following special Rules, shall apply to four-ball stroke play

b. In four-ball stroke play two competitors play as partners each playing his own ball.

c. The lower score of the partners is the score of the hole

If one partner fail to complete the play of a hole, there is no penalty.

(Wrong score — Rule 41-8a.)

d. The marker is required to record for each hole only the gross score of whichever partner's score is to count. The partners are responsible for the correctness of only their gross scores for each hole. The Committee is responsible for re cording the better-ball score for each hole, the addition and the application of the handicaps recorded on the card.

e. Only one of the partners need be responsible for com plying with Rule 38.

2. Ball Influencing Play

Any competitor may have any ball (except the ball about to be played) lifted or played, at the option of the owner, if he consider that it might interfere with or be of assistance to a competitor or side, but this may not be done while any ball in the group is in motion.

If the owner of the ball refuse to comply with this Rule when required to do so, *his side shall be disqualified.*

3. Balls to be at Rest

While the competitor's ball is in motion after a stroke on the putting green, any other ball shall not be played or touched

. Ball Struck by Another Ball

When the balls concerned lie on the putting green, if a competitor's ball strike any other ball, *the competitor shall incur a penalty of two strokes* and shall play his ball as it lies. The other ball shall be at once replaced.

In all other cases, if a competitor's ball strike any other ball, the competitor shall play his ball as it lies. The owner f the moved ball shall replace his ball, without penalty.

. Order of Play

Balls belonging to the same side may be played in the order he side considers best.

. Wrong Ball

If a competitor play any strokes with a wrong ball (Def. 5) except in a hazard, *he shall add two penalty strokes* to his score or the hole and then play the correct ball (Rule 21-3).

If the wrong ball be a ball in the competition, its owner shall place a ball on the spot from which the wrong ball was played.

. Maximum of Fourteen Clubs

The side shall be penalized for a violation of Rule 3 by either partner.

. Disqualification Penalties

a. FROM THE COMPETITION

A competitor shall be disqualified from the competition for a breach of any of the following, but the penalty shall not apply to his partner:—

Rule 8-3—Practice before Round.
Rule 37-5—Time and Order of Starting.

A side shall be disqualified from the competition for a breach of any of the following:—

Rule 2—The Club and the Ball.
Rule 4—Agreement to Waive Rules Prohibited.
Rule 37-2—Caddie and Forecaddie.
Rule 37-7—Undue Delay (repeated offense).
Rule 37-8—Refusal to Comply with Rule.
Rule 37-9—Artificial Devices.
Rule 38-2—Checking Scores.
Rule 38-3—No alteration of scores, i.e., when the recorded lower score of the partners is lower than actually played. If the recorded lower score of the partners is higher than actually played, it must stand as returned.

Rule 41-2—Ball Influencing Play, Refusal to Lift.

By both partners, at the same hole, of a Rule or Rules the penalty for which is disqualification either from the competition or for a hole.

b. FROM THE REMAINDER OF THE COMPETITION

A competitor shall be disqualified for the hole in question and from the remainder of the competition for a breach of Rule 37-6a (Discontinuance of Play), but the penalty shall not apply to his partner.

c. FOR THE HOLE ONLY

In all other cases where a breach of a Rule would entail disqualification, *the competitor shall be disqualified only for the hole at which the breach occurred.*

(Modification of penalty—Rule 36-5.)

9. Infringement Assisting Partner

If a competitor's infringement of a Rule or Local Rule assist his partner's play, *the partner incurs the relative penalty in addition to any penalty incurred by the competitor.*

10. Penalty Applies to Competitor Only

In all other cases where, by the Rules of Golf, a competitor would incur a penalty, the penalty shall not apply to his partner.

Appendix I
LOCAL RULES

Rule 36-7 provides:

"The Committee shall make and publish Local Rules for abnormal conditions, having regard to the policy of the Governing Authority of the country concerned as set forth in Appendix I attached to these Rules.

"A penalty imposed by a Rule of Golf shall not be waived by a Local Rule."

Among the matters for which Local Rules or other regulations may be advisable are the following:

1. Lateral Water Hazards

Clarifying the status of sections of water hazards which may be lateral under Definition 14c and Rule 33-3.

2. Obstructions

a. CLARIFYING STATUS: Clarifying the status of objects which may be obstructions under Definition 20 and Rule 31.

b. WHEN INTEGRAL PART OF COURSE: Declaring not an obstruction any construction which the Committee considers an integral part of the course (Definition 20c); e.g., built-up sides and surfaces of teeing grounds, putting greens and bunkers.

3. Defining Bounds and Margins

Specifying means used to define out of bounds, hazards, water hazards, lateral water hazards, and ground under repair.

4. Ball Drops

Establishment of special areas on which a ball may be dropped when it is not feasible to proceed exactly in conformity with the Rules for ball unplayable (29-2b) and for water hazards and lateral water hazards (33-2, -3).

5. Provisional Ball, Water Hazard

Permitting play of a provisional ball for a ball which may be in a water hazard of such character that it would be impracticable to determine whether the ball is in the hazard or to do so would unduly delay play. In such case, if a provisional ball is played and the original ball is in a water hazard, the player may play the original ball as it lies or continue the provisional ball in play, but he may not proceed under Rule 33-2 or 33-3.

6. Preservation of Course

Preservation of the course, including turf nurseries and other parts of the course under cultivation on which play is prohibited.

7. Temporary Conditions—Mud, Extreme Wetness

Temporary conditions which might interfere with proper playing of the game, including mud and extreme wetness warranting lifting an embedded ball on specific individual days (*see detailed recommendation below*) or removal of mud from a ball through the green.

8. Accumulation of Leaves

9. Unusual Damage To the Course (other than as covered in Rule 32.)

10. Roads and Paths

Providing relief of the type afforded under Rule 31-2b from roads and paths not having artificial surfaces and sides if they could unfairly affect play.

11. Priority On the Course (see Etiquette)

12. Practice Areas (see Rules 8 and 36-4b)

13. Automotive Transport

Specifying whether automotive transportation may or may not be used by players.

Lifting an Embedded Ball

On the putting green, Rule 35-1c permits a ball to be lifted to repair damage caused by the impact of a ball.

Through the green (Definition 35), when permission to lift an embedded ball would be warranted on specific days, the following Local Rule is suggested:

"Through the green," a ball which is embedded in its own pitch-mark in ground other than sand may be lifted without penalty, cleaned, and dropped as near as possible to the spot where it lay and must come to rest not nearer the hole. *(See Rule 22.)*

("Through the green" (Definition 35) is the whole area of the course except:—

a. Teeing ground and putting green of the hole being played;

b. All hazards on the course.)

Practice at Putting Green of Hole Played

When it is desired to prohibit practice on or to a putting green of a hole already played, the following Local Rule is recommended:

A player during a round shall not play any practice stroke on or to the putting green of any hole he has played in the round. (For other practice, see Rules 8 and 36-4b.)

PENALTY FOR BREACH OF LOCAL RULE:
Match play—Loss of hole; Stroke play—Two strokes.

Marking Position of Lifted Ball

When it is desired to require a specific means of marking the position of a lifted ball on the putting green, the following Local Rule is recommended:

When a ball on the putting green is to be lifted, its position shall be marked by placing an object, such as a small coin, immediately behind the ball; if the object interfere with another player, it should be moved one or more putterhead-lengths to one side. (This supersedes Rule 35-1k.)

PENALTY FOR BREACH OF LOCAL RULE:
Match play—Loss of hole; Stroke play—Two strokes.

Prohibition against Touching Line of Putt with Club

When it is desired to prohibit touching the line of putt with a club, the following Local Rule is recommended:

The line of putt shall not be touched with a club for any purpose except to repair ball marks or during address. (This modifies Rule 35-1b.)

PENALTY FOR BREACH OF LOCAL RULE:
Match play—Loss of hole; Stroke play—Two strokes.

Temporary Obstructions

When temporary obstructions are installed for a competition, the following Local Rule is recommended:

1. Definition

Temporary immovable obstructions include tents, scoreboards, grandstands, refreshment stands, lavatories and, provided it is not mobile or otherwise readily movable, any piece of equipment for photography, press, radio, television and scoring services.

Excluded are temporary power lines and cables (from which relief is provided in Clause 4) and mobile or otherwise readily movable equipment for photography, press, etc. (from which relief is obtainable under Rule 31-1).

2. Interference

Interference by a temporary immovable obstruction occurs when (a) the ball lies in or on the obstruction or so close to the obstruction that the obstruction interferes with the player's stance or the area of his intended swing or (b) the obstruction intervenes between the player's ball and the hole or the ball lies within one club-length of a spot where such intervention would exist.

However, if the player cannot play a stroke toward the flagstick because of interference by anything other than a temporary obstruction, he may not apply Clause 3a or 3b below.

3. Relief

A player may obtain relief from interference by a temporary immovable obstruction, without penalty, as follows:—

a. THROUGH THE GREEN

Through the green, the nearest point shall be determined (without crossing over, through or under the obstruction) which (a) is not nearer the hole, (b) avoids interference as defined in Clause 2 of this Local Rule and (c) is not in a hazard or on a putting green. He shall lift the ball and drop it within two club-lengths of the point thus determined on ground which fulfils (a), (b) and (c) above.

Note: The prohibition against crossing over, through or under the obstruction does not apply when the ball lies in or on the obstruction.

b. IN A HAZARD

If the ball lie in a hazard, a ball shall be dropped either:

(i) In the hazard, without penalty, on the nearest ground affording complete relief within the limits specified in Clause 3a above or, if complete relief is impossible, on ground within the hazard affording maximum relief, or

(ii) Outside the hazard, under penalty of one stroke, as follows: The player shall determine the nearest point which (a) is not nearer the hole, (b) avoids interference as defined in Clause 2 of this Local Rule and (c) is not in the hazard. He shall lift the ball and drop it within two club-lengths of the point thus determined on ground which fulfils (a), (b) and (c) above.

4. Temporary Power Lines and Cables

The above Clauses do not apply to temporary power lines and cables. If such lines and cables are readily movable, the player, may obtain relief under Rule 31-1. If they are not readily movable, the player may obtain relief under Rule 31-2. If a ball strikes an elevated line or cable, it must be replaced and replayed, without penalty. (Exception: Ball striking elevated junction section of cable rising from the ground shall not be replayed.)

PENALTY FOR BREACH OF LOCAL RULE:
Match play—Loss of hole; Stroke play—Two strokes.

"Preferred Lies" and "Winter Rules"

The USGA does not endorse "preferred lies" and "winter rules," and recommends that the Rules of Golf be observed uniformly. Ground under repair is provided for in Definition 13 and Rule 32. Occasional abnormal conditions which might interfere with fair play and are not widespread should be defined accurately as ground under repair.

However, adverse conditions are sometimes so general throughout a course that the local Committee believes "preferred lies" or "winter rules" would promote fair and pleasant play or help protect the course. Heavy snows, spring thaws, prolonged rains or extreme heat can make fairways unsatisfactory and sometimes prevent use of heavy mowing equipment.

When a Committee adopts a local rule for "preferred lies" or "winter rules," it should be in detail and should be interpreted by the Committee, as there is no established code for "winter rules." Without a detailed local rule, it is meaningless for a Committee to post a notice merely saying "Winter Rules Today."

The following local rule would seem appropriate for the conditions in question, but the USGA does not endorse it and will not interpret it:

A ball lying on a "fairway" may be lifted and cleaned, without penalty, and placed within six inches of where it originally lay, not nearer the hole, and so as to preserve as nearly as possible the stance required to play from the original lie. After the ball has been so placed, it is in play, and if it move after the player has addressed it *the penalty shall be one stroke*—see Rule 27-1f.

If the adverse conditions extend onto the putting green,

above local rule may be altered by adding the words "or
e putting green" after the word "fairway."

If it is desired to *protect* the course, the above local rule
ould be reworded to make it mandatory rather than per-
issive to move the ball from certain areas. The above rule
oes not require a player to move his ball if he does not want
o do so.

Before a Committee adopts a local rule permitting "pre-
rred lies" or "winter rules," the following facts should be
onsidered:

1. Such a local rule conflicts with the Rules of Golf and the
ndamental principle of playing the ball as it lies.

2. "Winter rules" are sometimes adopted under the guise
f protecting the course when, in fact, the practical effect is
ust the opposite—they permit moving the ball to the best turf,
om which divots are then taken to injure the course further.

3. "Preferred lies" or "winter rules" tend generally to lower
cores and handicaps, thus penalizing the players in compe-
tion with players whose scores for handicaps are made under
he Rules of Golf.

4. Extended use or indiscriminate use of "preferred lies"
r "winter rules" will place players at a disadvantage when
ompeting at a course where the ball must be played as it lies.

Handicapping and "Preferred Lies"

Scores made under a local rule for "preferred lies" or "winter
ules" may be accepted for handicapping if the Committee
onsiders that conditions warrant.

When such a local rule is adopted, the Committee should
nsure that the course's normal scoring difficulty is maintained
s nearly as possible through adjustment of tee markers and
elated methods. However, if extreme conditions cause ex-
ended use of "preferred lies" or "winter rules" and the course
management cannot adjust scoring difficulty properly, the club
should obtain a Temporary Course Rating from its district
golf association.

Appendix II
DESIGN OF CLUBS (DEF. 36)

Rule 2-2a provides in part:—

"The golf club shall be composed of a shaft and a head,
and all of the various parts shall be fixed so that the club is
one unit; the club shall not be designed to be adjustable,
except for weight."

Note: *Playing characteristics not to be changed during
a round—Rule 2-2b.*

"The club shall not be substantially different from the traditional and customary form and make, and shall conform
with the regulations governing the design of clubs."

The following are the regulations governing the design of
clubs:—

a. SHAPE OF HEAD

The length of a clubhead shall be greater than the breadth.

Length shall be determined on a horizontal line, five-eighths
of an inch above the sole, from the back of the heel to the end
of the toe or a vertical projection thereof.

Breadth shall be determined on a horizontal line between
the outermost points of the face and the back of the head or
vertical projections thereof.

b. FACE OF HEAD

The club shall have only one face designed for striking the
ball, except that a putter may have two faces if the loft of both
faces is substantially the same and does not exceed ten degrees.

Club faces shall not embody any degree of concavity on
the hitting surface.

Club faces shall not have any lines, dots or other markings
with sharp or rough edges, or any type of finish, for the purpose of unduly influencing the movement of the ball.

Markings on the face of a club shall conform with the specifications in Appendix III at page 61. The face of an iron club
shall not contain an inset or attachment.

c. SHAFT

The shaft shall be designed to be straight from the top to
a point not more than five inches above the sole. The shaft,
including any inserted plug, shall be generally circular in cross-
section and shall extend to the upper end of the grip.

The shaft shall be fixed to the clubhead at the heel (as
illustrated in Figure A on page 59). The shaft may be attached
directly to the clubhead or to a neck or socket of the clubhead;
any neck or socket shall not be more than five inches in length
measured from the top of the neck or socket to the sole. The
shaft and the neck or socket shall remain in line with the heel,
or with a point to right or left of the heel, when the club is
soled at address. The distance between the axis of the shaft
(or the neck or socket) and the back of the heel shall not
exceed five-eighths of an inch in wood clubs and five-sixteenths
of an inch in iron clubs.

Exception for Putters:—The shaft or neck or socket of a
putter may be fixed at any point in the head and need not
remain in line with the heel. The axis of the shaft from the top
to a point not more than five inches above the sole shall diverge
from the vertical by at least ten degrees in relation to the
horizontal line determining length of head under Appendix IIa.
The shaft in cross-section shall be generally circular or otherwise symmetrical.

The grip consists of that part of the shaft designed to be
held by the player and any material added to it for the purpose
of obtaining a firm hold. The grip shall be substantially straight
and plain in form, may have flat sides, but shall not have a
channel or a furrow or be molded for any part of the hands.

*The following are examples of grips which have been ap-
proved and some which have been disapproved:—*

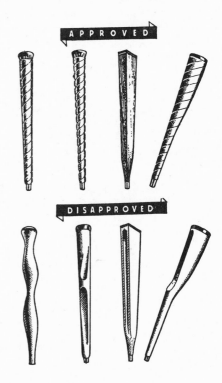

Appendix III
MARKINGS ON CLUBS (DEF. 36)

Rule 2-2a provides in part:—

"The golf club shall be composed of a shaft and a head, and all of the various parts shall be fixed so that the club is one unit; the club shall not be designed to be adjustable, except for weight.

"**Note:** *Playing characteristics not to be changed during a round—Rule 2-2b.*

"The club shall not be substantially different from the traditional and customary form and make, and shall conform with the regulations governing the design of clubs at Appendix II and the specifications for markings on clubs."

Appendix IIb provides in part:

"Club faces shall not have any lines, dots or other markings with sharp or rough edges, or any type of finish, for the purpose of unduly influencing the movement of the ball. Markings of the face of a club shall conform with the specifications."

Sharp or rough edges of markings may be determined by a finger test. A different problem is presented, however, by the detailed Specifications for Markings on Clubs. These are manufacturing specifications. For the guidance of players and Committees, following are a layman's interpretation of some essential parts of the specifications:

In general it is required that the face of a club shall present a smooth, flat surface on which a limited percentage of the area may be depressed by markings.

When the depressed area is in the form of grooves, each groove may not be wider than .035 inch (approximately one thirty-second of an inch), the angle between the flat surface of the club face and the side of the groove may not be less than 135 degrees. Except as provided elsewhere, the distance between grooves may not be less than three times the width of the groove.

When the depressed area is in the form of punch marks, the markings must not exceed .075 inch (a little over one-sixteenth of an inch) in diameter.

The complete specifications are:—

Specifications

In general a definite area of the surface is reserved for scoring. All the sections contained in this specification shall refer to this particular scored area. With regard to an iron club, reasonably-sized areas of the heel and the toe shall not be scored—see illustration of "Golf Head Scorings" below. This restriction does not apply to wood clubs.

This specification is divided into three sections: Section 1 refers to golf clubs where grooves are used; Section 2 refers to golf clubs scored with punch marks; Section 3 includes a combination of groove and punch markings.

Section 1-a Wood Clubs

Wood clubs shall not have any markings on the face for the purpose of unduly influencing the movement of the ball. Where the loft or face angle exceeds 24 degrees, grooves shall be generally straight with a maximum width measured in the face plane of .040 inches. The depth of any groove shall not be greater than 1-1/2 times the width. At no place on the face shall the distance between the edges of the grooves be less than three times the width of the adjacent groove.

Section 1-b Iron Clubs

1. A series of straight grooves in the form of V's may be put in the face of the club. The side walls of the grooves shall be essentially flat and the included angle shall be equal to or greater than 90 degrees. The bisector of the angle shall be normal to the face of the club. (See illustration of "Golf Head Scorings.")

2. The width of a groove shall be generally consistent and not exceed .035 inches along its full length. This width shall

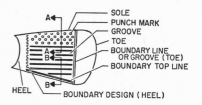

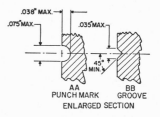

Golf Head Scorings

be measured in the plane of the face of the club between the two points where the planes of the groove meet the face o the club. The widths of grooves in any club face shall be generally consistent.

3. At no place on the face of the club shall the distance between edges of the grooves be less than three times the width of a groove, with the minimum distance between the edges of any two grooves being .075 inches.

4. Lines may be used to define the toe, heel and top boundaries of the scored area. Such a line must be no wider or deeper than .040 inches. Designs may be used to indicate the toe and heel boundaries of the scored area. They must be no deeper than .040 inches. Designs and lines must have smooth edges and shall not be designed in any way to influence unduly the movement of the ball.

5. The scored area shall be considered as that portion of the face within boundary lines or designs. In the case where such lines or designs do not exist, the scored area shall be that portion between the extremities of the grooves.

6. The center or intended impact center of the face may be indicated by a design which shall fit within the boundary of a square whose sides are .375 inches in length. Such a marking shall not in any way be designed to influence unduly the movement of the ball.

7. The face of the club shall be smooth and flat over the full surface. No sharp edges or lips due to die impression of any type will be permitted. For decorative purposes only, it is permissible to sandblast the scored area not to exceed a roughness of 180 microinches, with 15% tolerance. The relative roughness shall be determined in accordance with USA standards (ASA B46.1-1962) for surface texture. The direction of measurement shall be parallel to the grooves.

The above conditions for smoothness apply also to Sections 2 and 3.

Section 2

Punch marks may be used in the place of grooves. The area of such a mark, in the plane of the face, may not exceed .0044 square inches. A mark may not be closer to an adjacent mark than 0.168 inches measured from center to center. The depth of a mark may not be greater than .038 inches with centerline normal to the face. Punchmarks must be evenly distributed throughout the scored area.

ection 3

In the event punch marks in combination with grooves are sed within the scored area, groove specifications govern as Section 1 if grooves are adjacent. Punch mark specifications overn if punch marks are adjacent. At no place may a punch ark be closer to a groove measured from center to center an .168 inches.

Appendix IV
MISCELLANEOUS

How to Decide Ties in Handicap Events

Rule 36-3 empowers the Committee to determine how and hen a halved match or a stroke play tie shall be decided. he decision s'.ould be published in advance.

The USGA recommends:

. Match Play

A handicap match which ends all even should be played ff hole by hole until one side wins a hole. The play-off should art on the hole where the match began. Strokes should be llowed as in the prescribed round.

. Stroke Play

A handicap stroke competition which ends in a tie should e played off at 18 holes, with handicaps. If a shorter play-off e necessary, the percentage of 18 holes to be played shall be pplied to the players' handicaps to determine their play-off andicaps. It is advisable to arrange for a percentage of holes hat will result in whole numbers in handicaps; if this is not easible, handicap stroke fractions of one-half or more shall ount as a full stroke, and any lesser fractions shall be dis- egarded. *Example:* In an individual competition, A's handicap 10 and B's is 8. It would be appropriate to conduct a nine- ole play-off (50% of 18 holes) with A receiving 5 strokes and 4 strokes.

Pairings for Match Play

General Numerical Draw

For purposes of determining places in the draw, ties in quali- ying rounds other than those for the last qualifying place shall e decided by the order in which scores are returned, the first core to be returned receiving the lowest available number, etc. f it be impossible to determine the order in which scores are eturned, ties shall be determined by a blind draw.

Upper Half	Lower Half	Upper Half	Lower Half
64 Qualifiers		32 Qualifiers	
1 vs. 33	2 vs. 34	1 vs. 17	2 vs. 18
17 vs. 49	18 vs. 50	9 vs. 25	10 vs. 26
9 vs. 41	10 vs. 42	5 vs. 21	6 vs. 22
25 vs. 57	26 vs. 58	13 vs. 29	14 vs. 30
5 vs. 37	6 vs. 38	3 vs. 19	4 vs. 20
21 vs. 53	22 vs. 54	11 vs. 27	12 vs. 28
13 vs. 45	14 vs. 46	7 vs. 23	8 vs. 24
29 vs. 61	30 vs. 62	15 vs. 31	16 vs. 32
3 vs. 35	4 vs. 36	16 Qualifiers	
19 vs. 51	20 vs. 52	1 vs. 9	2 vs. 10
11 vs. 43	12 vs. 44	5 vs. 13	6 vs. 14
27 vs. 59	28 vs. 60	3 vs. 11	4 vs. 12
7 vs. 39	8 vs. 40	7 vs. 15	8 vs. 16
23 vs. 55	24 vs. 56	8 Qualifiers	
15 vs. 47	16 vs. 48	1 vs. 5	2 vs. 6
31 vs. 63	32 vs. 64	3 vs. 7	4 vs. 8

Par Computation

"Par" is the score that an expert golfer would be expected o make for a given hole. Par means errorless play without flukes and under ordinary weather conditions, allowing two strokes on the putting green.

Yardages for guidance in computing par are given below. They are not arbitrary, because allowance should be made for the configuration of the ground, any difficult or unusual con- ditions, and the severity of the hazards.

Each hole should be measured horizontally from the middle of the tee area to be used to the center of the green, following the line of play planned by the architect in laying out the hole. Thus, in a hole with a bend, the line at the elbow point should be centered in the fairway in accordance with the architect's intention.

	Yardages for Guidance	
Par	Men	Women
3	up to 250	up to 210
4	251 to 470	211 to 400
5	471 and over	401 to 575
6		576 and over

Handicapping

Par as computed above should not be confused with Course Rating as described in the USGA Golf Handicap System. USGA Handicaps must be based on Course Rating rather than par. See the booklet "Golf Committee Manual and USGA Golf Handicap System."

Flagstick Dimensions

The USGA recommends that the flagstick be at least seven feet in height and that its diameter be not greater than three- quarters of an inch from a point three inches above the ground to the bottom of the hole.

Protection of Persons against Lightning

As there have been many deaths and injuries from lightning on golf courses, all players, caddies, and sponsors of golf are urged to take every precaution for the protection of persons against lightning.

The National Bureau of Standards points out:

"If golf clubs could be impressed with the necessity of calling off matches *before the storm is near enough to be hazardous,* the cases of multiple injury or death among players and spectators could be eliminated."

Raising golf clubs or umbrellas above the head adds to the element of personal hazard during electrical storms.

Metal spikes on golf shoes do little to increase the hazard, according to the Bureau.

Taking Shelter

The following rules for personal safety during thunderstorms are based on material in the Lightning Protection Code, NFPA No. 78-1975; ANSI C5. 1-1975 available from the National Fire Protection Association, 470 Atlantic Ave., Boston, Mass. 02210, and the American National Standards Institute, 1430 Broadway, New York, N.Y. 10018:

(a) *Types of Shelter*

Do not go out of doors or remain out during thunderstorms unless it is necessary. Seek shelter inside buildings, vehicles, or other structures or locations which offer protection from lightning, such as:

1. Dwellings or other buildings protected against lightning.
2. Large metal-frame buildings.
3. Large unprotected buildings.
4. Automobiles with metal tops and bodies.
5. Trailers with metal bodies.
6. City streets shielded by nearby buildings.

When it is not possible to choose a location that offers better protection, seek shelter in:

1. Dense woods—avoid isolated trees.
2. Depressed areas—avoid hilltops and high places.
3. Small unprotected buildings, tents and shelters in *low*

areas— avoid unprotected buildings and shelters in *high* areas.

(b) *What to Avoid*

Certain locations are extremely hazardous during thunderstorms and should be avoided if at all possible. Approaching thunderstorms should be anticipated and the following locations avoided when storms are in the immediate vicinity:

1. Open fields.
2. Athletic fields.
3. Golf courses.
4. Swimming pools, lakes and seashores.
5. Near wire fences, clotheslines, overhead wires and railroad tracks.
6. Isolated trees.
7. Hilltops and wide open spaces.

In the above locations, it is especially hazardous to be riding in or on any of the following during lightning storms:

1. Tractors and other farm machinery operated on the golf course for maintenance of same.
2. Golf carts, scooters, motorcycles, bicycles.

Discontinuing Play during Lightning

Attention is called to Rules 36-4c, 37-5 and 37-6.

The USGA especially suggests that players be informed that they have the right to stop play if they think lightning threatens them, even though the Committee may not have specifically authorized it by signal.

The USGA uses the following signals and recommends that all local committees do similarly:

Discontinue Play: Three consecutive notes of siren, repeated.

Resume Play: One prolonged note of siren, repeated.

Lightning Protection for Shelters

Shelters on golf courses may best be protected by standard lightning protection systems. Details on the installation of conductors, air terminals, and maintenance requirements are included in the Lightning Protection Code.

An alternate method of protection of such shelters is through what is known as providing a "cone of protection" with grounded rods or masts and overhead conductors as described in Section 31 of the Lightning Protection Code. Such a system is feasible for small structures, but probably would be more expensive than a standard lightning rod system.

Down conductors should be shielded with non-conductive material, resistant to impact and climatic conditions to a height of approximately 8 feet to protect persons from contact with down conductors. Shelters with earthen floors which are provided with lightning protection systems should have any approved grounding electrodes interconnected by an encircling buried, bare conductor of a type suitable for such service, or, such electrodes should be provided with radial conductors run out to a distance of at least 10 feet from the electrode, away from the shelter.

★   ★   ★

It is recommended that several notices similar to this be posted at every course. Copies of this notice in poster form may be obtained from the USGA.

Rules of Amateur Status

Any person who considers that any action he is proposing to take might endanger his amateur status should submit particulars to the United States Golf Association for consideration.

Definition of an Amateur Golfer

An amateur golfer is one who plays the game as a nonremunerative or non-profit-making sport

Rule 1
Forfeiture of Amateur Status at Any Age

The following are examples of acts at any age which violat the Definition of an Amateur Golfer and cause forfeiture c amateur status:

1. Professionalism

a. Receiving payment or compensation for serving as professional golfer or identifying oneself as a professiona golfer.

b. Taking any action for the purpose of becoming a pr fessional golfer.

Note: *Such actions include applying for a professional's p sition; filing application to a school or competition conducte to qualify persons to play as professionals in tournaments entering into an agreement, written or oral, with a sponsor o professional agent; agreement to accept payment or compe sation for allowing one's name or likeness as a skilled golfer t be used for any commercial purpose; and holding or retainin membership in any organization of professional golfers.*

2. Playing for Prize Money

Playing for prize money or its equivalent in a match, tourn ment or exhibition.

Note: *A player may participate in an event in which priz money or its equivalent is offered, provided that prior t participation he irrevocably waives his right to accept priz money in that event. (See USGA Policy on Gambling fo definition of prize money.)*

3. Instruction

Receiving payment or compensation for giving instruction in playing golf, either orally, in writing, by pictures or by othe demonstrations, to either individuals or groups.

Exception: Golf instruction may be given by an employee o an educational institution or system to students of the insti tution or system and by camp counselors to those in their charge, provided that the total time devoted to golf instruction during a year comprises less than 50 percent of the time spent during the year in the performance of all duties as such employee or counselor.

4. Prizes and Testimonials

Acceptance of a prize or testimonial of the following cha acter (this applies to total prizes received for any event o series of events in any one tournament or exhibition, includin hole-in-one or other events in which golf skill is a factor):

(i) Of retail value exceeding $350; or

(ii) Of a nature which is the equivalent of money or makes it readily convertible into money.

EXCEPTIONS:

1. Prizes of only symbolic value (such as metal trophies) anything, whether or not used in or appertaining to golf, except as the author of golf books or articles as permitted by Rule 1-7

Note: *An advertisement may contain a player's name or likeness when it is customary to the business of such a player and contains no reference to the game of golf.*

6. Personal Appearance

Because of golf skill or golf reputation, receiving payment or compensation, directly or indirectly, for a personal appearance

Exception: Actual expenses in connection with personal appearances may be paid or reimbursed provided no golf competition or exhibition is involved.

7. Broadcasting and Writing

Because of golf skill or golf reputation, receiving payment or compensation, directly or indirectly, for broadcasting concern ing golf, a golf event or golf events, writing golf articles or books or allowing one's name to be advertised or published as the author of golf articles or books of which he is not actually the author.

Exceptions:
1. Broadcasting or writing as part of one's primary occupation or career, provided instruction in playing golf is not included (Rule 1-3).
2. Part-time broadcasting or writing, provided (a) the player is actually the author of the commentary, articles or books, (b) instruction in playing golf is not included and (c) the payment or compensation does not have the purpose or effect, directly or indirectly, of financing participation in a golf competition or golf competitions.

Sale of Golf Merchandise
Because of golf skill or golf reputation, receiving payment or compensation, directly or indirectly, for selling or promoting the sale of golf merchandise, at either wholesale or retail. (*The term "golf merchandise" does not include clothing, shoes or olf carts.)*

Golf Equipment
Accepting golf balls, clubs, golf merchandise, golf clothing r golf shoes from anyone dealing in such merchandise without ayment of current market price.

0. Membership and Privileges
Because of golf skill or golf reputation, accepting membership or privileges in a club or at a golf course without full ayment for the class of membership or privileges involved r indirectly, from anyone manufacturing such merchandise ithout payment of current market price.

. Membership and Privileges
Because of golf skill or golf reputation, accepting membership or privileges in a club or at a golf course without full ayment for the class of membership or privileges involved nless such membership or privileges have been awarded (1) s purely and deservedly honorary, (2) in recognition of an utstanding performance or contribution to golf and (3) without a time limit.

0. Expenses
Accepting expenses, in money or otherwise, from any source ther than one on whom the player is normally or legally ependent to engage in a golf competition or exhibition.
Exceptions: A player may receive a reasonable amount of xpenses as follows:
1. JUNIOR COMPETITIONS
   As a player in a golf competition or exhibition limited exclusively to players who have not reached their 18th birthday.
2. INTERNATIONAL TEAMS
   As a representative of a recognized golf association in an international team match between or among golf associations when such expenses are paid by one or more of the golf associations involved or, subject to the approval of the USGA, as a representative in an international team match conducted by some other athletic organization.
3. USGA PUBLIC LINKS CHAMPIONSHIPS
   As a qualified contestant in the USGA Amateur Public Links Championships proper, but only within limits fixed by the USGA.
4. SCHOOL, COLLEGE, MILITARY TEAMS
   As a representative of a recognized educational institution or of a military service in (1) team events or (2) other events which are limited to representatives of recognized educational institutions or of military services, respectively. In each case, expenses may be accepted from only an educational or military authority.
5. INDUSTRIAL OR BUSINESS TEAMS
   As a representative of an industrial or business golf team in industrial or business golf team competitions, respectively, but only within limits fixed by the USGA.

Note 1: *A player is not considered to be "normally or legally dependent" upon an employer, a partner or other vocational source, and acceptance of expenses therefrom is not permissible.*

Note 2: Business Expenses—*It is permissible to play in a golf competition while on a business trip with expenses paid provided that the golf part of the expenses is borne personally and is not charged to business. Further, the business involved must be actual and substantial, and not merely a subterfuge for legitimizing expenses when the primary purpose is golf competition.*

Note 3: Private Transport—*Acceptance of private transport furnished or arranged for by a tournament sponsor, directly or indirectly, as an inducement for a player to engage in a golf competition or exhibition shall be considered accepting expenses under Rule 1-11.*

12. Scholarships
Because of golf skill or golf reputation, accepting the benefits of a scholarship or any other consideration as an inducement to be a student in an educational establishment.
Exception: A scholarship or grant-in-aid awarded and administered by the establishment concerned and not in excess of commonly accepted educational expenses as defined by the National Collegiate Athletic Association or the Association of Intercollegiate Athletics for Women.

13. Conduct Detrimental to Golf
Any conduct, including activities in connection with golf gambling, which is considered detrimental to the best interests of the game.

Rule 2
Advisory Opinions, Enforcement and Reinstatement
1. Advisory Opinions
Any person who considers that any action he is proposing to take might endanger his amateur status may submit particulars to the staff of the United States Golf Association for advice. If dissatisfied with the staff's advice, he may request that the matter be referred to the Amateur Status and Conduct Committee for decision. If dissatisfied with the Amateur Status and Conduct Committee's decision, he may, by written notice to the staff within 30 days after being notified of the decision, appeal to the Executive Committee, in which case he shall be matter be referred to the Amateur Status and Conduct Committee for decision. If dissatisfied with the Amateur Status and Conduct Committee's decision, he may, by written notice to the staff within 30 days after being notified of the decision, appeal to the Executive Committee, in which case he shall be given reasonable notice of the next meeting of the Executive Committee at which the matter may be heard and shall be entitled to present his case in person or in writing. The decision of the Executive Committee shall be final.

2. Enforcement
Whenever information of a possible violation of the Definition of an Amateur Golfer by a player claiming to be an amateur shall come to the attention of the United States Golf Association, the staff shall notify the player of the possible violation, invite the player to submit such information as the player deems relevant and make such other investigation as seems appropriate under the circumstances. The staff shall submit to the Amateur Status and Conduct Committee all information provided by the player, their findings and their recommendation, and the Amateur Status and Conduct Committee shall decide whether a violation has occurred. If dissatisfied with the Amateur Status and Conduct Committee's decision, the player may, by written notice to the staff within

30 days after being notified of the decision, appeal to the Executive Committee, in which case the player shall be given reasonable notice of the next meeting of the Executive Committee at which the matter may be heard and shall be entitled to present his case in person or in writing. The decision of the Executive Committee shall be final.

Upon a final decision of the Amateur Status and Conduct Committee or the Executive Committee that a player has violated the Definition of an Amateur Golfer, such Committee may require the player to refrain or desist from specified actions as a condition of retaining his amateur status or declare the amateur status of the player forfeited. Such Committee shall notify the player, if possible, and may notify any interested golf association of any action taken under this paragraph.

3. Reinstatement

The Executive Committee shall have sole power to reinstate a player to amateur status or to deny reinstatement.

Each application for reinstatement shall be decided on its merits.

In considering an application for reinstatement, the Executive Committee shall normally be guided by the following principles:

a. PROBATION

The professional holds an advantage over the amateur by reason of having devoted himself to the game as his profession; other persons violating the Rules of Amateur Status also obtain advantages not available to the amateur. They do not necessarily lose such advantage merely by deciding to cease violating the Rules.

Therefore, an applicant for reinstatement to amateur status shall undergo probation as prescribed by the Executive Committee.

Probation shall start from the date of the player's last violation of the Definition of an Amateur Golfer unless the Executive Committee decides that it shall start from the date when the player's last violation became known to the Executive Committee.

b. PROBATIONARY PERIOD

A probationary period of two years will normally be required. The Executive Committee, however, reserves the right to *extend* or *shorten* such period. Longer periods will normally be required of applicants who have played extensively for prize money; shorter periods will often be permitted in the cases of applicants who were in violation of the Rules one year or less and did not play for prize money more than three times.

Players of national prominence who have been in violation for more than five years shall not normally be eligible for reinstatement.

c. ONE REINSTATEMENT

A player shall not normally be reinstated more than once.

d. STATUS DURING PROBATION

During probation an applicant for reinstatement shall conform with the Definition of an Amateur Golfer.

He shall not be eligible to enter competitions limited to amateurs except that he may enter competitions solely among members of a club of which he is a member, subject to the approval of the club. He may also, without prejudicing his application, enter, as an applicant for reinstatement, competitions which are not limited to amateurs but shall not accept any prize reserved for an amateur.

e. FORM OF APPLICATION

Each application for reinstatement shall be prepared, in duplicate, on forms provided by the USGA.

The application must be filed through a recognized amateur golf association in whose district the applicant resides. The association's recommendation, if any, will be considered. If the applicant is unknown to the association, this should be noted and the application forwarded to the USGA, without prejudice.

USGA Policy on Gambling

The Definition of an Amateur Golfer provides that an amateur golfer is one who plays the game as a non-remunerative or non-profit-making sport. When gambling motives are introduced, problems can arise which threaten the integrity of the game.

The USGA does not object to participation in wagering among individual golfers or teams of golfers when participation in the wagering is limited to the players, the players may only wager on themselves or their teams, the sole source of all money won by players is advanced by the players and the primary purpose is the playing of the game for enjoyment.

The distinction between playing for prize money and gambling is essential to the validity of the Rules of Amateur Status. The following constitute golf wagering and not playing for prize money:

1. Participation in wagering among individual golfers.
2. Participation in wagering among teams.

Organized amateur events open to the general golfing public and designed and promoted to create cash prizes are not approved by the USGA. Golfers participating in such events without irrevocably waiving their right to cash prizes are deemed by the USGA to be playing for prize money.

The USGA is opposed to and urges its Member Clubs, all golf associations and all other sponsors of golf competitions to prohibit types of gambling such as: (1) Calcuttas, (2) other auction pools, (3) pari-mutuels and (4) any other forms of gambling organized for general participation or permitting participants to bet on someone other than themselves or their teams.

The Association may deny amateur status, entry in USGA Championships and membership on USGA teams for international competitions to players whose activities in connection with golf gambling, whether organized or individual, are considered by the USGA to be contrary to the best interests of golf.

CHANGES SINCE 1978
Appendix I
Local Rules

Lifting an Embedded Ball — Preamble amended to provide that, if conditions generally are such that permission to lift an embedded ball is warranted, a Committee is justified in adopting the Local Rule for an entire competition or season and not just on specific days.

Relief from Temporary Obstructions — Language amended. New language is simpler, similar to language of immovable obstruction Rule (Rule 31-2b(i)) and provides same procedure for relief for line-of-sight interference as for interference with stance or swing. Thus, necessity for sequence of drops in certain situations eliminated.

These are the only official *Rules of Golf* recognized by the governing bodies of golf in the United States and in every part of the world in which golf is played. The *Rules of Golf* are approved by the United States Golf Association and the Royal and Ancient Golf Club of St. Andrews, Scotland. Golf—whether in competition or not—played by any other rules (excepting local rules, see below) is *not* golf. Many beginning golfers, who have not had the opportunity to study the official rules of the game, erroneously tend to regard these rules as restrictive and designed primarily for the tournament player. The more experienced player, regardless of his golfing ability, will always vouch for the fact that playing by the rules adds much to the enjoyment of the game.

It is impossible for the *Rules of Golf* to anticipate the special physical peculiarities of individual golf courses, with the result that it is often unfair, undesirable, or actually impossible to follow these rules literally. In such cases, local rules are recommended by the USGA and should be made, printed on the scorecard, and posted at the first tee. Where practical, limits of zones to which local rules apply should be marked with stakes. The USGA has made specific recommendations regarding local rules in the appendix to the *Rules of Golf.*

GOLF ETIQUETTE

Etiquette is your observance of the code for correct behavior in respect to other players and to the course itself. The rules of golf etiquette, as stated in Section I of the *Rules of Golf,* should govern your conduct on the course whether you are playing competitive golf or not. This code for correct behavior is a pleasant one, easily understood, and designed for all-round enjoyment of the game. The principle of the etiquette of golf is consideration for fellow players, be they opponents or partners.

It is pleasant to possess skill at golf, and a degree of skill may be attained by all willing to strive for it. But the degree of skill attained is not of greatest importance; golf's chief contribution to the enjoyment of living is the means it provides for making friends, playing in the outdoors, improving health, and developing a high reputation for honor through the observance of the following points of etiquette of the game of golf.

1. *No one should move, talk, or stand close to or directly behind the ball or the hole when a player is addressing the ball or making a stroke.* Unexpected movements and noises tend to disturb a golfer making a stroke. Also, most golfers are thrown off by having someone standing directly behind them when they are swinging or putting. Thus, you are expected to make yourself as unobtrusive as possible while another player is playing. In addition, remember that no attempt, however indirect, should be made to hamper the play of your opponent. In this respect, golf differs from most other competitive sports. In baseball, for example, it is considered part of the game to jockey or needle the opposing players and try to force them into making mistakes. In golf, this strategy should *never* be employed.

2. *The player who has the honor should be allowed to play before his opponent or fellow competitor tees his ball.* Give your fellow player the whole tee to himself when it is his turn to play. It helps him to concentrate. Also, when a golfer hits a tee shot out of bounds, he should step aside and not shoot again until all his fellow players have driven. This is really a good rule to follow, since if you have driven out of bounds, you will have time to compose yourself and probably make a better second try.

3. *No player should play until the players in front are out of range.* Never underestimate your hitting limits. A golf ball is hard and travels with tremendous speed. Many golfers have been severely injured by players

who did not know they could "hit so far." Do not be impatient to drive; you will catch up. When you hit a ball, and there is the slightest chance of its hitting someone, immediately and loudly cry, "Fore."

4. *In the interest of all, players should play without delay.* According to the *Rules of Golf,* a competitor who by delay in play unfairly interferes with the play of any other competitor shall be disqualified in either match play or stroke play. As you approach your ball, plan your upcoming shot: what club you should use, where you want to put the ball, and how hard to hit it. This will eliminate unnecessary delay and perhaps forestall annoyance on your fellow competitors' part. If the group behind is obviously playing faster than yours, or if they have fewer players, of course, invite them to play through.

5. *Players searching for a ball should allow other players coming up to pass them; they should signal to the players following them to pass and should not continue their play until those players have passed and are out of range.* If it appears that your original ball may be difficult to find, it is a good idea to play a provisional one. This saves the time required to walk back and play another ball if the original one is not found. Also, if your opponent hits a ball toward a difficult location, help him by following the shot and visually marking its position by some kind of landmark. Remember that nothing indicates a sportsman golfer quicker than his willingness to help find an opponent's lost ball. All in the group should co-operate. In all cases, the *Rules of Golf* allow only five minutes for a search for a ball.

6. *Before leaving a bunker, a player should carefully fill up all holes made by him therein.* In other words, upon leaving a sand bunker, always take the time to smooth your tracks. It is difficult enough to play efficiently from loose sand without having to dig your ball from a depression as you strike at it. Remember the other fellow, and fill in your heel marks. And the considerate golfer enters a trap where the bank is lowest, since he does less damage there than if he clambers down a steep sand slope.

7. *Through the green, a player should ensure that any turf cut or displaced by him is replaced at once and pressed down, and that,* after *the players have holed out, any damage to the putting green made by the ball or the player is carefully repaired.* Out of consideration both for those playing behind you and for those on the days to follow, you should take pride in preserving the turf as carpetlike as possible. Nothing is more exasperating than to find that your ball has ended in a divot scar after a perfect shot. Also, you have an obligation as a golfer to help maintain the course in as good a condition as possible. Divot marks and loose divots lying around are unsightly as well as injurious to the course.

8. *Players should ensure that, when dropping bags or the flagstick, no damage is done to the putting green, and that neither they nor their caddies damage the hole by standing close to the hole or in handling the flagstick or in removing the ball from the hole. The flagstick should be properly replaced in the hole before the players leave the putting green.* Perhaps the most frequent and flagrant abuses of etiquette occur on the putting green. With the use of caddies on the decline, golfers in the same group are frequently called upon to tend flagstick for a partner or opponent. Proper etiquette here simply calls for being as considerate of your opponents as of your partner—or as you would expect to be treated yourself. Do not step in the line of a putt. Ask whether the player would prefer to have the flagstick tended or removed. Take note of the fact that if the player is shooting from the fringe of the green, rather than the actual putting surface, he is entitled to have the pin left in the cup and will not incur a penalty if the ball hits the flagstick. If he is fairly close to the hole despite being off the putting surface, he may want the flagstick tended, taken out, or left in the cup. Ask him what his preference is. On the putting green, remember not to drag, twist, or scuff your golf shoes, as this will mar the green and may affect a following player's putt. Pick up your feet so that everyone will have a fair chance to putt. Also do not get into the habit of leaning heavily on your putter as you stand on the green or reach for your ball in the hole. This will produce indentations on the green that may affect another player's putt. Remember that the *Rules of Golf* prevent pressing down the surface of the green to give yourself a smoother line to the hole. You may, however, remove any

loose objects between the ball and the hole, either by picking them up or by brushing them aside with the putter. But in the latter case, use the putter in a brushing motion across the line of your putt, with no downward pressure exerted with its head. Also, you may, under the *Rules of Golf*, repair ball marks on your line left by balls hitting on the putting green, but you are only permitted to repair the pit mark, not to improve your line to the cup. To repair a ball mark on the green, insert a sharp-pointed object (a peg tee or knife) just outside the area; at several positions (1) tend to lift the center of the ball mark; then (2) tend to pull the turf toward the center of the pit mark; and (3) smooth the area after the repair. Smoothing may be done in any reasonable manner.

9. *When the play of a hole has been completed, players should immediately leave the putting green.* Be sure to place bags or golf carts on the side or back of the green nearest the next tee; never in front of the green. Record scores on the way to the next tee or on the tee itself. Remember that delays on the putting green will obstruct the flow of play and interrupt the pace of players behind you.

Good golf etiquette is really nothing more than common courtesy on the course. Sure, there are times when the temptation to break golf ethics and etiquette exists. However, since the golfer is completely on his honor, he must police himself as carefully and thoroughly when he is not being observed as when he is. If he moves the ball by accident, or grounds his club in a bunker, he should at once call the proper penalty on himself. He should never attempt to improve his lie in the fairway or rough by exerting downward pressure behind the ball with his foot or the sole of his club. When he marks his ball on the green, he should replace it exactly and not try to gain an inch in the direction of the hole or take a better lie to one side or the other of his spot. Generally, a golfer who slyly cheats hurts his own game most since the time he spends gaining unfair advantage could be more effectively applied to making better shots himself.

The simple rules of etiquette just mentioned serve three main purposes: (1) to reduce the probability of personal injury on the course; (2) to sustain the enjoyment of the game; and (3) to speed up play. Today, slow play is a major problem at most clubs and a concern of all golf committees. To guard against this major breach of golf etiquette, give yourself the following self-examination:

1. On the putting green, am I overcareful in reading the line from several angles? Do I imagine I see things that are not really there? Do I pick up unimportant things? Do I lift the ball to "clean" it when it could not possibly need it? Do I have other balls lifted needlessly, as a matter of routine, or only when they might really interfere? In stroke play, do I putt out whenever feasible, instead of lifting and marking my ball? Do I retry putts while others wait?

2. Before starting, do I know the handicap allowances and local rules?

3. Do I always know when it is my turn to play? And am I ready to play?

4. While others are playing, do I size up my shot and decide what club to use? Or am I indecisive in selecting clubs?

5. When I hit one off the fairway, do I line it up with objects in the area where it went and thus save time in searching?

6. With a double caddie, when I go a different way from the player sharing the caddie, do I take two or three clubs with me to speed my selection?

7. Do I have a second ball handy in case I need it?

8. Do I practice-swing or waggle unnecessarily?

9. Do I let following players through whenever there is an open hole ahead or when I am looking for a ball?

10. Does my idle chatter distract and delay others?

11. Do I try to give a lesson to others during a round?

12. After a bad shot, do I analyze it for my companions' edification and re-examine my swing needlessly?

13. If I use a cart, do I park it in the right place for saving time without hurting the course?

14. Do I waste time between nines?

Priority on the Course. In the absence of special local rules, singles (two players) should have precedence and should be entitled to pass any other kind of match. A single player has no standing and should give way to a match of any kind.

Any match playing a whole round (eighteen holes) is entitled to pass a match playing a shorter round. If a match fails to keep its place on the course and loses more than one clear hole on the players in front, it should allow the match following to pass.

The Caddie and the Golfer

The dictionary says that a caddie is "one who assists a golfer especially by carrying his clubs." With a good caddie, it is the "assists" that is important, and carrying the clubs is only incidental to his main purpose: helping his golfer any way he can. The player and his caddie make up "the side," and it is the one trace of teamwork in an otherwise individual sport.

Ideally, of course, the caddie should *help,* but it is up to the golfer to use him wisely. In the first place, it is true that except for a few notable exceptions, most touring pros do not make extensive use of their caddies except as psychological buffers from the pressures of the play and the galleries. They may perhaps exchange a few words to relieve tension, but they do not tend to ask for advice. Their example is a misleading one for the beginner, however. Professionals know the game so well that they have formed habits of self-reliance in situations requiring critical decisions. The tyro, on the other hand, cannot have the same self-knowledge at his disposal. He does not necessarily know the course or his own game.

A good caddie can be invaluable even to a pro. Arnold Palmer has attributed much of his success in the Masters to his "teammate" Ironman; and Jack Nicklaus, when he plays at the Firestone Country Club, has a boy who goes out and charts the course with a tape measure before play begins. Gary Player likes to use his caddies to help him line up putts, and Doug Sanders has his caddie travel with him, serving as a chauffeur and valet when he is not on the course. Some tournaments may have been *won* by caddies. Gene Sarazen thinks that his British Open victory in 1932 was due in a large part to the efforts of his seventy-year-old caddie, Dan Daniels, who gave Sarazen all he had and died a few months later.

Try to evaluate your caddie. If you think he is capable and knowledgeable, ask his advice, but ask it before you voice your own decision, so he will be objective. In quizzing him about distances to the green, ask him how many yards it is, not what club he thinks you need. Only *you* know how far you can hit with each club; only *you* know whether you are going to hit the shot full or punch it. Above all, remember that you may ask advice only of your caddie or your playing partner and his caddie, and you are permitted by the *Rules of Golf* to have only one caddie.

The player may send his caddie ahead to a hill to mark the line to the green, but he may not have him drop the bag there and go on ahead. Similarly on the putting green, the caddie may point to the desired line and even remain pointing at it while the player putts, but he may not touch the line with a club or other marker to indicate how much break should be played. Anything that the player is forbidden to do, such as repairing spike marks on the green, his caddie is prohibited from doing also. If the golfer's shot hits his caddie, he loses the hole in match play and is penalized two strokes in medal play. If this situation occurs in best-ball, only the offending player is affected. He is disqualified for the hole, but his partner is not penalized.

Caddies around the world are a colorful group, ranging from the wise old Scottish caddies who always say "we" when talking about their player, to the lovely geishas of Japan and the formidable women of Belgium. In the United States, several former caddies have become Open champions (Ouimet, Hagen, Sarazen, Hogan, Nelson, and Mangrum), and many have become excellent golfers.

Golf Cars and the Golfer

Electric golf cars and hand-drawn pull carts are replacing the caddie in many areas of the United States. While the caddie always added a trace of camaraderie to a sport that is basically lonely, the new vehicles are less expensive over all and are more readily available (the proliferation of wealth and high standards of living have stopped the flow of new caddies to a great degree). Proper handling of a golf cart or car is essential to course

Five ways to speed up golf by using golf cars: (A) *Drop off short hitter first.* Do not carry more than two sets of clubs on a car. Save valuable time by letting the shortest hitter of the two select club first, then go to longer ball. (B) *Follow signs on strange courses.* If you are playing a strange golf course, you will find that you can complete your round much quicker by paying attention to the signs that guide you from hole to hole. (C) *Do not be a nuisance.* Just because you are using a car does not mean you should travel from fairway to fairway visiting all your friends. You may disturb others. (D) *Be ready to go.* Once you have finished hitting your tee shot, take a place in the car instead of wandering around. This way you will be set to go when your playing partner completes his shot. (E) *Where to park the car.* One of the simplest ways to save time when you use a golf car is to park it on the side of the green closest to next tee while you are putting.

maintenance, pace of play, personal safety, and, of course, golf etiquette. Here are some points to keep in mind when handling a golf car:

1. On starting out, check to see if your car is in gear to go forward and not backward.

2. Do not start until everyone has driven from the tee.

3. Do not drive out ahead of the ball which is closest to the tee. If you have a gasoline car, turn off the engine while your companion is addressing and playing the ball. Never keep driving ahead when someone is playing a shot.

4. When appropriate, advance to your own ball. Always stop even with the ball and park to the side on which your clubs (or your companion's clubs) are carried.

5. Always park reasonably close to the ball so the player can size up his shot, make his selection of clubs, and even change clubs without undue delay.

6. If you have to park a distance from your ball, size up the distance to the green from your car as best you can. Then take one or two extra clubs with you so as to save a trip back and forth to the car.

7. When hunting for a lost ball, park your car in the rough; do not leave it in the fairway in the way of the following group.

8. In driving a car, be careful not to injure fairways, greens, or traps. Never drive close to traps or greens.

9. Never park in front of a green while putting. If possible, park high on the side of the green nearest the next tee, out of the way of the next group.

10. Never drive a car in muddy places, through puddles of water, or in any place that might injure it.

11. Do not drag your feet outside the car. Keep them inside until the car is stopped.

12. Do not get in or out of the car when it is moving.

13. Do not drive parallel to the top of a hill or rise in such a way that the car will be on a pronounced slant. It might overturn.

14. When you are going up or down, always approach a hill or rise in a straight line. If you want to turn at the bottom of a hill, keep going straight for a time after you have reached the bottom. Then turn slowly and at a big angle.

15. Never make a sharp turn, even on a straightaway.

16. Never ride with a companion you consider an inexperienced or incompetent driver.

17. Try to avoid holes or slight bumps on the fairway.

18. Be sure to set brakes before you leave the car.

Etiquette and the Spectator

Because more people are attending tournaments, it is important that golfing galleryites know the rules of being good spectators. If you recognize the following rules and obey them, you will enjoy the game more, and so will the players. Like the rules of etiquette for players, the ones for golf spectators are based on common courtesy and fairness.

1. Do not talk or move when someone is making a shot. Any distraction can break a player's concentration.

2. Do not speak to the players during their rounds unless they speak to you first.

3. Stay behind the gallery ropes which surround the tees and greens, and do not crowd the players. Cross fairways only at places where crosswalks are indicated.

4. Never call out loudly, even though no one in the group you are following is making a shot. There may be players in adjoining fairways.

5. Obey the commands of the marshals at all times. They are there for your protection as well as that of the players.

6. Remember that there may be players behind and in front of the group you are following, so watch out for them. Do not leave a green until all players have holed out.

7. Give all players the same courtesy. Actually, one of the worst breaches of spectator etiquette occurs when a particular gallery favorite, or golf star, is paired with some player in whom the spectators are less interested. The gallery tends to wait only until the favorite has putted out and then rush away to find a vantage point for watching the next hole. Quite often this leaves the other player putting while the crowd is streaking pell-mell toward the next tee and noisily discussing its favorite's performance on that hole. This is grossly unfair to the other player and leaves him at a distinct disadvantage in the competi-

Golf spectators often revert to artificial aids to view the play. Cardboard periscopes afford an acceptable substitute for direct vision.

tion. Stay in place until all have finished the hole. Be silent and immobile while a shot is being played, regardless of who is playing it.

8. Groups with little or no gallery deserve the same courtesies as the other players. They are playing for a living, too.

9. Keep the circle around the green or tee as large as possible. In this way more people will have a chance to enjoy each shot.

10. Show consideration to your fellow spectators by kneeling if you are in the front row and the gallery is large.

11. Do not walk through traps or on tees and greens.

12. Do not roam the course aimlessly, or you may be hit.

13. Never run, or you may create a stampede and someone may get hurt.

14. Wear low-heeled shoes or golf shoes. Ladies should never wear high heels, as they damage the golf course.

15. Do not be a litterbug. Use the litter baskets at all times.

16. Leave the camera at home, unless you are watching a practice round. Don't try to conceal a camera in your pocket—it might be confiscated.

17. Display your admission ticket or badge conspicuously.

18. Treat the players as you would want to be treated if you were in their golf shoes.

All over the world, golf grows ever greater in popularity. Ability to play the game, heeding its code of sportsmanship, is an asset in health, temperament, and social and business life. And the finest of golf's benefits is the fun you will have in the open air, on the rich turf, at the "game of a lifetime." But remember that the old-timers expect the beginning golfer to maintain the high standard the game has attained by observance of the etiquette and the spirit which prevail in American golf. Watching a golf tournament might be compared to owning a business or plunging into matrimony in that the more you put into it, the more you get out of it.

It is necessary to formulate a plan to achieve optimum value from watching a major golf tournament. For instance, if you are lucky enough to attend a four-day tournament, the formula is simple. The first two days, when the crowds are smaller, afford excellent opportunity to get to know the course by walking, say, four or five holes with different groups. Only by understanding and evaluating the architecture can you appreciate the merit of the leading scores. To illustrate, a par 72 at Augusta during the Masters, with its subtle layout and fast, tricky greens, may represent finer golf than, say, a 68 on a shorter, more straight-away course elsewhere on the tour circuit.

By walking the entire course you have an opportunity to study the pros' psychology. If you watch carefully you will find many of the seasoned campaigners playing well within themselves off the tees, perhaps even reverting to a three-wood on a hole within a particularly narrow fairway or where accuracy pays greater dividends than length. You will find that they will loosen the reins when it comes to a long par-5 in the hope of picking up a birdie.

You get a chance to study the way they attack the flagstick, not merely selecting a club which will reach the green; how they make use of, or allow for, the wind; how they have a routine on the green which seldom varies. Also during the first two days, before the guillotine falls, it is often profitable to follow some of the younger players. Although they may not have acquired the necessary consistency to bridge the big money gulf, they are still great shot-makers and courageous strikers of the ball—often, in itself, a joy to watch.

The last two days of the tournament, when the galleries, especially those following the leaders, grow dense, hole-by-hole watching becomes more difficult. The vital spot at any hole, of course, is the green. Consequently, as soon as the players have holed out you should head for the next green. Usually you will find that you will be down about level with their drives by the time they have all driven off, and can stop for a moment to contemplate their next shot. You ought to be well in position at the green on a par-4 by the time they hit their second shots. While you are waiting for the players to reach the green, move around so that you are in the most advantageous position to head for the next hole.

Some well-banked greens offer natural grandstands. These are the best spots at which to take a breather or wait for other pairings to come by. If you are short, and skeptical about your chances of seeing much in a large crowd, we offer these suggestions. A light three-legged stool is no trouble to carry and forms an ideal portable grandstand; or better still, there are, on the market, aluminum, three-legged seat-sticks which have been used on many occasions to see over the heads of galleries even twenty-deep. They act as walking-sticks when closed, a seat while waiting, and are prefectly balanced to stand on when necessary. If neither of these is available, cardboard periscopes are the next best thing to direct vision.

Being a spectator at golf is a highly individual pastime. No two people can nip in and out of a crowd or break away as quickly as one. One may want to watch a tee shot, the other to make for the green. You lose one another momentarily, and a couple of thousand people have reached a bottleneck ahead of you. The only way, therefore, to see what *you* want is to be a lone wolf. You are there to watch golf, and there is nothing guaranteed to spoil a perfect friendship more quickly than listening to your neighbor stating the obvious when you want to be off elsewhere.

Most tournament programs carry a map of the course so you can see at a glance how best to flit from one vantage point to another to pick up players two or three holes away. When you join a new group always look for the official scorer's board to find out how the players stand in relation to par. Never take the word of a "know-all" for you can bet your bottom dollar that he will be wrong.

If you can only spare one day at a tournament, then plan to get there really early. All the competitors at one time or another will be warming up in the practice area, and here is where you can really study their methods in detail. Do not just stand idly by watching where the balls go—take that for granted. Concentrate on one player and watch each particular facet of his swing in turn and in detail. At no time should a spectator interfere with or talk to a competitor even on the practice ground. This is his one opportunity to tune up his concentration as well as his game, and it is a gross breach of etiquette to question him at such a time.

A great deal can be gleaned from watching the top players, amateur or professional, if one goes in the right frame of mind and digests what one sees. Conversely, a knowledgeable gallery can give a tremendous boost to the morale of a player if they show they are rooting for him. Whether a player is leading the field or not, he appreciates the recognition of a good shot, but he is either appalled or embarrassed by a ripple of applause for a shot which is clearly inadequate, or for the completion of a tap-in putt. A golf tournament is not meant primarily as an entertainment. It is an exhibition of skill, and as with any subject, the more acquainted one is with it, the more one can appreciate the finer points.

Safety First on the Golf Course

Safety should come first on the golf course. Carelessness, overzealousness, ignorance of the rules—all can lead not only to embarrassment but to serious injury or worse. Accidents will happen, but most can be avoided if the player exercises common sense. The safety checkpoints below cover common situations encountered on the golf course.

Playing

In Range. Never hit a golf ball if others are within range.

Workers. If workers are ahead, warn them before you take your stroke.

Blind Hole. If a hole is blind (either dogleg or overhill), do not hit until you are certain that the party ahead is out of range.

Practice. Save your practice shots for the practice tee; you may hit an unwary companion. Besides, practice shots during play of a hole are against the rules. Do not practice-swing when it is not your turn to play.

Stand Away. Stand well away from a player making a shot, preferably to the right (if he is right-handed); do not get ahead of the ball; some of us *do* shank.

Anger. Anger can hurt your game; club-throwing can hurt your companions.

Shagging. If a caddie is shagging for you, avoid having him face the sun; it may blind him to a falling ball.

Wood and Stones. Warn others nearby when you play from woods or stony rough. Play a safety shot if the ball might bounce back at you.

Lightning

Get Off! If a thunderstorm threatens, get off the golf course if at all possible.

Sheltering. If you cannot leave the course, find a shelter, a grove of trees (never a single one), or below ground level protection in a ditch or bunker (sand trap).

Golf Cars

Hills. Never drive a golf car on a sidehill or up a steep slope. It can topple over.

Turns. Avoid sharp turns, even where the ground is level.

Legs. Keep your feet and legs in the car.

Common Sense. Drive sensibly: not too fast or too close to other players.

General

Insects. Beware of bees and hornets; some people are allergic to their sting.

Pets, Children. Pets and young children belong at home. Golf courses are not nurseries.

Sun. Wear a hat when the sun shines brightest; salt tablets may help.

Act Your Age. Remember—and act—your age.

COMPETITIVE GOLF

One of the most important features of golf, accounting in large measure for its almost universal popularity as an outdoor participating sport, is its adaptability to competition between players of varying abilities. In almost every other sport, there is seldom any real contest when one player is distinctly better than another. But in golf, the "duffer," or beginner, can play on equal terms with the expert golfer, thanks to a handicapping system.

Over the years many handicap systems have been devised, but today the United States Golf Association handicap system is almost universally used. Even this system, as fair as it is, is subject to annual review and revision by the Handicap and Executive committees of the USGA and must meet the needs of the more than ten million golfers of varying ability in the United States. Complete details regarding the USGA Golf Handicap System are contained in the USGA golf booklet, *Golf Committee Manual and USGA Golf Handicap System with USGA Course Rating System for Men and Women,* which costs

40 cents a copy and is available from the United States Golf Association, Golf House, Far Hills, New Jersey 07931.

Computation of Handicaps

In computing a USGA handicap, scores must be made for 18-hole rounds under the *Rules of Golf* in either match or stroke play. Scores must be made during the current playing season or calendar year and the immediately preceding playing season or calendar year. Scores on all courses, at home and away, should be reported by the player, along with the course rating. As you can see, accurate handicapping requires accurate scoring records of every 18-hole round played. Actually, most handicaps are based on the ten lowest "differentials" of the player's most recent twenty games.

A handicap "differential" is the difference between a player's gross score and the course rating of the course on which the score was made. If a player shot a 95 for a round on a course with a rating of 71.5, his handicap differential for that round would be 23.5; if he shot a 69 on the same course, his differential would be −2.5.

A USGA handicap is computed from the lowest ten handicap differentials of the player's last twenty rounds, as follows: (*a*) Total the ten lowest differentials. (*b*) Apply the total to the USGA Handicap Differential Chart. (*c*) Locate the group within which the total falls. (*d*) The player's handicap is opposite this group in the Handicap column at the right. (*Note:* The figures in the Handicap column were determined by taking 96 per cent of the average of the ten lowest differentials.)

USGA Handicap Differential Chart

Total of Lowest 10 Handicap Differentials		Handicap
From	*To*	
−36.4	−26.1	+3
−26.0	−15.7	+2
−15.6	− 5.3	+1
− 5.2	+ 5.2	0
+ 5.3	+15.6	1
15.7	26.0	2
26.1	36.4	3
36.5	46.8	4

Total of Lowest 10 Handicap Differentials		Handicap
From	*To*	
46.9	57.2	5
57.3	67.7	6
67.8	78.1	7
78.2	88.5	8
88.6	98.9	9
99.0	109.3	10
109.4	119.7	11
119.8	130.2	12
130.3	140.6	13
140.7	151.0	14
151.1	161.4	15
161.5	171.8	16
171.9	182.2	17
182.3	192.7	18
192.8	203.1	19
203.2	213.5	20
213.6	223.9	21
224.0	234.3	22
234.4	244.7	23
244.8	255.2	24
255.3	265.6	25
265.7	276.0	26
276.1	286.4	27
286.5	296.8	28
269.9	307.2	29
307.3	317.7	30
317.8	328.1	31
328.2	338.5	32
338.6	348.9	33
349.0	359.3	34
359.4	369.7	35
369.8	380.2	36
380.3	390.6	37
390.7	401.0	38
401.1	411.4	39
411.5 and over		40

A USGA handicap will not be issued to a player who has returned fewer than five scores. The following methods may be employed when at least five 18-hole-round scores but fewer than twenty are available:

1. Determine the number of differentials to be used from the following table:

Column I	Column II
5	Lowest 1
6	Lowest 2
7	Lowest 3
8 or 9	Lowest 4
10 or 11	Lowest 5
12 or 13	Lowest 6
14 or 15	Lowest 7
16 or 17	Lowest 8
18 or 19	Lowest 9

2. Average the lowest differentials to be

used (Column II). If this results in a decimal in the thousandths, round off to the nearest hundredth. (*Example:* If the average differential is 8.834, round off to 8.83; if the average differential is 8.835, round off to 8.84.)

3. Multiply the average of the differentials to be used by 10.

4. Locate the group within which the result falls.

5. The player's handicap is opposite this group in the Handicap column at the right.

Example: 9 differentials available (Column I)

Total of lowest 4 differentials (Column II)	103.5
Average (103.5 divided by 4)	25.875
Convert average to	25.88
Multiply converted average by 10	258.8
258.8 applied to Chart gives Handicap of	25

The USGA Slide Rule Handicapper eliminates the need for any number of differentials from 5 up and is available from the United States Golf Association for 35 cents.

The score should be returned every time a player completes an 18-hole round, no matter where he plays it. Fair handicapping depends on full, accurate information of a player's ability as reflected by his scores. Every golfer interested in fair play should make sure that all his scores, good and bad, are recorded. Incomplete records lead to unfair handicaps. Proper handicap records are very important to a club's well-being.

The following information should be given about each round:

(*a*) Player's name
(*b*) Date
(*c*) Name and rating of course
(*d*) 18-hole adjusted gross score or differential
(*e*) Course rating
(*f*) Handicap differential

Scores may be returned in total and need not be recorded hole by hole. Scores should be returned promptly, so that they may be used when handicaps are next revised. Handicap revisions should be made regularly, at least once a month. Scoring records should

be maintained continuously from year to year, adding new scores to old.

Recently, the USGA adopted what is known as "Equitable Stroke Control." Under this provision of the handicap system, a score for any hole is reduced to a specified number of strokes over par for handicap purposes only, as follows:

Handicap	Limitation on Hole Score
Plus or scratch	Limit of one over par on any hole.
1 through 18	Limit of two over par on number of holes equal to handicap. Limit of one over par on balance of holes.
19 through 36	Limit of three over par on as many holes as the handicap exceeds 18 strokes. Limit of two over par on balance of holes.
37 through 40	Limit of four over par on as many holes as the handicap exceeds 36 strokes. Limit of three over par on balance of holes.

If a player starts but fails to complete a hole, he shall, for handicap purposes only, record a score for the hole in accordance with the formula for "Equitable Stroke Control." Scores for such incompleted holes should be preceded by an "X" to indicate what they are, such as X-5, X-6, or X-7. There is no limit on the number of incompleted holes in a round provided incompletion is not for the purpose of controlling the handicap.

Par. "Par" is the score that an expert golfer would be expected to make for a given hole. Par means errorless play without flukes and under ordinary weather conditions, allowing two strokes on the putting green.

Yardages for guidance in computing par are given below. They are not arbitrary, because allowance should be made for the configuration of the ground, any difficult or unusual conditions, and the severity of the hazards.

Each hole should be measured horizontally from the middle of the tee area to be used to the center of the green, following the line of play planned by the architect in laying out the hole. Thus, in a hole with a bend, the line at the elbow point should be centered in the fairway in accordance with the architect's intention.

Yardages for Guidance

Par	Men	Women
3	up to 250	up to 210
4	251 to 470	211 to 400
5	471 and over	401 to 575
6		576 and over

Par as computed above should not be confused with Course Rating as described in the USGA Golf Handicap System. USGA Handicaps must be based on Course Rating rather than par.

Course Rating. Course rating is the evaluation of the playing difficulty of a golf course compared with other rated courses, for the purpose of providing a uniform, sound basis on which to compute handicaps. This rating is based on yardage and the ability of a scratch golfer, since handicaps are used to adjust players' scoring ability to a scratch level. Incidentally, courses are rated by golf associations, not by individual clubs.

Yardage rating is the first step in arriving at the course rating. Yardage rating is the evaluation of the playing difficulty of a course based on yardage only. It is the score scratch golfers when on their game are expected to make when playing an average course. Distance is the primary consideration in rating because it is the only factor which can be accurately measured on all courses.

Yardage ratings are obtained by using the following formulae:

a. Yardage Rating for Men

$$\text{Yardage Rating} = \frac{\text{Length of Course}}{200} + 38.25$$

Deduct a Relative Length Factor of 0.001 stroke for each yard the course is below 6,000 yards in length.

Example 1: If the length of the course is 6,419 yards, Yardage Rating is calculated as follows:

$$\text{YR} = \frac{6,419}{200} + 38.25 = 32.095 + 38.25$$

$$\text{YR} = 32.10 + 38.25 = 70.35 \text{ or } 70.4$$

(*Note 1: It is recommended that the division by the divisor 200 be carried three places of decimals and rounded off to the nearest hundredth before being added to 38.25.*)

(*Note 2: If the yardage rating under the formula is a figure with a fraction in the hundredths, round off to the nearest tenth.*)

Example 2: If the length of the course is 4,900 yards, Yardage Rating is calculated as follows:

$$\text{YR} = \frac{4,900}{200} + 38.25 = 24.50 + 38.25 = 62.75$$

Less: Relative Length Factor

$$6,000 - 4,900 = 1,100 \times .001 = \frac{1.10}{61.65 \text{ or } 61.7}$$

b. Yardage Rating for Women

$$\text{Yardage Rating} = \frac{\text{Length of Course}}{180} + 40.1$$

Deduct a Relative Length Factor of 0.001 stroke for each yard the course is below 5,500 yards in length.

Once the Yardage Rating has been determined as above, then that Yardage Rating is the Course Rating unless it is modified by the Rating Committee in the light of the factors below. (Any modification of the Yardage Rating should be made only for the entire course as a whole and should be expressed in tenths of a stroke.)

Modification of the Yardage Rating normally should not exceed one stroke for the entire course, either plus or minus, thus allowing a two-stroke spread. Any modification in excess of this suggested limit should be applied only on a very unusual course. In any case, the Rating Committee's judgment is final.

The possible variations in the extent to which a particular type of problem may affect the play of a hole are so great that no exact numerical modification can be suggested for specific situations. It is the responsibility of the Committee to decide what effect each variance will have on normal play by a scratch golfer.

Every effort should be made to eliminate errors arising from personal prejudices of a member of the Rating Committee. There is a real danger in overlooking compensating factors on other parts of the course which offset problems on some one particular hole. Over-stressing one or more holes, rather than considering the course as a whole, may result in overrating, which makes handicaps too low. It is as necessary to reduce Yardage Ratings for some courses as it is to increase them for others.

Adjustment Factors: The USGA Yardage Rating Formula is based on the assumption that that course is a normal one. After evaluating any unusual conditions, the Committee should decide whether any yards should be added to or subtracted from the effective playing length of the course and whether any abnormality of the putting greens should be taken into account. If so, the Yardage Rating for the course should be adjusted. Following are factors to be considered in determining whether adjustment of the Yardage Rating in arriving at the Course Rating is necessary:

1. General condition and upkeep. Thin fairways which result in longer rolls than the normal 25 yards could result in a Course Rating less than Yardage Rating; lusher fairways would reduce roll and could result in a Course Rating higher than Yardage Rating.

2. Wetness or dryness could have a similar effect on distance.

3. Overall tightness of course. On narrow holes it may be necessary to sacrifice distance to achieve greater control, or wide open fairways may invite power strokes with little concern for accuracy.

4. Fairway target areas: width, slope, general condition. Again, distance may be sacrificed for control. The normal fairway width of 40 yards offers a fair target for a full tee shot.

5. Difficulties near target areas: amount and nature of rough, proximity of out of bounds, and number and location of water hazards, bunkers, trees, and bushes. Even the scratch golfer cannot avoid trouble on some shots.

6. Putting greens: size, location, visibility, contours, general location. It may be more difficult to hit the ball onto the greens and make it stay. Larger greens may result in more than two putts. Subtle breaks which are difficult to read may increase the average number of putts per round.

7. Prevailing wind. Even though there may be as many holes with the wind as against, a constant wind, as on a seaside course, makes play of any hole more difficult.

8. Ground slope. On a hilly course, uphill and downhill holes tend to balance out, but there may be more hanging lies and greater control may be required if the ball tends to run to the right or left of the fairway because of the contours.

9. Altitude above sea level. It is a fact that balls will carry greater distances in higher altitudes and Course Ratings should be adjusted below Yardage Ratings to compensate.

Rating committees of golf associations generally are booked up months in advance, depending upon their regions. If a club is unable to obtain a rating by a district association, then the club is authorized to establish its own temporary ratings based solely on the Yardage Rating Formulae.

Proper course measurement is an integral part of course rating. Permanent markers should be imbedded in the middle of the tee and the hole measured from this point to the center of the green. Measurements should be horizontal (air-line) with steel tape or surveying instruments along the planned line of play (usually down the center of the fairway). If more than one set of tees are in common use, separate measurements and rating markers should be established for each. The yardage markers should be of the same color as the tee markers which will be balanced around them. Where men's tees are used by women, there must be a women's course rating from those tees in order for scores to be used for handicap purposes. There is no equitable way of automatically adjusting women's course rating from women's tees to any other set of tees.

The USGA recommends the following standard colors and terms for tee markers; the club scorecard should show the course rating from each set of markers, as in this example:

USGA Course Ratings

Tees	Terms	Rating
Back	Blue (or Championship) Course	72.0
Middle	White Course	71.3
Women's	Red Course	73.1

A single set of markers used on any hole to designate two courses should show both colors, half and half.

On a 9-hole course, if separate tees or markers are used for each nine of an 18-hole round, separate measurements and permanent rating markers shall be established for each nine. The yardage markers (and their respective tee markers) should be identified with "1" or "I" for the first nine and "2" or "II" for the second nine.

Stroke Holes. The higher-handicapped players receive the full difference between handicaps. For example, when a golfer with a 12 plays a golfer with a handicap of 7 strokes, he gets a handicap of 5 strokes. In match play these strokes must be taken on the holes indicated on the local scorecard. Each hole has been rated according to its difficulty. (Note the italicized numbers on the sample card shown here.)

A handicap stroke is in the nature of an equalizer and should be available on a hole where it most likely will be needed. In allocating the order of handicap strokes to the 18 holes of a course, consideration should be given to the likelihood of the strokes' being of use as equalizers and not solely as winning strokes to the one receiving them. To do this, you should assign the odd-numbered strokes to the holes on the first nine and the even-numbered strokes to the holes on the second nine. This equalizes as nearly as possible the distribution of handicap strokes over the entire 18 holes. (In a case in which the second nine is decidedly more difficult than the first nine, consider allocating odd-numbered strokes to the second nine.)

Allocate the first stroke to the hole on the first nine on which the higher-handicapped player most needs a stroke as an equalizer and the second stroke to the hole on the second nine on which the higher-handicapped player most needs a stroke as an equalizer. Continue alternating in this way for the full 18 holes.

It is felt that the higher-handicapped player most needs strokes as equalizers on difficult par-5 holes, followed in sequence by difficult par 4s, other par 5s, other par 4s, and finally par 3s. An exceptionally difficult par 3 might warrant being allocated a stroke before an exceptionally easy par 4 or par 5.

A difficult par 5 is one on which a majority of golfers normally cannot reach the green in three strokes. A difficult par 4 is one on which a majority of golfers normally cannot reach the green in two strokes. An exceptionally difficult par 3 is one on which a majority of golfers normally cannot reach the green in one stroke.

In our example, the player would receive three handicap strokes on the first nine, the other two on the second nine, on the holes listed 1, 2, 3, 4, and 5, in the order of need of an equalizing stroke. On the sample card, the five strokes would apply on holes 5, 16, 2, 13, and 1.

Handicapping the Unhandicapped. The USGA Golf Handicap System is the approved method for determining handicaps, but it will not solve unusual problems such as that of determining fair allowances for convention and resort tournaments which attract novice and occasional players. Obviously, the man who never plays except during his vacation or at an annual trade tournament wants a fair chance in the competition for net prizes.

A standard way of solving such a matter is

Sample Scorecard

Hole	1	2	3	4	5	6	7	8	9	
Par	4	5	4	4	5	3	4	3	4	36
Yards	444	525	380	391	572	177	401	228	368	3,486
Handicap	*5*	*3*	*11*	*9*	*1*	*17*	*7*	*15*	*13*	OUT

Hole	10	11	12	13	14	15	16	17	18	
Par	4	3	4	5	3	4	5	4	4	36
Yards	378	167	435	499	210	410	568	358	428	3,453
Handicap	*12*	*18*	*6*	*4*	*16*	*10*	*2*	*14*	*8*	IN
								Total Yards		6,939
								Total Par		72

to conduct a kickers' tournament (see page 351). Each player selects his own handicap and then shoots at a score which has been drawn blind.

Another method for stroke play is the Callaway Handicap System, devised by Lionel F. Callaway. It is not adaptable to match play tournaments and is not a substitute for the USGA Golf Handicap System.

Under the Callaway System a player's handicap is determined after each round by deducting from his gross score for 18 holes the scores of the worst individual holes during the first 16 holes. The table below shows the number of "worst hole" scores he may deduct and the adjustment to be made, based on his gross score. For instance, if his gross score for 18 holes is 96, he turns to the table and opposite that score finds that he may deduct the total for his 3 worst holes scored on Holes 1 through 16, inclusive. Thus, if he has one 9, one 8, and a 7, his handicap totals 24. From this total further plus or minus adjustment is then made according to the adjustment shown at the bottom of each column. For a gross score of 96 the adjustment requires a deduction of 2, resulting in a final handicap of 22.

Thus 96 minus 22 handicap equals a net score of 74.

Another one-round system is the Peoria handicapping system. While no golfer in Peoria knows who gave birth to the notion, it is simple and works fairly well in events where players have no playing records on which handicaps are based. After the players tee off, six holes are selected for handicap computation purposes. A player's scores on these six holes are selected and multiplied by 3, and par is subtracted to determine the handicap.

There are various other systems in use, including the famous Palm Beach Old Guard method, but the Callaway and Peoria systems of one-round handicapping are generally considered the fairest when one-day tournaments are played by golfers who have no formal handicaps.

Types of Play

As was stated in Section I, there are two basic types of play.

Callaway Handicap System

If Your Score Is					Deduct
		70	71	72	scratch; no adjustment
73	74	75	—	—	½ worst hole and adjustment
76	77	78	79	80	1 worst hole and adjustment
81	82	83	84	85	1½ worst holes and adjustment
86	87	88	89	90	2 worst holes and adjustment
91	92	93	94	95	2½ worst holes and adjustment
96	97	98	99	100	3 worst holes and adjustment
101	102	103	104	105	3½ worst holes and adjustment
106	107	108	109	110	4 worst holes and adjustment
111	112	113	114	115	4½ worst holes and adjustment
116	117	118	119	120	5 worst holes and adjustment
121	122	123	124	125	5½ worst holes and adjustment
126	127	128	129	130	6 worst holes and adjustment Maximum Handicap: 50

		Adjustment			
−2	−1	0	+1	+2	Add to or Deduct from Handicap

Notes: 1. No hole may be scored at more than twice its par.
2. Half strokes count as a whole.
3. The 17th and 18th holes are never deducted.
4. In case of ties, lowest handicap takes preference.

Stroke Play. In stroke play (formerly called medal play) scoring is based on the number of strokes a player requires to complete 18 holes, or one full round of golf. This form of play is used principally for one-day competitions and in the qualifying rounds of tournaments lasting for longer periods, where it is necessary to reduce a large field of competitors to a certain number of players. In tournaments of this kind, all who enter play 18 or 36 holes of stroke play, and the 8, 16, 32, or 64 players with the lowest scores then continue at match play. One-day tournaments are usually on a handicap basis to equalize the playing abilities of the golfers entered. Actually, stroke play competition is the most severe test of golf, for when a player has trouble on one or two holes in a good field of players, he has a very serious problem to overcome.

Match Play. Individual competition is involved in match play. There may be one player or two or more players on a side. In most tournament play a match is between two players only. In such a match the player who wins the greatest number of holes from his opponent wins the match; the total number of strokes involved does not count. Thus a player may require several strokes more on the entire round than his opponent and still beat him in the number of holes won. Each hole counts one point and is decided by the number of strokes required to complete the individual hole. If both players get identical scores on a hole, that hole is said to be "halved."

Match play is used in most tournaments following the qualifying round. The 8, 16, 32, or 64 players having the lowest scores at stroke play in the qualifying round continue at match play. The names of these players are placed in a hat and drawn and are listed in the order drawn and paired or bracketed. Players are paired by number for matches as follows:

Upper Half		Lower Half	
64 Qualifiers			
1 vs. 33	3 vs. 35	2 vs. 34	4 vs. 36
17 vs. 49	19 vs. 51	18 vs. 50	20 vs. 52
9 vs. 41	11 vs. 43	10 vs. 42	12 vs. 44
25 vs. 57	27 vs. 59	26 vs. 58	28 vs. 60
5 vs. 37	7 vs. 39	6 vs. 38	8 vs. 40
21 vs. 53	23 vs. 55	22 vs. 54	24 vs. 56
13 vs. 45	15 vs. 47	14 vs. 46	16 vs. 48
29 vs. 61	31 vs. 63	30 vs. 62	32 vs. 64
32 Qualifiers			
1 vs. 17	3 vs. 19	2 vs. 18	4 vs. 20
9 vs. 25	11 vs. 27	10 vs. 26	12 vs. 28
5 vs. 21	7 vs. 23	6 vs. 22	8 vs. 24
13 vs. 29	15 vs. 31	14 vs. 30	16 vs. 32
16 Qualifiers			
1 vs. 9	3 vs. 11	2 vs. 10	4 vs. 12
5 vs. 13	7 vs. 15	6 vs. 14	8 vs. 16
8 Qualifiers			
1 vs. 5	3 vs. 7	2 vs. 6	4 vs. 8

If there are insufficient players to complete a flight, byes may be used for the last places (or highest numbers) in the general numerical draw. The lowest score is No. 1, the second lowest score No. 2, and so on until the names of all qualifiers are listed. Thereafter, byes are added to complete the flight. If the defending champion is exempted from qualifying and the general numerical draw is used, it is customary for him to be given the No. 1 position in the draw. The matter should be settled in advance.

Tournaments and Competitions

One of golf's appeals is that so many different types of competitions can be arranged. Just a few of the more popular types are given here.

Age Contest

Twenties	Ages 20–29
Thirties	Ages 30–39
Forties	Ages 40–49
Fifties	Ages 50–59
Sixties	Ages 60 and over

All enter under the same conditions, play on the same day on the same course, and use their full handicaps. Each may choose his partner, who must be in the same class as himself. There are 18 holes of stroke play, and prizes are awarded in each class.

Alibi Event. Contestant may replay the same number of shots as allowed by his handicap, but not more than one on any single hole and with the exception of putts.

Average Score. Stroke play. Partners average their gross scores for each hole and deduct half their combined handicap from their 18-hole total. Half-strokes count as whole strokes after totaling.

Best-Ball and Aggregate (Low-Ball, Low-Total). This is a variation of the regular four-ball match. Two points are involved on each hole, one point for the best ball and one point for the low aggregate score of a side.

Best-Ball Match. Each player plays his own ball. Two of the contestants are partners and play their best ball against the score of a third and generally better player.

Best-Ball Twosome. Taking handicaps as they fall on the card, two players play as a team. The lowest score recorded on each hole, with handicap, counts toward the team's best-ball score for the round. Although both players play their own ball, only the lowest score on each hole is counted. The team having the lowest best-ball score wins the event.

Best-Ball Foursome. This is the same as the best-ball twosome, except that the teams are now composed of four players. The lowest score, with handicap, on each hole counts as the team's score. This can also be played using the best two-ball or best three-ball scores of the foursome where the two low scores or three low scores, respectively, are used in determining the team's total.

Bingle-Bangle-Bungle. Three points on each hole. One point to player whose ball first comes to rest on clipped surface of green. A second point to the player whose ball is nearest the cup after all players are on the green. The third point to the player who first sinks his putt. On short holes, where it is possible to reach the green from the tee, no point is awarded for first on the green, since the player with the honor has too great an edge; instead, this point goes to the player whose ball is second nearest to the pin after all balls

are on the green. In settling up, each player wins the difference between his total points and the total points of each player with fewer points.

Blind-Holes Tournament. The winning score is based on only 9 holes, selected individually from among the 18 to be played. The holes are not selected until after all players have left the first tee, so that the players have no knowledge of the holes that will count until they have finished play. Half-handicap is generally used to compile net totals.

Blind Low-Net Foursome. Contestants play 18 holes with whom they please. At conclusion of play, committee draws names from hat and groups players into foursomes; net scores are added to determine winning foursome.

Blind Partners. This is an 18-hole stroke play round with 100 per cent handicaps. Players may play with anyone of their choice, but partners are not drawn until the last group has teed off, so a player does not know his partner until he has finished. Winner is the team with the lowest better-ball score after deducting both handicaps.

Breakfast Team Tourney. All interested golfers assemble at the club for breakfast, then are split by handicaps into two equal teams. Low-handicap golfer of Team A plays against low man of Team B, and so on until all contestants are paired. Play is in four-somes, stroke play, no handicaps. Use Nassau scoring (see Nassau) to determine victors in each foursome, who get their breakfasts bought by losers.

Caddie Tourney. Open to all boys who are regular caddies. Generally scheduled on a Monday late in the season, but before school vacation ends. Boys play 18 holes in the morning for a variety of prizes and are given a picnic, athletic contests, and souvenirs to round out the day. At some clubs, where caddies come from poorer neighborhoods, members donate clothing and shoes their sons have outgrown. Other members make a cash donation toward a large array of prizes that boys like.

Choice Score. The best score of the partners on each hole is used in arriving at their 18-hole total. Full or three-quarter handicaps are allowed, and players enter their net scores in computing their round total.

Blind Choice Score. Same as above, except only half of the holes of the course (and the players do not know which ones) are used in determining the winners.

Class and Club Championships. Class and club championships may be played on either a match play or stroke play basis. No handicaps are figured. If the championship is to be played on a match play basis usually a qualifying round of 18 or 36 holes is played with either the low 8 or the low 16 players qualifying for match play. If the championships are to be decided on a stroke play basis this can be done by playing either 72 holes or 36 holes. Some clubs decide their championships on one day with the contestants playing 36 holes; others decide theirs on 72 holes, over four weekends of play. Some clubs match their players according to handicaps without a qualifying round.

Consolation Tournament. This is held at the end of the season on any basis desired. The only players eligible to compete, however, are those who have not won a tournament prize during the season. Some clubs give a prize to every player in the tournament.

Costume Tournament. Mixed Scotch Foursomes. Each player dresses in some sort of costume of his own selection. Prizes can be awarded for best costumes as well as best scores.

Drop-Out Tournament. This is similar to the match play vs. par tournament. Each player is allowed his full handicap, the strokes to be taken as they come on the card. The player then plays against par. The difference is that a player remains in the contest only until he loses a hole to par. The winner is the player going farthest around the course.

Fewest Putts. Only strokes taken with a putter on the putting surface are counted. No handicaps are used. The winner is the player using fewest putts.

Flag Tournament. Each player is given a small flag, with his name attached to the flagstick. Using his full handicap, he plays until he has used the number of strokes equaling par plus his handicap. He plants the flag after using his quota of strokes, playing an extra hole or two if necessary. The winner is the player who plants his flag farthest around the

course. A variation is to award equal prizes to all players who hole out at the 18th green within their allotted number of strokes. The United States flag should never be used as a marker in such tournaments.

Four-Ball Handicap vs. Par. Allow each player 100 per cent of his full handicap, the strokes to be taken as they come on the card. (When a player has a plus handicap, par is allowed 100 per cent of the player's plus handicap.)

Four-Ball Stroke Play. This is similar to individual handicap stroke play except that players are paired in two-man teams, and their better ball on each hole is the team score. Allow each player 100 per cent of his handicap, the strokes to be taken as they come on the card. Many of the other tournaments listed above for individuals can be adapted to four-ball play.

Get-Acquainted Tourney. Eighteen-hole stroke play with handicaps. Each entrant must play with a partner with whom he has never before been teamed.

Goat Tournament. Each member of the club is given an inexpensive token in the form of a goat, with his name on the reverse side. Any player may then challenge another to a handicap match, the winner to get the loser's "goat." After a player has lost his goat, he may continue to challenge in an attempt to get another player's goat. However, if he should lose and not have a goat with which to pay, he must purchase a "kid" for a nominal amount from the professional and give up the kid. The kid is convertible into merchandise in the professional's shop. Only players with a goat in their possession may be challenged, and players usually are not required to accept a challenge more often than once a week. Records of goat play and the current location of each goat are usually posted so that a player may know who has his goat and who has the most goats. The winner is the player holding the most goats at the end of the season.

Handicap Stroke Play. Players play 18 holes at stroke play. Prizes may be awarded for best gross and net scores. Full handicaps are used.

High and Low Ball. Two points are involved on each hole. One point is scored for the best ball and one for the better of the two poorest balls, in regular four-ball match. For example, A and B are partners, and C and D are partners. A scores 5 and B scores 3 on a hole. C and D each score 4 on the same hole. A and B win a point for the best ball, and C and D win a point because their second best ball is better than A.

Husband and Wife Two-Ball Match. This is to be played the same as a Two-Ball Mixed Foursome, but the partners must be husband and wife.

Individual Handicap vs. Par. Allow each player his full handicap. (When a player has a plus handicap, par is allowed the player's full plus handicap. Strokes are taken as they come on the card.) It is helpful if the card is marked at the start of play. The player then plays the full 18 holes against par, using the handicap strokes. The winner is the player most "up" on par at the finish.

Intra-Club Matches. Members of a club are divided into teams, and matches are played on a point system with a regular schedule. These leagues are proving more and more popular. They serve the purpose of allowing the less-skilled golfer the enjoyment of playing in team competition.

The following is the set-up of a league; variations can be made depending on the club or the organization: Players are divided according to classes. Each team should have one member from A, B, C, and D classes. In this way, a player plays against an opponent of his own class and reduces the number of strokes given to a minimum. Play is on a point basis, with the Nassau Point System recommended.

In some cases, the league is divided into five-man teams, with the fifth man acting as alternate. The alternate member of the team plays when one of the other members of the team is absent. A new alternate should be designated for each team match.

Junior Tourney. Open to sons and wards of members below the age of eighteen. Stroke play, 18 or 36 holes, no handicap. In addition to an award for low score among the entire field, it is a good idea to have several flights by age groupings. Where enough daughters are regular club players, a junior tourney for them is suggested.

Kickers' Tournament (sometimes called Blind Bogey). The committee draws a number, advising players that it was, for example, between 60 and 70. Players select their own handicaps without knowing exactly the number drawn. The player whose net score equals, or is closest to, the number drawn is the winner. This is a good type of tournament to schedule when accurate handicap information for a large percentage of the players is not available.

Kickers' Replay Tournament. Each player is allowed to replay any (and only) two shots in a round. The player must continue with the replayed ball once it is called. Full handicap to apply.

King's Tournament. This is a refinement—actually an expanded variation—of the pyramid tournament, in which the tournament "board" is composed of several pyramids placed on various levels of a scale of rating. The challenging procedure here is vertical within any pyramid and horizontal between pyramids. Unlike the regular pyramid tournament, play does not begin with the challenging of players on the same level; instead, each entry may challenge any other entry on the level directly above. When the challenger wins, he exchanges places in the pyramid with the loser. All other rules applicable to the ladder and pyramid tournaments apply here.

Ladder Tournament. The names of all players are listed in order, according to handicaps, at the start of the season, those having the same handicap being listed alphabetically. A player may challenge any one of the three players immediately above him to an 18-hole match. If he wins, they exchange places. If he loses, he may not challenge again until he has defended his own position against a challenge from below. Play is usually carried out without handicaps.

Long and Short Tourney. Many players have good long games and poor short games, and vice versa. This event combines the abilities of these two types of golfers. One player does the driving and long work; his partner does the approaching and putting. Players select their own partners.

Low-Net Foursome. The total score of the four players, less handicaps, determines the winning foursome in the field of contestants.

Match vs. Par. Players, using their handicaps as they fall on the card, play against par. For example, if a player's net score on a hole is 7 and par is 4, the player would be 1 down to par. The winner of the event is the player who is most "up" on par at the finish of the round.

Medal Sweepstakes. Players play 18 holes, and the winner is the player with the lowest net score. Also, a prize may be given to the player with the lowest gross score in order to encourage participation of low-handicappers.

Million Dollar Tournament. For this event the club has printed sufficient scrip in units of $100 and $500 each (the majority in the $100 denomination) to furnish each entrant with $10,000 in scrip at the first tee on the day of the tournament. Usually one can get a local printer to make up this scrip with his small advertisement on the back.

Each entrant pays 25 cents, or any amount you may designate, for use of the scrip, with a chance at the grand prize that goes to the player finishing with the most money.

The members may make up their own foursomes or ask the pro to arrange them. Each foursome will divide itself into teams and use the following system of scoring:

2 points for low ball
1 points for low total
3 points for a birdie
5 points for an eagle

(If eagle or birdie is scored, low ball does not count.)

Each foursome will elect a captain who is to decide all bets and arguments and to keep time on lost balls. Captain will turn in money after the 18th hole, recording the total of high man in the foursome.

Players incurring one of the following penalties must pay the sum named to each of the other players in his foursome:

$100 for playing into rough.
$200 for playing into wrong fairway or hitting tree and bouncing into right fairway.
$300 for missing ball entirely.
$300 for swearing.
$100 for stopping to look for tee.
$300 for loss of ball, to be paid to each member who helps look for it. Hunting time, two minutes limit.
$300 from each member of foursome to player whose ball is: first on the green; first down.

Players are to be admonished not to borrow nor to give away money to a big winner, but to play fair. Only scrip counts for the prize, which can be an article of merchandise or credit for merchandise from the pro shop.

This is another very fine tournament to either start or wind up the season.

Miniature Tourney. A 36-hole event. Contestants, using three-quarters of their handicaps, play 9 holes in morning to qualify. Entire field then divided into flights of eight players each, the eight low net players forming the first flight, the next eight low net players forming the second flight, and so on. Three match play rounds of 9 holes each are then played to determine a winner and runner-up for each flight.

Mixed Foursomes. These are a standard Sunday afternoon feature at many clubs, and they are now played in three ways. The official way is for the partners to alternate driving from each tee and then to play alternate shots until the ball is holed. The game is perhaps more enjoyable for average golfers if both partners drive from each tee and select which ball to play thereafter. In a third method, the partners both drive from each tee, and then each plays a second shot with the other's ball. After the second shots, a choice is made regarding the ball with which the hole will be completed, alternate shots being continued, of course.

Selective Drive. Same as above, except both man and woman drive from each tee. Either ball is continued in play; the other ball is picked up.

Mixed Foursome, Point Competition. Selective drive, alternate shots; one-half combined handicaps to be used just as they come on the card.

Most 3's. Or 4's or 5's. Use net or gross scores, as you prefer. Can also be used in combination with other events.

Mystery Event. Send players out without telling them what type of contest they are entering, except that it is either match or stroke play. After all scores are in, release news of what the event was, and determine winner.

Nassau Tournament. This is similar to the handicap stroke play except that handicap strokes are taken hole by hole as they fall on the card and prizes are awarded for the best first nine, the best second nine, and the best 18 holes. The advantage is that a player making a poor start or tiring at the finish may still win a prize for his play on the other nine.

No Alibi Tournament. Instead of deducting his handicap at the end of the round, each player is allowed to replay during the round the number of shots equaling three-quarters of his handicap. A stroke replayed must be used even if it is worse than the original; it cannot be replayed a second time.

Odd and Even Tournament. This tournament is played in foursomes, two players making up one team. One player to play all even holes and the other all odd holes. Use one-half of combined handicap; no more than 10 strokes difference in handicap of partners. Low net is the winner.

One-Ball Events. Very interesting events are those where only one ball is used by the partners, the two players stroking alternately between tee and green and driving alternately from successive tees. Such one-ball events can be just about anything listed under individual play, but most effective novelty is secured by requiring special pairings. Among the combinations are: father and son, pro and amateur, mother and daughter, brothers, brother and sister, man and wife, member and guest, member and caddie. This last event is particularly recommended to clubs interested in fostering caddie good will. A spirit of friendliness and understanding cannot be more easily secured.

Par Battle. Played under full handicap. Advise players that on a certain ten holes of the course 5 points will be won if par or better is shot. On three other holes award 10 points for par or better. On three other holes there is a 5-point penalty for players who do not score par or better, and on the remaining two holes, the penalty is 10 points for failing to make par. Winner is player with most points at end of round.

Parent and Child Tournament. Parent may play with one or more children. Selected drive, alternate strokes; one-half combined handicap is used for 18 holes. A nominal entrance fee may be charged each team, which may be used toward purchase of prizes.

This tournament is best held on Sunday, after regular play, not to start later than four o'clock. It can be followed by a buffet supper, at which prizes can be presented.

Pari-Mutuels. Play in these events is in foursomes with full handicaps. Score for each hole is determined by the two best balls on each hole (net). The score of the best two balls is used rather than the score for the best ball, as the two-ball procedure keeps more players in the competition, playing out each hole.

Usually a one-dollar entry fee is charged for this event, and this is used to buy the merchandise prizes for the winning foursome. When it is legal, bets on the foursomes to win, place, or show are taken in units of one dollar. After the last foursome has left the first tee, the betting is closed and the total money, less 10 per cent (the pro's cut for running the event), is divided into forty parts. The money is then split as follows:

	Win	Place	Show
Winning foursome	16 parts	8 parts	4 parts
Second-place foursome		6 parts	3 parts
Third-place foursome			3 parts

All the betters who have bet on the winning foursome to win divide the win-money. For instance, if the win-money was $100 and 8 men had bet $1 on them to win and one man had bet $2 on them to win, the $1 betters would receive $10 each and the $2 betters would receive $20.

Point Accumulation Tournament. To be scored as follows:

Any score equaling par or better, 5 points

Any score from 1 to 4 strokes inclusive over par, 3 points

Any score from 5 to 7 strokes inclusive over par, 1 point

The 18th fairway is measured off at 150 yards, 175 yards, 200 yards, and 250 yards.

A player with a handicap of 12 or less scores:

5 points for driving over 250 yards
4 points for driving over 200 yards
3 points for driving over 175 yards
1 point for driving in fairway

A player with a handicap of 13 or more scores:

5 points for driving over 200 yards

4 points for driving over 175 yards
3 points for driving over 150 yards
1 point for driving in fairway

(All drives, in order to score points, must be in the fairway.) Player scoring largest number of points is naturally the winner, but second and third prizes may also be given.

Point Tournament. Players use full handicaps, taking the strokes as they come on the card. Eight points are awarded for an eagle, six for a birdie, four for a par, and two for a score one over par, on a net basis. The winner is the player with the highest number of points. The origin of this event is credited to the Tin Whistles, an organization of Pinehurst golfers, and it is known there as a Par-Bogey tournament.

Pro-Am. Of the many new and exciting tournament ideas developed in the past decade, none has clicked with as much popularity and success as the pro-am event—that charitable arrangement whereby the unknown golfer has his day in the spotlight, or more correctly, shares it with someone who is used to it. Actually, the vast majority of pro-ams precede 72-hole PGA tour events and are, to a large degree, sponsored promotions. To induce golfers to enter these pro-ams at fees generally ranging from $100 to $200 a head, the sponsor uses a sales pitch that is difficult for any self-respecting golfer to turn down. The lure is: "Wouldn't you like to play with Arnold Palmer, Billy Casper, or Gene Littler?" Try to say No to that, especially when it is combined with a good cause to support.

For the pro, a pro-am event may serve as a practice round if it precedes a tournament, and in addition, he may win himself enough to meet his expenses for a tournament week. The PGA has a money breakdown for prize distribution in the pro-ams. In all the pro tour pro-ams, there is an individual pro competition that carries with it more than half the prize money and a team (best ball) competition. Pros believe that the team competition is largely a matter of the luck of the draw and of having the best partners. Since the pros rate individual skill as most important, they prefer to have most of the prize money go for individual rather than for team performance.

In a pro-am, the pro may have anywhere from one to three partners. One of the partners usually has an A handicap; one, a B; and one, a C. Play can be for best ball of a foursome, best ball of a threesome, two pros and two amateurs. Or you can have a foursome comprising three teams, the pro playing with each as a partner.

Pros vs. Members. The club professional agrees to play a handicap match against each member as he is challenged, making a nominal charge for each round. The professional plays from scratch. The member making the best showing in his match receives a prize from the professional at the end of the season.

Putting Tournament. The two men making fewest putts in 18 holes each win a bag of shag balls. Entrance fee, 3 old balls.

Pyramid Tournament. This is another form of the ladder tournament, featuring a different arrangement of the tournament board used. Entries are arranged in pyramidal form, with one name at the peak, two names in the next lower level, three names in the third level, etc. The pyramid can be as large or as small as the number of entries requires.

At the very beginning of the tournament, each entry must challenge and defeat at least one player on his own level before being eligible to challenge entries on the next higher level. After this initial win, all challenges are to the next higher level. The challenger, if he wins, exchanges places on the pyramid with the loser of the match. In all other respects, the rules of play are the same as required for the ladder tournament.

Relay Event. Partners select one of their scores for the first nine, the other score for the second nine, to get their 18-hole total. Allow one-half or three-eighths combined handicap.

Relay Tournament. In this tournament a player's score for the first nine holes is added to his partner's score for the second nine holes, with an allowance of three-eighths of their combined handicaps, to arrive at a net score for 18 holes.

Replay Tournament. This is a variation of the No Alibi Tournament. Instead of allowing a player to replay a given number of his worst strokes, an opponent is designated for each player and the opponent is allowed to recall a given number of the player's best shots and ask that they be replayed. For Class

A players, 9 strokes may be recalled; Class B, 6 strokes; Class C, 3 strokes. If the competition is conducted at stroke play, each opponent must, of course, exercise all his recall options.

Remorseful Golf. In this contest each player has the privilege of making his opponent play over any four shots during the round. These may be shots which he considers lucky or feels cannot be duplicated. For example, a player may hole out a 20-foot side-hill putt, at which point his opponent can say, "I respectfully request you to replay that shot," and he must replay it.

Ringer Tournament. A player builds his total over the season by posting his lowest score on each hole. Scoring is on a gross basis.

Round Robin Tournament. Each entrant plays every other entrant at handicap match play during the season; allow the full difference between handicaps in each match. A time limit is usually set for completion of each round; a player who cannot meet an opponent within the time limit forfeits the match, but may continue in the tournament. The winner is the player winning most matches.

Scorefest. Two teams, of any size. Losing team is the one that scores the least points on following system:

Net scores over 100	2 points
Net scores 90 to 100	5 points
Net scores 85 to 89	10 points
Net scores 80 to 84	15 points
Net scores 75 to 79	25 points
Net scores 70 to 74	40 points
Net scores under 70	75 points

Scotch Foursome. Two players to a side. On each hole, there is a point for low ball and a point for low aggregate score of a side. Holes may be halved by all players making the same score, or by one side winning low ball and losing the aggregate. On some holes, only one point may be won, as for example, if a side wins low ball and ties the aggregate. This event is sometimes played with low ball worth two points and aggregate, one.

Scratch and Scramble Tournament. Play is at four-ball stroke play. On each hole, partners' scores are added and divided by two to obtain the team's score. Play is more interesting if players with high and low handi-

caps are paired. The handicap of each team is usually obtained by totaling the two handicaps and dividing by two.

Example: A and B are partners. A's handicap is 10, B's handicap is 15, total combined handicap 25; divide by two and you have a handicap for each of 12½.

On each hole the scores of the two players are added and then divided by two, the result being the score of each for the hole. For instance, A scores 5 and B scores 4, making a total of 9. This is divided by two, making the score of each for the hole 4½.

It will be most interesting if the committee will draw the teams without regard for personal preferences of the members, combining a high-handicap man with a low-handicap man. This will bring together players who have never played together before. It will also give the poor players an opportunity to play with the better players and to learn more about the game and its rules.

Scrip Tourney. Furnish each player with $10,000 in stage money. Each player has a partner; play in foursomes. Pair with the most scrip after play is over wins. Wins and losses settled whenever incurred during round. Awards are such matters as: low ball each hole, $100; low aggregate each hole, $200; birdies, $300; eagles, $500; first ball on each green, $100; first putt sunk, $200; and so on, as the ingenuity of the committee can devise. Penalties include: ball in rough, $100; ball in wrong fairway, $300; ball hitting tree and rebounding into fairway being played, $500; ball in water, $200; fanning, $300; swearing, $400; swearing at caddie, $1,000, and so forth.

Selected Score. Each player plays 36 holes. From his two cards, he selects his best score on each hole. The winner is the player with the lowest total score for the selected 18 holes. If net prizes are awarded, three-quarters of handicaps are usually enough. This event may be completed in a day or extended over a weekend.

Senior Tourney. Stroke play, 18 holes. Open to players fifty or more years of age. Played without regular club handicaps, but older players get a stroke advantage as follows: fifty to fifty-four years old, scratch; fifty-five to fifty-nine, 2 strokes; sixty to sixty-four, 4 strokes; sixty-five to sixty-nine,

6 strokes; seventy and over, 8 strokes. There should be a prize for low gross player, no matter what his age.

Shotgun Tournament. At least one team is stationed on each tee of the 18 holes at a specific time; the longer holes may accommodate two teams. The start of play for everyone is signaled by a shotgun blast or a suitable substitute that can be heard throughout the course. All groups should finish playing the 18 holes at about the same time.

Six- or Twelve-Hole Elective. Either 9 or 18 holes stroke play, at the end of which each player selects as his score the total scores made on his 6 or 12 best holes. Two-thirds of the regular club handicap is used for 18 holes; one-third for 9 holes.

Six-Point Match. Six points are at stake on each hole. In reality there are two points being fought for by each pair in the threesome; A vs. B, B vs. C, and A vs. C. Low score each hole wins 4 points, middle score wins 2 points, high man wins nothing. If all tie, 2 points apiece. Two players tie for low, 3 points each. One player low, other two tied, the split is 4–1–1. Generally the point allocation is obvious, but when a player gets a stroke from one of his opponents and not from the other one, it is harder to figure the number of points each player wins. In such cases, merely compute results of each match (AB, BC, and AC) separately and the point split is readily determined.

Speck Tournament. Players are teamed as in four-ball match play. Each team is credited on each hole with one speck (*a*) for the longest drive in the fairway, (*b*) for getting the first ball on the green, (*c*) for having the closest ball to the pin on the approach shot, (*d*) for a one-putt green, and (*e*) for the lowest score on the hole. The team having the most specks at the end of the 18 holes wins an appropriate token, usually in golf balls, from the team with which it was paired.

Splash Contest. No entry fee, but players must contribute one new ball for every time they play into a water hazard during the round. A player entering contest but failing to turn in his score is charged 3 balls, on suspicion. Award balls to the three low net players on a 60–30–10 split-up.

String Tournament. Each player or each side is given a piece of string in lieu of handi-

cap strokes. The string is measured to allow one foot for each handicap stroke. The player or side may advance the ball by hand to a more favorable spot at any time, measuring the distance the ball was moved with the string and cutting off the length used. When the string is used up, the player is on his own. The string may be used on the putting green to advance the ball into the hole, or it may be used to inch away from a difficult lie through the green or in a hazard.

Sweepstakes. Stroke (or medal) play, full handicap. Each player in tourney signs up for one new golf ball. Golfer with low net score wins half the balls, second best net takes one-third, third place wins one-sixth.

Syndicate Tournament. The field is divided into classes according to handicaps: Class A may be men with handicaps of 7 and under; Class B, 8 to 15; Class C, 16 to 24; and the like. The player who makes the lowest score in his class on a hole wins a syndicate. Syndicates may be cumulative; in the event that one or more holes are tied, those syndicates go to the player next winning a hole. Each player pays an entry fee of one golf ball; the total balls in each class are divided by 18 to determine the value of a single syndicate, and each player's prize is determined by the number of syndicates he has won.

Cumulative Syndicates. Same as above, except that points not won on tied holes carry forward and go to the first player to win a low ball. Thus a player may not have been a party to the tying on two consecutive holes, yet on the third hole have low ball and thus win the points of all three holes.

Syndicate Tourney. Played with full handicap. Golfers post their scores, then put a ring around their score on each hole where they are entitled to a stroke by their handicap. This is to aid the committee, who looks over the scores of the entire field and picks the man whose net score is lowest for the first hole. If no one has tied him, he wins the hole from the entire field and wins 1/18th of the prize money. If two or more players tie for low on the first hole, the committee examines the second hole, and so on, until a hole is reached where one golfer has a clear net win. Tied holes carry forward to next win hole. Suggested entry: 5 cents per hole (90 cents). On eighteenth hole, if no syndicate is won, tying low players split whatever entry money remains.

Team Match—Nassau System. Regular 18-hole matches are played by two or more teams, but the scoring is on the Nassau System basis: 1 point for the first nine holes and 1 point for the second nine holes and 1 point for the match. This is a good method of scoring in that it gives a player a chance to salvage something after he may have had a very bad start.

Three-Ball Matches. In this match three players play together. Each may play against both of the others, or where one player is better than either of the other two he will play against the best ball of the two poorer players.

One-Half Aggregate Score. This is a variation of the Three-Ball Match described above and is used where the players are of equal playing ability and one of them is not enough better than the other two to justify his playing their best ball. In this case the scores of the two partners are added, and one-half thereof counts against the odd player's score. For example, one of the partners takes a 4 and the other a 3, making a total of 7, their score for the hole being 3½. The odd player must beat this in order to win.

Threesome Match. One player, hitting every shot, opposes two players who stroke alternately at a single ball. A traditional event in the British Isles, this contest does not seem to have much popularity this side of the ocean.

Tin Whistle Tournament. This competition is on a match play basis, and points are awarded as follows:

One point for each hole made in 1 over par, 3 points for par, 5 points for each birdie.

The player having the greatest number of points at the end of the round wins.

This is played on a handicap basis, and strokes are taken at the hole specified on the scorecard. A par scored, less a handicap stroke, counts as a birdie.

Turkey Tournament. This event is the same as a Kicker's Tournament, except that a turkey is awarded to each of three winners. A small entry fee may be charged to cover the cost of the turkeys.

Two-Ball Foursome. Two players constitute a team, and one ball only is used by each team; the partners alternate in playing the shots. One partner drives from all the even-numbered tees and the other partner drives from all the odd-numbered tees, regardless of which one made the last stroke on the previous hole. If this event is played on a handicap basis, one-half of the combined handicaps is used.

White Elephant Tournament. Each contestant brings some useful article that he is willing to give as an entry fee. This article is to be wrapped up and a number attached to it, starting with No. 1 and running up as high as the number of entries.

Play is on a low net basis, and the winner receives package No. 1, second place wins package No. 2, and so on. In this way each entrant receives a prize.

Special or Novelty Events

Approaching and Putting Contest. This is a very popular form of competition for a Sunday or holiday afternoon as it can be played in front of the clubhouse either on the 9th or 18th hole, or both. Each contestant approaches and holes out three balls from 25, 50, and 100 yards off the green. In each case each ball should be played from a different direction. The winner is the one holing out the three balls in the fewest number of strokes.

Bloopers Tournament. To qualify for this tournament a player must do one of the following:

Take more than 4 putts on any one hole.
Take more than 4 shots in sand trap.
Take 10 or more strokes on one hole.
Use unnecessary language on at least 9 holes of the round, and so on.

As many prizes may be offered as is felt necessary. You may also have a blind bogey between 65 and 75 and between 100 and 110.

"Can You Take It?" Tournament. This tournament is played in foursomes using regular handicaps, and how some of the fussy boys need that handicap after such a hectic round! The idea is to create noise and disturbance throughout the round to disturb and distract your partners. It is advisable to place one practical joker in each foursome to start the fireworks and get the other three members of the party into the right spirit. This is particularly good training for the fussy type of golfer. Contestants are not allowed, however, to interfere with the actual swinging of the club or with the lie or flight of the ball.

Any contestant who cannot take it good-naturedly is fined according to his misbehavior. These fines are set before the match and are applied, when paid, to the tournament fund to buy more prizes for the winners. A crooked-shafted club or badly scuffed golf balls are appropriate booby prizes.

Consecutive Club Tourney. Each player allowed only four clubs: brassie, No. 5 iron, No. 8 iron, and putter. All players use the brassie off the first tee, thereafter they must use No. 5 iron, No. 8 iron, and putter in that sequence for all subsequent shots, no matter what the lie of the ball. Player may find himself driving with an 8 iron and putting with a brassie. To even up player ability, allow only half handicaps, so poorer players to whom one club may be almost as good as another will not run away with the event.

Cross-Country Tournament No. 1. Start about a mile from the course and play directly across country, finishing on one of the greens of the course near the clubhouse, if possible, but designated in advance. The ball must be played from wherever it lies. If found in an unplayable position, the player is permitted to lift and tee up with the loss of two strokes. This contest furnishes many exciting and unusual situations.

Cross-Country Tournament No. 2. This contest is played entirely on the golf course, skipping about, however, from one hole to another, not in the usual rotation. Play might start at the 1st tee and go to hole No. 6, then start at the 7th tee and go to hole No. 14, and so on, until at least nine holes have been played.

Cross-Country Tournament No. 3. Nine holes are enough for this one. Course is not played in usual order; instead, tournament directions supplied each player read something like this:

> 1st Hole: From 1st tee to 3rd green
> 2nd Hole: From 4th tee to 10th green
> 3rd Hole: From 11th tee to 7th green

and so forth.

Played without handicap. Note that the tee to start each hole is the one normally following the green just played, to save long walks between green and tee.

Driving Contest. Pick a wide-open flat fairway. Each contestant gets five drives, with only the best three counting. Only shots ending in fairway count. For quick determination of distance, erect marker flags each 25 yards from 125 yards to 300 yards. Judges stationed down the fairway can estimate yardage beyond nearest marker. A variation of this event allows only three drives and deducts 10 per cent from the distance for all shots ending up in the rough.

Forfeit Round. This is not for serious play. At each green, post directions for a forfeit to be paid during the play of the next hole by the player whose score for the hole just completed is highest. Suggested: (*a*) take off shoes and play shots with shoes dangling between arms, laced around neck; (*b*) carry all clubs out of bag; (*c*) use only putter, tee to green; (*d*) at the "drink" hole, treat the foursome; (*e*) walk backward, tee to green; (*f*) laugh from instant of finishing drive until ball is holed out; (*g*) whistle (or sing) from tee to green; (*h*) low man, not high scorer, pays penalty prescribed for previous hole; (*i*) play all shots standing on one foot. No forfeit is paid on holes where high score is tied.

Inch or String Contest. Event is played without handicap. Players are given a specified number of inches of string, according to their handicaps, at the first tee as follows: players with handicaps up to 8 get 10 inches of string; those with handicaps between 9 and 15 get 25 inches; handicaps over 15 get 50 inches. These inches of string may be used by the player to call a close-missed putt sunk or to shift the ball from a bad lie, and so on. Low stroke score wins. Knots tell the player how much string he has used.

Monkey Foursome. Each member of the foursome carries a single club, those used being generally a wood, a 2 iron, a 5 iron, and a putter. One ball is played. Each member of the foursome, in rotation, plays the ball from wherever it happens to lie and with whatever club he has chosen to carry. Thus a player may be forced to putt with a 5 iron or drive with a putter.

Monkey Foursome, Captain's Choice. Played as above, except that each foursome elects a captain who selects the player to make each shot as the strategy of the hole dictates.

Obstacle Tourney. Played with or without handicap. Each hole presents some obstacle, such as a stake off to one side of the fairway that must be played around, or a barrel just short of the green that must be played through.

One-Club Event. Each player carries only one club, which must be used for all shots. Club may be specified by committee or selected by player. Low net wins. Variation may permit two clubs or even three.

Putting Contest. A putting contest is played entirely on a putting course or green. A qualifying round is played, and then the qualifiers compete on a match play basis. The whole tournament can be run off in one afternoon. An obstacle putting contest is one where obstacles are placed around the putting green.

Putting Tourney. An 18-hole event on the practice putting green. Winner determined by total putts. In case of ties, all tying contestants play extra holes at Sudden Death; That is, player is out on first hole he fails to halve. If club has no practice green, use the "clock" method on one of the regular greens near the clubhouse by marking off 9 "tees" at varying distances around edge of green; each player putts from these 9 tees to cup.

Razzle-Dazzle Tournament. Two teams are picked by the club professional from the field of players that shows up on the day of play. A captain is selected by each team. Each team numbers its players from 1 up with a cardboard pinned on back or chest of each player. Only one ball is played by each team. Player No. 1 shoots first, then No. 2, and so on, until every player has shot. Then start over again with No. 1. This keeps the entire field of both teams together, and many players meet new members they have never met before.

Play with regular Razzle-dazzle rules; that is, make all the noise you want, at any time you want to razz the opposing team, without touching them.

Shimby-Shamby. Holes are laid out in various shapes and sizes and located in out-of-the-ordinary spots on the greens: in a corner, on a steep ridge, and so forth. On the tees, the markers are not placed to make the problems of the golfers any easier. Anything goes by way of noise, by mouth, horns, or bells; and a player can dance and tease while another is making his shot. Contestants are not permitted, however, to interfere with the actual swinging of the club or alter the lie of a ball. Not an event for a fussy golfer.

Solo-Club Team Match. Two teams, each with twelve men and a nonplaying captain, are chosen. The players are numbered, and each player uses only the club assigned to him as follows:

> Player No. 1 uses Driver
> Player No. 2 uses Brassie
> Player No. 3 uses Spoon
> Player No. 4 uses No. 2 Iron
> Player No. 5 uses No. 3 Iron
> Player No. 6 uses No. 4 Iron
> Player No. 7 uses No. 5 Iron
> Player No. 8 uses No. 6 Iron
> Player No. 9 uses No. 7 Iron
> Player No. 10 uses No. 8 Iron
> Player No. 11 uses No. 9 Iron or Wedge
> Player No. 12 uses Putter

The captain directs the team and decides the club to be used on each shot, the club specified to be used only by the man assigned to it. In other words, each man carries and uses only one club. If desired, a qualifying round may be held to determine the members of the teams, or they may be selected by the committee or the professional.

Throw-Out Tournament. At the conclusion of play, each player is allowed to reject his three (or any designated number) worst holes. Handicaps usually are reduced in proportion to the number of holes which may be rejected. The winner is the player with the lowest score for the 15 holes (or the designated number) finally selected.

How to Win Golf Matches

Confidence and bold playing win golf matches. To gain confidence, it is essential to have and follow a plan of action. Think out the course you are going to play beforehand, and decide such things as where you will go strong off the tee and where you will just keep the ball in play. Having devised your plan, do not deviate from it unless, of course, it means losing the hole.

Now that you have a plan of attack thought out, let us consider the match itself. Here are twelve golden rules for success:

1. Know your own game. Never count on doing better than your average. You will have some good holes and some bad holes. Your opponent will, too. This sort of thinking will keep you from blowing up when things go wrong or being too elated when they are right.

2. Study the course conditions: they will radically affect your play. On a dry course, play run-up shots. On a wet day, play pitch shots right to the hole. On a windy day, you again want to play low, bouncing shots. Remember that the speed of the greens can change during the day. In the early morning the dew will make them slow. In the afternoon, when the sun has dried them out, they will be faster.

3. Play the shot you know you can make— not a fancy shot out of a book. In other words, forget trying to hit your "career shot" and play it safe and sane. Always plan one shot *ahead* to make your next shot easier.

4. Study your opponent's style during the first few holes. It can often give you a lot of confidence! A player with several faults will surely come ungrooved before the end. Also, in the psychology department, it is well to study your opponent to determine his little idiosyncrasies. Some players cannot stand to be outhit, in which case if possible let it fly on the first few holes to get him pressing. If you drive for equal distance, it may be a good idea to ease up just a little so that you get the first shot at the green. Seeing you on there, particularly if you are close, can burst a lot of them apart at the seams.

5. Disregard your opponent's shots as much as humanly possible and concentrate on playing your own game. That is, play your game shot by shot, and do not worry about your bad shots. Remember that a bad shot in match play can, at worst, mean *one* lost hole. Never give up on a hole and waste strokes. In singles many a hole is won with a bogey. It is important, too, to keep comments about your play to yourself. If you goof a shot and it still comes off, do not let anybody know

you blew it, but let them think you simply have a wide variety of shots. Your opponent may get a mental lift if you start complaining about your game, and, even worse, you may convince yourself.

6. Play position with *every* shot. Disregarding your opponent's shots from tee to green is, of course, virtually impossible. Yet you can conquer this to some extent by not even watching when he hits, but going about the business of mentally planning your own shot. Do everything in your power to concentrate merely on shooting the best score you can. Naturally you will be aware of the fact when an opponent hits the ball out of bounds or, as an example, into a water hazard. This is going to give you shots to play with, and your first instinct is to put the crusher on him by flogging it far down the fairway. Do not do it. In such a case, sacrifice distance for accuracy. Take the club with which you are dead certain you can keep the ball straight and safely in play.

7. Do not let the opposition profit from your club selection, but, if possible, learn from their shots. Much of the time an alert opponent will be watching you to profit from how much club you use on a short hole or on your approaches. To foil the fellow who makes a habit of looking in your bag, you can cross him up by hitting half or three-quarter shots. And if you are addicted to the same practice you will see how far down the grip he holds the club and how much of a swing he takes; otherwise he may be giving you the same business.

8. Do everything you can to keep the pressure on your opponent and off yourself. For example, try to hole everything from 30 yards in. Not that you *will* hole all of them, but because this positive attitude will leave you closer to the hole than a wishy-washy effort. Once in a while, one will drop and really shake your opponent.

9. Play away from trouble. We know this sounds obvious; but many players will dispatch a beautiful drive straight into a fairway bunker, when with a little care they could have been in good shape.

10. Do watch your opponent carefully when he putts, and keep the putting pressure on him at every opportunity. While this may sound like a contradiction of Rule 5,

remember this: If you have the same line and are inside of him you can "go to school" on how his ball rolls, but also be sure to watch how firmly he strokes the putt. Also be certain to observe the putt as it slides past the cup so that you can get a line on how the green will break coming back.

11. Always play at your own pace. If you usually play slowly, do not allow your opponent to speed up the game and throw you off your normal pace. If you normally play fast and your opponent is playing slowly, keep yourself in motion by walking forward and studying your next shot some more.

12. Do not let up when you are ahead. This is *fatal*. Keep playing each hole according to your plan.

Now, when it comes to playing a four-ball, you and your partner should start from the first tee with the idea of playing for birdies. A slow start can be very costly, because in this type of match it mostly takes a birdie to *win* a hole. Holes are very seldom won with pars. Also, at the start elect a captain for the side, usually the player with more experience. It is this player's job to make the tactical decisions. Here are three golden rules that will surely help in four-ball play:

1. Never stop building your partner's confidence.

2. Find out such seemingly trivial things as whether your partner likes to hit first. Many players prefer to have the other team member hit first, finding it comforting to know that he is on the fairway. This helps particularly on the 3-pars if your partner likes advice as to what club you used and how well you hit it.

3. Give your opponents fits!

All other considerations flow from these three.

On par-3's the better iron player should shoot first. Having the accurate iron player already on the green can give the weaker iron shooter confidence. If you have the honor, this puts the pressure on your opponents. Actually, before teeing off on *any* key hole, the side's strategy should be discussed and decided. Of course, the state of the match will sometimes reverse your original plans for any key hole.

One of the things amateurs forget is that if your side is away *either* of you can shoot next.

Do not confine your use of this option to the putting green. It can work in your favor on *any* approach shot, or even on seconds on par-5's. Remember: the idea is to give your partner confidence. So, when your side is away, *the player with the best chance of making the shot should play first.* A successful shot on his part will encourage his partner to make a success of the more difficult shot. And two successful shots can really put the pressure on your opponents.

While we are on this subject of options, there may be times when you prefer not to surrender the option. By this we mean have the player who is nearer the hole play first, regardless of the difficulty of the shot. The thinking here is to get two shots near the hole before your opponents have the chance to match your shots. Where options and the matter of giving confidence to your partner conflict, each case will have to be decided on its merits. But always think about the situation before making a decision. A clear plan can give each partner a better picture of what he has to do and increase his chances of making a successful shot.

Confidence will not come from ignorance, but will be fostered by planned knowledge. Playing bold does not mean playing with the blinders on, but rather knowing what you must do and then doing it!

Why Golfers Bet—and How

Why do people bet at golf? Almost everyone bets on sports events, but the peculiar thing about golf wagers is that the *participants* in the game do most of the betting. This situation is almost unique in sports, for the people who play a game do not as a rule have something staked on the outcome. Sports such as baseball, basketball, boxing, and football, which are ideal for spectator gambling, do not seem to produce betting by the players themselves. Then, why is the bet a *seemingly* necessary part of golf?

The answer seems to lie in the very nature of sport itself. Competition is a natural concomitant of most sports, but golf is an exception since, for all practical purposes, it can really be played alone, with only the course and one's best previous score as the opponent. People bet when they play golf to produce that element of competition with a tangible opponent that is inherent in most other sports. Without the wager, two players often feel that they are only randomly involved in any sort of game, and each of them may actually feel that he is playing by himself. The bet is the connecting link between the two golfers. It establishes the competition, creates it so that no longer is the player struggling only with himself, but with a flesh-and-blood rival. Any game that can be played alone generally *requires* a wager to state the competition. Thus, people bet on pool, free-throw shooting, and golf, but not on ping-pong, basketball, and tennis. Betting on golf also relieves the frustrations of the game, for the player is no longer fighting himself, but a palpable challenger. And so betting is a paradoxical factor in golf. It is the element that makes golf unique (because it is the participants who are doing the betting), but at the same time, it is the catalyst that makes golf like other sports because it establishes the competition with another player. Remember that we are always referring to casual, weekend golf in this write-up, and not tournament play.

On a less philosophical level, the high incidence of betting in golf is surely attributable to the game's admirable handicapping system. It is necessary for a good bet that the opponents be roughly equal in ability so that there is some doubt as to the outcome of the contest; golf's handicapping techniques effect such an equality, even between two players of disparate skills.

If you are going to bet at golf, you had better be like a poker player and know the house rules before you start. Most wagers are won or lost on the first tee when the game is made up, so know what you are playing, and above all, know your opponents. Here is a brief guide to the types of bets you may encounter:

Nassau. The most common kind of bet. At match play, as previously mentioned in this section, three points are scored: one for the first nine, one for the second, and one for the 18. If a golfer is playing a "one-dollar Nassau," he has three individual one-dollar bets.

Bisque. A handicap stroke that may be taken on any hole at the player's option. Strictly speaking, a stroke that is given to an opponent must be taken at the hole indicated on the scorecard as being that particular handicap number. Thus, if a player is given "five strokes," he must use those strokes on the holes marked one to five on the card. The handicap numbers are usually circled to differentiate them from the hole numbers. A bisque, on the other hand, may be taken anywhere.

Skins. A skin is awarded to the winner of each hole, provided that he is not tied by another player. If two tie, all tie. A deadlier version of this game (and not one for those who play a steady, unspectacular game) is called cumulative skins. In this little hairraiser, holes not won by anyone because of ties are accumulated and awarded to the first winner of a hole. Also called "scats" or "syndicates."

Greenie. This is a shot that ends up closest to the hole on par-3's. Again, the winner collects from the other members of the foursome.

Team Skins. Those loyal partners who do not wish to win greenies and skins from one another play for team skins. If either member wins a skin, it is awarded to the team and not to the individual.

Bobs and Birds. Bobs are points scored for closest to the pin on par-3 holes only. Birds are points scored for birdies on any hole; double for eagles.

Bingle-Bangle-Bungle. A fast-paced item with lots of action. Three points on each hole: one for the player who reaches the green first, one for the player nearest to the cup after all are on the green, and one for the player who first holes out.

Low Ball and Total. A four-ball team bet in which the best ball of each team wins one point, and the low total of the partners wins another. This game is a method of getting a good bet out of the situation in which there is one very good player with a poor one against two average players.

Low and High Ball. A four-ball team bet in which two points are scored on each hole; low score wins a point, and high score loses a point. If both partners score lower on a hole than their opponents, they can win two points.

Calcutta Pool or Auction. A once popular type of tournament which is seldom employed today. A calcutta is played according to the usual rules and regulations that always apply to a tournament. All competitors are registered according to their official handicaps. Then, on the eve of the tournament, the calcutta auction is held. Each twosome is sold to the highest bidder, with the result that after a percentage of the total pool has been taken out, usually for a charitable cause, the rest goes to winning team and their "owner or owners."

Press or Extra. A new bet on the remaining holes. If someone wants to take a "dollar extra" on the 17th tee, he wants to play the last two holes for the dollar.

The best advice on betting is never to wager more than you can comfortably afford to lose, or else you may be putting yourself under unnecessary pressure that will probably hurt your game. Do not rush into an extra bet when you are losing unless you have been playing unusually badly and have suddenly discovered the cure, or you have been hitting the ball well, but have been unlucky.

Country Club Membership

Say the words "country club" to someone, and he will more than likely conjure up a certain dreamy image: Suddenly, it is the days of F. Scott Fitzgerald, and men immaculately dressed in long white ducks, straw boaters, and blue blazers with the crest of their club emblazoned prominently over their chest pockets, stroll with elegant women about the grounds; here and there a few are playing golf on a green course that seems to run right up to the blue-pooled sky; the tennis courts are full; the veranda of the clubhouse is crowded with sports clustering around a portable bar; and at night the clubhouse becomes a ballroom, and the men and the women, even more elegant than before, are swirling on the floor under papier-mâché streamers soaked with sprinkling lights. Ah yes, the country club!

The image is no longer intact, for many country clubs exist today primarily as *golf clubs,* and they fulfill that function very well. A golfer who is thinking of joining a private club should be aware that he will be paying his money for several privileges and advan-

tages. Immediately upon joining, he is no longer a public links player, but one of the exclusive 15 per cent of golfers who play at private clubs. This exclusiveness is of more than nominal value, too. Public course players make up 85 per cent of the total number of golfers in the country, but only 54 per cent of the courses are open to them, and those are usually as crowded as subways. The skimpy 15 per cent who are club members, on the other hand, play on 46 per cent of the country's courses, and for them, five-hour waiting lines are unheard of.

The club golfer gets some more things for his money, too. Inevitably, private club courses are in better condition and are more challenging than the average municipal layout. The clubs spend an average of nearly $4,000 per hole every year to maintain their courses, and their maintenance job is made easier by the absence of crushing traffic that the public courses must withstand.

Another advantage for the club player is the type of course he will be playing on. A golfer who wants to develop a top-flight game must play and practice on championship courses, and "championship courses" means private clubs. There is still another inducement to membership for the talented player. There are more than 4,000 golf clubs in the United States, and more than 3,500 of these are members of the United States Golf Association (USGA), the ruling body of United States golf. To be eligible for participation in the U.S. Amateur, a golfer *must* be a member of one of these USGA clubs.

Country clubs are expensive, and statistics of New York metropolitan area clubs reveal how much. In 1977, the range of yearly dues of these clubs was $1,200 to $2,000; the initiation fee ranged between $1,500 and $2,500; the annual assessment was between $50 and $200; and the cost of a bond required for purchase by a new member was in the $1,000-to-$5,000 range. The cost of first-year membership averaged out to almost $5,000, but in recent years many clubs have been allowing new members to spread some of this initial cost over a two- or three-year period.

The aspirant club member should not be put off by what appear to be princely expenses. There is a club for every taste. There are many clubs where the dues are as low as

$50 a year, and the initiation fee is $50 or less. On the other hand, there are clubs so wealthy that they extract no dues at all, waiting until the end of the year, when they figure the total deficit and divide it evenly among their members—each of whom writes a check for whatever is needed. There are small clubs with less than 100 members, and large ones with more than 700. And there are all kinds of memberships. Nongolfing members enjoy every privilege of the club except golf, and they can usually play by paying a greens fee, though there may be a limit to the number of rounds they can play a year. There are also special memberships for widows, clergy, seniors, nonresidents, and juniors (usually for members' sons who are over twenty-one, but have not yet reached the requisite age for full, regular membership, normally between twenty-five and thirty). All of these special memberships go at a reduced rate and are bargains.

A golf club member should remember that membership is a privilege which involves certain responsibilities. A private golf club does not pay its operating costs with social status. Everybody has to pay cash in carrying a share of the financial load.

The clubs may not be as elegant as they were in the past, when they were the bastions of the nabobs of the community. But the golf courses are better and harder, and the golfers are more enthusiastic than ever. If a new member, wistfully searching for past glories and faded dreams, were to don his white ducks and blazer, he would probably be stared at, but if you do join and happen to run into Scott Fitzgerald's ghost lurking about the old place, you will know it is a country club.

SECTION VII

Championship Golf Courses

The phrase "championship golf course" is so broadly used that one would expect a clean-cut knowledge of the meaning, but that is not the case. To say it is one on which a championship can be played is not enough. Championships have been played on both good and bad golf courses. One could assume that a course of extreme length would be classified as a championship golf course, but this also is not the case. Extreme length alone does not make a championship golf course. One could also expect that large greens would be a requirement, but this is not necessarily so. One would naturally expect that a profusion of trapping would also be required in a championship course, but this, too, is not always the case.

When one analyzes the characteristics of some of the well-known and accepted-as-great championship golf courses of the country, the points above are easily proved. Merion, near Philadelphia, is not a long golf course in the modern sense: only 6,694 yards. Augusta National, while having length, is not profusely trapped; there are only 23 traps on its full 18 holes.

Big greens alone do not make a great golf course. Merion's greens are small, averaging only about 6,000 square feet, though some are smaller and some much larger, often being as large as 9,000 square feet. Pinehurst No. 2 has relatively small greens, as have

famed Pebble Beach and the Olympic Club in San Francisco. Conversely, St. Andrews in Scotland, probably the most famous of all championship golf courses, has mammoth greens, almost acre-sized, primarily due to the fact that seven greens are in reality two greens each, being played with two pin settings, thus becoming different holes from the opposite directions.

Scenic beauty does not necessarily make a championship course, although it does add to the enjoyment and pleasure of playing the course. Consider the contrast between Pebble Beach along the blue Pacific, Augusta National in a natural arboretum horticultural amphitheater, and Pinehurst No. 2 in its pine-tree-framed sand dunes. All of these courses have in common one basic quality: *character*.

Character in the golf course sense is similar to character in the individual sense in that character is attributed to those who have strong individual points making them stand out over and above others. While great golf courses should necessarily have beauty, they should, above all else, have great playing value.

Great shot value and playing value are linked arm in arm. The tee shot must be hit straight as well as long within the scope of well-laid-down limitations. The perfect shot on a given hole can be considered as in the "white" area. When the shot takes on a de-

Some courses have *real* difficult hazards—bears at Jasper Park Golf Club, Canada, and an alligator at Sea Pines Golf Club, South Carolina.

gree of error, it goes into the "gray" area. If the shot becomes exaggerated in its degree of error, the color becomes a deeper tone of gray until the badly missed shot goes into the "black" area. The values of a hole should be emphasized so that the player can see at a glance what he must conquer to avoid penalty: traps, rough, out of bounds, water, trees, or just plain lack of position. The position of the trapping, the position of the ponds and creeks, the tilt or contour of the fairways, and the width as well as the narrowness of the fairways are all part of the formula making demands upon the player, rewarding for accuracy and penalizing for lack of it.

The green, of course, is the ultimate target. What is more enjoyable than to play a shot to a well-placed, beautifully designed green where the guarding traps as well as the contours are in harmony and with a subtle pin position demanding from the golfer the greatest possible shot! The variety of green design is infinite. Elevated greens, terraced greens, tilted greens, mounded contours, flanked trapping on the sides, direct trapping in the front, creeks or water ponds to carry—these many varied green designs contribute to the

joy of playing a great golf course and to the miseries of failing to meet the persistent demands.

Golf course architecture theory has changed over the years. In Herbert Warren Wind's book, *The Complete Golfer,* the world's premier golf course architect, Robert Trent Jones, reveals the development of course architecture theory in the United States. To quote him at some length:

"As we are indebted to the Scots and English for the game, we are also indebted to them for our principles of architecture. There is no doubt that early golf and its growth in the United States owed much to the interest, enthusiasm, initiative and fine conception of design of Charles Blair Macdonald, our first Amateur Champion, who learned the game when he was being educated at St. Andrews, Scotland. Macdonald was responsible for the first course in Chicago, in 1893, but it was not until the National Links at Southampton, Long Island, New York, was built by Macdonald in 1907 that our golf began to come out of the 'cow-pasture' stage of golf-course architecture.

"Macdonald became obsessed with the idea

of building a truly classical golf course in America, incorporating in this course the best features of the most famous holes of England and Scotland. In this way he felt that he could obtain an eighteen-hole golf course with each hole of outstanding quality, for although certain holes on most English and Scottish links were outstanding, these did not usually exceed two or three per course, with the remaining holes falling into the 'fair' category. In 1902, Macdonald went abroad to gather material. This consisted of playing on most of the courses, observing them studiously, and discussing them with golfing friends. From these investigations he decided that his plan was entirely feasible.

"For four years he proceeded to gather ideas, and in 1904 he made a second trip to study foreign courses. This time he made a detailed survey of the more famous holes, such as the Alps at Prestwick, the Redan at North Berwick, the Eden and the Road Hole at St. Andrews. He also drew twenty to thirty sketches of holes that embodied distinct features that in themselves seemed misplaced, but which could be utilized in principle to harmonize with certain characteristics of un- dulating ground, and so serve as the foundations of outstanding holes.

"The work of Macdonald and his disciples was unquestionably one of the chief factors behind the spread of golf throughout the United States. Many of the holes that Macdonald brought over were copied at other places. In addition, the emigration of English and Scottish professionals added to the growth of golf in this country. While many of the professionals laid out mediocre courses— 'eighteen stakes on a Sunday afternoon'— some did very fine work, such as the late Donald J. Ross, who became nationally famous in the United States as a designer of golf courses.

"The influence of British architecture was also felt in the next era of our golf-course design, when the course at Pine Valley in Clementon, New Jersey, was built by George Crump, a Philadelphia sportsman. With the advice and assistance of the English architect, H. S. Colt, Crump laid out one of the world's ranking golf courses.

"In the twenties American courses fell into the 'penal' pattern of architecture which

Robert Trent Jones is one of best known golf course architects in the world.

punishes the golfer for the slightest error. This undoubtedly was produced by attempts to emulate Pine Valley, a basically penal course. As a result, our fairways became overcluttered with traps and our greens became extremely small target areas. The high cost of maintenance necessary to keep such a course well groomed, as well as the dissatisfaction felt by the average golfer, led to the next revolution in golf-course architecture in the United States.

"In the late twenties, Dr. Alistair Mackenzie, the Scottish golf architect, came to America and began designing golf courses. The main principle of Mackenzie's design was to revert from the 'penal' to the 'strategic' theory of design implicit in the best British courses and to bring about the elimination of the overabundance of traps. (In this same period, Stanley Thompson, a well-known Canadian golf-course architect, was paralleling the Mackenzie idea at Jasper Park in the Canadian Rockies. It was at this time that Thompson and I became partners, because of our basic agreement on this philosophy of golf-course design.) It took the greatest name in American golf, Robert Tyre Jones, Jr., to give this new theory impetus.

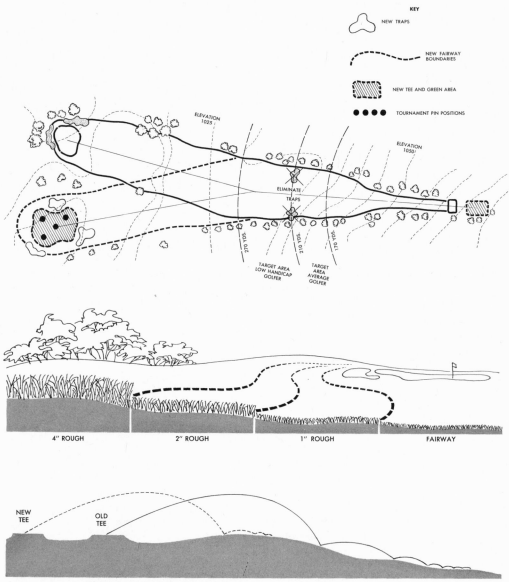

Diagram of the 18th hole at Firestone Country Club before and after Robert Trent Jones redesigned the hole. Jones recommended that the rough be cut (center) to allow gradual increase in severity. The new design eliminated the advantage of the downhill slope, thus greatly reducing roll (bottom).

With Dr. Mackenzie, he created the Augusta National golf course. Jones had some theories of his own which modified some of Mackenzie's extremes. Jones believed that a course had to require thought as well as sheer technical skill to test a player's true ability. Furthermore, it was his conviction that a really great course must be a source of pleasure to the greatest possible number of players, giving the average golfer a fair chance and at the same time demanding the utmost from the expert who tries to break par. Jones' theory of design was influenced by his love for the Old Course at St. Andrews.

"In the next decade, the post-depression thirties and early forties, a very few new courses came into being in the United States. Those that did were built under Government programs for states, municipalities, counties, and the like. These courses were the finest public courses built during any period in the history of American golf-course architecture, but they were, of necessity, modified somewhat to meet their special mass-play conditions.

"Since [World War II], golf has been on the upswing, and our golf-course architects have been busy from coast to coast developing new courses. During this period, I have had the opportunity of working with Robert Tyre Jones, Jr., on the second Jones course, the Peachtree Golf Course in Atlanta, Georgia, Jones' home town. Since it exemplifies, we believe, the best principles of modern golf-course architecture, I should like to describe it in some detail.

"Peachtree differs from the Augusta National particularly in the basic principle of green design. Each green has five or six definite pin positions, of which at least four are ideal for tournament play. These pin positions represent the target area for the better golfer, whereas the whole green represents the target area for the average golfer. The greens are undulating in character, but not as severe nor as continuous as the slopes at Augusta, the undulations at Peachtree being folds between the various pin positions.

"Another feature of Peachtree is exceptional flexibility, brought about through the extreme length of the tees and the numerous possible variations in pin positions. In some cases the tees are as much as eighty yards long. The course can fluctuate from 6,300 to 7,400 yards in length, and yet, by the proper positioning of the pins, the holes are never made tricky in character. By combining these two factors, the number of green positions and the number of tee positions, it is possible to give an infinite variety to the layout.

"While there is no hole on the course that a golfer would recognize as a copy of one of the classic English or Scottish holes, some British holes did play a part in the design. For example, Bob Jones asked if we could not work in a Sahara-type trap (after the one at Sandwich) on one of our holes, and this we were able to do on the tenth, which we consider has now become an excellent par five. The hole plays from the top of a hill into a valley, then up to a green nestled punch-

Bobby Jones, Jr., and Dr. Alistair Mackenzie, the famous British golf architect, going over the blueprints and looking the ground over during the building of "the perfect course" at Augusta.

bowl-like in the hillside. The left-hand side of the green is guarded by an awesome-looking trap about eight or nine feet deep, and the green is well undulated and large, being about 11,000 square feet. The left side of the fairway is clear. At the right side of the fairway, we devised a long Sahara-like maze of trapping, which the bigger golfer, attempting to get home in two, must carry.

"On the sixteenth hole of the course, Bob Jones said that he would like to have the principle of the fourteenth at St. Andrews developed into the strategy, as he had always found that hole very fascinating to play. The tilt of the green was the point he wanted to bring out, and we worked this in with a plateau-type green at the crest of a hill. The green is elevated on the left, behind a mound that protects the left-hand pin position, and then drops to the right through two foundation mounds. The tilt of the green is not continuous, but is broken by two little valleys, one running out through the right, the other through the front."

OUTSTANDING GOLF COURSES

There are many golf courses throughout the world that have "character." The Editors of *Golf* magazine, in association with their professional golf consultants, have selected the following courses as the most outstanding in the world.

United States

Shinnecock Hills Golf Club, Southampton, New York. This club is one of the oldest and most revered in America. It was host to the second United States Open and Amateur in 1896. In the Pleistocene days the Open and the Amateur were played in tandem at the same place on succeeding dates. Willie Dunn came to America from Scotland in 1891 for one purpose: to design and to build a golf course near Southampton, about a hundred miles from New York City on the south shore of Long Island. In laying out the course, he actually attempted to alter the ground contours and create holes with some character. Not here did Dunn walk off a straight line, cut a hole in the turf, and declare it a golf hole, as did some other "architects" of the period. The course soon became relatively congested, and the club put in an additional nine holes for the exclusive use of lady players. This somewhat awkward arrangement was soon abandoned in favor of a single 18-hole course. Today Shinnecock measures 6,429 yards, with a par of 35–35–70.

Merion Golf Club (East Course), Ardmore, Pennsylvania. Under present standards, the course is a short one. Its over-all length is 6,694 yards, and its nines are unbalanced: par 36 out, 34 home. But the charm and the quality of Merion cannot be captured in figures. It looks as if it had simply grown out of the gently rolling landscape, as indeed it has, for almost sixty years. Its daily condition is usually championship condition. From the first drive, it calls upon the golfer to control the ball to prescribed areas rigorously guarded. Its putting greens have pace and are subtly contoured, requiring close reading. That is, Merion can be punitive. You must weave your way among 128 bunkers—the "white faces"

of Merion, into which 800 tons of sand have been poured this year, as is done every third year; Scotch broom and tall grasses fringe many bunkers. There are important boundaries on six holes and unlikely boundaries on five others. There is water on six holes. On three holes you play across a rough depression which, while no longer recognizable as an abandoned quarry, is thought-provoking.

Oak Hill Country Club, Rochester, New York. At first appearance, this course does not look tough. It is not loaded with traps, and the length is not back-breaking: 6,902 yards and a par 70. But looks can be deceiving, and they are here. Oak Hill's greens are comparatively small and have little subtle breaks that are a product of time and harsh winters. Although the rough is not long, it is wiry and thick and demands a club of higher loft to recover. Because of its undulating fairways, Oak Hill will put a premium on shot-making rather than distance. The long-ball hitters who rely too much on distance to score will be at a disadvantage here, where a stray tee shot can hit many of the overhanging limbs or catch a slope and role into the wiry rough. Although each nine consists of one par-5 and two par-3 holes, the heart of the course is its six par-4's, each measuring over 440 yards. These will yield few birdies. And it is difficult for any golfer to finish the last six holes with a string of birdies. Even par on these holes would be commendable. Anything better than that would be supergolf.

Pinehurst Country Club, Pinehurst, North Carolina. Pinehurst's No. 2 Course was designed and carefully engineered by Donald J. Ross, one of America's foremost golf architects. Its 7,051 yards stretch out through dogwood and pine forests in the heart of North Carolina's sand-hill section. One of this course's most striking aspects is the isolation of the separate holes. Each becomes an individual unit, due to the fact that the pine trees planted early in the development now frame the holes completely. This framing accords the holes a third dimension which adds immensely to their character and creates an aesthetic background that emphasizes the

The last three holes at Merion Golf Club. The 16th, the famous "Quarry Hole," is a treacherous 445-yard, par four. The rugged 17th hole measures 230 yards and requires a wood shot or long iron. The home hole, a long four par, is played over the arm of the quarry and requires a long, accurate tee shot.

flowing lines of the architecture. Another feature of the architecture is the small greens, perhaps the smallest of any on United States championship courses. They are nicely formed, with their rhythmic sweeps carrying well out into the approach areas. This particular type of architecture makes the greens difficult to hit and at the same time makes for a chipping course that has no equal.

Pine Valley Golf Club, Clementon, New Jersey. This course is frequently alluded to as the most difficult course in the world, and this reputation is justified. Describing Pine Valley, Robert Trent Jones stated:

What makes this course unlike any other on the globe is the basic principle of its design: the island. From the tee, the fairway targets are islands of grass surrounded by sandy wastes and forests. The sandy wastes are terrifying, for, unlike ordinary trap-land, they bristle with small pines, low-growing juniper, and other troublesome bushes and shrubs. Moreover, the sand is mottled with footprints. Since there is too much sand at Pine Valley for all of it to be raked, none of it is. If you do not hit the fairway island off the tee, you must play brilliantly to finish the hole only two strokes over par. The greens are islands too, smaller ones, of course, and they rank among the best-molded, best-textured

greens on the continent. Like the fairways, the greens are surrounded by sandy horrors. There is no compromise house on the approach shots: you either make or break. One must really see Pine Valley to appreciate it, play it to enjoy it, assault it to relish the combat, laugh at one's own desperation, thrill with one's pars, be satisfied with a bogey, and continue on far from downcast after a double bogey.

Seminole Golf Club, Palm Beach, Florida. The Atlantic Ocean is close enough to bathe this course with spray occasionally. The sea breezes, which are not ordinarily cruel winds like those found in some of the more inland areas of Florida, are considered one of Seminole's hazards. A sudden gust of wind from off the ocean, and the ball will not hover for long; rather, it may settle into one of many bunkers that give "character" to this course. Another architectural feature of Seminole is that it has more rolls and knolls than the usual Florida course. Its fairways are a velvety grass called Ormond Bermuda, and the Bermuda greens are fast but true. It is not an overly long course—6,890 yards—but the trickiness of the course gives Seminole its character.

Baltusrol Golf Club, Springfield, New Jersey. Founded only seven years after the

The Pinehurst Country Club was the prototype for hundreds of United States courses in the early days of golf. The ponderous clubhouse serves all four courses of the Country Club. Behind it are the first two holes of the famed Number Two course (left). The Cathedral Hole on Number Four course (right) is breathtakingly beautiful when dogwood, which interlaces the pines, is in springtime bloom.

original American golf club, St. Andrew's, it is one of the venerable clubs in the country, encrusted with a patina of traditions, a cachet of grace. In 1920, the original course was torn up, and two entirely new layouts built instead. The standard of play was improving precipitately, and the old course was inadequate to challenge the new giants. Baltusrol's members reacted swiftly, commissioning A. W. Tillinghast (the Robert Trent Jones of his day) to design two new courses. The result is essentially what one sees today: the Upper (with its woods, sharp slopes, and tricky greens), and the Lower (deceptive by appearing to be wide open, but whose hazards spring up to catch a careless player). Both courses are roughly 7,000 yards and play to a par of 72. *Sports Illustrated* picked the Lower's par-3 fourth as one of its "best 18 holes in America," and Bobby Jones says that 17 and 18 (both par-5's) are two of the finest finishing holes in the world. The 623-yard 17th at present is the longest hole in Open history. And the 542-yard 18th provides the setting for a dramatic conclusion, since any time the last hole is a par-5, there can be expectations of a birdie finish. The course is beautiful as Tillinghast designed it and, above all, eminently fair. There will be no tricks at Baltusrol; the course is enough.

The Country Club, Brookline, Massachusetts. This club, like Baltusrol, obtains some of its character from tradition. It has been in the forefront of golf leadership in America ever since, as a charter member, it helped create the United States Golf Association in 1894. But the Country Club's course also has a great deal of character. Its greens are not overly large, and all are well trapped. It is a course that requires a lot of shot-making ability and thinking. It is not unusual for a player to use every club in his bag on this 6,870-yard par-71 course. But if you stay out of the rough and keep the ball in play, you have a good chance to score at the Country Club. This, of course, is good advice at any country club.

Augusta National Golf Club, Augusta, Georgia. Is the home of the Masters a tough course? The touring professionals think so, including Jack Nicklaus, whose 17-under-par 271 in 1965 established the Masters scoring record. "The Augusta course is made to play tough for the Masters," Nicklaus explained, "just like the courses are toughened up for the U.S. Open and the British Open. Actually, it's the pin placements that make Augusta a difficult course. Most courses on the tour play about the same for the pros as for the club members. Augusta with wide fairways

A close-up at the green area on the par 4, 439-yard 13th hole at Pine Valley Golf Club.

and few bunkers might not be too difficult for everyday play. In fact, a 15-handicap player at most of the courses we play might be an 11 or 12 at Augusta, but not during the Masters."

Arnold Palmer, who has won four Masters titles, agrees with Nicklaus, but adds, "There are challenges at Augusta like 13 and 15 where you have to decide whether to gamble with your second shots with that water in front of the greens. Even with the wide-open fairways, you still have to drive in the right places to be in position to get up close to the pins. That's very important at Augusta because if you do not get fairly close and on the right sides of the pins on most greens, you are going to have trouble putting. Yet, without a doubt, it is one of the finest golf courses in the world."

Olympic Country Club (Lakeside Course), San Francisco, California. At Olympic, a player must be able to place his ball, for this is a course requiring an ability to maneuver the ball as well as a keen golf sense. The demand is for a definite pattern on every hole, from tee to green, and every tee creates drive choices which will be costly to the man who strays or errs. Many courses today are built for gorillas who can tee it high and let it fly as far as possible. But at Olympic there are a number of 425- to 440-yard holes on which many golfers do not even use a driver, but will strike off with a spoon. This is because there are so many dog-legs that, if played properly, length is no factor whatsoever. In other words, the Olympic may not be Olympian in size (6,727 yards, par 71), but it is far from being a pushover.

Pebble Beach Golf Links, Monterey, California. When asked about Pebble Beach, Robert Trent Jones replied:

If Pine Valley is the most dramatically

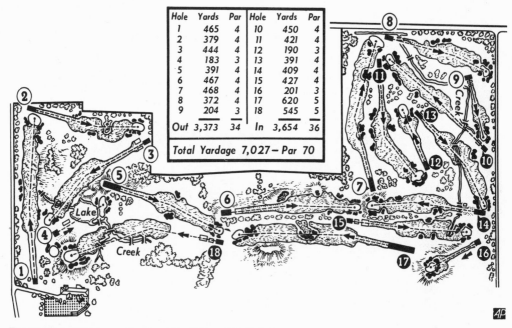

Hole	Yards	Par	Hole	Yards	Par
1	465	4	10	450	4
2	379	4	11	421	4
3	444	4	12	190	3
4	183	3	13	391	4
5	391	4	14	409	4
6	467	4	15	427	4
7	468	4	16	201	3
8	372	4	17	620	5
9	204	3	18	545	5
Out	3,373	34	In	3,654	36

Total Yardage 7,027 — Par 70

The diagram of the Lower Course at the Baltusrol Golf Club.

beautiful pine-and-lakeland course in the United States, then this Monterey Peninsula affair is its unrivaled counterpart among our oceanside courses. I say oceanside and not seaside, because "seaside" has come to imply low-lying links land, and Pebble Beach is quite the reverse. It is routed along the craggy headlands that drop abruptly into Carmel Bay. I think you can best visualize the superlative qualities of this setting if we briefly describe the eighth hole. The simple deceptive facts are that it is a par four, 425 yards long. Strategically, it is a cousin of the thirteenth at Pine Valley, a dog-leg to the right this time, instead of to the left; in the place of the sandy waste, an elbow of Carmel Bay commands the tactics for the second shot. The tee sits at the base of a hill, and it is only after one has driven (blindly) and scaled the slope that he realizes what a tartar he is tackling. From his perch at the top of the headland, after his drive, he sees the green in the distance, and yawning between his ball and the green is an elbow of Carmel Bay, 180 yards wide, lined with precipitous cliffs. Here again, it is up to the golfer to decide for himself how much of the hazard he wants to bite off. The fairway curves around the rim of the cliffs to succor the conservative. For my tastes, this second shot on the eighth is every bit as awesome, and wonderful, as the tee-shot on the more famous sixteenth hole at the neighboring Cypress Point course.

Oakland Hills Country Club, Birmingham, Michigan. "Water, water, everywhere, nor any drop to drink." That famous line from the pen of Samuel Taylor Coleridge has a special meaning for the members of famed Oakland Hills in Birmingham, Michigan—but in a paraphrased version that goes: "Sand, sand, everywhere, and golfers all did shrink." The reason for this should be obvious: Oakland Hills has sand, lots of sand, in fact, 400 tons of medium-sharp sprinkled liberally throughout 113 traps on this beautiful and historic course. The original course was built in 1918, but was remodeled by Robert Trent Jones in 1950. This course is now most deceptive in appearance. The course looks quite open, almost inviting. But one must take another look. That lonesome oak you see out there is in exactly the right spot to cause trouble. So is that willow. Every tree that has been planted since 1951, every bush, has been carefully placed to enhance the playing quality. The modern Oakland Hills is a tough but fair eighteen holes.

Surely, there are many that will disagree with our selection of the so-called "outstand-

Accuracy, not distance, is the determining factor on The Country Club's narrow sloping fairways and small greens.

ing" golf courses of the United States. There are so many good ones in our country. Oakmont, Winged Foot, National Golf Links, Pine Tree, Cypress Point, Medinah No. 3, Cherry Hills, Bellerive, Broadmoor, Scioto, Colonial, Prairie Dunes, The Dunes, Quail Creek, Greenbrier, Champions, Desert Inn, Doral, Congressional, and Royal Kaanapoli are just some of the other courses that could easily fall into this category.

Canada

Banff Springs Hotel Golf Course, Banff, Alberta. This course is a 6,704-yard, par-71 dazzler. Great groves of northern pine line the fairways, and everywhere on the horizon are the snow-capped peaks of the Rockies. From the moment you drive across a raging mountain torrent on the first tee, you are in-

volved in a delicious adventure of shot-making and scenery gazing. Designed by Stanley Thompson, a renowned Canadian golf course architect, it was built under enormous constructional difficulties. One hole—the seventh —had to be literally carved out of the face of Mount Rundle. But out of this rocky wilderness arose one of the most splendid golf courses in the world.

In the immense space encompassed by the mountains, distance is quickly swallowed up and one's perspective may be thrown off. Even such a sharp-eyed player as Gene Sarazen found that his eyes played tricks on him when he rejected his caddie's advice to play a long-iron for what looked to be a short approach shot. Positive that he would hit the ball over a mountain if he used the club the caddie suggested, he picked his own club and proceeded to plop the ball halfway

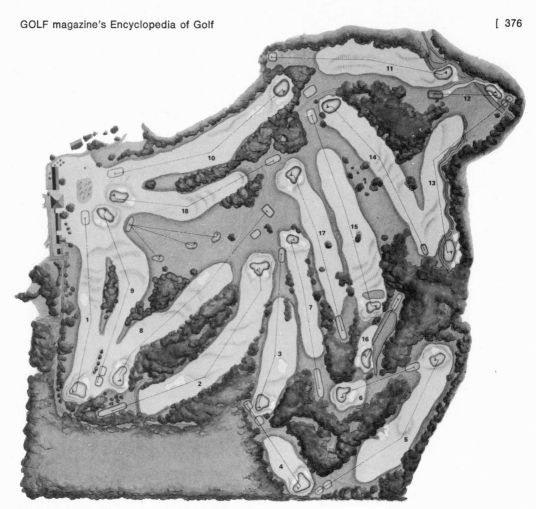

The layout of the Augusta National Golf Club.

THE CHALLENGE

No. 1. White Pine	400 yards Par-4	
No. 2. Woodbine	555 yards Par-5	
No. 3. Flowering Peach	355 yards Par-4	
No. 4. Palm	220 yards Par-3	
No. 5. Magnolia	450 yards Par-4	
No. 6. Juniper	190 yards Par-3	
No. 7. Pampas	365 yards Par-4	
No. 8. Yellow Jasmine	530 yards Par-5	
No. 9. Carolina Cherry	420 yards Par-4	
Totals: OUT	3,485 yards Par-36	
No. 10. Camellia	470 yards Par-4	
No. 11. Dogwood	445 yards Par-4	
No. 12. Golden Bell	155 yards Par-3	
No. 13. Azalea	475 yards Par-5	
No. 14. Chinese Fir	420 yards Par-4	
No. 15. Fire Thorn	520 yards Par-5	
No. 16. Red Bud	190 yards Par-3	
No. 17. Nandina	400 yards Par-4	
No. 18. Holly	420 yards Par-4	
Totals: IN	3,495 yards Par-36	
Over-all Totals:	6,980 yards Par-72	

to the green. Of the incident, Sarazen remarked, "I can't play Banff; the scenery won't allow me to concentrate."

There are many other superlative tests in Canada. Digby Pines, Royal Montreal, Kanawaki, Scarboro, Mississaugua, Jasper, Fraser River, and Capilano are the leaders in this department.

England

Royal Lytham and St. Anne's Golf Club, St. Anne's on the Sea, Lancashire. This course does not seem like one of those famous English seaside courses because it is fully a mile from the sea and is bounded by a railroad

An aerial view of the Olympic Club's Lakeside course. The test of this 6,727-yard course is its trees (15,000 of them) the tight fairways, the rolling terrain, and small greens. It has relatively little sand.

and a housing development. But the turf and the wind are certainly seaside, and there

are enough bunkers for every day of the year. Royal Lytham, like all British seaside links,

View overlooking the 18th fairway at Pebble Beach.

abounds in undulating fairways, towering sand hills, tufted grasses in the rough, and deep pot bunkers. It takes a lot of knowing and an ability to control the ball when the wind gets up. Though not excessively long (6,657 yards, par 74), it is a good test demanding great accuracy. It was here at Royal Lytham in 1926 that Bobby Jones won the first of his three British Open titles. A plaque in the face of a bunker on the dog-leg 17th hole commemorates Jones's 175-yard mashie-iron shot to the green in the final round which virtually won him the championship.

Royal Liverpool Golf Club, Hoylake, Cheshire. Hoylake, as this course is commonly called, is considered by many experts to be the greatest test of golf in Britain. It also enjoys the reputation of being the best groomed. While the course (6,673 yards, par 75) architecture has plenty of character itself, tradition lends some, too. To delve into the history of Hoylake would take a complete book by itself. It was the Hoylake members who instituted both the British Amateur Championship in 1885 and the English Close Championship in 1925. The club negotiated the first amateur international between England and Scotland in 1902 and played host to the first amateur international between Great Britain and the United States in 1921, the prelude to the Walker Cup Matches. It

produced such great names as John Ball, Horace Hutchinson, and John Laidlaw, who dominated the Amateur in its early years. Harold Hilton, the only Britisher to win the U.S. Amateur (in 1911), was also a Hoylake stalwart. So golf-mad were the Royal Liverpool members in the early days that the fabulous John Ball, eight times Amateur Champion and once Open Champion, refused to forgo his golf even on his wedding day. After reaching the ninth, not far from the church, he asked his three astonished fellow golfers to accompany him to his wedding. After the ceremony all four returned to the links to complete their round. Incidentally, Hoylake is not only a golfer's haven but a bird sanctuary, too. The flat, muddy Dee Estuary, once a seaport from which William III's troops set out for the Battle of the Boyne, is famous in ornithological circles as a temporary stopover for migratory birds. Many species rare to the British Isles have been seen seeking temporary shelter on the sandy wasteland.

Walton Heath Golf Club, Tadworth, Surrey. Set in the High Heathland covered with heather, Walton Heath Golf Club offers a course that follows the natural undulations of the terrain. The link is laid out on the heath, about 600 to 700 feet above sea level and exposed to the breezes. The ground is fine and dry and playable even after a violent rain. Since Walton Heath lies open to the winds, it has the feel of a seaside links even though it is only twenty miles from London. It is not an easy course, as many expert golfers can testify. The greens are big and the shots longer, the bunkers deeper and steeper; it is golf on a grand scale, although it should not frighten away the less expert player. Golfing here will give him the feel of a large course, where each player is absolutely on his own to play as he sees fit. The accurate player will stand a better chance than the wild swinger who goes strictly for distance. This is true of most English championship courses. If scores are high here, there is no reason for embarrassment. Some of the finest stroke play produces high scores.

England is a golfer's paradise. Nowhere else in the world are there such a variety of challenges in a relatively compact area. Other championship golf courses worthy of note

Historic St. Andrew's, where any golfer can take on the challenge of this most famous course in the world for a green fee of approximately one dollar.

are: Royal Birkdale, Princes, Royal North Devon, Wentworth, Sunningdale, Southport & Ainsdale, and Royal St. George's.

Scotland

Royal and Ancient Golf Club of St. Andrews, St. Andrews, Fife. Although St. Andrews may not actually be the cradle of golf, as far as the game's disciples are concerned it is Jerusalem, Rome, and Mecca rolled into one, and no one would have it any differently. Situated thirty miles northeast of Edinburgh on the North Sea, St. Andrews and its Old Course embody everything that could reasonably be expected of the game's birthplace, and if golf was not first played there, it must have been some place quite like it. The ancient cathedral and university town of 10,000 inhabitants originated in the seventh century as the site of a Celtic monastery and developed into the ecclesiastical capital of Scotland. The earliest documented record

of golf at St. Andrews was in 1552, but it is known that the game was played there at least a hundred years earlier. The St. Andrews Society of Golfers was founded in 1754 and is the second golf club on record, the Honourable Company of Edinburgh Golfers having been founded in 1744. The club became the Royal and Ancient in 1834 after the king accepted an invitation to become its patron. St. Andrews also was responsible for today's standard round of 18 holes—and quite by accident. The course originally was played as 11 holes out and the same 11 home, but in 1764 two holes each way were combined, making a total of 18. For more than four hundred years the course has been open to anyone and everyone, and only in fairly recent years has a small green fee been charged.

What can one say about St. Andrews that has not been said a thousand times before? Perhaps in golfing circles the Old Course could be termed the ultimate in sophistication. That is to say, a true appreciation of its subtleties has to be acquired. Anyone who walks off the eighteenth green for the first time and raves about the course is as naïve as a teenager pretending to like her first Martini. When Bobby Jones first saw it he called it a "cow pasture." But six years later he described it as "the most fascinating course I have ever played."

Mastering the Old Course is not just a pastime; it is an art. There is no set way to play this 6,936-yard, par-73 course with its rolling fairways and hidden bunkers; that is determined by the elements. And even the wind can be a mean and scheming enemy. Many a player has battled his way out to the 7th in the teeth of the blast, mentally counting the minutes till he completes the four-hole loop to start home with the wind at his back, only to find that with the turn of the tide the wind has veered a full 180 degrees and is still his No. 1 opponent. The fact that it poses such a challenge, that it is a thinker's course, is 75 per cent of its fascination. Some of the Old Course caddies make up the other 25 per cent. Often they will give you the line without even looking up, as on one occasion when a visitor stood on the twelfth tee, a mile and a half from the town, and was told to play "a foot to the right of the church spire." He looked townward only to see a blanket of mist restricting visibility to a quarter of a mile!

Carnoustie Golf Club, Carnoustie, Angus. After the Old Course, almost anything else would be anticlimactic. But as a test of golf, Carnoustie, on the other side of the Firth of Tay, measures up nearly as well. The Championship course, perfected by James Braid, one of Scotland's greatest golf course architects as well as one of its greatest players, has been ranked by leading professionals as among the best three in the world. It has the seaside's typical rolling fairway, and when the winds blow, Carnoustie is plain murder. To add to the problems of the golfer, the burns (creeks) are a major menace. They meander all over the course, popping up at the most unlikely places and contributing to what is conceded to be the most dangerous finish in Scottish golf—Carnoustie's last two holes, on each of which the burn must be crossed twice.

In some ways, Carnoustie seems the least typical of seaside Scottish courses. The rough and traps are not quite as bothersome as they are elsewhere, and you see trees here and there at Carnoustie—a few stands of pine break the wind. There is also a decidedly different sort of clubhouse from the grim, dark old buildings found on most Scottish courses. Carnoustie's clubhouse is a new and incongruously modern structure with an enormous picture window in the lounge.

Honourable Company of Edinburgh Golfers, Muirfield, East Lothian. As previously stated, Muirfield is recognized as the world's oldest golf club. The course is considered by many experts to be the toughest in Scotland and possibly in the world. The course is laid out in an interesting way in that nearly every hole forms an enclave or pocket of its own, often completely out of sight of the surrounding holes thanks to the roll of the terrain. Fairways are rather narrow and hazards generally are readily visible. But, to the player, it seems as though the course knows every move he is going to make and is ready to defend itself against him. Its treacherous bunkers and roughs combine with heavy gusts of wind blowing in from the sea to test to the limit the skills of the best golfers.

The Honourable Company is steeped in its own traditions that shuns some of the conventions of the world of golf. A pro? The Honourable Company would not think of having one. Even something as seemingly basic as par is not employed here; at any rate, Muirfield does not have any par. There is a scorecard, but it simply lists the holes in numerical order and leaves a blank for your score on each hole.

Gleneagles Hotel Golf Courses, Gleneagles, Perthshire. This is Scotland's glorious golf oasis. Designed by James Braid, there are two excellent courses, the King's and Queen's. (The King's is the championship course, 6,597 yards, par 71; Queen's is 6,012 yards, par 69.) Carved from moorland under the Ochil Hills, with the foothills of the Grampians in the distance, both courses are immaculately kept and provide a change of pace after the rigors of seaside golf.

The Queen's course is rated as the more picturesque of the two, but the King's is more challenging and definitely no orphan when it comes to visual splendor. In fact, Gleneagles is rated one of most scenic *sets* of courses in the world. From every hole on both courses

Gleneagles, the pride of the Scottish Highlands in the heart of Perthside, boasts two noble courses in glorious settings.

you get a picture-postcard view of the surrounding mountains and trees and the sky—an endlessly stunning panorama. Every hole is secluded in its own valley or grove, and the privacy is even more pronounced than at the similarly designed Muirfield course, because the hilly terrain at Gleneagles offers more valleys into which to set the holes.

Troon (Old Course), Royal Aberdeen, Turnberry (Ailsa Course), Gullane, North Berwick, and Prestwick—the list of courses with "character" could go on and on. Scotland was the birthplace of modern golf and is still in the forefront for great golf courses.

Ireland

Portmarnock Golf Club, Portmarnock, County Dublin. This course is to Irishmen what St. Andrews is to the rest of the golfing world. The fabulous course, a few miles along the coast from Dublin, is like a Jekyll and Hyde. The greens there are like billiard tables. However, in direct contrast with the fabulous greens is the tiger rough that borders the fairways. It is so high in places that players have

been known to lose their golf bags in it. In fact, caddies have gone astray in it. Big hitting will not help you here if you are not extremely accurate, especially off the tee. Also, the wind is likely to whip up across Dublin Bay, and it is not unusual to have to play against the wind on the way out and the way in, because the wind keeps changing points all the time. But on a fine day, with the larks singing up there in the clear blue sky and the wind toned down to a gentle breeze, you have the type of golf you read about in holiday golf brochures. In other words, sea, wind, weather, terrain, and design all combine at Portmarnock to make it a test of course vs. craft.

Royal Portrush Golf Club, County Antrim, Northern Ireland. The first professional tournament ever held in Ireland was run by Royal Portrush in 1895, seven years after its establishment. It was won by the famous Sandy Herd, who beat Harry Vardon in the final. In July, 1951, this famous County Antrim club had the distinction of being the first Irish course to house the British Open Championship, the winner being Max Faulkner with a score of 285 for the four rounds. Royal Portrush today has three courses, the Dunluce course being the championship links. With a total length of 6,809 yards, it provides a relentless test for the best of golfers. The narrow curving fairways allow no room for errors, with great sand hills always looming near and the roughest of rough an additional hazard. Portrush is laid out in a marvelous stretch of true golfing country. A remarkable feature of the links is the formation of the dunes in two, and sometimes three, distinct levels, from which the prehistoric sea receded, leaving parallel lines of high sand hills with plateaus and valleys between. Portrush is truly a championship course, spectacular in parts, subtle in others. Accurate driving is essential, with the undulating greens offering a rare test of pitching and putting skill.

Royal County Down Golf Club, Newcastle, Northern Ireland. Here you will play with "the Mountains of Mourne sweeping down to the sea" beside you, for Newcastle is laid out on the shores of Dundrum Bay, and sand, heather, and sea are major features. Newcastle is a stiff test even for the top-class golfer. Though tees are built up on the top of ridges and greens are wonderfully true (they say that the man who cannot putt on Newcastle greens cannot putt!), the course is a subtle one. Sand hills are an ever-present hazard; ridges and valleys mean trouble for a crooked shot. Playing on this course keeps you figure-conscious. In addition to two 500-yarders, there are two 470-yarders and half a dozen or so 415- to 430-yarders. There are four par-3 holes, and the shortest of the par-4's are the three holes between 370 and 380 yards. Incidentally, a mile or two east of the course is the famous Giant's Causeway: great columns of black basalt jutting out to sea. And who is to say that they were not built by giant leprechauns in this ethereal land of make-believe?

The list of outstanding Irish courses for a small country is rather lengthy: Rosslare, County Wexford; Rosses Point, County Sligo; Lahinch, County Clare; Ballybunion, County Kerry; Galway, County Galway; Baltray, County Louth; and, of course, the one and only Killarney in County Kerry. They say at Killarney that you can be an angler without knowing it since one of its members, slicing his drive into the lake at the 18th, stunned a leaping salmon. In wading in to retrieve his ball, he emerged with a fair-sized fish!

There are other golf courses in Europe that can be considered of championship class. These include Club de Golf (Spain), Royal Belgique (Belgium), Penina (Portugal), Golf de Saint-Nom-la-Bretèche (France), Crans-Sur Sierre (Switzerland), Halmstad (Sweden), Club de Campo (Spain), Pau (France), Cologne (Germany), Circolo Golf Olgiata (Italy), Estoril (Portugal), The Hague (Holland), Villa d'Este (Italy), St. Cloud (France), Engadine (Switzerland), and Rungsted (Denmark).

Japan

Kasumegaseki Country Club, Kasahata Kawagoe-ski, Saitama. This championship layout has a par 72 on both the East course, stretching 6,913 yards, and the West course, measuring 6,590 yards. (The West course is the one selected by *Golf* magazine's Editors to be the outstanding one.) The fairway turf is heavy, which discourages bounce and roll, making the holes play longer than the actual

yardage would indicate. (This is true for most Japanese golf courses.) The greens are composed of korai grass, similar to but coarser than Bermuda and requiring a more solid whack when putting. Kasumegaseki is possibly one of the best-conditioned courses in the world. Hand-tended care—and this is not an exaggeration—is the reason for the superb fairways and greens. Japanese women laborers actually weed, reseed, and clip the grass by hand. Another reason for the excellent condition is the exceptional care taken by the girl caddies. These efficient girls not only replace divots but carefully reseed them from small bags they carry.

Included among Japan's other championship courses are Tokyo Yomiuri, Tokyo Country Club, Fuji, and Hirono.

Australia

Royal Melbourne Club, Melbourne. The club was formed in 1891; land was secured, and incredible as it may seem now, the course was ready in a few weeks. Royal Melbourne lies in the Melbourne "sand belt" area—the area considered the most perfect for golf courses in Australia. The soil is particularly sandy, grows a thick cover of couch and other grasses, and is naturally well drained. Native tea-trees—bushy, coastal trees that grow about 15 to 20 feet high with rambling branches that reach to the ground—line most of the fairways. These trees penalize off-line shots very heavily, but they are also most attractive and provide good windbreaks when the strong sea breezes blow. This 6,642-yard-long course is covered with a mixture of Bermuda, bent, Kentucky blue, and Poa Annua grasses, and is watered from bores sunk in the great depth of sand below the fairways. So skilfully did Alex Russell, who designed the course in 1930–1931, make use of the sandy soil and native vegetation that the Royal Melbourne East Course (par 74) is regarded by a majority of the experts as the most difficult in Australia.

The huge greens are extremely fast, and are heavily and deeply trapped. Actually, its spacious bunkers have caused more than one international player to wish he had never heard of the word "sand." Because of the light sand base, there has never been a need to bring in sand for the traps.

The Royal Melbourne Club also has a 6,563-yard, par-3 West Course. Other outstanding golf courses of Australia include the Royal Canberra, the Victoria, the Royal Adelaide, and the Kooyonga.

MOST INTERESTING GOLF HOLES IN THE WORLD

After making a survey of the outstanding golf courses, the staff of *Golf* magazine next selected 72 holes—36 from the United States and 36 from the remaining golfing countries of the world—as the most interesting in the world. These holes were not selected on difficulty alone, but rather because they offered a colorful panorama of grass, water, trees, bunkers, sand, and other features to rest, refresh, and challenge the golfer. The holes listed here meet these tests and the intent is not to compare but to give the reader a cursory introduction to some of the finest and most interesting golf holes in the world. While several of the great courses of the world have more than one interesting hole, only one was selected from a club.

Hole	1st Eighteen Course[a]	Yards	Par	2nd Eighteen Course[a]	Yards	Par
1	Spyglass Hill GC	602	5	Peachtree GC	388	4
2	Scioto CC	436	4	Eisenhower GC	567	5
3	The Country Club	440	4	Mauna Kea Beach GC	215	3
4	Baltusrol GC	194	3	Firestone CC	465	4
5	Colonial CC	459	4	Coral Ridge CC	195	3
6	Seminole GC	388	4	Olympic CC	437	4
7	Pine Valley GC	554	5	Hazeltine National GC	605	5
8	Concord Hotel & GC	399	4	Prairie Dunes GC	424	4
9	Doral CC	186	3	Charlotte CC	369	4
	Out	3,658	36		3,665	36
10	Pinehurst CC	596	5	Winged Foot GC	191	3
11	Merion GC	378	4	Oyster Harbor GC	430	4
12	Augusta National GC	155	3	Southern Hills CC	465	4
13	Oak Hill CC	602	5	Dunes G & BC	560	5
14	Shinnecock Hills GC	434	4	Champions GC	430	4
15	Oakmont CC	458	4	Warwick Hills GC	456	4
16	Cypress Point GC	222	3	Oakland Hills CC	405	4
17	Pleasant Valley CC	402	4	Medinah CC	201	3
18	Congressional CC	465	4	Pebble Beach GL	530	5
	In	3,712	36		3,668	36
	Total	7,370	72		7,333	72

[a] Location of courses can be found on pages 364–369.

Hole	Course	Yards	Par	Course	Yards	Par
1	Crans-sur-Sierre GC (Switzerland)	585	5	Royal Lytham & St. Anne's GC (England)	208	3
2	Walton Heath GC (England)	445	4	Valley GC (Philippines)	460	4
3	Gleneagles Hotel GC (Scotland)	393	4	Prestwick GC (Scotland)	505	5
4	Doral Beach GC (Puerto Rico)	205	3	Royal Johannesburg GC (South Africa)	476	4
5	Mid-Ocean GC (Bermuda)	433	4	Royal Portrush GC (Northern Ireland)	392	4
6	Glyfada GC (Greece)	435	4	Cotton Bay GC (Bahamas)	539	5
7	Club de Golf Mexico (Mexico)	575	5	Royal Dublin GC (Ireland)	352	4

Hole	1st Eighteen Course	Yards	Par	2nd Eighteen Course	Yards	Par
8	Banff Springs Hotel GC (Canada)	175	3	Troon GC (Scotland)	125	3
9	Royal County Downs GC (Northern Ireland)	426	4	Turnberry Hotel GC (Scotland)	475	4
	Out	3,672	36		3,532	36
10	London Hunt & CC (Canada)	550	5	Royal Cinque Ports—Deal— GC (England)	385	4
11	Laguneta CC (Venezuela)	188	3	Fuji CC (Japan)	550	5
12	Kooyonga GC (Australia)	391	4	Monte Carlo GC (Monaco)	175	3
13	Club de Campo (Spain)	466	4	Wentworth Club (England)	437	4
14	County Sligo GC (Ireland)	440	4	Portmarnock GC (Northern Ireland)	385	4
15	North Berwick CC (Scotland)	203	3	Royal St. George's CC (England)	435	4
16	Royal Liverpool GC (England)	532	5	Royal Melbourne Club (Australia)	215	3
17	Carnoustie GC (Scotland)	423	4	St. Andrews (Scotland)	453	4
18	Wack Wack G & CC (Philippines)	422	4	Capilano G & CC (Canada)	575	5
	In	3,615	36		3,610	36
	Total		72			72

THE MOST CHALLENGING COURSES IN THE UNITED STATES

The selection of the most challenging courses in the United States is almost as difficult as it would be to play them. The staff of the *Encyclopedia of Golf,* from the suggestions of the professional golfers who contribute to *Golf* magazine, has compiled the following listing of over two hundred of the most difficult courses in the United States. For full information on how a course rating is obtained, see page 344. Sure, we may have left out your favorite "tough" course (sorry!), but here are the ones selected by our experts:

Location	Course	Yardage/ Par/Rating
Alabama		
Birmingham	CC of Birmingham	7,004/71/72
Dauphin Island	Isle Dauphin GC	7,000/72/73
Point Clear	Lakewood GC	6,429/70/71
Tuscaloosa	Indian Hills CC	6,900/71/71
Arizona		
Carefree	Desert Forest CC	6,929/72/72
Litchfield Park	Goodyear G & CC	7,220/72/74
Tucson	Tucson National GC	7,200/72/71
Arkansas		
Cherokee Village	Cherokee Village GC	7,051/72/72

Location	Course	Yardage/ Par/Rating
Fort Smith	Hardscrabble CC	6,823/72/73
Hot Springs	Hot Springs G & CC (No. 3)	6,915/72/72
Texarkana	Texarkana CC	6,613/72/72
California		
Apple Valley	Apple Valley CC	6,765/71/71
Carlsbad	La Costa CC	7,013/72/73
La Jolla	Torrey Pines GC	7,011/72/72
Los Angeles	Los Angeles CC (North)	6,433/71/73
Pacific Palisades	Riviera CC	6,536/72/71
Palm Springs	La Quinta CC	6,904/72/72
Palo Alto	Stanford University GC	6,605/72/72
Pauma Valley	Pauma Valley	7,001/71/73
Pebble Beach	Cypress Point Club	6,506/72/71
Pebble Beach	Pebble Beach GL	6,747/72/75
Pebble Beach	Spyglass Hill GC	7,035/72/75
San Francisco	California GC	6,655/71/72

Looking back on the 13th hole at Dunes Golf and Country Club.

Location	Course	Yardage/Par/Rating	Location	Course	Yardage/Par/Rating
San Francisco	Olympic Country Club (Lakeside)	6,727/71/75	Palm Beach Gardens	PGA National GC	7,027/72/74
South Laguna	El Niguel CC	6,804/72/73	Pompano Beach	Palm Aire Lodge & CC	7,120/72/73
Yorba Linda	Yorba Linda CC	6,696/72/73	Ponte Vedra Beach	Ponte Vedra CC	6,786/72/72
Colorado			Sarasota	De Soto Lakes GC	6,927/72/73
Air Force Academy	Eisenhower GC	7,158/72/72	West Palm Beach	West Palm Beach CC	6,475/72/72
Colorado Springs	Broadmoor GC (East)	7,131/72/73	**Georgia**		
			Atlanta	Atlanta CC	7,053/72/72
Denver	Cherry Hills CC	7,042/71/72	Atlanta	East Lake CC (No. 1)	7,000/70/71
Evergreen	Hiwan GC	7,114/70/71	Atlanta	Peachtree GC	7,219/72/72
Connecticut			Augusta	Augusta National GC	6,980/72/73
Darien	CC of Darien	6,800/72/73	Sea Island	Sea Island GC	6,873/72/72
Darien	Wee Burn CC	6,713/72/72	**Hawaii**		
Greenwich	Stanwick Club	7,179/72/73	Kaanapoli Beach	Royal Kaanapoli GC	7,179/72/75
New Haven	Yale University GC	6,628/70/72	Kamuela	Mauna Kea Beach GC	7,016/72/74
Delaware					
Wilmington	Wilmington CC (South)	6,841/71/71	**Idaho**		
			Boise	Plantation GC	6,522/72/72
Florida					
Boca Raton	Boca Raton Hotel & CC	6,777/71/71	**Illinois**		
			Chicago	Beverly CC	6,997/71/73
Delray Beach	Pine Tree GC	7,210/72/73	Flossmoor	Flossmoor	6,707/72/73
			Glencoe	Skokie CC	6,790/72/72
Fort Lauderdale	Coral Ridge CC	7,280/72/72	Glenview	North Shore CC	6,595/72/73
Fort Meyers	Cypress Lake CC	7,048/72/75	Highland Park	Bob O'Link CC	6,731/72/73
Miami	CC of Miami (West)	6,927/72/73			
Miami	Doral CC (Blue)	7,028/72/74	Lemont	Cog Hill GC	7,224/72/73
Miami	Miami Lakes CC	7,030/72/72	Medinah	Medinah CC (No. 3)	7,110/72/73
North Palm Beach	Lost Tree CC	6,839/72/72	Olympia Fields	Olympia Fields CC (North)	6,722/71/72
Palm Beach	Seminole GC	6,890/72/72	Pekin	Pekin CC	6,895/72/72

Left, Art Wall, Jr., smacks a two-iron to the famed 222-yard 16th hole at Cypress Point Country Club during a recent Bing Crosby tournament. Right, here is what may happen if you do not make the green of this hole.

Location	Course	Yardage/Par/Rating	Location	Course	Yardage/Par/Rating
Wheaton	Chicago GC	6,545/70/72	**Massachusetts**		
Indiana			Brookline	The Country Club	6,870/71/72
Bristol	Elcona CC	7,002/72/73	Bolton	International GC	7,040/72/74
Columbus	Otter Creek GC	7,054/72/74	Mashpee	CC of New Seabury	7,122/72/74
Dyer	Longwood CC	6,575/70/71	North		
Indianapolis	CC of Indianapolis	6,800/70/71	Swansea	Swansea CC	6,855/72/72
Indianapolis	Speedway GC	7,179/72/72	Osterville	Oyster Harbors GC	6,770/72/72
La Porte	Beechwood GC	6,674/72/73	Peabody	Salem CC	6,796/72/72
Iowa			Sutton	Pleasant Valley CC	6,713/71/72
Davenport	Emeis Park GC	7,000/72/72	Winchester	Winchester CC	6,659/71/71
Des Moines	Wakonda GC	6,897/72/72	**Michigan**		
Iowa City	Finkbine GC	6,905/72/72	Ann Arbor	University of Michigan	
Waterloo	Gates Park GC	7,210/72/72		GC	6,770/72/72
Kansas			Benton	Point O'Woods G &	
Hutchinson	Prairie Dunes CC	6,522/70/70	Harbor	CC	6,990/71/75
Shawnee			Birmingham	Oakland Hills CC	6,910/72/72
Mission	Kansas City CC	6,435/70/71	East		
Kentucky			Lansing	Forest Acres GC	6,834/71/71
Fort Knox	Lindsey GC	6,528/72/73	Grand		
Lexington	Spring Valley CC	6,813/72/72	Blanc	Warwick Hills GC	7,001/72/72
Louisiana			Grosse Point		
New Orleans	Timberlane CC	7,200/72/74	Farms	CC of Detroit	6,915/72/72
Maine			**Minnesota**		
Bar Harbor	Kebo Valley GC	6,709/70/72	Chaska	Hazeltine National	
Orono	Penobscot Valley CC	6,700/72/72		GC	7,410/72/75
Maryland			Duluth	Northland CC	6,950/72/72
Baltimore	Baltimore CC (Five		**Mississippi**		
	Farms)	6,796/70/71	Jackson	CC of Jackson	7,005/72/71
Baltimore	Mount Pleasant GC	6,730/71/74	Laurel	Laurel CC	6,709/72/72
Bethesda	Congressional CC	7,169/72/74	**Missouri**		
			Creve Coeur	Bellerive CC	7,191/71/72

HOLE	YARDS	PAR
1	405	4
2	449	4
3	176	3
4	425	4
5	362	4
6	508	5
7	576	5
8	420	4
9	151	3
Out	3472	36
10	432	4
11	348	4
12	390	4
13	376	4
14	204	3
15	341	4
16	183	3
17	402	4
18	565	5
In	3241	35

Yards	6713
Par	71

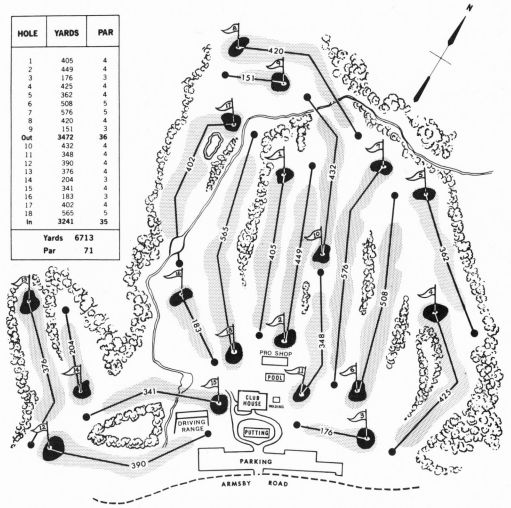

The layout of the Pleasant Valley Country Club is one of the toughest tests in New England.

Location	Course	Yardage/Par/Rating
Kansas City	Blue Hills CC	7,410/72/72
Ladue	Old Warson CC	7,168/71/73
Montana		
Billings	Yellowstone CC	7,000/72/72
Nebraska		
Omaha	Chapel Hill CC	7,150/72/73
Nevada		
Incline Village	Incline Valley CC	7,116/72/72
Las Vegas	Desert Inn CC	7,209/72/73
Las Vegas	Paradise Valley CC	7,069/72/73
Las Vegas	Sahara-Nevada CC	6,581/71/71
New Hampshire		
Greenland	Portsmouth CC	7,107/72/73

Location	Course	Yardage/Par/Rating
New Jersey		
Absecon	Seaview CC (Pines)	6,900/72/72
Clementon	Pine Valley GC	6,703/70/74
Jamesburg	Forsgate CC	6,526/70/71
Medford	Sunny Jim GC	7,235/72/75
Plainfield	Plainfield CC	6,817/72/72
Springfield	Baltusrol GC (Lower)	7,031/72/72
Summit	Canoe Brook GC	7,063/72/73
Tuckerton	Atlantis CC	7,085/72/73
Vineland	Buena Vista CC	7,031/72/73
New Mexico		
Albuquerque	Paradise Hills G & CC	7,185/72/72
Albuquerque	University of New Mexico GC	7,258/72/75

Plenty of "beach," as they call traps in golf, faces the player who pushes a short off-line on the 12th hole of the Winged Foot Golf Club.

Location	Course	Yardage/Par/Rating
New York		
Farmingdale	Bethpage GC	6,873/71/73
Hamburg	Bethlehem CC	7,100/72/72
Kiamesha Lake	Concord Hotel	7,205/72/75
Mamaroneck	Winged Foot GC (West)	6,881/72/72
New Rochelle	Wykagyl CC	6,700/72/72
Rochester	Oak Hill CC (East)	6,902/70/72
Scarsdale	Quaker Ridge GC	6,745/70/72
South Fallsburg	Tarry Brae GC	7,180/72/74
Westbury	Meadow Brook CC	7,122/71/71
West Point	West Point Officers GC	6,323/70/73
White Plains	Century CC	6,464/71/71
White Plains	Fenway GC	6,800/70/70
White Plains	Metropolis CC	6,790/71/71
North Carolina		
Charlotte	Charlotte CC	6,774/72/72
Charlotte	Quail Hollow CC	7,109/72/73
Lenoir	Cedar Rock CC	7,149/72/74
Pinehurst	CC of North Carolina	7,040/72/74
Pinehurst	Pinehurst CC (No. 2)	7,051/72/73
Southern Pines	Pine Needles CC	6,905/72/72
Tryon	Red Fox CC	7,139/72/75
Whispering Pines	Whispering Pines CC	7,151/72/74
North Dakota		
Fargo	Fargo CC	6,627/72/72

Location	Course	Yardage/Par/Rating
Grand Forks	Grand Forks CC	7,000/72/72
Ohio		
Akron	Firestone CC	7,165/70/70
Alliance	Tannerhauf GC	7,006/72/72
Aurora	Aurora CC	6,800/72/71
Cleveland	Canterbury CC	6,936/71/71
Cincinnati	Coldstream CC	6,674/71/72
Cincinnati	Kenwood CC	6,798/71/71
Columbus	Columbus CC	7,120/72/71
Columbus	Scioto CC	7,067/72/73
Dayton	National Cash Register Club	6,910/71/72
Indian Hill	Camargo Club	6,527/70/71
Milford	Terrace Park CC	6,671/72/71
Toledo	Inverness Club	6,719/72/72
Oklahoma		
Checotah	Fountainhead State Park	7,023/72/72
Oklahoma City	Quail Creek CC	7,042/72/74
Tulsa	Southern Hills CC	6,980/71/74
Tulsa	The Oaks CC	6,609/71/72
Oregon		
Canby	Willamette Valley CC	6,614/72/72
Hillsboro	Meriwether National GC	7,042/72/72
Pennsylvania		
Ardmore	Merion GC (East)	6,694/70/71
Bushkill	Tamiment GC	7,110/72/73
Fleetwood	Moselem Springs CC	7,117/72/72
Flourtown	Philadelphia Cricket Club	6,815/71/74
Havertown	Llanerch CC	6,700/70/71
Hershey	Hershey CC	6,988/72/73
Ligonier	Laurel Valley GC	7,100/71/71
Newtown Square	Aronimink GC	7,045/70/71
Oakmont	Oakmont CC	7,050/72/72
Philadelphia	Whitemarsh Valley CC	6,670/72/72
Pittsburgh	Fox Chapel GC	6,633/71/72
Sewickley	Sewickley Heights CC	7,160/72/72
Shawnee-on-Delaware	Shawnee CC	6,720/72/72
Rhode Island		
Newport	Newport CC	6,850/71/71
West Barrington	Rhode Island CC	6,900/71/71
South Carolina		
Aiken	Palmetto CC	7,100/72/73
Columbia	Columbia CC	7,192/72/72
Columbia	Spring Valley CC	6,824/72/73
Greenville	Green Valley CC	7,105/72/74
Myrtle Beach	Dunes G & BC	7,180/72/74
South Dakota		
Sioux Falls	Elmwood Park GC	7,100/72/73

Location	Course	Yardage/Par/Rating
Tennessee		
Knoxville	Holston Hills CC	7,107/72/72
Memphis	Memphis CC	6,870/70/71
Nashville	Belle Meade CC	7,600/72/72
Texas		
Dallas	Dallas AC	6,789/71/72
Dallas	Preston Trail GC	7,113/71/71
Fort Worth	Colonial CC	7,021/70/71
Houston	Champions GC	7,250/71/72
Houston	Houston CC	7,056/72/72
Houston	Memorial Park GC	7,122/72/73
Houston	River Oaks CC	6,583/71/72
San Antonio	Pecan Valley CC	7,223/70/72
San Augustine	Fairway Farms GC	7,352/71/71
Utah		
Salt Lake City	The ·Country Club	6,984/72/73

Location	Course	Yardage/Par/Rating
Virginia		
Falls Church	International CC	6,914/71/73
Hot Springs	Homestead GC (Lower)	7,140/72/72
Washington		
Tacoma	Firecrest GC	6,470/71/71
West Virginia		
Charleston	Berry Hills CC	6,593/71/72
Morgantown	Lakeview CC	6,850/71/71
White Sulphur Springs	The Greenbrier Club	6,534/70/71
Wisconsin		
Fontana	Big Foot CC	6,490/72/72
Madison	Cherokee CC	7,022/72/73
Milwaukee	Brown Deer GC	7,030/71/73
Mukwonago	Rainbow Springs CC	7,135/72/74
West Bend	West Bend CC	7,071/73/74

THE WORLD'S TOUGHEST HOLES

Selecting the world's toughest holes is a difficult task. We have studied thousands of candidates for this honor and talked with hundreds of professionals who have played them and the architects who designed many of the holes. The front nine holes were selected from courses in the United States, while the back nine were from courses in the other golfing nations of the world. This truly world championship course, as is the case in any good championship course, requires that the player be able to hit every shot in the game and that good shots are always rewarded and poor shots are always penalized. Now let us go out and play *Golf* magazine's 18 toughest holes in the world.

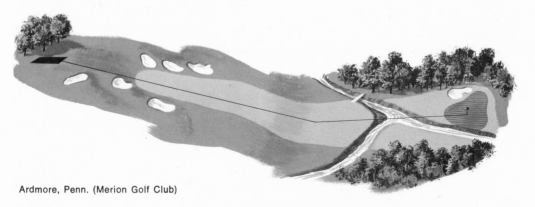

Ardmore, Penn. (Merion Golf Club)

Hole 1: The Eleventh at Merion Golf Club, Par 4, 378 Yards. At first blush, this hole does not look difficult, with its relatively short yardage. Actually, all too many golfers, including the touring pros, do not respect this hole and end up paying dearly for their disrespect. From the tee there appears to be plenty of fairway for the drive. But less than 100 yards down the fairway the terrain dips rather abruptly to a lower level which is not totally visible from the tee. Unfortunately for the unsuspecting golfer, this lower level abounds with trees and bunkers. The green is far back in a shaded setting of trees and shrubs and is embraced, front, right, and back by Baffling Brook. This rocky-bed creek has an entrance from the left and winds around to the right, forming a moat in front of the green. If the tee shot is played short of the creek bed and straight, you will be in good position for the second stroke, which is usually a pitch ap-

proach. But it must be a near "perfect" pitch; hit just a bit short, or you will be in the water. Hit a bit strong or to the right, the ball will get a washing. To the left is trouble also. The second shot must be a high, well-aimed, back-spinning short iron to the middle of the green, if you plan to par or birdie No. 11 at Merion.

The Dunes Golf and Beach Club

Hole 2: The Thirteenth at the Dunes Golf and Beach Club, Par 5, 560 Yards. This hole, aptly named "Waterloo," is a horseshoe-shaped affair that loops around Singleton Lake, one of the largest water hazards in the United States. The tee shot, which must be taken in a general direction away from the green, has to be straight and long, coming to rest approximately 220 to 240 yards out and near the lake's edge. Such positioning is necessary if the second shot is to be from an ideal setup. If you slice your drive, the ball will go into the water or the stand of bushes and trees that grow on the lake's edge. A hooked drive takes you too far away for a correct second shot. This second shot is a daring one since it requires a fairway wood (generally a No. 3) to make it across the water. The next

shot, depending on how brave you were on the second, is anything from a No. 3 iron to a No. 7 or No. 8 iron. This approach shot to the rolling 13th green is also demanding. In other words, to be on the green in three, you must hit three "perfect" shots in a row—a rare requirement today in America where we are presently faced with a dearth of honest par-5's. Actually, many experts consider the Dunes' 13th the most difficult par-5 in the United States.

Hole 3: The Twelfth at Augusta National Golf Club, Par 3, 155 Yards. "The meanest little hole in the world," according to Lloyd Mangrum, is *the* hole at the Augusta National, if you ask Arnold Palmer. A bare 155 yards long, the 12th appears to be a simple one-shotter to a wide, shallow green, with only the

Augusta, Georgia

seemingly easy carry over Rae's Creek to possibly cause concern. But standing on the elevated tee, the player cannot feel or judge the capricious winds that swirl down the creek, changing speeds and reversing directions within the space of a few seconds and varying the choice of clubs from a No. 4 iron to a No. 8. Throughout the tournament, the pin is almost invariably cut into the right side of the green, and although an approach to the left side is safer and avoids the sand, it sets up a huge putt across a lightning-fast green. In 1958, Palmer took advantage of a local rule allowing a free drop from soft areas to salvage a par at the 12th and win his first Masters. But the very next year, he went directly for the pin tucked on the right side, landed in the creek, and took a triple bogey six. As Nicklaus puts it, "That 12th hole has jumped up and grabbed a lot of people."

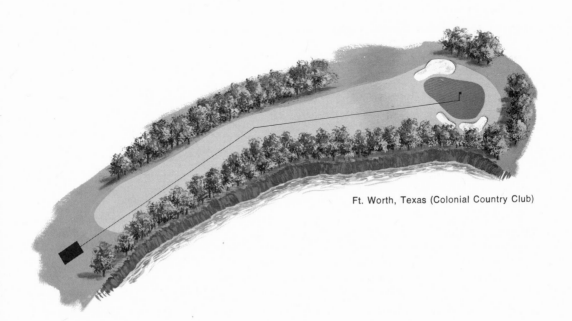

Ft. Worth, Texas (Colonial Country Club)

Hole 4: The Fifth at Colonial Country Club, Par 4, 459 Yards. To get home in two strokes, your drive must be almost perfect, a slight fade, and about 230 to 250 yards out. To the left of the fairway are trees, rough, and a drainage ditch, while to the right is Trinity, a murky stream that runs from tee to green. In other words, a little off the straight and narrow, and you are in bad trouble. If you have positioned your tee shot in the bend of the fairway, you can reach the large, well-bunkered green with either a No. 2 or a No. 3 iron.

Springfield, N. J. (Baltusrol Golf Club)

Hole 5: The Fourth at Baltusrol Golf Club, Par 3, 194 Yards. According to PGA Executive Director Joe Dey, this hole has as much playing value as any par-3 in the world. A 3-foot-high stone wall girds the front of the green, threatening to ricochet a low shot back into the water, and directly behind the extremely large putting surface are three sand traps. Also the two-level green slopes toward the water hazard and narrows sharply to the right making the hole even more difficult when the pin is placed in that location. Hitting against the prevailing breeze into the double-tiered green can call for as little as a No. 4 iron or as much as a No. 3 wood. Most pros agree that a golfer should hit for the traps in back, for more pars will be made from there than from the pond. Golf architect Robert Trent Jones, who redesigned the 4th for the 1954 Open, made a hole in one with his first shot on his new hole, leading him to observe to his detractors who had complained about the hole's severity, "Gentlemen, as you can see, this hole is not too tough." But Jones hit his shot from the front of the tee and got home with a No. 7 iron. During the 1954 Open, Ben Hogan consistently faded a No. 4 wood to the green, and Snead was in the water—with a No. 3 iron. This hole will ambush the unwary.

Hole 6: The Seventh at Pine Valley Golf Club, Par 5, 554 Yards. As was stated earlier in this section, this course is one of the most difficult in the world, and this hole is considered the course's most difficult. If you slice or hook on a shot you are in bad trouble. The best rule for the player who finds himself in trouble at Pine Valley is to play directly out of it and onto the fairway. This may even call for a backward shot. On the 7th, your tee shot must be straight down the fairway, but not more than 260 yards. If your drive is more than this, you will land in Hell's Half Acre, the world's largest sand hazard. Your next shot should be made with a fairway wood and hit straight over the sand and brush of Hell's Half Acre. Then a short iron to the green, which is actually an island amid a sea of brush and sand. No one has ever been recorded as having reached this green in two.

Hole 7: The Sixteenth at Cypress Point Club, Par 3, 222 Yards. This hole requires a

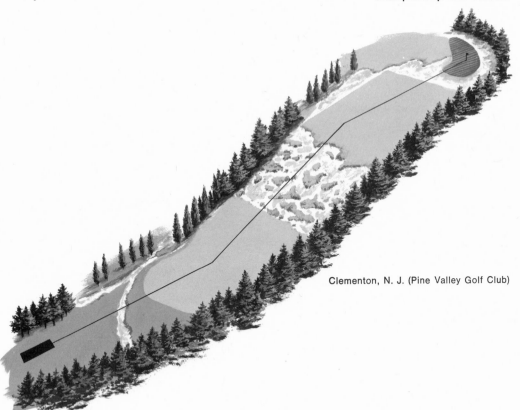

Clementon, N. J. (Pine Valley Golf Club)

Cypress Point

strong shot into a frequently strong wind by a golfer with a strong heart. The hole plays directly into the Pacific Ocean, a carry of 210 yards over a cove, with the prevailing wind in the golfer's face. Depending on the wind conditions, a shot to the putting green requires at minimum a No. 3 iron ranging up to a brassie or driver. Penalties for inaccuracy are extremely severe. A hooked shot often carries into the cove that juts in to the left front of the putting green. A shot pushed to the right catches either the water or the beach and rocks at the base of the steep cliff. A too strong shot can encounter one of three bunkers at the back of the green or the wild, entangling ice plant that seems to defy recovery. For those who choose not to gamble, a No. 4 or No. 5 iron can be played over a shorter carry of about 150 to 160 yards to the left front fairway, leaving a No. 9 iron or a wedge to the green and hopes of one putt for a par 3.

Hole 8: The Sixteenth at Oakland Hills Country Club, Birmingham, Michigan, Par 4, 405 Yards. Placement of the tee shot is extremely important on this hole. The rough is very heavy on both sides of the relatively narrow fairway, and attempts to hit out of it and over the large expanse of water quite often meet with disaster. A good drive should leave the golfer with a No. 4 or No. 5 iron shot to the green, though long hitters may only need a No. 6 or No. 7 iron to get home. The green is actually on a peninsula jutting out into the lake and is protected at the rear by four large traps. The putting surface has a devilish ridge running across its middle, and the placement of the pin can make for a harrowing session with the putter. And, oh yes, there are four rather large sand traps just behind the green to discourage gamblers.

Hole 9: The Eighteenth at Pebble Beach Golf Links, Par 5, 530 Yards. To play this hole, a timid approach is the wise one. That is, hit your tee shot well to the right. Just be sure that your shot does not go too far right and get among the trees that are located on that portion of the fairway. Then your second shot should again be kept to the right and well short of the green. This will leave a wedge shot to the well-trapped green. Sounds easy, but most golfers, including the pros, try the short-cut method to a birdie or par and end up with more trouble than ever can be realized.

The first nine is par 36, 3,457 yards.

Birmingham, Michigan (Oakland Hills Country Club)

Monterey, Cal. (Pebble Beach Golf Links)

Hole 10: The Thirteenth at Club de Campo, Madrid, Spain, Par 4, 466 Yards. The trick on this hole is to cut the dog-leg by aiming your drive down the right side from the elevated tee. But if you push it too far to the right, you are in the trees and bad rough, and it will cost you an extra shot. There are bunkers at 200 and 230 yards out on the left, at the point of the dog-leg. You hit your approach with anything from a No. 6 to a No. 8 iron. The green is good-sized and undulating, and it is guarded by two large bunkers at the right front and the left rear.

Madrid (Club de Campo)

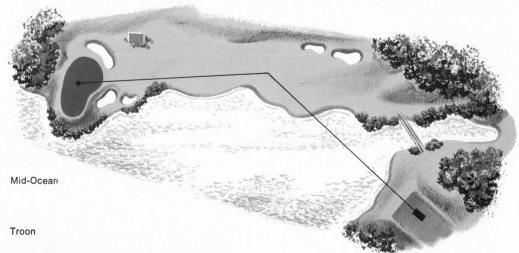

Mid-Ocean

Troon

Hole 11: The Fifth at the Mid-Ocean Golf Club, Tuckerstown, Bermuda, Par 4, 433 Yards. Also known as the "Cape," this hole gives you a choice, but only a small one. From an elevated tee, either you can hit your drive across the small finger of water that is 165 yards wide at its narrowest point (it also leaves you far back on the fairway with a long approach shot) or you can hug the water bordering the left side of the fairway, a shot calling for a carry of approximately 250 yards. A lot of great golfers have tried this and left their ball in the drink. The best shot is a right-to-left shot, but if you push your drive, you can take as much as a seven on this hole. Depending on where you have landed, you can take anything from a No. 2 to a No. 7 iron for your approach. In any event, the hole dog-legs slightly left to a green contoured over Bermuda grass, naturally.

Hole 12: The Eighth at Troon Golf Club, Troon, Scotland, Par 3, 125 Yards. This is the famed "Postage Stamp" hole, because of the size of the green. It is an accurate description. What faces you when you stand on the tee is a long, narrow green, with a high mound guarding the left side and a deep drop into a bunker on the right. Depending on how the wind is blowing, you can use anything from a pitching wedge to a No. 6 iron here. The trick is to land on the green and to hold. Otherwise, you might wind up having a game of ping-pong. If you hit the mound, your ball is very likely to run off the other end into the bunker. Blasting out, you can again hit the mound and come back.

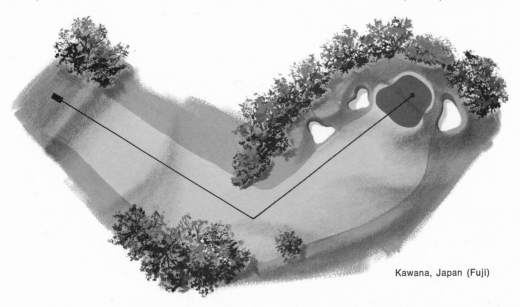

Kawana, Japan (Fuji)

Hole 13: The Eleventh at Fuji Country Club, Kawana, Ito, Japan, Par 5, 550 Yards. The tee on this hole was named the Eisenhower Tee when they played the World Amateur Golf Team Championship here back in 1962. It is a high hilltop tee overlooking a fairway that swings sharply to the left. Although some sluggers try it, and sometimes make it, there is really no point in attempting to shave the dog-leg. The best route is toward a single pine tree straight ahead in the fairway below, about 280 yards away. It is possible to reach the green with a wood, but even if you do not, you are left with a little pitch. The green is two-level, so when the pin is in the raised rear part, it can very easily turn into a three-putt green for you.

Hole 14: The Fourteenth at Portmarnock Golf Club, Portmarnock, Ireland, Par 4, 385 Yards. Known as "Ireland's Eye," this hole plays across flat terrain into a fairway that bends sharply to the left about 240 yards out. Tall, marshy grass that reaches up to your kneecaps guards both sides of the fairway, and if you land in it, it is like trying to chop your way out of straw. If you try to take the

Portmarnock, Ireland (Portmarnock)

Turnberry

short route by cutting off the dog-leg, you will be faced with a difficult second shot because there is a bunker to carry just short of the green. A wedge can get you home if you hit a perfectly placed drive here. But if you take the long way by hitting out to the right, you have a relatively clear shot to the green —with a longer club, of course. It is slightly uphill to a real small, exposed green that pitches from back to front. The approach is made even tougher because there is no background behind the green to help you judge the distance. Henry Cotton calls this the finest par-4 in the British Isles.

Hole 15: The Ninth at Turnberry Hotel Golf (Ailsa) Course, Turnberry, Scotland, Par 4, 475 Yards. To many experts, this is the toughest par-4 in the world. Your drive has to carry 200 yards over a rocky inlet, with water below and a stiff wind hitting you in the face. The fairway off in the distance is camel-backed, and for your second shot you usually have to play as much as a No. 4 or No. 5 iron. The green is small and slopes away from you, so you really have to make your approach shot bite. The undulations in the green make it even more perilous.

Hole 16: The Eighth at Banff Springs, Hotel Golf Course, Banff, Canada, Par 3, 175

Yards. They call this hole "The Devil's Cauldron" because of the twisting winds that blow off the elevated tee overlooking the lake you must carry. About a No. 5 iron should get you across, but you are hitting to a tiny green, and you have to be careful of the wind. There is a slope on opposite sides of the green. This hole proves that you do not have to have 260-yard par-3's to make a great hole.

Hole 17: The Seventeenth at Royal and Ancient Golf Club of St. Andrews, St. Andrews, Scotland, Par 4, 453 Yards. This is the famous "Road Hole," which wind and the terrain have made into a par-4½. It has cost many a golfer a championship. Getting your par calls for hitting a perfect tee shot; if you try to play it safe, it will put great pressure on your second shot. If you are in good position, you can get home with a No. 5 or No. 6 iron, but you have to guard against hitting over the green. There is nothing but gravel behind, and if you wind up there, you are in deep trouble. No, this is one hole you cannot play safe. That is what makes a great hole.

Hole 18: The Eighteenth at Capilano Golf and Country Club, Vancouver, Canada, Par 5, 575 Yards. Distance and a tricky 45-degree dog-leg right to an elevated green are what make this hole so fascinating and challenging.

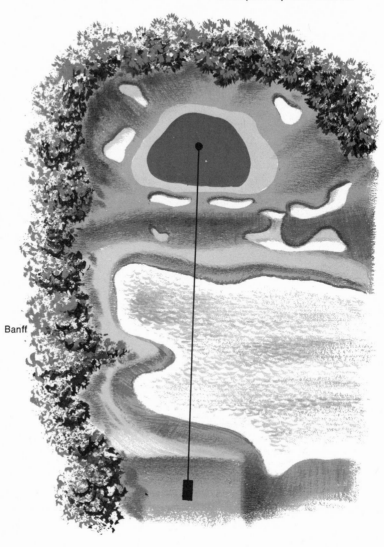

Banff

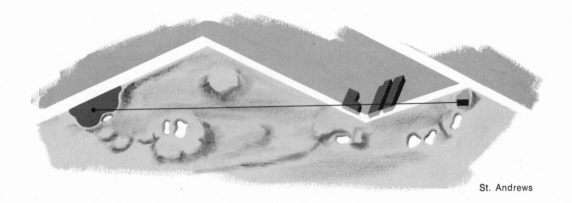

St. Andrews

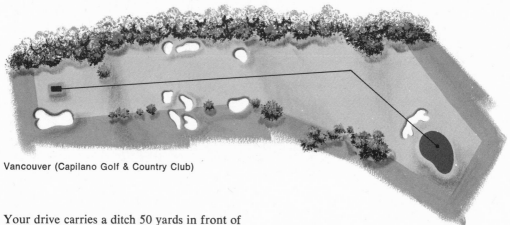

Vancouver (Capilano Golf & Country Club)

Your drive carries a ditch 50 yards in front of the tee to a fairway lined left and right by bunkers. The best thing here is to keep the ball out in the center. A No. 3 wood should lay it up close enough for a short pitch to the green. But you have to be careful of trees on the right at the point of the dog-leg and a rockery which guards the right side of the green and is out of bounds. Three sprawling bunkers protect the front.

The second nine is par 36, 3,637 yards. Total is par 72, 7,094 yards.

GOLF RESORTS

United States

For the golfer who is searching for new courses to conquer, there are unlimited opportunities on the fairways of the United States. As was stated in Section I, there are over ten thousand regulation golf courses in the United States, and every year the number increases by approximately 125. Thus this country is the land where golf flourishes in all its glory.

In the following listing, you will find the leading and most interesting resort, public, and semiprivate courses in the United States. Strictly private clubs have been omitted from this directory for obvious reasons. The costs of green fees and course range greatly. It is a good thing to write to the local Chambers of Commerce of cities and state travel department of areas you plan to visit. Your local travel bureau will also be of great assistance in planning golf vacations.

Course	Location	Par	Yard-age
Alabama			
Alabama International CC	Talladega	71	6,646
		71	6,682
Grand Hotel	Point Clear	35	3,171
		35	3,246
		36	3,177
Gulf State Park Resort	Gulf Shores	72	6,822
Jetport GC	Huntsville	72	6,470
Joe Wheeler Resort	Rogersville	72	7,200
Lake Forest	Daphne	72	6,700
Lakepoint Resort GC	Eufaula	72	7,026
Lakewood GC	Point Clear	70	6,417
		35	3,119
Langan Park GC	Mobile	72	6,383
Olympia Spa Golf & CC	Dothan	72	7,318
Pin Oaks GC	Auburn	72	6,018

Course	Location	Par	Yard-age
Point Aquarius Hotel & CC	Alpine	72	6,274
		72	6,296
Point Mallard GC	Decatur	72	7,113
Still Waters	Dadeville	72	6,513
Alaska			

There are only three public courses in Alaska, two of which are military, located in Fairbanks and Anchorage. The Million Dollar Golf Course is operated on City of Juneau land by the Juneau Sandblasters Golf Club and is open to guests. Holes, 9; par, 32; yardage, 2,300.

Course	Location	Par	Yard-age
Arizona			
Antelope Hills GC	Prescott	72	6,750
Apache Wells	Mesa	70	5,717

Course	Location	Par	Yard-age
Arizona Biltmore	Phoenix	72	6,783
		35	3,022
Boulders GC	Carefree	72	6,148
Camelback Inn & CC	Scottsdale	72	6,140
Century CC	Scottsdale	72	6,438
Desert Forest GC	Carefree	72	6,543
El Rio GC	Tucson	70	6,013
Encanto GC	Phoenix	70	6,245
Fountain Hills GC	Fountain Hills	71	5,600
Golden Hills CC	Mesa	71	6,540
Kino Springs	Nogales	72	6,002
Lake Havasu G & CC	Lake Havasu	72	6,382
		36	3,133
Maryvale GC	Phoenix	72	6,223
McCormick Ranch GC	Scottsdale	72	7,000
		72	7,000
Mesa CC	Mesa	72	6,750
Moon Valley CC	Phoenix	72	6,600
Mountain Shadows	Scottsdale	56	3,000
Papago Park GC	Phoenix	72	6,628
Pima Golf Resort	Scottsdale	72	7,000
San Marcos Resort & CC	Chandler	72	7,175
Scottsdale CC	Scottsdale	70	6,200
Sierra Estrella GC	Goodyear	71	6,370
Skyline Resort & CC	Tucson	70	6,400
Sun City (Del Webb's)	Sun City	—	—
Thunderbird CC	Phoenix	71	6,375
Valley CC	Scottsdale	72	6,150
The Wigwam	Litchfield Park	72	7,220

Arkansas

Course	Location	Par	Yard-age
Arlington Hotel	Hot Springs	72	6,828
		72	6,799
		34	2,929
Belvedere CC	Hot Springs	72	6,685
Cherokee Village	Cherokee Village	72	7,045
		72	6,775
Dawn Hill CC	Siloam Springs	72	6,880
Diamondhead	Hot Springs National Park	72	6,900
Eden Isle GC	Heber Springs	36	3,376
Hot Springs G & CC	Hot Springs	72	6,828
		72	6,799
Hot Springs Village CC	Hot Springs	72	6,770
Paradise Valley GC	Fayetteville	71	6,503
Rebsamen Park GC	Little Rock	71	6,207
Red Apple Inn & CC	Heber Springs	36	3,363

California

Course	Location	Par	Yard-age
Alameda GC	Alameda	71	6,417
Alisal	Solvang	72	6,400
Alondra Park CC	Lawndale	72	6,200
Anaheim Hills Public CC	Anaheim	72	5,939
Apple Valley Inn	Apple Valley	71	6,804
Brookside GC	Pasadena	72	6,611
		70	5,429
Canyon Racquet & Golf Resort	Palm Springs	71	6,700
Carlton Oaks GC & Lodge	Santee	72	—

Course	Location	Par	Yard-age
Catalina Island GC	Avalon	64	—
Cathedral Canyon	Palm Springs	72	6,700
Circle R Resort	Escondido	71	6,300
Corona National GC	Corona	72	6,463
Costa Mesa GC	Costa Mesa	71	6,118
		70	5,005
Cottonwood CC	El Cajon	73	6,719
		72	6,037
Del Monte GC	Monterey	72	6,200
Del Monte House	Monterey	72	6,200
Del Monte Lodge	Pebble Beach	72	6,806
Del Safari CC	Palm Desert	72	7,106
Desert Air CC	Palm Desert	72	6,398
Fallbrook G & CC	Fallbrook	72	6,169
Half Moon Bay Golf Links	Half Moon Bay	72	7,105
Harding Municipal GC	Los Angeles	71	6,340
Harding Park GC	San Francisco	72	6,651
		32	2,500
Hesperia CC & Golf Resort	Hesperia	72	7,000
Ironwood CC	Palm Desert	72	7,150
La Costa & Spa	Carlsbad	72	6,835
Laguna Seca Golf Ranch	Monterey	71	6,380
Lake Cabot GC	Oakland	72	6,180
Lake Shastina Golf & CC	Weed	72	6,600
Las Positas GC	Livermore	72	6,590
Lew F. Galbraith GC	Oakland	72	6,312
Les Robles Greens GC	Thousand Oaks	70	6,400
Massacre Canyon Inn & Golf Resort	Gilman Hot Springs	36	3,294
		36	3,397
		36	2,885
Master Hosts Inn, Stardust CC	San Diego	72	6,587
Mission Hills G & CC	Rancho Mirage	72	6,454
Mission Lakes	Desert Hot Springs		7,100
Murrieta Hot Springs Hotel & CC & Spa	Murietta	72	6,901
Navajo Canyon CC	San Diego	71	6,000
Ojai Valley Inn & CC	Ojai	70	6,800
Pala Mesa Golf & Tennis Resort	Fallbrook	72	6,461
Palm Desert CC	Palm Desert	72	6,800
Palo Alto Municipal GC	Palo Alto	72	6,439
Pasatiempo GC	Santa Cruz	71	6,281
Peacock Gap CC	San Rafael	71	6,369
Pebble Beach GC	Pebble Beach	72	6,806
Pleasant Hills GC	San Jose	72	6,950
		54	2,900
Quail Lodge at the Carmel Valley Golf & CC	Carmel	72	6,756
Rancho Bernardo Inn	San Diego	71	6,460
Rancho California Golf Resort	Temecula	72	6,800
Rancho Canada GC	Carmel	72	6,613
		71	6,401
Rancho Murietta CC	Sloughhouse	72	6,997

The burn that makes the old Prestwick links a real championship test is seen here with a typical sand bunker in the rear. Several of Prestwick's bunkers are bolstered up with railroad ties. They help keep the sand in its place.

Course	Location	Par	Yard-age
Rancho Park GC	Los Angeles	71	6,600
Rancho Santa Fe	Rancho Santa Fe	72	6,660
Recreation Park GC	Long Beach	72	6,457
Ridgemark	Hollister	72	6,500
Salinas Fairways GC	Salinas	72	6,555
San Bernadino Public GC	San Bernadino	71	6,100
San Diego Country Estates	Romona	72	6,630
Sandpiper GC	Goleta	72	6,977
San Jose Municipal GC	San Jose	72	6,450
San Luis Bay Inn & GC	Avila Beach	71	6,341
San Vicente CC	Romona	72	6,630
Seven Hills GC	Hemet	72	6,326
Silverado CC & Resort	Napa	72	6,680
		72	6,562
Singing Hills CC & Lodge	El Cajon	73	6,800
		72	6,400
		61	4,200
Soboba Springs CC	San Jacinto	72	6,726
Spyglass Hill GC	Pebble Beach	72	6,810
Stallion Springs– Horsethief G & CC	Tehachapi	72	6,559
Sunnyvale Municipal GC	Sunnyvale	70	6,406
Sunol Valley GC	Sunol	72	6,681
		72	5,819
Torrey Pines GC	La Jolla	72	6,317
		72	6,649

Course	Location	Par	Yard-age
Valencia GC	Valencia	73	6,801
Walnut Creek GC	Walnut Creek	72	7,000
Warner's Golf Resort	Warner Springs	72	6,345
Western Avenue GC	Los Angeles	70	6,084
Westward Ho	Indio	72	6,666
Whispering Palms CC & Lodge	Rancho Santa Fe	36	3,270
		36	3,177
		35	2,194
Wilson Municipal GC	Los Angeles	72	6,945
Colorado			
The Broadmoor	Colorado Springs	72	6,550
		72	7,036
		72	6,935
Cimarron Hills GC	Colorado Springs	72	7,072
Eagle Vail GC	Vail	72	6,800
Heather Ridge CC	Denver	70	5,896
		32	2,230
Hiwan GC	Evergreen	71	7,142
Pagosa Pines GC	Pagosa Springs	36	3,694
Snowmass	Snowmass Resort	71	7,029
Stramboat Village Inn and CC	Steamboat Springs	72	6,925
Tamarron	Durango	72	7,000
Vail	Vail	71	7,004
Winter Park Resort	Winter Park	—	—

Course	Location	Par	Yard-age
Connecticut			
Lyman Meadow GC	Middlefield	72	6,319
Norwich Inn GC	Norwich	71	6,320
Shennecossett CC	Groton	72	6,128
Tunxis Plantation CC	Farmington	36	3,250
		36	3,250
		36	3,250
Florida			
Alhambra Golf & Tennis Club	Orlando	72	6,600
Amelia Island Plantation	Amelia Island	36	2,942
		35	2,738
		35	2,572
Arrowhead CC	Ft. Lauderdale	71	6,190
Atlantis CC	Lantana	72	6,534
Babe Zaharias GC	Tampa	71	6,142
Bardmoor	St. Petersburg	70	6,200
		71	6,600
		72	7,100
Bay Hill Lodge & CC	Orlando	72	7,092
		36	2,957
Bay Point Yacht & CC	Panama City	33	2,960
		72	6,913
Bay Shore GC	Miami Beach	72	6,985
The Beach Club Hotel	N. Naples	72	6,500
Belleview Biltmore Hotel	Clearwater	71	6,338
		72	6,350
Biltmore GC	Coral Gables	71	6,173
Bobby Jones GC	Sarasota	72	6,388
		72	6,080
Boca del Mar Golf & Tennis Club	Boca Raton	71	6,600
		70	6,000
Boca Lago Golf & Racquet Club	Boca Raton	72	6,400
		70	6,000
Boca Raton Hotel	Boca Raton	—	—
Boca Rio GC	Boca Raton	72	6,508
Boca Teeca CC	Boca Raton	35	3,070
		37	3,573
		36	3,077
Boca West	Boca Raton	72	7,085
		72	6,574
		72	6,805
Bonaventure CC	Ft. Lauderdale	72	6,952
The Breakers	Palm Beach	70	6,008
		71	6,388
Briar Bay	Miami	31	2,000
The Bridge Hotel	Boca Raton	—	—
Burnt Store GC	Punta Gorda	72	6,364
Cape Coral Golf & Racquet Club, Cape Coral CC Inn	Cape Coral	72	6,865
Carlton House Resort Hotel	Orlando	—	—
Clearwater CC	Clearwater	72	6,100
Clearwater Golf Park	Clearwater	63	4,282
Cocoa Beach Golf Club	Cocoa Beach	72	6,700
Colony West CC	Tamarac	72	6,610
Conquistador Bay CC	Bradenton	72	6,400
Continental CC	Wildwood	72	6,200
Costa Del Sol G & CC	Ft. Pierce	72	6,240

Course	Location	Par	Yard-age
Costa Del Sol Golf & Racquet	Miami	72	5,931
Countryside CC	Clearwater	72	6,511
Cove Cay G & TC	Clearwater	70	5,693
Crystal Lago GC	Pompano Beach	72	6,730
Cypress Creek CC	Boynton Beach	72	6,880
Cypress Creek Golf & Tennis Club	Orlando	72	7,006
Cypress Lake CC	Ft. Myers	72	6,362
Days Lodge of Orlando	Alamonte Springs	—	—
Daytona Beach G & CC	Daytona Beach	72	6,080
		71	5,950
Deer Creek CC	Deerfield Beach	72	6,439
Delray Beach CC	Delray Beach	72	6,987
		36	3,270
Deltona G & CC	Deltona	72	6,917
Diplomat Resort & CC	Hollywood by the Sea	72	6,964
		72	6,702
Dodger Pines CC	Vero Beach	73	6,209
Doral Hotel & CC	Miami	71	7,258
		71	6,480
		72	6,726
		72	7,065
Dunedin CC	Dunedin	72	6,292
Dutch Inn Resort Hotel	Lake Buena Vista	72	6,540
Eastpointe CC	Rivera Beach	73	6,450
Errol Estate G & CC	Apopka	108	9,595
Fontainebleau CC	Miami	72	6,800
Fort Myers CC	Ft. Myers	71	6,105
Fountains Golf & Racquet Club	Lake Worth	—	—
Foxcroft Golf & Tennis Club	Miramar	72	6,511
Frenchman's Creek	N. Palm Beach	70	6,130
		72	6,406
Golden Gate Inn	Naples	72	6,602
Golf Hammock CC	Sebring	72	6,774
Grand Bahama Hotel & CC	West Palm Beach	72	6,800
		36	3,600
Grenelefe Golf & Racquet Club, A. Radisson Resort	Cypress Gardens	72	7,325
The Hamlet	Delray Beach	72	6,208
Harbor City Municipal CC	Melbourne	72	6,400
Harder Hall Golf & Tennis Resort	Sebring	72	6,850
Hidden Valley GC	Miami	60	3,800
Holiday Inn of Fort Walton Beach	Ft. Walton Beach	—	—
Holiday Inn–Hollywood Lakes CC	Hollywood	72	6,659
		72	6,579
Holiday Springs	Margate	72	6,324
Holiday Springs Village, Holiday Springs GC	Margate	72	6,940
Hollywood G & CC	Hollywood	70	6,500
Hollywood Lakes CC	Hollywood	72	6,238
		72	6,160

The old Miami Biltmore in its heyday was typical of the opulence associated with golf.

Course	Location	Par	Yard-age
Hotel Royal Plaza	Orlando	—	—
Howard Johnson's at Florida Center	Orlando	—	—
Indian Rocks GC	Largo	62	6,166
Indian Spring CC	Boynton Beach	72	6,635
Indigo Golf & Tennis Resort	Daytona Beach	72	6,849
The Inn at Sandestin	Destin	72	6,782
The Inn on the Beach	Daytona Beach	72	6,858
Innisbrook Resort	Tarpon Springs	70	6,087
		36	3,588
		35	3,443
		36	3,393
Isla Del Sol G & CC	St. Petersburg	71	6,105
Jacaranda CC	Plantation	72	7,355
		72	6,680
Jacksonville Beach	Jacksonville Beach	72	6,700
Jacksonville Beach GC	Jacksonville Beach	72	6,270
Kendal Lakes G & CC	Miami	72	6,335
		36	3,188
Key Biscayne GC	Key Biscayne	72	6,212
Killearn G & CC	Tallahassee	72	6,336

Course	Location	Par	Yard-age
King's Inn Golf & Racquet Club	Sun City Center	72	6,704
Lago Mar Hotel	Ft. Lauderdale	72	6,800
Land O'Lakes Golf & CC	Casselberry	70	6,001
Lehigh CC	Lehigh	72	6,498
Leisure Village at Seven Lakes	Ft. Myers	60	3,597
Lely G & CC	Naples	72	6,201
Lochmoor CC	N. Ft. Myers	72	6,492
Longboat Golf & Tennis Club	Sarasota	72	6,158
Magnolia Valley CC	New Port Richey	70	6,011
Marco Beach Hotel & Villas	Marco Island	72	6,976
		72	6,691
Martin County G & CC	Stuart	72	6,305
Mayfair CC	Sanford	72	6,480
The Meadows	Sarasota	72	7,073
Melreese le Jeune GC	Miami	72	6,452
Miami Lakes Inn & CC	Miami Lakes	72	7,059
Miami Springs G & CC	Miami Springs	72	6,900
Mirror Lakes CC	Lehigh Acres	72	7,100
Mission Inn & CC	Howey in the Hills	72	6,640

Course	Location	Par	Yardage
Mission Valley G & CC	Venice	72	6,438
The Moorings Golf & Tennis Club	Vero Beach	63	4,440
Normandy Shores GC	Miami Beach	71	6,055
Oak Ridge CC	Ft. Lauderdale	72	6,264
Oak Ridge G & CC	Dunedin	72	6,292
Palm-Aire at Sarasota	Sarasota	72	6,487
Palm Beach Lakes GC, Ramada Inn on the Green	W. Palm Beach	68	5,500
Palm Beach Nat'l G & CC	Lake Worth	72	6,400
Palm Coast GC, Sheraton Palm Coast Resort Inn	W. Palm Beach	68	5,500
Palm River CC	Naples	72	6,421
Palma Sola GC	Palma Sola	71	6,352
Palmetto GC	South Miami	71	6,669
Pasadena GC	St. Petersburg	72	6,132
Perdido Bay Inn CC	Pensacola	72	6,871
Placid Lakes Inn & CC	Lake Placid	72	6,802
Plantation GC	Ft. Lauderdale	72	6,424
Plantation Inn	Crystal River	72	6,838
Poinciana Golf & Racquet Club	Kissimmee	72	6,700
Pompano Beach CC	Pompano Beach	71	6,150
		72	6,527
Ponce de Leon Lodge & CC	St. Augustine	71	6,226
Port Charlotte CC	Port Charlotte	72	6,900
CC of Port Charlotte	N. Port Charlotte	72	6,266
Port Malabar CC	Palm Bay	71	6,708
Punta Gorda	Punta Gorda	72	6,200
Quail Hollow GC	Tampa	72	6,100
Quail Ridge	Delray Beach	71	6,300
Quality Inn West	Orlando	—	—
Red Carpet International	Orlando	—	—
Redlands G & CC	Homestead	72	6,302
Riverside Villas	Homosassa	—	—
Riviera G & CC	Ormond Beach	71	6,308
Rocky Point GC	Tampa	72	6,122
		32	2,456
Rodeway Inn	Orlando	—	—
Rogers Park GC	Tampa	71	6,677
Rolling Hills G & CC	Wildwood	72	6,043
Rolling Hills Golf & Tennis Club	Ft. Lauderdale	72	7,122
Rosemont G & CC	Orlando	72	6,142
Rotunda West CC	Rotunda West	72	6,622
Royal Oak CC & Resort	Titusville	71	6,880
Royal Palm Beach Golf & CC	Royal Palm Beach	72	7,200
		72	7,200
San Carlos Golf & CC	San Carlos Park	72	6,815
Sandalfoot Cove CC	Boca Raton	72	6,841
Sandpiper Bay Resort	Port St. Lucie	72	6,587
Santa Rose Shores CC	Gulf Breeze	72	7,140
Sarasota GC Inc.	Sarasota	72	6,621
Sawgrass	Ponte Vedra Beach	72	6,500
Seascape Golf & Racquet Club	Destin	72	6,150
1776 Resort Inn	Orlando	—	—
Sheoah GC	Winter Springs	71	6,298
Sheraton Homosassa Springs Inn	Homosassa Springs	—	—
Silver Springs Shores Resort & CC	Ocala	72	7,050
South Seas Plantation	Captive Island	36	3,021
Spruce Creek GC	Daytona Beach	72	6,650
Sugar Mill CC & Estates	New Smyrna Beach	72	7,003
Sun City Center	Sun City Center	72	6,700
		72	6,800
Sun N Lake of Sebring	Lake Placid	72	7,001
Sunrise CC	Ft. Lauderdale	72	6,750
Sunrise National GC	Sarasota	72	6,098
Sunset GC	St. Petersburg	72	6,250
Tampa Air Resort Golf & Racquet Club	Tampa	72	6,704
Tarpon Springs GC	Tarpon Springs	72	6,445
Tarpon Woods Golf & Tennis Club	Palm Harbor	72	—
Tides Hotel & Bath Club	Redington Beach	72	6,285
Tomoka Oaks Golf & CC	Ormond Beach	72	6,725
Travel Lodge Tower	Lake Buena Vista	72	6,540
Turtle Creek C	Tequesta	72	6,550
Tuscawilla GC	Winter Springs	72	6,360
The Village of Royal Palm Beach	W. Palm Beach	72	6,600
		72	6,600
Vista Royale GC	Vero Beach	70	6,200
Walt Disney World Golf Resort	Lake Buena Vista	72	6,577
		72	6,540
West Palm Beach CC	W. Palm Beach	72	6,675
Wilderness CC	Naples	71	6,200
Wildwood CC	Wildwood	72	6,200
Williston Highlands	Williston	72	6,304
The Woodlands CC	Pompano Beach	72	6,487
		72	6,285
Woodmont	Tamarac	70	5,400
		72	6,747
World of Palm-Aire	N. Pompano Beach	72	6,773
		71	6,774
		72	6,526
		72	7,064
		60	3,619
Zellwood Station	Zellwood	72	6,900

Georgia

Course	Location	Par	Yardage
Bacon Park GC	Savannah	71	6,318
Big Canoe	Big Canoe	72	6,043
Browns Mill	Atlanta	72	6,535
Callaway Gardens	Pine Mountain	72	7,040
		72	6,392
		70	6,006
		31	2,096

Course	Location	Par	Yard-age
Chattahoochee GC	Gainesville	72	6,343
The Cloister,	Sea Island	72	6,876
Sea Island		72	6,591
Francis Lake CC	Valdosta	72	6,766
Island Club	St. Simons		
	Island	72	—
Jekyll Island GC	Brunswick	72	6,261
King & Prince Beach	St. Simons		
Hotel	Island	72	6,214
Kingswood CC	Clayton	70	5,348
Pine Isle Resort Hotel	Buford	72	6,500
Savannah Inn & CC	Savannah	72	7,100
Sea Palms Golf &	St. Simons		
Racquet Club	Island	72	6,781
Snapfinger GC	Atlanta	72	6,400
Stone Mountain Park	Stone Mountain	72	6,831
GC			

Hawaii

Course	Location	Par	Yard-age
Ala Wai GC	Honalulu	71	6,281
Hawaii Country Club	Kunia	71	5,601
Hawaii Kai GC	Honolulu	72	6,562
Hilo Municipal GC	Hilo	72	6,270
Kapa Lua (The Golf	Maui	72	6,831
Club at)		72	6,145
		72	5,520
Kauai Surf Golf & CC	Kauai	72	6,808
Keauhou Kona CC	Kailua-Kona	72	6,814
Kona Surf Resort	Kailua-Kona	72	6,814
Kuilima Hyatt Resort	Oahu	72	6,383
Hotel			
Makaha Inn & CC	Waianee	72	7,250
Makaha Valley Towers	Waianee	72	6,427
Ted Makalena	Waipahu	71	6,296
Maui Surf	Lahaina	72	6,336
		64	4,300
Mauna Kea Beach Hotel	Kamuela	72	7,000
Naniloa Surf	Hilo	35	2,745
Olomana Golf Links	Oahu	71	6,000
Pali Golf Course	Oahu	72	6,493
Pearl CC of Hawaii	Aiea	72	6,481
Princebille of Hanalei	Hanalei	36	3,460
		36	3,436
		36	3,488
Royal Kaanapali GC	Maui	72	6,305
		72	6,250
Seamountain Ninole GC	Pahala	72	6,492
Sheraton-Maui Hotel	Lahaina	—	—
Sheraton Molokai	W. Molokai	72	6,200
Uplands Golf Club	Victoria	70	6,228
Volcano GC	Hilo	72	6,219
Waikoloa Village GC	Kamuela	72	6,850
Waiehu GC	Waiehu	72	6,565
Wailea	Maui	72	6,700
Wailua GC	Kauai	72	6,665

Idaho

Course	Location	Par	Yard-age
Avondale on Hayden	Coeur d'Alene	72	6,328
Lake GC			
Bigwood	Sun Valley	36	3,300
Elkhorn Golf Resort	Sun Valley	72	7,200

Course	Location	Par	Yard-age
Highlands GC	Pocatello	72	6,435
McCall Municipal GC	McCall	70	6,026
Pinecrest Municipal GC	Idaho Falls	72	6,430
Purple Sage GC	Caldwell	71	6,564
Sun Valley	Sun Valley	69	6,300
		72	7,200

Illinois

Course	Location	Par	Yard-age
Cog Hill G & CC	Lemont	72	6,332
		72	6,341
		72	6,431
		72	6,540
Galena Territory	Galena	72	6,527
Macktown GC	Rockton	72	5,935
Marriott's Lincolnshire	Lincolnshire	71	6,600
Resort			
Nordic Hills CC	Itasca	71	6,114
Pheasant Run Lodge	St. Charles	68	6,043

Indiana

Course	Location	Par	Yard-age
Christmas Lake G & CC	Santa Claus	72	6,500
French Lick–Sheraton	French Lick	71	6,800
Hotel & Resort		71	6,100

Kentucky

Course	Location	Par	Yard-age
General Burnside State	Burnside	71	5,905
Park			
Lake Barkley State	Cadiz	72	6,405
Resort Park (Boots			
Randolph GC)			

Maine

Course	Location	Par	Yard-age
Bethel Inn GC	Bethel	36	3,069
Kebo Valley C	Bar Harbor	70	6,209
Poland Spring GC	Poland Spring	71	6,464
Shawmut Inn	Kennebunkport	—	—
Webhannet GC	Kennebunk		
	Beach	70	6,200
York Golf & Tennis	York Harbor	70	6,203
Club			

Maryland

Course	Location	Par	Yard-age
Dwight D. Eisenhower	Annapolis	71	6,320
GC			
Hunt Valley Inn & GC	Hunt Valley	72	6,588
Martingham GC	St. Michaels	70	5,948
Needwood GC	Rockville	71	6,400
Northwest Park GC	Wheaton	72	7,320
Ocean Pines G & CC	Ocean City	72	6,391
Pine Ridge GC	Lutherville	72	6,449
Washington GC	Gaithersburg	72	6,400
		70	6,640

Massachusetts

Course	Location	Par	Yard-age
Bass River GC	S. Yarmouth	72	6,000
Chatham Bars Inn	Chatham	34	2,325
Clauson's Inn & Golf	N. Falmouth	72	6,593
Resort			
Cranberry Valley GC	Harwich	72	6,400
Dennis Pines GC	Dennis	72	6,500
The Dunfey Family's	Hyannis	—	—
Hyannis Resort			

The short par-3, 8th hole at the Mountain Shadows Golf Club in Arizona.

Course	Location	Par	Yardage
Falmouth CC	Falmouth	72	6,400
The Inn & CC of New Seabury	New Seabury	72	7,175
The Island CC	Martha's Vineyard	70	6,018
Jug End	S. Egremont	67	5,080
Pleasant Valley CC	Sutton	72	6,857
Pocasset GC	Pocasset	72	6,300
Sea Crest Motel & Motor Inn	N. Falmouth	—	—
Trull Brook GC	Tewkesbury	72	6,275

Michigan

Course	Location	Par	Yardage
Bay Valley GC	Bay City	71	6,600
Boyne Highlands GC	Harbor Springs	71	7,200
		72	7,200
Boyne Mt. Alpine CC	Boyne Falls	72	7,181
Kingdom of Schuss	Mancelona	36	3,230
McGuire's Motor Lodge & Resort	Cadillac	72	6,010
Michaywe Hills GC	Gaylord	72	6,467
Shanty Creek Lodge	Bellaire	72	6,197
White Deer CC	Prudenville	72	6,428

Minnesota

Course	Location	Par	Yardage
Bemidji Town & CC	Bemidji	72	6,278
Coon Rapids– Bunkerhill GC	Coon Rapids	72	6,600
Enger Park GC	Duluth	72	6,105
Gross GC	Minneapolis	71	6,343
Keller GC	St. Paul	72	6,557
Madden Resorts at Gull Lake	Brainerd	72	5,920
		67	5,028
		28	1,341
Maple Valley G & CC	Rochester	72	6,975
Meadowbrook GC	Hopkins	72	6,474
Sundance G & CC	Osseo	71	6,489

Mississippi

Course	Location	Par	Yardage
Biloxi Hilton Resort & Convention Center	Biloxi	71	6,500
Broadwater Beach Hotel & GC	Biloxi	71	6,000
Diamondhead Yacht & Country Club	Louis	36	3,388
		36	3,430
		36	3,410
Gulf Hills Inn & GC	Ocean Springs	72	6,294
Hickory Hill CC	Pascagoula	72	7,049
Howard Johnsons	Biloxi	72	6,424
		72	6,202
		72	6,314
		71	6,285
		72	6,500
		72	7,049
Marsh Islands GC	Ocean Springs	71	6,285

Course	Location	Par	Yard-age
Pass Christian Isles GC	Pass Christian Isles	72	6,424
Pete Fountain's Buena Vista Hotel & Motel	Biloxi	—	—
Rodeway Inn	Biloxi	—	—
St. Andrew's Golf & CC	Ocean Springs	72	6,449
Sheraton Motor Inn	Gulfport	72	6,780
Sunkist	Biloxi	72	6,579
Tramark GC	Gulfport	72	6,045
Missouri			
Chapel Woods GC	Lee's Summit	72	6,306
Dogwood Hills GC	Osage Beach	71	5,986
Howard Johnsons Motor Lodge	Lake Ozark	71	6,200
Lake Valley G & CC	Camdenton	70	6,041
Lodge of the Four Seasons Spa & Golf Resort	Lake Ozark	71	6,607
Shamrock Hills GC	Lee's Summit	71	6,100
Tan-Tar-A Golf & Tennis Resort	Lake of the Ozarks	35	2,842
Montana			
Big Sky	Big Sky	72	6,725
Glacier View GC	West Glacier	68	5,200
Whitefish Lake GC	Whitefish	72	—
Nevada			
Black Mountain G & CC	Henderson	72	6,397
Brookside GC	Reno	70	6,500
Graig Ranch CC	Las Vegas	70	6,138
Desert Inn & CC	Las Vegas	72	7,089
Dunes Hotel & CC	Las Vegas	72	7,240
Edgewood Tahoe GC	Lake Tahoe	72	7,546
Fairway-to-the-Stars	Las Vegas	70	6,335
Incline GC	Incline Village	58	3,440
Lake Ridge GC	Reno	72	6,352
Las Vegas GC	Las Vegas	72	6,325
Paradise Valley CC	Las Vegas	72	6,568
Reno Brookside GC	Reno	72	6,295
Hotel Sahara	Las Vegas	71	6,800
Sierra Sage GC	Reno	72	6,250
Spring Creek GC	Elko	72	6,536
Tropicana Hotel	Las Vegas	70	6,647
Washoe County GC	Reno	72	6,600
Winterwood GC	Las Vegas	71	6,427
New Hampshire			
Bald Peak Colony C	Melvin Village	72	6,211
Balsams Hotel & CC	Dixiville Notch	72	6,800
		32	2,100
Chase Sport Resort	Bethlehem	72	6,300
Crawford House GC	Crawford Notch	35	3,400
Five Chimneys Golf & Tennis Resort	Province Lake	37	6,600
Jack O'Lantern Resort	Woodstock	35	3,010
Lake Sunapee CC Inc.	New London	71	6,600
Mount Washington Hotel	Bretton Woods	71	6,200

Course	Location	Par	Yard-age
Mountain View House	Whitefield	70	5,807
Pleasant Valley CC	Sutton	72	6,857
Waterville Valley Golf & Tennis	Waterville Valley	32	2,407
Waumbek Inn & CC	Jefferson	71	6,001
Wentworth by the Sea	Portsmouth	70	6,100
Whitemountain CC	Ashland	71	6,700
New Jersey			
Atlantis CC	Tuckerton	72	6,575
Forsgate CC	Jamesburg	72	6,620
		71	6,401
Playboy Resort & CC at Gt. Gorge	McAfee	35	3,457
New Mexico			
Angel Fire CC	Angel Fire	72	6,401
Inn of the Mountain Gods	Mescalero	72	6,352
Paradise Hills CC	Albuquerque	72	7,200
Rio Rancho G & CC	Albuquerque	72	6,600
New York			
Bergen Point GC	Bergen Point	72	7,030
Concord Hotel	Kiamesha Lake	72	7,672
		71	6,500
		31	2,200
Dyker Beach GC	Brooklyn	71	6,502
Grossinger Hotel & CC	Grossinger	71	6,780
		36	3,240
Kutshers CC	Monticello	72	7,157
Lochmor GC	Sheldrake	71	6,470
Montauk Golf & Racquet Club	Montauk	72	6,860
Nevele CC	Ellenville	71	6,600
Otesaga Hotel	Cooperstown	72	6,554
Peek 'N Peak Resort GC	Clymer	72	6,475
Ransom Oaks CC	Amherst	72	6,315
River Oaks GC	Grand Island	72	7,200
Riverton GC	Henrietta	72	6,800
Sagamore GC	Bolton Landing	72	6,400
Saratoga Spa GC	Saratoga Springs	72	6,319
7 Keys GC	Loon Lake	70	5,600
Stevensville	Swan Lake	71	6,980
Tarry Brae GC	S. Fallsburg	72	6,615
Tennanah Lake Golf & Tennis Club	Roscoe	72	6,700
Thousand Islands Club Resort	Alexandria Bay	72	6,452
Whiteface Inn GC	Whiteface	72	6,300
North Carolina			
Beaver Lake GC	Asheville	72	6,556
Beech Mountain	Banner Elk	72	6,017
Bermuda Run G & CC	Clemmons	72	6,427
Black Mountain GC	Black Mountain	71	6,087
Blowing Rock CC	Blowing Rock	70	6,100
Boone GC	Boone	71	6,388
Carolina Trace	Sanford	72	7,007

Looking towards the 6th green and 7th tee on the Torrey Pines Golf Club near San Diego, California.

Course	Location	Par	Yard-age
The Chalet Lodge	Little Switzerland	72	6,267
		72	6,475
Chatuge Shores GC	Hayesville	72	6,647
Cypress Lakes GC	Hope Mills	36	7,245
Duck Woods GC	Kitty Hawk	72	6,600
Eagle Crest GC	Garner	71	6,253
Eseeola Lodge	Linville	72	6,800
Fairfield Mountains	Lake Lure	72	7,085
Foxfire Golf & CC	Pinehurst	72	6,919
		36	3,523
Grandfather Gold & CC	Linville	72	6,888
Great Smokies Hilton Resort & Conference Center	Ashville	70	5,597
Green Valley GC	Greensboro	71	5,710
High Hampton Inn & CC	Cashiers	71	5,904
High Meadows G & CC	Roaring Gap	72	7,097
Hound Ears Club	Blowing Rock	72	6,165
Hyland Hills G & CC	Southern Pines	72	6,420
Lake Surf CC	Vass	72	7,000
Linville GC	Linville	72	6,750
Maggie Valley CC & Motor Lodge	Maggie Valley	71	6,500

Course	Location	Par	Yard-age
The Magnolia Inn	Pinehurst		
The Manor Hotel	Pinehurst		
The Mid Pines Club	Southern Pines	72	6,500
Oak Island & Beach Club	Southport	72	6,135
Pine Crest Inn	Pinehurst	—	—
Pine Needles Lodge & CC	Southern Pines	71	6,626
Pinehurst Hotel, GC, Villas & CC	Pinehurst	72	7,025
		72	6,905
		71	6,013
		72	7,051
		70	6,129
Roaring Gap Club	Roaring Gap	72	5,870
Sapphire Valley, The Fairfield Inn	Sapphire	72	6,850
Seascape GC	Kitty Hawk	71	6,300
Seven Devils Mountain Resort	Banner Elk	71	6,240
Seven Lakes CC	West End	72	6,934
Southern Pines GC	Southern Pines	71	6,500
		34	3,000
Springdale CC	Canton	72	6,783
Star Hill G & CC	Cape Carteret	71	6,837

Course	Location	Par	Yardage
Tanglewood Park	Clemmons	70	7,050
Waynesville CC Inn	Waynesville	71	6,058
Whispering Pines CC	Whispering Pines	70	5,458
Wolf Laurel	Mars Hill	72	6,145
Ohio			
Avalon Lakes	Warren	71	6,102
Granville GC	Granville	71	6,756
Hueston Woods State Park	Oxford	72	7,373
Jack Nicklaus Golf Center, Kings Island Inn	Mason	71	6,185
Oxbow G & CC	Belpre	71	6,780
Sawmill Creek	Huron	70	6,948
Whetstone River GC	Caledonia	72	6,256
Oregon			
Alderbrook GC	Bay City	71	5,810
Battle Creek GC	Salem	71	5,800
Black Butte Ranch	Sisters	72	6,600
Bowman's Mt. Hood Resort	Wemme	70	6,100
Broadmoor GC	Portland	72	6,155
Colwood GC	Portland	72	6,432
Eastmorland GC	Portland	72	6,142
Forest Hills GC	Cornelius	72	6,244
Gearhart By-the-Sea	Gearhart	72	6,100
Glendover National GC	Portland	74	6,368
		72	6,066
Kah-Nee-Tah Vacation Resort	Warm Springs	70	6,370
McNary GC	Salem	72	6,350
Oakway GC	Eugene	61	3,052
Pleasant Valley GC	Clackamas	72	6,500
Progress Downs GC	Beaverton	71	6,149
Rock Creek CC	Somerset West	72	6,432
Rose City GC	Portland	72	6,376
Salem GC	Salem	70	6,205
Salishan Lodge	Gleneden Beach	72	6,500
Santiam GC	Stayton	71	6,245
Sunriver Lodge	Sunriver	72	7,019
Tokatee GC	Blue River	72	6,327
West Delta Park GC	Portland	72	6,400
Pennsylvania			
Bedford Springs Hotel & GC	Bedford Springs	74	6,753
Buck Hill Inn & GC	Buck Hill Falls	36	3,282
		36	2,893
		34	2,858
Downington Inn & GC	Downington	72	6,500
Fernwood Resort & CC	Bushkill	72	6,710
Glen Brook CC	Lehigh Valley	72	6,805
Hershey CC	Hershey	73	6,928
		71	7,240
Hershey Parkview GC	Hershey	71	6,135
Host Farm & Coral Resorts	Lancaster	72	6,890

Course	Location	Par	Yardage
Hotel Hershey	Hershey	71	7.240
		73	6,928
		71	6,135
		33	2,316
		34	2,680
Mt. Manor Inn & GC	Marshall Creek	36	3,186
		35	3,109
		36	3,206
Overlook GC	Lancaster	70	6,290
Pocono Farms CC	Tobyhanna	36	3,200
Pocono Manor Inn & GC	Pocono Manor	72	6,460
		72	6,855
Riverside Inn & Resort	Cambridge Springs	70	6,104
Seven Springs Resort	Champion	71	6,685
Shadow Brook CC	Tunkhannock	70	6,200
Shawnee Inn & CC	Shawnee-on-Delaware	36	3,390
		36	3,230
		36	3,480
Sheraton-Picasso Inn & Resort	White Haven	72	6,090
Skytop Club	Skytop	71	6,370
Spring Creek GC	Hershey	36	2,316
Standing GC	Huntingdon	70	6,698
Tamiment Resort & CC	Tamiment	72	7,110
Toftrees CC & Lodge	State College	73	6,800
South Carolina			
Azalea Sands GC	N. Myrtle Beach	72	6,550
Bay Tree Golf Plantation	N. Myrtle Beach	72	7,200
		72	7,200
		72	7,200
Beachwood GC	N. Myrtle Beach	72	6,752
The Breakers	N. Myrtle Beach	—	—
Cabana Terrace Motor Inn	N. Myrtle Beach	—	—
The Caravelle Resort Motel	Myrtle Beach	—	—
Carolina Shores	N. Myrtle Beach	72	6,704
Chesterfield Inn & Motor Lodge	Myrtle Beach	—	—
Chickasaw Point	Fairplay	72	6,573
Cypress Bay GC	N. Myrtle Beach	72	6,502
Darlington CC	Darlington	72	6,800
Dear Track G & CC	S. Myrtle Beach	72	7,057
Dunes Golf & Beach Club	Myrtle Beach	72	7,007
Eagle Nest GC	N. Myrtle Beach	72	6,917
Fripp Island GC	Fripp Island	71	6,777
Hilton Head Plantation, Dolphin Head	Hilton Head Island	72	6,654
Holiday Downtown	Myrtle Beach	—	—
Holiday Inn North	N. Myrtle Beach	—	—
Howard Johnsons Ocean Resort	Myrtle Beach	—	—
Hyatt on Hilton Head Island at Palmetto Dunes	Hilton Head Island	—	—

BLUE COURSE

Hole	Yards	Par	Hole	Yards	Par
1	533	5	10	496	5
2	366	4	11	361	4
3	402	4	12	608	5
4	225	3	13	246	3
5	374	4	14	419	4
6	437	4	15	183	3
7	427	4	16	379	4
8	528	5	17	426	4
9	181	3	18	437	4
Out	3,473	36	In	3,555	36

Par 72, Total Yards 7,028

RED COURSE

Hole	Yards	Par	Hole	Yards	Par
1	372	4	10	338	4
2	437	4	11	220	3
3	394	4	12	406	4
4	141	3	13	537	5
5	492	5	14	465	4
6	476	5	15	408	4
7	340	4	16	381	4
8	174	3	17	186	3
9	336	4	18	501	5
Out	3,162	36	In	3,442	36

Par 72, Total Yards 6,604

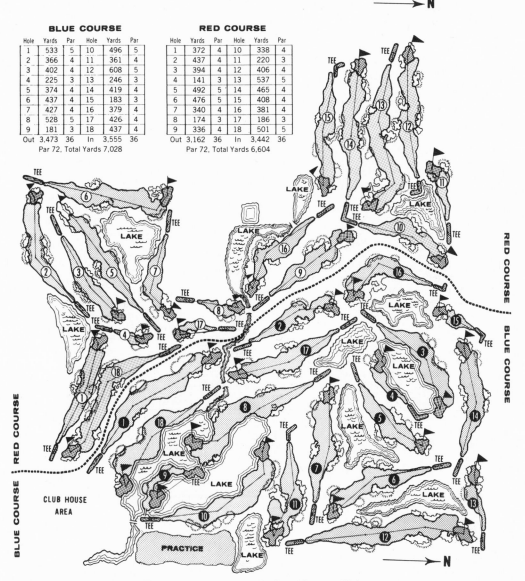

Layout of the two well-known Florida resort courses at the Doral Country Club.

Course	Location	Par	Yard-age
Internationale Inn	N. Myrtle Beach	—	—
Kiawah Inland Resort	Charleston	72	6,600
Landmark Resort Hotel	Myrtle Beach	—	—
Litchfield CC	Pawleys Island	72	6,858
Midland Valley CC	Aiken	72	6,800
Moss Creek Plantation	Hilton Head Island	72	6,851
Myrtle Beach Hilton, Arcadian Shores GC	Myrtle Beach	72	6,950

Course	Location	Par	Yard-age
Myrtle Beach National GC	Myrtle Beach	72	6,650
		72	6,900
		71	6,264
Myrtle Beach Ramada Inn	Myrtle Beach	—	—
Myrtlewood GC	Myrtle Beach	72	6,406
		72	6,965
Ocean Dunes Resort Motel	Myrtle Beach	—	—

Course	Location	Par	Yard-age
Oristo Golf & Racquet Club	Edisto Island	72	6,750
Palmetto Dunes Resort	Hilton Head Island	72	6,707
		70	6,873
Pine Lakes International CC	Myrtle Beach	71	6,600
Pineland CC	Nichols	72	6,900
Pineland Plantation Golf & Hunt Club	Mayesville	72	7,080
Pocalla Spring	Sumter	71	5,800
Port Royal Inn Golf & Tennis Club	Hilton Head Island	72	6,643
		72	6,791
Possum Trot GC	N. Myrtle Beach	72	6,966
Quail Creek GC	Myrtle Beach	72	6,800
Quality Inn Caribbean	N. Myrtle Beach	—	—
Quality Inn on Hilton Head Island	Hilton Head Island	—	—
Ramada Inn North	N. Myrtle Beach	—	—
Robbers Roost GC	N. Myrtle Beach	72	7,055
St. John's Inn	Myrtle Beach	—	—
Santee-Cooper Resort	Santee	72	6,900
Save Inn Lake Harwell	Fairplay	—	—
Sea Crest Motel	Hilton Head Island	—	—
Sea Gull GC	Pawley's Island	72	6,910
Sea Mist Resort	Myrtle Beach	—	—
Sea Pines Plantation	Hilton Head Island	71	6,655
		72	6,433
		72	6,443
		72	6,654
Seabrook Island	John's Island	72	6,852
Sheraton Myrtle Beach Inn	Myrtle Beach	—	—
Shipyard Plantation– Hilton Head GC	Hilton Head Island	72	6,300
Skyway GC	Myrtle Beach	36	3,265
		36	3,365
		36	3,240
Snee Farm CC	N. Myrtle Beach	72	6,859
Swamp Fox Motor Inn	Myrtle Beach	—	—
Thunderbird Motor Inn	Myrtle Beach	—	—
Tryon Seville Motel	N. Myrtle Beach	—	—
Wedgefield CC	Georgetown	72	6,724
The Wellman Club	Johnsonville	72	7,000
Yachtsman Resort Inn	Myrtle Beach	—	—

Tennessee

Course	Location	Par	Yard-age
Brainerd GC	Chattanooga	72	6,453
Dead Horse Lake GC	Knoxville	71	6,225
Fairfield Glade Resort	Fairfield Glade	70	6,100
Fall Creek Falls GC	Pikeville	72	6,700
Gatlinburg GC	Gatlinburg	72	6,440
Henry Horton State Park	Chapel Hill	72	6,570
The Inn at Cobbly Nob	Gatlinburg	72	6,456
Ironwood GC	Cookeville	72	6,105

Texas

Course	Location	Par	Yard-age
April Sound	Conroe	35	7,079
		32	7,079
		35	7,079
Bear Creek Golf World	Houston	72	6,485
		72	7,100
Clear Lake CC	Galveston	72	6,821
Columbia Lakes	W. Columbia	72	7,198
Corpus Christi Golf Center	Corpus Christi	72	6,668
Fairway Farms Golf & Hunt Resort	San Augustine	71	6,740
Galveston CC	Galveston	72	6,291
Hilltop Lakes Resort City	Hilltop Lakes	72	6,316
Horseshoe Bay CC	Marble Falls	72	6,900
Lake Travis World of Resorts	Lake Travis	72	6,181
		27	1,387
Lakeway Inn & GC	Austin	72	6,873
Memorial Park GC	Houston	72	7,150
Monte Cristo CC	Edinburg	72	6,700
Padre Isles CC	Corpus Christi	71	—
Pecan Valley GC	San Antonio	71	6,564
The Pirates GC	Galveston	72	6,255
Plano Municipal Golf Course	Plano	72	6,400
Rancho Viejo CC	Olmito	70	6,823
Sierra Blanca CC	Sierra Blanca	72	7,000
Tenison Park Mem. GC	Dallas	70	6,578
Valley International CC	Brownsville	70	6,875
Waterwood National Resort & CC	Huntsville	71	6,997
Woodland Hills GC	Nacognoches	72	6,566
Woodlands CC	Houston	72	6,566
World of Resorts Inn	Lago Vista	72	6,500
		72	6,500

Utah

Course	Location	Par	Yard-age
Davis Park GC	Kaysville	72	6,029
Glendale Park Municipal GC	Salt Lake City	72	6,432
Logan G & CC	Logan	71	5,800
Patio Springs CC	Ogden	72	6,600
Park City Resort	Park City	72	6,700
Timpanogos	Provo	72	6,573
Tri-City GC	American Fork	72	6,752
Wasatch Mountain State Park GC	Wasatch Mountain State Park	72	6,765
		36	3,525

Vermont

Course	Location	Par	Yard-age
Basin Harbor Club	Vergennes	72	6,018
Equinox Hotel & CC	Manchester	72	6,558
Lake Morey Inn & CC	Fairlee	69	5,900
Manchester CC	Manchester Center	72	6,724
Mount Snow	Mount Snow	72	6,443
Quechee Club	Quechee Lakes	72	6,778
Stowe CC	Stowe	72	6,200
Stratton Mountain	Stratton Mountain	72	6,655

The beautiful million-dollar Sea Pines Golf Course at Hilton Head Island, South Carolina, is spread out amongst lagoons, creeks, the Atlantic Ocean on one border, and trees a hundred or more years old on the other.

Course	Location	Par	Yard-age
Sugarbush GC	Warren	72	6,800
Woodstock CC	Woodstock	69	6,915
Virginia			
Bow Creek Municipal GC	Virginia Beach	71	6,200
Bryce Resort & CC	Basye	71	6,300
Caverns CC	Luray	72	6,743
The Homestead	Hot Springs	72	6,769
		71	5,922
		71	6,565
Ingleside Augusta GC	Staunton	72	6,609
Kempsville Meadow G & CC	Virginia Beach	72	6,013
Kingsmill GC	Williamsburg	71	6,014
Lake Wright GC	Norfolk	70	6,131
Lakeview GC	Roanoke	67	5,000
Olde Mill GC	Groundhog Mountain	72	6,266
Ole Monterey GC	Roanoke	71	6,387
Redwing Lake GC	Virginia Beach	72	6,534
Shenvalee Lodge	Newmarket	70	6,050
Sheraton Motor Inn	Fredericksburg	72	7,140
The Tides Inn	Irvington	72	6,950
The Tides Lodge	Irvington	72	6,370
Williamsburg Inn & Golden Horseshoe	Williamsburg	71	6,950

Course	Location	Par	Yard-age
Washington			
Alderbrook Inn	Union	73	6,182
Cedarcrest GC	Marysville	69	5,165
Indian Canyon GC	Spokane	71	6,380
Meadow Park GC	Tacoma	72	6,158
		31	1,775
Ocean Shores	Ocean Shores	71	6,021
Port Ludlow GC	Seattle	72	6,800
Tumwater Valley GC	Olympia	72	6,800
Veterans Memorial GC	Walla Walla	72	6,400
West Virginia			
Cacapon State Park GC	Berkeley Springs	72	6,410
Canaan Valley Resorts Inc.	Davis	72	6,911
Glade Springs	Daniels	72	6,850
The Greenbriar	White Sulphur Springs	70	8,852
		70	6,435
		70	6,289
Lakeview Inn & CC	Morgantown	72	6,650
Oglebay Park Speidel GC	Wheeling	71	6,500
Pipestem State Park GC	Pipestem	72	6,215
Twin Falls State Park GC	Mullens	72	6,756

Course	Location	Par	Yard-age
Wisconsin			
Abbey Springs GC & Hotel	Fontana	72	6,600
Alpine Resort & GC	Egg Harbor	70	5,913
Lake Lawn GC	Delavan	71	6,100
Lawsonia Links	Green Lakes	72	6,620
Maxwelton Braes Resort & GC	Bailey's Harbor	71	6,045
Olympia Village Resort	Oconomowoc	72	7,250
Peninsula State Park	Fish Creek	71	6,945
Playboy Resort & CC at Lake Geneva	Lake Geneva	71	6,880
		72	7,258
Scotsland GC	Oconomowoc	72	6,700
Wyoming			
Jackson Lake Lodge	Moran	72	7,066

Canada

A look at Canadian golf should start on the country's eastern coast. *Prince Edward Island,* an unspoiled island resort area, has two fine courses at Summerside Golf and Country Club and Cavendish Golf Club. Perhaps the finest Prince Edward Island course, though, is Green Gables, with its two contrasting nines: one on hilly, wooded terrain, the other directly flanking the open Atlantic.

The province of *Nova Scotia* has some thirty courses. Notable are the Canadian Pacific-created Digby Pines course, a beautifully scenic layout, and the challenging Highlands Course at Keltic Lodge. In the Halifax area, Ashburn and the Dartmouth golf clubs are worthy of a visit.

New Brunswick offers an outstanding layout at St. John's Riverside Golf Club, where two Canadian Amateur Championships and one Canadian Open have been played. Edmonton provides another unusual course.

Bolstered by a staunch Scottish community, Montreal became the first city on the North American continent to form an organized golf club. Founded in 1873, the Royal Montreal Golf Club is a bastion of tradition and a terrific test of golf. The 45-hole private club is situated on Ile Bizard, just north of Montreal. Located around Expo city are several other landmark clubs, many of them private, but not impossible to play with a little thought and direction. Montrealers are a hospitable lot. In all, the *Province of Quebec* has some

120 courses. Kanawaki, built on an Iroquois reservation, is one of the finest-conditioned layouts anywhere. Laval-sur-le-Lac is perhaps the world's foremost French-speaking club and a magnificent test over superb parkland. Beaconsfield, Mount Bruno (a Willie Park creation), Islesmere, Summerlea, and Elmridge are a few other outstanding Montreal district courses.

Situated between Montreal and the Canadian capital, Ottawa, is the storied Seignory Club. Here is another Canadian Pacific product and one of the most unusual resorts in Canada. The Seignory course is not exhaustingly long. It provides the ultimate in condition, and its accompanying log-style lodge is one of the luxury watering spots of North America.

The ancient capital of the New World, Quebec City, has a number of enjoyable layouts. Outstanding is the resort course at Lac Beauport, thirteen miles from the picturesque Citadel City. Royal Quebec, one of the oldest courses in America, is situated at Boischatel, close to the trenches occupied by Wolfe's Highlanders in 1759.

Ontario is Canada's largest golfing province. Nine resort districts offer 79 courses. Toronto, a city of 1,500,000, has played host to more major championships than any other in Canada. Superlative tests such as Scarboro Golf Course, Mississaugua Golf & Country Club, Toronto Golf Club, the ultra Boxgrove, Summit, and Lambton rate with the finest.

The scenic Thousand Islands region on Ontario's section of the St. Lawrence River has a number of fine courses. In the Muskoka district, Bigwin Inn has long been a summer rendezvous for keen golfers. Far north, in the hard-rock mining district, clubs such as Sudbury's Idlwylde and the inviting French River Club attract many traveling players. Ottawa's Gatineau, Glenlea, and Chaudière Clubs are open to visitors.

Manitoba has four courses of the resort variety. They are Falcon Lake Golf Course, a 6,789-yard Provincial Park course; Wasagaming Golf Course located at Clear Lake in Riding National Park; Minaki Lodge Course (actually in Ontario) right on the Manitoba border; and Victoria Beach Golf Course, situated on the eastern shore line of scenic Lake Winnipeg.

Year-round golf at the Dorado Beach Hotel and Golf Club in Puerto Rico.

Saskatchewan's Prince Albert National Park, far to the north, has a club known as Waskesiu, dating back to the early thirties. It is surrounded by good motels and cottages. The golfing visitor may find it interesting to visit some of the Provincial Park Clubs in Saskatchewan, which in many cases still provide the now-unusual sand greens.

Two of the finest resort courses in Canada, Banff Springs and Jasper, are found in Alberta. Both are located in Canada's Mountain National Parks. The Banff Springs Hotel Golf course was selected as one of the twenty-five outstanding courses in the world and was described earlier in this section.

Some four or five hours of driving north of Banff is Canadian National Railways' Jasper Park Lodge. This resort is also a train stop for CN's transcontinental trains from east and west. Jasper's course is an 18-hole, 6,590-yard, par-71 layout. Arguments rage about which course is better: Banff or Jasper. But this is flagrant hairsplitting. Both are landmarks in the diary of any golfer. Other fine courses for the visiting player can be found in Calgary, Edmonton, Medicine Hat, and Waterton Lakes National Park.

British Columbia golf, played virtually the year round, concentrates heavily around Vancouver, scenically situated against the coastal mountain range. Clubs such as Capilano in West Vancouver, Marine Drive, and Shaughnessey Heights, overlooking the busy Fraser River, have all housed national Canadian Championships. So has the narrow, testing Point Grey Layout.

Victoria, a touch of "jolly old England" on Vancouver Island, ninety miles from the mainland, offers the Victoria Golf Club, known as Oak Bay. Royal Colwood, for many years the home of the Empress mid-winter championships, is a real beauty and open to the public. Gorge Vale, overlooking the Juan da Fuca Straits, offers some of the most exciting scenery of any course in North America.

Some rules of thumb when visiting Canada for golf are: (*a*) make inquiries to provincial tourist bureaus; (*b*) if moving about, ask for information from leading hotels in the area;

(*c*) living costs in Quebec and Ontario are the highest in Canada. Everything grades slightly downward from costs in these two regions. Each Canadian province has its own golf association, with the whole fabric well knit through the Royal Canadian Golf Association. For complete information, write Canadian Government Travel Bureau, 150 Kent Street, Ottawa 4, Ontario, Canada.

Course	Location	Par	Yardage
Alberta			
Banff Springs Hotel	Banff	71	6,729
Jasper Park Lodge	Alberta	71	—
Waterton Lakes National Park	Alberta	71	6,103
British Columbia			
Fairmont Hot Springs	Hot Springs	72	6,510
Victoria GC	Victoria	70	5,961
Uplands Golf Club	Victoria	70	6,228
Nova Scotia			
Highlands Golf Links	Igonish Beach	71	6,475
Oakfield CC	Grand Lake	73	6,781
Pines Resort Hotel	Digby	71	6,141
Prince Edward Island			
Belvedere Golf & Winter Club	Charlottetown	72	6,372
Brudenell	Cardigan	72	6,500
Green Gables GC	Cavendish	72	6,269
Quebec			
Carling Lake GC	Laurentian Foothills	72	6,650
Gray Rocks	St. Jovite	72	6,403
Le Chanecler	Ste. Adele	70	6,060
Le Chateau Montebello	Montebello	69	6,110
Manoir Richekieu Auberge des Gouveneurs	Pointe-au-Pic	70	6,100

Bahamas, Bermuda, Caribbean Islands, and Mexico

Golfing on the many islands of the Caribbean and off the East coast is coming into its own. From the championship courses on Bermuda, the Bahamas, and Puerto Rico to the nine holes on some of the smaller islands, golfers are finding challenging play. Even the nongolfers in the family will agree that your golfing vacation takes them to some of the world's finest playgrounds, which, until the advent of low-cost air transportation, catered only to the very rich. Sailing, swimming, and just lying around the beach in that West Indian sun will keep the family satisfied while you are out trying to crack par on some of the most spectacular golf courses to be found anywhere.

Generally, these courses fall into two categories. First is the resort course operated in conjunction with a hotel; and second is the privately owned golf club run basically for the permanent residents of the island. Without exception, you will be welcomed at either one. At the present time, only one small course in the Caribbean is limited to a strictly private basis.

Private or resort, each has its advantages. The resort courses are designed with the American tourist in mind. Long, wide fairways, liberally lined with palms and mango and mahogany trees and abounding in sand and water, are commonplace. On the other hand, the private courses have usually been in existence a great number of years. Fairways are narrow, and the greens are exceptionally tight. On most of these courses, a premium is placed more on accuracy than length.

A visiting golfer should not hesitate to arrive at a private club alone, for it is frequently possible to join in play with the locals, and many a lasting friendship has been made this way.

		Par	Yardage
Bahamas			
Ambassador Beach Hotel & GC	Nassau	72	7,040
Bahama Reef CC	Grand Bahama Island	72	6,768
Bahama Princess Hotel, Beach & Tennis Club	Grand Bahama Island	72	7,500
Bahamas Princess Tower	Grand Bahama Island	72	7,500
		72	7,500
Balmoral Hotel	Nassau	—	—
Cape Eleuthera Resort	Eleuthera	71	6,982
Coral Harbor GC	Nassau	70	6,710
Cotton Bay Resort	Eleuthera	72	7,068
Emerald Beach Hotel	Nassau	—	—
Fortune Hills GC	Freeport	36	3,250
Lucaya Park Golf CC	Grand Bahama Island	72	6,477
Paradise Island	Nassau	72	6,562
Shannon Park Golf CC	Grand Bahama Island	72	6,810

South Ocean Beach Hotel & GC	Nassau	72	6,800
Treasure Cay GC & Resort	Abaco	72	7,012
Xanadu Princess Yacht & Tennis Club	Grand Bahama Island	72	7,500
		72	7,500
Bermuda			
The Belmont Hotel Golf & Beach Club	Warwick	70	5,700
Castle Harbour	Tuckerstown	71	6,485
Holiday Inn CC	St. Georges	27	1,201
Inverurie Hotel	Paget	—	—
Ocean View GC	Devonshire	35	2,736
Port Royal GC	Southampton West	71	6,380
Riddell's Bay G & CC	Warwick West	68	5,476
Rose Hill GC	St. Georges	34	2,455
Southampton Princess Hotel, Golf, Beach & Tennis Club	Hamilton	—	—
Barbados			
Sandy Lane Hotel & GC	St. James	72	6,896
Dominican Republic			
Casa de Campo-Hotel Romana	La Romana	72	6,750
		71	6,198
Jamaica			
Caymanas GC	Spanish Town	72	6,515
Constant Spring GC	Kingston	70	5,474
Half Moon Hotel & Cottage Colony, Half Moon Rose Hall GC	Montego Bay	72	7,130
Hotel Inter-Continental Rose Hall	Montego Bay	72	6,598
Ironshore G & CC	Montego Bay	72	6,615
Runaway Bay Hotel & GC	Runaway Bay	72	6,884
Tryall Golf & Beach Clubs	Hanover	72	6,680
Upton Plantation & GC	Ocho Rios	71	6,600
Mexico			
Acapulco Princess Hotel & GC	Acapulco	72	6,355
Bosques de San Isidro GC	Guadalajara	72	6,819
El Tapatio	Guadalajar	72	6,161
		72	6,720
		—	6,617
Las Hadas	Manzanillo	36	3,494
Pierre Marques y Club de Golf	Acapulco	72	6,723
Puerto Rico			
Cerromar Beach Hotel	Dorado	72	7,080
Dorado Beach Hotel	Dorado	72	6,950
Dorado Del Mar CC	Dorado	72	7,254

El Conquistador Hotel & Club	Las Croabas	—	—
Palmas de Mar	Humacao	72	6,660
Rio Mar Resort	Palmer	72	—
St. Maarten			
Mullet Bay Beach Hotel	Philipsburg	70	5,757
Tobago			
Mount Irvine Bay Hotel	Mount Irvine	72	6,887
Trinidad			
St. Andrews GC	Maraval	72	6,705
Virgin Islands			
The Bucaneer Hotel	St. Croix	71	6,492
Cane Bay Plantation	St. Croix	72	6,909
Estate Carlton Hotel & CC	St. Croix	36	3,173
Fountain Valley GC	St. Croix	72	6,909
The Reef	St. Croix	35	—

Packaged Golf Vacations

Packaged golf vacations are very popular, but before purchasing any plan, keep the following in mind:

1. Only "unlimited golf" means as much play as you like. "Free golf" might be hedged by restrictions on dates, number of rounds, and places.

2. Check which courses are included in the deal. You might be required to play one of your rounds on a nine-holer or at a place that does not interest you. Remember that unless specifically included, golf cars are extra.

3. Check into the number of days and nights advertised. If your room is for six nights, a seventh day's free golf is academic if you have a plane to catch.

4. To save money, travel in off-season. Happily, it is almost always off-season somewhere. Many hotels offer packages only during their slow season (or what used to be the slow season before they had golf packages). Avoid traveling solo: package prices on single rooms are 30 per cent higher.

5. To get the best rates and the smallest crowds, avoid holidays and weekends. Some resorts have special weekend-type packages for midweek. To compare packages, make a

chart showing what is offered in each category: rooms (what kind, how long), meals (which, how many), rental car (mileage included), green fees.

6. Have the hotel or packager specify the type of room you will get. You can check the desirability of the room by asking what its regular rate is and comparing it to other regular rates.

7. Do not be swayed by such inexpensive extras as free cocktails or golf hats.

8. Bring along your membership card from your own golf club. Even where everything is prearranged, you may be asked for proof of membership. Nonmembers: get your travel agent to spell out how you will be affected by this—in writing.

9. Get everything in writing from whoever sells you your package. Carry the correspondence with you, so that you will have something to wave in the face of anyone giving you less than was promised.

SECTION VIII

Glossary of Golf Terms

The language of golf is almost as romantic and interesting as the history and play of the game itself. True, many words (those that can be printed) of the golfer are self-explanatory and do not require lengthy definitions. But there are others whose derivations, like the early history of the sport, are lost in antiquity. For instance, no one is sure where the word "golf" itself comes from. Many historians of the sport believe it was taken from a game that has little to do with its present namesake. The original "kolf" or "kolfen" was a Dutch game played on ice with hockey-like sticks and was closer to curling, croquet, or hockey than the 18-hole sport described in this book.

As a matter of fact, there is even some controversy over why 18 holes constitute a round of golf. Sure, there are any number of counterfeit theories. One of the more spurious is based on the notion that there are approximately eighteen shots of whisky in a fifth of Scotch. As golfers plied their way across the Scottish moors centuries ago—so the story goes—they celebrated the completion of each "hole" by imbibing a swig. Hence, when the bottle had been emptied, the round was considered finished.

Actually, golf became an 18-hole game at St. Andrews, Scotland, a little less than 200 years ago, according to Robert Browning (among other authorities), who, after forty-

five years as editor of the British magazine *Golfing,* authored his monumental *A History of Golf* (E. P. Dutton: New York).

During the latter half of the eighteenth century, the rules, standards, and fashions of golf were set by the Honourable Company of Edinburgh Golfers, who played their golf over the Links of Leith. However, this leadership was gradually taken over by the members of the Royal and Ancient Golf Club, who played their golf over the links of St. Andrews. Until the middle of the eighteenth century, golf had been played over courses of no established length. Leith, for example, had only 5 holes. Blackheath, another ancient club, had 7, which was the most fashionable number; but other courses had as many as 25. Possibly 7 would have remained the traditional number for a round had it not been for the example of St. Andrews.

At the time, St. Andrews had 12 holes. The first 11 traveled straight out to the end of a small peninsula. After playing these, the golfers returned to the clubhouse by playing the first 10 greens backward, plus a solitary green by the clubhouse. Thus, a "round" of golf at St. Andrews consisted of 22 holes. In 1764, however, the Royal and Ancient resolved that the first 4 holes should be converted into 2. Since this change automatically converted the same 4 holes into 2 on the way back, the "round" was reduced from 22 holes to 18. And since St. Andrews was the arbiter of all that was correct about golf, 18 holes soon came to be accepted as standard throughout Scotland and England and, eventually, the world. Thus, this is the accepted reason why a round consists of 18 holes.

We know the derivations of many other golf terms. In 1891, in England, for example, one Hugh Rotherman suggested that a certain "ground score" be established for each golf course so that players could compete against a fixed and certain score. At the Great Yarmouth Club, the secretary, Dr. T. Browne, initiated a series of matches based on a relatively stable score for each hole, and the device proved to be eminently popular. For the first time, players could devise systems of handicapping and course comparisons and, at the same time, roughly analyze how they were performing on particular days. During this same year, a popular music-hall song was sweeping Britain, and the words were catchy and naggingly unforgettable: "Hush, hush," it went, "here comes the Bogey Man." And so quite naturally, as such stories go, a Major C. Wellman grew especially angry after a bad round and fired at Dr. Browne the immortally mordant remark, "That score of yours is a regular 'Bogey Man.' "

In those days, the term "bogey" became synonymous with our "par," meaning the score that an average good player should make on a given hole. But unlike American "par," "bogey" might change from day to day according to weather conditions and other influences. Eventually, there evolved a more demanding standard—"Old Man Par," as Bobby Jones was wont to call it. Par was and is an unvarying score: it never takes three putts, and never gets down in one. It is immutable and impervious to any mere change in conditions. And therein lies its terror—and its challenge.

The word "birdie," meaning one under par, had a similarly unusual birth in the United States. In 1903, A. H. Smith of Atlantic City, after holing out, is said to have commented, "That's a bird of a shot." The terms "eagle," for two under par, and "albatross," for three under par, came about by natural amplification of Smith's original metaphor, but "double eagle" has completely replaced the awkward "albatross."

The term "caddie," for bag carrier, can be traced back to the days of Mary, Queen of Scots. An avid golfer, the queen played the game while attending school in France, using cadets (pronounced ka-day), younger sons of nobility who served as pages, to carry her unwieldy clubs. The close cognate was transposed, with the French pronunciation intact, and it has lasted since the seventeenth century.

Here are some of the more common phrases that are frequently used in golf:

Ace. A hole made in one stroke. Same as a hole in one.

Address. The position taken by a player in preparing to start a stroke. Same as *addressing the ball*.

Advice. Counsel which could influence how a shot is played or what club is used.

Albatross. Score for a hole of three strokes under par. See *double eagle*.

Amateur. One who plays golf as a sport, without monetary compensation.

Approach. A stroke played to the putting green, or to the pin if possible. Usually refers to a medium- or short-iron shot.

Apron. Grass area immediately bordering the putting surface, generally mowed about halfway. Same as *fringe*.

Automatics. An extra Nassau bet permitted any time a player is two points behind.

Away. The ball farthest from the hole when more than one golfer is playing. The golfer whose ball is "away" shoots first.

Back door. The rear of the hole. A putt that "drops in the back door" is one that goes all the way around the hole and at the moment when it seems to have no chance to fall in, plops in the back of the cup.

Back side. The second 9 holes in an 18-hole course.

Backspin. A reverse spin put on the ball to make it stop on the putting green.

Backswing. The backward portion of the swing starting from the ground and going back over the head.

Baffy. No. 5 wood with loft comparable to a No. 3 or No. 4 iron.

Bail out. Holing out a long putt to avoid losing a hole.

Ball. The round object struck by the golf club. The USGA golf ball is 1.68 inches in diameter and has a weight of 1.62 ounces. The R&A golf ball is 1.62 inches in diameter and has a weight of 1.62 ounces: same as the *British small ball*.

Ball deemed to move. A ball is deemed to have

"moved" if it leaves its position and comes to rest in any other place.

Ball holed. A ball is "holed" when it lies within the circumference of the hole and all of it is below the level of the lip of the hole.

Ball in play. A ball is "in play" as soon as the player has made a stroke on the teeing ground. It remains in play as his ball until holed out, except when it is out of bounds, lost, or lifted or when another ball is substituted in accordance with the official rules or local rules.

Ball lost. A ball is "lost" if (1) it cannot be found within five minutes after the player's side or his or their caddies have begun to search for it; (2) it be declared lost by the player without searching five minutes; (3) after a search of five minutes the player is unable to identify a ball as his ball. Time spent in playing a wrong ball is not counted in the five-minute period allowed for search. Play of a wrong ball does not constitute abandonment of the ball in play.

Ball marker. A small coin or facsimile used to spot a ball position on the putting green.

Banana ball. A flagrantly bad slice, curving to the right in the shape of a banana.

Barber. A talkative player.

Barranca. A deep ravine.

Beach. Any sand hazard on the golf course.

Belt one. To hit a ball well while applying a little extra power.

Bend one. To hook or slice.

Bent. Type of grass primarily used on northern courses.

Bermuda. Type of grass primarily used on southern courses.

Best-ball. A match in which one plays against the better ball of two or the best ball of three players. Also the lower score by either of two match partners.

Birdie. One stroke under the designated par of a hole.

Birds. Competition in which points are scored for birdies on any hole; double points for eagles.

Bisque. A handicap stroke allotted to an opponent which he may use at his own discretion on any hole he chooses, although he must so declare before teeing off on that hole. Strictly speaking, a stroke that is given to an opponent must be taken at the hole indicated on the scorecard as being that particular handicap number. Thus, if a player is given "five strokes," he must use those strokes on the holes marked one to five on the card. The handicap numbers are usually circled to differentiate them from the hole numbers. A bisque, on the other hand, may be taken anywhere.

Bite. Backspin imparted to a ball.

Blade. A type of putter.

Blade one. To hit a topped shot. See *top*.

Bladesman. An admiring description applied to an excellent putter.

Blast. Hitting out of a sand trap and taking large quantities of sand with the shot. Same as *explode*.

Blind Bogey. A competition in which a score is drawn out of a hat, and the player coming closest to it wins.

Blind hole. A hole is said to be "blind" when its putting green cannot be seen by the player as he approaches.

Block. To manipulate the swing to force a clubhead arc from inside to outside at impact.

Bogey. In the United States, one stroke over the designated par of a hole. In Great Britain, the number of strokes which an average player should make on a hole (thus, on easier holes, par and bogey might be the same).

Bold. Strong, too long, as in "he was bold with the putt, and it went six feet past." Also a firmly played approach to a well-protected flagpin in a difficult position. Often refers to a daring player.

Borrow. In putting, to play to one side or the other from a direct line to the hole in order to compensate for slope or curve in the green.

Brassie. No. 2 wood. Usually used on a fairway where maximum distance is required. Received this name because it was originally equipped with a brass sole plate.

Bulger. A pear-shaped driver with a convex face. Now largely obsolete.

Bunker. An area of bare ground, often a depression, which is usually covered with sand. It falls under the category of "hazard" in the *Rules of Golf*, although grass-covered ground bordering or within a bunker is not part of the hazard. Oddly enough, "bunkers" were once havens, but only for sheep. The original bunkers in Scotland were holes hollowed out by flocks of sheep for protection against the strong winds on seaside courses.

Bunt. Hitting an intentional short shot.

Burn. A Scottish term for a creek or stream.

Bye. The holes remaining after the match has been decided. Also a term used in tournament pairings. Those who draw a "bye" advance to the next round without having to play an opponent.

Bye holes. Unplayed holes after a match has been won.

Caddie. A person who carries or handles a player's clubs during play and otherwise assists him in accordance with the rules. Properly spelled with an "i" and an "e," according to Fowler. So spelled, it is also the first choice of Webster. A "caddy" is something in which you carry a spare supply of tea.

Can. To hole a putt.

Cap. Top end of a club grip and shaft.

Carry. Distance from the place where the ball is struck to the place where it first strikes the ground.

Casting. A swing-damaging error of starting the downswing with the hands dominating the action. Same as *hitting from the top*.

Casual water. Any *temporary* accumulation of water which is visible before or after the player takes his stance and which is not a hazard of itself or is not in a water hazard. Snow and ice are "casual water" unless otherwise determined by rules. A player may lift his ball from "casual water" without penalty. Sometimes called a *casual lie*.

Championship. A tournament representing title to a trophy offered for competition, usually annually, by a recognized golfing body, such as the United States Golf Association or the Royal and Ancient Golf Club of St. Andrews, Scotland.

Chip-and-run. A controlled stroke used just off the green and played with a less-lofted club than the pitch and run. It is played almost like a putt, with the loft of the club doing the work.

Chipping iron. A special iron employed primarily for making chip shots.

Chip shot. A short approach of low trajectory, usually from near the putting green, hit with overspin or bite, depending on the distance from the putting green, or from the cup.

Choke. To grip down farther on the handle. Also, to collapse under great pressure.

Chop. To hit a ball with a hacking motion to impart extra spin.

Chump. An easy opponent.

Cleek. No. 4 wood. Originally the least-lofted iron club except for a putter. Later developed as a wooden club with loft comparable to a No. 1 or No. 2 iron.

Closed stance. The left foot extends over the line of flight while the right foot is back.

Club. Used to hit a golf ball. Also a group of golfers.

Clubbing a player. To advise a partner which club to use for a particular shot.

Club head. The hitting portion of the club.

Clubhouse. A building that houses such facilities as lockers, restaurant, bar, and meeting rooms.

Clubhouse lawyer. An over-officious caller of the *Rules of Golf;* or a self-appointed arbiter.

Cocked wrists. The bend of the wrists in the swing.

Collar. Edge of a sand hazard.

Come up empty. To lose a hole or miss a carefully planned shot.

Committee. The "committee" is the group in charge of the competition.

Competitor. A player in a stroke competition. A "fellow competitor" is any player with whom the competitor plays. Neither is partner of the other. In stroke play, foursome, and four-ball competitions where the context so admits, the word "competitor" or "fellow competitor" shall be held to include his partner.

Controlled shot. A stroke made for a definite purpose. Same as an *intentional stroke*.

Course. The whole area within which play is permitted. A "golf course" usually indicates 9 or 18 holes, each hole consisting of a tee, fairway, and putting green.

Course Rating. The evaluation of the playing difficulty of a course compared with other rated courses. It is expressed in strokes and decimal fractions of a stroke, and is based on yardage and the ability of a scratch golfer.

Cross-bunker. A narrow bunker that crosses a hole at a right angle to the player's line of flight to the putting green.

Cup. See *hole*.

Cuppy. A lie in which the ball is positioned in a small depression in the ground.

Cut-one-in. To play a precision approach or pitch shot with backspin, to a flagpin lying in a guarded position.

Cut shot. A controlled stroke that results in a high, soft shot that sits (stops rolling) almost immediately when it hits the green.

Dead. A ball is said to be dead when it lies so close to the hole that there is no doubt that it will be sunk with the next stroke. Also a ball which lands on the green with so much backspin it stops without running forward.

Deuce. A hole made in two strokes.

Dimple. Round, scientifically made indentations in the cover of a ball which keep its flight through the air steady and true.

Divot. Piece of turf cut out by a club head during a stroke (always to be replaced and pressed down).

Dog-it. To play poorly under stress.

Dog-leg. A bend in the fairway either to the right or to the left.

Dormie. When a player or side is as many holes ahead as remain to be played in a match. Opponent(s) must win every remaining hole to tie the match.

Double bogey. A score of 2 over par for a single hole.

Double eagle. A score of 3 under par.

Down. The number of holes (match play) or strokes (stroke play) a player is behind an opponent.

Draw. A controlled "hook" stroke used to gain shot-making position or get out of trouble. Also the pairing for match play.

Drive. To hit a ball from a tee.

Driver. No. 1 wood. Usually used only off the teeing surface when maximum distance is required.

Driving iron. No. 1 iron. This iron is seldom used today.

Dub. A poorly executed shot; a missed shot. Same as a *foozle*.

Duck hook. A violent hook caused either by an over-closed club face or by severe pronation of the hands. Ball normally travels low and hits the ground quickly.

Duffer. An unskilled golfer. Same as a *hacker*.

Dunk. To hit a ball into a water hazard.

Eagle. Two strokes under the designated par for a hole.

Equipment. This is anything used, worn, or carried by or for the player except his ball in play.

Explode. Hitting out of a sand trap and taking large quantities of sand with the shot. Same as *blast*.

Extra. A new or additional bet on the remaining holes. If someone wants to take a "dollar extra" on the 17th tee, he wants to play the last 2 holes for the dollar. Same as a *press*.

Face. Hitting surface of the club head.

Fade. A term used to indicate a slight turn from left to right at the end of the ball's flight. Also a controlled "slice" shot.

Fairway. The well-kept portion of terrain between the tee and putting green, affording the player a favorable lie for the ball. Same as a *fairgreen*.

Fan. To miss the ball completely. Same as *whiff*.

Fat shot. Refers to the club first hitting the ground behind the ball. Ball should be struck first with ensuing divot in front. Causes high or low shots and loss of distance.

Feather. To hit a long high shot with a gentle left-to-right flight which brings the ball down very lightly and without much roll.

Field. All the contestants in a tournament or championship.

Flagstick. A movable marker placed in the hole on the green to show its location. Same as *flag* or *pin*.

Flange. Additional surface of the club head which protrudes at the sole.

Flash trap. A small, shallow sand bunker.

Flat. A very obtuse angle between the sole of a club and the shaft.

Flat swing. Occurs when the club head is carried back in a flat manner, usually in an inside-out manner.

Flier. A ball that leaves the club face without spin and travels farther than normal.

Flier lie. A "lie" in clover or tufted grass. Also a good "lie" in the rough.

Flight. A division of players for tournament play. Players of equal ability are placed in the same flight. The flights may consist of any number of players; however, sixteen is the usual number. Also a term given to a ball hit into the air.

Floater. A ball that soars high and lightly in the air. Also a special ball that is light enough to float on water.

Floater lie. A "lie" in the grass, usually in the rough, that is not just high but thick. The ball is buried—almost out of sight.

Flub. A poor shot, usually caused by hitting the ground before hitting the ball.

Follow-through. The continuation of the swing after the ball has been struck.

Fore. An expression called out in warning to those in danger from the flight of the ball. From the British phrase, "Look out before!"

Forecaddie. A person employed by the committee to indicate or mark the position of a player's ball on the course.

Four-ball. A match in which two play their better ball against the better ball of two other players.

Foursome. A match in which two play against two, and each side plays one ball. Often erroneously used to describe a four-ball match. Used most often in international competition, such as the Walker, Ryder, and Curtis Cups. Also a term given to four players playing together.

Fried egg. See *plugged lie*.

Fringe. See *apron*.

Frog hair. Short grass bordering the edge of the green.

Front side. The first 9 holes of an 18-hole course.

Gimme. A putt so short that it will most likely be conceded by an opponent.

Gobble. A boldly hit putt that unexpectedly finds the hole.

Go-to-school. To help determine the roll of a green by observing the path of a prior putt over the same area.

Go-to-the-hill. To move to the practice area, usually after an unsatisfactory round.

Go-to-the-window. To collect money in a professional tournament.

Grain. The direction in which grass on a putting green grows, and therefore lies, after it is closely cut.

Grasscutter. A hard-hit ball, traveling low and skimming the grass.

Green. The whole links or golf course. A "putting green," on the other hand, is all the ground of the hole being played which is specially prepared for putting or otherwise defined by the committee. Hence, the terms "green fee," "green committee," "greenkeeper," and so on should always be used in the singular rather than the plural. While this is true according to the *Rules of Golf*, the term "green" popularly means the putting surface, the closely cut area which contains the hole or cup, and means the same as *putting green*.

Green fee. The fee paid for the privilege of playing on the golf course.

Grip. The part of the shaft, covered with leather or other material, by which the club is grasped. Also the grasp itself.

Groove. The slot in which the club always travels in the repeating, consistent swing.

Gross. A player's score before his handicap is deducted. That is, the total number of strokes taken to complete a designated round.

Ground under repair. Any portion of the course so marked by order of the committee. It includes material piled for removal and a hole made by a greenkeeper, even if not so marked. Stakes and lines marking such an area are not in such ground.

Hacker. An unskilled golfer. Same as *duffer*.

Halfswing. A swing in which the club head is brought back just halfway. Same as *half shot*.

Halved. A hole is "halved" when each side has played it in the same number of strokes. Also to play a match to no decision.

Handicap. The stroke or strokes which a player may deduct from his gross, or actual, score. Actually, it is the number of strokes a player receives to adjust his scoring ability to the common level of a scratch or zero-handicap golfer.

Handicap allowance. The portion of the handicap usable in a given form of play.

Handicap differential. The difference between a player's gross score and the course rating of the golf course on which the score was made.

Handicap player. A player whose average round is above par golf and who thus is given a handicap.

Hanging lie. A ball resting on a downhill slope.

Hazard. A "hazard" is any bunker or water hazard. Bare patches, scrapes, roads, tracks, and paths are not "hazards." (1) A "bunker" is an area of bare ground, often a depression, which is usually covered with sand. Grass-covered ground bordering or within a bunker is *not* part of the hazard. (2) A "water hazard" is any sea, lake, pond, river, ditch, surface drainage ditch, or other open watercourse (regardless of whether or not it contains water), and anything of a similar nature. All ground or water within the margin of a water hazard, whether or not it be covered with any growing substance, is part of the water hazard. (3) A

"lateral water hazard" is a water hazard or that part of a water hazard running approximately parallel to the line of play and so situated that it is not possible or is deemed by the committee to be impracticable to drop a ball behind the water hazard and keep the spot at which the ball last crossed the hazard margin between the player and the hole.

Head. Part of the club with which the ball is struck, consisting of the sole, heel, toe or nose, neck, and face.

Heel. Part of the club head nearest the shaft. Also to hit from this part and send the ball at right angles to the line of play.

Hole. A round receptacle in the green, 4¼ inches in diameter and at least 4 inches deep and usually metal-lined. Same as *cup*. Also units of play from tee to putting green; a *round* consists of 18 holes or units.

Hole-high. A ball even with the hole, but off to one side.

Hole in one. A hole made in one stroke. Same as *ace*.

Hole out. To put the ball into the cup to complete the play for one hole.

Home. The green.

Home pro. A professional who maintains his position at a golf club to teach and plays only in local events. Same as *club professional*.

Honor. The right or privilege of hitting first from the tee, which goes to the winner of the preceding hole or the last hole won (or, on the first hole, by tossing a coin).

Hook. To hit a ball in a curve to the left of the intended target. This is caused by the counter-clockwise ball rotation.

Hosel. The hollow part of the iron club head into which the shaft is fitted.

Hustler. An adept golfer who purposely maintains a higher handicap in order to make more favorable wagers.

In. An expression used to describe the second nine of golf course, as opposed to *out*—the first nine holes.

Insert. Part of the club face of wooden clubs.

In-the-leather. A term in friendly matches allowing (or giving) a putt that lies no farther from the cup than the length of the leather wrapping on the player's putter.

Iron. Club with a metal head. Irons are usually classified long irons (Nos. 1, 2, 3), middle irons (Nos. 4, 5, 6), and short irons (Nos. 7, 8, 9, and wedge). Progressing from the No. 1 through the wedge, the iron face becomes larger and more lofted.

Jigger. An iron, now obsolete, with a narrow blade that had approximately the loft of a No.

4 iron. It was used for recovering from bad lies and for chipping, in addition to normal fairway shots.

Lag. Putting with the intention of leaving the ball close to the hole in a position for surely holing out with the next stroke.

Lateral hazard. Any water hazard running approximately parallel to the line of play. Same as *parallel hazard*.

Lie. The position in which the ball rests on the ground. Also the angle which the shaft makes with the ground when the club is sitting in its natural position.

Lie-alike. Players have taken the same number of strokes. Same as *like-as-we-lie*.

Line. The direction in which the player *intends* the ball to travel after it is hit. Same as *line of flight* or *line of play*.

Links. A term originally given to a seaside golf course; now, any golf course.

Lip. The top edge or rim of the hole or cup.

Lob shot. An extremely high and soft type of of shot requiring a good deal of "feel" in the hands. It goes straight up and comes almost straight down with a minimum of overspin or forward momentum. Very useful in tight situations where not much green is available to work with.

Loft. The elevation of the ball into the air. Also the angle at which the club face is set from the vertical and is employed to lift the ball into the air.

Lofter. A highly lofted iron club that was a forerunner of the niblick. It is now obsolete.

Long game. Any of those shots in which considerable distance is important.

Looping. A backswing error in which the head and shoulders move forward and to the left so that they are more over the ball than is correct. This makes the club head return to the ball from the outside and causes shanking.

Loose impediments. Natural objects that are not fixed or growing or adhering to the ball. Includes stones that are not solidly imbedded, twigs, leaves, branches, and the like, molehills, dung, worms, and insects, and the casts or heaps made by them.

Low ball and total. A four-ball team bet in which the best ball of each team wins one point, and the low total of the partners wins another. This game is a method of getting a good bet out of the situation in which there is one very good player playing with a poor one against two average players.

LPGA. Abbreviation for Ladies' Professional Golf Association.

Luck-it. To drop a putt that the player did not deem well hit.

Make-the-cut. To score well enough in allocated number of rounds to qualify for final one or two rounds in professional tournament competition.

Marker. An object on the tee which determines the forward limits from which to drive. Same as *tee marker*. Also a scorer in stroke play who is appointed by the committee to record a competitor's score. He may be a fellow competitor. He is not a referee. A marker should not lift the ball or mark its position and, unless he is a fellow competitor, should not attend the flagstick or stand at the hole or mark its position.

Marshal. A person appointed by the committee to handle spectators and keep order during a tournament.

Mashie. No. 5 iron. The name probably comes from the French *massé*, the same term still used today in billiards to describe extreme backspin.

Mashie iron. No. 4 iron.

Mashie niblick. No. 7 iron.

Match. A golf competition played by holes—each hole is a separate contest—rather than the total score. The team or player winning the greatest number of holes is the winner.

Match Play. Competition by holes. The winner of the first hole is said to be "one up," and even if he wins that hole by two or more strokes, he is not more than "one up." He can increase his lead by one every time he wins another hole. A competition decided according to match play ends when one player is more holes "up" than there are left to play—as in 4&3, four up with three to play.

Medal. The low qualifying score for a match-play tournament or championship.

Medalist. The player with the lowest qualifying score in a tournament.

Medal Play. A competition decided by total, overall score, with every stroke counting and being significant. Same as *stroke play*.

Midiron. No. 2 iron.

Mid mashie. No. 3 iron.

Mixed foursome. A foursome with two pairs of golfers, each consisting of a male and a female player.

Mulligan. A second shot, usually off the first tee, that is sometimes permitted in a casual social game, but never in a competition played strictly by the *Rules of Golf*. Same as a *Shapiro*.

Nassau. A competition, either match or stroke play, in which a point is allotted for the first 9 holes, another point for the second 9, and still another for the over-all 18.

Neck. The part of the club where the shaft joins the head. Same as *socket*.

Needle. Gibing an opponent into making an extra bet or causing him to over-try. Also describes the making of an extra bet at an even point in a match.

Net. A player's score after his handicap is subtracted.

NGF. Abbreviation for National Golf Foundation.

Nose. See *toe*.

Observer. A person appointed by the committee to assist the referee, to decide questions of fact, and to report to the referee any breach of the rules. An observer should not attend the flagstick, stand at or mark the position of the hole, or lift the ball or mark its position.

Obstruction. Anything artificial, whether erected, placed, or left on the course, except objects defining course boundaries or artificially constructed roads and paths.

Odd. Indicates a term for the player who has already played one stroke more than his opponent.

Open. A tournament open to both amateurs and professionals.

Open stance. The left foot is dropped back of the imaginary line of the direction of the ball, enabling the golfer to face more in the direction toward which he wishes to hit.

Out. An expression used to describe the first nine of a golf course, as opposed to *in*—the second nine holes. See *side*.

Out of bounds. The ground outside of the course, on which play is prohibited. This area requires a penalty of "stroke" and "distance" each time a player hits into it. In other words, the player has to replay the shot with a one-stroke penalty.

Outside agency. Any agency not part of the match or, in stroke play, not part of a competitor's side; includes marker, observer, referee, or a forecaddie.

Overclubbing. Use of a club giving too much distance; for example, a midiron when a mashie should have been used.

Par. The theoretical number of strokes a player should take for a hole; golf's standard of good performance. The par for each hole is usually indicated on the scorecard.

Partner. A player associated with another player on the same side in a match.

Part shot. This phrase describes the swing used in playing shots of less distance than could be obtained with the most lofted club carried in the modern sets. As an example, if a full wedge or No. 9 iron would travel a distance of 90 yards, a shot of 50 yards would be considered a "part shot."

Penalty stroke. A stroke added to a player's score for violation of certain rules.

PGA. Abbreviation for Professional Golfers Association.

Pin. See *flagstick*.

Pinehurst. Partners play each other's drive, then select one ball with which to finish the hole. Usually in stroke play.

Pitch. A short shot up to the putting green, generally made by lofting the ball in a high arc and landing with backspin.

Pitch and run. The same shot as the pitch, but executed with a lower-numbered club, thus preventing the high arc and backspin and thereby permitting the ball to run after it hits the putting green.

Pitcher. A form of niblick, usually with the loft of a contemporary No. 8 iron. Now largely obsolete.

Pitching niblick. No. 8 iron.

Pitching wedge. An iron designed primarily for making short pitching shots. It has a heavy flange on the bottom.

Play club. An ancient driver; now obsolete.

Playing through. Occurs when a group of players are permitted to pass another group playing ahead.

Plug. A cut piece of whole turf used to repair any break or divot.

Plugged lie. A "lie" generally in a bunker in which the ball is buried in the sand. Same as a *fried egg*.

Plus handicap. The number of strokes a player gives to adjust his scoring ability to the common level.

Pole one. To hit a long shot.

Pot bunker. A small, deep sand trap.

Preferred lie. Under local rules which permit a player to improve the lie of the ball in a specified way without penalty.

Press. To swing the club so hard that the player cannot hit the ball with accuracy. Also, an extra bet.

Pressing. Attempting to hit the ball beyond one's normal power.

Professional. Usually called a *pro*. A player who teaches (the *teaching pro*) or plays in tournaments (the *touring pro*) for monetary compensation.

Pro shop. A place to buy golf equipment; it is operated by the club professional.

Provisional ball. A ball played after the previous ball has been lost or is out of bounds.

Pull. A ball, when hit, that goes to the left of the target with little or no curving.

Punch. A low, controlled shot straight into the wind, executed by slamming the club down into the ball with a short swing.

Push. A ball, when hit, that goes to the right of

the target with little or no curving. Also a controlled shot in which the ball is hit straight with a low trajectory, good against strong winds, yet using the wind to bring the ball into the desired line.

Putt. Stroking the ball toward the hole when on the putting green.

Putter. No. 10 iron; used on the putting green.

Putting green. The "putting green" is all the ground of the hole being played which is specially prepared for putting or otherwise defined as such by the committee.

Quail high. A long shot that has low trajectory.

R & A. Abbreviation for Royal and Ancient Golf Club of St. Andrews.

Rabbit. A topped shot that bounces erratically. Same as a *scooter*. Also refers to a touring professional who must attempt to play his way into each event in a Monday morning qualifying round.

Rating Marker. A permanent indicator of the starting point from which each hole is measured for yardage rating placed at the side of the tee.

Referee. A person who has been appointed by the committee to accompany players to decide questions of fact and of golf law. He shall act on any breach of rules which he may observe or which may be reported to him by an observer. In stroke play, the committee may limit a referee's duties. A referee should not attend the flagstick, stand at or mark the position of the hole, or lift the ball or mark its position.

Ringer score. The cumulative scores of a player's lowest number of strokes per hole set on a given course over a given period of time.

Roll-on-a-shot. To turn the wrists too much at impact.

Rookie. A former amateur golfer on his first year of playing the professional tour.

Rough. Areas, usually of relatively long grass, adjacent to the tee, fairway, putting green, or hazards.

Round. See *hole* (last sentence).

Round robin. A controlled tournament in which every player plays one match against every other player.

Rub of the green. A "rub of the green" occurs when a ball in motion is stopped or deflected by an outside agency, which is any agency not part of the match or, in stroke play, not part of a competitor's side, and includes a referee, a marker, an observer, or a forecaddie employed by the committee. Also, golfese for "tough luck," or "that's the way the ball bounces."

Run. The distance the ball rolls after striking the ground or on the ground.

Running iron. An iron used primarily for short running shots.

Run-up. An approach shot in which the ball travels close to the ground or on the ground. Sometimes referred to as a *running-shot*.

Sand trap. A hazard containing sand.

Sand wedge. An iron designed primarily to get out of sand traps. It has a heavy flange on the bottom.

Scare. That portion of a wood club where the head and shaft are spliced together, usually protected with a whipping.

Sclaff. The name given to the error of hitting the ground behind the ball. Also referred to as hitting too "fat" or "heavy."

Scoop. An improper swing in which the clubhead has a dipping or digging action.

Scoring lines. The corrugations on the face of irons.

Scotch foursome. A match in which partners alternate hitting one ball, alternately driving regardless of which one holed out on the previous hole. A "mixed" Scotch foursome refers to a man and woman as partners.

Scrape. Describes a slightly topped fairway or bunker shot. Also an old Scottish term for a hole made by a burrowing animal.

Scratch. In the United States, to play at par.

Scratch player. One who receives no handicap allowance.

Scruff. Scraping or cutting the turf with the club head, generally before making impact with the ball.

Scuffing. The name given to the error of hitting the ground behind the ball.

Set. A full complement of golf clubs.

Shaft. That part of the club which is not the head.

Shagging. Gathering of golf balls hit from practice tees.

Shank. That part of the hosel nearest the face. Also, to hit a ball on the shank causing it to go sharply off line, generally to the right.

Short game. The shots of pitching, chipping, and putting.

Side. A player, or two or more players who are partners. Also when speaking of the 18 holes on a golf course, "side" can mean the first 9 holes (*front side,* or "out"), or last 9 holes (*back side,* or "in").

Single. A match in which one plays against another. Often erroneously referred to as one playing alone.

Skulling. An error, generally in a chip or pitch shot, of hitting the ball too hard and obtaining too great distance.

Sky. To hit underneath the ball, sending it higher than intended, like a "pop fly" in baseball. Same as a *rainmaker*.

Skywriting. A swing error in which the club head describes or makes a loop or a circle at the top of the backswing. It generally causes shanking.

Slice. A shot which curves to the right of the target. This is caused by the clockwise rotation of the ball.

Slider. A low-hit shot that takes erratic bounces.

Smothered ball. One that is hit down as a result of pressing.

Snake. A very long putt, usually one over several breaks in the green.

Snipe. A sharply hooked ball that dives quickly.

Socket. The opening in the neck of an iron club into which the shaft is fitted. Also, in Great Britain, to shank a shot. See *neck*.

Sole. The bottom of the club head. Also the act of placing the club on the ground at address.

Sole plate. The metal plate located on the bottom of wooden-head clubs.

Spade mashie. No. 6 iron.

Spoon. No. 3 wood. Generally employed where distance plus loft is required.

Spray. To hit a ball far off line.

Square. A match that is all even.

Square stance. A stance in which both feet are in a line parallel to the direction in which the player wishes to hit the ball.

Stab. A half-hearted swing, or one lacking the proper arc.

Stance. Position of the feet when addressing the ball.

Stand please. The shout used to request spectators to remain motionless and silent while a player is shooting.

Stipulated round. Playing all 18 holes of a course in their correct sequence.

Stony. To hit it "stony" is to hit a ball close to the flagstick.

Stroke. Any forward motion of the club head made with intent to hit and move the baseball, successful or not.

Stroke hole. The hole on which a player applies a handicap stroke. The numerical order in which handicap strokes are allocated to the holes of the golf course should be shown on the scorecard.

Stroke play. Competition in which the winner is determined by the low number of strokes taken for one stipulated round; or for the number of stipulated rounds constituting a given tournament. Same as *medal play*.

Stymie. In match play, a situation in which an opponent's ball is in the line of a player's putt. Since the stymie is no longer played (the blocking ball may be lifted), the word is used generally when there is a tree in the way of a shot to the green; such a golfer would be "stymied." The term comes from an old Scotch word meaning "the faintest form of anything."

Sudden death. The continuation of a match or stroke competition that is deadlocked at the end of the allotted number of holes. Competition continues until one or the other of the players wins a hole.

Summer rules. Ordinary playing rules of golf apply.

Sweet spot. Dead center of the face of the club. Used to define the reason for a well-hit shot.

Swing. The action by a player in stroking the ball.

Take-the-pipe. Collapsing under tension at critical stage of golf competition.

Takeway. The beginning of the backswing.

Tee. A wood or plastic device on which the ball is placed for driving. Also the area from which the ball is driven on the first shot of each hole. Same as *teeing ground*.

Tee marker. See *marker*.

Texas wedge. The putter, when used to roll the ball up to the putting green from a chipping distance, or for playing a ball out of a trap.

Thread. A shot on which the ball steered through a narrow opening.

Three-ball. A match in which three play against one another, each playing his own ball.

Threesome. A match in which two players play alternate strokes with the same ball and oppose a single player. Also, a colloquialism for three players engaged in stroke play.

Through the green. The whole area of the course except the teeing ground, putting green, and hazards.

Tiger. A player having a good scoring streak.

Toe. The portion of the club head farthest from where it joins the shaft. Same as *nose*.

Toe job. A shot hit too far toward the toe of the club.

Top. To hit a ball above center, causing it to roll or hop rather than to rise off the ground.

Tournament. A competition at either match or stroke play. A tournament is said to be "open" when both amateurs and professionals may form the field.

Track iron. A club with a small, round head, used in the early days of golf, mainly to extricate the ball from cart tracks; club is, of course, now obsolete.

Trouble shot. A recovery stroke taken from a trouble position such as a bunker or rough, or from behind trees.

Turn. Starting the second or back nine.

Twosome. A colloquial expression for a single, or for two players engaged in stroke play.

Underclubbing. Using a club giving too short distance; for instance, a mashie when a mid-iron should be used.

Unplayable lie. A ball in a position where it cannot be played; for example, between rocks or in a thicket of trees.

Up. The number of holes or strokes a player is ahead of his opponent.

Upright. That angle between the head of a club and its shaft which is less obtuse than a flat lie.

Upright swing. A swing in which the club head is carried more directly backward and upward from the ball with little deviation from center.

USGA. Abbreviation for United States Golf Association.

Waggle. The preliminary action before hitting the ball of flexing the wrists, causing the club to swing forward and backward.

Water hazard. See *hazard.*

Water hole. A hole which has a stream or pond adjacent to it or in the middle of it, usually forcing the players to shoot over it.

Wedge. A special club that has a heavy flange on the bottom. Can be a "pitching" wedge or a "sand" wedge.

Whiff. To miss the ball completely. Same as *fan.*

Whins. A British term for heavy rough or brush.

Whipping. The thread or twine used in wrapping the space where the head and shaft are joined. Plastic ferrules are sometimes used for this purpose.

Wind cheater. An intentionally low-hit ball into the wind.

Winter rules. Rules used when the players are permitted to improve the lie of their ball on the fairway. They are usually local golf rules.

Wood. A club with a wooden head.

Yardage Rating. The evaluation of the playing difficulty of a hole or a course based on yardage only.

Yips. Convulsive shakes that cause the player to badly miss a short putt.

Illustration Credits are listed by page numbers. All other illustrations courtesy of Universal Publishing and Distributing Corp.

7 Acme Newspictures
12 Geo. S. Pietzcker
17 Copyright by International News Photo
18 *Top left:* Wide World Photo
   Bottom right: Julian P. Graham, Photo
19 *Top left:* United Press International Photo
20 *Left:* Wide World Photo
   Right: P. & A. Photo
21 *Top left:* N. Y. Times
   Bottom: United Press International Photo
22 *Top right:* Copyright by International News Photos, Inc.
23 *Top:* Wide World Photo
   Bottom right: Copyright by International News Photos
24 *Top left:* Copyright by International News Photos, Inc.
   Bottom right: Wide World Photo
25 *Top left:* Associated Press Wirephoto
   Bottom right: Wide World Photo
26 *Top left:* United Press International Photo
   Bottom right: Wide World Photo
29 United Press International Photo
33 *Top right:* United Press International Photo
   Center left: Wide World Photo
   Bottom right: United Press International Photo
49 Wide World Photo
50 Wide World Photo
54 Wide World Photo
58 *Top right:* United Press International Photo
   Center: Wide World Photo
64 *Top left:* United Press International Photo
   Top right: Acme Photo
77 Acme Photo
   Center left: L.P.G.A. Publicity Bureau Photo

Bottom left: L.P.G.A. Publicity Bureau Photo
   Bottom right: Wide World Photo
79 *Left:* United Press Photo
97 Copyright United Press International (UK) Ltd.
99 *Left:* Wide World Photo
   Right: Wide World Photo
103 *Left:* Copyright Photo Illus. Co.
116 *Center:* Copyright United Press International (UK) Ltd.
117 Wide World Photo
128 *Right:* Rotofotos Incorporated
130 *Right:* Photograph Kadel & Herbert News Feature Photos
131 *Left:* United Press International Photo
   Right: Radel & Herbert News Photo
133 *Left:* Acme Photo
   Right: Newsphotos
134 Rotofotos Incorporated
136 United Press Interantional Photo
137 *Left:* Rotofotos, Inc.
   Right: Wide World Photo
139 *Right:* H. J. Chachowski
140 *Right:* Wide World Photo
141 Wide World Photo
142 Acme Photo
143 *Left:* Acme Photo
144 Wide World Photo
145 Wide World Photo and Associated Press Wirephoto
147 *Left:* L.P.G.A. Publicity Bureau Photo
   Right: Wide World Photo
148 Cal-Pictures
149 *Right:* Acme Newspictures
152 *Left:* Wide World Photo
156 Acme Photo
157 United Press International Photo
159 United Press International Photo
160 *Left:* Will Hertzberg
   Right: L.P.G.A. Publicity Bureau Photo
161 *Left:* United States Golf Association

162 *Right:* Wide World Photo
163 Copyright by International News Photo
164 *Right:* Wide World Photo
170 *Bottom:* Peter Dazeley
171 *Right:* United Press International Photo
172 *Left:* Wide World Photo
214 Morgan Fitz Photographers, Inc.
217 Artist, Dom Lupo
221 Rubber Age
237 *Top left:* Wisler Photography, Inc.
250 Copyright A. G. Spalding & Bros.
265 Artist, Dom Lupo
276 H. J. Chachowski
289 Artist, Lealand Gustavson
366 *Left:* Canadian National Railways
367 Alex Bremner
369 Hamilton M. Wright, "Newspaper Feature News"
374 Wide World Photo
375 Artist, Dom Lupo
377 Wide World Photo
378 United Press International Photo
379 Wide World Photo
386 *Top right:* Wide World Photo and Associated Press Widephoto
389 Artist, Dom Lupo
390 Artist, Dom Lupo
391 *Top:* Artist, Dom Lupo
   Bottom: Artist, Dom Lupo
392 Artist, Dom Lupo
393 *Top:* Artist, Dom Lupo
   Bottom: Artist, Dom Lupo
394 Artist, Dom Lupo
395 *Top:* Artist, Dom Lupo
   Bottom: Artist, Dom Lupo
396 *Top:* Artist, Dom Lupo
   Bottom left: Artist, Dom Lupo
397 *Top:* Artist, Dom Lupo
   Bottom: Artist, Dom Lupo
398 Artist, Dom Lupo
399 *Top:* Artist, Dom Lupo
   Bottom: Artist, Dom Lupo
400 Artist, Dom Lupo
415 Dorado Beach Hotel and Golf Club

Index

Abandoned-as-lost balls, 317
Accessories, 237–238, 240–241
Adair, Rhona, 12
Adams, Robert, 208
Addressing the ball, 248, 249, 306
Advice, 306, 311
Age contest, 348–349
Agrippa (ball), 208–209
Alibi event, 349
All-American Collegiate Team, 87–88
All-American Team, *Golf Magazine*, 204–205
All-time leading money winners, 195, 196
All-time records
 Hall of Fame (LPGA), 198–199
 Hall of Fame (PGA), 197–198
 LPGA, 197
 PGA, 196–197
 World Golf Hall of Fame, 199
Aluminum shafts, 215–216
Amateur Golf Association of the United States, 9
Amateur Public Links Championship, 47–48
Amateur status, rules of, 331–332
Americas Cup, 26
Anderson, Jamie, 7
Anderson, John G., 13, 15
Anderson, Willie, 11, 125, 126
Appel, Joseph, 13
Approaching and putting contest, 357–359
Argentine Open, 103–104
Armour, Estelle, 17–18
Armour, Thomas Dickson (Tommy), 16, 17, 18, 19, 21, 125–127
Artificial devices, 324
Assistance, 311

Auchterlonie, Lawrence, 11
Auction, 362–363
Augusta National Golf Club, 19, 369, 372–373, 390–391
Australia, golf in, 22, 29, 30, 382–383
 Open, 104
Average score, 349
Award winners. *See* Trophy and award winners

Backspin, 269, 272, 277
Backswing, 251–252. *See also* Iron shots; Wood shots
Bad lies, 283
Baffy, 217
Bags, 236, 240
Bahamas, 416–417
Ball, John, 7, 127
"Balloon ball," 210
Ball(s)
 care of, 240
 compression, 234–236
 evolution of, 4, 207–211
 manufacture of, 220–223
 Rules of Golf concerning, 306–307, 309, 310, 312–323, 325–326
 selection of, 234–236
Baltusrol Golf Club, 371–372, 392
Banff Springs Hotel Golf Course (Canada), 375–376, 398, 399, 415
Barbados, 417
Barber, Jerry, 121
Barnes, James M. (Long Jim), 14, 16, 17, 50, 127–128
Behavior during play, 306
Belgium, golf in, 1, 29, 382
Bell, Andrew, 8
Beman, Deane, 22
Ben Hogan Trophy, 202
Bent grass, 287–288

Berg, Patricia Jane (Patty), 20, 24, 25, 77, 128
Bermuda
 golf in, 416, 417
 grass, 287, 288
Best-ball and aggregate (low–ball, low total), 349
Best-ball foursome, 349
Best-ball match, 349
Best-ball twosome, 349
Betting, 332, 361–363
Bing Crosby National Pro-Am, 54
Bingle-bangle-bungle, 349, 362
Bishop, Ted, 25
Bisque, 362
Blind bogey, 351
Blind choice score, 350
Blind holes, 341
 tournament, 349
Blind low-net foursome, 349
Blind partners, 349
Bloopers tournament, 357
Bobby Jones Award, 203
Bobs and birds, 362
Body action, 243, 246–254
Bogey competition, 325
Bolivia, golf in, 30
Bolt, Tommy, 22
Boros, Julius Nicholas, 22, 128–129
"Bounding billies," 209
Bounds, defining, 324, 327
Brady, Michael Joseph, 129
Braid, James, 7, 129–130, 380
Brantford Golf Club (Canada), 8
Brassie, 217, 254
Brazil, golf in, 29
Brazilian Open, 104–105
Break, judging, 288–290
Breakfast team tourney, 349
Brewer, Gay, 116
British Amateur, 7, 100–102
British balls, 210

British Ladies' Amateur, 102–103
British Open, 6–7, 22, 98–100, 213
Brown, C. S., 41
Brown, Mrs. Charles, 10, 11
Browne, Mary K., 16
Bulla, Johnny, 23
Bunkers, 334
Burke, Billy, 19
Burke, Jack, 22, 130
Burkemo, Walter, 22
Burma, golf in, 30
Burns, Miriam, 16
Byrd, Sam, 22

Caddie(s), 307, 324, 336
  tourney, 349
Caesarea, golf in, 28
Calcutta pool, 362–363
Callaway, Lionel F., 347
Callaway Handicap System, 347
Campbell, Dorothy, 12
Canada, golf in, 7, 29, 375–376, 398, 399, 400, 414–416
Canada Cup, 26, 121
Canadian Amateur, 105–106
Canadian Open, 54, 105
Canadian Open Amateur, Women's, 106
"Can you take it?" tournament, 357–358
Capilano Golf and Country Club (Canada), 398, 400
Carner, JoAnne Gunderson, 23, 82, 117, 130–131
Carnoustie Golf Club (Scotland), 380
Carter, Garnet, 20
Carts, 29, 236–237, 241, 306, 336–338, 341
Casper, William Earl, Jr. (Billy), 22, 58, 116, 121, 131–132
Casual water, 307, 319–320
Ceylon, golf in, 29
Championship Challenge Belt, 6
Championship of the Professional Golfers' Association of America, 14
Championships. See International golf events, major; International team matches; United States championships
Chapman, Dick, 22, 25, 99
Charles I, King of England, 4
Charles Bartlett Award, 203
Chicago Golf Club, 9
Chipping iron, 218, 269
Chip shots, 269–272, 298
Choice Score, 349–350
Choulla (game), 1
Claims, 311
Cleaning balls, 314–315, 321
Cleek, 217
Clothing, 237–238, 240–241
Club de Campo (Spain), 395
Clubs
  care of, 238–240
  covers, 238

Clubs (continued)
  evolution of, 4–5, 211–216
  gripping of, by player, 243–246, 291
  grip size and type, 228–230
  irons. See Irons
  loft and lie of club head, 230–232
  manufacture of, 219–220
  putters, 213–214, 218, 227, 230, 231, 233–234, 309
  Rules of Golf concerning, 309–310, 327, 328–329
  selection of, 224–234
    flexibility, 224–226
    length, 226–227
    swing weight, 227–228
  types of, 216–218
  woods. See Woods
Coe, Charles, 22, 99
College Golfer-of-the-Year Award, 203
Collett, Glenna (Mrs. Edwin H. Vare), 16, 20, 22, 132, 164, 200
Collins, Bill, 121
Colonial Country Club, 392
Colt, H. S., 367
Committees, 307, 323–324
Committee's decision, 311
Competitive golf, 341–364
  country clubs, 363–364
  gambling, 332, 361–363
  handicapping, 342–347
  Rules of Golf concerning, 310–329
  special or novelty events, 357–359
  tournaments and competitions, 348–357
  types of play, 347–348
  winning, 359–361
Competitor, defined, 307
Complete Golfer, The (Wind), 366–369
Compression, ball, 234–236
Confidence, 359, 361
Conley, Peggy, 117
Consecutive club tourney, 358
Consolation tournament, 350
Cooper, Harry E., 19, 132–133
Corcoran, Fred, 19, 23–24, 120
Cossar, Simon, 212
Costume tournament, 350
Cotton, Henry, 20, 133–134, 136, 398
Country Club, The, 9, 372
Country club membership, 363–364
Courses, 365–418
  care of, 306
  evolution of architecture, 366–369
  most interesting holes, 383–384
  number of, 27–28
  outstanding, 370–383
  rating of, 344–346
  resorts, 400–418
  Rules of Golf concerning, 306, 307, 323–324, 327
  toughest holes, 389–400

Courtesy, 306, 335
Crawford, McGregor & Canby Company, 214
Croome, A. C. M., 142
Cross-country tournaments nos. 1, 2, and 3, 358
Cruickshank, Robert Allan (Bobby), 16, 17, 18, 134–135
Crump, George, 367
Cummings, Edith, 16
Cumulative syndicates, 356
Cupit, Jacky, 58
Curtis, Harriot, 12, 115, 116
Curtis, Margaret, 12, 115, 116
Curtis Cup Match, 26, 115–117
Curtiss, Julian W., 213–214
Custom clubs, 222–223
Cut stroke, 273–274
Cypress Point Club, 392–394
Czechoslovakia, golf in, 28–29

Daily fee courses, 28
Daniels, Dan, 336
Darwin, Bernard, 14, 136, 142
Dawson, Johnny, 22
Decision by equity, 311
Deflected balls, 315–316, 322
Demaret, James Newton (Jimmy), 20, 22, 135–136
Denmark, golf in, 29, 382
Depression years, 17–20
Dettweiler, Helen, 24
DeVincenzo, Roberto, 65
Dey, Joe, 392
Dickson, Andrew, 212
Didrikson, Babe. See Zaharias, Mildred Didrikson (Babe)
Diegel, Leo, 16, 18, 19, 136
Dill, Mary Lou, 23
Dimples, ball, 223, 236
Disputes, 311
Distance, judging, 288–290
Dodd, Betty, 26
Doherty Tournament, 89
Dominican Republic, golf in, 417
Dorset Field Club, 9
Doubt as to procedure, 311–312
Downhill lie, shots from, 282
Downswing, 252–253. See also Iron shots; Wood shots
Drivers, 4, 212, 217, 254
Driving, 255–257, 297, 298
  contest, 358
  iron, 218
Drop-out tournament, 350
Dropping balls, 314, 320, 327
Dudley, Edward Bishop, 19, 120, 136–137
Dunes Golf and Beach Club, 390
Dunn, Jamie, 5
Dunn, Willie, 5, 213
Dutch Open, 106–107
Dutra, Olin, 19, 137–138

Eclipse (ball), 209
Egan, Chandler, 12

Eisenhower, Dwight D., 27, 28
Eisenhower Trophy, 26
England. *See* Great Britain
Ennever, G. C., 13
Equipment, 207–241
  See also Accessories; Bags;
    Balls; Carts; Clothing;
    Clubs
Espinosa, Al, 16, 17, 18
Espinosa, Jo, 17
Espirito Santo Trophy, 26, 118
Etiquette, 333–341
  caddies and, 336
  care of the course, 306
  courtesy on the course, 306,
    335
  golf carts or cars and, 306,
    336–338, 341
  priority on the course, 306,
    335–336
  rules of, 306, 333–335
  safety checkpoints, 341
  spectators and, 338–341
Evans, Charles, Jr. (Chick), 12,
    32, 137, 138
Exemption point system, 53
Explosion shot, 275–280
Extra, 363

Fairway wood shots, 257–258
Farrell, John J., 16, 138–139
Faulk, Mary Lena, 23, 65
Feather-ball period, 4, 207–
    208, 211–212
Ferguson, Bob, 7
Ferrules, 219
Fewest putts, 350
Fiberglas shafts, 215
Fifty Years of American Golf
    (Martin), 7–8
Findlay, Alex 8
Finland, golf in, 29
Finsterwald, Dow, 22, 121,
    139–140
Firestone Country Club, 368
Fishwick, Diana, 20, 103
Flagstick, 307, 321, 330
Flag tournament, 350
Fleck, Jack, 27, 32
Follow-through, 254, 282
Footwork, 243, 246–249
Ford, Douglas (Doug), 22,
    121, 140
Ford, Gerald R., 199
Forecaddies, 307, 324
Forfeit round, 358
Forgan, Robert, 208, 212–213
Forgan, Thomas, 213
Forward press, 251
Fotheringham, George, 13
Foulis, Dave, 209
Four-Ball handicap vs. par, 350
Four-ball stroke play, 326, 350
Foursomes, 312, 349, 351, 352,
    355, 357, 358, 359
Fownes, William C., Jr., 12,
    210
Foxburg Country Club, 9
France, golf in, 1, 30, 382
French Golf Federation, 118
French Open, 107

Fuji Company Club (Japan),
    397
Full-finger grip, 243, 244, 245–
    246
Fundamentals of golf, 243–254
Furgol, Ed, 27

Gambling, 332, 361–363
Gardner, Robert, 12, 100
Geiberger, Al, 273
German Open, 107–108
Germany, golf in, 382
Get-acquainted tourney, 350
Ghezzi, Victor, 20, 140–141
Giles, Marvin, 22
Gillespie, J. Hamilton, 8
Girls' Junior Championship, 26,
    48–49
Glass shafts, 215
Gleneagles Hotel Golf Courses
    (Scotland), 380–381
Glennie, George, 5
Glossary of golf terms, 419–429
Gloves, 241
Goalby, Bob, 65
Goat tournament, 350
Golf
  bags, 236, 240
  balls. *See* Balls
  cars or carts, 29, 236–237,
    241, 306, 336–338, 341
  courses. *See* Courses
  etiquette. *See* Etiquette
  fundamentals, 243–254
  history of, 1–30
    in Australia, 22, 29, 30
    balls, evolution of, 4, 207–
      211
    between the wars, 14–20
    clubs, evolution of, 4–5,
      211–216
    courses, evolution of, 366–
      369
    current international
      growth, 28–30
    depression years, 17–20
    forerunners of game, 1
    in Great Britain, 1–7, 14–
      16, 20, 21, 29
    inception of game, 1
    in Japan, 28, 29–30
    LPGA, 24
    modern era, 21–28
    money prizes, growth of,
      27
    PGA, 13–14
    players, increase in, 27–29
    pre-World War I, 11–14
    professionalization, 13–16
    professional tours, 17–20
    roaring twenties, 15–17
    USGA, 11
    war years, 21–22
    women players, 12, 16, 20,
      23–26
    WPGA, 22–23, 25
  principles of, 243–303
  strategy, 295–302
Golf Club Grand-Ducal de
    Luxembourg, 28

*Golf Committee Manual and
    USGA Golf Handicap
    System with USGA
    Course Rating System
    for Men and Women,*
    341–342
Golfcraft Incorporated, 215
Golfers. *See* Players
Golf Magazine
  All-American Team, 204–205
  College Golfer-of-the-Year
    Award, 203
  Golf's Player-of-the-Year
    Award, 203
Golf Professional-of-the-Year
    Award (PGA), 201
Golf's Player-of-the-Year
    Award, 203
Golf Writers' Association of
    America, 197, 199
  trophies and awards
    Ben Hogan Trophy, 202
    Brunswick-MacGregor
      Charles Bartlett Award,
      203
    Player of the Year (men),
      203
    Player of the Year
      (women), 203
    William D. Richardson
      Trophy, The, 202
Golf Writers' Association of
    America Brunswick-
    MacGregor Charles
    Bartlett Award, 203–204
Goodman, Johnny, 18, 20
"Gourlay," 208
Gourlay, Douglas, 208
Graphite shafts, 216
Grassed drivers, 4–5
Grass types, 287–288
Great Britain, golf in, 1–7, 14–
    16, 20, 21, 29, 376–379
Greenie, 362
Greens. *See* Putting greens
Gripping, of clubs, by player,
    243–246, 291
Grips, of clubs
  defined, 309
  Rules of Golf concerning,
    330
  size and type, 228–230
Ground under repair, 307, 319–
    320
Guldahl, Ralph, 20, 120, 141
Gunderson, JoAnne. *See*
    Carner, JoAnne Gun-
    derson
Gutta-percha ball period, 4,
    208–209, 212–213
Gwinner, Alice, 65

Hagen, Walter Charles, 15, 17,
    18, 120, 141–143, 211,
    336
Hagge, Marlene Bauer, 25, 65
Half-shot, 268–269
Hall of Fame
  LPGA, 198–199
  PGA, 197–198
  World Golf, 199
Hand action, 243–254, 259

Handicap(s)
  computation of, 342–347
  events, 324, 328
  Rules of Golf concerning, 324
  stroke play, 350
Handmacher, Alvin, 24
Hanson, Beverly, 25, 65
Harbert, Melvin R. (Chick), 143
Harlow, Bob, 18
Harper, Chandler, 143–144
Harris, W. W., 13
Harrison, Ernest Joe (Dutch), 20, 144
Harry E. Radix Trophy, 199
Haskell, Coburn, 209
Haskell balls, 209, 210
Hawes, Theodore, 117
Hazards, 307, 320–321
Heafner, Clayton, 23
Herbert, Jay, 22, 121
Hepburn, James, 13
Herd, Alex "Sandy," 7
Herd, Fred, 164
Hezlet, May, 12
Hickory shafts, 213, 215
Hicks, Helen, 16, 20, 23
High and low ball, 350–351
Hilton, Harold H., 7, 378
Hiskey, Jim "Babe," 58
History of golf. See Golf, history of
Hobens, Jack, 13
Hogan, William Benjamin (Ben), 11, 20, 22, 27, 32, 144–146, 170, 336, 392
Holbrook, Harry, 9
Holbrook, Warren, 8
Holes
  defined, 307
  most interesting, 383–384
  toughest, 389–400
Holland, golf in, 1, 382
Hollins, Marion, 16
Hong Kong, golf in, 29, 30
Hong Kong Open, 108
Honor, 307, 312, 333
Honourable Company of Edinburgh Golfers (Scotland), 5, 379, 380
Honourable Company of Golfers at Blackheath (Scotland), 4
Hooks, 259–261
Hopkins, John Jay, 121
Horton Smith Trophy, 202
Hoyt, Beatrix, 12
Hurd, Dorothy. See Campbell, Dorothy
Husband and wife two-ball match, 351
Hutchison, Jock, 15, 16, 17, 146, 152, 215

Identification of ball, 314
Inch or string contest, 358
India
  golf in, 29
  Open, 108
Individual handicap vs. par, 351

Insets, 213
Interference
  by ball, 320, 322, 323
  by immovable obstruction, 319
Interlocking grip, 243, 244, 245
International Golf Association, 121
International golf events, major, 98–113
  Argentine Open, 103–104
  Australian Open, 104
  Brazilian Open, 104–105
  British Amateur, 7, 100–102
  British Ladies' Amateur, 102–103
  British Open, 6–7, 22, 98–100, 213
  Canadian Amateur, 105–106
  Canadian Open, 54, 105
  Canadian Open Amateur, Women's, 106
  Dutch Open, 106–107
  French Open, 107
  German Open, 107–108
  Hong Kong Open, 108
  India Open, 108
  Italian Open, 108–109
  Japanese Open, 109
  Korea Open, 109
  Malaysian Open, 109
  New Zealand Open, 109–110
  Philippine Open, 110
  Portuguese Open, 110
  Singapore Open, 110
  South African Open, 110–111
  Spanish Open, 111
  Swiss Open, 111–112
  Taiwan (China) Open, 112
  Thailand Open, 112
  World Match Play Championship, 113
  World Senior Amateur Championship, 112
  World Series of Golf (men), 112–113
International team matches, 113–123
  Curtis Cup Match, 26, 115–117
  Ryder Cup Match, 26, 119–121, 210
  Walker Cup Match, 16, 26, 113–115, 210, 378
  Women's World Amateur Team Championship, 118–119
  World Amateur Team Championship, 117–118
  World Cup Match, 26, 121–123
International Trophy Championship, 26, 123
Intra-Club Matches, 351
Ireland, golf in, 7, 381–382, 397–398
Iron(s)
  care of, 239–240
  defined, 309
  evolution of, 5, 211–214
  manufacture of, 220

Iron(s) (*continued*)
  no. 1, 217, 218, 227, 230, 231, 254, 263–265
  no. 2, 217, 218, 227, 230, 231, 254, 263–265, 272
  no. 3, 217, 218, 227, 230, 231, 263–265, 272, 283
  no. 4, 217, 218, 227, 230, 231, 265–267, 269, 271, 272, 283
  no. 5, 218, 227, 230, 231, 265–267, 280
  no. 6, 218, 227, 230, 231, 265–267, 269, 271
  no. 7, 218, 227, 230, 231, 269, 271, 272
  no. 8, 218, 227, 230, 231, 271
  no. 9, 218, 227, 230, 231, 272, 275, 277, 280
  normal distance for, 217
  Rules of Golf concerning, 329
  shots, 263–286
    chip, 269–273, 298
    common errors, 283–286
    long iron, 263–265
    middle (medium) iron, 265–267
    pitch, 269–275
    short iron, 267–269
    standards for, 297
    trouble, 275–283
Israel, golf in, 28
Italian Open, 108–109
Italy, golf in, 382

Jamaica, golf in, 417
James II, King of England, 2
James VI, King of Scotland, 207
Jameson, Betty, 20, 25, 65, 77, 146, 147, 200
Japan, golf in, 28, 29–30, 382, 397
Japanese Open, 109
Jaques, Herbert, Jr., 210
Jasper Park Golf Club, 366, 367, 415
Jigger, 218
Jones, Col. Robert T., 58
Jones, Robert Trent, 28, 366–369, 371, 373–374, 392
Jones, Robert Tyre, Jr. (Bobby), 11, 17, 18, 19, 20, 22, 100, 146–147, 367–369, 372
Junior championships
  USGA, 25–26, 48–49
  Western, 92, 93
Junior tourney, 351

Kasumegaseki Country Club (Japan), 382
Keeler, O. B., 147
Kempshall Golf Ball Company, 209
Kickers' replay tournament, 351
Kickers' tournament, 351
King's tournament, 351
Kinnan, Alexander P. W., 8, 9
Kirk, Peggy, 26

Kirkby, Oswald, 15
Kirkwood, Joe, 16
Knight, A. W., 214
Kolf (game), 1
Korea Open, 109
Kroll, Ted, 22
Kuala Lumpur, golf in, 30

Lacoste, Catherine, 49
Ladder tournament, 351
Ladies Golf Union, 12, 23, 115
Ladies' Professional Golf Asso-
    ciation of America
    (LPGA), 45, 78–85
  all-time records, 197
  Hall of Fame, 198–199
  inception of, 24
  LPGA Championship, 79–80
  LPGA Tour, 80–85
    money-winning records,
        195–196
    1955, 186
    1956, 186
    1957, 187
    1958, 187
    1959, 187
    1960, 187
    1961, 187
    1962, 187–188
    1963, 188
    1964, 188
    1965, 188–189
    1966, 189
    1967, 189
    1968, 189
    1969, 189–190
    1970, 80, 190
    1971, 80–81, 190
    1972, 81, 190
    1973, 82–83, 190–191
    1974, 83, 191
    1975, 83–84, 191
    1976, 84–85, 191
    1977, 85, 191–192
  Teaching Committee, 201
  trophies and awards
    Player-of-the-Year Award,
        200–201
    Teacher-of-the-Year
        Award, 201–202
    Vare Trophy, 200
LaGorce Open, 18
Lard, Allan, 214, 215
Lateral water hazards, 307,
    320–321, 327
Lawrence, W. G., 10
Le Fiell Products, Inc., 215
Leitch, Cecil, 12, 103
Lema, Tony, 268
Lenczyk, Grace, 65
Lengfield, Helen, 24
Lesser, Patricia, 23
Lessons, 302–303
Lie
  of ball
    Rules of Golf concerning,
        312
    See also Iron shots; Wood
        shots
  of club, 230, 232, 234
Lifting balls, 314, 327

Lightning, 330, 341
Line of play, improving, 312–
    313
Links of Leith (Scotland),
    2–3, 5
Little, William Lawson, Jr., 18,
    20, 24, 32, 126, 148
Littler, Gene Alec, 22, 27, 121,
    148–149, 266–267
Local rules, 327–328
Locke, Arthur D'Arcy
    (Bobby), 22, 149–150
Lockhart, Bob, 9
Loft angle, 230, 231, 234
Long and short tourney, 351
Long irons, 217, 263–264, 297
Loose impediments, 307, 313
Los Angeles Open, 18
Lost balls, 317, 320
Low and high ball, 362
Low ball and total, 362
Lowell, William, 211
Low-net foursome, 351
LPGA. *See* Ladies' Professional
    Golf Association of
    America
L-shafts, 222
Luxembourg, golf in, 28

Macapagal, Diosdado, 30
MacClain, E. M., 215
McCormack, Mark H., 113,
    157
McDermott, John J., 11–12,
    151
Macdonald, Charles B., 8, 10,
    36, 366–367
McEwan, Douglas, 211, 212
McEwan, James, 212
McEwan, Peter, 212
MacFarlane, Willie, 136
MacFie, A. E., 7
McIntire, Barbara, 23, 82, 117
Mackenzie, Alistair, 19, 367–
    369
Mackie, Jack, 13
McLean, Edward B., 18
McLeod, Frederick Robertson,
    11, 146, 152
McNamara, Tommy, 17
McSpaden, Harold "Jug," 20,
    21–22, 24
Maiden, James, 13
Malaysian Open, 109
Manero, Tony, 120
Mangrum, Lloyd Eugene, 22,
    150–151, 336, 390
Manufacture of golf equipment
  balls, 220–223
  clubs, 219–220
Margins, defining, 324, 327
Marker, 307
Marking position of lifted balls,
    327
Markings on clubs, 328–329
Marr, Dave, 99, 270–271, 274
Marston, Max R., 15
Martin, H. B., 7–8
Mashie iron, 218
Mashie niblick, 218
Masters Tournament, 19, 77–78

Match
  play, 308, 310–329, 348
  vs. par, 351–352
May, George S., 21, 192
Mayer, Dick, 22
Mayne, William, 211
Medal sweepstakes, 352
Medium irons, 217, 265–267,
    297
Mehlhorn, Wild Bill, 18, 21
Melvill, James, 207
Men's North and South
    Amateur, 93–94
Mental aspects of game, 295
Merion Golf Club, 365, 370,
    389–390
Metropolitan Golf Association,
    11
Mexico, golf in, 29, 417
Middlecoff, Cary, 22, 32, 152–
    153
Middle irons, 217, 265–267, 297
Midiron, 218
Mid mashie, 218
Mid-Ocean Golf Club
    (Bermuda), 396
Mill, Henry, 212
Miller, Johnny, 22, 153
Million dollar tournament, 352
Miniature golf, 20
Miniature tourney, 352
Mixed foursome(s), 352
  point competition, 352
Money prizes
  increases in, 27
  total and average purses:
      1950–1977, 192
Money winners, leading
  men, 192–195
  women, 195–196
Monkey foursome, 358
  captain's choice, 359
Montague, Russell W., 8
Morris, Thomas (Old Tom), 5,
    153–154, 208, 213
Morris, Thomas, Jr. (Young
    Tom), 6, 98, 154, 212,
    213
Morrison, Fred, 22
Most 3's, 352
Moving balls, 315
Municipal courses, 28
Mystery event, 352

Nassau (bet), 362
Nassau Tournament, 352–353
National Amateur Public Links
    Championship, 17
National Collegiate Athletic
    Association (NCAA)
    Championship, 86–87
National Intercollegiate
    Championship, Wom-
    en's, 88
National Links, 366
Nelson, John Byron, Jr., 20,
    21–22, 24, 50, 120, 154–
    155, 170, 336
Newport (R.I.) Golf Club, 8,
    9, 10, 31, 36
New Zealand, golf in, 22
New Zealand Open, 109–110

Niagara-on-the-Lake Golf Club (Canada), 8
Niblick, 218
Nicholls, Gilbert, 13
Nicklaus, Jack William, 15, 22, 29, 79, 97, 99, 155–156, 243, 372, 390
No alibi tournament, 353
North and South Amateur Championships
 Men's, 93–94
 Seniors', 95
 Women's, 94–95
Norway, golf in, 29
Novelty events, 357–359

Oak Hill Country Club, 370
Oakland Hills Country Club, 374–375, 394
O'Brien, Jack, 18
Observer, 308
Obstacle tourney, 359
Obstructions, 308, 318–319, 327
Odd and even tournament, 353
Oliver, Porky, 22
Olympic Country Club, 365, 373
One-club event, 359
One-half aggregate score, 357
Open Championship Cup, 31
Orcutt, Maureen, 16, 20
Ouimet, Francis Desales, 12, 13, 32, 156–157, 336
Out of bounds, 308
Outside agency, 308
Overlapping grip, 244–245
Overswinging, 259
Overturning, 259

Pacific Northwest Golf Association, 11
Packaged golf vacations, 417–418
Pairings for match play, 328–329
Pakistan, golf in, 29
Palmer, Arnold Daniel, 22, 29, 58, 121, 155, 157–158, 170, 216, 336, 373, 390
Palmer, Johnny, 22, 58
Par, 1, 329–330, 343–344
 battle, 353
Parent and child tournament, 353
Pari-mutuels, 353
Park, Mungo, 6
Park, Willie, 6
Park, Willie, Jr., 6, 212
Parks, Sam, Jr., 23
Partner, 308
Paterson, John, 2
"Paterson's Patent," 208
Patton, Billy Joe, 22
Pau Golf Club (France), 4
Peachtree Golf Course, 369
Pebble Beach Golf Links, 365, 373–374, 394, 395
Penalties, 311
Penalty stroke, 308
Peru, golf in, 29
Peters, Richard, 10

PGA. See Professional Golfers' Association of America
Philippine Open, 110
Philippines, golf in, 30
Philp, Hugh, 211, 212
Picard, Henry G., 20, 120, 158–159
Pinehurst Country Club, 199, 365, 370–371, 372
Pine Valley Golf Club, 371, 392, 393
Pitch
 and-run shot, 269–272
 shots, 269–275
Pitching niblick, 218
Pitching wedge, 230, 231, 277
Placing balls, 314
Planning shots, 295–296
Plas/Steel Products, 215
Play clubs, 4, 212
Player, Gary Jim, 16, 22, 79, 159, 215, 336
Player-of-the-year awards
 Golf Magazine, 203
 Golf Writers' Association of America, 203
 LPGA, 200–201
 PGA, 200
Players
 all-time records
  Hall of Fame (LPGA), 198–199
  Hall of Fame (PGA), 197–198
  LPGA, 197
  PGA, 196–197
  World Golf Hall of Fame, 199
 current touring professionals
  men, 174–177
  women, 177–178
 great, of all time, 125–174
 LPGA Tournament winners, 80–85
 money winners, leading
  men, 192–195
  women, 195–196
 PGA Tournament winners, 53–57
 Rules of Golf concerning, 324
 trophy and award winners. See Trophy and award winners
Playfair, Sir Hugh, 5
"Playing within yourself," 296
Point accumulation tournament, 353–354
Point Tournament, 354
Porter Cup Tournament, 88
Portmarnock Golf Club (Ireland), 381, 397–398
Portugal, golf in, 382
Portuguese Open, 110
Practice, 327, 341
 ground, 323
 Rules of Golf concerning, 311
 strategy, 301–302
Pratt, Bob, 58
Preferred lies, 328
Press (bet), 363

Prestwick Golf Club (Scotland), 6, 7
Preuss, Phillis Ann, 117
Principles of golf, 243–303
Priority on the course, 306, 335–336
Private clubs, 28
Prize money. See Money prizes; Money winners, leading
Pro-Am, 354
Professional Golfers' Association of America (PGA), 50–78
 all-time records, 196–197
 Executive Committee, 201
 Hall of Fame, 197–198
 inception of, 13–14
 Masters Tournament, 19, 77–78
 National Advisory Committee, 201, 202
 National Press List, 200
 PGA Championship, 50–52
 PGA Seniors' Championship, 53
 PGA Tour, 53–77
  average purse, 27
  money winning records, 192–195
  1955, 54–55
  1956, 55–56, 178–179
  1957, 56–57, 179
  1958, 57–59, 179
  1959, 59, 179–180
  1960, 59–60, 180
  1961, 60–61, 180
  1962, 61–62, 180–181
  1963, 62–63, 181
  1964, 63, 65, 181
  1965, 65, 181–182
  1966, 65–66, 182
  1967, 66–67, 182
  1968, 67–68, 182–183
  1969, 68–69, 183
  1970, 69–70, 183
  1971, 70–71, 183–184
  1972, 71–72, 184
  1973, 72–73, 184–185
  1974, 73–74, 185
  1975, 74–75, 185
  1976, 75–76, 185–186
  1977, 76–77, 186
 Special Awards Committee, 198
 trophies and awards
  Golf Professional-of-the-Year, 201
  Horton Smith Trophy, 202
  Player of the Year, 200
  Vardon Trophy, 199–200, 297
Professionalism, 331
Professional tours, early history of, 17–20
Pros vs. members, 354
Provisional balls, 317–318, 328
Public Links Championship, 47–48
Puerto Rico, golf in, 417
Pulls, 262
Pulver, P. C., 13
Punch shot, 273–274

Pung, Jackie, 26
Pushes, 261–262
Putnam, Kingman, 9
Putters, 213–214, 218, 227, 230, 231, 233–234, 309
Putting, 286–295
    contest, 359
    greens, 286–288, 308, 321–323, 327, 334–335, 365, 366
    judging distance and break, 288–290
    reading the greens, 286–288
    standards for, 297
    strokes, 291–295
    tournament, 354
    tourney, 359
Pyramid tournament, 354

Quast, Anne, 23

Rainsford, William, 10
Rankin, Judith Torluemke (Judy), 159–160
Ravenscroft, Gladys, 12
Rawlins, Horace, 11, 31, 32
Rawls, Elizabeth Earle (Betsy), 25, 160
Ray, Edward (Ted), 12, 16, 32, 160–161
Razzle-dazzle tournament, 359
Records. See All-time records
Recovery shots, 298
Reddy Tee, 211
Referee, 308
Referee's decision, 311
Reid John, 8, 9
Relay
    event, 354
    tournament, 354
Remorseful golf, 355
Replay tournament, 354–355
Resorts, 400–418
Revolta, John, 20, 120, 161–162
Rhythm, 254
Rice, Grantland, 197
Riegel, Skee, 22
Ringer tournament, 355
Roaring twenties, in golf, 15–17
Robertson, Alan, 5, 153–154, 162, 208, 212, 213
Rodgers, Phil, 58
Rogers, Jason, 13
Rogers, John, 22
Romack, Barbara, 23, 65
Rosburg, Bob, 243
Ross, Aleck, 11
Ross, Donald J., 367
Roth, Nancy, 117
Rough, shots from, 280–282
Round robin tournament, 355
Royal and Ancient Club of St. Andrews (Scotland), 3, 7, 13, 100, 117, 118, 210, 213, 215, 365, 379–380, 398, 399
Royal Bangkok Sports Club (Thailand), 30
Royal County Down Golf Club (Ireland), 381–382

Royal Hong Kong Golf Club, 30
Royal Island Golf Club (Singapore), 30
Royal Liverpool Golf Club (England), 7, 100, 378
Royal Lytham and St. Anne's Golf Club (England), 376–378
Royal Melbourne Club (Australia), 382–383
Royal Montreal Golf Club (Canada), 8
Royal Portrush Golf Club (Ireland), 381
Royal Quebec Golf Club (Canada), 8
Royal St. Georges Golf Club (England), 7
Royal Singapore Golf Club, 30
Rubber-ball period, 4, 209–211, 213–215
Rub of the green, 308
Rules of Golf, 305–333
    definitions, 306–308
    etiquette, 306
    flagstick dimensions, 330
    grip, nature of, 330
    lightning, protection against, 330
    local rules, 327–328
    markings on clubs, 328–329
    pairings for match play, 328
    par computation, 329–330
    rules of amateur status, 331–332
    rules of play, 308–327
Run-up iron, 218
Runyan, Paul, 20
Russell, Alex, 382
Ryder, Samuel A., 119
Ryder Cup Match, 26, 119–121, 210

Safety, 341
St. Andrew's Golf Club of Yonkers, 7–10
St. Andrews Society of Golfers, 3, 5, 7, 211
"St. Andrews swing," 211
St. Maarten, golf in, 417
St. Paul Chamber of Commerce, 18
Sanders, Doug, 22, 292, 336
Sand traps, shots from, 275–280
Sand wedge, 230, 231, 277
Sarazen (Saraceni), Gene, 16, 19–24, 32, 79, 120, 142, 162–163, 215, 243, 336
Sayers, Ben, 213
Scorefest, 355
Scorekeeper, 1
Scoring records
    LPGA, 197
    PGA, 196–197
Scotch foursome, 355
Scotland, 1–4, 7, 29, 207–213, 378–381, 396, 398, 399
Scott, Lady Margaret, 12
Scratch and scramble tournament, 355
Scrip tourney, 355

Sea Pines Golf Club, 366
Seignious, Hope, 23
Selected score, 355
Selective drive, 352
Seminole Golf Club, 371
Seniors' championships
    North and South, 95
    PGA, 53
    U.S., 89–90
        National Open, 90
    USGA
        Amateur, 26, 49
        Women's Amateur, 26, 49–50
    World, 112
Senior tourney, 355–356
Shafts, 309
    evolution of, 211–216
    flexibility of, 224–226
    length of, 226–227
Shakespeare Company, 215
Shanking, 283–286
Sharkey, Hal, 18
Shimby-shamby, 359
Shinnecock Hills Golf Club, 9, 370
Shoes, 237–238, 240–241
Short irons, 217, 267–269
Shotgun tournament, 356
Shotts, John C., 9
Shute, Herman Densmore (Denny), 16, 19, 20, 120, 163–164
Sides, 308
Singapore
    golf in, 30
    Open, 110
Six-hole elective, 356
Six-point match, 356
Skins, 362
    team, 362
Skying, 263
Slices, 258–259
Smothering, 262–263
Smith, Alex, 11, 17, 164
Smith, Horton, 16, 18, 19, 58, 120, 164–165, 215
Smith, Macdonald, 16, 19, 165–166
Smith, Marilynn, 25
Snead, Samuel Jackson, 20, 22, 23, 32, 50, 120, 166–167
Soft pitch shot, 272
Solo-club team match, 359
Sorenson, Carol, 117
Souchak, Mike, 22, 121
South Africa, golf in, 22, 29
South African Open, 110–111
South America, golf in, 30
Southern Amateur, 96–97
    Women's, 97
Southern Golf Association, 11
Spade mashie, 218
Spain, golf in, 382, 395
Spalding & Bros., A. G., 11, 209, 211, 213–215
Spalding Wizard (ball), 209
Spanish Open, 111
Special irons, 218
Speck tournament, 356
Spectators, etiquette and, 338–341

Splash contest, 356
Spoons, 4, 5, 212, 217, 254
S-shafts, 224
Stableford competition, 325
Stance, 246–249, 308, 312, 313, 320. *See also* Iron shots; Wood shots
Standing above the ball, 283
Standing below the ball, 282–283
Steel-shaft club, 20, 214–215
Stewart, Marlene, 23
Stipulated round, 308
Stirling, Alexa, 16
Stoddard, L. B., 10
Stopped balls, 315–316, 322
Strafaci, Frank, 79
Stranahan, Frank, 22, 79
Strategy, 295–303
    lessons, 302–303
    practice, 301–302
    weather conditions, 298–301
Striking at ball, 313
String tournament, 356
Stroke(s), 308
    holes, 346
    play, 310–328, 348
    taken, information as to, 311
Strong, Herbert W., 13
Suggs, Louise, 23, 25, 167
Sullivan, Ed, 162
Sunnehanna Amateur Championship, 88–89
Surlyn, as cover for ball, 223
Sweden, golf in, 29, 382
Sweeny, Robert, Jr., 25
Sweepstakes, 356
Sweetser, Jess, 16, 100
Swing, 249–254
    weight, 227–228
    See also Iron shots; Wood shots
Swiss Open, 111–112
Switzerland, golf in, 382
Syndicate tournament, 356
Syndicate tourney, 356–357

Taft, William H., 214
Taiwan (China) Open, 112
Tallmadge, Henry O., 9, 10
Tam O'Shanter Open, 21, 192
Tap putt, 295
Taylor, John Henry, 7, 167, 168, 171
Taylor, William, 209
Teacher-of-the-Year Award (LPGA), 201–202
Team match—Nassau System, 357
Team matches. *See* International team matches
Team skins, 362
Teeing, 308
    ground, 308
Tee(s), 210–211, 255, 296
    shot, 255–257
Teplow Club, 13
Texas Open, 18
Thailand
    golf in, 30
    Open, 112
Thompson, Stanley, 367

Thompson, W. J., 15
Thomson, Jimmy, 20, 22
Thomson, Peter, 7, 22, 99, 167–169
Three-ball matches, 357
Three-ball match play, 325–326
Threesome(s), 312, 357
    match, 357
Through the green, 308
Throw-out tournament, 359
Ties, 323, 328
Tillinghast, A. H., 13, 372
Timing, 254
Tin whistle tournament, 357
Tobago, 417
Tolley, Cyril, 100
"Tom Thumb" golf, 20
Topping, 262
Toronto Golf Club, 8
Toski, Bob, 22
Tournament types, 348–357
Tournament winners. *See* International golf events, major; International team matches; United States championships
Trajectory of ball, 236, 255
Trans-Mississippi Amateur, 95–96
Trans-Mississippi Golf Association, 11, 95
Trans-National Amateur, Women's, 96
Travers, Jerome, 12, 15, 164, 169
Travis, Walter J., 12, 100, 169–170, 209, 214
Trees, shots near, 283
Trevino, Lee, 22, 116, 170
Troon Golf Club (Scotland), 211, 396
Trophy and award winners, 199–205
    Ben Hogan Trophy, 202
    Bobby Jones Award, 203
    Charles Bartlett Award, 203
    College Golfer-of-the-Year Award, 203
    Golf Magazine All-America Team, 204–205
    Golf's Player-of-the-Year Award, 203
    Golf Writers' Association of America Brunswick-MacGregor Charles Bartlett Award, 203–204
    Horton Smith Trophy, 202
    LPGA Player-of-the-Year Award, 200–201
    LPGA Teacher-of-the-Year Award, 201–202
    LPGA Vare Trophy, 200
    PGA Golf Professional-of-the-Year Award, 201
    PGA Player-of-the-Year Award, 200
    PGA Vardon Trophy, 199–200, 297
    Player of the Year (men and women), 203
    William D. Richardson Trophy, 202

Trouble shots, 275–283
Tufts, Richard S., 201
Tunku Abdul Rahman, 30
Turkey tournament, 357
Turnberry Hotel Golf (Ailsa) Course (Scotland), 398
Turnesa, Joe, 16, 24
Turnesa, Willie, 22, 24, 25
Turnesa family, 24
Tuxedo Club, 8
Twelve-hole elective, 356
Two-ball foursome, 357

Umbrella, 238, 240
Unauthorized attendance, 321
Undue delay, 324
Union Hardware Company, 215
United States
    championships
        All-American Collegiate Team, 87–88
        Doherty Tournament, 89
        LPGA competitions. *See* Ladies' Professional Golf Association of America
        National Collegiate Athletic Association (NCAA) Championship, 86–87
        North and South Amateur, 93–95
        PGA competitions. *See* Professional Golf Association of America
        Porter Cup Tournament, 88
        Southern Amateur, 96–97
        Women's, 97
        Sunnehanna Amateur Championship, 88–89
        Trans-Mississippi Amateur, 95–96
        USGA competitions. *See* United States Golf Association
        U.S. National Senior Open, 90
        U.S. Seniors' Championship, 89–90
        Western Golf Association. *See* Western Golf Association
        Women's National Intercollegiate Championship, 88
        Women's Trans-National Amateur, 96
    history of golf, 7–30
    outstanding golf courses, 370–375
    resorts, 400–414
United States Golf Association (USGA), 31–50, 113, 115, 213
    Amateur Public Links Championship, 47–48
    ball specifications and, 210, 223
    Bobby Jones Award, 203
    country clubs, 363

United States Golf Association
   (USGA) (*continued*)
   early history of, 9–11, 17
   Executive Committee, 341
   Girls' Junior Championship,
      26, 48–49
   Handicap Committee, 341
   Handicap Differential Chart,
      342
   Junior Amateur Champion-
      ship, 25–26, 48
   membership, 26
   rules of amateur status, 331–
      332
   Senior Amateur Champion-
      ship, 49
   Senior Women's Amateur
      Championship, 49–50
   U.S. National Amateur
      Championship, 10,
      36–40
   U.S. National Open Cham-
      pionship, 10–12, 27,
      31–36
   U.S. Women's Amateur
      Championship, 11,
      40–45
   U.S. Women's Open Cham-
      pionship, 45–47
U.S. National Amateur Cham-
   pionship, 10, 36–40
U.S. National Open Champion-
   ship, 10–12, 27, 31–36
U.S. National Senior Open, 90
U.S. Seniors' Championship,
   89–90
U.S. Women's Amateur Cham-
   pionship, 11, 40–45
U.S. Women's Open Champion-
   ship, 45–47
Unplayable balls, 317
Upham, John B., 8
Uphill lie, shots from, 282
USGA. *See* United States Golf
   Association

Vanderbeck, C. H., 82
Van Wie, Virginia, 16, 20, 82
Vardon, Harry, 7, 11, 12, 16,
   22, 170–171, 199, 243–
   244
Vardon Flyer (ball), 11, 209
Vardon Trophy, 199–200, 297
Vare, Edwin H., Jr., 16
Vare, Glenna Collett. *See*
   Collett, Glenna
Vare Trophy, 200
Venezuela, 29
Venturi, Ken, 22
Virginia C. Lord Award, 200

Virgin Islands, 417
Von Elm, George, 20

Waggle, 251
Walker, George H., 114
Walker Cup Match, 16, 26,
   113–115, 210, 378
Wall, Art, Jr., 22, 121, 243, 386
Walsh, Thomas, 50
Walton Heath Golf Club
   (England), 378–379
Wanamaker, Rodman, 13, 50
Ward, Bud, 20
Ward, Harvie, 22
Warren, Herbert, 25
Water
   casual, 307, 319–320
   hazards, 307, 320–321, 327
   shots from, 280
Watson, Thomas, 171–172
Weather conditions, 298–301
Weight distribution, 248–249
Western Golf Association
   (WGA), 11
   Western Amateur, 90–91
   Western Junior, 92
   Western Junior Girls', 93
   Western Open, 54, 91–92
   Western Women's Amateur,
      92–93
Wethered, Joyce (Lady
   Heathcoat-Amory), 16,
   22, 23, 172
Wet-weather play, 299–300
WGA. *See* Western Golf Asso-
   ciation
Wharton, Frank, 58
White, Barbara Fay, 117
White, Harold, 212
White, Robert, 13
White elephant tournament,
   357
Whitworth, Kathrynne Ann
   (Kathy), 25, 172
William D. Richardson Trophy,
   202
Williams, Dave, 58
Wilson, Enid, 20
Wilson, James, 212
Wind, Herbert Warren, 366–
   369
Windy-day strategy, 301
Winter rules, 328
Women's Canadian Open Ama-
   teur, 106
Women's golf, history of, 12,
   16, 20, 23–26
Women's National Inter-
   collegiate Championship
   88
Women's North and South
   Amateur, 94–95

Women's Professional Golfers'
   Association (WPGA),
   23–24, 25, 45–47
Women's Southern Amateur, 97
Women's Trans-National
   Amateur, 96
Women's World Amateur Team
   Championship, 118–119
Wood, Craig Ralph, 19, 172–
   173
Woods
   care of, 238–239
   defined, 309
   drivers, 4, 212, 217, 254
   early, 211–214
   facing of, 232–233
   finishes of, 238–239
   manufacture of, 219–220
   no. 1, 217, 227, 230, 231
   no. 2, 217, 227, 230, 231,
      257, 258
   no. 3, 217, 227, 230, 231,
      257, 258, 280, 281
   no. 4, 217, 227, 230, 231,
      254, 257, 258, 280, 281
   no. 5, 217, 227, 230, 254,
      258, 280, 281
   no. 6, 217, 227, 230, 254
   normal distance for, 217
   Rules of Golf concerning,
      329
   shots, 254–263
      common errors, 258–263
      fairway, 257–258
      tee, 255–257
   tees, 211
   types of, 216–217
Work, Bertram G., 209
World Amateur Golf Council,
   26
World Amateur Team Cham-
   pionship, 117–118
   Women's, 118–119
World Cup Match, 26, 121–123
World Golf Hall of Fame, 199
World Match Play Champion-
   ship, 113
World Senior Amateur Cham-
   pionship, 112
World Series of Golf (men),
   112–113
Worsham, Lew, 22, 58
Wright, Mary Kathryn
   (Mickey), 25, 173–174
Wrong ball, 313–314

Yardage rating, 344–346

Zaharias, Mildred Didrikson
   (Babe), 22–26, 126, 174